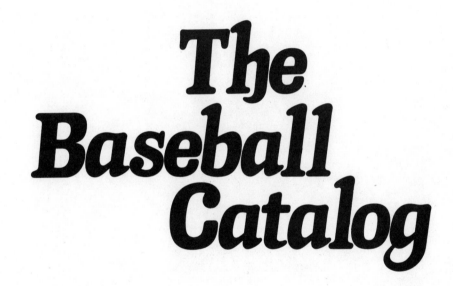

# The Baseball Catalog

# The Baseball Catalog

**By Dan Schlossberg**

JONATHAN DAVID PUBLISHERS, INC.
MIDDLE VILLAGE, N.Y. 11379

# The Baseball Catalog

## By
## Dan Schlossberg

Copyright © 1980, 1983, 1989
by
Jonathan David Publishers, Inc.

No part of this book may be used without the prior written permission of the publisher. Address all inquiries to:

**JONATHAN DAVID PUBLISHERS, INC.
68-22 ELIOT AVENUE
MIDDLE VILLAGE, N.Y. 11379**

**Library of Congress Cataloging in Publication Data**

Schlossberg, Dan.
　The baseball catalog.
　1. Baseball--Miscellanea--Addresses, essays, lectures.　2. Baseball--History--Addresses, essays, lectures.　I. Title.
GV867.3.S34　　　　796.357　　　　77-29025
ISBN 0-8246-0227-7

Jacket and Book design by Louis Mercurio

*Production by Nancy C. Mercurio*

*Printed in the United States of America*

# Acknowledgements

The author wishes to thank the following for their invaluable assistance in the preparation of this book:

**Editors** — Walter Anderson, *Parade;* Rick Cerrone, *Baseball Magazine* Irwin Cohen, *The Baseball Bulletin;* Joyce Jack, *Vista/USA;* Murray Olderman, Newspaper Enterprise Association; Phil Patton, East/West Network sports; Milton Richman, United Press International sports; Linda Roberts, *Carte Blanche;* C.C. Johnson Spink, *The Sporting News;* Burdett C. Stoddard, *Detroit News.*

**Artists** — John Anderson, Bob Laughlin, and Charlie McGill.

**Photographers** — Laura Gaynor, Barbara Morgen.

**Calligrapher** — Cheryl Harlan.

**Baseball personalities** — Moe Drabowsky, Ernie Harwell, Waite Hoyt, Billy Hunter, Ralph Kiner, Clyde King, Frank Lane.

**Baseball executives** — Seth Abraham and Rick White, Major League Baseball Promotion Corporation; John Dittrich, National Association; Monte Irvin, Office of the Commissioner of Baseball; Blake Cullen and Katy Feeney, National League; Bob Fishel and Phyllis Merhige, American League; and Clifford Kachline and Ken Smith, National Baseball Hall of Fame and Museum.

**National League publicists** — Don Davidson, Astros; Bob Hope and Randy Donaldson, Braves; Buck Peden, Cubs; Steve Brener, Dodgers; Stu Smith, Giants; Arthur Richman and Tim Hamilton, Mets; Bob Chandler and Andy Strasberg, Padres; Larry Shenk and Chris Wheeler, Phillies; and Bill Guilfoyle, Pirates.

**American League publicists** — Mel Franks, Angels; Howie Starkman, Blue Jays; Tom Skibosh, Brewers; Hal Childs, Mariners; Bob Brown, Orioles; Bill Crowley, Red Sox; Dean Vogelaar, Royals; Tom Mee, Twins; Don Unferth, White Sox; and Mickey Morabito, Yankees.

**Corporate publicists** — N.P. Allerup, Pabst Beer; Sy Berger, Topps Chewing Gum Company; Judy Bradley, Rawlings Sporting Goods; Bennett Curry, Hillerich & Bradsby Company; J.Y. Foster, Fair Play Scoreboards; Jim Johnston, Descente Sporting Goods; David Maurer, Insty-Prints; and Lynn A Small, United Air Lines.

**Collectors** — Kevin Barnes, Duke Hott, John Kain, Bill Mazeika, Michael Mercurio, Tom Reid, and A. Kent Sykes.

**Others** — L. Robert Davids, president, Society for American Baseball Research; James E. Holland, attorney, Office of the Commissioner of Baseball; Ed Lucas, broadcaster, WJLK radio, Asbury Park, N.J.; Robert D. Opie, publisher, San Jose, California; Dr. Jim Parkes, team physician, New York Mets; Personalized First Day Covers, Lemon Grove, California.

**Special Mention** — A leading contributor to this book and long-time friend of the author was Larry Chiasson, the late public relations director of the Montreal Expos, whose sudden death in 1978 was a great loss to baseball.

# Contents

FOREWORD BY MILT RICHMAN

AUTHOR'S INTRODUCTION

## CHAPTER ONE
### BEGINNINGS OF BASEBALL     *1*

*Origin, American founders, first teams and leagues, birth of the majors, labor relations and other problems, schedule changes*

## CHAPTER TWO
### HOW SOME RULES APPLY     *9*

*Rule changes through the years, home run records, the designated hitter, balks, famous rules violations, the rain rule, unusual postponements, forfeits*

## CHAPTER THREE
### UMPIRES     *23*

*The basic job, all-time greats, umpiring teams, arguments, unusual decisions, tough calls, stances, recruiting, the umpire today*

## CHAPTER FOUR
### PLAYING THE GAME     *33*

*Keeping score, running and stealing, fielding and defensive strategy, hitting and bunting, strange home runs, pinch-hitters, playing the percentages, pitching, sign-stealing, legal tricks, bench-jockeying*

## CHAPTER FIVE
### EQUIPMENT     *65*

*Uniforms, numbers, shoes, glasses, bats, balls, umpire's equipment*

## CHAPTER SIX
### BALLPARKS     *77*

*Early parks, sites, home run distances, famous old parks, modern stadiums, scoreboards, groundskeeping tricks*

## CHAPTER SEVEN
### THE GAME     *91*

*Sunday ball, night ball, weather, marathons, big scores, the war years, the color line, travel conditions, roommates, fines and fights, injuries, player size and sex, prolonged careers, stunts, benefits*

## CHAPTER EIGHT
### FAMOUS FACES     *119*

*Hank Aaron vs. Babe Ruth, awards, year and career leaders, famous families, "little shots," two-sport stars, baseball's funny men*

## CHAPTER NINE
### MANAGERS     *135*

*Hazards of managing, player-managers, great managers, modern managers, strategy, handling pitchers, coaches*

## CHAPTER TEN
### THE BRASS     *155*

*Government of baseball, commissioners, team executives*

## CHAPTER ELEVEN
### TRADES     *173*

*The art of trading, big deals, unusual transactions, inter-league trading*

# CHAPTER TWELVE
## THE SUPPORTING CAST 185

*Stadium announcers, organists, scoreboard operators, equipment managers, batboys, batting practice pitchers, mascots, wives, concessionaires, vendors, doctors, scouts*

# CHAPTER THIRTEEN
## MEDIA 195

*Writers, changing reporting style, J.G. Taylor Spink, publicists, broadcasting, famous announcers, bloopers, home run calls, the influence of television*

# CHAPTER FOURTEEN
## BIG MOMENTS 207

*Most memorable moments, pennant races, World Series highlights, All-Star Games*

# CHAPTER FIFTEEN
## LANGUAGE OF BASEBALL 233

*Origin of key phrases, famous quotes, baseball slang, team nicknames, player nicknames*

# CHAPTER SIXTEEN
## SUPERSTITIONS & OTHER TRADITIONS 251

*Common superstitions, famous traditions, retired uniform numbers, holding out, the art of chewing, Opening Day, Presidents at the ballpark, farewells, the Hall of Fame*

# CHAPTER SEVENTEEN
## SPRING TRAINING 263

*Sites, accommodations, camps, on and off the field, training in war years, barnstorming home*

# CHAPTER EIGHTEEN
## OTHER LEAGUES, OTHER LANDS 273

*National Association, top teams of the minors, minor league problems and changing map, playing conditions, famous minor-leaguers, major-minor relations, the Federal League, Mexican League, Latin winter leagues, Negro leagues, barnstorming teams, baseball in Japan*

# CHAPTER NINETEEN
## FANS 287

*Promotions and promoters, attendance records, field crowds, the advent of ushers, famous fans, cards and collectors*

# CHAPTER TWENTY
## BASEBALL TODAY 297

*Franchise shifts, expansion, amateur draft, labor unrest, fall of the reserve clause, runaway salaries, how contracts changed, why trading is tougher, player agents, major changes in baseball, modern record-breakers, unusual achievements*

# Foreword

As a boy growing up in the Bronx, my most frequent trips would be to Yankee Stadium – first because it was closest to my home and second because I was passionately in love with the St. Louis Browns, who were so downtrodden and generally forsaken at the time they could do with any little affection they could get.

Now and then, when the Giants were in town, I'd wander over to the horseshoe-shaped Polo Grounds, which had a peculiar fascination for me because of its uncommonly short fences in right and left field. I always thought of the Polo Grounds as a ballpark bounded on the east by the Harlem River, on the west by Coogan's Bluff and on the north and south by the home run.

It was also perpetually surrounded by eager, excited young boys looking for some way to get in and see the ball game.

Such a boy – I am reasonably sure – was little Danny Schlossberg, author of **The Baseball Catalog.** The reason I am so sure is because in writing this book, he has poured into it not only all his energies but all his love for the game of baseball as well.

Watching the uncommon enthusiasm and vigor he puts into his work covering the major league beat, I am not in the least surprised at all the ground he was able to cover in the pages immediately following these.

What he does is almost literally take you out to the ball game, starting appropriately enough with a vivid panorama of the ballparks past and present. More than that, he conjures up visions of what it would've been like had the left handed-hitting Ted Williams spent his career in Yankee Stadium and Joe DiMaggio in Fenway Park. Interestingly, both Williams and DiMaggio have often thought about this same thing themselves.

I remember going out to Yankee Stadium with DiMaggio while it was in the process of being refurbished and remodeled some years ago. There were huge piles of dirt where the infield and outfield once were and the stands were being dismantled, but DiMaggio focused his attention on one particular sector – the left field fence.

He asked the workmen if they were moving it in, as he had heard they had planned to, and when he was given an affirmative answer, DiMaggio nodded and said:

"Now they're bringing it in! Where were they 30 years ago?"

Joe DiMaggio's celebrated 56-game hitting streak is included in these pages for everyone to consider and marvel over again, and such other notable achievements as Roger Maris' 61 homers, Bob Feller's Opening Day no-hitter and Johnny Vander Meer's back-to-back no-hitters also are re-examined under Schlossberg's keen eye for detail.

The title of the book fulfills its promise. It is, indeed, a catalogue of baseball, with everything crammed into it that any red-blooded baseball fan could ask. The ballparks, the equipment, the players, the managers, the owners, the language and the traditions are all there, and more.

Space is even devoted to the hot dog, without which no game ever really is complete. The author talks about how the hot dog first was introduced in the ballparks and then goes into some of the players' eating habits.

One story he does not include, however, has to do with Babe Ruth and a hot dog. It concerns one of the Boston Red Sox relief pitchers summoned in from the bullpen in a game with the Yankees back in the '30s.

The pitcher hadn't figured he'd be called in – not at that precise moment, anyway – and, being hungry, had only a moment or so earlier purchased a frankfurter from one of the passing vendors.

He had taken only one bite out of the hot dog when he suddenly got the call from the dugout to hurry in. Looking toward home plate, he saw Ruth was the next batter and there were two men on base.

"Here," he said, turning the hot dog over to his bullpen catcher. "Hold it for me. I'll be right back."

He was, too.

Dan Schlossberg missed that one, but he didn't miss much else.

**The Baseball Catalog,** like some thing of beauty, is a joy forever. Now go read it, and have the same delightful time that I did.

**Milton Richman**
*Sports Editor*
*United Press International*

AUTHOR'S NOTE: *Milton Richman passed away since writing this foreword. His wit and his wise counsel are missed by those who knew him.*

# Introduction

The Baseball Catalog *was not just written – it was assembled. Gathering the graphics, conducting the interviews, transcribing the tapes, and doing the research consumed hundreds of hours. Sorting the material into chapters was difficult; the writing turned out to be the easiest part of the project.*

*It took nearly two years of concentrated effort to produce this book. At the end, it would have been possible to write a full book on every subject covered.*

*My office became a miniature Hall of Fame, filled with borrowed materials from clubs, friends, and fans. The mailman was especially burdened – bringing an endless avalanche of envelopes for months on end.*

*Without the cooperation of many editor friends and people inside baseball, this volume could not have reflected the true history and scope of the game. Fortunately, the response to my appeals for material was good – both in quality and quantity.*

*During the 1977 National League Championship Series, I combed the files of the Philadelphia Phillies and Los Angeles Dodgers, unearthing such priceless photos as a 1916 shot of Grover Cleveland Alexander and a 1955 picture of Brooklyn's Sandy Koufax trying to locate the strike zone in spring training.*

The Baseball Catalog *meant sitting in a sunny hotel lobby in Hawaii, talking to Monte Irvin about life in the old Negro Leagues. It involved a detailed discussion with New York Mets' team physician Dr. Jim Parkes about proper conditioning and other aspects of baseball medicine.*

*Clyde King provided special insights about train travel during the war years, "spring" training for the Dodgers in Bear Mountain, N.Y., and strategy conferences on the mound.*

*Ralph Kiner, cornered in the lounge of a transcontinental 747, talked about barnstorming, broadcasting, and the trials of being the top star on a bad ballclub.*

*Baltimore super-scout Jim Russo revealed the behind-the-scenes process of big-league trading. Paul Richards, long-time manager and front office figure, and Frank (Trader) Lane supplied specifics on the same subject.*

*Billy Hunter talked about the secrets of the third-base coach – and his extreme importance to a ballclub.*

*So much more went into the pages which follow: sign-stealing, bench-jockeying, traditions, superstitions, pennant races, unusual home runs, handicapped ballplayers, changing salary structure, ballparks, uniforms, transportation to the ballpark, strategy, fights, fines, equipment, the home-field advantage. The list is almost endless. Pulling it all together was a task akin to preparing a volume on American history.*

*A personal favorite is the behavior of celebrities connected with the game: Bing Crosby, James T. Farrell, Ernest Hemingway, James Michener, Danny Kaye, Ring Lardner, Zane Grey, Gene Autry, Sophie Tucker, Hubert Humphrey.*

*Former Chief Justice Earl Warren, in an interview during the 1973 World Series, said, "Baseball is truly the great national pastime. There is always some excitement and a fan can see the values of clean competition, sportsmanship, as well as a display of physical skills and athletic talent that calls for precision and speed."*

*Presidents Herbert Hoover and Dwight D. Eisenhower were fans of the game – and Eisenhower's grandson, David, actually covered baseball as a columnist for a Philadelphia daily.*

*At age 89, Hoover wrote National League President Warren Giles, "I shall tell my doctors baseball has more curative powers than all their medicine."*

*Said Eisenhower: "The more baseball the better. It is a healthful sport and develops team play and initiative, plus an independent attitude."*

*To this writer, assembling* The Baseball Catalog *was a labor of love. It required the skills of a reporter, writer, editor, and even historian.*

*Because I follow no other sport, friends often apply the needle, "You eat, drink, and sleep baseball." In this case, they were right. I turned down invitations to parties, missed the openers of both New York clubs for 1978, and cut short conversations with anyone who dared call while I was working. My concentration on this project was as important to me as Hank Aaron's concentration was to him as he neared Babe Ruth's home run record.*

*My only hope now is that the reader will find as much pleasure reviewing it as I did preparing it.*

**DAN SCHLOSSBERG**

*To Ezra Schlossberg,*
*in loving memory*

# CHAPTER ONE
# BEGINNINGS OF BASEBALL

# BRITISH ORIGIN OF BASEBALL

In Spalding's *Base Ball Guide of 1903*, English-born editor Henry Chadwick traced the origin of the game to the British sports of rounders, town ball, and one old cat:

"More than seventy years ago, when I was a schoolboy in England," he wrote, "my favorite field sport was the game of rounders. This was played with an ordinary ball and with stout, round sticks as bats.

"After schooltime, we boys would proceed to the nearest playing field, select a smooth portion of it, and lay out the ground for a contest. This was easily done by placing four stones, or posts, in position as base stations, and by digging a hole in the ground where the batsman had to stand.

"We then tossed for sides and innings and started the game. Custom made the rules of play, as there was no written code to govern the game."

In the eighteenth century, shortly before the American Revolution, a poem called "Base Ball" appeared in *A Little Pretty Pocket Book*. It was first published in Great Britain in 1744 and reprinted in Worcester, Massachusetts in 1787. It read:

> The ball once struck off,
> Away flies the boy
> To the next destined point,
> And then home with joy.

These early accounts cast considerable doubt on the long-standing theory that Abner Doubleday "invented" baseball at the sleepy village of Cooperstown, New York in 1839. Though a 1907 special commission lent credence to the Doubleday story—perhaps in an attempt to give America credit for the game's origin—later research indicates Doubleday was a plebe at West Point in 1839 and probably did not get to Cooperstown that year.

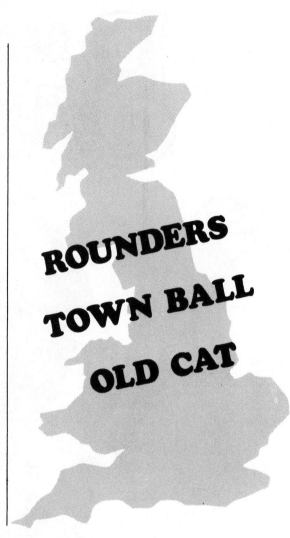

ROUNDERS
TOWN BALL
OLD CAT

# ALEXANDER CARTWRIGHT: FATHER OF BASEBALL

The Baseball Hall of Fame in Cooperstown gives Alexander Cartwright the title, "Father of Modern Base Ball." That inscription decorates his plaque in the Hall of Fame's gallery.

Cartwright was a teller at the Union Bank of New York in 1845 when he organized the first regular team, the Knickerbockers, and wrote rules to govern the sport. A talented draftsman, he set bases 90 feet apart, established nine players on a side, three outs per inning, and an unchangeable batting order.

The loosely-organized games played at the time consisted of teams with eleven to twenty players each. Bases were made of stakes, stones, or sand-filled sacks that could be kicked away by fielders. Runners were put out—literally—when fielders plunked them in the middle of the back with the baseball. ☞

Cartwright developed the concept of a nine-inning game later. The first game played under his rules ended when the New York Nine scored its 21st run (then called an ace) in the fourth inning (called a hand). New York added two more, the Knickerbockers took their final turn at bat, and the game ended in a 23-1 defeat for the home team. The site was the Elysian Fields, Hoboken, New Jersey, on June 19, 1846.

A talented pitcher, Cartwright served as umpire in that first game. His goal was to make both sides understand the new rules, and he succeeded. Cartwright was fair but stern; he fined a New York Nine player named Davis six cents for swearing.

By 1849, the Knickerbockers had reached such a level of respectability that they wore uniforms for the first time, and in 1857, the nine-inning format replaced the 21-run rule.

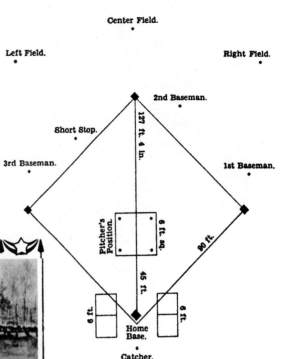

## BASE BALL AT HOBOKEN

NEW YORK, July 6, 1853.

*Friend P.*—The first friendly game of the season, between the Gotham and Knickerbocker Base Ball Clubs was played on the grounds of the latter. The game was commenced on Friday the 1st, but owing to the storm had to be postponed, the Knickerbockers making nine aces to two of the Gotham.

# THE FIRST LEAGUE

The National Association of Baseball Clubs, the first league, was organized in New York in 1857, and the Fashion Race Course in Jamaica, New York was declared the site for all games. The season ran from July to October because the players felt it was too warm to play in May and June. Perhaps the weather pattern has changed, but the "dog days of August" have wilted pennant hopes of contenders throughout the modern era, which began in 1901.

In 1858, there was evidence that baseball was catching fire with the fans. Spectators paid 50 cents each to see Brooklyn and New York clash at the Fashion Race Course; attendance was 1500.

Two years later, the Excelsiors of Brooklyn became the first team to go on tour. Twice during a five-game swing upstate, they scored more than 50 runs in a game, and they returned home undefeated.

Championship Boston team of 1874 included Harry Wright (center), who founded first professional team, Cincinnati Red Stockings of 1869. Standing to his left is Al Spalding, who posted 57-7 record in 1875 and helped found the National League a year later.

## Abe Lincoln Played Baseball

*Abraham Lincoln was playing in a closely contested baseball game in 1860 when a message arrived for him. He told the messenger not to interrupt him during the game. Afterward, he found out he had been nominated for President by the Republican Party.*

TCMA

Some baseball historians insist this old ball was used by youths who "invented" baseball at Cooperstown, N.Y. in 1839.

## THE FIRST PROFESSIONAL TEAM

Baseball fever boomed in 1860, when the Olympic Town Ball Club of Philadelphia, organized in 1833, decided to abandon the imported British sport of town ball and play baseball instead.

By 1869, Harry Wright, originally a cricket player, had gathered nine other top players to form the Cincinnati Red Stockings, the first professional team. Though the average player did not earn much more than $1,000 that season, the Red Stockings were more concerned with pride than price; they went undefeated in 69 games (there was one tie) and launched an amazing 130-game winning streak that did not end until June 14, 1870.

Only once did Cincinnati fail to score 16 or more runs in a game, and one of their decisions was a 103-8 triumph over the Buckeyes. The team was so popular that President Ulysses S. Grant received them in the White House.

The Red Stockings, named for their scarlet hose, kindled the establishment of the National Association of Professional Baseball Players in 1871, but the first pro league was riddled with constant franchise and player shifting, plus the influence of gamblers and other unsavory characters in the ballparks. Tinged with dishonesty, the league lost its fans and folded.

### Lopsided Scores

*Early handicaps on hurlers helped hitters immensely. Forest City, based in Cleveland, beat the Brooklyn Atlantics 132-1 in a five-inning game in 1870. In another game that year Forest City scored 90 runs in the first inning, and had the bases loaded with nobody out, when rain halted play at Utica, New York.*

### Spalding's Sensational Season

*In 1875, one year before the formation of the National League (and several years before modern pitching rules were established), A.G. Spalding of Boston (National Association) posted a 57-7 record, using only fastballs and curves.*

## THE NATIONAL LEAGUE

William A. Hulbert, owner of the Chicago National Association club, and Boston pitcher A.G. Spalding then laid the groundwork for the National League, with authority concentrated among the team owners and a strong constitution to protect the game's integrity.

A 70-game schedule was drawn up for the eight-club circuit, but the New York Mutuals and Philadelphia Athletics were expelled before season's end for failing to take their final western roadtrips. Admission to games was 50 cents, or 10 cents to those who arrived after the third inning.

Well into the 1880s, batters ordered their pitches, and runners interfered with fielders trying to make plays. Pitchers were obliged to throw underhand until 1881 and faced numerous other restrictions that remained in force until 1884. Their distance from batters was much closer until 1893, when the current standard of 60 feet, 6 inches was introduced—quite by accident.

Pitching distance had been 45 feet until 1881, then 50, then "60 feet, 0 inches." The surveyor misread the "0" as a "6" and the mistake was never corrected.

In the early days of the game, proximity to home plate allowed hurlers to work more and win more. Old Hoss Radbourn won 60 and lost 12 for Providence of the National League in 1884. In the modern era, it would take a star pitcher three seasons to win that many.

SINCE 1876
NATIONAL LEAGUE
OF PROFESSIONAL BASEBALL CLUBS

# EARLY PROBLEMS IN THE GAME

One of the National League's biggest problems was constant player movement between seasons. In 1879, the first reserve rule was invoked. Clubs were allowed to place five men "on reserve" so that other teams would not sign them for the following year. The list gradually grew from five to fifteen and, finally, to the entire roster.

The best test of the reserve clause was the creation of a second major league, the American Association, in 1882. At first, it competed for the Nationals' players, as did the Union Association (which lasted only for the 1884 season), but the AA eventually came to terms with the older NL.

National League president Abraham Mills was hailed as "the Bismarck of baseball" when he signed the first National Agreement with the American Association in 1883. The pact set up an 11-player reserve list, guaranteed territorial rights, set minimum salaries at $1000, and even created a post-season series between league champions—the first "World Series."

Players deemed it an honor to be placed on reserve because those who weren't were not considered valuable by their teams. But the reserve clause allowed owners to deal out arbitrary salary cuts because it forbade free movement of players between teams.

# LABOR VS. MANAGEMENT

Player-owner friction, which reached an explosive climax with the demolition of the reserve clause in 1975, is almost as old as the game itself. Noting that owners were using the reserve clause to keep salaries of stars at low levels in the 1880s, law school graduate John Montgomery Ward, top star of the New York Giants, started a union called the Brotherhood of Professional Base Ball Players.

Among other things, Ward wanted each team to lift its arbitrary salary ceiling. Following the 1888 season, the owners agreed, and a delighted Ward set sail with Albert Spalding on a round-the-world baseball tour. When he returned in March 1889, he found the players about to strike because the owners had reneged on their promises. Ward urged them to play that year with an eye out for investors in a new league.

In 1890, many of the game's stars drifted to the new Players League, which put teams in seven of eight National League cities. The exodus of players crippled the American Association and weakened the National, which coaxed many of its players to return the following year. Several Players League backers bought into the NL.

Because National League owners took an estimated $500,000 bath when the Players League drained it of top talent, economy became mandatory. Ed Delahanty's salary was slashed from $2100 to $1800 and lefthanded catcher John Clements went from $3000 to $1800.

## Red Stockings Were Nonchalant

*The Cincinnati Red Stockings took winning so matter-of-factly that when pitcher Asa Brainard spotted a rabbit on the field during a game, he threw the ball at it as two runners scored.*

## Strong-Armed Pitcher

*One-armed Cleveland pitcher Hugh Daily no-hit Philadelphia, 1-0, in 1883.*

## Old Hoss Was Warhorse

*Old Hoss Radbourn, who won 309 games in eleven seasons, was the winning pitcher in the most lopsided shutout of all time—a 28-0 win for Providence over Philadelphia on August 21, 1883.*

In 1896, New York Giants' pitcher Amos Rusie sat out the entire season because the team attempted to deduct a $200 fine from his contract. A series of lawsuits eventually persuaded the league to cough up the $3000 he had demanded.

Teams were understood to have a per player salary limit of $2400 and a club ceiling of $30,000. They were not bound to pay injured or ill athletes, and the Baltimore Orioles were commended for a "humanitarian" gesture after they paid John McGraw $1200 upon his return from a long bout with typhoid fever.

The collapse of the Players League and American Association left the National with an unwieldy 12-club structure dissimilar from that created by the second wave of expansion in 1969. The original 12-team format was not broken into divisions, thereby enabling a team to suffer the ignominy of a 12th-place finish. Four NL teams were dropped after the 1899 campaign, restoring the league to eight members.

# THE AMERICAN LEAGUE

What was to become the American League surfaced for the first time in 1900 as the American Association. When this new circuit began, it announced goals of fostering honest competition without the reserve rule and supporting itself by luring big crowds with low ticket prices.

Created from the remains of the Western League, which Ban Johnson served as president, the American League took its present name on November 14, 1900, with a lineup that included Baltimore, Buffalo, Chicago, Cleveland, Detroit, Milwaukee, Philadelphia, and Washington.

Eight AL teams played a 140-game schedule with 14-man rosters in 1901. The Chicago White Sox recorded the best attendance—354,350—as the circuit drew a combined total of 1,683,584. Both Chicago and Boston drew more fans than National League rivals in those cities.

League players came primarily from National League teams. The prize was Napoleon Lajoie, who jumped crosstown from the Phils to the A's and hit .422, highest in league history. The star second-baseman was later barred from playing in Philadelphia because of the intra-city squabble over his services, and was sold to Cleveland. When the Indians visited Philadelphia, Lajoie languished on the beach in nearby Atlantic City, New Jersey.

More than 110 of the American League's 185 players had National League experience, including Baltimore player-manager

---

*CLEVELAND PLAIN DEALER*

# THE SEASON IS OPEN

## Cleveland and Chicago Had the Day to Themselves

### HOFFER'S WILDNESS LOST THE GAME

Philadelphia-Washington, rain
Baltimore-Boston, rain
Detroit-Milwaukee, rain
Chicago 8-Cleveland 2
*Special to the Plain Dealer*

CHICAGO, April 24—McAleer's men had two disastrous innings today, the first and second, then steadied down and played hard ball, but Comiskey's aggregation had turned into the home stretch and the game was won and lost. Hoffer could not control the ball in these two innings, apparently unable to get it far below the shoulder. He steadied wonderfully in the third and pitched good ball the remainder of the game. The season opening was a great success.

Resplendent in their new white suits and marching with proud steps to strains of music by the Rough Riders' Band, the champion White Stockings were led by Clark Griffith from their club house to the field, encircled it twice and assembled about the flagpole on the extreme northeast corner of the park, where the championship pennant, won by hard and consistent playing last year, was flung to the breeze.

When the ceremonies at the flagpole were concluded and the White Stockings had pulled the bit of white bunting to the top, the two teams—Comiskey's champions and McAleer's Clevelanders—marched abreast to the diamond. Robert E. Burke arose and delivered a short speech to the ball tossers, complimenting the local aggregation on their prowess of last year and wishing them the same good fortune for the season on 1901. He then tossed a new ball into the diamond. Umpire Connolly handed it to pitcher Patterson, who did the club honors for the White Sox, and at 3:35 o'clock the first game of the season was on.

The grandstand was decorated with flags and bunting, draped gracefully about the boxes and the entire front of the stand. Back of the decorations and filling the stand to the utmost, as well as the bleachers, 9,000 "fans" were assembled. With critical eyes, they marked the playing of last year's stars, as well as the new acquisitions from the National League—Mertes, Jones, Sullivan, Bradley and McCarthy. In practice just prior to the game, these men were greeted with rounds of applause.

The weather could not have been more ideal for a ball game. The bright sun dried the diamond and made the outfield hard and fast. It was warm and balmy and a light refreshing breeze blew across the park from the lake. Roy Patterson and "Boston" Sullivan were chosen by Manager Griffith as the battery to represent the champions in the opening game, while Hoffer and "Bob" Wood were the battery for the visitors.

Pickering was the first Clevelander up; and he caught the second ball Patterson pitched, sending a long fly to "Dummy" Hoy in center field. McCarthy, the ex-National Leaguer, was given a cane and umbrella and he answered by swatting a sizzling grounder to Hartman. The third baseman tried to get it, but it struck his foot and caromed off; Shugart finally picked it up, but McCarthy reached first. Then Genins sent an easy fly to Hoy, and LaChance went out on a grounder to Brain. Chicago, aided by Hoffer, started to win the game in the first inning. In this act he gave three men bases on balls and allowed Hartman to single, netting three runs.

### CLEVELAND

|  | AB | R | H | PO | A |
|---|---|---|---|---|---|
| Ollie Pickering, rf | 4 | 0 | 1 | 0 | 0 |
| John McCarthy, lf | 4 | 0 | 2 | 4 | 0 |
| Frank Genins, cf | 4 | 0 | 0 | 1 | 0 |
| George LaChance, 1b | 4 | 1 | 1 | 13 | 0 |
| Bill Bradley, 3b | 4 | 0 | 0 | 2 | 5 |
| Erve Beck, 2b | 3 | 0 | 2 | 0 | 4 |
| Bill Hallman, ss | 3 | 1 | 0 | 1 | 3 |
| Bob Wood, c | 4 | 0 | 1 | 2 | 2 |
| Bill Hoffer, p | 4 | 0 | 0 | 1 | 1 |
| Totals | 34 | 2 | 7 | 24 | 15 |

### CHICAGO

|  | AB | R | H | PO | A |
|---|---|---|---|---|---|
| Billy Hoy, cf | 5 | 0 | 1 | 3 | 0 |
| Fielder Jones, rf | 2 | 2 | 1 | 4 | 0 |
| Sam Mertes, lf | 3 | 2 | 1 | 4 | 0 |
| Frank Shugart, ss | 3 | 2 | 0 | 4 | 4 |
| Frank Isbell, 1b | 2 | 1 | 1 | 8 | 0 |
| Fred Hartman, 3b | 4 | 0 | 1 | 0 | 5 |
| Dave Brain, 2b | 4 | 0 | 0 | 1 | 3 |
| Billy Sullivan, c | 4 | 1 | 2 | 2 | 0 |
| Roy Patterson, p | 4 | 0 | 0 | 1 | 1 |
| Totals | 31 | 8 | 7 | 27 | 13 |

| Cleveland | 000 010 100—2 |
| Chicago | 250 000 10x—8 |

E—Hartman, LaChance, Hallman. 2b—Beck. DP—Brain, Shugart and Isbell; Hoffer, Hallman and LaChance. LOB—Cleveland 3, Chicago 5.
BB—Patterson 2, Hoffer 6. SO—Hoffer 1.
Umpire—Connolly. Time—1:30.

John McGraw. Early in the year, McGraw discovered a talented black secondbaseman, Charlie Grant, and attempted to circumvent the unwritten "color line" by informing rivals that Grant was a full-blooded Cherokee named Tokomoma. The ruse failed.

In a rough-and-tumble season, the AL's best-educated battery belonged to the Athletics: lefthanded pitcher Eddie Plank, from Gettysburg College, and Dr. Mike Powers, a catcher from Notre Dame.

By January 1903, the American achieved major status when a new National Agreement was drawn and ratified in Cincinnati. Two AL franchises had shifted—Baltimore to New York and Milwaukee to St. Louis—and Boston had replaced Buffalo. The National of that year had Boston, Brooklyn, Chicago, Cincinnati, New York, Philadelphia, Pittsburgh, and St. Louis.

There were no further changes in the baseball map until 1953, when the Boston Braves shook the sports world by moving to Milwaukee. (The outlaw Federal League of 1914-15 failed in its brief challenge to the majors.)

With the 1903 agreement between leagues, the reserve rule was tightened. It read, "Contracts with players must be respected under the penalties specified. The right and title of a major league club to its players shall be absolute, and can only be terminated by release or failure to reserve under the rules of the agreement by the club to which a player has been under contract."

# PROTECTION OF THE MINORS

The agreement also guaranteed the independence of minor league teams and prohibited a big-league club from "farming" a player to the minors. Branch Rickey, a colorful and innovative executive, later reversed that concept.

The major-minor relationship in 1903 stipulated that big-league teams could purchase players from the minors (called the National Association) between August 15 and October 15 for the following prices: $750 from Class A (the highest minor league), $500 from Class B, $300 from Class C, and $200 from Class D.

Though those prices seem low from the perspective of the late 1970s—where the minimum major league salary was $21,000—money was low in volume but high in value in the early days of the game. A little went a long way.

Consider this: the first National League franchises, in 1876, sold for $100 each. Five years earlier, National Association franchises went for just $10. Umpires worked gratis until 1883, then were paid $5 per game by the home team. In 1888, visiting clubs received 15 cents from each paid admission to the ballpark. And clubs deducted from player salaries $30 per season for uniform costs and 50 cents per day for meal money.

When the champion Boston club of the National Association made a season's profit of $2,261.07 in 1875, other team executives were startled. Baseball was not known as a profit-making business.

Once the major leagues solidified, however, profits climbed as clubs in both circuits played constant schedules under practical rules that stabilized at the same time as the two leagues.

# HOW THE SCHEDULE CHANGED

When the National League began operation in 1876, its eight members played schedules of 70 games each. As the league's size and membership varied, so did the schedule, finally climbing to 112 games in 1884 and 126 two years later.

By 1901, when the American shattered the National's monopoly on big-league baseball, the two circuits were playing 140 games each. That increased to 154 games in 1904. Each club played its rivals 22 times—11 home and 11 away.

With expansion to ten-team leagues in 1961-62 came extension of the schedule to 162 contests—nine home and nine away for each team against each rival. The advent of divisional play in 1969 did not destroy the 162-game concept but did jettison the idea that each team should play a constant number of games against each rival.

Under divisional schedules, intra-division clubs, such as the New York Mets and Philadelphia Phillies, play each other 18 times—nine home and nine away—but face inter-division clubs, such as the Los Angeles Dodgers, only 12 times—six and six.

All games count in the standings, with a best-of-five championship series to determine the league's pennant-winner.

The first unbalanced 162-game schedule was created with American League expansion to 14 clubs in 1977. It lasted only two seasons.

In 1979, the league adopted a slate that called for each team in the two seven-team divisions to play each opponent 12 times—six home and six away—for a total of 156 games. Clubs then play each intra-divisional rival one additional game.

## BATTING RECORD
### Of Clubs Members of the National League of Professional Base Ball Clubs,
### SEASON OF 1876.

| NAME OF CLUB. | WHERE LOCATED. | No. of Games played. | No. of Games won. | Times at bat. | Runs scored. | Average per game. | Runs earned. | Average per game. | 1st Bases. | Percentage of base hits per time at bat. |
|---|---|---|---|---|---|---|---|---|---|---|
| Chicago | Chicago, Ill. | 66 | 52 | 2,818 | 624 | 9.45 | 267 | 4.03 | 926 | .328 |
| Hartford | Hartford, Conn. | 69 | 47 | 2,703 | 429 | 6.22 | 154 | 2.23 | 711 | .264 |
| St. Louis | St. Louis, Mo. | 64 | 45 | 2,536 | 386 | 6.03 | 109 | 1.70 | 642 | .253 |
| Boston | Boston, Mass. | 70 | 39 | 2,780 | 471 | 6.73 | 167 | 2.38 | 723 | .260 |
| Louisville | Louisville, Ky. | 69 | 30 | 2,594 | 280 | 4.06 | 107 | 1.55 | 641 | .247 |
| Mutual | Brooklyn, N.Y. | 57 | 21 | 2,202 | 260 | 4.55 | 72 | 1.26 | 494 | .223 |
| Athletic | Philadelphia, Pa. | 60 | 14 | 2,414 | 378 | 6.30 | 145 | 2.41 | 646 | .267 |
| Cincinnati | Cincinnati, O. | 65 | 9 | 2,413 | 238 | 3.66 | 77 | 1.18 | 555 | .230 |
| | Total | 520 | 257 | 20,460 | 3066 | 5.89 | 1098 | 2.11 | 5338 | .261 |

Tie Games Played—LOUISVILLE, 8; ATHLETIC, 1; HARTFORD, 1

## A Towering Achievement
On August 25, 1894, Chicago NL catcher William Schriver became the first player to catch a ball thrown from the top of the Washington Monument.

# CHAPTER TWO

# How Some Rules Apply

Boston Braves double-play partners Alvin Dark (left) and Eddie Stanky knew the rules
so well that both became major league managers.

# RULES AND RECORDS

Baseball rules are constantly changing and, because of that fact, old records that are broken must be viewed in light of rule changes that have been made.

In 1879, a pitcher had to throw nine balls to give up a walk and, in 1887, it took four strikes to get a man out. At one time, the catcher stood 20 or more feet behind the batter, and the pitcher got credit for a strike even when his pitch bounced before passing through the strike zone. The batter (called striker) received credit for a hit when he walked, and the runner got a stolen base each time he advanced on a teammate's hit.

For a while, bases on balls counted as hits, inflating batting averages of early players.

# SUDDEN DEATH HOME RUNS

Rule changes had a great effect on home run kings Babe Ruth and Hank Aaron. Did Ruth actually hit 714 lifetime home runs or 716? And did Aaron really have 714 to his credit when he broke Ruth's record on April 8, 1974?

On September 8, 1918, Ruth was a hard-hitting pitcher for the Boston Red Sox. With a man on first in the bottom of the ninth inning of a tie game, he came to bat against Cleveland and hit the ball over the fence. Under present-day rules that would be a home run—but it wasn't then.

A sudden death rule was in effect in 1918. Once the winning run scored, the game was automatically over. So Ruth was given only a triple, since it took three bases to force home the decisive tally.

Little more than a year later, on September 20, an overflow crowd was standing behind a roped-off area in front of the bleachers at Boston's Fenway Park. The Red Sox and White Sox agreed before the game that any ball hit into the crowd would be a triple. Ruth hit a ball over the crowd and into the bleachers, but it struck something hard and bounced back into the crowd. The umpire couldn't tell whether the ball cleared the wall, and incorrectly awarded three bases to Ruth—even though he had actually hit a home run.

Babe Ruth and Hank Aaron (opposite) were the only men in baseball history to hit more than 700 home runs. Though the records list their career totals as 714 and 755, respectively, varying interpretations of the rules leave those figures open to debate.

## THE 325-FOOT FENCE RULE

Rule 1.04, Official Baseball Rules, 1978 edition, stipulates that any playing field built after June 1, 1958 shall have a minimum distance of 325 feet from home plate to the nearest fence and 400 feet from home to the center field fence. It also says that remodeling of existing fields after June 1, 1958 may not include shortening of fences below the 325-foot standard.

## The 210-Foot Fence Rule

In 1884, the National League passed a rule mandating a minimum distance for outfield fences at 210 feet. Since the Chicago White Stockings' fence was located just 196 feet from home plate, balls hit over the fence became automatic doubles.

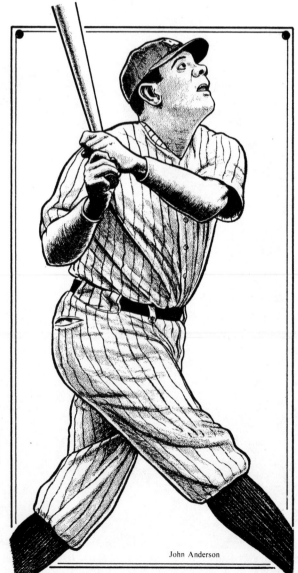

John Anderson

## HOW THE GAME CHANGES

*Each game is different. Red Sox hurler Hub Leonard proved that in 1916, when he pitched a no-hitter against the Browns one day after the same club had knocked him out in the first inning!*

## YOUNGEST PERFECT GAME PITCHER

*Jim (Catfish) Hunter had just turned 22 when he pitched a perfect game against the Minnesota Twins for the Oakland A's in 1968. He was the youngest man to pitch a perfect game.*

Atlanta Braves

# HOME RUNS AFTER 1954

By 1954, nearly twenty years after Ruth's retirement, rules governing home runs had changed in certain respects, some beneficial to Ruth and others to Hank Aaron, who started his career that season.

Balls that cleared the fence fair but landed foul were considered nothing more than long strikes for Ruth, but counted as home runs for Aaron. Conversely, balls that bounced over the wall on one hop were homers for Ruth but ground-rule doubles for Aaron.

The new home run king, who ended his career in 1976 with a career count of 755, missed a definite homer on August 18, 1965 when his clout onto the roof of Sportsman's Park, St. Louis, was ruled an out by umpire Chris Pelekoudas.

Aaron was particularly incensed, since his victim was crafty lefthander Curt Simmons, a long-time nemesis. Pelekoudas made the call when Cardinal catcher Bob Uecker pointed out that Aaron's back foot was out of the batter's box when he took his stance.

A rule dictates that the batter must remain in the box until the pitcher delivers the ball—but Uecker wisely kept quiet about it until the appropriate moment. The umpire is not obligated to cite the batter for such an infraction unless the opposing team appeals.

There is no way to document how many home runs Ruth and Aaron hit without credit because of rained-out games (anything less than five innings, or four-and-a-half with the home team ahead). Baseball historians have settled on final figures of 755 for Aaron and 714 for Ruth.

These figures reflect only regular-season games, with All-Star and World Series totals excluded.

# THE DESIGNATED HITTER

A hitter may be designated to bat for the starting pitcher and all subsequent pitchers in any game without otherwise affecting the status of the pitcher(s) in the game. A Designated Hitter for the pitcher must be selected prior to the game and must be included in the lineup cards presented to the Umpire In Chief.

It is not mandatory that a club designate a hitter for the pitcher, but failure to do so prior to the game precludes the use of a Designated Hitter for that game.

Pinch hitters for a Designated Hitter may be used. Any substitute hitter for a Designated Hitter becomes the Designated Hitter. A replaced Designated Hitter shall not re-enter the game in any capacity.

The Designated Hitter may be used defensively, continuing to bat in the same position in the batting order, but the pitcher must then bat in the place of the substituted defensive player, unless more than one substitution is made, and the manager then must designate their spots in the batting order.

A runner may be substituted for the Designated Hitter and the runner assumes the role of Designated Hitter. A Designated Hitter may not pinch run.

A Designated Hitter is "locked" into the batting order. No multiple substitutions may be made that will alter the batting rotation of the Designated Hitter.

Once the game pitcher is switched from the mound to a defensive position this move shall terminate the Designated Hitter role for the remainder of the game.

Once a pinch hitter bats for any player in the batting order and then enters the game to pitch, this move shall terminate the Designated Hitter role for the remainder of the game.

Once the game pitcher bats for the Designated Hitter this move shall terminate the Designated Hitter role for the remainder of the game. (The game pitcher may only pinch-hit for the Designated Hitter.)

Once a Designated Hitter assumes a defensive position this move shall terminate the Designated Hitter role for the remainder of the game. A substitute for the Designated Hitter need not be announced until it is the Designated Hitter's turn to bat.

*—Official Baseball Rules, 1978*

The most radical baseball rule change of the twentieth century was the introduction of the designated hitter by the American League in 1973. Though it was first suggested by National League president John A. Heydler in 1928, and formally presented to baseball's Rules Committee by Pacific Coast League president Dewey Soriano in 1961, the recommendation lay dormant until the International League adopted it as an experiment in 1969. AL owners finally adopted the DH as a three-year experiment late in 1972, after eight of the twelve league clubs lost money and nine failed to draw 1,000,000 customers.

The rule allows a specified player to take the batting turn of the weakest hitter in the lineup (usually the pitcher) without entering the contest. The player who yields his batting spot to the DH does not have to leave the game—though a man who yields to a traditional pinch-hitter must.

# WHAT THE CRITICS SAY

Critics contend that the rule denies good-hitting pitchers the built-in edge they normally have over weak-hitting rival pitchers. They say it interferes with managerial strategy, such as whether to use a late-inning pinch-hitter for the pitcher, whom to choose, and what relief pitcher should be called into action.

Another anti-DH argument is that the rule extends the careers of "over-the-hill" stars and allows "incomplete" players (hitters who can't run or throw) to remain in the majors.

Supporters suggest the DH improves the offense and makes the game more exciting. When the International League tried the rule in 1969, the overall batting average of its top team climbed 17 points. Designated hitters batted .261 with 108 homers and 472 runs batted in. A year earlier, pitchers hit only .160 with 24 home runs and 204 runs batted in.

In 1975, both major leagues proved almost equal in overall batting average (.257 for the NL and .258 for the AL) though playing under different rules. Because of the DH, American League clubs outscored NL counterparts, averaging 8.6 runs per game against 8.2. AL hitters averaged 1.52 home runs per game, as opposed to 1.27 in the NL. The designated hitters produced 222 home runs and 960 runs batted in on a .254 batting average, while NL pitchers hit just .150 with 10 home runs and 284 RBI.

In the first three years of the DH rule, the overall American League batting average was .258. In 1972, the last year pitchers hit in that league, it was .239.

# VIEWS OF THE LEAGUE PRESIDENTS

Naturally, the two major league presidents had opposite viewpoints as to the value of the DH rule. National League chief executive Chub Feeney said, "Baseball is a game of teams which emphasizes individuals in competition. Use of the DH takes something away from the game. Baseball has always been the hardest game to play because any player must be a whole athlete—able to do everything." ☞

## SLUGGERS "ESCAPED" DH

*Four sluggers who reached the Hall of Fame might not have attained stardom had the designated hitter rule applied when they played. The four—Babe Ruth, George Sisler, Ted Williams, and Stan Musial—all began their careers as pitchers.*

The hitting talent of Ted Williams, Babe Ruth, and Stan Musial might have remained a secret if the designated hitter rule were in force when they played.

Lee MacPhail of the American said the rule restored balance to a game which had begun to overemphasize pitching and defense. He also noted that league attendance had jumped since its inception. "While it would be preferable if both leagues followed identical playing rules," he explained, "the situation in the National League with respect to offensive/defensive balance is dissimilar to ours because most of their parks have artificial turf—an innovation which has changed the game as much as the designated hitter rule."

# THE DH IN THE WORLD SERIES

Though the designated hitter rule was adopted in time for the 1973 season, agreement to use it in World Series games (or even meaningless spring training games) was not reached for several years. The AL wanted it, the NL did not, and Commissioner Bowie Kuhn had to settle the stalemate. He ruled that the DH can be used in years that the World Series begins in the home park of the American League club. It was first used in 1976, but backfired on the AL Yankees when Dan Driessen, the first National League DH, helped the Cincinnati Reds to a four-game sweep.

# REACTION TO THE DH

When the designated hitter rule was first enacted, several pitchers objected. Terry Forster, then with the Chicago White Sox, had the strongest argument after he hit .519 (10-for-19) in 1972, and knocked in the winning run as a pinch-hitter for third baseman Hank Allen in a late-season game.

In 1973, Oakland A's manager Dick Williams prepared for the World Series by using four pitchers as pinch-hitters in one game. Catfish Hunter singled, Ken Holtzman walked, Darold Knowles hit a sacrifice fly, and Vida Blue struck out.

The following season, Texas Rangers pitcher Ferguson Jenkins, the only pitcher to appear in an AL lineup as a hitter that year, singled in the sixth to break up a no-hitter and scored the first run as he beat Minnesota, 2-1, to win his 25th game.

The DH prolonged the careers of Orlando Cepeda, Tommy Davis, Billy Williams, Rico Carty, Harmon Killebrew, and even Hank Aaron, who hit his 755th and last home run in that role in 1976.

# THE BALK RULE

8.05 If there is a runner, or runners, it is a balk when—
(a) The pitcher, while touching his plate, makes any motion naturally associated with his pitch and fails to make such delivery;
(b) The pitcher, while touching his plate, feints a throw to first base and fails to complete the throw;
(c) The pitcher, while touching his plate, fails to step directly toward a base before throwing to that base;
(d) The pitcher, while touching his plate, throws, or feints a throw, to an unoccupied base, except for the purpose of making a play;
(e) The pitcher makes an illegal pitch;
(f) The pitcher delivers the ball to the batter while he is not facing the batter;

## DH DIDN'T HINDER HOLTZMAN

*Though he did not bat during the season because of the American League's designated hitter rule, Oakland A's pitcher Ken Holtzman hit well during World Series play in 1973-74. His pair of doubles in '73 led to rallies which helped Oakland beat the Mets, while his double and home run contributed to another world title the following fall.*

## SLUGGER CATFISH

*Among pitchers who objected to the designated hitter rule was Jim (Catfish) Hunter, who once received a $5,000 bonus from Oakland A's owner Charley Finley for his hitting ability.*

## WILHELM COULD HAVE USED DH

*Hoyt Wilhelm, who worked most of his record 1,070 games as a pitcher in the American League, could have used a designated hitter. He homered in his first at-bat for the 1952 New York Giants, but never homered again in a twenty-one-year career.*

(g) The pitcher makes any motion naturally associated with his pitch while he is not touching the pitcher's plate;

(h) The pitcher unnecessarily delays the game;

(i) The pitcher, without having the ball, stands on or astride the pitcher's plate or while off the plate, he feints a pitch;

(j) The pitcher, after coming to a legal pitching position, removes one hand from the ball other than in an actual pitch, or in throwing to a base;

(k) The pitcher, while touching his plate, accidentally or intentionally drops the ball;

(l) The pitcher, while giving an intentional base on balls, pitches when the catcher is not in the catcher's box;

(m) The pitcher delivers the pitch from Set Position without coming to a stop.

—*Official Baseball Rules*, 1978

The first balk rule was enacted in 1898 and refined two years later, ostensibly to provide protection for base-runners who were constant victims of deceiving movements by pitchers.

The basic balk is a motion to deliver the ball to home plate or first base that is not followed through. When it occurs, base-runners are entitled to move up one base. If a batter hits a ball delivered during a balk, play proceeds without penalty. Nor does the rule apply when bases are clear.

When he is ready to deliver the ball, the pitcher must have his back heel in contact with the rubber, a 24 x 6-inch slab imbedded in the pitcher's mound. A balk may be called if a pitcher touches the rubber when he does *not* have the ball.

In 1963 and 1978, National League umpires were ordered by the league to enforce the balk rule to the letter. Minor "balk wars" ensued as pitchers charged the arbiters were overstepping their bounds.

Variations between leagues in interpreting the balk rule caused a minor controversy prior to the 1975 World Series because Red Sox star Luis Tiant had developed a tricky pick-off move which, according to NL standards, seemed to be a balk. Tiant still won two of his club's three triumphs against the Reds that fall.

Rare calls of the balk rule occur when a pitcher drops the ball by accident. This happened to Red Sox reliever Sparky Lyle against the Yankees in 1969, and a run scored as a result. It also happened to Boston's Diego Segui, who balked home the winning run in May 1974 when hitter Jerry Terrell of Minnesota reached down to pick up some dirt and Segui stopped his motion.

# RULES VIOLATIONS

Violation of baseball rules often proves costly—to both team and individual. Under pennant pressure, mistakes happen and the most fundamental rules are not followed.

For example, it is illegal to pass preceding runners on the bases. Runners must touch all bases in order (or reverse order when forced to return *except* on a home run or ground-rule "automatic," which requires the runner to start at his original route).

Runners may not return to missed bases if a following runner has scored. Runners must touch the next base safely when forced to advance. All plays must be completed.

The defensive team may appeal that a runner has missed a base and, if correct, the umpire will call the runner out when the defensive team tags the base while in possession of the ball.

Boston Red Sox

Controversial pickoff move—which might have been considered a balk by some National League umpires—did not prevent Boston's Luis Tiant from winning two games in the 1975 World Series.

# "MERKLE'S BONER"

The most famous rules violation in baseball history was "Merkle's boner" of September 24, 1908. The New York Giants and Chicago Cubs, fighting for the National League pennant, were locked in a 1-1 tie in the ninth inning at New York when the Giants put Moose McCormick on third and Fred Merkle on first with two outs.

Al Bridwell drilled a hit to center field and McCormick raced home with the apparent winning run. But Merkle, seeing him score, stopped short of touching second and headed for the clubhouse. Cub first baseman Frank Chance saw what happened and screamed for the ball; he knew he could touch second and make Merkle the victim of a force play, thus ending the inning with the score still tied.

Giants' pitcher Joe (Iron Man) McGinnity heard Chance, sprang off the bench, and tackled him before he could reach second. Meanwhile, the fans—thinking the game was over—had spilled onto the field in a rush for the exits.

McGinnity grabbed the ball and threw it into the crowd. Chance appealed to umpire Hank O'Day, who ruled Merkle out because of interference from McGinnity. The game ended in a tie and had to be replayed when the two teams finished the season with identical 98-55 records.

The Cubs won the replay and the pennant, but 19-year-old Merkle, perpetrator of the costliest blunder in baseball history, actually received a raise from Giants' manager John McGraw and went on to become an excellent player.

# TOUCHING ALL BASES

Base-running blunders are common. Touching all bases is one of baseball's primary rules, but mishaps occur on the basepaths.

In 1916, pitcher Ernie Koob of the St. Louis Browns was deprived of victory while "scoring" in the fifteenth inning; he had missed third base and was called out when the opposition appealed. The game was called for darkness two innings later, with the score 0-0.

Red Sox starter Howard Ehmke got a "gift" no-hitter against the Philadelphia A's near the end of the 1923 season, when rival pitcher Slim Harriss failed to touch first on an apparent double off the right field fence. He too was called out on an appeal play.

Yankee slugger Lou Gehrig, trotting around the bases after hitting the ball over the fence, lost the 1931 home run crown when teammate Lyn Lary—on base at the time—proceeded from third base to the dugout rather than completing the circuit to home plate. Gehrig, who didn't see the play, was ruled out for passing Lary and was credited with a triple, as he had only touched three bases safely. That year, Gehrig and Babe Ruth each hit 46 home runs to share the home run title.

Hank Aaron was involved in the strange ending of Harvey Haddix's twelve-inning perfect game, which he pitched for Pittsburgh against Milwaukee in May 1959.

In the last of the thirteenth, Felix Mantilla was safe on an error by Don Hoak (ending the perfect game). Eddie Mathews sacrificed him to second and Aaron was intentionally walked to set up a potential

Brooklyn's Jimmy Wasdell steals third. Boston Braves third baseman Sibi Sisti leaped to prevent catcher Phil Masi's throw from going astray.

## MERKLE'S BONER COST MATHEWSON VICTORY CROWN

*Because Christy Mathewson was deprived of a certain victory when Fred Merkle forgot to touch second base in a late-season Giants-Cubs contest of 1908, he ended his career with 373 victories, a total later equaled by long-time Phillies star Grover Cleveland Alexander. No NL pitcher ever won more. It's possible Mathewson would rank alone at the top if victory hadn't become a tie because of "Merkle's boner."*

**Wild toss by third baseman Travis Jackson gets past Bill Terry of New York Giants as Jake Powell of the Yankees crosses first in 1936 World Series.**

15

inning-ending double-play. But Joe Adcock foiled the strategy by slamming the ball over the fence, an apparent three-run homer and the only hit off hard-luck Haddix.

Mantilla scored, but Aaron, rounding second, saw the ball disappear over the wall and was so stunned that he forgot to continue his circuit of the basepaths. He headed directly for the dugout, and Adcock, making a grand home run trot, was ruled out when he passed the spot where Aaron had made his departure. Instead of a 3-0 victory, the Braves wound up 1-0 winners—and Adcock had a double instead of a home run.

A strange footnote to the game was the pitching of Lew Burdette, who yielded twelve hits but no runs in thirteen innings to win. Haddix gave up one and lost.

Base-runners must stay alert at all times. On August 15, 1926, Babe Herman tripled into a double-play when he didn't.

In the seventh inning, with one out and the bases loaded, Herman slammed a pitch toward the right field fence. The ball might have been caught—and the runners had to wait and see if it would be—but Herman put his head down and ran.

The Dodger runner scored from third, but pitcher Dazzy Vance, running from second, mysteriously slowed down as he rounded third on his way home. Chick Fewster, running from first, had caught up to Vance but knew he couldn't pass him on the basepaths.

Herman, closing in on Fewster and Vance, looked like he would pass both runners. Coach Mickey O'Neil yelled "Back! Back!" to Herman, but Vance—not used to running the bases—answered the cry. He turned back toward third and slid in from the home-plate side. Herman slid in from the second base side. Fewster stood stock still on the base and watched.

Thirdbaseman Eddie Taylor grabbed the ball and tagged all three runners. The umpire ruled Vance entitled to the bag but called Fewster and Herman out, ending the inning.

Brooklyn manager Wilbert Robinson was beside himself. But it wasn't as bad as the time Herman stole second while runners were at second and third.

Gary Geiger of the Red Sox suffered an embarrassing moment in 1961 when he hit a run-scoring triple in the bottom of the eleventh inning against the California Angels. Thinking his hit had won the game, Geiger headed for the clubhouse. An Angel infielder tagged him for the first out of the inning. Geiger's hit had actually tied the game and he would have been on third with nobody out.

# THROWING A GLOVE AT THE BALL

Fielders are penalized for throwing gloves, caps, or other parts of their uniform at balls in flight. Rule 7.05 (c) provides three bases for a hitter if a fielder throws his glove at, and touches, a fair ball.

In 1947, the same rule applied to foul balls as well. On July 27, Boston's Jake Jones got credit for a triple on a foul ball with two out and the bases empty in the sixth inning against the St. Louis Browns. He hit a roller inside the third base line that looked like it *might* go fair. Pitcher Fred Sanford, realizing Jones would have a certain infield hit if that happened, threw his glove to keep the ball foul. The glove and ball met and Jones immediately had an automatic triple.

In 1954, the rule was amended to apply only to fair balls.

## WAGNER SOUGHT CHANGES

**In 1904, Pittsburgh shortstop Honus Wagner asked for a ban on freak deliveries and suggested the standard pitching distance of 60 feet, 6 inches was too short.**

The 12-inning perfect game of Harvey Haddix in 1959 had an unexpected finish in the 13th when Hank Aaron failed to complete his circuit of the bases after Joe Adcock's homer. The final score was 1-0.

# WARM-UP PITCHES

8.03 When a pitcher takes his position at the beginning of each inning, or when he relieves another pitcher, he shall be permitted to pitch not to exceed eight preparatory pitches to his catcher during which play shall be suspended. A league by its own action may limit the number of preparatory pitches to less than eight preparatory pitches. Such preparatory pitches shall not consume more than one minute of time. If a sudden emergency causes a pitcher to be summoned into the game without any opportunity to warm up, the umpire-in-chief shall allow him as many pitches as the umpire deems necessary.

*—Official Baseball Rules, 1978*

In 1911, the American League instituted a short-lived rule forbidding pitchers to take warm-up pitches between innings. Boston's Ed Karger was doing just that—and the outfielders were taking their time returning to their positions—when Stuffy McInnis, part of the Athletics' famed $100,000 infield, stepped into the batter's box and hit a warm-up pitch far over the fielders' heads. It was an easy home run, and the umpire said it was perfectly legal under prevailing rules.

---

## THE SUBMARINE DELIVERY

*Carl Mays, Yankee ace in the '20s, used a submarine (underarm) delivery. During his motion, he often scraped the ground as he delivered to the plate.*

---

National League

# MISSED THIRD STRIKE

A strikeout is incomplete if the catcher does not catch the ball (Rule 10.17). The batter may advance to first base, provided there is no runner there before two are out. Should the catcher retrieve the ball and tag the batter, or throw the ball to first base before his arrival, the batter is out. A batter who bunts foul on the third strike is also a strikeout victim. In all cases, the pitcher is credited with a strikeout even if a defensive lapse by the catcher allows a runner to reach base.

There have been multiple instances of pitchers striking out four men in one inning because one of the strikeout victims reached base when the catcher missed the third strike. Only once, however, has a pitcher fanned *five* in one inning.

Joe Niekro of the Houston Astros, whose knuckleball is as difficult to catch as it is to hit, did it during a 1977 exhibition game. The ball twice eluded catcher Cliff Johnson on third strikes, allowing runners to reach base.

Semaphore signals are used to indicate strike calls. The practice of raising the right arm to call strikes, one of baseball's oldest traditions, began around the turn of the century after Dummy Hoy, a deaf-mute, requested a sign instead of a sound.

# TWO BALLS IN PLAY

Baseball rules stipulate that the game be played with one ball at a time. The ball is often changed—when it becomes discolored or roughed up—but never is a new ball entered by the umpire until the old one is removed.

On June 30, 1959, however, the Chicago Cubs threw two balls to second base simultaneously in a bid to erase base-runner Stan Musial of the St. Louis Cardinals.

Musial was at bat with a three-ball, one-strike count when Chicago pitcher Bob Anderson delivered a pitch that home plate umpire Vic Delmore called ball four. But Cub catcher Sammy Taylor argued that the ball hit Musial's bat and was therefore foul, increasing the count to three balls and two strikes.

Taylor did not give chase as the ball bounced toward the backstop. Delmore contended the ball hit Taylor's glove, glanced off the umpire's arm, and rolled toward the screen. ☞

## BENDING THE RULES

*Free substitution is banned in baseball, but rules against it were bent during a Pirate-Cub game in 1952. Pittsburgh catcher Clyde McCullough was forced out by injury, and reserve receiver Ed Fitzgerald had already appeared as a pinch-hitter.*

*Cub manager Phil Cavarretta said he did not mind if Fitzgerald reentered the game and the umpires permitted the unusual maneuver. The Pirate home crowd cheered the sportsmanlike decision of the visiting manager.*

When Musial reached first, he heard teammates yell, "Run! Run!" He took off for second. If Delmore's call was correct, the ball was still in play. Third baseman Alvin Dark raced in and threw to shortstop Ernie Banks. At the same instant, pitcher Anderson took a new ball—which the umpire absent-mindedly gave him during the argument over the ball four call—and threw to second.

Anderson's throw sailed into center and Musial, seeing the error, headed for third base. He had gone only a few steps when Banks, holding the original ball, tagged him out.

Umpire Bill Jackowski ruled Musial out because he was tagged with the original ball. The Cardinals protested the decision, then dropped their protest after winning, 4-1.

## IS THERE A DIFFERENCE BETWEEN LEAGUES?

*Many pitchers say the strike zone is eight to ten inches higher in the American League than in the National. They also say NL hitters are more aggressive—an opinion substantiated by the fact that they hit 184 more home runs and had a batting average nine points higher than AL counterparts in 1972, last year before the American League adopted the designated hitter.*

## BASEBALL'S ONLY RAIN-IN

*The only rained-in game in baseball history occurred in Houston on June 15, 1976, when torrential rains flooded the city with up to 10 inches of water. The Houston Astros and Pittsburgh Pirates managed to get to the rain-proof Astrodome, but the umpires, fans, and most stadium personnel did not.*

## THE FIRST DH

*Ron Blomberg of the Yankees was the first designated hitter.*

# THE RAIN RULE

3.10 (c) The umpire-in-chief shall be the sole judge as to whether and when play shall be suspended during a game because of unsuitable weather conditions or the unfit condition of the playing field; as to whether and when play shall be resumed after each suspension; and as to whether and when a game shall be terminated after such suspension. He shall not call the game until at least 30 minutes after he has suspended play. He may continue the suspension as long as he believes there is any chance to resume play.     —*Official Baseball Rules,* 1978

Because baseball rules do not mandate completion of all games, there have been 19 no-hitters of less than nine innings since 1900. There have also been "official" games shortened by rain, hail, fog, snow, gnats, darkness (before night baseball), and power failure (after the advent of night play).

For a variety of reasons—some of which will be explained here—the "rain rule" (which allows unfinished games to go into the record as if they were played to completion) is ridiculous.

Basically, the rule makes it legal for a game to be called after five complete innings, or after four-and-a-half if the home team is ahead. If an inning is in progress and the game is called at any time after the fifth inning, the game is suspended if (1) the visitors have tied the score and the home team has not scored or (2) if the visitors have taken the lead while an inning is in progress and the home team has not scored.

If a tie game is called after completion of an inning, all records count but the game must be replayed from the beginning.

One notable exception: if the home team ties the game at any time from the fifth inning onward—and the game is called by the umpire at that time—the score does *not* revert to the previous completed inning. Instead, the game becomes a tie, all records count, but the game must be replayed from the beginning.

If a game is called *before* five innings are completed (four-and-a-half with the home club leading), none of the records count. Roger Maris lost one home run to the rain in 1961, when he slammed 61 homers in 162 games and suffered the indignity of an asterisk (*) after his record because it was accomplished in an expanded schedule.

To illustrate the rain rule, suppose Pittsburgh is playing in Atlanta and leading, 4-2, when rain cancels the contest after four-and-a-half innings. The game and its records would not count. If Atlanta led by the same score, they would.

This hypothetical example—and many real-life examples—underline the importance of playing all major league games to completion. Games stopped by curfew, pre-arranged time limits, light failure, and darkness (if law prevents turning on the lights) are considered suspended contests and must be completed from point of interruption. But some games stopped by weather are treated differently

## WHY PHILS FAILED TO CHEAT THE CURFEW LAW

*On June 8, 1947, the Philadelphia Phillies lost an estimated $10,000 because an unthinking reserve catcher, just back from the minor leagues, failed to stall long enough to allow the Pennsylvania curfew to stop a game between the Pirates and Phils.*

*The game was tied 4-4 after eight complete innings in Philadelphia, but the Pirates took a 5-4 lead in the ninth on Ralph Kiner's home run. If the 6:59 p.m. Sunday curfew had stopped the game before the Phils had completed the home half of the ninth, it would have ended in a tie, since the score would have reverted back to the end of the previous completed inning. A tie would have forced a replay as a future doubleheader, guaranteed to bring out 10,000 more fans than a single game.*

*In the top of the ninth, Hank Greenberg of Pittsburgh allowed himself to be tagged on the basepaths after he followed Kiner's two-out homer by getting hit with a pitch.*

*In the bottom of the inning, Phillies' manager Ben Chapman told his players to delay as much as possible. The first man popped out, but the second, Charley Gilbert, was a pinch-hitter who deliberately took excessive time to select a bat. He argued with the umpire, fouled off a series of pitches intentionally, but then struck out. One more out and the Phillies would lose the game and the $10,000 additional they would make if it ended in a tie.*

*Chapman called for catcher Hugh Poland, stationed 300 feet away in the bullpen. To the dismay of his teammates, Poland ran in. Had he walked, he would have saved valuable time. Minutes remained on the clock. When he reached the batter's box, the delaying tactic suddenly dawned on Poland. He argued briefly with umpire Babe Pinelli, who hurried him back into the batter's box. Poland took two strikes, then lofted a lazy fly that Wally Westlake caught—just 52 seconds before curfew.*

# PROBLEMS WITH THE "RAIN RULE"

Bill Terry, one-time slugger of the New York Giants, lost the 1931 batting crown by three-thousandths of a percentage point because he lost a base-hit in a game canceled by darkness.

Playing a double-header in Brooklyn, Terry singled in his first at-bat of the second game. Confident he had won the batting title in a tight three-way race with Jim Bottomley and Chick Hafey, he retired from the lineup.

But Fresco Thompson of the Dodgers—the Giants' arch-rivals—set fire to several scorecards as a signal that it was too dark to continue. Umpire Bill Klem spent considerable time looking for the culprit, then called the game. None of the records counted.

In the days when clubs depended on 10-hour train trips to travel around the league, it was often necessary to stop a game early to coincide with local railroad schedules. This was done by previous agreement between clubs—and such games were terminated at the appointed hour, rather than suspended.

In the early '50s, when Satchel Paige was the ace relief man for Bill Veeck's St. Louis Browns, the Browns were nursing a one-run lead late in the game and due to catch a train in less than an hour. Veeck told Paige to get the opposition out quickly for fear the game would revert to the previous inning and plunge the Browns into a tie.

Paige accomplished his mission by striking out the side with only 10 pitches. "The umpire missed one," he told Veeck as they boarded the train.

# STALLING TO TWIST THE RULES

Crafty Clark Griffith, manager of the New York Highlanders (later Yankees) in 1907, was one of many big-league pilots who tried to twist the rain rule to their advantage by using stalling tactics.

White Sox hurler Ed Walsh had a 4-1 lead in the fifth inning as rain—and even hail—fell steadily. Griffith, hoping the game would be called and have to be replayed, inserted himself as a relief pitcher for New York and took his time warming up. When he pronounced himself ready, rain fell hard and play was held up.

To Griffith's dismay, play resumed 10 minutes later. Sox runners were at first and third when Griffith walked Billy Sullivan and then served an easy pitch to Walsh, who socked a two-run double. Chicago suddenly realized the situation and tried to end the inning quickly.

Sullivan waltzed home on Walsh's double, but allowed himself to be tagged out short of the plate. Ed Hahn hit a ground ball and waited out infielders who were in no mood to tag him out. Fielder Jones, White Sox manager, then tapped the ball to Griffith, but the pitcher let it go through his legs for a deliberate error.

Kid Elberfeld retrieved it and threw to firstbaseman Hal Chase, but Jones refused to touch first and Chase would not make the putout to end the inning.

Umpire John Sheridan finally ordered the Yankees to make the plays or face a forfeit. Griffith had no choice. The game continued until the last of the sixth, when the deluge broke and terminated play. Chicago won, 8-1, and Walsh was credited with a no-hitter—one of the two he threw in his career.

# FOG-OUTS AND OTHER UNUSUAL POSTPONEMENTS

On May 20, 1960, the Cubs and Braves were victims of the first fog-out at Milwaukee County Stadium. Umpire Frank Dascoli, having trouble seeing the outfielders from home plate, took his three crew members and headed into the outfield, where the Cubs' three men were already stationed. Frank Thomas of the Cubs hit a fungo and none of the seven could see it. That clinched it. The game, 0-0 in the last of the fifth, was wiped out.

The only previous fog-out in National League records also involved the Cubs—at Brooklyn in 1956. The Cubs had previously lost a game to the elements when gnats descended on Ebbets Field in the sixth inning of a doubleheader nightcap on September 15, 1946. The sun was out, but the gnats so irritated the fans that they waved their white scorecards to shoo them away and created a hazard for players' vision. The Dogers were awarded a 2-0 win since five innings had been completed.

Records of the Pacific Coast League, a Triple-A circuit, show (1) an Oakland game in the '40s, called because mounted Army troops had churned up the turf during maneuvers, (2) a seismic shock in Seattle that occurred during a game and forced cancellation, (3) a midday game in Ventura, California, called because of a total eclipse, and (4) a 24-inning 1-1 tie in Sacramento, forced because wind blew a neighbor's thick black smoke (from burning trash) over the playing field.

# FORFEITS

## From *Official Baseball Rules*, 1978:

4.15 A game may be forfeited to the opposing team when a team—
(a) Fails to appear upon the field, or being upon the field, refuses to start play within five minutes after the umpire has called "Play" at the appointed hour for beginning the game, unless such delayed appearance is, in the umpire's judgment, unavoidable;
(b) Employs tactics palpably designed to delay or shorten the game;
(c) Refuses to continue play during a game unless the game has been suspended or terminated by the umpire;
(d) Fails to resume play, after a suspension, within one minute after the umpire has called "Play";
(e) After warning by the umpire, willfully and persistently violates any rules of the game;
(f) Fails to obey within a reasonable time the umpire's order for removal of a player from the game;
(g) Fails to appear for the second game of a double-header within twenty minutes after the close of the first game unless the umpire-in-chief of the first game shall have extended the time of the intermission.

4.16 A game shall be forfeited to the visiting team if, after it has been suspended, the orders of the umpire to groundkeepers respecting preparation of the field for resumption of play are not complied with.

4.17 A game shall be forfeited to the opposing team when a team is unable or refuses to place nine players on the field.

A team may forfeit a game to an opponent if it does not abide by an umpire's ruling, if it cannot control unruly fans, or if it knowingly violates the rules.

When a game is forfeited, it goes into the books as a 9-0 victory, but batting and pitching records count if the contest has survived the minimum five-inning standard for "official" games. ☞

## THREE KNOTTY PROBLEMS

*Because the unexpected is expected in baseball, umpires must have thorough knowledge of baseball rules. Here are three problems that have happened before and may happen again.*

*1. An outfield fly strikes a bird in flight. The centerfielder catches the ball and the right-fielder catches the stunned bird. The correct ruling? The ball is in play because it is no longer "in flight" once it hits the bird. The batter may advance at his own risk.*

*2. Another touchy situation occurs when a base-runner attempts to score and anticipates a close play at home. He slides but misses the plate—while the catcher fails to tag him as he whizzes by. Since umpires are not bound to monitor missed bases for the defensive team, the right ruling is "safe" until an appeal is made. Then the call would change to "out."*

*3. Proper interpretation of the rules makes it possible for a team to get six hits in the same inning without scoring. For example, the first two batters hit singles. One is thrown out trying to steal third, the other is picked off. Three infield hits follow. The next hitter's grounder strikes the runner moving from first to second; the batter gets credit for a hit, but the runner is out for interference. No runs, six hits, no errors.*

## CREDITING THE PITCHER PROPERLY

*A starting pitcher must go five innings in a game to be eligible for the victory—with one exception. Should a game be stopped after it has become an "official" game (five full innings, or four-and-a-half with the home team ahead), but before it has gone six innings, the starter is eligible for victory after pitching four innings.*

Stalling tactics by the Phillies robbed St. Louis slugger Joe Medwick of sole possession of the 1937 home run crown. Medwick's homer had helped the Cards take a 3-0 lead in the third inning of the nightcap of a double-header, but the game began late because of a heavy shower that began just as the first game ended.

It would have been hard to squeeze in the required five innings before curfew curtailed the game, and Philadelphia manager Jimmy Wilson began a deliberate effort to delay when St. Louis jumped off to the early lead. He had failed to heed several warnings from umpire Bill Klem before Klem decided to award the game to the Cardinals by forfeit.

Since five frames had not passed, Medwick lost the home run and finished in a tie with Mel Ott of the Giants at 31 each.

# ROWDY FANS FORCE FORFEITS

Unruly crowds have contributed to many forfeits in baseball. As early as 1905, Brooklyn fans stormed the field with their team on the short side of a 16-0 score, and umpires handed victory by forfeit to the New York Giants.

Rowdy Philadelphia fans caused a forfeit of the Phillies' 1907 opener when they pelted umpire Bill Klem with snowballs. Detroit fans, angered when a Tiger was hit by a pitch, caused a disturbance that resulted in a forfeit to the Yankees in 1924.

The Philadelphia faithful were at the scene of the 1937 forfeit, caused by stalling, that robbed Cardinal Joe Medwick of the home run crown; but one of the more famous forfeits in baseball annals occurred two years later in Boston.

With Sunday curfew approaching in the second game of a Sunday double-header between the Red Sox and Yankees, New York tallied twice in the top of the eighth to take a 7-5 lead. Only 20 minutes remained before curfew would stop the game.

After looking at the clock, the Yankees began to make deliberate outs so that the top AND bottom of the inning could be completed. If the entire inning were not completed, the score would revert to the previous complete frame, leaving the game a 5-5 tie.

Seeing the farce, normally staid Boston fans showed their disgust by hurling straw hats, soda bottles, seat cushions, and other objects onto the field. Fenway Park was quickly covered with debris and therefore not in playing condition. Hence, the forfeit—and accompanying $1000 fine for the Red Sox.

Boston was on the receiving end of a 1941 forfeit in Washington when the Senators' notoriously inept groundcrew failed to cover the field on time during a rain delay in the top of the eighth. The umpires ruled their delay was deliberate since the Senators held a 6-3 lead at that time.

Stalling by manager Eddie Stanky caused the St. Louis Cards to forfeit to the Phils—following a brawl between the clubs—in 1954; but fans caused forfeits in the early '70s, at Washington in 1971 and Cleveland in 1974.

The Senators had been leading the Yankees in their final game in the capital before moving to Texas for the 1972 campaign, but souvenir-hungry fans couldn't wait for game's end to storm the field. The transplanted Senators, as Texas Rangers, recouped the '71 forfeit when they benefited from Cleveland's Beer Night Promotion three years later. Overindulgent fans made play impossible.

## WHEN WALKS WERE HITS

For one season—1887—walks were counted as hits. Tip O'Neill led the American Association with a .492 batting average. With the rule removed the following year, O'Neill again led the league. This time, he hit .332.

## RELIEVERS FORCED CHANGE IN ERA RULE

When baseball rule-makers realized the growing importance of relief pitching, they changed the qualifications governing the earned run average title. Previous to 1950, eligible pitchers had to throw at least ten complete games. Under the revised rule, they had to work as many innings as their team played games (162). Hoyt Wilhelm became the first reliever to win the ERA crown in 1952, when he worked 159 innings under the 154-game schedule.

## THE SACRIFICE FLY

Rules regarding the sacrifice fly have changed several times. In 1908, the present sacrifice fly rule was created: no time at bat is charged to a batter for a fly ball (with less than two outs) that enables a runner to score from third base. In 1926, the rule was expanded to award a sacrifice fly when any runners moved up a base. The rule was abandoned in 1939, but the 1908 version was restored in 1954.

# ACROSS THE YEARS WITH THE RULE BOOK

Following is a list of the major rules additions and changes that have occurred since the first set of rules was compiled in 1845, by Alexander Cartwright.

In 1857, the game, previously decided when one side scored 21 aces, became a contest of nine-innings duration, regardless of the score. This, too, has not changed.

In 1858, the pitcher could make a short run in his delivery and was relieved of the "called ball" penalty; called strikes were introduced; a batsman was out on a batted ball, fair or foul, if caught on the fly or first bounce, and the base runner was not required to touch each base in order.

In 1859, the catcher was first tried standing close behind the batter. Catchers complained that it hindered their powerful throws to second base.

In 1863, the bat was regulated in size; the pitcher's box was now 12 feet by 4 feet; no step was allowed in the pitcher's delivery and he had to pitch with both feet on the ground at the same time; home base and the pitcher's box were marked; no base could be made on a foul ball; base runners were required to return to base and could be put out in the same manner as the striker when running to first base.

In 1864, the "out on a fair bound" was removed and the "fly catch" of fair balls adopted. Then the rule was added that each base runner must touch each base in making the circuit, and Henry Chadwick introduced the first system of scoring.

In 1865, official averages were first introduced.

In 1867, the pitcher's box was made a six-foot square and the pitcher was permitted to move about as he wished; the batter was given the privilege of calling for a high or low ball, and the first curve ball was introduced by Candy Cummings.

In 1872, the ball specifications as to size and weight were changed into what they are to this present day.

No further rules changes per se were introduced until the National League's first season of 1876.

The years and major changes follow in chronological order:

**1877**—Canvas bases 15 inches square were introduced, the same measurement as today; home plate was placed in the angle formed by the intersection of the first and third base lines, as today, and the hitter was exempted from a time at bat if he walked.

**1879**—Player reserve clause was for the first time put into a contract; the number of "called balls" became 9 and all balls were either strikes, balls or fouls; the pitcher had to face a batsman before pitching to him, and a staff of umpires was first introduced.

**1880**—Base on balls was reduced to 8 "called balls"; the base runner was out if hit by a batted ball, and the catcher had to catch the pitch on the fly in order to register an out on a third strike.

**1883**—The "foul bound catch" was abolished and the pitcher could deliver a ball from above his waist.

**1884**—All restrictions on the delivery of a pitcher were removed; six "called balls" became a base on balls, and championships were to be decided on a percentage basis, as today.

**1885**—One portion of a bat could be flat (one side); home base could be made of marble or whitened rubber, and chest protectors worn by catchers and umpires came into use.

**1887**—The pitcher's box was reduced to 4 feet by 5½ feet; calling for high and low pitches was abolished; five balls became a base on balls; four "called strikes" were adopted for this season only; bases on balls were recorded as hits for this season only; the batter was awarded first base when hit by a pitch; home plate was to be made of rubber only (dropping the marble type) and was to be 12 inches square, and coaches were recognized in the rules for the first time.

**1888**—Player reserve clause was written into the contracts of minor leaguers for the first time; the base on balls exemption from a time at bat was restored, and a batsman was credited with a base hit when a runner was hit by his batted ball.

**1889**—Four balls became a base on balls, as today, and a sacrifice bunt was statistically recognized.

**1891**—Substitutions were permitted at any point in the game, and large, padded mitts were allowed for catchers.

**1893**—Pitching distance increased from 50 feet to 60 feet, six inches, as today; the pitching box was eliminated and a rubber slab 12 inches by 4 inches was substituted; the pitcher was required to place his rear foot against the slab; the rule exempting a batter from a time at bat on a sacrifice was instituted, and the rule allowing a flat side to a bat was rescinded and the requirement that the bat be round and wholly of hard wood was substituted.

**1894**—Foul bunts were classified as strikes.

**1895**—Pitching slab was enlarged to 24 inches by 6 inches, as today; bats were permitted to be 2¾ inches in diameter and not to exceed 42 inches; infield-fly rule was adopted, and a held foul tip was classified as a strike.

**1901**—The American League became a major league and rules from this point on occasionally were instituted for one league only, as the foul strike rule, used only by the National League. Catchers, under protest, were compelled to remain continuously under the bat, but they complained that the base runner received too much of an advantage this way.

**1903**—Foul strike rule was adopted by the American League.

**1904**—Height of the mound was limited to 15 inches higher than the level of the baselines.

**1908**—Pitchers were prohibited from soiling a new ball; shinguards were reintroduced, this time by Roger Bresnahan, and the sacrifice fly rule was adopted, exempting the batter from a time at bat when a runner scored after the catch.

**1910**—The cork center was added to the official baseball, the start of the new ball (which today can be cork, rubber or similar material).

**1917**—Earned-run statistics and definitions were added to the rules.

**1920**—All freak deliveries, including the spitball, were outlawed, but registered spitballers were allowed to play out their string; the failure of a preceding runner to touch a base would not affect the status of a succeeding runner; the batter was given credit for a home run in the last of the ninth inning if the winning run was on base when the ball was hit out of the confines of the playing field; the number of runs batted in were to be included in the official score, and frivolous "ninth-inning uncontested steals in one-sided games" were discarded.

**1925**—Pitcher was allowed to use a resin bag, and the minimum home-run distance was set at 250 feet (existing parks with shorter fences were exempted).

**1931**—Sacrifice fly rule was wiped completely off the books; glass buttons and polished metal was forbidden on uniforms, and the distance from the plate to the backstop was reduced from 90 feet to 60 feet (existing parks not conforming were exempted).

**1954**—The sacrifice fly rule was brought back, this time with a man scoring after the catch only; defensive interference was changed from an offense solely by a catcher to one by a fielder as well; the quick-return pitch, squeeze play and wild pitch were defined; players were to remove their gloves from the field when batting and no equipment was to show on the field at any time; no fielder could take a position in line with a batter's vision with the deliberate intent to in any way distract the batter; regulations referring to a batter contacting his own ball were clarified as was the area of bases awarded a batter and/or base runner when a defensive player threw his glove or other equipment at a batted or thrown ball or in the case of spectator interference.

**1959**—Regulations were set up for minimum boundaries for all new parks, 325-400-325 feet.

**1968**—The anti-spitball rule was rewritten and tightened up because of the wave of moistened pitches that floated plateward the prior season.

**1969**—The pitcher's mound was dropped five inches and the strike zone was shrunken to the area from the armpits to the top of the batter's knees to assist the hitters against the pitching dominance, and the save rule was added to the official rules for the first time.

**1971**—All major league players were ordered to wear protective helmets at bat and all Class A and Rookie League players were required to wear ear-flap type helmets at bat in the 1971 season.

**1973**—With the influx of so many new gloves and shapes and colors, the rule on glove size and color was minutely outlined for standardization, specific guildelines were set out to determine cumulative performance records, and the American League began using designated hitters for pitchers on an experimental basis.

**1974**—The save rule was rewritten, and minimum standards for individual championships were outlined.

**1975**—The ball, always covered with horsehide, was permitted to be covered with cowhide because of the shortage of horses and their hides; suspension for three days became mandatory if batter were to hit a fair ball with a filled, doctored or flat-surfaced bat, and the save rule again was changed.

**1976**—The American League's designated hitter experimental rule was put into the official rules on an optional basis.

# CHAPTER THREE
# Umpires

Frankie Crosetti (1) of the Yankees argued too vehemently in this 1940 game and was thumbed out by the umpire.

# THE JOB OF AN UMPIRE

Umpires are paid by their leagues to officiate impartially at all games. Among other duties, they decide whether a field is in playable condition, call runners safe or out on the bases, and pass instant judgments on balls and strikes at home plate. Umpires are "the law" on the diamond and their decisions are final.

Umpiring was informal in the early days of baseball. When John Gaffney, unable to coax an apology from Giant manager John Montgomery Ward, refused to take the field for an 1886 contest, Pittsburgh pitcher Pud Galvin, sitting in the stands, replaced him.

Umps often risked life and limb—especially when the roughhousing Baltimore Orioles were in town. John Heydler, a pre-1900 umpire who later became National League president, said of the Orioles, "They were mean, vicious, and ready at any time to maim a rival player or umpire if it helped their cause."

A little-enforced rule of 1881 empowered arbiters to fine pitchers for deliberately throwing at hitters, but the rule—since reinstated—proved immensely unpopular and had to be dropped.

# THE STRIKE ZONE

The strike zone has always been the chief concern of the umpire. The calls of the home plate umpire make or break no-hitters, preserve or ruin shutouts, win or lose games, and even decide championships.

In 1887, the strike zone was defined as the area from the top of the shoulders to the bottom of the knees, but was changed to "armpits to knee-tops" in 1950. From 1963-68, however, the zone resumed its original definition and batting statistics fell in all categories.

The current standard, the same one in use from 1950-62, was reinstituted in 1969.

St. Louis Cardinals

Lou Brock, stolen base king, was also a fine hitter with excellent knowledge of the strike zone.

## THE FIRST UMPIRES

*Early umpires sat in rocking chairs 20 feet behind home plate.*

## A STRIKEOUT TO REMEMBER

*In his only major league appearance, Arliss Taylor of the A's yielded seven hits in two innings against the Indians on September 15, 1921. His only strikeout victim was Joe Sewell, the toughest batter to strike out in major league history! Sewell averaged only one strikeout per 63 at-bats in his long career.*

## EVANS ENJOYED HIMSELF

*Umpire Billy Evans was behind the plate when Al Schacht was pitching a game for the Senators. "Have you thrown your fastball yet?" Evans asked. "Yes," Schacht replied, "about 10 times." Evans then pressed the button, letting the air out of his chest protector. "Good," he said, "I guess I won't need this."*

# BILL KLEM:
# MOST FAMOUS MAN IN BLUE

Five umpires have done their jobs so well that they are now enshrined in the Hall of Fame: National Leaguers Bill Klem and Jocko Conlan plus American Leaguers Cal Hubbard, Billy Evans, and Tommy Connolly.

Klem, whose thirty-five-year career as a field official began in 1905, ranks at the top of the list. He was the first arbiter to use exaggerated gestures to call balls and strikes. He developed the style while taking leisurely horseback rides in the quiet of the seashore pines near Lakewood, New Jersey.

Two Klem quotes sum up his legacy to the sport: "I never missed one in my heart," and "Baseball is more than a game to me—it's a religion."

Klem worked exclusively behind the plate for his first sixteen seasons—even after the two-umpire system came into general use around 1920. He had an established reputation for excellence at calling balls and strikes and won a record number of World Series assignments (18 in all) as a result.

Umpiring crews were increased to three in the '30s, and later to the present-day four. World Series games had only two arbiters—one from each league—when the classic began in 1903. Regular-season games that year had only one ump.

## HOW CONLAN GOT HIS JOB

*Jocko Conlan, a so-so outfielder in two seasons with the White Sox in the '30s, became an umpire by accident. Emmett Ormsby, one of the regular umpires, was overcome by heat one afternoon and Conlan—out of the lineup with a broken finger—was drafted into service. Though he was wearing his Chicago uniform, he called teammate Luke Appling out on a close play at third. The next year, American League president William Harridge got Conlan a job as an ump.*

A play at the plate is always a difficult call—especially when there is an attempted steal of home. Jackie Robinson, a master at this daring tactic, succeeded in this 1952 game between the Dodgers and Cubs.

# FROM FOUR TO SIX UMPIRES

In the Pittsburgh-Detroit series of 1909, four umpires were assigned, but worked in alternating pairs. Klem and Billy Evans of the American League sat in the stands for the opener, eating peanuts and keeping score, but a controversial hit by Max Carey of the Pirates stirred them to action.

The ball went into the stands, but a special ground rule set aside only a specified area as home run territory. If the ball landed elsewhere, the hit would count as a double. Neither Klem nor Evans could tell where the ball hit, and the umpires on duty weren't sure either. All four umpires, accompanied by two bewildered managers, marched out to the stands and let the crowd convince them that the ball was actually a two-base hit.

Evans decided fans shouldn't be allowed to substitute for professional umpires and immediately wired American League President Ban Johnson. The next day, all four arbiters were working. The World Series crew was later increased to six—with two umpires monitoring the foul lines.

Both Klem and Evans, plus their countless colleagues in blue, were the traditional victims of abuse from both sides. Umpiring is such a thankless job that NL arbiter Dolly Stark curtailed his career with this remark: "I'm sick of being in a profession in which the greatest compliment I can receive is the silence of the crowd."

St. Louis Cardinals

Tension shows on the faces of both infielder and umpire as Dal Maxvill sets to receive throw at second base.

## FAN ATTACKS UMPIRE

*The umpire accepts derision from men in uniform and jeers from fans as part of his profession. Sometimes he has to put up with more. In 1981, Mike Reilly was tackled from behind by an irate fan during the seventh inning of the American League East Division Series between the Milwaukee Brewers and the New York Yankees. The incident was witnessed by 54,000 fans at Yankee Stadium.*

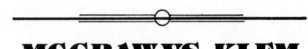

# MCGRAW VS. KLEM

Fiery umpire baiter John McGraw, long-time manager of the New York Giants, had a close relationship with Klem—fast friends off the field but arch-rivals when in uniform. One afternoon, McGraw blew his top after a Klem call went against his team.

A Chicago batter hit the ball against the left field scoreboard, but the sphere struck a section of board where the vertical line delineating foul territory from fair did not appear. McGraw sent a groundskeeper out to check for a dent in the scoreboard—only to learn Klem had made the right call.

In a game at Pittsburgh, years later, bespectacled pitcher Danny MacFayden, incredulous that Klem had called his last pitch "ball four," raced home with glasses in hand, shouting to the umpire, "Here, you need these more than I do!" The pitcher was promptly ejected—over the protests of Pirates' manager Frankie Frisch.

"I'm not ejecting him for questioning my eyesight," Klem said, "but for screaming so loudly that the crowd could hear him." At that, MacFayden replied, "The only reason I did that was I was afraid your ears might be as bad as your eyes!"

Anyone calling Klem "catfish" faced instant ejection. The remark was a personal affront because it reminded Klem of an argument he once had with Columbus manager Bill Clymer in the American Association. "Why you old catfish!" Clymer clamored after a close call went against him. "You can't talk, you can't smile, you can't do anything but move your gills!"

Klem, also quick with one-liners, put one over on Hack Wilson in 1930—the year Wilson set a National League standard with 56 home runs and a major league record of 190 runs batted in. ☞

When the slugger questioned a strike call by saying, "You missed that one, Bill," the ump answered, "If I had your bat in my hands, I wouldn't have."

Earlier in his career, Klem gave the heave-ho to mild-mannered Pie Traynor. Inquisitive reporters asked about it after the game. "He wasn't feeling well," Klem explained. "He told me he was sick and tired of my stupid decisions."

# THE HAZARDS OF UMPIRING

Sometimes the life of an umpire is threatened with more than the traditional cry of "Kill the umpire!" On September 6, 1907, Billy Evans was struck on the head by a bottle thrown from the stands in St. Louis. He suffered a fractured skull and nearly died.

In 1921, at age 37, Evans had to rely on his boxing know-how when 35-year-old Ty Cobb—as great an agitator as he was a hitter—challenged him to a fight under the Griffith Stadium stands in Washington. The only pre-condition to the match, which was ruled a draw by witnesses, was that league president Ban Johnson would not be informed of proceedings.

## PUTTING HIS FOOT IN IT, AGAIN

NEA

There are many documented cases of illegal "umpire bumping" by players, brief on-field bouts, and a celebrated 1961 shin-kicking exchange between Dodger coach Leo Durocher and Jocko Conlan. The basic routine of an umpire continues to be an endless battle of words and wits, most of them involving challenges to the arbiter's eyesight.

After John McGraw referred to him as "a blind robber," umpire Robert Emslie showed up at the Giants' practice with a rifle. He marched out to second base, split a match, and inserted a dime. Then he walked to home plate, aimed and fired, sending the dime spinning into the outfield with his first shot. McGraw argued with him again —but never challenged his eyesight.

Pitcher Babe Ruth challenged umpire Brick Owens so vehemently on a ball-four call to the first Washington hitter on June 23, 1917 that the umpire ejected him. Reliever Ernie Shore came on to retire 26 men in a row, plus the man Ruth walked, who was thrown out trying to steal second. Because of an umpire's decision, Shore managed to record the only perfect game that was not a complete game.

To ward off challenges to his vision, Southern Association umpire Harry (Steamboat) Johnson actually carried a card, signed by an eye doctor and certified by a notary public, stating that his vision was 20/20 in both eyes.

When Charlie Grimm was in one of his three terms as manager of the Chicago Cubs, umpire Charlie Moran called a Cub out on a close play. Grimm led a protest posse out of the dugout. He put his hand on the umpire's head and said, "The first man to touch this blind old man is fined fifty bucks!"

Fresco Thompson of the Brooklyn Dodgers, with a rule book thrust in his face by an umpire seeking to silence his protest, came up with this gem: "How can I read that? If it's yours, it must be in braille."

On a day when the Cincinnati Reds were particularly rough on Al Barlick, he finally took action—giving the thumb to second baseman Johnny Temple. Infuriated, Temple asked how bigger stars on the team can say the same thing without ejection. "I don't mind taking it from the lions and tigers," Barlick replied, "but I ain't about to take it from the gnits and gnats."

On occasion, an entire bench sends a steady stream of insults in the umpire's direction. Unable to pinpoint the chief source, the arbiter may eject the entire dugout. That's exactly what Frank Dascoli did to the Brooklyn Dodgers on September 27, 1951, the last week of the Giant-Dodger pennant race that ended in Bobby Thomson's miracle home run for New York.

One of the fifteen players Dascoli banished that day was rookie outfielder Bill Sharman, a minor-leaguer added to the Dodger roster for the final days of the season. Sharman, who later achieved stardom in basketball, thus became one of the handful of players in the history of baseball to be a manager's whim away from playing, but never to get the call.

# ABUSING THE UMPIRE

Repartee between catcher and umpire generally centers on the same subject—though umpires report that almost all catchers have smaller strike zones when they're hitting than they do while catching. Not in the umpire's eyes, however.

When star Yankee receiver Yogi Berra was especially unhappy with Cal Hubbard's calls one day, the veteran arbiter stopped the game and said, "Look, there's no point in both of us umpiring. One of us has to go." Berra, agreeing to be quiet, answered, "Cal, don't you know when I'm kidding and when I'm being ferocious?"

Berra's successor, Elston Howard, complained about a ball-four call to Harmon Killebrew, who had homered, tripled, and doubled twice in four previous trips to the plate one evening. "You sure put him on that time," said Howard to the umpire. The reply was quick: "Yeah, but I held him to one base."

## UMPS CONTROL BALLS

*Prior to 1906, the home team manager was in charge of supplying new baseballs. Charges were frequent that freshly introduced balls were "doctored" to help the home club and the leagues decided to place control of the balls with the umpires.*

## SEMAPHORE SIGNALS

*Umpires began raising their right arms to indicate strikes at the request of Dummy Hoy, outfielder who played 14 seasons, mostly before the turn of the century. Hoy was a deaf-mute who could not hear the umpire call strikes at the plate.*

## RECORD WIN STREAK

*Rube Marquard of the Giants won 19 consecutive games, a single-season record, in 1912.*

# UNUSUAL PLAYS AND DECISIONS

Calling time and deciding plays not necessarily in the rule book are also duties within the province of an umpire.

When Frankie Frisch was running the Pirates in the early '40s, his club was a run behind the Phillies in the ninth, with Frankie Zak at second and Babe Russell the potential winning run at the plate.

Zak called time to tie his shoes and umpire Scotty Robb complied, waving his arms for temporary suspension of play. But the pitch was on its way and Russell hit a home run that would have won the game if time had not been called. The home run didn't count and Russell, given the chance to bat again, made an out to end the game. The next day, Zak appeared with zippers on his spikes instead of laces.

In an International League game in 1963, Rico Carty homered twice in the same at-bat because time had been called just before he hit the first one. When play resumed, Carty calmly proceeded to hit the next pitch out of the Toronto ballpark.

One of the most unusual plays in the annals of umpiring occurred during a Federal League game in 1914. One of the two umpires failed to appear, so the other stood behind the pitcher in order to see home plate and to be closer to all the bases. When the hitters started fouling off too many balls, the umpire, Bill Brennan, stacked a pile of fresh baseballs behind the pitcher's mound. (In those days, umpires did not carry a fresh supply in special coat pockets, as they do now.)

No sooner did Brennan set up his pile than batter Grover Lund lined a pitch into the stack, scattering the balls around the infield. Since no one knew what to do, Lund circled the bases while the infielders tagged him with every ball in sight.

No one could prove which was the batted ball, so Brennan ruled the 70-foot shot a home run—undoubtedly the shortest one ever hit.

Bill Summers went against the script too—literally. The veteran umpire, working on a Hollywood movie set, got into his crouch, then called, "Strike One!" The director stopped the shooting and said, "Bill, that was supposed to be 'Ball One.'" The ump responded, "Tell the pitcher. I call them as I see them."

# STRANGE GRIPE

Umpires expect arguments on certain calls, but they never expect a pitcher to argue *against* a strike call. But, to prove anything can happen in baseball, St. Louis Browns' pitcher Jim Walkup did just that during the Rogers Hornsby regime of the mid-'30s.

Hornsby had warned his pitchers they would be subject to a $50 fine if they threw a pitch over the plate after having a no-ball, two-strike count on a hitter. (Hornsby followed the baseball theory that wise pitchers "waste" a pitch with an 0-2 count in the hope that the anxious batter will swing wildly and strike out.)

On the day Walkup had the proscribed 0-2 count, his third pitch just nipped the corner of the plate. The umpire yelled, "Strike three!" Walkup argued, but the umpire refused to reverse his call and the pitcher was out $50.

## SPITBALL OR SINKER?

*Dodger firstbaseman Norm Larker complained to umpire Frank Secory that Milwaukee pitcher Lew Burdette was throwing spitballs in a game in the early '60s. Secory replied that they were sinkers. Larker responded, "Oh, yeah? One of them sinkers just splashed me in the right eye."*

## "FISHERMAN" CONVINCED UMP TO HALT PLAY

*Hall of Fame umpire Tommy Connolly was behind the plate for a Cleveland-Detroit game of 1908 vintage when steady rain began to fall. Tiger infielder Germany Schaefer appealed for suspension of play several times, but to no avail.*

*Finally, Schaefer took the field in high rubber boots, raincoat, Gloucester fisherman's hat, and umbrella. Connolly's attention was focused on the player. "I have a very bad cold," said Schaefer, "and it's now bordering on pneumonia. If I get rid of my rubber boots, my raincoat, and my umbrella, I will be in the hospital in less than two hours, and I will certainly sue you and the league."*

*Connolly suspended play.*

Gene Mauch, one of baseball's best umpire-baiters, pleads his case—to no avail.

# HOW MANAGERS VIEW UMPIRES

Though they tend to argue loud and long, managers and players generally respect umpires.

Clyde King, one-time Brooklyn Dodgers' pitcher who saw Leo Durocher bait umpires, and later became a manager himself, conceded, "Overall, umpires do a good job. They're conscientious. Most umpires are human beings who make mistakes and know that. Ninety-five per cent of the time, an umpire knows when he's missed a play. But there's a limit as to how long you can argue.

"Leo could argue louder and more vehemently than any manager I knew without getting thrown out. I really believe some of the umpires enjoyed having confrontations with Leo. Umpires respect good managers, others they don't respect.

"As a manager, I never went out to argue if I didn't think an umpire missed a play. There were a few instances where I've talked an umpire into changing his call because he asked another umpire. But most of them are too stubborn to do that.

"Consistency by an umpire is what managers look for—in handling the game, calling balls and strikes, and calling the bases. We should get the best umpires behind the plate every other day instead of every fourth day. That way they'll be sharper. It's just like the extra man on the bench who claims he can't get his hitting stroke because he doesn't play regularly."

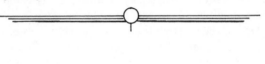

## WHY FREAK PITCHES WERE BANNED

*The spitball, emery ball, and other deliveries which involved doctoring of the ball were outlawed in 1920 as officials tried to "clean up" the game in the wake of the Black Sox scandal of 1919. Team and league executives thought heavier emphasis on offense would make fans forget the scandal quickly.*

Umpire Bill Summers debates a swarm of angry Yankees after a close call went against New York.

# THE UMPIRE TODAY

As the 1980 season opened, there were 32 umpires in the American League and 28 in the National, both divided into crews of four men and working for an escalating salary that has a minimum of $17,500.

Umpires make their own travel and hotel arrangements and handle their own equipment. They dress and shower at the ballpark in a special room far removed from team dressing rooms; all these practices stem from innovations by Bill Klem early in the century.

Current equipment includes a mask, uniform (blue blazers in NL and red in AL), and chest protector, worn inside by National League umpires but either way by their counterparts. The balloon protector, which must be adjusted before each pitch, gives more protection, but the pad, which can be worn inside, is far more comfortable.

Because of the great variety of pitches, and number of pitchers used per game, modern umpires like to know what each man has in his repertoire. They exchange information often.

# THE TOUGHEST CALLS

Among the most difficult calls an ump faces every day is the call of interference. This would apply to the base runner who aims for the infielder rather than the base in an attempt to break up a double-play. To avoid approaching runners, fielders attempting to pivot at second and make a relay to first often throw the ball before touching the base or step off the base before getting the ball.

The "phantom double-play" was accepted for years—only because the runner's slide at the fielder was accepted. The man with the glove was forced to cheat a little or risk amputation.

Previous to 1978, when American League umpires were ordered to enforce the rules strictly, such illegal tactics as the slide at the fielder and the phantom double-play were overlooked with a knowing wink.

Beanballs—intentional pitches at batters' heads—were also an accepted, though scoffed upon, part of the game. Umpires were empowered to take strict measures against both pitchers and managers believed to be practicing this forbidden but traditional art.

Other tough calls are application of the rules governing postponements and suspensions of play (especially because of foul weather) and the batter's half-swing. Lightning-fast reflexes of players make it tough to tell whether a hitter has taken a swing or held back. Umpires watch the wrists; the batter must "break his wrists" to be charged with a swinging strike when the ball is out of the strike zone.

# HOW UMPIRES POSITION THEMSELVES

Umpires must be agile to make correct calls on fastballs that come in high on the outside corner of the strike zone. National League umpires work on the right side of the catcher and look over his right shoulder when a righthanded hitter is up. They go the opposite way for a lefthanded hitter. ☞

St. Louis Cardinals

Lou Brock slides into second with another stolen base. Umpire signaled his safe arrival.

## THE UMPIRES WEREN'T THIRSTY

In 1957, Pittsburgh manager Bobby Bragan, while arguing with the umpires, tried to make peace by offering them a drink of orange juice. He was banished to the clubhouse and, shortly thereafter, replaced by Danny Murtaugh. Murtaugh had four terms with the Pirates and became one of the club's most successful managers.

31

In the American League, umpires stand directly behind the receiver and look over his head.

NL umpires, with the inside protector, shield their bare hands behind the catcher, while AL arbiters keep them grasped behind their backs to provide a better fit for their cumbersome balloon protectors, which fit tightly under the chin.

Each ump has his own stance and some, like National Leaguer Jerry Crawford and father Shag before him, actually touch the catcher. The Crawford style involves a hand placed between the catcher's hip and rib cage. Most players don't object.

# RECRUITING OF UMPIRES

Umpires are recruited from the high minors—and get jobs there after graduating from umpire schools. Veteran National League arbiter Ed Sudol, who lasted more than 30 seasons, began his career during the bitter winter of 1941, when he was a construction worker in Passaic, New Jersey.

"One wintry night I got home, opened up *The Sporting News,* and it was like a divine inspiration," he recalled. " I opened right up to a full-page ad for Bill McGowan's Umpire School. There was a picture of a girl in a bikini leaning up against a palm tree and I decided that was for me. I answered the ad and went to the school in Daytona Beach, Florida. I met my wife there, started my career there, and that's where I live now."

When umps are scouted in the minors, major league officials look for knowledge of fundamentals, technique, mobility, and control of managers, players, and even themselves in pressure situations. Conditioning is also important, since umpires stay on the field until the game ends—even if it takes twenty-five innings, the length of one game Sudol handled.

Stop-action cameras showing "instant replay" have helped the profession, according to American League Supervisor of Umpires Dick Butler, because the video invention gives umpires a 99 per cent rating for accuracy. Scoreboards which show such replays seconds after the call are taboo, however; if the umpire's judgment is wrong, the replay could rile a crowd—which already dislikes the umpire simply because it's baseball tradition.

# AN ERROR
# FOR THE UMPIRE

Umpires do make occasional mistakes. In a pre-1900 game between Baltimore and Washington of the National League, umpire Jack Kerns kept the game going in fast-approaching darkness.

Oriole catcher Wilbert Robinson held a strategy conference with pitcher John Clarkson. During the meeting, Robinson slipped Clarkson a lemon and told him to throw it on his next pitch. Clarkson stuck the baseball into his back pocket and threw the lemon to the plate.

"Strike One!" roared the umpire. Robinson called time, then turned around to face the umpire. He opened his glove to reveal the lemon.

"When you can't tell the difference between a baseball and a lemon, it's time to stop," he said. The embarrassed umpire capitulated.

This lineup card is identical in content to the one submitted by Kansas City manager Whitey Herzog to the umpire for the game played on 9/15/77.

## 1977 OFFICIAL BATTING ORDER
### KANSAS CITY

DATE 9/15/77

| | ORIGINAL | POS. | CHANGE |
|---|---|---|---|
| 1 | WILSON | 8 | B |
| | | | C |
| 2 | McRAE | DH | B |
| | | | C |
| 3 | BRETT | 5 | B |
| | | | C |
| 4 | COWENS | 9 | B |
| | | | C |
| 5 | MAYBERRY | 3 | B |
| | | | C |
| 6 | ZDEB | 7 | B |
| | | | C |
| 7 | PORTER | 2 | B |
| | | | C |
| 8 | PATEK | 6 | B |
| | | | C |
| 9 | WHITE | 4 | B |
| | | | C |
| P | SPLITTORFF | 1 | B |
| | | | C |
| | | | D |
| | | | E |

Manager's Signature ........Whitey Herzog (sig.)........

### 3.00—Game Preliminaries.

3.01 Before the game begins the umpire shall—

(a)  Require strict observance of all rules governing implements of play and equipment of players;

(b)  Be sure that all playing lines (heavy lines on Diagrams No. 1 and No. 2) are marked with lime, chalk or other white material easily distinguishable from the ground or grass;

(c)  Receive from the home club a supply of regulation baseballs, the number and make to be certified to the home club by the league president. Each ball shall be enclosed in a sealed package bearing the signature of the league president, and the seal shall not be broken until just prior to game time when the umpire shall open each package to inspect the ball and remove its gloss. The umpire shall be the sole judge of the fitness of the balls to be used in the game;

(d)  Be assured by the home club that at least one dozen regulation reserve balls are immediately available for use if required;

(e)  Have in his possession at least two alternate balls as needed throughout the game. Such alternate balls shall be put in play when—

   (1) A ball has been batted out of the playing field or into the spectator area;

   (2) A ball has become discolored or unfit for further use;

   (3) The pitcher requests such alternate ball.

The umpire shall not give an alternate ball to the pitcher until play has ended and the previously used ball is dead. After a thrown or batted ball goes out of the playing field, play shall not be resumed with an alternate ball until the runners have reached the bases to which they are entitled. After a home run is hit out of the playing grounds, the umpire shall not deliver a new ball to the pitcher or the catcher until the batter hitting the home run has crossed the plate.

—*Official Baseball Rules,* 1978

# CHAPTER FOUR

# Playing the Game

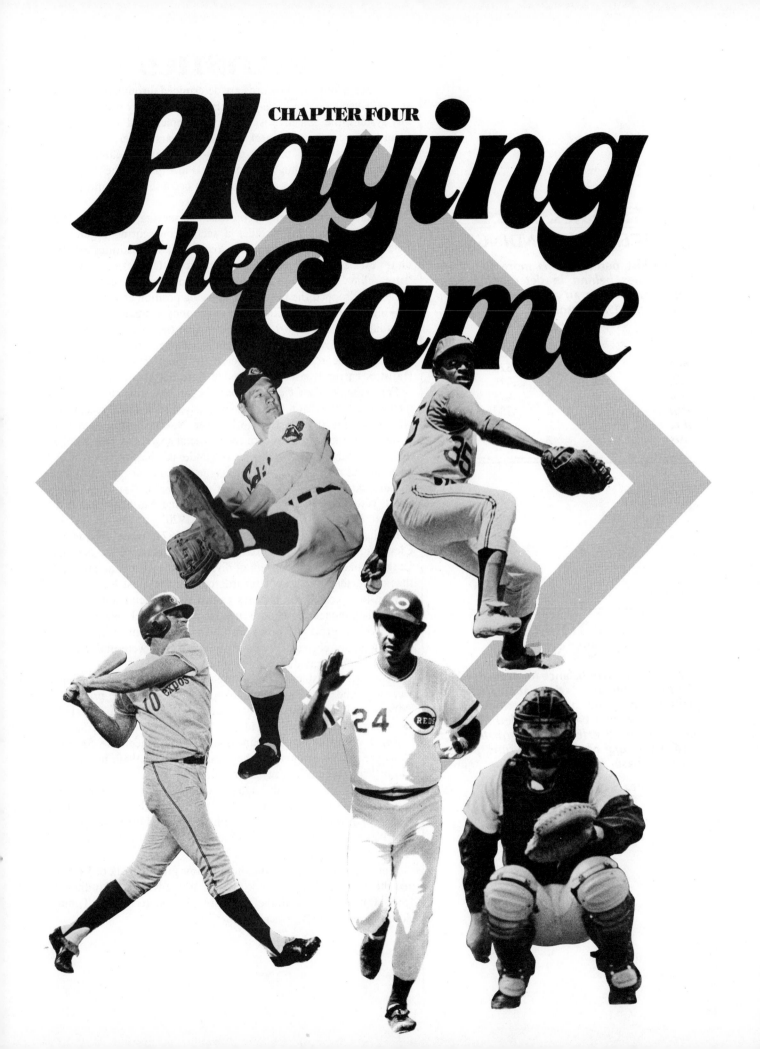

## STATISTICS

Baseball's individual records are determined through the daily box scores. Keeping score is easy, but there are a variety of methods. In any system, the objective is to keep a complete and accurate game record that can be read weeks—or even years—later.

Scorebooks come in two styles—with blank squares or with smaller squares within the squares. Fans prefer the first (and ballpark scorecards are made this way) because there's more room to write.

To guarantee uniformity in professional scoring, the Offical Playing Rules of baseball includes a section on scoring regulations. Under any system, it is essential to keep track of substitutes, position changes, and all pitching statistics. Unfortunately, the "streamlined" box score adopted by the major wire services in the early '70s dropped the practice of showing position changes, thereby making it impossible for the avid fan to follow the game as closely as he would like. *The Sporting News* became the sole source of boxes showing defensive movement of players during the game.

Modern records are "unofficial" in many cases because key statistics currently used in the game were not always recognized.

For example, the *Chicago Tribune* began reporting runs batted in during the 1880 season, but the idea received such a cool reception it was discontinued until 1891, when the National League and the American Association ordered their official scorers to keep track of RBIs. By June, NL scorekeepers abandoned the practice; the AA men obeyed their orders, but the league folded after that campaign.

Runs batted in returned in 1907 at the urging of *New York Press* sports editor Jim Price, but the American and National League did not give RBIs official recognition until 1920!

Batting averages were not used until 1871, when Boston and Cleveland of the National Association (forerunner to the National League) conceived the concept of dividing hits by times at bat. Up to that point, teams had kept records only of the most hits.

Won-lost records for pitchers gained semi-official status only in 1887, when pioneer baseball writer Henry Chadwick began keeping such records. Previously, pitchers who worked the most innings in a winning game received the victory—even if they were out of action when the game was decided.

Records of complete games weren't kept until National League secretary (and later president) John Heydler began the practice in 1909, long before the American League followed suit. In 1912, Heydler also introduced the idea of ERA (earned run average).

Relief pitchers' saves began—unofficially—when *The Sporting News* created its Fireman of the Year Awards in 1960, but did not win official recognition by the majors until 1969.

Historians, thumbing through old records, have attempted to include all major-leaguers, 1876 to the present, in the game's official register, but the process proved both tedious and difficult. Because pre-1900 rules were quite different, most historians consider true records to be those made in this century.

When Pete Rose put together his 44-game hitting streak of 1978, he tied the National League mark of Wee Willie Keeler, who did it in 1897. But he surpassed the "modern" league record of Tommy Holmes, who hit in 37 straight games in 1945.

## DECEPTIVE STANDINGS

*Won-lost percentage is more important than games behind in determining team standings. Here is an actual example from early in the 1978 season:*

National League East

|        | W | L | Pct. | GB |
|--------|---|---|------|----|
| Phila. | 5 | 3 | .625 | ½  |
| N.Y.   | 8 | 5 | .615 | —  |
| Chi.   | 6 | 5 | .545 | ½  |
| Mont.  | 5 | 5 | .500 | 1  |
| St.L.  | 5 | 7 | .417 | 2  |
| Pitts. | 3 | 7 | .300 | 3  |

## HOW TO PROVE A BOX SCORE

*A box score is in balance (or proved) when the total of the team's times at bat, bases on balls received, hit batters, sacrifice bunts, sacrifice flies and batters awarded first base because of interference or obstruction equals the total of that team's runs, players left on base and the opposing team's putouts.*

# LEARN TO SCORE AND ENJOY BASEBALL MORE.

Much of the fun at a ball game is keeping your own scorecard.
Fans can enjoy baseball to its fullest extent by keeping score as it allows you to trace the complete progress of the game and pinpoint those crucial plays that bring victory or defeat.

All you need is a basic knowledge of baseball's rules. Although there are countless scoring methods, experts use a simple code based on numbering players by position and tracing action through the use of symbols.

It's easy and fun. In fact, why not devise your own scoring system with the basic suggestions on this page. Part of the fun of scoring is improvising a system which you can decipher after the game is over.

One suggestion on player substitutions is to use a heavy or wavy line under or over a box to indicate a change, either of a pitcher or a batter. Another is if a batter flies to the right fielder, merely use the figure 9. If it is a foul fly – 9F.

Just number the players as follows:

| | |
|---|---|
| Pitcher | 1 |
| Catcher | 2 |
| First Baseman | 3 |
| Second Baseman | 4 |
| Third Baseman | 5 |
| Shortstop | 6 |
| Left Fielder | 7 |
| Center Fielder | 8 |
| Right Fielder | 9 |
| Designated Hitter | DH |

And use these simple symbols for plays:

| | |
|---|---|
| Single | — |
| Double | = |
| Triple | ≡ |
| Home Run | ≣ |
| Error | E |
| Foul Fly | F |
| Double Play | DP |
| Fielder's Choice | FC |
| Hit by Pitcher | HP |
| Wild Pitch | WP |
| Stolen Base | SB |
| Sacrifice Hit | SH |
| Sacrifice Fly | SF |
| Caught Stealing | CS |
| Passed Ball | PB |
| Balk | BK |
| Struck Out | K |
| Base on Balls | BB |
| Force Out | FO |
| Intentional Walk | IW |

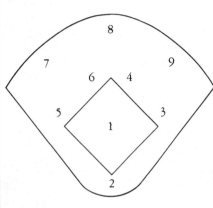

In this example, the hitter reached first base on a walk, stole second, advanced to third on pitcher's balk, scored on pitcher's wild pitch. Be sure to trace a player's complete progress around the bases. Indicate scoring plays by encircling or boxing symbol.

| Team | Pos. | 1 | 2 |
|---|---|---|---|
| Rightfielder | 9 | 4-6 W | |
| Second Baseman | 4 | 3 FC | |
| First Baseman | 3 | = | |
| Centerfielder | 8 | SF8 | |
| Designated Hitter | DH | K | |
| Leftfielder | 7 | | 4-6 — |
| Catcher | 2 | | DP 6-3 |
| Third Baseman | 5 | | ≣ |
| Shortstop | 6 | | 7 |
| Pitcher | 1 | | |
| | | | |
| | | | |
| | | | |
| Totals R/H | | 1/1 | 1/2 |

Inning 1
Walked and was forced out at second (2nd baseman to shortstop)
Reached first on fielder's choice when runner was forced out, advanced to third on double by third-place hitter, scored on fourth-place hitter's sacrifice fly
Doubled and did not advance further
Flied out to center field scoring runner on third
Struckout – end of inning

Inning 2
Singled, later forced out at second (2nd baseman to shortstop in first half of double play)
Hit into double play (2nd baseman to shortstop to 1st baseman)
Hit home run
Flied out to left fielder – end of inning

# HOW TO FIGURE AVERAGES LIKE AN EXPERT

**Individual Batting**—Divide the total number of times a player has been at bat into the total number of hits he has made. Example: Player White has 361 official times at bat and has been credited with 92 hits. Dividing 92 by 361 results in a batting average of .255.

To win a batting championship in the major leagues, a player must have a total of 502 appearances at the plate (at-bats, sacrifice flies, sacrifice hits, walks and hit-by-pitcher) . . . The number 502 was set as the qualifying standard because it is the product of games scheduled (162) multiplied by 3.1 (the average number of times a player goes to bat during a game).

**Slugging Average**—Divide the total number of times a player has been at bat into the total number of bases he has accumulated. Example: Player Green has 534 official times at bat and is credited with a total of 382 bases (home run four, triple three, double two, single one). Dividing 534 into 382 gives a slugging percentage of .715.

**Earned Run Average**—The number of earned runs a pitcher has allowed is multiplied by nine, the number of innings in a game. The product is then divided by the number of innings he has pitched. Example: Pitcher Black has allowed 63 earned runs in 174 innings. The formula is 63 times 9, divided by 174. The result is an earned run average of 3.26.

A pitcher must hurl 162 innings in a season to qualify for the earned run average championship. The number was selected to represent one inning pitched for each game scheduled.

**Fielding Average**—The total number of putouts, assists and errors on a player's record are added. Also add the number of putouts and assists he has. Then, divide the first sum (putouts, assists, errors) into the second sum (putouts, assists). Example: Player Brown has 167 putouts, 67 assists and three errors. The formula is 167 plus 67 plus 3, divided into 167 plus 67. That results in a fielding average of .987. A fielding champion must appear in 108 games at his position, except a catcher, who must appear in 81 games.

**Won-lost percentage** is reached by dividing the number of victories by the total games won and lost.

The **number of games behind the leader** in the standings is determined by comparing the leading team's record with the trailing team's figures on a minus-plus basis—12 victories and 4 losses, against 7 victories and 8 losses is a difference of 5 victories and 4 losses . . . The total of nine is then divided by two—indicating a difference of 4½ games.

To determine the "**magic number**" in a pennant race, compute the number of games yet to be played, add one, then subtract the number of games ahead in the loss column of the standings, from the closest opponent.

# RUNNING

Running the bases well presents an easy path to victory. Not only is speed important, but also instinct. A base-stealer must get the best jump and make the best slide or he won't be successful. Proper slides can break up double-plays, keep big innings alive, and avoid injuries for the base-runner. ☞

## A's SWINDLE INDIANS

On July 25, 1930, the Philadelphia Athletics twice executed rare triple-steals against the Cleveland Indians. It was the only time the triple-steal has been used twice in the same game.

## CRAFTY CAREY WAS CAPABLE CULPRIT

Pittsburgh's Max Carey was thrown out only twice in 53 steal attempts in 1922. That success ratio remains a major league record.

Ty Cobb      Maury Wills

"I practiced running as hard as I practiced anything," Ty Cobb conceded, years after he had retired from the game. "When I was a kid; I bought all the 'How to Sprint' books advertised in *The Police Gazette.* I spent hours out in the field learning to pump my knees high and especially to break into a fast start.

"I would jog 10 steps, break into a sprint, slow down, and start all over. I spent many hours learning to run in a straight line at top speed with my head over my right shoulder, so that I could watch what the outfielders were doing with the ball.

"I didn't have a lot of natural speed on the bases, but I knew how to run."

Cobb's 1915 record of 96 stolen bases stood until 1962, when Maury Wills stole 104 times in the first year of the expanded 162-game schedule. Lou Brock topped both men when he swiped 118 bases in 1974. Brock also surpassed Cobb's lifetime total of 892 steals—a record once considered as safe as Babe Ruth's 714 home runs.

Mastery of bunt and slide techniques contributed greatly to Cobb's game. He compiled the all-time batting mark of .367 largely because he reached base often on bunts. Cobb taught himself pinpoint bunting control by putting a sweater down on the field and trying to make the ball come to a stop on the sleeve. As a sliding aid, he learned to "read" the eyes of the man covering second as the throw came in. He then aimed his slide away from the tag.

Even slow-footed runners can win games on the basepaths. In close plays, they can knock the ball out of a fielder's mitt with a well-placed kick. "If you're coming home and the ball is going to beat you, your only shot is to knock the ball loose," conceded Bob Boone, a catcher who has been on the receiving end of many collisions.

Kicking helps in the infield too. During the 1951 World Series, Eddie Stanky of the New York Giants knocked the ball out of Phil Rizzuto's glove as the Yankee shortstop attempted a tag. After the game, Rizzuto told the media Stanky had made a smart play.

Straying from the baseline is illegal, but officials generally look the other way when runners dump infielders trying to pivot during a double-play.

"As soon as the second baseman or shortstop catches the ball, I'm out, so I disregard the base," admitted Hal McRae, an aggressive Kansas City Royal of the '70s. "The fielder becomes the base. And the best way to keep him from relaying the throw is to knock him down. He can't throw when he's on his back."

Smart infielders learn to jump as well as pivot.

## STEALING HOME

*Stealing home is one of the most difficult feats of baseball. Ty Cobb did it a record 35 times, and even 30 pitchers have done it since 1900. Maury Wills tried it once, but batter Frank Howard missed the sign and slammed a hard liner that just missed the startled runner. Lou Brock also disdained the idea. But Rod Carew liked it, and made it seven times in 1969. Pitcher Nolan Ryan—who once lost a game when Amos Otis stole home—called the play "humiliating."*

Maury Wills dives back to first on attempted pickoff as Giants' Willie McCovey reaches for throw. The wily Wills, more than anyone else, reintroduced the stolen base as a key offensive weapon.

# STEALING BASES

Before the lively ball era began in 1920, base-stealing was an important part of baseball offense. One run often made the difference in a game where home runs were unlikely, and swift players could turn a walk, single, or error into a double by picking an opportune moment to steal.

Increased emphasis on the home run convinced most big-league managers to play for "the big inning," and to stack their batting orders with lumbering sluggers rather than speedy base-runners. The hit-and-run became a favorite tactic as the tendency toward stealing declined in direct proportion to the absence of fast, cunning runners.

Ty Cobb's old standard of 96 steals was achieved in 1915, but Babe Ruth's bat triggered an offensive boom five years later and base thievery declined. Even Cobb's game changed. In the ten years he played after 1918, he never stole more than 28 bases and had less than 15 six times.

By 1938, the National League leader in stolen bases, Stan Hack of the Cubs, had only 16 to his credit. As late as 1950, Dom DiMaggio paced the American with 15.

Gradually, things began to change. Players like Jackie Robinson and Willie Mays proved the value of speed plus power, and Luis Aparicio proved that teams could win with a combination of pitching, speed, and defense—even if they didn't have power.

Maury Wills, who reached the majors in 1959, showed that herculean performances by a base-stealer could be just as important as consistent production from a home run hitter. In 1962, his exploits on the bases were almost enough to offset a late-season drive by the San Francisco Giants, who repeated their miracle finish of 1951.

Ironically, 1962 was also the year Lou Brock was playing his first full season in the National League. He stole 16 bases for the Cubs—and 24 the next season—but drew more recognition for a prodigious home run clout into the distant center-field bleachers at New York's Polo Grounds.

Only the St. Louis Cardinals saw Brock's immense potential and, in 1964, they traded veteran starter Ernie Broglio and two other players to get him. At the time, the deal looked like a "steal" for the Cubs, but it turned out to be just the opposite.

In his first 16 seasons (not counting an 11 at-bat trial with the '61 Cubs), larcenous Lou stole 900 bases. It took Ty Cobb 24 seasons to reach his mark of 892.

"He had great speed and utilized it well," said Wills of Brock after the former had left the playing field for the broadcast booth. "He got a great jump despite the fact he didn't take a big lead."

Brock, who said he ran only when reasonably sure of making it, became baseball's best base-stealer because he studied the pitchers. "The thing I looked for," he said, "was how they released the ball—quick, fast, moderate, or slow. That determined when I could go."

Joe Torre, a former catcher and Brock teammate who later became a manager, recalled his technique of stealing. "When Brock got on," said Torre, "the catcher tried to get the ball out of his glove before it even got to him. The game is all rhythm and when you don't have that, you end up watching people like Lou Brock steal bases. When he was on base, he made the infielders play out of position and messed up the pitcher's timing. The pitcher kept looking over his shoulder and trying to throw to the plate at the same time."

Ty Cobb took a long lead and used a hook slide, but Brock—with greater speed than Cobb or Wills—got away with a short lead and

Joe Medwick of St. Louis creates controversy with hard slide into Detroit's Marv Owen in 1934 World Series.

Speed demon Willie Davis of the Dodgers slides home long before Houston's John Edwards receives the ball.

pop-up slide—almost no slide at all. That helped preserve his body from the painful "strawberries" which afflict so many base-stealers.

Injury can cripple the team that depends on a one-man running show, but a collection of base thieves can often overcome the absence of a single individual. The 1976 Oakland A's finished tenth in batting with a .246 team average, but wound up second—just two-and-a-half games from the top—because they established an American League record with 341 steals.

In finding success 73 per cent of the time, the A's missed by six of tying the major league mark of the 1911 New York Giants. But Oakland did become the first team to have three players with 50 or more stolen bases: Don Baylor, Bill North, and Bert Campaneris.

"They throw some pressure on you—no doubt about that," said catcher Thurman Munson of the Yankees, American League champions that year. "Most of those guys are so good that if they get a jump, they're going to steal."

With the exception of the delayed steal—where the runner breaks after the relaxed catcher throws the ball back to the pitcher—most steals are achieved against the pitcher—especially a man who neglects to hold runners close to the bases.

A flaw in the pitcher's motion may alert runners about his intentions—is he throwing to first or pitching to the batter? Top runners can tell by watching the movement of the shoulder.

Base-stealing is a more hazardous trade than hitting home runs because the runner risks injury every time he slides—which is often. Many of the most serious accidents of baseball history occurred during slides (especially when players changed their minds after committing themselves). One such accident, in March 1954, knocked Bobby Thomson out of the lineup and gave an obscure youngster named Hank Aaron the chance to play every day. Except for his own sliding fracture—suffered that fall—Aaron stayed in the lineup twenty-one years, long enough to become baseball's new home run king.

# FIELDING

Many baseball managers believe the best offense is a good defense.

Teams built around speed, defense, and pitching have won numerous championships, while power-laden clubs that were weak in defense often failed to play well. ☞

## SPEED PLUS POWER

*With 42 home runs and 40 stolen bases during the 1988 season, Oakland Athletics outfielder Jose Canseco became the charter member of the 40/40 Club (that many homers and steals in the same season). Ten previous players, including Bobby Bonds five times and Willie Mays twice, had reached the 30/30 plateau.*

## RECORD ROBBERS

*The World Champion Cincinnati Reds of 1975, led by Joe Morgan, were successful base-stealers 82 per cent of the time, a major league record.*

## WILD BILL RUNS WILD

*Detroit pitcher Wild Bill Donovan singled, then stole second, third, and home (on a double-steal), in beating Cleveland, 8-3, on May 7, 1906. He also hit a triple in the game.*

## WHEN ST. VRAIN RAN WRONG WAY

*Weak-hitting pitcher Jimmy St. Vrain of the 1902 Cubs, hitting lefthanded for the first time, hit a grounder to Pittsburgh shortstop Honus Wagner and was so startled he made contact that he ran to third.*

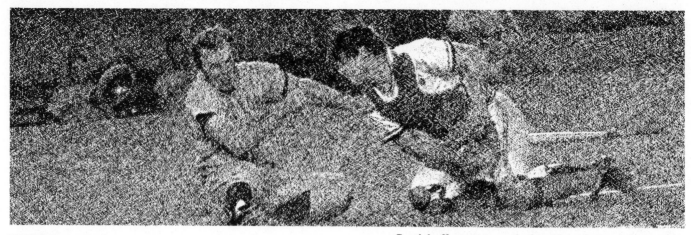

FIELDING *continued*

Special effect captures the intensity of play at home plate.

Leo Durocher was criticized heavily when he traded several sluggers to secure such players as Alvin Dark and Eddie Stanky, who provided stability around second base that helped the New York Giants stage their 1951 "miracle."

The 1959 Chicago White Sox, led by the double-play team of Nellie Fox and Luis Aparicio, won the American League pennant for the first time in forty years.

Championship teams are invariably strong "up the middle"—catcher, shortstop and second base, and center field. Hall of Famer Frankie Frisch, a second baseman in his playing days, once said, "The muscle men who sweep the ball over the wall attract the attention, but the skillful artists who operate around the second base bag win the pennant. The voters should pick more infielders for the Hall of Fame."

Phil Rizzuto, one-time American League Most Valuable Player who played short for the Yankees before taking to the airwaves, is an excellent example of a highly-regarded infielder who had trouble entering the Hall. Rizzuto, instrumental in many New York championships, was a World Series hero in 1951. "They never would have done it without that little pest," said Herman Franks, coach of the losing Giants, in reference to Rizzuto.

Honus Wagner, also a shortstop, was the most sure-handed fielder of his era—and perhaps of all time. Wagner, one of five charter Hall of Famers elected in 1936, began a seventeen-year career with the Pittsburgh Pirates in 1900.

According to *Baseball Magazine* of August 1943, "Perhaps the greatest pair of hands baseball has ever seen dangled at the end of the long arms of Hans Wagner. They, indeed, were more like twin steam shovels than human hands, literally ploughing under National League infields. The Flying Dutchman of the Pirates never fielded the ball alone. He would blithely scoop a handful of dirt too and ball and dirt would go flying over to first base impartially. It left Old Honus hidden behind a smoke screen of his own raising."

Lou Boudreau, Cleveland shortstop at the time the Wagner article appeared, was not only a capable fielder but also a shrewd tactician who became the club's player-manager at age 24. In 1946, he devised the radical Ted Williams shift—designed to thwart the Boston pull-hitter's amazing success against the Tribe.

After Williams had hit three homers—one with the bases loaded—to give the Red Sox an 11-10 victory in the opener of a doubleheader on July 14, Boudreau stationed six fielders on the right side of the diamond—where the lefthanded Williams placed nearly all of his hits. ☞

## LOPES CATCHES CAREY

*Dave Lopes of the Dodgers stole safely 38 straight times in 1975 to erase Max Carey's 1922 record.*

## STEALERS CAN SLUMP

*"Stealing is like hitting—you can go into slumps," said George Case, who swiped 61 bases for the 1943 Senators. "I remember being thrown out three or four times in a row. Clyde Milan was coaching for us and said, 'You're not taking your good lead, and you're too tensed up, too afraid of being picked off. Relax and it'll come back.'"*

Ron Santo . . . good glove at third

The leftfielder, playing deep shortstop, was the only man on the left side of the infield.

Williams, a student of hitting, could have overcome the shift by bunting or slicing the ball to the opposite field, but such strategy would have reduced his power. Though other clubs copied the Williams shift (though none so radically as the Indians), the slugger decided to overpower the defense. He said later that the shift probably deprived him of 20-30 points on his lifetime batting average, which was an excellent .344.

The Red Sox slugger did get even with Lou Boudreau on September 13, 1946. In the first inning at Cleveland, he belted the only inside-the-park home run of his career—a 400-foot drive to left center that proved to be the only run of the game. The 1-0 win gave Boston the pennant.

Radical defenses had been tried before Ted Williams reached the majors. Branch Rickey, the great executive who managed the Cardinals in the early '20s, concocted a shift against Cy Williams, the Phillies' lefthanded slugger who also hit to right field with consistency. Ken Williams of the Browns, who played at the same time, also was a lefthanded pull-hitter and also inspired opponents to shift to right.

Babe Ruth hit lefthanded too, but a shift tried on him by Cleveland's Tris Speaker was unsuccessful. Later, Luke Appling—a righthanded hitter who hit to right—overcame a Yankee shift.

In 1937, the Chicago Cubs shifted to left against Wally Berger of the New York Giants. In a critical doubleheader in late summer, however, the value of the shift was questioned when Berger slammed a ball to Billy Herman, a second baseman playing in the shortstop's spot. Herman couldn't reach first, though strong-armed Billy Jurges —who might have made the play if not for the shift—stood only a foot away.

Herman's miscue opened the gates for the Giants, who reversed a 7-2 deficit and went on to sweep both games. They knocked the Cubs out of the race and went on to win the National League pennant.

# DEFENSIVE STRATEGY

In the seventh game of the 1962 World Series at San Francisco, the New York Yankees loaded the bases with nobody out in the fifth inning of a scoreless game. Manager Alvin Dark of the Giants had two choices: (1) play the infield in to try to cut off a run at the plate if the batter hit a grounder, or (2) play the infield back to decrease the chance of the ball going through—possibly igniting a big inning—

## SUN FIELD

It's debatable whether Brooklyn pitcher Billy Loes ever lost a ground ball in the sun, but it's a fact that the sun plays havoc with outfielders in search of fly balls. Fenway Park has always been especially rough in the fall. "In Boston," a verse goes, "the sun rises in the east and sets in the eyes of the right-fielder."

## MULTIPLE MISCUES

The 1901 Detroit Tigers and 1903 Chicago White Sox share the embarrassing record of most errors in one game: 12.

41

The Sporting News

**Leo Durocher, best known as a manager, was an excellent shortstop for the St. Louis Cardinals.**

and to hope for a double-play on a ground ball. The second choice involves conceding a run unless the DP is infield-to-home-to-first.

Dark, confident his team would get the run back quickly, selected the second choice and did get the desired double-play grounder. However, that was the only run of the game as the Yankees won the World Championship.

In the 1977 World Series against the Yankees, Dodger manager Tom Lasorda faced a similar situation: runners on second and third, one out, in a 3-3 game in the fourth inning of Game 3. With Mickey Rivers the batter, Lasorda's choices were: play the infield in, play it back, or walk Rivers in the hope the next man would hit into an inning-ending double-play.

Like Dark, Lasorda played the infield back, got the grounder, but gave up the run. He too was confident his team would score and he did not want to risk a big inning, which might have resulted from a two-run hit over a drawn-in infield.

Defensive decisions contribute just as much to a victory or defeat as insertion of the proper relief pitcher or pinch-hitter. The five-man infield can save a tie game for the visiting team after the home club loads the bases with less than two out.

Usually, the centerfielder is brought into the infield between the second baseman and shortstop. The left and rightfielders are brought closer together and drawn toward the plate, since a long fly will score the winning run anyway.

From their new position, the outfielders can throw home on short fly balls, keeping the runner at third base, or try to nail him at home if he attempts to score. The transplanted centerfielder guards against balls going up the middle.

Such an alignment greatly increases the chances of a double-play grounder or a force-play at the plate.

Not all infields are good defensive units, however. Zeke Bonura, with the White Sox in the '30s, once allowed four runs to score on a game-ending third out. With the bases loaded and two down, the batter grounded to Bonura. He picked it up, dropped it, repeated the routine, then kicked it some more. When he looked up, all three runners had scored and the batter was en route to third. Bonura threw the ball in that general direction, but it wound up in the dugout.

Slightly more than twenty years later, Dick Stuart proved so erratic at first base that he was called "Stonefingers" and other less-than-complimentary nicknames. When he took a wife, he beamed with pride and told a writer, "Behind every successful man there stands a good woman." The newsman responded, "...with a first-baseman's glove?"

For on-the-field embarrassment, Houston's Norm Miller won't soon forget the day he tried to score on a passed cast. Atlanta catcher Bob Didier caught a low, outside fastball from sidearm reliever Cecil Upshaw. The ball knocked off a small, plastic cast Didier had been wearing on a sore finger, and the white plastic device went spinning toward the backstop. Houston's third base coach, Salty Parker, mistook the cast for the ball and sent Miller home.

Halfway there, Miller looked up to see Didier waiting for him with the ball. "Talk about a look of total disbelief!" said Atlanta pitcher Gary Neibauer. "Miller's eyes got big as saucers and he just stood there as Didier tagged him out."

## WILLIE MAYS
## WAS FLAWLESS FIELDER

*Former teammate Monte Irvin on Willie Mays: "I've talked to many players, black and white, who say that no one could play center field like Willie Mays. Not only was he so great going back to field the fly ball or catch a line drive, but he was terrific coming in too. He could catch the low liner like there was nothing to it. He saved many games for the Giants.*

*"There was a period where he could have been Most Valuable Player eight or nine years in a row; he was that valuable to the club. He could cut the ball off in left or right center and keep it to a single. He would always make the big catch in a crucial situation.*

*"One year in Pittsburgh, he went back on a ball hit directly over his head. By the time he got to where the ball was going to fall, the wind had carried it over to the right so he couldn't bring his glove across his body. So all he did was catch the ball in his bare hand on a dead run. He always got a great jump on the ball, had huge hands, and great reflexes."*

Hank Aaron and Willie Mays, representing the cities (but not the teams) of their big-league births, enjoyed a nostalgic meeting at Hall of Fame Day in Cooperstown.

Bob Bartosz

# FREAKS OF FIELDING

Anything can happen in baseball and usually does.

In 1905, Jack McCarthy of the Cubs threw out three Pittsburgh runners at the plate in a single game. No other player has performed that feat.

Twenty-two years later, an unassisted triple play—the most unusual defensive play in the game—occurred on successive days, May 30-31.

In 1945, second baseman Irvin Hall of the Athletics smashed a Dutch Leonard pitch right back to the Washington moundsman. Leonard got his glove on the ball, but then lost it. A hasty search revealed that the ball had lodged inside the pitcher's pants!

A's shortstop Eddie Joost played the comedic role in '48 when a grounder from Boston's Billy Goodman literally went up his sleeve, then dropped to the waist inside his uniform shirt. Ted Williams, the runner at third base, was so overcome with laughter he couldn't run home.

Philadelphia was victimized again when a Washington player socked a long ball to center in old Griffith Stadium. It rolled into the small doghouse-type box where the flag was stored. Socks Siebold poked his head and shoulders into the box in a vain search for the ball while the surprised Senator circled the bases with an inside-the-doghouse home run.

A real dog had the last bark during an American Association game in 1886. Chicken Wolf, batting for Louisville in the last of the eleventh, hit a line drive to right for a base-hit. Cincinnati's Abner Powell gave chase, but a dog—which had been sleeping near the fence when the action started—chased Powell and grabbed his leg just as he was about to throw the ball toward the infield. The dog let go just as Wolf crossed the plate with the winning run.

★ ★ ★ ★

# FIELDING FACTS

There are no lefthanded catchers in baseball primarily because there are no lefthanded catchers' gloves. In the early days of the game, almost all batters were righthanded (lefthanded batters were converted) and it was easier for a righthanded catcher to whip a throw to first or second without a batter standing in his way.

A notable exception was John Clements, hard-hitting receiver for the Phillies and several other clubs shortly before the turn of the century. Joe Wall and John Donahue were lefthanded catchers who played briefly in 1901-02, and Dale Long of the Cubs caught several games in 1958. On one occasion, Long used a first baseman's mitt because the team had no lefthanded catcher's glove.

While first basemen may throw from either side, teams prefer to have a lefthander at that position—the glove would be closer to the other infielders—while righthanders must be stationed elsewhere in the infield. The tough double-play pivot would be difficult for a southpaw, and a third baseman needs to have his glove hand facing into the infield.

Ironically, superstar third baseman Brooks Robinson, who retired in 1977 after more than 20 seasons with the Orioles, is a natural lefthander who was righthanded only when fielding and batting. Eddie Mathews, Hall of Fame third baseman of the Braves, was a lefthanded batter who threw from the right side. ☞

## THE IRON HORSE

Most trivia fans can give you the details of Lou Gehrig's consecutive games record, which likely will never be broken. Baseball's Iron Horse played 2130 games for the New York Yankees between 1925 and 1939.

He replaced Wally Pipp at first base on June 2, 1925, and played in every New York game until May 2, 1939, when manager Joe McCarthy replaced Gehrig with Babe Dahlgren. Gehrig's name never appeared in another Yankee lineup. He died of multiple sclerosis sixteen years to the day after he had replaced Pipp.

However, Gehrig's astonishing playing streak actually started the day before he replaced Pipp as he was inserted into the lineup by manager Miller Huggins as a pinch-hitter for shortstop Pee Wee Wanninger.

Longevity by position, according to statistics computed over the years, ranks catchers first, pitchers second, outfielders third, and infielders last. Though catching is the most difficult position physically, the demand for capable catchers is the major reason receivers can expect the longest survival spans in the majors.

# HITTING

Babe Ruth reached base 54 per cent of the time he came to bat during the 1923 season. Reaching safely 375 times in 592 appearances, the powerful Yankee outfielder hit .393 with 41 home runs, 151 runs scored, and 131 runs batted in. But the secret to his success was his patience at the plate; he walked a record 170 times.

Baseball teams treasure batters who can get on base—whether they do it by hitting, walking, or being hit by pitches. Good contact hitters are also valued. A strikeout gains nothing, but a ground ball or timely fall may produce a run or move previous runners into scoring position.

Hitting a baseball is one of the most difficult jobs in sport. The ball takes only 5/10ths of a second to travel from pitcher to hitter—and the hitter has only 2/10ths of a second to move his bat from his shoulder to the contact zone. That leaves 3/10ths of a second for him to:

- pick up the ball visually,
- determine what kind of pitch is coming,
- decide if it will be a ball or strike,
- decide whether to swing or take the pitch.

It is simply amazing that Joe Sewell, playing a full schedule, struck out only four times in 1925 and tied that record in 1929. In 1930, Pat Caraway of the White Sox fanned Sewell twice on May 26. The Cleveland shortstop did not strike out again that season.

Nellie Fox of the 1958 White Sox went a record 98 games without a strikeout because he followed a simple philosophy at the plate: "Meet the ball," he said. "Keep your eye on the ball. A big swing has more arc, but doesn't follow the baseball."

Power-hitters have a tendency to strike out because they swing hard. Babe Ruth held the lifetime strikeout record for years until Mickey Mantle passed him. Willie Stargell later passed Mantle.

Joe DiMaggio, who struck out only once per 18.48 at-bats and homered once per 18.89 at-bats, was a notable exception to the rule that long-ball hitters strike out often. Mantle, DiMaggio's successor in center field, went down on strikes once per 4.74 at-bats. ☞

**Babe Ruth's records weren't all positive. For years, he held the mark for most strikeouts by a hitter.**

Robert D. Opie

In one of Mantle's big years, however, he teamed with Roger Maris to give the Yankees the finest 1-2 batting punch for a single season. With Maris hitting 61 homers and Mantle 54 in 1961, the Yankees ran up a record total of 240 and won the pennant and World Series. The 1947 Giants and 1956 Reds share the NL mark at 221.

The best lifetime home run tandem consisted of Hank Aaron and Eddie Mathews, who belted 863 during their days as teammates with the Braves.

Aaron, who had an unorthodox cross-handed batting style as an amateur, was one of many successful hitters whose pose at the plate defied basic batting rules. Al Simmons, the Philadelphia A's star of the '30s, was another with a unique style.

Simmons stood deep in the batting box with feet close together. When he swung, he took a long step with his left (front) foot—but toward third base rather than the pitcher. Though experts said he was hitting "with his foot in the bucket," Simmons did shift his hips and weight into the pitch and hit with authority—often to the opposite field.

Lefthanded hitter Stan Musial, like Simmons a Hall of Fame outfielder, also stood deep in the box and often hit to the opposite field. In 1948, he missed the opportunity by one home run to lead the National League in batting, base-hits, doubles, triples, homers, runs, runs batted in, and slugging.

With 230 hits, Musial hit .376 and had a slugging average of .702, based on 46 doubles, 18 triples, and 39 homers. He scored 135 runs and knocked in 131. Moreover, he fanned just 34 times in 611 at-bats.

Musial's corkscrew stance was marked by the position of his feet —close together, as in the style of Babe Ruth. The Yankee slugger stood taller in the box, however, and had a classic swing that made writers of the time suggest that he looked as good striking out as he did hitting a home run.

Ty Cobb crouched and choked up on the bat while batting, and induced Harry Heilmann to do the same with the Tigers. The latter kept his feet six inches apart and a foot from the plate. With his hands two inches up the bat handle, Heilmann bent over to get a good view of every pitch.

Lou Boudreau's "hunchback" stance also involved an obvious bend that was effective but dangerous; pitched balls came close to the Cleveland player-manager.

Rogers Hornsby stood far from the plate and stepped into the pitch. Joe DiMaggio kept his feet spread far apart. Heinie Groh kept his toes facing the mound and used a short "bottle bat" which helped him hit fastballs consistently.

Without question, the most unusual stance was Mel Ott's. The powerful lefthanded slugger lifted his front foot several inches off the ground just before he unleashed his swing.

"I got my main power from my back foot," he explained. "With my right foot off the ground, I wouldn't be caught flat-footed. I had a better chance to wait on the pitch."

The patient Ott slammed 511 homers for the Giants.

**Eddie Mathews teamed with Hank Aaron to produce the most home runs by teammates—863.**

**Stan Musial, long-time bane of National League pitchers, kept his feet close together when he batted—a style used with success by Babe Ruth.**

## DODGER DONS COULD HIT AND PITCH

*Don Newcombe, Dodger star of the '50s, hit and ran well—and stole home during the 1955 Brooklyn pennant drive. Don Drysdale, who succeeded Newk as the club's crack righthander, hit .300 with seven homers and 19 runs batted in over 130 at-bats in 1965. Drysdale and Newcombe had good power at bat, but were best known for their outstanding achievements on the mound.*

# KNOW THEM BY THEIR STANCE:

THEY TOSSED AWAY THE BOOK ON CORRECT HITTING...

HEINIE GROH, USED A "BOTTLE BAT"... STOOD WITH BOTH TOES FACING THE MOUND...

TY COBB, ONE OF THE GAME'S GREATEST HITTERS, USED A CROUCH, CHOKED HIS BAT... LED A.L. BATTERS 11 OUT OF 12 YEARS...1907 TO 1919

STAN LOPATA, HAS A "SQUAT" WHICH HAS UPPED HIS BATTING AVERAGE FROM .220 TO .290 FOR THE SEASON!

BABE RUTH... WITH THAT STAND-UP,- FEET-TOGETHER STANCE THAT SYMBOLIZED HIS GREAT HOME RUN POWER...

# BUNTING

The bunt is an offensive maneuver with multiple purposes. It is most often used as a sacrifice, to move a runner into scoring position (second or third base). It may be used in a squeeze play to score a runner from third. Or it may be employed by a speedy batter hoping to reach first base—and gain an infield hit—before a play can be made on him.

Dickie Pearce, shortstop of the champion Brooklyn Atlantics in 1864-65, dropped the very first bunt—moving his hand along the bat, easing it back, and softening the impact of ball against wood. The ball rolled a short distance in fair territory and died, while Pearce raced to first base with an infield hit.

By 1910, a full decade before the dawn of the home run era, the bunt was widely used. Napoleon Lajoie once beat out six bunts in a doubleheader. Ty Cobb and George Sisler helped themselves to .400 batting years by bunting often. When the infield played in, looking for the bunt, they swung away. With the defense back, they bunted—always trying to keep the ball away from the pitcher.

Hall of Fame pitcher Lefty Grove hated the bunt. "I don't have too much trouble with the guys who swing from their heels," he said. "The hitters who get under my skin are the pests who bunt and drag, or poke at the ball. They're hard to fool."

Heinie Manush, a heavy hitter of the late '20s and '30s, became a superb bunter who taught the technique to several other players. Johnny Pesky, Phil Rizzuto, Eddie Stanky, and Cookie Lavagetto mastered the bunt and helped their clubs win games with seemingly harmless infield dribblers.

In September 1951, Rizzuto and Joe DiMaggio, the runner at third, worked a perfect squeeze play for the Yankees against the Indians.

With the bases loaded and one out in the last of the ninth, Rizzuto batted against Cleveland ace Bob Lemon in a tie game. If Rizzuto had hit away, he might have grounded into an inning-ending double-play. The first pitch was low, but the umpire called it a strike. Rizzuto staged a big argument on purpose, hoping to convince the Indian infield he wanted a better pitch because he would be swinging.

The trick worked because none of the infielders moved in. DiMaggio, an excellent runner, made the squeeze work by not breaking for home too soon—a runner who does may alert the pitcher in time for him to make a pitch-out that will allow the catcher to tag the runner coming home.

"Lemon had no idea Joe was coming until it was too late," Rizzuto recalled. "Suddenly, with the pitch on its way and Joe breaking for home, I dumped the ball down, and that was the ballgame."

When bunting for a hit, Rizzuto made a practice of laying the ball down almost after the pitch was past him. A righthanded batter, he was also capable of pushing the ball toward first base. This was the drag bunt, executed while the batter is in motion toward first base. ☞

## RULES ROBBED TED WILLIAMS

In 1954, Ted Williams lost the batting title because he fell 14 official at-bats shy of the required total of 400. Williams, a feared slugger who received 136 walks, hit .345, four points higher than spray hitter Bobby Avila, who walked only 59 times. But bases on balls are not counted as official at-bats. Qualifications for the batting crown subsequently were changed to count plate appearances rather than official trips.

## HOW WILLIAMS HIT .406

Ted Williams, last man to hit .400, reached the figure by banging out six hits in eight trips during an end-of-season doubleheader between his Red Sox and the Philadelphia A's in 1941. He wound up with a .406 mark for the season. Going into the twinbill, Williams' average was .39955.

Joe DiMaggio's bat and glove were so outstanding that his excellent instincts on the bases were often overlooked.

The suicide squeeze—the most difficult bunt play—can make the manager look like a genius or a goat. If the batter misses the ball, the runner coming home from third is certain to be tagged out by the catcher. If he bunts the ball, he must push it far enough from the plate so that the catcher can't reach it, yet out of reach of the pitcher or any infielder.

On the safety squeeze, the runner from third breaks for home only after the ball is bunted.

Pete Rose, long-time Cincinnati infielder, used the bunt to win the 1969 batting title from Roberto Clemente on the last day of the season and, nine years later, bunted for a base-hit to keep his long hitting streak alive.

# STRANGE HOME RUNS

The home run—the grandest achievement in baseball—is usually a mighty shot over a distant fence. But not always.

When Babe Ruth was with the Boston Red Sox in 1919, he was credited with a home run on an infield fly. "It must have been the highest popup ever hit," said Ruth's victim, pitcher Lefty Leifield of the St. Louis Browns. "The infielders were running around like chickens with their heads cut off, yelling that they couldn't see the ball.

"When that ball came down, Babe had already rounded third. There wasn't any chance to make a play on him and three runs scored."

On June 19, 1942, Dom DiMaggio of the Red Sox sliced the ball down the right field line. White Sox outfielder Wally Moses watched it roll under the bullpen bench, where he parted the feet of the occupants in frantic search. By the time he found the sphere, DiMaggio had scored the only run of the game.

Earlier in the century, Cascade held a 1-0 lead over Buckhorn with two out in the last of the ninth when the Buckhorn batter sent the ball toward the left field fence. Just as it got there, however, it broke in two. Half completed the journey into home run territory, while the leftfielder caught the other half. After a protracted argument, the umpire ruled the game over, with Cascade the victor by a score of 1-½.

Then there was the time Cleveland's Jimmy McAleer hit a ball into an empty tomato can at the base of the outfield wall. Hugh Duffy, unable to pry the ball loose, threw the whole can toward the infield, which relayed it home. Tagged with ball in glove, McAleer would have been out. But tagged with ball in can was something else. The umpire ruled him safe. ☞

## TWO SLUGGERS IN ONE LINEUP

*Probably the best seasons enjoyed by slugging teammates occurred in 1927 and 1932. Babe Ruth and Lou Gehrig powered the Yankees to the '27 title—Ruth with 60 homers, 164 runs batted in, and a .356 average. Gehrig slugged 47, knocked in 175, and hit .373. Five years later, Al Simmons of the Athletics hit 35 homers, knocked in 151 runs, and batted .322, but was overshadowed by Jimmie Foxx, with 58 homers, 169 RBI, and a .364 mark. The A's also won.*

## GAVVY CRAVATH, EARLY HR KING

*Dead-ball slugger Gavvy Cravath of the Phillies won six home run titles by learning to hit to the opposite field in cozy Baker Bowl, with its 280-foot line in right. In 1915, he slammed 24 homers—more than 10 per cent of the National League's total.*

## EARLY & LATE

*Rusty Staub and Ty Cobb were the only players to homer in the majors before their 20th and after their 40th birthdays.*

## RUTH FOOLED DEFENSE IN FINAL FLURRY

*Babe Ruth's last great home run display—three in a game for the Boston Braves at Pittsburgh's Forbes Field on May 25, 1935—also featured a solid single through the shortstop hole. The Pirate shortstop had shifted to the right side of second in a common shift used against the aging lefthanded pull-hitter.*

---

## TALENTED TED

*Experts who insist that Ted Williams was the best hitter in baseball history have evidence to back them up: he was the only man to win more than two titles in each of the three major hitting categories—batting average, home runs, and runs batted in. Here is how the top hitters fared:*

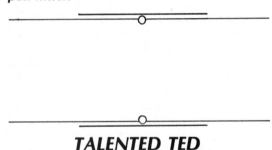

| Name | Led in Batting | HRs | RBIs |
|------|----------------|-----|------|
| Ted Williams | 6 | 6 | 4 |
| Ty Cobb | 12 | 1 | 4 |
| Babe Ruth | 1 | 12 | 6 |
| Rogers Hornsby | 7 | 2 | 4 |
| Jimmie Foxx | 2 | 4 | 3 |
| Joe DiMaggio | 2 | 2 | 2 |
| Mickey Mantle | 2 | 4 | 1 |
| Willie Mays | 1 | 4 | 0 |
| Honus Wagner | 8 | 0 | 3 |
| Hank Aaron | 2 | 4 | 4 |
| Stan Musial | 7 | 0 | 2 |
| Lou Gehrig | 1 | 3 | 5 |

---

**STRANGE HOME RUNS** *continued*

The longest home run was produced by a spontaneous combination of long ball and hopper. Joe Hauser, with Baltimore of the International League, deposited the ball in the passing coal car, which hauled it 32 miles.

Pitcher Wes Ferrell, an excellent hitter, homered in the eighth to tie and in the twelfth to win for the Red Sox, 3-2, over the White Sox on August 22, 1934.

Light-hitting Joe Niekro hit the first home run of his ten-year career in 1976—a game-winning blow off brother Phil, a good hitter.

Hoyt Wilhelm, even a lighter hitter than Joe Niekro, homered in his first at-bat as a rookie with the '52 Giants, then tripled in his second. But he never hit another home run or triple over the rest of his twenty-one-year career as a relief specialist.

Pitcher-outfielder Johnny Cooney of the Boston Bees in the '30s hit his first homer after playing fifteen years, then hit another the next day. He played five more years without hitting any more.

Many players have homered in their first at-bat, but Bob Nieman of the 1951 Browns was the only man to hit home runs in his first two plate appearances in the majors.

Eight years later, a pinch-runner homered for the Red Sox. Gene Stephens, inserted as a runner for Ted Williams during a Boston uprising, was cut down in a force-play, but the rally continued and his batting turn came up again. Manager Billy Jurges let him bat and Stephens responded with a grand-slam homer. Boston won the contest from New York, 13-3.

Six players have hit two grand-slams in the same game—pitcher Tony Cloninger in the National League, plus American Leaguers Tony Lazzeri, Jim Gentile, Jim Tabor, Rudy York, and Jim Northrup. Two teams have hit slams in the same inning—the 1962 Minnesota Twins (Bob Allison and Harmon Killebrew) and the 1969 Houston Astros (Denis Menke and Jim Wynn). The Braves, Indians, and Twins all hit four consecutive home runs—in 1961, 1963, and 1964, respectively.

Home run history illustrates the unpredictable nature of the game.

# LEFTY-RIGHTY PERCENTAGE

Lefthanded hitters have an advantage over righthanded pitchers and an overall edge over righthanded batters. For these reasons, and because a majority of pitchers are righthanded, many natural righthanders become southpaw swingers or switch-hitters.

When a lefthanded batter faces a righthanded pitcher, he has an excellent vantage point. The ball will be delivered in his direct line of sight and the curve will break toward him rather than away from him.

The lefty-lefty match is more difficult, but Ty Cobb believed it could be conquered. "What I did," explained Cobb, a lefthanded batter who baffled pitchers of all types, "was stand as far back in the batter's box as I could. That gave me an extra split second to watch the ball and a chance to hit it after it had broken. I also tried to hit it in the direction it was breaking—often to left field (the opposite field) instead of pulling it to right." ☞

Curveball pitchers pose particular problems for hitters, who must decide instantly whether the ball will curve or hit them in the head. Batters who bat from the opposite side than the pitchers throw get a better viewpoint, but the rule doesn't apply to the screwball. A righty's screwball behaves like a lefty's curve and breaks away from the lefthanded hitter. For that reason, switch-hitter Frankie Frisch batted lefthanded against lefthanded screwball pitcher Carl Hubbell.

Normally, the all-southpaw match is difficult. Even Stan Musial conceded, "You don't know when to pull the trigger against a southpaw. A righthander may fool you and you still can hit the pitch. You're dead if you guess wrong against a southpaw."

The great Cardinal star, strictly a lefthanded batter, never enjoyed the luxury of a perfect view at all times. Switch-hitters do. Robert Ferguson, second baseman-manager of the New York Mutuals (later Giants) in 1871, led the way, and Max Carey, Frisch, Mickey Mantle, Red Schoendienst, and Pete Rose perfected the practice.

Mantle, a natural righthander converted to the left side by his righthanded-throwing grandfather, was the most powerful switch-hitter in baseball history. Ten times, he hit a home run righthanded and a home run lefthanded in the same game.

Frisch and Rose compiled the best batting marks for switch-hitters. Each had a .348 season.

The Los Angeles Dodgers of the '60s drove pitchers batty with an infield comprised entirely of switch-hitters: Wes Parker, Jim Lefebvre, Maury Wills, and Junior Gilliam from first to third.

Anyone batting from the left side has an advantage because he is several feet closer to first base and, when completing his swing, is directly facing the bag. A righthander stands on the third base side of the plate and must uncoil, turning himself halfway around, before he can begin his race to first.

In 1947, an enterprising sportswriter from *The New York Sun*—using 1946 statistics—calculated that lefthanders enjoyed an 18-point advantage over righthanders at the plate. The figure wavers from year to year, but there's no doubt southpaw swingers have an edge on their righthanded counterparts.

# PINCH-HITTING

Pinch-hitting is an art which several players have refined to a science. It involves coming off the bench in a crucial situation—invariably with no previous warm-ups except for batting practice—and making or breaking a team's fortunes.

Because pitchers are generally weak hitters, they often depart for pinch-hitters in the late innings of close games. The American League's introduction of a designated hitter in 1973 reduced the role of the pinch-hitter because the DH batted whenever the pitcher's batting turn came up.

Managers in both leagues who play percentage baseball frequently substitute lefthanded pinch-hitters for righthanded batters (and vice versa) after the defensive team makes a pitching change. If a righthander replaces a lefthander on the mound, a manager may yank a righthanded batter for one who swings from the left side.

Top stars are seldom removed for pinch-hitters unless they are hurt or the score is lopsided when their batting turn comes up. After striking out twice and popping up against Lefty Grove on Opening Day of the 1927 season, Babe Ruth was removed for Ben Paschal,

## STAN MUSIAL'S PEEKABOO STANCE

Pitcher Ted Lyons once said that Stan Musial's batting stance reminded him of a kid peeking around the corner to see if the cops were coming.

## HOW TO HIT WITHOUT A BAT

Hall of Famer Napoleon Lajoie singled twice in 1906 without holding a bat. He was able to rap hits over first base by tossing his bat at the ball.

## MOST TOTAL BASES

Joe Adcock, first baseman for the Milwaukee Braves, racked up 18 total bases —a major league record—when he slammed four home runs and a double at Brooklyn on July 31, 1954.

who stroked a run-scoring single to help the Yankees beat the A's, 8-3. That was the year Ruth hit 60 home runs.

Smoky Burgess, a rotund catcher of the '50s, was the most prolific pinch-hitter of baseball history until Manny Mota exceeded his record 144 pinch-hits in 1979. Jerry Lynch swatted 18 pinch-homers in his career, and Johnny Frederick hit six in a season for Brooklyn. Frenchy Bordagaray, also with Brooklyn, hit a record .465 in emergency roles in 1938.

In 1976, third-string catcher Jose Morales of the Montreal Expos found his niche as a pinch-hitter. He set records for pinch-hits (25), at-bats (78), and games (82) by an emergency batsman in one season.

Early baseball rules discouraged the use of pinch-hitters. In fact, NL clubs could not make any substitutions before the fourth inning in 1876, that circuit's first season.

Dode Criss of the St. Louis Browns was the first heavy-duty pinch-hitter, when he registered 12 hits in 41 at-bats—twice the workload of any previous batting substitute—in 1908. The following year, John McGraw of the Giants began using Moose McCormick and Otis Crandall as pinch-hitters.

In 1911, the same year he earned the nickname "Doc" for saving "sick" ballgames as the first regular relief pitcher, Crandall was the hero of Game 5 of the World Series against the Athletics. With two outs in the ninth and the Giants behind, 3-1, Crandall doubled home a run, scored the tying run himself, then pitched a scoreless tenth. The Giants scored a run to win, 4-3.

Two years later, Ham Hyatt of the Pirates made quite a splash by socking three pinch-hit homers with the dead ball then in use. A pitcher, Ray Caldwell of the Yankees, hit pinch-homers in consecutive games in June 1915.

Red Lucas, a pitcher with a strong bat, collected 114 hits in pinch-batting roles—fourth on the all-time list—and Wes Ferrell, Red Ruffing, Don Newcombe, Don Drysdale, and Ken Brett also proved adept at pinch-hitting, usually for their fellow pitchers.

Tommy Davis, two-time National League batting king for the Dodgers, became an excellent pinch-hitter in his later years. His lifetime emergency average was .320. Dave Philley (.299) once collected nine straight pinch-hits for the Phillies.

Other outstanding pinch-hitters were Gates Brown, Vic Davalillo, Tito Francona, Johnny Mize, Red Schoendienst, Enos Slaughter, and Elmer Valo.

# PITCHING

The 1947 New York Giants and 1956 Cincinnati Reds share the National League record for most home runs by a team—221—but neither won the pennant. Their pitching wasn't up to championship caliber.

Many baseball insiders insist that pitching is 75 to 90 per cent of the game. Light-hitting teams with good pitching, backed by good defense and often good speed, have won pennants many times. Heavy-hitting teams with weak pitching haven't.

In 1930, the Philadelphia Phillies had a team batting average of .315. Each of the eight regulars hit .300. Yet the club finished last because its pitchers allowed the opposition to score a record average of 6.71 earned runs per game! ☞

## STRANGE HOME RUN RECORDS

*Dale Long of the 1956 Pirates and Don Mattingly of the 1987 Yankees homered in eight consecutive games. Frank Howard of the 1968 Senators hit 10 in six games. Stan Musial (Cardinals) and Nate Colbert (Padres) each hit five home runs in a doubleheader.*

## WHY WHITE SOX WARNED APPLING

*Shortstop Luke Appling, a specialist at tiring a pitcher by hitting countless fouls, was warned by the White Sox to cease and desist because he was losing too many balls.*

Ernie SHORE
BOSTON RED SOX

PITCHED A PERFECT GAME ON JUNE 23, 1917 VS WASHINGTON... WON A TOTAL OF 3 WORLD SERIES GAMES FOR THE RED SOX IN 1915 AND 1916..... WON 18 REGULAR SEASON GAMES IN 1915 AND 15 THE FOLLOWING YEAR

Hall of Fame pitchers Walter Johnson, Grover Cleveland Alexander, and Carl Hubbell (left to right) had excellent control, full command of their pitches, and expert knowledge of enemy hitters.

"When you get consistently good pitching," said Walter Alston, long-time manager of the pitching-rich Dodgers, "you keep the score low and have a chance in every game. You can try to use all the ways there are to score a run, and benefit from any error or lucky break. You're never out of the game.

"But if your pitching gives up a lot of runs, there will be times when you're out of business early, where the only way to get back is with a lot of slugging of your own. So it's pretty hard to be lucky when your pitching is bad."

Good control and a variety of pitches are invariably hallmarks of baseball's best pitchers. Southpaw Carl Hubbell, who won a record 24 straight games for the Giants in 1936-37, was always right around the plate. On July 2, 1933, he didn't walk a batter while pitching a six-hit, 1-0 victory over the Cardinals in a game that took eighteen innings.

Cy Young, who would go on to post a record 511 lifetime victories, illustrated the importance of good control when he worked for the Red Sox in 1904; he walked only 28 in 380 innings pitched.

Before the advent of the lively ball in 1920, pitchers worked more often, primarily because relief pitching was not widely practiced and also because they did not have to bear down as hard on the collection of slap hitters who then populated the majors. Many old-timers worked doubleheaders—Iron Man McGinnity winning three of them in August 1903 and Ed Reulbach tossing a double shutout five years later.

The four biggest winners of baseball history were Young (511), Walter Johnson (404), and Christy Mathewson and Grover Cleveland Alexander (373 each). All were active at the same time, though Young had reached the end of the line when Alexander was a sophomore in 1912.

Speaking from a hitter's viewpoint, Casey Stengel, a 1912 rookie, later recalled his memories of that era. "Johnson was the most amazing pitcher in the American League and Alexander in the

## WHY WANER CLOBBERED THE CURVE

*Lloyd and Paul Waner—Pittsburgh's "Big Poison" and "Little Poison"—played corncob baseball as youths on an Oklahoma farm. Baseballs were hard to come by. "The constant practice of hitting the strange curves of the corncob did more than anything else to build up my batting," said Paul, owner of a .333 lifetime average. "You had to keep your eye on the cob because it would blind you if it hit you in the eye or hurt if it hit your head. There were more curves in those corncob games than I have ever seen in a real baseball game."*

## LONGEST RELIEF STINT

*Zip Zabel of the Cubs worked 18 1/3 innings of relief in beating the Dodgers, 4-3, in 19 innings on June 17, 1915. It was the longest relief stint in baseball history.*

National," he said. "Alexander had to pitch in that little Philadelphia ballpark (Baker Bowl) with that big tin fence in right field and he pitched shutouts—which must mean he could do it. He had a fastball, curve, change of pace, and perfect control. With Johnson, you knew what was coming but you couldn't hit it. He had perfect control too."

Ty Cobb said Johnson might have been even more effective. "If he had been willing to throw a few dusters and keep the batters on edge worrying about that cannonball he threw," suggested Cobb, "nobody knows how many more games he might have won. But obviously he was afraid of his own speed and what he might do to the batter."

Warren Spahn, a lefthander who mastered the screwball after his fastball faded, won more games than any pitcher of the lively ball era: 363. Spahn, who retired in 1965, probably would have joined Johnson and Young at the 400 level had he not lost four youthful years to wartime military service. Spahn was 26 when he won his first game for the Braves.

# PITCHING FEATS

Pitchers with a high ratio of strikeouts to walks are usually successful, but high strikeout totals are not necessary for victory. In the '20s, Cleveland's Emil Levsen pitched a doubleheader victory over the Red Sox, 6-1 and 5-1, without a single strikeout.

By contrast, Roger Clemens fanned a record 20 Seattle Mariners in a nine-inning game on April 29, 1986. Several previous pitchers had whiffed 19 in a game.

An obscure righthander named Tom Cheney fanned 21 in a sixteen-inning, 2-1 triumph for Washington over Baltimore in 1962.

Johnny Vander Meer was not as overpowering as Clemens or Cheney, but the first use of lights in Brooklyn's Ebbets Field helped him record his second consecutive no-hitter for Cincinnati on June 15, 1938. Allie Reynolds, Virgil Trucks, Jim Maloney, Dean Chance, and Nolan Ryan were others who tossed two no-hitters in the same season—but not back-to-back.

The Trucks feat was especially remarkable because his two 1-0 gems comprised 40 per cent of his victory total in 1952. Without the no-hitters, Trucks would have had a 3-19 record for last-place Detroit!

When Reynolds threw his second no-hitter the previous September, catcher Yogi Berra threw a scare into the Yankee Stadium crowd when he dropped a foul pop that would have ended the game. That error gave the hitter—Ted Williams—another chance. But Reynolds made him pop to Berra again.

Ryan, who fanned a record 383 batters in 1973, broke by one the old standard of Sandy Koufax and later duplicated Koufax's feat of hurling four no-hitters. In 1966, Sandy's last season, he pitched his only perfect game, blanking the Cubs. Chicago pitcher Bobby Hendley pitched a one-hitter himself.

The Koufax-Hendley duel might have been the best-pitched complete game to be played in the regulation nine innings, but a battle between Fred Toney of the Reds and Hippo Vaughn of the Cubs on May 2, 1917 was far more gripping. At the end of nine, both pitchers had pitched no-hitters! Vaughn yielded two hits in the tenth to lose, 1-0, while Toney kept his no-hitter intact. ☞

National League

**Warren Spahn won more games than any pitcher who performed after World War II. He won 20 or more 13 times —including a remarkable 23-7 season at age 42.**

## Types of Pitches
## Thrown to Baffle Batters

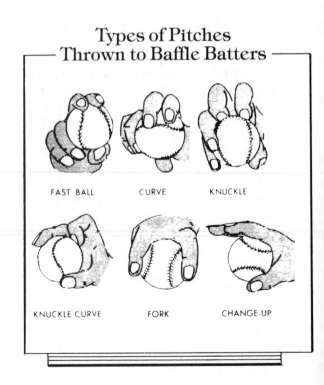

FAST BALL    CURVE    KNUCKLE

KNUCKLE CURVE    FORK    CHANGE-UP

Cincinnati's Doc Parker was guilty of the worst pitching performance in history on June 21, 1901, when he yielded 21 runs on 26 hits to Brooklyn. But the Philadelphia Athletics made an effort to corner the market on bad pitching.

In 1916, Bruno Haas walked 16 Tigers in his debut. In 1932, reliever Ed Rommel allowed 14 runs on 29 hits in a seventeen-inning relief job against Cleveland, but won, 18-17. Four years later, Howard Lisenbee yielded 26 hits in a 17-2 rout at the hands of the White Sox.

Lisenbee might have been better off walking a few hitters—but don't tell that to Milt Pappas. The Cubs' righthander missed a perfect game in 1972 when he walked Larry Stahl on a 3-2 pitch with two outs in the ninth.

Early Wynn won 300 games, but allowed more walks than any other pitcher, while Bill Fischer would be totally forgotten if not for his ability to throw strikes. Fischer, spot-starting with the Kansas City A's in 1962, pitched a record 84 1/3 innings without yielding a walk. His record that year was 4-12.

Many pitchers are effective even though they give up many hits and walks. Yankees Lefty Gomez, in 1941, and Mel Stottlemyre, in 1970, pitched 11-walk shutouts, and Larry Cheney of the Cubs stopped the Giants, 7-0, on a 14-hitter in the World War I period.

Fingers of Eddie Rommel reveal knuckleball grip. Veteran hurler had enough stamina to endure 29-hit, 14-run onslaught in a 1932 relief outing—and win, 18-17!

# WHAT PITCHERS THROW

The repertoire of the major league pitcher consists of much more than fastball and curve. Only overpowering pitchers—Walter Johnson and Sandy Koufax, for example—could survive with such a limited assortment.

Legal deliveries currently in use include the fastball, curveball, slider, sinker, forkball, knuckleball, palm ball, screwball, change-up, and knuckle curve. The spitter, emery ball, shine ball, grease ball, and sandpaper ball occasionally pop up too—despite the fact that such tricky pitches were banned in 1920.

Though Candy Cummings threw the first curve in 1864, skeptics had to be convinced six years later that a ball would actually curve. The National Bureau of Standards has since decided that a baseball can curve no more than 17½ inches.

Curves pose problems for young pitchers because they place a strain on the elbow. Improperly thrown, they become "hanging curves" and often result in a home run or extra-base hit. Proper grip of the curve is up to the individual pitcher, but in all cases, the index finger guides the ball and the middle finger pulls.

Like the curve, the fastball is held across the seams. Wrist flexibility gives the ball movement, as well as velocity, and the good fastball will, in effect, act as a mini-curve; it will tail to one side or the other, and may even rise—especially when thrown by a side-armer.

The slider approaches the plate like a fastball, but suddenly slides a few inches to the side. It may also break downward. A derivation of the slip pitch once taught by catcher-turned-manager Paul Richards, the slider came into widespread use in the early '60s. Whitey Ford didn't throw one until 1961. The pitch is popular among pitchers because it is easy to throw and hard for batters to identify. ☞

## THE SWITCH-PITCHER

Noted baseball executive and manager Paul Richards was a switch-pitcher in high school. As a pro at age 20 in 1928, Richards was playing third for Muskogee of the Western Association when he was inserted as a relief pitcher. Topeka sent switch-hitting Charlie Wilson to the plate. Richards, determined to throw from the side opposite the way Wilson was batting, staged a standoff with the batter, who kept switching in the batter's box as Richards switched gloves on the mound. Finally, Richards let Wilson choose the side he preferred.

## TIMING MAKES GOOD HITTERS

Swinging a heavy bat does not guarantee home run production. A man who swings a lighter bat but has good timing will get better distance on the ball than the player with a heavy bat but poor timing. The objective is to let bat meet ball at the moment of greatest power in the swing.

Hoyt Wilhelm, first reliever to win the ERA Crown, was king of the knuckleballers. He floated his way to more than 1,000 career appearances—leaving the majors just short of his 49th birthday.

## WHAT MADE KOUFAX A WINNER

*Sandy Koufax became a star when he learned to throw his fastball slower. Second-string catcher Norm Sherry, later a manager, suggested he master the curve, shorten his stride, and conceal his intentions from batters and coaches.*

**WHAT PITCHERS THROW** *continued*

Both the forkball and the sinker drop sharply when they reach the plate. The former is often called a "split-fingered" fastball because of the way it is usually held.

Like the slider, the palm ball is a pitch that traces its origin to the slip pitch. It breaks down across the plate. It is gripped with the palm and pushed toward the plate.

The change-up can be any pitch that will balance a pitcher's primary delivery, usually his fastball. The change must look exactly like the other pitch when thrown, but must arrive at a different speed. The change, off a fastball, is thrown with a locked wrist.

The screwball, once known as the fadeaway, is a reverse curve. It helps make a lefthanded pitcher effective against a righthanded batter and vice versa. The good screwball, like a slider, should look like a fastball en route to the plate. But, like the forkball and the knuckleball, it's a tough pitch to throw properly. It involves "turning the ball over" with a quick snap of the wrist.

Knuckleball pitchers place their nails or knuckles on the ball and throw it with locked wrist. There's no rotation and the ball floats to the plate, riding the wind currents on the way.

The spitball, developed by Elmer Stricklett around the turn of the century, is thrown by wetting the first and second fingers and holding the ball so those fingers do not touch the seams. The ball slips from the fingers without any spin and floats to the plate with seams clearly visible. But the pitch will break very sharply at the last minute.

Carl Hubbell, long-time ace of the New York Giants, explained the overall theory of pitching: "The whole art is in the wrist. You use the body, the shoulder, and arms in getting power behind the throw but the twist of the wrist determines just what the ball will do."

Every unusual pitching delivery became the primary weapon for pitchers who found it easy to throw.

Christy Mathewson, Carl Hubbell, and Warren Spahn were masters of the screwball—and relievers Mike Marshall and Tug McGraw found late-inning success with the same delivery.

Sparky Lyle, who joined Marshall as the only bullpen ace to win the coveted Cy Young Award for pitching excellence in its first 22 seasons, depended heavily on the slider.

Hoyt Wilhelm, first relief pitcher to win the earned run average title (1952), was primarily a knuckleballer. So were Ed Rommel, Jesse (Pop) Haines, Freddie Fitzsimmons, Schoolboy Rowe, Wilbur Wood, and Phil Niekro.

ElRoy Face, who posted an 18-1 record for the 1959 Pirates and won 22 relief victories in a row over two seasons, called on the forkball, the same pitch which later helped Bruce Sutter of the Cubs.

Burt Hooton, an original Cub who later went to Los Angeles, was the creator of the knuckle curve, a spinning pitch that is easier to catch than the straight knuckleball.

According to his catcher, Sandy Koufax threw a curve that "collapsed at the plate like a folding chair."

Walter Johnson, Bob Feller, and Koufax were among the top fastball pitchers in baseball history.

Johnny Podres, Brooklyn World Series hero of 1955, had a clever change-up; Grover Cleveland Alexander and one-time Yankee reliever Wilcy Moore mastered the sinker; and Hall of Famer Eddie Plank threw the palmball.

Among successful spitballers before the pitch was outlawed were Jack Chesbro, Ed Walsh, and Burleigh Grimes.

Satchel Paige, whose pitching career spanned forty years, threw a bee ball (snapping fastball), jump ball (a hopper that jumped 4-6 inches), and a hesitation pitch (slow curve), in addition to other things.

The hesitation pitch was so good it was banned by the American League. "Will Harridge, the president of the league, said I was tricking the batters and umpires," Paige reported. "He said I had the batters swinging at the ball when I still had it in my hand. And he said the umpires were calling strikes when the catcher thumped his empty glove."

Of all the pitches, the knuckler places the least strain on the arm. But catchers have as much trouble holding it as hitters do hitting it. In 1966, the Braves shipped Phil Niekro to the minors because they didn't have a catcher who could handle the pitch.

"There are two ways to catch a knuckleball," said Charlie Lau, a catcher-turned-coach. "Unfortunately, neither of them works."

The pitch is so slow when matched against the standard fastball that it fouls up the timing of free-swinging sluggers. When Hoyt Wilhelm was in the American League, Minnesota manager Bill Rigney admitted, "I hate to see my guys bat against him. They swing three times before the first knuckleball is halfway to the plate."

As a rookie with the Giants, Wilhelm dared any of his teammates to catch three out of five knucklers. None—including Willie Mays—could do it. Relying strictly on the knuckleball, Wilhelm lasted in the majors until he was just shy of age 49. For five straight years, when he was already in his 40s, Wilhelm allowed fewer than two earned runs per game.

## RUTH WAS TOP PITCHER

*Babe Ruth, pitching 44 games for the Boston Red Sox, led the American League with a 1.75 earned run average in 1916. One of his 23 victories was a 1-0 defeat of Walter Johnson in a thirteen-inning game at Fenway Park.*

## O'DOUL WAS CHASED AS PITCHER

*In seven seasons as an outfielder, starting in 1928, Lefty O'Doul hit .349, but he first came to the majors as a pitcher. After losing to Cleveland, 27-3, on July 7, 1923, the Boston southpaw began a five-year hiatus from the majors.*

## FOUR 20-GAME WINNERS

*The 1920 White Sox and 1971 Orioles were the only teams to produce four 20-game winners in the same season.*

Cleveland player-manager Lou Boudreau gives ball to rubber-armed reliever Satchel Paige. The 42-year-old rookie —marooned for years in the Negro Leagues—was a key man in his club's 1948 pennant drive. His pitching repertoire was extraordinary.

# THE PICKOFF

Successful pitchers are often good hitters and excellent defensive players—men who can win their own games with bat or glove in crucial situations. Many have mastered the pickoff play.

"I depend on deceiving the runner," said Warren Spahn, the great lefthander for the Braves, at the height of his career. "The move to first must have coordination. I try to get the movement with my head and my right knee exactly as I do when throwing to the plate. The difference is that, at the last moment, I have to step toward the base instead of the plate.

"The runner is looking for the pitcher to tip his move, but I try hard to confuse him. I look at home plate, then to first base a couple of times. If the runner starts looking at my head, I know I've confused him. When I pick somebody off, it's the runner who has tipped *himself* off."

# SIGN-STEALING

Baseball larceny is legal. Base-stealing is an important aspect of offensive play, while sign-stealing plays a lesser—though often important—role. The "miracle" New York Giants of 1951, for example, raced from last to first because of an elaborate spy network that gave advance warning on upcoming pitches to such hitters as Willie Mays.

There are no rules against stealing the signs of the opposing catcher (or coaches)—provided that no mechanical device is used in the process. Even that regulation is often overlooked.

"There's no excuse for anybody stealing signs if you work at it," suggested Ralph Kiner, a daily observer of baseball as player and announcer since 1946. "You can set up a system like a war and code your messages so nobody will pick them up. You can change your signs with every pitch. The fault is not with the people stealing the signs, but with the people giving them. You can code them so they can't be stolen."

Religious athletes frown on the practice of sign-stealing, but it's been part of the game since the National League was born in 1876.

That very first season, the Hartford club was accused of stealing signals. Not many years later, catcher Morgan Murphy of Philadelphia rigged an elaborate buzzer system from the clubhouse —where he studied enemy signs with binoculars—to third base coach Bull Childs. One buzz signaled fastball, two buzzes a curve. Childs, feeling the vibrations under foot, then relayed the information to batters with a pre-arranged word code.

When the American League began play in 1901, the Philadelphia Athletics followed the lead of the Phillies. Dan Murphy, a club employee, stationed himself on a rooftop beyond the center field wall and used high-powered field glasses to watch the rival catcher's fingers. He then twirled a weathervane to signal A's batters. One windy day, however, he was unable to control the vane and the club had to do without his help.

Pittsburgh's Chief Zimmer, a fine catcher who happened to be the head of the Ball Players' Association at the turn of the century, was caught red-handed when stealing signs from a large billboard at old Exposition Park. Several Cincinnati players noticed the sign moving while the Pirates batted. They rushed the spot and found Zimmer with binoculars tucked under his arm. ☞

## Signals . . . Secret Language of Baseball

## Signals ... Secret Language of Baseball

**ACE "O·S·S" MAN**

{OUTSTANDING SIGNAL STEALER}
Charley DRESSEN
HAD THE TABLES TURNED ON HIM IN THE '52 SERIES WHEN BILLY MARTIN SPOTTED HIS SIGNAL...AND A "RALLY-KILLING" "OUT" WAS MADE AT THE PLATE!! BY THE YANKS..!

AW.. C'MON.. SIGN..! NOPE! I'M HAPPY HERE!
CRACK "O·S·S" MAN ..ART FLETCHER.. PREFERRED THE COACH'S BOX TO MANAGING..!

TED CARROLL
From Gillette Cavalcade of Sports    NP

"DECODERS" OF ENEMY SIGNALS..ARE OFTEN THE DIFFERENCE BETWEEN VICTORY AND DEFEAT..!

Frank CROSETTI    Billy HERMAN    Del BAKER
Eddie COLLINS

..THESE BASEBALL OSS MEN!.. {OUTSTANDING SIGNAL STEALERS} ..AS PLAYERS AND COACHES.. PLAYED BIG PARTS IN THE SUCCESSES OF THEIR VARIOUS TEAMS FOR MANY YEARS!

TED CARROLL

..THEY WERE AMONG THE TOP EXPERTS AT USING AND "DECODING".. SIGNALS.. BASEBALL'S SECRET LANGUAGE..!..
From Gillette Cavalcade of Sports    NP

In New York, manager George Stallings of the Highlanders (later Yankees) of 1909-10, rented an apartment overlooking right center field and planted an agent there. He used field glasses and mirrors to "telegraph" instructions to the plate.

When the plot was discovered, Stallings put his man inside the "O" of a colorful whisky billboard on the rim of the outfield. The spy held out his hand as a signal—right for a fastball and left for a curve.

Determined to overcome the New York sign-stealers, Washington catcher Gabby Street instructed ace pitcher Walter Johnson to work an entire game without signals. Street, not knowing what was coming at any time, kept himself braced for Johnson's powerful fastball. He made passed balls on several unexpected curves, but the Senators won, 3-2.

In 1912, fleet Eddie Collins of the A's twice stole six bases in a game in a period of 11 days. Chief Bender's ability to read the enemy catcher was the major factor in his success.

Not only do sign-stealers watch the catcher to learn defensive signals of the opposition, but also the first and third base coaches, who flash such signals as "take the next pitch," "hit-and-run," "steal," or "suicide squeeze." The sign-stealers can set their defense accordingly.

In 1957, *The Sporting News* polled a panel of experts in a search for the best dozen sign-stealers since World War I. This list was produced: Del Baker, Eddie Collins, Frank Crosetti, Charley Dressen, Leo Durocher, Freddie Fitzsimmons, Art Fletcher, Mike Gonzalez, Billy Herman, John McGraw, Merv Shea, and Rudy York.

Baker called nearly every pitch for Hank Greenberg, Detroit's star slugger of the '30s and '40s, but nearly got him killed when he signaled a curve and the pitcher threw a high, inside fastball. Greenberg listened for a code word from Baker. If the coach shouted, "Come on Hank, paste this one," the word "come" told Hank a fastball was coming. But if Baker yelled, "All right, Hank, get one now," the word "get" told him the pitch would be a curve.

Sign-stealing backfired on one of the masters, Charley Dressen, during the Brooklyn-New York World Series of 1953. Yankee infielder Billy Martin, later a manager himself, intercepted Dressen's sign for the squeeze bunt because the Dodger manager had carelessly used the same sign that he had used as Martin's manager in the Pacific Coast League several years before.

Dressen was so adept at sign-stealing that he bragged about it. Managing the 1953 National League All-Stars, the manager held a pre-game meeting. Asked what signals he would use, the Dodger pilot said, "Don't worry about it, men. I'll give each of you the signals used on your own team."

Though he could pick off enemy signs as well as hide his own, Dressen blew a 13½-game lead in the closing months of the 1951 season because Leo Durocher had also turned the art of sign-stealing into a science. Coaches Fred Fitzsimmons and Herman Franks were also expert spies, but the key agent for the Giants was the man who watched the enemy from a peephole in the center field clubhouse. A buzzer rang once for fastball, twice for curve, but several Giants disdained the advance signals. They were leery of being crossed up.

Among the game's great hitters, Hank Aaron, Joe DiMaggio, Rogers Hornsby, Stan Musial, Babe Ruth, and Al Simmons refused to heed sign-stealers, while Greenberg and Willie Mays liked to have a sneak preview. ☞

Ty Cobb had access to pitch-by-pitch tips, but ignored it. Many of his Detroit teammates didn't. In an outfield billboard that read THE DETROIT NEWS, BEST NEWSPAPER IN THE WEST, a Tiger spotter opened the slots in the "B" to indicate what pitches were coming. With the top slot open, a fastball followed. If the bottom slot opened, the pitch would be a curve.

With sign-stealing so rampant, did Bobby Thomson have advance knowledge of the high, inside pitch he hit for "the shot heard 'round the world" in 1951? No, said Thomson, teammate Monte Irvin, and manager Leo Durocher years later. The three-run blast in the home ninth, which erased a 4-2 Dodger lead to give the New York Giants a 5-4 victory and the pennant, was hit without help. Had Thomson known what Ralph Branca was throwing, Durocher insisted, he would have swung at the first pitch—a fastball down the middle. He had hit a Branca slider for a homer earlier in the series.

Some pitchers inadvertently "telegraph" their pitches through quirks in their deliveries, or by allowing hitters to see the way they grip the ball. Two notable examples were Walter Johnson and Sandy Koufax. The Tigers "read" Johnson and the Astros "read" Koufax, but both men were so overpowering that they managed to win anyway.

# LEGAL TRICKS

Shrewd players and managers employ a variety of trick plays to help win games.

The best-known deception is the hidden ball trick, the simple ruse of a fielder tagging an unsuspecting runner with a ball thought to be in the hands of the pitcher.

One-time Yankee shortstop Frank Crosetti was a master of the play, but he needed the full cooperation of the pitcher to make it work. While Crosetti concealed the ball in the back of his glove—exposing the bare palm to convince his victim that he doesn't have it—the pitcher pretends that he does.

Lefty Gomez and Red Ruffing were expert at feigning possession, while making sure not to step on the pitching rubber—a move which would blow the strategy and produce a balk call. Ruffing maintained a constant dead-pan expression, while Gomez manicured the mound as if getting ready to pitch.

Without wasting too much time—a delay would tip off the runner or, more likely, the third base coach—Crosetti would talk to the nearest umpire in an effort to get his attention. The runner, thinking the pitcher was ready, would take a lead of several steps, giving Crosetti his cue. A lunge and a quick tag produced a most humiliating putout.

Lou Boudreau, shortstop-manager of the Indians in the '40s, told a radio interviewer one night that there was no excuse for any player to be caught by the hidden ball trick. But, the next day, the season's opener, Boudreau himself was the victim of White Sox third baseman Tony Cuccinello.

One of Cuccinello's predecessors in Chicago had been a specialist in setting hidden ball traps. Willie Kamm, who played in the '20s and '30s, hid the ball under his armpit in a wrinkled sweat shirt that formed a perfect pocket. He could even flap his arms without losing it. ☞

## NL BID FOR DH FAILED

In 1928, National League president John Heydler suggested the designated hitter idea to John McGraw of the Giants and Wilbert Robinson of the Dodgers. The managers liked it, but the concept failed when the American League showed no interest.

## McCORMICK LOST GAME-WINNING HIT

Moose McCormick stroked Grover Cleveland Alexander's first pitch to right for a game-winning hit one day, but umpire Bill Klem ordered the three runners back to their bases. The arbiter's back was turned—he was announcing McCormick's pinch-hitting appearance—and he did not see the play. Batting again, McCormick rapped into an inning-ending double-play and the Giants lost to the Phillies in the twelfth inning.

## HOME RUN BALL FOUND OUTFIELD HOLE

The American League's first pinch-hit grand slam home run was hit by Cleveland's Marty Kavanagh in a 5-3 victory over the Red Sox in 1916. The ball rolled through a hole in the outfield fence and could not be recovered in time to make a play.

## HOW COMPLEX ARE SIGNALS?

Signals must be simple enough for the slowest thinker on a team to remember them. But they must also be concealed in such a way that the sharpest thinker on the opposite bench cannot decipher them. Some clubs use different signs for each player. Many use a sequence of signals with only one serving as the key. The catcher and pitcher may agree to follow only the second sign flashed.

## SCOREBOARD DECEPTION

When Marty Marion managed the White Sox in the '50s, scoreboard spy Del Wilber told batters what was coming by moving the number 10 in the Chicago lineup. When the number moved slightly, the batter could expect a fastball. If it stood still, a curve was on the way.

Two of the more embarrassing moments of hidden ball history involved the Red Sox. In the late '30s, Crosetti caught shortstop-manager Joe Cronin—the man who taught the play to the Yankee infielder when both were in San Francisco.

Nearly twenty years later, the Sox had the tying run on second and the winning run on first with two outs in the ninth against Chicago. The White Sox led, 3-2, as shortstop Chico Carrasquel conferred with pitcher Sandy Consuegra. He returned to his position, slipped behind Sammy White, who had taken a short lead off second, and tagged him for the final out.

The hidden ball trick is almost as old as the game itself. According to the late Arlie Latham, who began his pro career before the century changed, it was frequently used in the early days of the majors. It was even banned briefly because players hoping to pull it off took too much time trying to complete the trick play.

Since Ty Cobb was an outfielder, he wasn't involved in the defensive end of the hidden ball trick—but he had plenty of other slick maneuvers.

Cobb, whose .367 lifetime average has not been surpassed, actually practiced limping. "It's a great help to stumble deliberately at first base and come up lame, or seem to be hurt by your slide," he once said. "If your act is good enough, the pitcher and catcher relax and it's no trick at all to steal second."

Because many managers follow "percentage baseball," which dictates that righthanded hitters perform better against lefthanded pitchers (and vice versa), manager Bucky Harris of the Washington Senators succeeded in getting John McGraw of the New York Giants to list a lefthanded lineup for Game 7 of the 1924 World Series.

Harris had righthander Curly Ogden warm up in plain sight and start the game, while star southpaw George Mogridge—winner of Game 4—cranked up in secret under the stands. In the first inning, Ogden walked one and fanned one before he was lifted in favor of Mogridge. Washington went on to win, 4-3.

# TALKING IT UP AND BENCH-JOCKEYING

Talk is an important element of the game. Unsettling the opposition can force mistakes that will win games, and constant jabber on the field or on the bench helps keep all team members involved in the contest.

Former pitcher Moe Drabowsky said he was oblivious to comments from the stands or rival dugouts, but he remembered hearing the infielders of other clubs.

"Rocky Bridges was a great one for yelling, and it really helped our pitchers," said former Brooklyn reliever Clyde King. "You'd be surprised at some of the things that were said. The infield chatter was geared to keep our pitchers on their toes.

"Jackie Robinson was always yelling encouragement too. Once in awhile, you could hear one of the infielders' comments through the crowd noise and it would give you a little jack-up on the mound. Pee Wee Reese might come in half-way from shortstop to the mound and just give you a little clenched fist gesture. He was saying, 'Bear down, you can get this guy out.' ☞

## OSCAR MELILLO HAD A BALL

Bill Rogell, Detroit infielder of the '30s, delivered milk in the Chicago area during the winter—an unexciting job except for one stop. Oscar Melillo, St. Louis Browns' infielder, was one of his customers. When Rogell arrived at his colleague's home—just as the sun was peeking over the horizon—he purposely rattled the bottles and bellowed, "Here's your milk, Melillo!"

The victim picked out a prime time for revenge. In a tie game the following spring, Rogell led off the tenth inning with a double. Confident he would soon score the go-ahead run, he took a three-step lead off second. That was Melillo's cue.

"Remember how you used to wake me up in the morning by shouting, 'Here's your milk?'" Oscar asked. Rogell broke into a wide grin. "Well," Melillo concluded, "here's the ball."

With a quick lunge, Rogell was tagged out—the victim of the oldest, and most humiliating, trick in the game.

## WATER MADE MITT CRACKLE

In an attempt to intimidate enemy hitters, catcher Ossie Schreckengost soaked his mitt in water before catching fastballer Rube Waddell. When the ball hit the mitt, a loud CRACK! could be heard all over the park.

## PEPPERPOT MANAGERS

The era of the late '30s featured three player-managers who doubled as head cheerleaders for their teams: Joe Cronin (Red Sox), Mickey Cochrane (Tigers), and Gabby Hartnett (Cubs).

## DUROCHER DISHED IT OUT

Veteran manager Leo Durocher was one of the all-time great bench jockeys. "He knew how to rile a guy," said Clyde King, a pitcher for Durocher in Brooklyn. "He wouldn't get personal; he'd always keep his remarks light and airy. But he could really get to you. He'd say some funny things to get your mind off whatever you were trying to do. He'd break your concentration whether you were at bat or in the field."

# WHO'S A BUM!

"One time, I came in to relieve against the Giants with the bases loaded. Eddie Stanky came over, took the ball, rubbed it up, and gave it back. Then he said, 'You're a college guy. You're supposed to be smart. Let's see how you get out of this.' Two pitches later, I got out of it."

The needle is invariably friendly among teammates, but hostile toward rivals. The Gashouse Gang Cardinals of Dizzy Dean, Pepper Martin, and Joe Medwick were masters at riling the opposition—as were John McGraw, Leo Durocher, and Billy Martin.

Bench-jockeying began a slow death with the influx of college-educated players into the majors after the Second World War. Interleague trading was also a factor, since former roommates and teammates often populate enemy benches.

"The game is not as rough as it used to be," said Ralph Kiner, who played in the '40s and '50s, then broadcast in the '60s and '70s. "In the old days, it was common knowledge that everybody was thrown at. I don't think a pitcher has that right."

Beanballs, always a factor in baseball, were decreased by regulation in the '70s, but rule-makers can't do anything about boos.

This form of bench-jockeying by fans bothered Bob Elliott so much at Pittsburgh that he never became a good player there. The deluge of derision began after he booted a ball at third base. Once traded to the Boston Braves, Elliott blossomed into the Most Valuable Player.

"Most bench-jockeying is done in a kidding sort of way," said Clyde King. "I remember one time when we were having trouble beating Sal Maglie. Some of our guys were yelling at him. He hit one of them with the bases loaded one day and that was the only run we got. Finally, we decided, 'Hey, maybe we shouldn't be getting on this guy.' "

An agitated opponent may become a more difficult adversary, but Billy Martin doesn't figure it that way. The veteran manager, once a scrappy infielder for some half-dozen clubs, subscribes to the theory that mad players lose their cool—and their skills.

Leo Durocher agreed. "He was the best bench-jockey," said former manager Danny Ozark, who is cool, calm, and collected by contrast. "His voice carried—it was piercing. He even got on his own players—not just the other guys.

Once, when Durocher made the mistake of offending the gentle giant, Frank Howard, he found himself held by the neck, several feet off the ground. Howard said, "Mr. Durocher, don't ever say that again."

Brooks Robinson, also of a gentle disposition, quieted the Oriole bench when the players overdid the razzing of an opposing pitcher. Robinson didn't want the man to be too agitated when his turn to bat came up. ☞

Catcher Roy Campanella handled Brooklyn's best pitchers, including (left to right) Ralph Branca, Carl Erskine, and Preacher Roe.

*Baseball Hall of Fame*

## MATHEWSON ON THE SECRET OF PITCHING

*"Next to control, the whole secret of big-league pitching is mixing 'em up. It means inducing a batter to believe that another kind of ball is coming from the one that is really to be delivered, and thus preventing him from getting set to hit it."*
—Christy Mathewson

*John Anderson*

Oriole pitcher Mike Cuellar was one of several stars who took a verbal pounding from Gene Mauch, fiery manager in several cities. Larry Bowa was Mauch's target when Gene was with Montreal.

Pete Rose, Philadelphia superstar, plays an aggressive brand of ball that includes constant chatter from the bench and from his position in the infield. Rose often visits opposing players before a game, then attacks the same "friends" after play begins.

"The defense can't yield to pressure," said Maury Wills, explaining the purpose of infield talk. "It must do all the little things—and do them steadily. All defensive players must think, at all times, 'What will I do in the event the ball is hit to me?' "

Jabbering players seldom use invective—though this was once standard operating procedure in the game—and shy away from questioning ability. But the needle is always there. Bob Gibson gave it to rivals and teammates on the Cardinals, and Tim McCarver, long-time batterymate, learned from him. McCarver later established his own reputation.

Gil Hodges, the slugging Dodger first baseman who later managed the Mets and Senators, never said much on the field. "He let his bat do the talking," said Clyde King.

Many other players followed suit, leaving the bench-jockey roles to players who seldom played and managers seeking to win at any cost.

Vicious bench-jockeying exploded into a fight between two contenders—the Braves and Dodgers—in June 1957. Milwaukee shortstop Johnny Logan, a leading protagonist, takes aim at Brooklyn manager Walter Alston as Eddie Mathews (41) piles onto battlers behind them. At far right, Gil Hodges tries to quell the fray.

## HOW CHATTER HELPS

*"Noise helps you hustle," said Eddie Dyer, manager of the Cardinals in the '40s. "If you feel a little down and perhaps are inclined to loaf a little, the guy playing next to you can pep you up by making a lot of holler. You hear him and invariably and immediately snap out of it. I know, because it's happened to me. Cardinal clubs have been noisy clubs and the record shows they've been winning clubs."*

## THE HIT-AND-RUN

*The hit-and-run play is a favorite weapon of managerial strategy, especially when a team does not have great speed on the bases. It is designed primarily to keep out of the double-play but also to advance a runner from first to third if the batter hits safely. On the hit-and-run, the runner at first breaks with the pitch and the batter swings no matter where the pitch is. On the run-and-hit play, the runner breaks but the batter does not have to swing. Either play is worked best when the pitcher has good control (the ball figures to be near the plate) and the hitter has good bat control (he might hit it through the defensive hole created by the man who moved over to cover second).*

## SLUGGING PITCHERS

*Hall of Famers Babe Ruth, George Sisler, Ted Williams, and Stan Musial began their pro careers as pitchers. Their batting abilities made them stars, but might have remained undiscovered had the designated hitter rule been in effect when they played.*

*Pitchers with 35 or more lifetime homers were Wes Ferrell (Indians-Red Sox), 38; Bob Lemon (Indians), 37; Red Ruffing (Yankees), 36; and Warren Spahn (Braves), 35.*

## NO-HIT DEBUT

*Bobo Holloman of the St. Louis Browns threw a no-hitter against the Philadelphia Athletics in his starting debut on May 6, 1953. He never pitched another complete game in the majors and was through before that season ended.*

## RELIEVER'S PERFECT GAME

*Baltimore Orioles reliever Dick Hall threw a "perfect game," retiring 28 batters over five straight appearances, in 1963.*

# Pitching Tandems

## Lifetime (300 wins minimum)

(records indicate years pitchers were teammates)

| | WINS | | | TEAM | YRS. | PENNANTS |
|---|---|---|---|---|---|---|
| Mathewson | 328-133 | Wiltse | 135-85 | 463 | NY (N) | 11 | 5 |
| Plank | 267-148 | Bender | 191-103 | 458 | Phi (A) | 12 | 5 |
| Spahn | 264-158 | Burdette | 179-120 | 443 | Mil (N) | 13 | 2 |
| Ruffing | 219-120 | Gomez | 189-101 | 408 | NY (A) | 13 | 7 |
| Newhouser | 200-147 | Trout | 161-153 | 361 | Det (A) | 14 | 2 |
| Hubbell | 204-121 | Schumacher | 154-117 | 358 | NY (N) | 12 | 3 |
| Lemon | 201-116 | Feller | 154-105 | 355 | Cle (A) | 11 | 2 |
| Drysdale | 177-134 | Koufax | 163-85 | 340 | LA (N) | 11 | 5 |
| Marichal | 202-97 | G. Perry | 134-109 | 336 | SF (N) | 10 | 1 |
| Walsh | 189-123 | White | 143-105 | 332 | Chi (A) | 10 | 2 |
| Grove | 195-79 | Walberg | 130-106 | 325 | Phi (A) | 9 | 3 |
| Mathewson | 178-69 | McGinnity | 145-81 | 323 | NY (N) | 6 | 2 |
| Friend | 176-190 | Law | 141-124 | 317 | Pit (N) | 13 | 1 |
| Lemon | 166-92 | Wynn | 149-83 | 315 | Cle (A) | 8 | 1 |
| Lemon | 186-106 | Garcia | 126-82 | 312 | Cle (A) | 9 | 2 |
| Roberts | 205-165 | Simmons | 107-97 | 312 | Phi (N) | 11 | 1 |
| Brown | 171-70 | Reulbach | 135-62 | 306 | Chi (N) | 8 | 4 |
| Leever | 157-65 | Phillippe | 148-79 | 305 | Pit (N) | 10 | 4 |

## Single Season

| YEAR | TEAM | | | | | WINS |
|---|---|---|---|---|---|---|
| 1904 | NY (N) | McGinnity | 35-8 | Mathewson | 33-12 | 68 |
| 1904 | NY (A) | Chesbro | 41-12 | Powell | 23-19 | 64 |
| 1903 | NY (N) | McGinnity | 31-20 | Mathewson | 30-13 | 61 |
| 1908 | NY (N) | Mathewson | 37-11 | Wiltse | 23-14 | 60 |
| 1908 | Chi (A) | Walsh | 40-15 | White | 19-13 | 59 |
| 1904 | NY (N) | McGinnity | 35-8 | Taylor | 21-15 | 56 |
| 1912 | Was (A) | Johnson | 32-12 | Groom | 24-13 | 56 |
| 1944 | Det (A) | Newhouser | 29-9 | Trout | 27-14 | 56 |
| 1916 | Phi (N) | Alexander | 33-12 | Rixey | 22-10 | 55 |
| 1920 | Cle (A) | Bagby | 31-12 | S. Covaleski | 24-14 | 55 |

## TOP LEFT-RIGHT TANDEMS

*The best left-right tandems in baseball history included Rube Marquard and Christy Mathewson (Giants); Babe Ruth and Carl Mays (Red Sox); Lefty Grove and George Earnshaw (Athletics); Warren Spahn and Johnny Sain (Braves); Spahn and Lew Burdette (Braves); Sandy Koufax and Don Drysdale (Dodgers); and Vida Blue and Catfish Hunter (A's).*

Indians/Giants

**Righthanders Gaylord Perry (top left) and Juan Marichal (top right) formed fearsome twosome as teammates in San Francisco before former was swapped to Cleveland.**

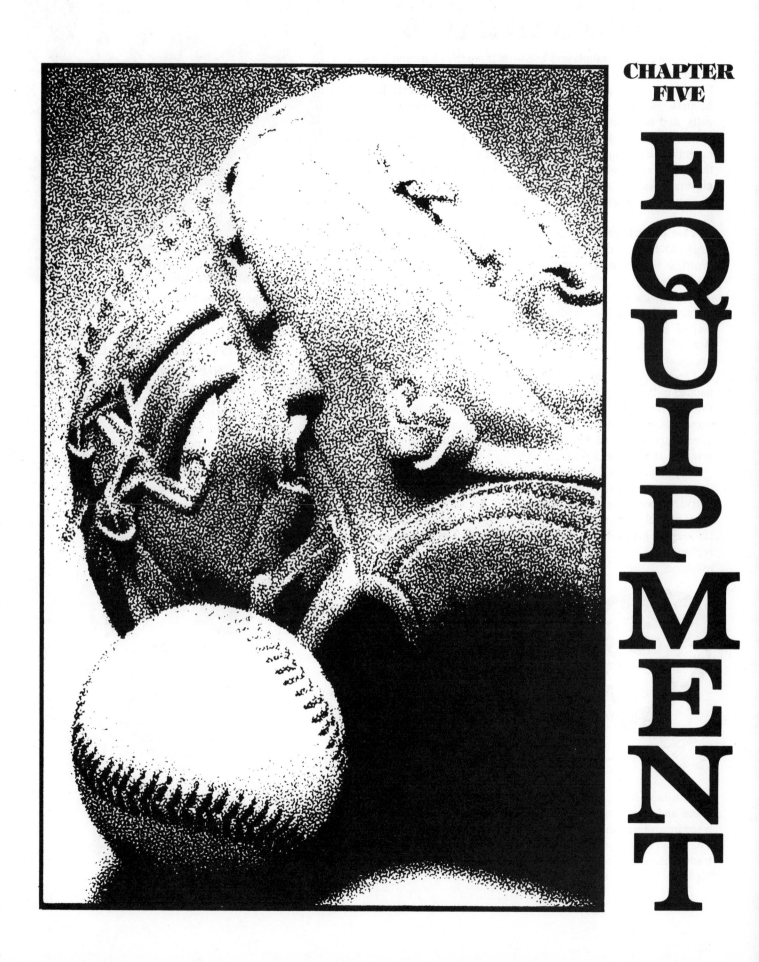

CHAPTER FIVE

EQUIPMENT

# MUCH MORE THAN BATS AND BALLS

Though country ballplayers had little more than bats and balls as equipment, professional baseball requires not only a full wardrobe for athletes, but also catcher's and fielder's equipment, batting helmets, mechanical pitching machines, the omnipresent bats and balls, and much more.

Gloves were unknown in the game until Charles White, first-baseman for champion Boston of the National Association, braved the jeers of rivals when he wore a thin, unpadded mitt in 1875. Other players picked up the idea, but the idea did not become universal until Providence shortstop Arthur Irwin broke a finger on his left hand in 1883.

Irwin protected his bandage with a buckskin diving glove several sizes too large and padded the insides. When John Montgomery Ward, a star of the era, copied the concept, manufacturers began mass production.

Catchers did not have adequate protection until 1908. Early gloves had little or no built-in padding, and Ossie Schreckengost of the A's stuffed his with goose feathers to cushion the blow of Rube Waddell's fastball early in the century. Other players used raw beefsteak to provide padding.

The first unpadded catcher's glove was used in 1875, but the padded mitt did not appear until Buck Ewing of the Giants wore one fifteen years later. The first chest protectors, primitive by modern standards, were worn by both catchers and umpires in 1885, 10 years after Harvard's Fred Thayer and a nameless Boston tinsmith co-invented the catcher's mask.

Thayer wanted his catcher to stand immediately behind the plate (a practice not adopted by the majors until 1893), but the reluctant Harvard receiver expressed concern for his facial features in the event of foul tip or missed pitch. Thayer took a fencer's mask to the tin man to get eyeholes cut in the wire mesh. The latter suggested replacing the mesh with wide-spaced iron bars—the first "bird-cage" mask.

With face, hand, and chest protectors, catchers still had exposed knees and legs. Roger Bresnahan of the Giants solved the problem when he invented shin guards in 1908. On September 24 of that year, *The New York Times* reported, "Roger Bresnahan makes an entrance, accompanied by a dresser who does him and undoes him in his natty mattress and knee pads." ☞

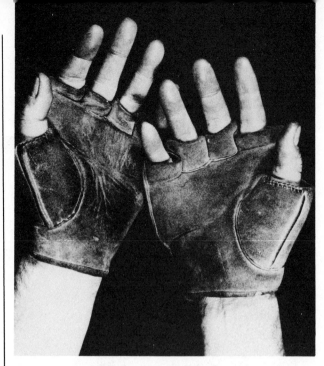

Early gloves provided no protection for fingers.

## THE OUTSIDE FINGER

*Yogi Berra, Hall of Fame catcher for the Yankees, began the custom of leaving one finger (usually the forefinger) outside the glove. He did it to reduce the wear-and-tear on his left hand by putting more padding between hand and ball. Many catchers copied his style, though fielders at other positions also borrowed it occasionally.*

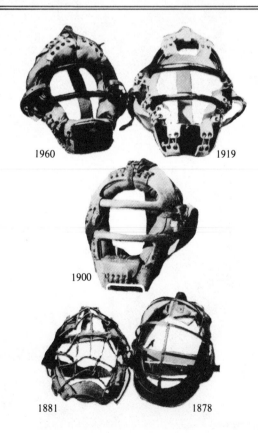

1960                                    1919

1900

1881                                    1878

Bresnahan also introduced the first helmet, which he designed after a serious beaning in 1907. The American League made helmets mandatory in 1957, but most players began to wear them after Ray Chapman of the Indians was killed by a fastball thrown by submarine pitcher Carl Mays of the Yankees in 1920.

Though Chapman was the only man killed in major league history, slugger Tony Conigliaro of the Red Sox narrowly missed a similar fate in 1967 when a pitch from Jack Hamilton of the Angels struck him just below the helmet, broke his left cheekbone, and caused blurry vision which shortened his career.

"I don't think there was anybody who was closer to death than I was the night I got hit," recalled Conigliaro, who managed comeback seasons in 1969-70 before his eyes failed again. "I said a couple of prayers just to stay alive. I wasn't even thinking about my future in baseball."

The untimely end to the career of Conigliaro, who had hit 104 home runs by age 22 when the incident occurred, caused other clubs to extend the standard helmet downward to include earflaps.

Protection of players changed dramatically throughout baseball's first century, but the basic ingredients—bats, balls, and gloves—remained the same. Guidelines for each were specified in the *Official Baseball Rules,* published by the Commissioner of Baseball.

Hank Greenberg-1940     Lou Gehrig-1939

Wally Pipp-1922

## GREENBERG'S GLOVE DREW CRITICISM

*Hall of Fame slugger Hank Greenberg used a big, fish-net style mitt at first base for the Tigers in the '30s, but angered opponents with the unusually large gear. As a direct result, a rule was passed limiting the size of the first baseman's mitt to 8 inches across and 12 inches lengthwise. Similar legislation was passed years later when Baltimore manager Paul Richards created an oversized catcher's mitt for Gus Triandos, who was having trouble handling the tricky knuckleball of Hoyt Wilhelm.*

## OBSOLETE EQUIPMENT

*Early baseball equipment included sliding gloves and sliding pads for base-runners and knee pads for catchers. Turn-of-the-century receivers wore strips of felt under their stockings to protect their legs from foul tips or missed pitches. The sliding pads—worn to avoid strawberries—were welcomed by those who slid in to a base with feet first, while sliding gloves were most appreciated by head-first sliders. The sliding glove came all the way up to the elbow.*

# UNIFORMS: COLORS AND STYLE

For many years, baseball teams wore flannel uniforms with conservative markings—white at home and gray on the road. But new materials and styles of the '60s—especially public acceptance of men wearing bright colors—returned the baseball uniform to the rainbow days of the nineteenth century.

The first uniformed team, the New York Knickerbockers of 1849, wore long cricket-style pants, but the first professional team, the Cincinnati Red Stockings of twenty years later, began the tradition of wearing shorter pants and long colored stockings.

In the National League's first year, the Chicago White Stockings had a different colored hat for each player, including a red, white, and blue topping for pitcher-manager Al Spalding.

At its winter meeting of 1881, the league voted to have its clubs wear stockings of different colors: Cleveland dark blue, Providence light blue, Worcester brown, Buffalo gray, Troy green, Boston red, and Detroit yellow. Position players had to wear shirts, belts, and caps as follows: catchers scarlet, pitchers light blue, first basemen scarlet and white, second basemen orange and blue, third basemen blue and white, shortstops maroon, leftfielders white, centerfielders red and black, rightfielders gray, and substitutes green and brown. Pants and ties were universally white and shoes were made of leather.

The plan caused too much confusion and was quickly dropped, but color remained part of the game. The Chicago White Stockings wore black uniforms and white neckties under Cap Anson in 1888 and had daily laundry service. The weekly *Sporting Life* complained that the pants were so tight they were "positively indecent."

Pittsburgh of 1889 wore new road uniforms consisting of black pants and shirt with an orange lace cord, an orange belt, and orange-and-black striped stockings. ☞

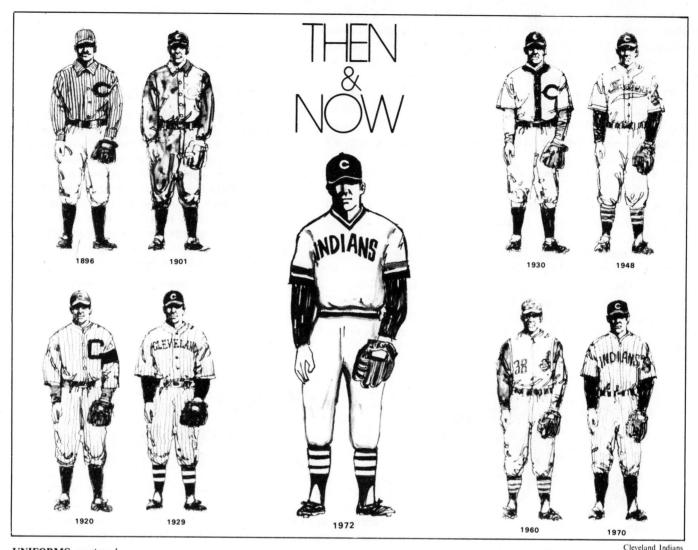

THEN & NOW

1896 1901

1920 1929 1972

1930 1948

1960 1970

Cleveland Indians

**UNIFORMS** *continued*

The St. Louis Browns, whose nickname changed to Cardinals when their uniforms took on more red, wore shirts with vertical stripes of brown and white, with matching caps.

Pre-1900 styles dictated laced shirts with collars and ties, open breast pockets, and occasionally red bandana handkerchiefs as good-luck tokens. John McGraw, manager of the Giants, was the first baseball official to order uniform shirts without collars, and he also discarded the breast pockets, which sometimes served as a resting place for a batted ball.

The Giants and Phillies started the trend of wearing white at home and dark, solid colors on the road and, in 1911, the concept of whites and grays became mandatory—partly because it was sometimes hard to tell the home club from the visitors.

In an effort to lure fans to the ballpark, Charley Finley outfitted his Kansas City Athletics in green, gold, and white suits in the '60s and invited the scorn of the baseball world. Some of his own players expressed embarrassment at playing in "softball uniforms." Others likened the suits to pajamas.

But the Finley concept of color—which included mix-and-match combinations of caps, shirts, and pants—caught on quickly. In 1971, the Pittsburgh Pirates introduced form-fitting double-knits, complete with pullover tops, and six years later designed three sets of uniforms—gold, black, and striped—that may be worn in nine different combinations.

## ORIGIN OF ROAD GRAYS

*According to several sources, Connie Mack instigated the practice of dressing his players in gray uniforms away from home. It seems his A's played hard, aggressive baseball before the home fans, but did not wish to spoil their clean uniforms away from home. Among other things, they wouldn't slide and risk getting dirty. Mack figured that his charges wouldn't mind dirtying a gray road uniform and began the practice of dressing his players that way.*

"The players certainly look better," said one-time Pirate slugger Ralph Kiner. "When you see pictures of players from the '50s in old baggy-looking pants, remember that was the style then. We wore wool flannels only because we never knew any better."

# ☆ 7 ☆ 3 ☆ 5 ☆ 9 ☆ 2
# NUMBERS

With the experiment of different colors for different positions a decided dud, several farsighted executives discovered a different way to facilitate fan identification with players.

The 1888 Cincinnati Reds wore numbers on their sleeves, but players complained about being a number instead of a person, and the numerals came off.

The Cleveland Indians repeated the Cincinnati experiment on June 26, 1916, when they wore sleeve numbers against the White Sox, and the St. Louis Cardinals tried the idea for two years in 1924-25, but the concept of numerals was not fully accepted until the New York Yankees donned large digits on uniform backs in 1929.

New York's original numbering system corresponded to the batting order. Since Babe Ruth hit third and Lou Gehrig fourth, Ruth received No. 3 and Gehrig No. 4.

Most players wear numerals between 1 and 50, but there have been many exceptions. Bill Voiselle, 21-game winner for the New York Giants in 1944, hailed from Ninety-six, South Carolina and wore No. 96. Willie Crawford wore No. 99 for the Oakland A's in 1977. Paul Dade asked the Indians to give him No. 00 that same year, and the team had to prepare a special uniform for him. Al Oliver, seeking "a new start" with the Texas Rangers in 1978 after nine years with the Pittsburgh Pirates, asked for and received No. 0.

Probably the most unusual number ever worn by a major league player was 1/8, the digits sewn on the back of Bill Veeck's midget, who walked for the 1951 St. Louis Browns in his only appearance.

# SHOES

The first baseball teams wore canvas shoes with cleats, but the Harvard College nine launched a trend toward leather in 1877. Heels and toeplates were sold separately until 1890, when they were combined to improve traction.

Spikes came into general use in 1888 and it wasn't long before Cleveland Spiders manager Patsy Tebeau ordered his men to file them before a big game. "Give 'em steel," he ordered. The Spiders won the fear and respect of rivals with spikes-high slides, and their aggressive style of play was quickly copied.

To counter the Cleveland running game, Pittsburgh pilot William Chase Temple had his players line up on the field, in full view of the Spiders, with files in hand. The deterrent factor forced the Cleveland nine to use moderation.

In the minors, Omaha manager Billy Fox suggested rounding off the corners and cutting deep, square notches into the sharp edges of the spikes. Fox said this shaping of the shoe-bottom would bruise an opponent's shin without breaking it open.

The danger of being cut by flying spikes brought sanitary hose into the game. Players feared infection from the dye in their colored hose, ☞

## COLORFUL ORIOLES

*The 1901 Baltimore Orioles wore pink caps, black shirts with a large yellow "O" on the left front, black baggy pants with yellow belts, yellow stockings, and double-breasted jackets with wide yellow collars and cuffs and two rows of pearl buttons. Glass and metal were not prohibited from the major league uniform until 1931.*

## PITCHERS LAST TO USE GLOVES

*Pitchers, as a group, were the longest holdouts against wearing gloves during games. Catchers wore the first gloves, followed by outfielders and infielders.*

## RUTH WORE WHITE MITT

*Babe Ruth wore a white glove while playing the outfield for the Boston Red Sox.*

## FINED FOR PLAY WITHOUT SPIKES

*Pittsburgh fined slugger Pete Browning for playing with spikeless shoes in 1891.*

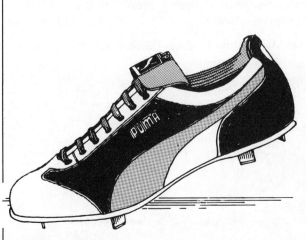

**Spikes, providing extra traction, came into general use well before the turn of the century.**

and began the practice of wearing white cotton stockings underneath.

The development of suitable spikes helped batters "dig in" at home plate and gain traction on the basepaths. Old-style cleats contained 5-7 ounces of steel, but modern spikes are much lighter, with each spike placed individually as opposed to the former single unit with protruding prongs.

Modern players own two pairs of shoes: one with metal cleats for standard fields and another with multiple cleats and soles made of heat-resistant polyurethane for artificial surfaces.

Shoe and spike design changed little through the years, though the advent of white shoes made from kangaroo leather (introduced by Adidas in 1967) brought color to the traditional black shoe.

Today's teams wear red, blue, brown, green, white, and other colors.

# GLASSES

In 1973, one of every seven big-leaguers wore glasses or contact lenses. Vision correction is an easy problem in the modern era, but old-time teams were reluctant to hire players with imperfect eyes.

William Henry White won 227 games as a bespectacled pitcher with three National League clubs from 1877 to 1886, but he was the lone major-leaguer to wear glasses until Specs Meadows joined the St. Louis Cardinals in 1915. Six years later, the Cards had the first fielder with glasses, George (Specs) Toporcer. He hit .279 in eight years as an all-position infielder.

St. Louis solidified its reputation as a home for four-eyed players when Clint (Scrap Iron) Courtney caught 119 games for the Browns in 1952. He was the first receiver to wear glasses, and proved his durability by lasting eleven years in the majors.

Fred Clarke of the Pittsburgh Pirates was the first ballplayer to wear sunglasses, shortly after the century changed. Today, no outfielder would be caught without them on a sunny afternoon.

Though the sight of umpires is often questioned by fans and players, arbiters are allowed to wear vision correction. Wise men in blue prefer contacts because they are not as obvious as glasses, but retired National League ump Larry Goetz did wear regular spectacles near the end of his 22-year career.

Several top sluggers of recent vintage have worn glasses. AL sluggers Dick Allen, Reggie Jackson, and Jeff Burroughs won consecutive Most Valuable Player awards, 1972-73-74, that they probably would have lost without the aid of their glasses.

**Pepper Martin of the St. Louis Cardinals had tight grip on the bat.**

**Special shoes, worn on artificial turf, are heat resistant and contain special spikes.**

## WILLIE MIRANDA'S SECRET GLOVE

*Slick-fielding Baltimore shortstop Willie Miranda, one of the American League's defensive stars in the '50s, used a "doctored" glove. It contained extra supports—wooden tongue depressors—and extra padding—pieces of white sanitary hose.*

## PLAYERS BOUGHT UNIFORMS

*Major-leaguers bought their uniforms until 1912. Price: $30.*

## FLANNELS CAUSED PROBLEMS

*Early baseball uniforms consisted of 8-ounce flannels that absorbed their weight in sweat and shrank after laundering. Players usually began the season with suits at least one size too large.*

# BATS

Hitters have always been choosy about their bats. Weight, length, grip, and even color is of concern, but the texture of the wood is most important.

Many players personally choose the wood for their bats. Ted Williams spent hours looking through timber stacks for a narrow grain, while Al Simmons looked for the widest grain. Both were slugging outfielders who made the Hall of Fame.

## ROUSH
## SWUNG 46-OUNCE CLUB

*Edd Roush swung a 46-ounce bat, one of the heaviest in baseball history. Asked why, he said he was used to hauling heavy objects as a country farm boy who rose every morning at 4:30.*

Simmons swung the longest bat—38 inches—and Wee Willie Keeler the shortest—30½—while Babe Ruth's 54-ounce club was by far the heaviest. Simmons needed the long bat to reach the ball because he batted with his "foot in the bucket," stepping away from the plate as he swung. Keeler was a place hitter who "hit 'em where they ain't" and wielded exceptional bat control. Ruth, who usually used a 44-ouncer, used a wide variety of bats during his career as a home run slugger.

Both Ruth and Hank Aaron, the new home run king, used similar bats, with the sole exception being weight. Ruth's basic weapon was a half-inch longer than Aaron's 35-inch brand, with a normal taper from barrel to handle. Aaron was the biggest star who never paid a personal visit to his bat manufacturer, Hillerich & Bradsby, makers of the Louisville Slugger. At the plate, however, he made good use of their product. He turned the bat in his hands until it felt comfortable. He paid scant attention to the trademark, though most hitters believe it should be on the topside because the bat is less likely to break if the ball hits a smooth surface. Once, when batting against the Dodgers, Aaron rotated the bat, then stepped in to hit with the trademark facing out. Catcher John Roseboro said, "Your bat is facing the wrong way!" Aaron delivered one of baseball's classic answers: "I didn't come up here to read!"

Because modern players prefer lighter bats to the "wagon tongues" used by earlier sluggers, most bats are now made from strands of straight ash from Pennsylvania, New York's Adirondack Mountains, or other woods in the northeast.

Ash, known for its resiliency and driving power, has been a favorite wood for years, but hickory and "Cuban timber" have fallen into disuse because they are too dense to facilitate the process of bat-building.

As in the game's early days, wood scouts judge a tree's bark, height, and age, and also determine strength, durability, and grain quality.

Trunks of selected trees are cut into bolts 40 inches long, sawed into squares or split, and turned into rounds for storage. Then they are naturally dried for up to two years and stacked for seasoning. Exposure to heat or improper drying can affect resiliency.

Bud Hillerich was 18 years old when he turned a new bat for Pete Browning, star slugger for a Louisville nine known as The Eclipse, and the athlete showed immediate results with a 3-for-3 performance the next day. Word spread and the simple wood-turning shop of J. F. Hillerich became a thriving bat-making plant.

Today, Hillerich & Bradsby makes its famed Louisville Sluggers at a new plant in "Slugger Park," a six-and-a-half acre complex in Jeffersonville, Indiana, eight miles from Louisville. The basic process is still the same.

Billets are turned on a lathe and sanded, with deadwood knocked off the ends. Wood is inspected and flame-treated, a process which hardens the outer surface. The trademark, code number, and player's signature are embossed on the sealed wood and a lacquer finish is applied. ☞

The process varies slightly in the Adirondack Company's plant, and that firm also caters to players who demand specific dimensions in their bats. The Adirondack "batmobile" visits spring training camps and manufactures bats in 35 minutes—meeting players' specifications precisely.

Both Hillerich & Bradsby and Adirondack are kept busy throughout the year because each player uses a number of bats per season. Babe Ruth once used 170 in a season because he gave many away to adoring young fans, but Lou Gehrig managed to get through a season with only six. Another slugger, Bill Terry, was even more frugal—using two en route to the 1930 batting championship with a .401 mark.

## Louisville Slugger Baseball Bats

For nearly half a century known as the best bat made wherever baseball is played.

Make your batting record this year with a Louisville Slugger.

**HILLERICH & BRADSBY CO.**

Louisville, Kentucky

Eddie Collins, a star in the early part of the century, ordered a half-dozen bats in late summer, took them home, and "seasoned" them by hanging them out in the winter winds. Collins borrowed the idea from an earlier Chicago star, Cap Anson, who had more than 200 bats hanging like salamis in his basement.

More than three million Louisville Sluggers are carved each year—most by mass production, but those ordered for professional players by hand. None are exactly alike; they differ in weight, balance, length, shape of barrel and handle, and taping.

To keep bats in prime condition, players treat them with tobacco juice, pine-tar, oil, and special sprays. Some have attempted to smooth the surface by rubbing Coke bottles against the wood.

Aluminum bats, popular in softball, are held together by rubber plugs and are stronger than wooden bats for that game; but the plugs sometimes fail and send the barrel flying off at high speed. The expression, "Don't fly off the handle," comes from a poorly-put-together baseball bat, which can become a lethal weapon.

## MODEL BATS HOUSED IN VAULTS

*Original copies of bats ordered by players are stored in fireproof vaults. When a player orders more bats, his model is used to carve duplicates.*

Heine Groh Bottle Bat — 1915

Charles Comiskey — 1886

Dan Brouthers — 1880

## HOW COBB CARED FOR BATS

*Ty Cobb treated bats with tobacco juice in an effort to keep dampness out of the wood. Using a chewing tobacco called Nerve navy-cut—an especially juicy brand—Cobb rubbed his bats for hours with the hollowed-out thigh of a steer. The bone was still chained to a table in the Detroit clubhouse years after Cobb retired.*

SPALDING        HEINIE GROH

## COLORED BALLS

*Larry MacPhail introduced yellow base-balls in 1938 and Charley Finley tried orange balls thirty-five years later, but neither idea caught on.*

## THE LIVELY BALL

*Washington pitcher Walter Masterson: "The ball has so much rabbit in it, you can hear the rabbit's heartbeat."*

## OUTFIELDERS PLAYED DEEPER IN 1920

*With the introduction of the lively ball in 1920, major league outfielders learned to play further back. Two of the top center-fielders of the day, Tris Speaker and Edd Roush, could no longer play shallow center and hope to reach hard-hit balls.*

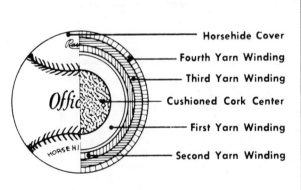

- Horsehide Cover
- Fourth Yarn Winding
- Third Yarn Winding
- Cushioned Cork Center
- First Yarn Winding
- Second Yarn Winding

## BALL WAS TOO LIVELY IN 1930

*The National League's souped-up baseball of 1930 had to be toned down after a season in which six of eight teams hit .300 and the other two topped .280. The pennant-winning Cardinals had eleven .300 hitters and the New York Giants hit a record .319. The Phils hit .315 but finished last—40 games from first—because their team earned run average was 6.71. Pitching was hurting all around the league; a 4.07 ERA ranked as the fifth best mark that season.*

# BALLS

Baseballs have been dead and lively, white and colored, horsehide and cowhide. In 1883, five million of them were used in the United States, and the number has quadrupled since.

In 1872, four years before the founding of the National League, balls were standardized, though a cushioned cork center was not introduced until 1926. The "rabbit ball" earned its nickname because of its great hop. Hitters nudged it a little; it hopped a lot.

When cowhide replaced horsehide in 1974, teams complained during spring training that the ball sometimes came apart at the seams. A new ball, with fewer but tighter stitches, was used the following year.

Since each ball's seams are hand-sewn, no two balls are alike. If a ball's seams are slightly raised, they will catch enough wind to make the curveball break more sharply.

Pitchers generally prefer to work with a lively ball because their teams will score more runs as a result. "With a few runs to work with," said Tommy Bridges in the '30s. "I'll take my chances of stopping the hitters even with a lively ball."

The issue of live *vs.* dead ball usually doesn't faze the slugger. Babe Ruth hit 29 home runs (topping the Gavvy Cravath mark of 24) in 1919, when the dead ball was still in use and freak deliveries were legal (unusual pitches were banned in 1920).

Statistics before 1920 reflect the nature of the dead-ball era: stolen bases, hit-and-run plays, bunts, choked-up swingers, spray hitters, and place hitters. Few, if any, went for the home run. The pennant-winning Chicago White Sox of 1906 hit six for the season and two years later had only three. But "the Hitless Wonders" won games.

When Ruth began to crack home runs with regularity, and the game needed a boost after the staggering Black Sox scandal of 1919, a livelier ball came into play and the game changed. But not everyone was happy.

"When you monkey with the ball, you monkey with the game itself," said New York Giants' manager John McGraw. "That's all right, of course, within reason. But you'd better make sure the ball is going to make the kind of game the fans want when you change it."

### THE BALL

Starting with the 1977 season, the Official National League Baseball was manufactured by the Rawlings Sporting Goods Company. The ball, like every phase of National League Baseball, is subject to rigorous standards and specifications. Listed here are the specifications and the process involved in making an official National League baseball (AL ball is similar):

### NATIONAL LEAGUE BASEBALL SPECIFICATIONS

The manufacturing of a National League baseball requires superior craftsmanship and quality materials to meet the rigorous standards and specifications set forth by the N.L.

The following outlines these specifications and standards:
1. Cushion cork center consisting of composition cork sphere surrounded by one layer black and one layer red rubber 7/8 oz.
2. Approximately 121 yards 4/11 blue-grey woolen yarn to make circumference 7-3/4" and weight 2-7/8 oz.
3. Approximately 45 yards 3/11 white woolen yarn to make circumference 8-3/16 and weight 3-11/16 oz.
4. Approximately 53 yards 3/11 blue-gray woolen yarn to make circumference 8-3/4" and weight 4-1/4 oz.
5. Approximately 150 yards 20/2 ply fine cotton yarn to make circumference 8-7/8" and weight 4-1/2 to 4-5/8 oz.
6. Yarn used with exception of cotton finishing yarn to be 99% wool, 1% other fibers, and of the wool, 75% to be virgin wool and 24% reprocessed.
7. Apply coat special rubber cement.

8. Special alum tanned leather sewn with double stitch 10/5 red thread. Weight of cover 1/2 to 9/16 oz. Thickness of cover .045 to .055, the whole to make size 9 to 9-1/4" and weight 5 to 5-1/4 oz.

The size of the ball shall be measured by a steel tape in graduations of 1/10th of an inch, with two pounds tension applied to the tape, measuring twice over two seams and once over four seams, and thereafter averaging three measurements, which shall establish the size of the ball.

9. When tested on an indoor driving machine (machine to be approved by the President of the National League) to determine and measure the resiliency of baseballs through the co-efficient of restitution with an initial velocity of 85 feet per second, the rebound of velocity shall be 54.6% of the initial velocity, with a tolerance of 3.2% plus or minus of said initial velocity.

NOTE: 85 feet per second is determined to be approximately equal to the velocity of a baseball which after being hit by a bat would carry 400 feet.

## MAKING A RAWLINGS NATIONAL LEAGUE BASEBALL

The following highlights the process of putting a National League baseball together:

The manufacture of a baseball starts with the cushioned cork center around which the ball is developed by successive stages of winding—first, a layer of blue-grey yarn; then, one of white wool; followed by a third layer of blue-gray. Each winding requires exacting tension control and, upon completion of each winding stage, the balls are inspected for size and weight. The final winding application consists of a layer of cotton finishing yarn. These four windings consume nearly one-quarter mile of yarn.

Next, the ball receives a coat of pure crepe rubber cement to form a permanent bond. The same cement is applied to the inside of the covers just before they are stitched on the ball. The alum tanned leather covers, before being stitched onto the ball, are dampened to permit a slight stretch. The covers are then stitched by hand, just as they have been ever since covers were first put on baseballs.

In the stitching process, a pair of covers (each cover is in the shape of a figure eight and encases only half the baseball) are stapled to the ball and then the covers are sewn together. There are 108 stitches in all with the first and last perfectly hidden. After the covers are sewn together, the staples are removed and the baseball goes through another of its many inspections. Then, it is placed in a rolling machine while the cover is still slightly damp. This rolling operation levels the stitches, assuring uniformity.

## THE DEAD BALL ERA

The period before 1920 was known as the "dead ball era." The ball had a different core than today's lively ball, moved more slowly, seldom took high bounces, and rarely reached the deep part of the outfield.

Heavier bats were used to push, rather than drive, the ball, and pitchers took short strides, emphasizing control rather than strikeouts. They let batters hit the ball and hoped fielders would catch it. At the same time, they saved wear-and-tear on their arms and were able to work often.

Home runs were so rare that in 1902, National League leader Wee Tommy Leach failed to hit one out of the park. All six of his "homers" were inside-the-park jobs.

## BREVITY BEST FOR CUBS

The late Phil Wrigley, owner of the Chicago Cubs, liked brevity on his team's jerseys. "I always preferred CHICAGO rather than CHICAGO CUBS on the uniform," he said. "CUBS ends up on the stomach and that emphasizes it. Just CHICAGO across the chest makes them look huskier. CHICAGO CUBS looks like JOE'S GARAGE."

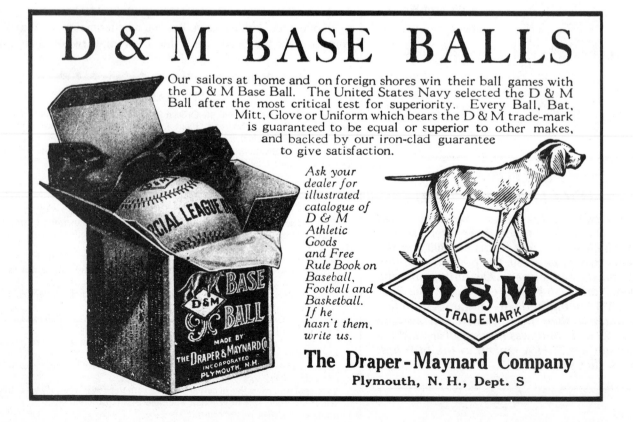

# A CHANGE IN NAME

### By C. C. JOHNSON SPINK
### Editor and Publisher of *The Sporting News*

ST. LOUIS—One thing is going to be different in the major leagues this season—the name on the baseball. It will say "Rawlings" instead of "Spalding."

With the name change, you can bet if home-run totals and batting averages go up, the pitchers will blame the new baseball. And, conversely, if homers and averages fall off, the batters will blame the ball.

Except they'll be wrong.

It may come as a surprise to the major leaguers, but they played with Rawlings-made baseballs for a number of years without knowing it.

Until this season, Spalding had provided the National League balls since 1879. A.J. Reach originally made the balls for the American League, but the company was acquired by Spalding, which eventually substituted its name for Reach's on the A.L. ball.

**RAWLINGS GOT INTO** the major league baseball production picture after Spalding bought the company in December, 1955. Following the merger, Rawlings made some of the baseballs for Spalding at its St. Louis plant, shipping them in blank boxes to Chicopee, Mass., where Spalding applied the final A. L. or N. L. stamps.

So, in those years, the major leagues used the products of both companies without anyone noticing any difference. Actually, there wasn't any because the Spalding and Rawlings balls were identical.

The government forced Spalding to divest itself of Rawlings and after the firms parted in 1968, Rawlings continued to make some of the Spalding baseballs. Even more, in 1971 and '72, Spalding sublet its ball manufacturing to Rawlings and most major league baseballs those two years were made by the St. Louis-based company, although each bore the Spalding name. The relationship ended in 1973.

Spalding now stitches its baseballs in Haiti. Rawlings has gone completely to Haiti and manufactures all of its baseballs there, using American materials, American machinery, American supervision and American quality control.

Starting this season, Rawlings will provide all major league baseballs under a 10-year contract, replacing Spalding as the supplier.

Frank Torre, who carries the imposing title of vice-president of professional, military and Asian sales for Rawlings, told us, "The fact that the name on the ball has changed won't make any difference."

Perhaps not, but Torre's claims for the Rawlings ball may make a difference. He said, "If there's anything that might be a plus, it would be the fact that our baseballs will retain their hardness longer than those in the last three years."

**AFTER THE INTRODUCTION** of cowhide instead of horsehide for the cover in 1974, major league players began to complain that some of the Spalding balls were "soft" and ripped easily. Torre said this condition had nothing to do with the cover but rather with the inner composition of the baseballs.

"Some of the windings inside the ball would break down and loosen the cover," he said. "Then it would tear under pressure."

(A spokesman for Spalding disagreed with Torre that the windings were at fault. He said, "When we did go to cowhide, there were some start-up problems, but that was to be expected. And after the initial experience, we had very little trouble.")

The Rawlings baseball, Torre asserted, is made under strict manufacturing control.

"The key to the whole thing is the automated windings," he explained. "The covers will tear only if the windings are not done properly. After each winding, we check the circumference of the ball to make sure it comes within the right specification."

The sewing of the cover—exactly 108 stitches—is the only operation still performed by hand.

**JUDGING FROM** everything Torre said, the Rawlings baseballs will be consistently and uniformly hard as compared with some of those made the last three years.

Will that make any difference? On the face of it, you would think that the batters will profit. A baseball that's hard can be driven farther than a soft one. But when we sought the opinion of a major league authority, he straddled the fence by saying:

"A uniform ball will benefit everyone. The batters, when they make contact, won't be hitting a soft ball and the pitchers will be more effective with a baseball that doesn't give."

It will be interesting to see what happens.

## THE CHANGES OF 1921

*Before the 1921 season began, baseball moguls mandated tighter winding of the ball, outlawed such trick deliveries as the spitball and emery ball, and told umpires to keep fresh, white balls in play. All three moves were designed to promote distance hitting, which Babe Ruth proved to be a great fan attraction.*

## SHOESTRINGS IN BOSTON

*The Boston National League club allowed players just one pair of shoestrings per year. If they lasted two years, the team paid the player's fare (one way only) on the horse-car to or from the park.*

## CABBAGE LEAVES IN THE CAP

*To avoid sunstroke, old-time players placed cabbage leaves under their caps.*

## BABE RUTH'S NO. 3

*Cliff Mapes wore No. 3 after Babe Ruth and No. 7 before Mickey Mantle. Mapes took No. 3 into retirement in 1948. When Mantle asked for No. 7, Mapes took No. 13. Mapes had a lifetime average of .242 with 13 home runs.*

## SANDLOT BAT FAVORED FAIN

*Ferris Fain, mired in a slump, watched a sandlot slugger hit several long drives in a game, then bought his bat for three times its value. He did well in a doubleheader the next day and sent the bat to Louisville, where he ordered a load of exact duplicates.*

## COLLINS SAVED BROKEN BATS

*One-time Cardinal Rip Collins couldn't bear to throw away broken bats. He brought them home and converted them into a fence in front of his house.*

# UMPIRE'S EQUIPMENT

In addition to his uniform, including mask and chest protector, the umpire has various other pieces of equipment.

The ball-and-strike indicator keeps track of the count and allows the arbiter to correct the scoreboard, which occasionally deviates from the actual count. The official count is the one shown on the umpire's indicator.

The mound measuring stick, a little-known device, is used by umpires before each series between teams. The pitching mound must be sloped one inch per foot, and must be uniform with the warm-up mounds in the same ballpark. Mounds may be no more than 10 inches from ground level and no greater than 18 feet in diameter. Umpires must make sure the measurements are within the rules.

Umpires also use whisk brooms heavily. They are used not only to dust off home plate but also as outlets for the umpire's temper. When the arbiter gets into an argument, he can get out of it gracefully by whipping out the whisk broom, marching over to home plate, and dusting it off—whether it's needed or not.

The least-known equipment used by the umpire is the mud supply from a South Jersey creek. The unusually smooth silt, discovered by Philadelphia Athletics coach Lena Blackburne, was first applied to baseballs in 1937 after umpire Harry Geisel complained about the slickness of new balls.

The mud, with the texture of cold cream, did not scratch the ball or darken it noticeably. Geisel liked it and word spread so quickly that in 1938, American League president Will Harridge ordered all league umpires to apply it before games. The job, which took 20 minutes, put Blackburne in business, as the National League, International League, and American Association soon followed the AL's lead.

## HARRY WALKER LIKED TWO-TONED BAT

*Harry (the Hat) Walker, 1947 NL batting king, was prowling the Louisville Slugger plant when he spotted a worker stirring stain with a bat. He liked the club, which had a brown barrel and white handle, and asked to buy it. Walker followed with a pinch-hit home run and placed the bat on permanent order.*

# CHAPTER SIX

# The Ballparks

Kansas City Royals

**Royals Stadium, featuring a three-tiered water display between the outfield fence and the scoreboard, hosted the All-Star Game in 1973, its first season of operation.**

# EARLY BALLPARKS

The first ballpark—Union Grounds in Brooklyn—existed seven years before the Cincinnati Red Stockings became the first professional team in 1869 and 15 years before the National League's first season in 1876. Admission was 10 cents.

Early stadiums were made of wood and had limited capacities. Often, there were no outfield fences, only a barrier at the end of the ballpark's property—a safeguard against freeloaders. Many parks had a special admission gate in this barrier for horse-drawn (and later horseless) carriages, which were allowed to park in the outfield. When fans exceeded a park's ability to seat them, they were also permitted to stand behind roped-off sections of the outfield—creating the need for special ground rules governing balls hit into the crowd.

In addition to uncomfortable seating on long, backless planks, wooden parks presented an obvious fire hazard. After a number of fires, concrete-and-steel stadiums began to replace wood ballparks. The last game in the old-style stadium was played at Robison Field, St. Louis, on June 6, 1920.

Another St. Louis stadium, Sportsman's Park (renamed Busch Stadium in 1953), enjoyed the longest lifespan of a major league field. First used by the Cardinals in the National League's initial 1876 season, it was reinforced with concrete and steel in 1908 and remained in regular service until May 8, 1966 (though it was unoccupied, 1878-84, when the city had no big-league club).

## TURNSTILES

*Turnstiles were used for the first time in Providence in 1878. More than 6,000 fans crammed the ballpark—many of them arriving by two special trains from Boston—and 300 carriages ringed the outfield. Boston won, 1-0.*

Hilltop Park was an early home of the Yankees, then called Hilltoppers. Its site is now occupied by the Columbia-Presbyterian Medical Center.

# SITES OF STADIUMS

Other than a fifty-year span from 1903-53, constant franchise shifting, expansion, and contraction changed the size, style, and location of major league ballparks.

Two modern clubs, the Brooklyn Dodgers and Chicago White Sox, borrowed a pre-1900 concept of playing "home" games at a neutral site to hike attendance. The Dodgers played seven games in Jersey City's Roosevelt Stadium in both 1956 and 1957 before moving to Los Angeles, while the Chisox occupied deserted Milwaukee County Stadium for nine games in 1968 and eleven in 1969.

A dozen championship games in 1902-03 were played outside major league cities which then banned Sunday baseball. The Indians left Cleveland for contests in such cities as Canton, Columbus, and Dayton, Ohio, and played two games in Fort Wayne, Indiana. The

## OLDEST FRANCHISE IN BASEBALL

*The Chicago National League franchise is the oldest in baseball. The Cubs, once known as the White Stockings, were the only club to spend a full century in the NL, 1876-1976. The American League did not begin play until 1901.*

Boston Braves played a "home" game in Providence, Rhode Island, and the Detroit Tigers visited Columbus and Toledo, Ohio and Grand Rapids, Michigan.

Broadcast baseball, the home run heroics of Babe Ruth, and the advent of night play mushroomed the popularity of the game and led to a building boom in stadiums after World War II. All but six of the 26 ballparks in the majors in 1978 were constructed after the war —17 of them since 1960.

The best illustration of the stadium building boom is Frank Robinson's home run record. Robinson, who played from 1956-76 and became the only man to win the Most Valuable Player award in both leagues, homered in record 32 different stadiums (a feat duplicated by Hank Aaron):

Anaheim Stadium, Atlanta Stadium, Baltimore Memorial Stadium, Fenway Park (Boston), Ebbets Field (Brooklyn), White Sox Park, Wrigley Field (Chicago), Crosley Field and Riverfront Stadium (Cincinnati), Cleveland Municipal Stadium, Tiger Stadium, Colt Stadium (Houston), Roosevelt Stadium (Jersey City), both Municipal Stadium and Royals Stadium (Kansas City).

Also, Dodger Stadium, the Los Angeles Coliseum, Milwaukee County Stadium, Metropolitan Stadium (Bloomington, Minnesota), Yankee Stadium, Shea Stadium and the Polo Grounds (New York), Oakland-Alameda County Stadium, Connie Mack Stadium and Veterans Stadium (Philadelphia), Forbes Field (Pittsburgh), Busch Stadium (St. Louis), San Diego Stadium, Candlestick Park and Seals Stadium (San Francisco), Arlington Stadium (Texas), and Robert F. Kennedy Stadium (Washington).

★ ★ ★ ★ ★ ★

## Current Major League Parks

| STADIUM | YEAR OPENED | CAPACITY |
|---|---|---|
| White Sox Park | 1910 | 44,492 |
| Fenway Park (Boston) | 1912 | 33,379 |
| Tiger Stadium | 1912 | 54,220 |
| Wrigley Field (Chicago) | 1914 | 37,741 |
| Yankee Stadium | 1923 | 57,545 |
| Cleveland Stadium | 1932 | 77,797 |
| Baltimore Memorial Stadium | 1949 | 52,137 |
| Milwaukee County Stadium | 1953 | 46,625 |
| Candlestick Park (San Francisco) | 1960 | 59,091 |
| Dodger Stadium | 1962 | 56,000 |
| Shea Stadium (New York) | 1964 | 55,101 |
| Arlington Stadium (Texas) | 1965 | 35,698 |
| Atlanta Stadium | 1965 | 53,043 |
| The Astrodome (Houston) | 1965 | 45,011 |
| Anaheim Stadium | 1966 | 43,250 |
| Busch Memorial Stadium (St. Louis) | 1966 | 50,126 |
| Oakland Coliseum | 1966 | 48,621 |
| San Diego Stadium | 1967 | 47,634 |
| Riverfront Stadium (Cincinnati) | 1970 | 51,726 |
| Three Rivers Stadium (Pittsburgh) | 1970 | 50,235 |
| Veterans Stadium (Philadelphia) | 1971 | 56,581 |
| Royals Stadium | 1973 | 40,762 |
| The Kingdome (Seattle) | 1977 | 59,059 |
| Olympic Stadium (Montreal) | 1977 | 59,511 |
| H.H. Humphrey Metrodome (Minn) | 1982 | 54,000 |
| The Skydome (Toronto) | 1989 | 54,000 |

(table applies through the 1989 baseball season)

**Brooklyn Dodgers played 15 "home games" across the river at Roosevelt Stadium in Jersey City, New Jersey.**

# HOME RUN DISTANCES

Without established standards, teams built parks to suit their own needs.

With lefthanded power-hitter Babe Ruth as their man batting threat, the New York Yankees built Yankee Stadium with a short right field porch—just 296 feet from home plate.

The park had long dimensions from home to center and left center field, but was called "the House that Ruth Built" with good reason. He hit most of his shots to right—as did Roger Maris in 1961, when he broke Ruth's one-season record by hitting 61 home runs.

Baseball rules established a minimum distance of 325 feet from home plate to the nearest fence, and 400 feet from home to center, as of June 1, 1958. The rules also barred clubs from remodeling existing fences to bring them closer to home than the minimum distance, but allowed fields with shorter fences to retain them.

An earlier fence rule, passed by the National League in 1884, set a minimum distance of 210 feet and ordered that balls hit over closer fences would be ground-rule doubles rather than home runs. The Chicago White Stockings, forerunners of the Cubs, then had a fence just 196 feet from the plate.

Failure by the major leagues to set standard dimensions for all parks has triggered endless controversy among fans and players alike. Advocates of standard fences argued that, without them, it was unfair to compare player records. Opponents said different dimensions in each park made the game more interesting.

Righthanded hitters benefit from a short left field fence, and lefthanded hitters like a short right field.

The righthanded hitting Joe DiMaggio had great power to left, but played home games in Yankee Stadium, with its short right field. Meanwhile, lefthanded batter Ted Williams, a dead pull hitter of the same era, had to cope with a long right field in Boston's Fenway Park—famous for its short left field wall, nicknamed "The Green Monster" by pitchers.

Had DiMaggio and Williams exchanged places, they probably would have rewritten the record book.

Many ballparks got into the record book with their unusual dimensions. The Polo Grounds was just 258 feet to right field and 280 feet to left—easy pickings for Bobby Thomson's pennant-winning "shot heard 'round the world" in 1951.

Brooklyn's Ebbets Field, tailor-made for such southpaw sluggers as Duke Snider, was only 297 feet to right, but 348 to left. The Dodgers' first home in Los Angeles, the football-designed Coliseum, was just 251 feet to the left field foul line and 320 feet to the left-center power alley, but 385 to right-center.

Baker Bowl's 280-foot right field line benefitted lefthand batter Chuck Klein of the Phillies—but helped visiting sluggers even more. In 1930, when the Phils hit .315 as a team, Klein hit 40 homers, knocked in 170 runs, and batted .386. But the team won only 52 times because its pitchers allowed rivals an average of 6.71 earned runs per game.

The average foul lines of parks built after World War II stretch 330 feet from home to the foul poles. Most modern stadiums are symmetrical, avoiding such shapes as the old Polo Grounds horseshoe. All—including the remodeled Yankee Stadium, opened in 1976—maintain fences at least 300 feet from home. Yankee Stadium's right field now stands at 310 feet.

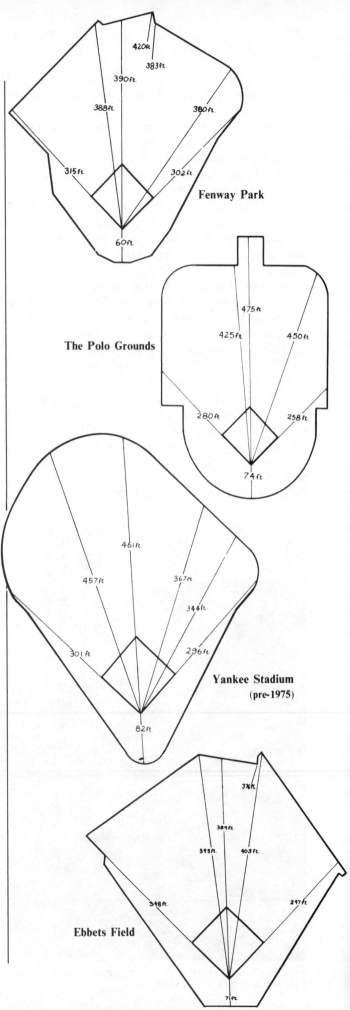

Fenway Park

The Polo Grounds

Yankee Stadium
(pre-1975)

Ebbets Field

# LONG HOME RUNS

## THE CROSLEY FIELD TERRACE

*Most ballparks, past and present, have dirt "warning tracks" to tell outfielders in pursuit of long flies that they are approaching the outfield wall. Cincinnati's Crosley Field (1912-70) had an incline, known as "the terrace." Any outfielder running uphill knew he was running out of room.*

## HOME RUNS FLY IN TIGER STADIUM

*The New York Yankees and Detroit Tigers combined for 11 home runs during a game at Briggs Stadium (now Tiger Stadium) on June 23, 1950. Detroit won, 10-9, before 51,400 partisan fans.*

Stadiums with difficult dimensions for home run hitters cause considerable excitement when a slugger defies the odds with a long home run. Insiders refer to long-distance shots as "tape-measure homers."

By far, the "longest" home run in baseball history was hit by Cincinnati catcher Ernie Lombardi in the '30s. His blast over the 387-foot center field fence in Crosley Field landed in a truck which carried it 30 miles.

The tape measure had to come out on successive nights at the Polo Grounds in 1963 when Lou Brock, then with the Cubs, and Hank Aaron of the Braves became only the second and third hitters ever to reach the center field bleachers in the Polo Grounds.

The ancient New York ballpark tantalized batters with short distances to the right and left field seats, and agonizingly long distances to center. Joe Adcock of the Braves was the first man to reach the bleachers with a 475-foot shot in 1953, but no one duplicated the feat until Brock—with only seven career home runs at the time—found the range. Aaron did it with the bases loaded.

While Mickey Mantle's 565-foot shot off Chuck Stobbs in 1956 at Washington's old Griffith Stadium was probably the most famous tape-measure home run, it is not regarded as the longest. Babe Ruth (twice), Frank Howard, and Norm Cash are considered to be authors of longer home runs—though no official records are kept on the subject.

One thing is known: Joe Adcock chose Ebbets Field to stage the mightiest power display by a hitter in a single game. On August 1, 1954, he hit four home runs and a double for the Braves against the Dodgers. His 18 total bases in one game is a major league record.

## FIRST HOME RUN IN ATLANTA STADIUM

*Home run king Hank Aaron hit the most famous home run in Atlanta Stadium—the one that pushed him beyond Babe Ruth's career mark of 714—but not the first one.*

*In a 1965 exhibition game against the Detroit Tigers, Tommie Aaron, Hank's younger brother, hit the first homer in the brand-new, circular ballpark. Hank hit 755 home runs in his career, Tommie 13.*

Atlanta Braves

Hank Aaron hits his 715th home run on April 8, 1974 against the Los Angeles Dodgers.

# MEMORIES OF OLD PARKS

Before 1900, major league stadiums shifted as frequently as the franchises. The Chicago White Stockings of 1884 were forced to open the season on the road because the Illinois Central Railroad had purchased Lakefront Park and announced plans to build a new depot there. Legal hassles followed and the team finally persuaded the railroad to allow play in Lakefront Park that year on the condition that the team would find new quarters for 1885.

In 1887, the Philadelphia Nationals opened their new Baker Bowl on April 30, when 14,500 fans watched the team beat New York, 15-9. Construction cost for the park was $80,000, the average major league player's salary in 1978.

Two years later, the New York Giants' Polo Grounds closed because of the extension of 111th Street, forcing the team to open the season on borrowed ground in Jersey City. Some home games were played on Staten Island before the "new" Polo Grounds, at 155th Street and 8th Avenue, was dedicated on July 8, 1889.

In 1890, however, the Players League put a franchise in New York and it built a park so close to the 155th Street Polo Grounds that Mike Tiernan of the Giants hit a home run from one park into the other! When the Players League collapsed, the Giants moved into their horseshoe-shaped park and remained there until leaving for San Francisco in 1958. The park saw two more years of major league service as home of the expansionist New York Mets in 1962-63.

When Ben Shibe and Connie Mack paid $150,000 for a brickyard, where they built Shibe Park (later Connie Mack Stadium) in 1909, they thought they might have ventured too far from downtown Philadelphia. But the city caught up with the park and virtually overran it, forcing the Phillies to build Veterans Stadium in time for the 1971 season.

The Phils were Baker Bowl tenants until 1938, while the Athletics played at Shibe Park. Shibe's right field fence was originally ten feet high, allowing tenants of apartments facing the park to have an unobstructed view. Fans in Shibe Park weren't so lucky; they often found themselves in seats behind steel support pillars.

## SULPHUR DELL

*Sulphur Dell, home of the Nashville Vols of the Southern Association for many years, had a longevity record as a stadium that may never be surpassed. The first game was played there in 1866 and the last in 1963, when the Vols folded and the ancient ballpark was demolished.*

*Its right field fence was just 266 feet from home plate and its proximity wasn't the only factor that plagued rightfielders who played there. They also had to play a steep embankment called "The Dump," which served the same purpose as the modern warning track. When the outfielder was going uphill, he knew he was near the fence.*

*The press box was so close to home that writers could confer with umpires while a game was in progress. A boy perched on the roof tried to keep foul balls from going out of the park, but occasionally lost his balance and rolled down the screen connecting the roof with the top of the backstop.*

*Assorted prizes were offered to Nashville players. The best known gimmick, used in other parks as well, was a tire company promotion which offered free tires to anyone who hit a ball through the hole in the firm's scoreboard advertisement.*

*Sulphur Dell was widely known in the southeast as Nashville's oldest landmark and baseball's most historic park.*

The Polo Grounds had an unusual horseshoe shape and close right field barrier.

## GREENBERG GARDENS

*The Pittsburgh Pirates, a bad ballclub in need of a gate attraction, shortened their home run distances when Hank Greenberg joined the team in 1947. Left field was reduced from 365 feet from home to 335 feet, and left center was cut by nearly 20 feet. The new section behind the wall was called Greenberg Gardens, then changed to Kiner's Korner when Ralph Kiner became the club's top slugger. When Kiner was traded in mid-season of 1953, Branch Rickey wanted to tear down the short barrier at once because the Pirates had no other slugger who could reach the wall, but a league rule prevented him from restoring the original distances in mid-year.*

## "POLO GROUNDS SWING"

*The unusual dimensions of the Polo Grounds, long-time home of the New York Giants, perplexed pitchers and batters alike. Dusty Rhodes learned to cope by pulling the ball. "In the Polo Grounds," he said, "you either pulled the ball 260 feet and got a home run or you hit it 490 feet straightaway for an out."*

*Rhodes went 3-for-3 as a pinch-hitter in the 1954 World Series. Two of the hits were singles, the other a three-run homer off Cleveland's Bob Lemon in the tenth inning of the opener. The ball drifted into the close right field stands, 260 feet from home. The disgusted pitcher threw his glove—and Rhodes said later he threw it farther than the ball was hit.*

During the Depression, the team added 40 feet to the height of the right field fence, ending the tradition of freebies for ballpark neighbors and "guests" who paid to share the rooftop view. The A's, in need of revenue, finally allowed the Phillies to escape rusting Baker Bowl and share the costs of running Shibe Park.

Boston also had two teams until the Braves left for Milwaukee in 1953. In 1914, when the "miracle" Braves won the National League pennant, they played their two home World Series games in Fenway Park, the two-year-old Red Sox home which had a larger capacity than the Braves' South End Grounds. But in 1915 and 1916, when the Red Sox won the American League flag, and the Braves failed to repeat, the Bosox opted for the new Braves Field—with 4300 extra seats—as their "home" park and won all five games from NL opposition, including Babe Ruth's 14-inning, 2-1 triumph over the Dodgers in October 1916.

In St. Louis, the Browns and Cardinals switched their tenant-landlord relationship when Anheuser-Busch bought the Cards in 1953. The Cardinals bought the ballpark from the Browns and immediately began a $400,000 facelift. The National Leaguers had been renting the stadium for $35,000 plus approximate annual maintenance costs of $100,000 (half the maintenance). Under the new deal, the Browns rented for $175,000 per year, with maintenance costs included.

Lights had become part of baseball (except in Chicago's Wrigley Field) by the '50s, but they didn't always work properly. In Washington, Detroit's George Kell remembered what happened when the arc lights failed.

"There was a 2-2 count and the pitcher was in his windup when all the lights suddenly went out," he said. "I quickly hit the dirt. I must have stayed down there a good minute when I began to feel foolish and started to get up. Just as I did, the lights came on again. It was quite a sight. Every outfielder and infielder, even the catcher, was flat on the ground. The only guy standing was the pitcher. He *knew* where the ball was."

Crosley Field, Cincinnati, hosted the first night game in the majors in 1935, but the Reds did little to improve their lighting system after that. Still, major league lighting was far superior to that found in minor league ballparks.

"When I played in the minor leagues," said Ralph Kiner, "it seemed to me like kerosene lamps could have done as good a job."

# MODERN BASEBALL STADIUMS

The major changes in baseball stadiums of today and those of the Babe Ruth era, some fifty years ago, are the introductions of lights, artificial turf, electronic scoreboards, and domes.

Night ball began in 1935 and played tricks on the eyes of batters for years—especially in its first twenty years, when teams played more often by day than by night. On June 15, 1938, Johnny Vander Meer of the Reds became the only man to pitch back-to-back no-hitters, but he was helped considerably in the second effort by the dim lights of Brooklyn's Ebbets Field. It was the park's first night game. ☞

**Cornerstone of Brooklyn's Ebbets Field survives at Cooperstown.**

Artificial turf, a necessity caused by the creation of the first covered park, the Houston Astrodome, made its debut during an exhibition game between the Astros and the New York Yankees on April 9, 1965. President Lyndon Johnson, a Texan, watched Mickey Mantle's homer lead the Yankees to a 2-1 victory in the $31.6 million ballpark.

In 1978, 10 fields had artificial turf—seven of them in the National League—and the number of domes in the majors had doubled and seemed on the verge of tripling. The $163 million Louisiana Superdome begged for a ballclub, while the $60 million Seattle Kingdome landed the expansion Seattle Mariners in 1977.

Both artificial turf and domed ballparks caused problems—just as the advent of lights did years earlier. Light failure became such a factor in the game that contingencies regarding it were written into baseball rules. Turf failure and dome failure had to be handled by individual clubs which opted for such features.

The Chicago White Sox, on orders from president Bill Veeck, replaced their artificial infield with natural grass. Veeck was one of many baseball insiders who felt that the true bounces and aesthetic appearance of plastic grass did not counterbalance the wear-and-tear on athletes on the hard, hot surface. Nor did he like the turf's tendency to rocket balls through the infield and tilt the traditional balance between hitter and pitcher.

## ASTRODOME THWARTS SCHMIDT

*Philadelphia's Mike Schmidt was deprived of a tape-measure home run when his 1974 blast in Houston struck a loudspeaker hanging from the Astrodome in center field. Under ground rules in the domed ballpark, such balls are in play; Schmidt had to settle for the longest single in baseball history.*

## NOVEL WAY TO BEAT THE HEAT

*To cool off from the scorching heat of artificial turf at St. Louis, Cardinal outfielder Jim Beauchamp soaked his feet—shoes and all—in cold water between innings. The plastic grass dried his socks quickly when he resumed his defensive position.*

# BIG PARKS SHORT FENCES

The Los Angeles Coliseum, built for football, had the largest capacity and most unusual dimensions in baseball during its brief tenure as home of the Dodgers, 1958-61. It held 93,600 for baseball —and nearly reached that figure three times during the 1959 World Series against the White Sox. The park's left field screen stood just 251 feet from home, and the left-center power alley was only 320 feet away. In right field, the distance down the line was 300 feet, but the right-center power alley was 385. ☞

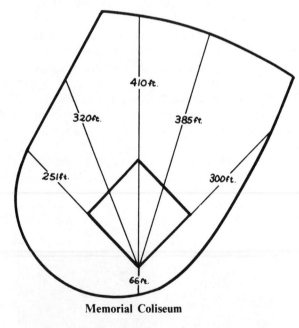

**Memorial Coliseum**

There is a remarkable contrast between the old and new homes of the Dodgers in Los Angeles. The Memorial Coliseum, used before Dodger Stadium opened in 1962, was built for football.

**Dodger Stadium**

Los Angeles Dodgers

The Houston Astrodome gives the game an entirely different perspective. Balls do not travel well inside and power-hitting teams often have trouble there.

In the Astrodome, the 4500 plastic skylights caused a glare which resulted in fielders "losing the ball" in the roof. After conditions deteriorated to a point where outfielders wore helmets for day games, the team painted the skylights and reduced the day lighting by 25 to 40 per cent. Since that time, electric lighting has been used for all games, day or night.

In a story on the Seattle Kingdome in 1977, columnist Mike Schuman of *The Baseball Bulletin* listed player complaints about the coloring of the dome, the proximity of bullpen mounds to the playing field, and high seams in the artificial turf near second base, where dirt meets carpet.

Olympic Stadium, which costs Montreal taxpayers an estimated $15,000 per day for maintenance, is the ballpark most in need of a dome (the Expos never open the season at home). Instead it has a "technical ring" with a central opening that measures 600 feet by 300 feet. Snowouts are still a problem.

Baseball executives who like intimate ballparks with unusual dimensions insist that such symmetrical parks as Riverfront and Three Rivers Stadiums, both opened in 1970, destroy the color of the game. They frown on horizontal yellow "home run lines" painted on the outfield wall, dislike artificial turf, and warn that fans who cannot see the game well enough to identify with the players will quickly lose interest.

It is a fact of life that the five oldest parks currently in use house healthy crowds consistently: Comiskey Park and Wrigley Field in Chicago, Fenway Park in Boston, Yankee Stadium in New York, and Tiger Stadium in Detoit.

All have undergone major face-liftings, notably Fenway Park in 1934 and Yankee Stadium in 1974-75. The Yankee Stadium project, originally projected at $24 million, wound up with a $100 million price-tag—more than triple the cost of building Royals Stadium, a particularly handsome baseball park that opened in Kansas City in 1973.

Remodeling Yankee Stadium was the only option open to New York City in 1972 when it appeared the team would join the football Giants in a baseball-football park in nearby Hackensack, New Jersey, less than five miles from Manhattan but far more accessible than Yankee Stadium. ☞

## RUTH PULLED PERFECT FAKE

*Babe Ruth was a good defensive outfielder. When Detroit's Tiger Stadium was called Navin Field in the late '20s, there was a board fence in left instead of double-decked stands. With one out and Charlie Gehringer of the Tigers on second, the batter hit a long fly ball to Ruth in left. Ruth knew he could catch the ball, but pretended it had cleared the wall. Watching the dejected Ruth, Gehringer left for home. The minute he left the base, Ruth came to life, caught the ball, and fired to second for the inning-ending double-play.*

## FLOODING IN PITTSBURGH'S PARK

*With water knee-deep in Pittsburgh's Exposition Park on July 4, 1902, a special ground rule was created: any ball hit into the water (named Lake Dreyfuss after the Pirate owner) would be an automatic double.*

The bitter irony of the project was the total bill. The team could have built two new parks, from the ground up, for the price of its two-year overhaul of a fifty-year-old field.

Dimensions were changed slightly in the "new" stadium: 312 to left, 310 to right, and 417 to dead center field. Formerly, it was 301 feet to left, 296 to right, and 461 to center.

Obstructing pillars were removed and aisles—and seats—widened, reducing capacity from 65,010 to 57,545. Blue paint was used in liberal doses and the famous ballpark looked years younger. Only the dismal Bronx neighborhood remained the same.

Troubled by similar environs around Comiskey Park in Chicago, Bill Veeck took steps to improve both the lighting and the outer appearance of his park.

# SCOREBOARDS

The baseball scoreboard, originally designed to tell spectators the score of the game they were watching, has become as much an attraction as the ballgame itself.

Old-style boards were manually operated, with run-markers put up by hand. When Dizzy Dean was pitching for Houston, then in the minor leagues, he hit a rare home run. Immediately afterward, he lost his control and walked three consecutive batters.

Taken from the game, Dean ran to the scoreboard and plucked the numeral "1" that represented his home run. The pitcher took the painted wooden square into the clubhouse, prompting a visit from the manager. "If I can't pitch," he said, "you can't have my run."

The St. Louis Cardinals, where Dean reached stardom, maintained an ancient scoreboard until 1938, when a $40,000 replace-

## SICKS STADIUM

*Sicks Stadium, Seattle, held 25,400 fans—more than adequate for Pacific Coast League play but below major league standards. Bad weather, bad financing, and the unavailability of a better facility forced the expansion Seattle Pilots of 1969 to abandon ship and stadium the following year. The team became the Milwaukee Brewers.*

## KAYCEE WATER SHOW

*Royals Stadium, part of the Harry S Truman Sports Complex in Kansas City, features a $3 million "Water Spectacular" behind the wall between center field and right field. The 322-foot-wide attraction, the world's largest privately-funded fountain, contains a 10-foot-high waterfall from an upper cascade pool, plus two lower pools that empty into five more 10-foot falls. Post-game water shows are accompanied by music and colored lights.*

Scoreboard at Veterans Stadium, Philadelphia, requires three operators and coordination of music and animation. The ballpark opened in 1971.

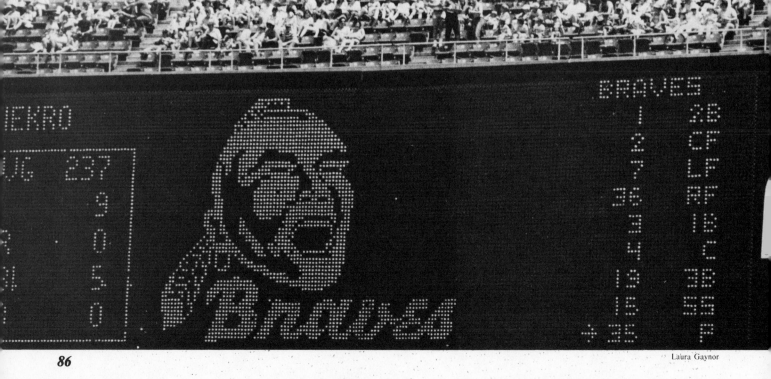

Laura Gaynor

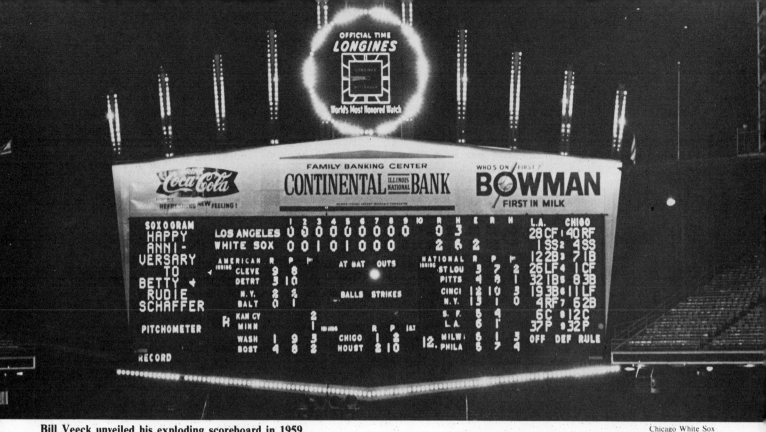

**Bill Veeck unveiled his exploding scoreboard in 1959.**

Chicago White Sox

ment, 136 feet long and 40 feet high, brought electricity into the picture. Inning-by-inning scores of out-of-town games were still posted by hand, but balls, strikes, hits, errors, numbers of players at bat, and other information was flashed in lights.

Multimillion-dollar boards broke into baseball with the wave of new stadium construction in the '70s, but Bill Veeck gave birth to the idea of using the scoreboard as an attraction to lure customers. In 1960, his exploding scoreboard delighted White Sox players and fans, but irritated the opposition so much that Cleveland centerfielder Jimmy Piersall once threw a ball at the noisy monolith.

Veeck's board still shoots off multicolored rockets and gyrates wildly when a Chicago player homers, or when the Sox win a game, and other clubs parroted the creative concept by using lights instead of fireworks.

Only Wrigley Field, home of the tradition-minded Cubs, retained a board which displayed inning-by-inning scores of all games. The team also refused to follow the mass stampede to night baseball; the park remains lightless.

Tradition did bend at Fenway Park, where an animated board was added to the compact, ancient stadium, and in Yankee Stadium, which received a new board during the 1974-75 refurbishing.

Modern boards feature "home run spectaculars," animated cheerleaders, and even advertising—which helps defray massive maintenance costs. The major victim, in many cases, was the listing of other scores. They are flashed only occasionally and sometimes— if the team has too many birthdays to post or promotions to announce—not at all. Since not everyone at the ballpark is a fan of the two teams on the field, the absence of scores annoys numerous patrons.

Probably the best new board appeared at Veterans Stadium, Philadelphia, in 1971. Three staffers work the board and coordinate activities with a public address announcer who shares their booth. The organist sits in another booth, separated by glass, but works closely with the scoreboard crew. ☞

## KOUFAX ON ASTROTURF

Hall of Fame pitcher Sandy Koufax on the St. Louis AstroTurf: "I know one thing. I was one of those guys who pitched without a cup. I wouldn't do it on this stuff."

## REDS DYED GRASS GREEN

In 1937, the Cincinnati Reds became the first club to artificially color its diamond. The team dyed sun-burned grass green with a product recommended by the United States Greens Association.

## NOVEL APPROACH

Long-time Sportsman's Park groundskeeper Bill Stockstick used a goat to help him trim the outfield grass for the St. Louis Cardinals. The goat was grazing in the outfield the morning after Frankie Frisch became the team's manager in 1933.

In Atlanta, the $1.5 million scoreboard came equipped with a TV capability that included "instant replay." The Braves nearly forfeited a game when umpires walked off the field after the board showed "instant replay" of a close call.

During rain delays, the board shows baseball movies, and flamboyant club owner Ted Turner joked that he could even hold baseball's first "Adult Night" and show X-rated films at the stadium.

The major gripe of baseball insiders against the new boards is their propensity to unnerve visiting teams by flashing giant "GO" or "CHARGE" signs, accompanied by blasts from the organ, in the middle of inning. Leo Durocher, as Cubs' manager in the late '60s, raised the cry against Houston scoreboard chief Bill Giles.

In the absence of directives from either league office, the idea spread. When Durocher became Houston manager in 1972, he found himself enjoying one of the game's most creative home run spectaculars.

# "FIXING THE FIELD" FOR THE HOME TEAM

Each major league club maintains its home field with meticulous care and a bag of tricks designed to help the home team and slow the opposition.

Groundskeepers may water the base-paths or slope the foul lines to thwart a bunt-and-steal team, or freeze baseballs to help a weak-hitting, good-fielding home club.

It was once common practice to place the visitors' dugout in line with the hot afternoon sun, but the prevalence of night baseball (except in Chicago's Wrigley Field) has diminished the value of that tactic. Many home dugouts—but not visiting dugouts—have heat and air-conditioning, and home clubhouses are invariably superior to those given the visitors. Bullpen lighting is generally better for the home team too.

Both Ty Cobb and Connie Mack were masters at freezing balls before slugging clubs came to town. Mack frightened visiting hitters by ordering his groundskeepers to build a 20-inch mound for ace pitchers Lefty Grove, George Earnshaw, Chief Bender, and Eddie Plank. Early Washington manager Joe Cantillion, taking the opposite approach, trained his pitchers to work on a flat mound; rival pitchers hated to pitch in the Senators' park.

The Yankees reached into their bag of tricks by raising or lowering a huge green curtain in center field of Yankee Stadium. If a power pitcher worked for New York, the curtain was up so that enemy batters had trouble picking up the ball against a sea of white shirts. If an ordinary pitcher was on the mound, the curtain was down to help Yankee batters.

The Yankee Stadium groundcrew had a reputation for speed in spreading the infield tarpaulin, but they prolonged the 10-minute job whenever New York was ahead in a game that had passed the minimum four-and-a-half innings. By moving slowly, the field could absorb enough water to make further play impossible. If the Yankees trailed, the crew worked as quickly as possible to keep the field dry and hope play would resume. ☞

## AN ANSWER TO VEECK

When the Yankees played at Chicago in 1960, the year Bill Veeck installed his exploding scoreboard, manager Casey Stengel and Yogi Berra, joined by other players, brought sparklers to the ballpark. When Mickey Mantle homered—and the partisan Veeck board was silent—the Yankees lit the sparklers and jumped up and down in the dugout.

## FABIAN SPENT FIFTY YEARS AS GROUNDSKEEPER

Henry Fabian was a groundskeeper for more than fifty years—half of them with the New York Giants. In 1914, ace Giant pitcher Christy Mathewson showed Fabian the value of a flat mound. The star pointed out that the average pitcher jerks his head back and fouls up his follow-through when working off a high mound. Fabian kept the Polo Grounds mounds low to the ground (a 9-inch slope), much to the delight of a later Giants' star, Carl Hubbell.

## CUBS' GROUNDSKEEPER CAUGHT BABE RUTH

Bobby Dorr, Chicago Cubs' groundskeeper for more than thirty seasons, was Babe Ruth's first warm-up catcher with the Baltimore Orioles of the International League. Dorr later created the concept of keeping fresh baseballs in a wooden box buried near home plate. Previously, new balls were thrown out from the bench or rolled down the screen behind the plate.

# "THE BEAUTIFUL CONFINES OF WRIGLEY FIELD"

*Hall of Fame slugger Ernie Banks, who spent his entire career with the Cubs, always lauded his home park, which he called "the beautiful confines of Wrigley Field." The Wrigley family, which owned the team, spent several million dollars on beautification but refused to install lights. They maintained that the green vines on the outfield wall looked more attractive by day, when people would equate a trip to the ballpark with a picnic. "We're aiming at people not interested in baseball," Phil Wrigley once said.*

National League

Groundskeepers sometimes work 16-hour days, paying special attention to the batter's box, pitcher's mound, and often the baselines. Hitters usually like smooth, flat ground and dislike holes which can break their stride and force them to swing under the ball. Pitchers have their own preferences as to height and texture of the dirt on the mound.

Washington's Camilo Pascual spent considerable time manicuring the mound whenever he pitched, earning the nickname "The Rake," and Catfish Hunter's well-known preference for a soft mound prompted Kansas City groundskeeper George Toma to pack the mound hard when Hunter came to town as a visitor with Oakland or New York.

"I make it as uncomfortable as the rules permit," he said. "He relies a great deal on the shape and condition of the mound. I did my best to help him when he was here and now I do whatever I can to hinder him."

During Ty Cobb's day as a great base-stealer, rival clubs trimmed their infield grass before Detroit came to town so that Cobb's bunts would reach fielders more quickly. When Maury Wills was en route to breaking Cobb's one-season record in 1962, the Giants tried to thwart the Dodger star by sanding the basepaths. The Dodgers tried a similar tactic against the bunt-and-steal Phillies during the 1977 National League Championship Series, but NL president Chub Feeney made them remove the excess dirt.

The Senators helped slow-footed third baseman Harmon Killebrew, their top slugger, by letting the infield grass grow enough to slow balls hit his way. Earlier, the Indians watered down third base territory—making it "the warm corner"—after slugger Al Rosen broke his nose nine times on hard-hit balls.

Richie Ashburn of the Phillies won the 1955 NL batting crown partly because his bunts down the third base line never rolled foul; they coasted to a stop in fair territory because of "Ashburn's Ridge," an inclined foul line raised slightly above the rest of the infield level. St. Louis manager Eddie Stanky tried to thwart the Philadelphia tactic by stamping down the ridge with his spikes before the game.

The "Go-Go" White Sox, a hit-and-run team that singled opponents to death en route to the 1959 AL pennant, were also accused of harboring a raised third base foul line. The Sox, and the pennant-winning Pirates of 1960, thrived on rock-hard infields in their home parks because line drives by their hitters got by enemy infielders quickly. ☞

## GROUNDCREW CHIEF LIVED IN BALLPARK

*Matty Schwab borrowed a minor league custom when he persuaded Horace Stoneham, owner of the New York Giants, to build him a house under the stands. The three-room cottage, under Section 31 of the left field grandstand, was the Schwabs' summer home for many years.*

## THE TARPAULIN

*The tarpaulin is used to cover infields when it rains. The old, heavy tarp absorbed moisture and required drying after the rain, thereby complicating the life of the groundcrew. A lightweight spun-glass tarp which weighed half as much, did not absorb water, and did not need drying was introduced by Cleveland's Emil Bossard in the '40s. By 1960, most tarps were similar to the 1,110-pound plastic-coated nylon cover used by the St. Louis Cardinals. Rolling and unrolling the tarp takes nine men.*

## BEFORE THE TARPAULIN

*Before canvas field covers were used to protect dirt infields from rain, groundskeepers resorted to other means of protection. Bill Stockstick, in St. Louis, poured gasoline over the field and burned it. If the field had excessive mud, he covered it with sawdust first, then poured on the gasoline and lit a match. Players complained of the fumes, but the method was often successful.*

Charges of partisan groundskeeping were hurled at the Houston Astros when they moved into the air-conditioned Astrodome in 1966. Ed Kranepool of the Mets noticed that the air-conditioning was blowing out when Houston hitters took their swings, but that the breeze stopped when the visitors came to bat. He made the deduction by watching the flag in the outfield.

Though most groundskeepers will swear that their only duty is to maintain their field in good condition, they make the remark with tongue in cheek. It's not really legal to fix the home field in favor of one club, but it's an accepted part of the game.

**Ebbets Field, with unusual dimensions, was the scene of countless hitters' battles.**

## THE EBBETS FIELD BULLPEN

*The bullpen in Brooklyn's Ebbets Field (1913-57) was a hazardous place to work. Squeezed between the left field foul line and the stands, pitchers were pelted with assorted debris from the stands. Another problem was line drives from hitters; pitchers warmed up in a tiny space facing the plate, with lefthanders on the outside and righthanders on the inside. An extra player stood behind bullpen catchers (who had their backs to home) to field balls hit in the pen's vicinity.*

## FIRST PA SYSTEM

*The New York Giants installed baseball's first public address system on August 25, 1929, in a game against Pittsburgh. Umpire Charles Rigler had a microphone inside his mask to broadcast ball-and-strike calls.*

National Leag

Fairchild Aerial Surveys

## FENWAY: A NIGHTMARE FOR PITCHERS

*Fenway Park has always been a nightmare for pitchers—especially lefthanders whose best pitches frequently bounce off "the Green Monster," the huge left field wall 315 feet from home. In 1950, the Sox beat the Browns 20-4 and 29-4 in consecutive games. They scored 17 runs in an inning against Detroit in 1953, winning 23-3, beat the Senators 24-4 in 1940, and lost to the Yankees by the same score in 1923.*

# CHAPTER SEVEN

# THE GAME

# SUNDAY BALL

In the early years of pro ball, Sunday was literally a day of rest. At one time, Sunday games counted only as exhibitions and most cities banned them completely.

In 1878, the National League decided to expel clubs or players who played on Sunday. Two years later, the rule was used to throw Cincinnati out of the circuit. The early Reds had made $4000 by leasing their park to a non-league club—and selling beer during games—on Sundays.

Cincinnati—restored to good graces—beat St. Louis, 5-1, in the league's first recognized Sunday game on April 17, 1892. But Sunday restrictions continued for years, forcing several clubs to play in such neutral cities as Columbus, Ohio. Cleveland's Addie Joss beat Clark Griffith of the Yankees in Columbus, 9-2.

Sunday ball began in New York in January 1917, when Charles Ebbets of the Dodgers staged a benefit concert preceding a National League game against the Phillies. He claimed tickets were being sold only to the concert, but he and manager Wilbert Robinson were arrested and fined $250 each.

The New York Giants used the guise of a military benefit to play a Sunday game the following year, and managers John McGraw of the Giants and Christy Mathewson of the Reds were arrested. Magistrate Francis X. McQuade, named a club official when Charles Stoneham purchased the franchise in 1919, laughed off the charges and blasted the police.

Mathewson's arrest was ironic because he and Branch Rickey, among others, had steadfastly refused to participate in Sunday baseball, even when it was permitted.

By the mid-1930s, Sunday ball was universal and baseball was concerned with a new development—night games.

# NIGHT BASEBALL

On May 24, 1935, the Cincinnati Reds defeated the Philadelphia Phillies, 2-1, in the first night game played in the major leagues. President Franklin D. Roosevelt, sitting in the White House, threw a special switch that turned on the power in the new light towers above Crosley Field, where 20,422 spectators watched.

Baseball executives and writers panned the advent of night play, which they dubbed "MacPhail's Madness" after pioneering Cincinnati general manager Larry MacPhail.

"There is no chance of night baseball ever becoming popular in the bigger cities," said Washington owner Clark Griffith. "People there are educated to see the best there is and will only stand for the best. High-class baseball cannot be played under artificial light."

Cincinnati's $50,000 lights were not the first in Organized Ball. In fact, MacPhail himself had installed lights at Columbus, Ohio, when he owned that American Association club several years earlier. Des Moines of the Western Association had announced its intention to install lights prior to the 1930 season, but Independence, Kansas of the same circuit got the jump on Des Moines by rigging a primitive illumination system and losing pro ball's first night game to Muskogee, 13-3. ☞

Light towers in Arlington, Texas.

## AMERICAN LEAGUE LIGHTS

The Cleveland Indians and Philadelphia Athletics were the first American League teams to install lights, and the Detroit Tigers —in 1948—the last. When Tiger owner Walter O. Briggs decided to light his park, he tested several lighting systems to avoid any which might be unflattering to female fans.

Des Moines made its arc-light debut May 2 with a 13-6 win over Wichita. The fan response was so enthusiastic that team president E. Lee Keyser announced the teams would play another night game the following day. He added that night ball would be the salvation of the minors because it attracted families and working people who could not attend day games.

The first night game on record was played between two amateur teams at Nantasket Beach, Massachusetts in 1880, and another was played three years later when the Quincy Pros met the M. E. Collegians at Fort Wayne, Indiana. The power failed twice, much to the satisfaction of skeptics.

Quincy won, 19-11, in a seven-inning game marked by sloppy fielding. But *Sporting Life* reported, "Not the least difficulty was found at the bat. With between 25 and 39 lights, there is no question but what electric light ball playing is an assured success." Only 17 lamps were used at Fort Wayne.

Night ball wasn't an idea that popped into somebody's head. Its origin was traced to a General Electric brochure advertising new lights at Boston Common. The State of Massachusetts had asked the company to provide lights with the power of daylight. The brochure which showed children playing baseball on Boston Common came to the attention of Lee Keyser at Des Moines.

GE employees at Lynn, Massachusetts played ball under the lights in 1923—twelve years before Larry MacPhail introduced the idea in the majors. MacPhail's original intent was to use night ball as a novelty; he urged baseball to restrict night games to seven per year. At first, this was done, but the number later doubled and eventually took over more than 50 per cent of the schedule. Fan reaction was enormous.

What had been branded "madness under moonlight" and "a passing fad" became an integral part of baseball.

# WEATHER

Bad weather often cancels or delays games. Sometimes it threatens the lives of the athletes.

Ray Caldwell of Cleveland carried a 2-1 lead against the Athletics into the ninth inning on August 8, 1919, and retired two batters. A bolt of lightning hit him, knocking him down. He recovered and—not wishing a repeat performance—made quick work of the last hitter.

First baseman Harold Jensen of Urbana, Ohio, in the Miami Valley League was struck and killed on August 7, 1949. Three other players and two umpires were knocked off their feet, and all five were treated at a nearby hospital.

Five years earlier, four persons were critically injured and 26 others less seriously when the east roof of the Milwaukee Brewers' grandstand collapsed during a sudden windstorm. Neighboring cars and houses were also damaged. Needless to say, the game against Columbus was blown away. It went down as a seven-inning 5-5 tie.

Early in the century, Washington was proving the slogan, "First in war, first in peace, and last in the American League." Trailing Detroit 1-0 early in the game, manager Joe Cantillon was ecstatic as the Senators broke through for five runs. Seeing the end of an 18-game losing streak, Cantillon celebrated prematurely. A fierce storm broke, washing out the potential victory, and the uniformed players raced for their horse-drawn bus. ☞

## LIGHTNING KAYOED BIG-LEAGUER

*New York Giants' outfielder Red Murray was knocked unconscious by lightning just as he caught a game-ending fly in the 21st inning of a 3-1 win over Pittsburgh, July 17, 1914. Murray was otherwise uninjured.*

## MACPHAIL LIT 2 NEW YORK PARKS

*Night ball pioneer Larry MacPhail installed lights when he became an executive with the Brooklyn Dodgers (1938) and New York Yankees (1946). Cincinnati's Johnny Vander Meer pitched his second straight no-hitter in Brooklyn's first night game on June 15, 1938.*

Famous portrait of umpires surveying the situation was painted by Norman Rockwell at Brooklyn's Ebbets Field.

Norman Rockwell

93

As the last man boarded, a lightning bolt struck and killed the two horses. Cantillon looked at his players, raised his hands skyward, and said, "What kind of justice is there in heaven that strikes those poor creatures dead and leaves these miserable vegetables sitting in here alive?"

Around the same period, lightning converted a single into a home run (or maybe a run home) during a semi-pro game in Cincinnati. The batter singled to right, lightning struck the ball, and the outfielder turned and ran. It was the only run of the game.

Lightning helped one-time home run king Gavvy Cravath hit one over the fence. The Phillies and Giants were still playing as a thunderstorm, preceded by strong wind, approached from the west. Visibility was poor. With the aid of a bright lightning flash, Cravath hit a Red Ames pitch deep into the outfield. Dark silence followed, then everyone in the park heard the ball rattle the wooden bleachers. It too was the only run of the game.

Willie Tasby, outfielder for the Orioles in the '60s, actually played center field barefoot in approaching storms. Apparently, he didn't like the idea of standing in puddles while wearing metal spikes.

Phil Rizzuto, who played several years before Tasby broke in, was another who was especially wary of electric storms.

Montreal encountered another problem when it entered the majors in 1969: late-season snows canceled games. Six inches fell on May 6, 1970. Later, Rusty Staub became the first man to homer into a snowbank. The ball cleared the right field fence, sank into the snowbank, and died.

# BASEBALL MARATHONS

The longest game in major league history (26 innings) was a 1-1 tie between the Brooklyn Dodgers and Boston Braves on May 1, 1920. The New York Mets played 25 innings in 1974, 24 in 1968, and 23 in 1964; the Philadelphia A's and Boston Red Sox also played 24, the American League high, in 1906.

Because baseball mandates completion of games if the teams are deadlocked after nine, marathon games are not uncommon. But consider this: those Dodgers of 1920 got no decision in their 26-inning contest against Boston. They lost to the Phillies in 13 innings the next day. Then the Braves beat them in 19 innings.

The Mets, whose early struggles recalled Brooklyn Dodger teams in lean years, could sympathize. They spent 10½ hours losing a doubleheader to the Giants in 1964, came up on the wrong side of a 1-0 score in the 24-inning game at Houston, and saw 50 players and 15 dozen balls used in the 25-inning match with St. Louis. The 23-inning game—the nightcap (literally) of a twinbill against the Giants on May 31, 1964—consumed 7 hours and 23 minutes, a record for a major league game.

Marathons were in vogue before the Mets were born in 1962. As recently as 1951, the Cardinals played two different teams on the same day. They narrowly avoided playing the first tripleheader since 1920.

The Cards and Giants played a doubleheader on Tuesday, September 11, with the first of those games a previous rainout

## RED SOX SQUEEZED CLEVELAND'S LEMON
**Cleveland's Bob Lemon led the American League with 23 wins in 1950, but missed a chance for No. 24 when he blew a 10-0 lead against the Red Sox at Fenway Park on August 28. The Sox won, 15-14.**

## BIG INNINGS
**Wholesale collapse of a pitching staff can result in big innings for the opposition. In 1952, the Brooklyn Dodgers scored 15 runs in the first inning against Cincinnati (final score, 19-1). A year later, the Boston Red Sox tallied 17 times in the seventh en route to a 23-3 win over Detroit.**

## REVERSING A LOST CAUSE
**On June 15, 1925, the Cleveland Indians led the Philadelphia Athletics, 15-4, as the play began in the last of the eighth. The A's scored 13 times to win, 17-15.**

transferred from New York. A single game slated for September 12 was rained out, but the Cardinals were scheduled to play the Boston Braves on September 13.

Because the Giants were in contention for the pennant, the game had to be played. But there were no other meetings planned between the two clubs. St. Louis owner Fred Saigh suggested a doubleheader —an afternoon game against the Giants and the regular night game against Boston.

Horace Stoneham, Saigh's counterpart, balked. He said the Giants "owned" the date and would exercise priority for the night game if rain prevented the afternoon contest. He added that should the sun prevail, a night game with Boston on the same date would hurt the afternoon gate.

Meanwhile, a suspended Braves-Cards game of August 2 was scheduled to be completed before the start of the September 13 night game against Boston. Keeping that date, and adding the Giants' afternoon game, would create a "tripleheader."

Commissioner Ford Frick was asked for assistance. He ordered the Giants to play the Cards in the afternoon and switched the completion of the suspended game to the following day. So the Cardinals did play two different teams on the same day.

Legitimate tripleheaders have been staged several times, all in the National League. On September 1, 1890, Pittsburgh swept Brooklyn, 10-9, 3-2, and 8-4. Six years later, Baltimore swept Louisville, 4-3, 9-1, and 12-1. On October 2, 1920, Cincinnati beat Pittsburgh, 13-4 and 7-3 before losing 6-0.

Brooklyn's 1890 tripleheader, featuring a mid-morning opener, was the only to include three nine-inning games. The last inning of the third game was lost to darkness in Baltimore, and the last three of the finale were blacked out in Pittsburgh.

Lou Gehrig welcomes Joe DiMaggio at plate after home run. The pair helped the Yankees ignite many late-inning explosions.

## MOST RUNS IN A GAME

*When the Cubs beat the Phillies, 26-23, on August 24, 1922, the two teams produced the most runs for a single game. Chicago took a 25-6 lead after four innings, then had to hang on for the win. In 1976, the Cubs led the Phils, 13-2, but Philadelphia came back for an 18-16 win in 10 innings.*

# LATE INNING EXPLOSIONS

The most overworked cliche in baseball concerns the uncertain nature of the sport: "The game isn't over until you get the last out."

Countless cases of ninth-inning lightning fill the record books. Bucky Walters of the Reds lost a game of brinksmanship against the New York Giants in 1940. Pitching in the Polo Grounds, Walters had a 3-0 lead in the ninth with two men out and a 3-2 count on Bob Seeds.

Walters walked Seeds, then went 3-2 on Burgess Whitehead. He hit a home run, cutting the lead to 3-2. Walters went 3-2 on Mel Ott, but walked him. Then, the pitcher got two quick strikes on Harry Danning. The next pitch left the park—a game-winning homer. Walters had missed four separate occasions to get the third strike across.

On July 16, 1920, Pittsburgh's Earl Hamilton suffered an even more agonizing defeat. He worked 16 scoreless innings against the Giants—then fell victim to a seven-run outburst in the 17th to lose, 7-0. A year earlier, the Reds ruined a string of 12 scoreless innings by Al Mamaux to blast Brooklyn, 10-0.

The American League twice featured nine-run rallies in the ninth with one out to go—both times in 1901. Cleveland trailed Washington, 13-5, on May 23, with two out and ☞

95

none on base when the hit parade started. Less than two weeks later, Boston did the same to Milwaukee, adding to a meager 4-2 lead.

Nine runs with an out to play represent the major league record, and the American League also has had eight-run explosions in that situation. The 1937 Yankees wiped out a 6-1 Boston lead at Yankee Stadium that way (the final three scored on a Lou Gehrig homer) and the 1961 Red Sox surprised Washington by overcoming a 12-5 deficit in the final frame.

The Yankees yielded a two-out, nine-run ninth to the Indians late in 1929 and blew another game by letting the St. Louis Browns score seven times with an out to go in 1922.

The National League record for last-ditch heroics stands at seven runs—a total achieved by the 1952 Cubs against the Reds. It began with the bases empty and the Reds coasting on the front end of an 8-2 score. ☞

## FIRST AL DRAFTEE KILLED

*Gene Stack of the White Sox, first American League draftee of World War II, was killed in action.*

# THE WAR YEARS

Baseball wasn't the same in wartime. Though the game maintained a full schedule and played the World Series throughout World War II, the 1945 All-Star Game was skipped. In 1918, the All-Star Game had not yet been established, but the nation's war needs superseded the interests of baseball teams. The final month was cut from the schedule.

During World War I, teams set aside one week per month as Red Cross Week and sent a percentage of the profits to the Red Cross for European War Relief. In 1918, baseball also sent some of its biggest names to the war. ☞

★ WIN THE WAR ★

# The Sporting News

### THE BASE BALL PAPER OF THE WORLD

112, NUMBER 24     ST. LOUIS, JANUARY 22, 1942     TEN CENTS

# STAY IN THERE AND PITCH--F.D.R.

## Best for Country to Keep Baseball Going, Roosevelt Tells Landis

*5,000 to 6,000 Players ... Are a Definite Recreational Asset to at Least 20,000,000 of Their Fellow Citizens'*

### 'Player of the Year'

*President Bestows a Signal Honor --and Responsibility--on Game*

#### By J. G. TAYLOR SPINK

WELL IN ADVANCE of the 1942 pennant season, baseball could designate Franklin Delano Roosevelt, President of the United States, as its Player of the Year. Without even waiting for the national executive to throw out the first ball in Washington in April, both major leagues would make no mistake in naming Mr. Roosevelt their most valuable man in all branches of their specialized endeavor. For in writing to Commissioner Kenesaw Mountain Landis that the White House wanted baseball to go right on through the war, in giving to our National Game that priceless executive sanction and presidential approval, F. D. R. already has done more for the game than any of its most brilliant exponents possibly could hope to contribute through the 1942 season—and the 1943 campaign to boot.

To Judge Landis, too, goes the accolade of the fans, for the Commissioner took the initiative and drew from Mr. Roosevelt an expression which the President doubtless wanted to have drawn from him. In a simple little note scribbled in pencil—and in the Judge's well-nigh illegible hand-writing, too—Landis stated the situation tersely and to the point. In effect, Judge Landis wrote that "Baseball is about to adopt schedules, sign players, make vast commitments, go to training camps. What do you want it to do? If you believe we ought to close down for the duration of the war, we are ready to do so immediately. If you feel we ought to continue, we would be delighted to do so. We await your order."

The President's answer came at once. He said in part: "I honestly feel that it would be best for the country to keep baseball going. There will be fewer people unemployed and everybody will work longer hours and harder than ever before. And that means that they ought to have a chance for recreation and for taking their minds off their work even more than before."

In effect, the President told baseball to keep on swinging—keep pitching—and keep fighting!

Just imagine the elation and the pride of baseball to be singled out above all other sports for Presidential approval and an executive sanction to go right on through the war!

To Mr. Roosevelt go not alone the thanks of all connected with baseball as players, executives, writers or onlookers. He deserves the highest praise for the sanest kind of outlook on the myriad problems which now confront this country. No man is more intense for an all-out war effort and war material production. But no man is more completely aware of the fact that not all of us can go into the fighting forces, not all of us can make planes and munitions.

In every war there is that vastly important great majority which must remain on the home front. These men and women, no less than the fighters, constitute the strength of the nation. Germany learned that in 1918 when a series of strikes broke down the support and morale of the still-aggressive armies of the Kaiser. No matter how great its military power in the field, no nation at war is stronger than the morale of its people at home. The President has recognized this in his sanction to baseball to go on playing.

Original material from *The Sporting News* tells the story: President Roosevelt wanted baseball to continue during the war as a morale booster.

## IKE ARRANGED BASEBALL BROADCASTS

*General Dwight D. Eisenhower arranged for broadcasts of the 1943 World Series between the New York Yankees and St. Louis Cardinals. He said baseball boosted the morale of his troops.*

**THE WAR YEARS** *continued*

Ty Cobb, Herb Pennock, Tris Speaker, George Sisler, Eddie Collins, and Christy Mathewson went overseas along with dozens of other players. The White Sox and Indians sent 19 players each into the military.

Cobb was a captain in the chemical warfare division, while Mathewson was the only manager to serve in the First World War. Then running the Reds, Mathewson endured poison gas attacks in France and never regained his health; he died prematurely in 1925.

Long-time catcher Hank Gowdy had the unusual distinction of serving in both world wars, while Ted Williams served in World War II and the Korean conflict.

The influence of the Second World War on baseball was far more obvious than the influence of the first war because its long duration and multiple battle theaters demanded more men.

Before they shortened the 1918 season to a September 1 finish, owners had debated playing out the schedule using players who were above or below draft age, but decided against it. In World War II, they were forced to use that policy or shut the game down.

More than 500 players helped the Allies against the Axis, starting with Phillies pitcher Hugh Mulcahy—the first draftee.

Cleveland's Bob Feller, who won 25 games and saved two others in 1941, began the exodus of top stars when he enlisted in the Navy shortly after the bombing of Pearl Harbor. Feller, Warren Spahn, and Ted Williams were three outstanding players whose records would have been even better had the war not intervened.

Ballplayers in service frequently got to play for military teams. When Ted Lyons of the White Sox pitched for his Navy team on Guam, his first game was against an Army squad starring Joe DiMaggio. "I left the country to get away from DiMaggio," Lyons quipped, "and here he is!"

An Army-Navy game in Cleveland, shortly before the 1942 All-Star Game, drew 62,094 fans—primarily because Feller was pitching for Mickey Cochrane's Great Lakes Naval Training Station team. The Cochrane crew won 63 games, including four over major league opposition.

Players and managers who stayed behind in the States often volunteered to visit the battle fronts under the auspices of the USO. Baseball shows featured films, autographs, amusing anecdotes, and bull sessions. When Yankee pitcher Hank Borowy returned from a trip to Alaska's Aleutian Islands with Frankie Frisch and Dixie Walker, he said, "We did some 200 shows there and they didn't want to let us go. I never realized there was so much heart-felt, deep-down interest in baseball. After twelve hours on the jump from camp to camp, we'd get back to our shack dog-tired to find a delegation of men waiting to talk to us until two or three o'clock in the morning."

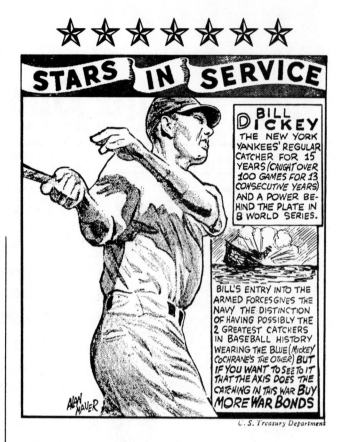

★ ★ ★ ★ ★ ★ ★
**STARS IN SERVICE**

BILL DICKEY THE NEW YORK YANKEES' REGULAR CATCHER FOR 15 YEARS (CAUGHT OVER 100 GAMES FOR 13 CONSECUTIVE YEARS) AND A POWER BEHIND THE PLATE IN 8 WORLD SERIES.

BILL'S ENTRY INTO THE ARMED FORCES GIVES THE NAVY THE DISTINCTION OF HAVING POSSIBLY THE 2 GREATEST CATCHERS IN BASEBALL HISTORY WEARING THE BLUE (MICKEY COCHRANE'S THE OTHER) BUT IF YOU WANT TO SEE TO IT THAT THE AXIS DOES THE CATCHING IN THIS WAR *BUY* MORE WAR BONDS

ALAN MAVER

*U.S. Treasury Department*

## FANS RETURNED BALLS

*Fans returned balls hit into the stands during the wars. These were given to servicemen.*

## TED WILLIAMS, AIR ACE

*Marine Corps Captain Ted Williams flew 39 combat missions during the Korean War.*

## NO NIGHT GAMES IN '43

*Night games were banned in 1943 because of blackout restrictions.*

The Baseball Bulletin

Depletion of the ranks in the majors opened the gates for such handicapped players as one-armed Pete Gray.

## CARDS SEARCHED FOR PLAYERS

*The St. Louis Cardinals advertised for players in 1943. The St. Louis organization lost more than 200 athletes to the military.*

Hank Greenberg retained his batting eye in the service, enabling him to be ready to play when his stint ended. His last-day grand slam in the ninth inning enabled the Tigers to win the 1945 American League pennant.

Five units of stars stumped military bases in the 1944-45 off-season. They went to Europe, the Mediterranean, the Middle East, the Far East (China-Burma-India), and the Pacific.

At home, baseball had deteriorated—understandably—into a comedy of errors. After receiving a "green light letter" from President Franklin D. Roosevelt in January 1942, baseball brass was determined to provide the morale-boosting entertainment that the chief executive sought. "Sports kept people occupied and helped them not to think of the war all the time," said pitcher Hal Newhouser. "Baseball had to continue."

More than 200 draft board rejects translated their 4-F classifications into major league jobs. More than a dozen of them played for the pennant-winning St. Louis Browns of 1944, but the most famous played for the same team the following year.

One-armed outfielder Pete Gray, 28, was purchased by the Browns after hitting .333 with five home runs and 68 stolen bases for Memphis, where he was voted Most Valuable Player in the Southern Association.

Originally righthanded, Gray lost that limb in a truck accident. As a lefthanded hitter with the '45 Browns, he hit .218 in 61 games. His fielding was below par for a normal player, but sensational for a man who had to catch and throw with the same arm.

Not to be outdone, a pitcher with a wooden leg—Bert Shepart—pitched five innings for the Washington Senators that season.

The quality of play was so poor that the players who finished second and third in the American League batting race—Tony Cuccinello and John Dickshot of the White Sox—were released after the season, even though they had hit .308 and .302, respectively. Batting king George (Snuffy) Stirnweiss of the Yankees hit .309 with 10 homers—then hit .246 with 10 homers *over the next seven seasons!*

Washington's 40-year-old catcher, Rick Ferrell, had the unenviable task of handling four knuckleball pitchers. Yankee outfielder Johnny Lindell spiked teammate Herschel Martin in the nose when the pair collided in pursuit of a fly ball. The leagues averaged about 1,500 errors more than usual.

Many clubs dumped their scouts because most able-bodied athletes were overseas, but the Dodgers didn't and began building toward their future "Boys of Summer" champions. Brooklyn also followed a pattern adopted by other clubs—activating old stars to fill out the roster. Babe Herman, out of the league since 1936, came back at age 42. Yankee pitcher Paul Schreiber, the same age, had been out since 1923 but stayed in shape by pitching batting practice.

The minor leagues were stripped bare. Thirty-two teams suspended operations. Those who continued—like Nashville of the Southern Association—turned to old-timers or teenagers. Ex-pitcher Red Lucas, always a good hitter, became a pinch-hitter at Nashville and hit .421 at age 43.

When the 1945 All-Star Game was scrubbed, the move was made not only because of travel restrictions (a good excuse) but also because there were no stars to represent the leagues. A two-day series of exhibition games was staged to raise money for war relief.

The stars began to return after the war ended in Europe, and later, in the Pacific. They had to play themselves back into shape—a task that is always difficult—but had maintained good condition in the military. Timing was the missing ingredient, but by season's end, Hank Greenberg had it. His last-day grand slam in the ninth inning gave the Tigers the American League pennant.

The 1946 Newark Eagles, loaded with talent of major league caliber, beat the Kansas City Monarchs for the championship of the Negro Leagues. Organized Ball did not drop its color line until 1947.

# THE COLOR LINE

Adrian (Cap) Anson was the greatest star of the National League's first quarter-century. A standout hitter and manager, he was also an excellent promoter. He had one flaw: he was prejudiced against blacks.

Though two brothers—Moses and Welday Walker—had already played in the majors at Toledo of the American Association, Anson slammed the door on any other blacks considering the profession. He is the man who drew the infamous "color line" that kept blacks out of Organized Ball until Jack Roosevelt Robinson signed with the Brooklyn Dodgers at the tail-end of the 1945 season.

There were 20 blacks in baseball—all but the Walkers in the minors—in 1882. (One of them, George Stovey, struck out 22 Bridgeport batters in a single game for Newark, New Jersey five years later.)

Neither Walker was a good ballplayer and they drifted out of the American Association to several minor league teams and eventually out of baseball. None of the blacks was made to feel welcome, and soon the game was devoid of dark-skinned players. Anson and other executives determined to keep it that way, and the tradition of segregation persisted.

Unrest over the color line was muted, to a degree, by the formation of professional Negro Leagues, but black players showed they

## SPRING SEGREGATION PERSISTED

*Though blacks were well-established in baseball by the early '60s, segregation still divided several major league clubs during spring training.*

## KLAN THREATENED DODGERS

*The Ku Klux Klan blasted the announcement that the integrated Brooklyn Dodgers would play three April 1949 exhibitions against the Atlanta Crackers of the Southern Association. Owner Earl Mann, backed by Atlanta's press and police, staged the games without a hitch.*

By opening its doors to black talent, the Brooklyn Dodgers developed a dynasty in the '50s. Among the team's stars were Duke Snider, Jackie Robinson, Roy Campanella, Pee Wee Reese, and Gil Hodges.

Many blacks became baseball's biggest stars. Among the best were (top to bottom) Roy Campanella, Ferguson Jenkins, Ernie Banks, Frank Robinson, and Roberto Clemente.

could hold their own during exhibitions with big-leaguers and a drive to admit them began.

The Los Angeles Angels of the Pacific Coast League invited three blacks for a tryout, then withdrew their invitation without explanation. Bill Veeck, owner of the Milwaukee franchise in the American Association, bid for the Philadelphia Phillies, with the intention of signing several black stars for the struggling club, but his purchase was not completed.

Also in 1944, the Red Sox gave a short Fenway Park tryout to three black stars—after two city councilmen threatened to strip the Sox and the Braves of exemptions from Sunday blue laws. One of the three was Jackie Robinson of the Kansas City Monarchs, a powerful Negro League team.

All three did well, and Boston manager Joe Cronin said he was impressed, but the blacks were informed that signing players after short tryouts violated Red Sox policy. They suffered the indignity of filling out applications—a step most athletes never take—and were given the standard line: "Don't call us, we'll call you." Not only did they never hear from the Sox, but Boston was the last team in the majors to integrate. Pumpsie Green finally broke the Boston barrier in 1959.

A year after the escapade in Boston, Branch Rickey was telling Jackie Robinson what problems he would face as the first black player in the major leagues. He also warned him that he wanted a ballplayer "with guts enough not to fight back."

Robinson, a gifted but outspoken athlete, wasn't sure he was the right man, but finally accepted Rickey's offer, reporting to the Dodgers' top farm at Montreal in 1946. "I had to do it for so many reasons," Robinson said later. "For black youth, for my mother, for Rachel [his wife], and for myself. I even felt I had to do it for Branch Rickey."

Rickey, who had spent considerable time and money recruiting baseball's first black of the modern era, was correct in anticipating trouble. Several Dodgers circulated a petition protesting Robinson's presence. The Cardinals and Phillies threatened strikes—stopped only when Commissioner Happy Chandler threatened lifetime suspensions. Hotels were always segregated during spring training, but sometimes during the regular season too.

## THE RACES MIX

*Bobby Grich, white infielder, and Don Baylor, black outfielder, were among the first interracial roommates in the game.*

## JACKIE HAD POWER WHEN NEEDED

*Jackie Robinson wasn't primarily a power-hitter—he twice hit 19 homers for his one-season high—but he produced when it counted. On the last day of the '51 season, the Dodgers and Giants were tied for the top. The Giants knocked off the Braves, and the Dodgers had to beat Philadelphia to force a playoff. Brooklyn was behind, 6-1, when word came of the Giant win. The Dodgers tied it, 8-8, but almost lost it in the twelfth. With two outs and the bases loaded, the batter hit a low liner to the right of second base. Jackie Robinson dove and speared it just above the ground, then crashed heavily on his shoulder. In the fourteenth, he found a fastball he liked and deposited it over the left field wall to win the game, 9-8.*

Incendiary taunts, including vicious name-calling, were hurled from every enemy dugout. But Robinson kept his word and his cool. He convinced the Dodgers—and their opponents—with a winning style of play that included aggressive base running, fine fielding, and steady contributions with the bat. He was an outstanding curveball hitter—a rarity for a rookie.

Robinson had been a second baseman, but moved to first during his first Dodger season. He returned to second on a full-time basis in 1949 and was named to the All-Star Major League Team by *The Sporting News* for four successive seasons.

He was an All-Star other years too, but played a variety of positions, including first, second, third, and the outfield. In 10 seasons, he hit .311, twice led the National League in stolen bases (he stole home 19 times), and won the batting title with a .342 mark in 1949.

Jackie Robinson was the recipient of baseball's first Rookie of the Year Award in 1947. He was named Most Valuable Player in the National League two years later.

"My main ambition," Robinson said, "was to get along well enough with whomever I was playing so they would realize there wasn't any friction because I was colored and they were white. I wanted them to know we *could* play together. It wasn't so important that *I* go to the major leagues, it was just important that *somebody* go."

Robinson's entry immediately opened the door for others. Larry Doby, one of 14 blacks signed by Bill Veeck's Cleveland Indians in those early years of integration, became the first American League black late in 1947. Other early blacks in the majors were Satchel Paige, Roy Campanella, Don Newcombe, and Monte Irvin.

Frank Robinson became the first black manager with Cleveland in 1975, and the first black manager to be fired in 1977. Larry Doby, who followed Jackie Robinson as the second black player, followed Frank Robinson as the second black manager. Bill Veeck hired him with the White Sox in 1978.

The end of the color line was hailed by some historians as the real beginning of major league baseball. Contributions by blacks have been numerous. Hank Aaron became the new home run king. Maury Wills, and then Lou Brock, set single-season stolen-base records. Brock surpassed Ty Cobb as the career leader.

Willie Mays became the third-ranking home run hitter in history. Bob Gibson, Juan Marichal, and Ferguson Jenkins were brilliant pitchers for years. Ernie Banks, Frank Robinson, and Willie McCovey joined Aaron and Mays in hitting at least 500 home runs.

The list of accomplishments is endless.

**Leo Durocher and Willie Mays**

# THE TRIALS AND TRAVAILS OF TRAVEL

Baseball teams have traveled by rail, bus, subway, automobile, trolley, airplane, and assorted other conveyances.

But the pioneering Cincinnati Red Stockings of 1877 came up with a new idea after three straight days of rain prevented their home opener. They obtained a barge and floated to Louisville, where it was dry enough to play.

Not long after, the same club reached the Arizona territory via rail and stagecoach.

In the early days of the American League, shortly after the turn of the century, teams made the Detroit-Cleveland run by overnight steamer on Lake Michigan. Indian third baseman Bill Bradley, assigned to a stateroom with a cocky rookie, was about to turn in one night when he hit upon an idea that would knock the first-year player down a peg.

He put on his nightshirt, then strapped a life preserver on top of it and lay down in the bottom bunk. The rookie, not knowing what to do, decided he would follow the older man's example.

As soon as the lights were out, Bradley quietly unzipped himself and went to sleep, while the rookie squirmed all night in an effort to make himself comfortable.

Neither man said a word until the return trip, when the freshman blurted, "Nix on those life preservers. I'd rather drown."

## TRAIN TRIPS

Baseball travel in the majors was primarily by rail until the early '50s. Though train trips consumed more time, players found them more relaxing. Forced to spend so much time together, teammates got to know one another well and unity resulted.

"Some players thought the trains had rough wheels and it was a rough ride," recalled ex-Brooklyn pitcher Clyde King, "but we enjoyed it. We'd have a Sunday afternoon game at Ebbets Field, then go down to the station. They'd have a dining car all set up for us, we'd go in and sit down to a nice meal. Then we'd play cards—I played bridge a lot. Usually, we'd have Monday off and, if we were going to St. Louis, we'd travel all day Monday. We played bridge and talked baseball."

Waite Hoyt remembered trains of the Babe Ruth era, twenty years before King played in the majors. "We made a railroad trip from Washington to St. Louis wearing just our underwear," he said. "You opened the windows when you were in the Pullman berth at night and in the morning you'd be covered with coal dust."

Star players had lower berths, average players the uppers. When the train reached the team's destination in the early hours of the morning, the baseball cars were uncoupled and shunted onto a siding. Players later hauled their own luggage down the tracks to the station, hailed cabs for the team hotel, and went back to sleep once they got there. Few players caught much sleep on trains.

Since writers, team executives, and sometimes even umpires shared the trains with athletes, impromptu interviews flowed during the course of a trip. The bar car was as thick with quotable stories as it was with smoke. ☞

## SOX PICK WRONG CAR

*Red Sox players Oscar Melillo and Eric McNair accidentally went to sleep on a train taking the Philadelphia Athletics out of Boston on July 4, 1937. Their teammates were on another train that left at the same time.*

**Boston Red Sox of 1912 board train for road trip.**

Cards kept players occupied on the road. New York Giants Clyde Castleman, Mark Koenig, and Harry Danning were frequent players.

TRAIN TRIPS *continued*

Only one player—Ed Delahanty in 1903—was killed in train travel, but there were several close calls.

Delahanty, the lone casualty, lost his life on July 2, 1903, when he fell from the International Bridge at Buffalo, New York, after his ejection from a train because of drunkenness. The train, from Detroit, had almost reached its destination: the Buffalo terminal.

During the Second World War, the Brooklyn Dodgers were en route from St. Louis to Chicago when a gasoline truck, loaded with an extra tank, was struck at a Joliet, Illinois grade crossing at four o'clock in the morning. It exploded, sending gas and flames all over the train and igniting a coalyard nearby.

The Dodgers had been sitting up—or sleeping on the floor—because train frequency and accommodations were limited in wartime. No one got burned because the train's momentum carried it through the burning remains of the truck, but the engineer and fireman lost their lives. The automatic brake stopped the train.

Clyde King, who was there, remembered the incident vividly. He described how the intense heat from the blast melted the train's thick double windows, and recalled the startled Luis Olmo—awakened from his position on the floor—running through the aisles, stepping on people, in the panic.

Despite that experience, the Dodgers made their preference for rail travel known several years later, after the team started to make some trips by air.

# AIR TRAVEL

Baseball teams began to travel by air because of bad weather on the ground. In 1938, a hurricane battered New England, leaving flood waters in its wake. The St. Louis Cardinals, stranded in Boston, had to get to Chicago to meet their schedule.

An enterprising club official chartered a mail plane, jammed 21 players inside, and took off for the Windy City. The official had wired Cardinal owner Sam Breadon for permission, but storm-snarled communications lines delayed the message. By the time Breadon answered WAIT FOR OTHER MEANS, the team was in flight.

The same hurricane, incidentally, washed out normal shore routes between New York and Boston, causing the New York Giants—the next opponent of the Boston Braves—to reach the city via overnight steamboat!

With the flight of the Cardinals, air travel began its long route to predominance over other means of transportation. It wasn't easy, however. Planes of the period were primitive by modern standards and flights were invariably long and bumpy.

The Dodgers flew for the first time in 1940, but Babe Phelps sometimes opted for the train instead. As late as 1947, pitcher Kirby Higbe was a bundle of nerves in the air. Pee Wee Reese tried to calm him. "If your number's up, you'll go," Reese said. That didn't satisfy Higbe. "Suppose I'm up here with some pilot and my number ain't up, but *his* is!"

The war returned ballclubs to the rails, but with victory in sight late in 1945, 11 major league teams signed "volume travel plan"

## ON THE ROAD

What do players do on the road? Clyde King, pitcher in the '40s-'50s and manager in the '70s, had an answer: "They play cards a lot in their rooms. We used to go to movies a lot. We looked forward to playing in Chicago, where they had only day games and we could go to movies at night. I went to two double-features many times in Chicago. Nowadays, players have business connections in so many towns. They also make more appearances on the road than they used to."

## FANS CATERED DODGER TRAIN

Dodgers Hugh Casey and Curt Davis called ahead when they found out where the team train would stop en route to their next game. In one town, fans brought barbecued ribs to the train. The players looked forward to that midnight feast.

## JET-LAG

Coast-to-coast air travel crosses four time zones and creates the problem of "jet-lag"—especially for anyone headed east to west. Roberto Clemente was one of many players who suffered, according to former Pirate coach Clyde King. "It's not as bad as you think it is," he said. "Most players can rise to the occasion."

The 1957 World Champion Milwaukee Braves used air travel extensively. The club posed for this picture before departure. Note superstars Warren Spahn (top of ramp), Hank Aaron (third from top), and Eddie Mathews (fourth from top).

contracts with United Air Lines. In 1946, the Yankees became the first team to travel extensively by air. But Red Ruffing—who had bitter memories of his days in the Army Air Force—was one of several players who declined to fly. Manager Joe McCarthy said he would leave the choice of transportation up to each player, but said he expected every man to attend every game.

After several particularly rough flights (the team used a four-engine C-54 transport), the majority of Yankee players balked at flying in 1947. They gradually became accustomed to the idea, and other clubs followed a pattern of mixing rail with air travel rather than switching suddenly.

As rail travel declined and air service improved, flying became widely accepted among players. Don Newcombe and Preacher Roe of the Dodgers and Jackie Jensen of the Red Sox never liked it, however.

After the Dodger plane was forced to land during an especially rough flight home from spring training in 1951, Roe got out, rented a car, and drove the rest of the way.

Several times in 1961, Jensen refused to accompany the Red Sox on plane hops. In June, he drove 850 miles from Boston to Detroit and played the following day. Two months later, after beating Washington with a tenth-inning home run, he lost $750 in salary when he would not board an airplane to Los Angeles.

"Fear of Flying" was more than a best-seller—it was a problem facing men of enormous strength and flexibility.

# ROOMMATES

Except for top stars, baseball players usually have roommates on the road. Sometimes, the matched pairs have trouble adjusting.

Early in the century, Philadelphia Athletics pitcher Rube Waddell actually signed a contract forbidding roommate Ossie Schreckengost from eating Animal Crackers in bed. The pact became known as 'The Animal Cracker Contract.'

Burly Ernie Lombardi, hard-hitting Cincinnati catcher of the '30s, kept roommate Chick Hafey awake with his snoring. Hafey tried to solve the problem by tying Lombardi's big toe to the bed.

The expansion Los Angeles Angels of 1961 paired 5-5, 140-pound Albie Pearson and 5-8, 170-pound Rocky Bridges in one room and 250-pound Steve Bilko with 245-pound Ted Kluszewski in another. In one hotel, they were across the hall from each other. Bridges phoned the traveling secretary and suggested he switch assignments. "If you don't, the hotel will tilt!" he said.

Fun-loving Babe Ruth liked to share his zest for high living. Whenever he ordered food from room service, he insisted roommate Jimmie Reese eat with him. "He'd order six eggs and I'd have two," Reese said, years later.

Many clubs like to put highly-rated rookies with experienced veterans, often matching pitchers with other pitchers, or sometimes pitchers with catchers. Players of similar temperaments or positions are grouped wherever possible.

When he first joined the Philadelphia Athletics, Mickey Cochrane was matched with incumbent catcher Cy Perkins. The latter's pointers paid off so well that Cochrane took his job. ☞

## FIRST CLUB TO FLY

The Hollywood Stars of the Pacific Coast League became the first professional team to fly in 1928.

## PLAYERS PAID FOR ROOMS

Early major-leaguers were charged 50 cents per game for rooms when on the road.

## GIANTS RODE BAROUCHES TO PARK

The 1905 world champion New York Giants, following the custom of their day, rode from their hotel to the ballpark in uniform. The players sat in handsome barouches—open carriages—drawn by horses wearing black-and-yellow blankets. The Giants were hated intensely by other teams because of an overaggressive style of play, and fans outside of New York sometimes stoned the carriages.

Brash freshman Ted Williams was placed in the same room with soft-spoken veteran Charley Wagner by Red Sox manager Joe Cronin, and the duet proved a perfect match. Williams calmed down and developed into a superstar.

Young Curt Simmons roomed with experienced Dutch Leonard, another Phillies pitcher, and Eddie Stanky was placed with double-play partner Alvin Dark by the Boston Braves. Simmons became an outstanding major league pitcher, while the Stanky-Dark tandem helped the Braves win the 1948 pennant.

Boston's Dom DiMaggio earned the nickname "the Little Professor"—perhaps because of the influence of roommate Moe Berg, a capable but light-hitting catcher who spoke seven languages and held almost as many college degrees.

Brothers on the same team were not necessarily roommates. The Deans of St. Louis—Dizzy and Daffy—were separated. Dizzy lived with Pepper Martin, "the Wild Horse of the Osage," and the Cardinal cutups frequently visited their teammates with midnight serenades on the guitar.

Luke Sewell and Joe Sewell of the Indians also slept in separate quarters.

Certain pairs were inseparable: pitching aces Lew Burdette and Warren Spahn of the Braves, drinking buddies Mickey Mantle and Whitey Ford of the Yankees, and long-time leaders Stan Musial and Red Schoendienst of the Cardinals. Starting in the '20s, Joe Judge and Sam Rice set a roommate record by sharing hotel rooms for 18 consecutive seasons with the Washington Senators.

It was an accident of fate that paired Yogi Berra and Bobby Brown of the Yankees. Brown, using his baseball salary to pay his way through medical school, was deep into a textbook one night when he suddenly slammed the cover shut. Berra, watching him, piped up, "How did it come out?"

## REDS LOST FREY IN '40

*The Cincinnati Reds lost second baseman Lonnie Frey for the 1940 World Series when the heavy lid to the dugout water cooler fell off and landed on his foot, breaking a bone, during a late-season game.*

## LOUD LAUGHS INJURED PLAYER

*As Red Sox roommates Dom DiMaggio and Sam Mele went to bed in May 1947, the former's bed collapsed. Mele laughed so loud he aggravated an old sacroiliac condition. He ached so badly that he was forced to leave the next day's game in the third inning.*

Milwaukee's Johnny Logan (23) vs. Brooklyn manager Walter Alston, 1957. They weren't posing for the camera.

# FINES, FIGHTS, AND FEUDS

Fines are baseball's primary way of punishing fighters. The game is supposed to consist of nine innings—not fifteen rounds—but tempers grow short when the heat of the pennant race begins to match the air temperature of mid-summer.

The game's best-known fighters were Ty Cobb, John McGraw, Leo Durocher, Clint Courtney, and Billy Martin, but almost every player in major league history has witnessed bench-clearing brawls.

Fights often begin over beanballs—deliberate brush-back pitches designed to keep a batter from "digging in" at home plate. A pitcher has a decided edge when the hitter is unable to relax at the plate.

Beanballs are serious business. Ray Chapman of Cleveland was killed by a pitch in 1920, Mickey Cochrane suffered a career-ending skull fracture when struck in 1937, and Tony Conigliaro's career ended prematurely when his vision failed as the result of a beaning.

Current baseball rules mandate an automatic $50 fine when an umpire warns a pitcher about throwing too close to batters. A second warning means ejection from the game. Umpires are even empowered to warn both teams about beanballs before a game begins, if circumstances warrant. ☞

Home-plate collisions, severe bench-jockeying, spikings of fielders by runners, hard tags of runners by fielders have also contributed to the game's history of fights and fines.

Umpires are often involved, and occasionally even fans. Ty Cobb received an indefinite suspension from the American League on May 15, 1912, after attacking a heckler in the stands at New York. His Tiger teammates wired the league office from Philadelphia the next day that they would strike until Cobb was reinstated. On May 18, Cobb took the field with his teammates and was ordered off by the umpires. All the Detroit players went with him.

Manager Hugh Jennings activated two coaches, recruited some semi-pros headed by pitcher Al Travers—later a priest—and lost to the A's, 24-2. Travers earned $25 for his one-day stand in the majors. He had batted fourth and pitched the whole game.

Two days later, American League executives held a special meeting to discuss the Cobb case. Detroit's players were ordered to return or face expulsion from the game. Each was fined $100—twice what Cobb paid when he was reinstated on May 25.

# BASEBALL FIGHTS

Though bench-clearing brawls represent the typical baseball fight, one-on-one encounters occasionally occur under the stands, in airplanes, or in hotel rooms.

It's hard to envision Casey Stengel in such a situation, but the fact is that the youthful Stengel, as manager of the Brooklyn Dodgers in the '30s, delivered a right hook that bloodied the lip of Leo Durocher, then St. Louis Cardinals shortstop, under the Ebbets Field grandstand.

Umpire George Moriarty battled several White Sox at Cleveland after a doubleheader defeat on Memorial Day 1932. Pitcher Milt Gaston, who started the melee beneath the stands, and Chicago manager Lew Fonseca were fined $500 each, catcher Charley Berry (later an umpire) $250, and catcher Frank Grube $100.

John McGraw, razzing rookie Phillies' third baseman Paul Sentelle from his third base coaching box during a 1906 game at Baker Bowl, precipitated a free-for-all that caused both to be ejected. They proceeded under the stands to continue their fight.

Boston player-manager Joe Cronin and the Yankees' Jake Powell clashed under the stands after an earlier go-round on the field in the '30s. Rico Carty and Hank Aaron battled on the Atlanta airplane in 1967. And Billy Martin, then managing Minnesota, kayoed pitcher Dave Boswell in a Detroit bar two years later after breaking up a battle between Boswell and teammate Bob Allison.

Ty Cobb won unanimous decisions over umpire Billy Evans under the stands and Buck Herzog of the Giants in a Dallas hotel. "I got beat," Herzog said, "but I knocked the bum down and he'll never forget a little guy like me having him on the floor."

On the field, Hall of Fame catcher Bill Dickey of the Yankees broke the jaw of Washington outfielder Carl Reynolds with a hard right after a rough collision at home plate on July 4, 1932. Reynolds was out six weeks and Dickey four; he was slapped with a 30-day suspension and $1000 fine. ☞

## TWO FABLED FEUDS

*Because of geographic proximity and location in the same leagues, the Dodgers and Giants of the National League and Red Sox and Yankees of the American League have always been intense rivals.*

*The Dodger-Giant rivalry was so strong that Dodger owner Walter O'Malley urged Horace Stoneham of the Giants to move west with him after the 1957 season and keep the competition going.*

*Brooklyn, actually a part of New York, was already engaged in a feud with the Giants in 1906, when New York's Arthur Devlin punched a Washington Park spectator. Dodger president Charles Ebbets appealed to the league "to protect my customers against rowdy New York players."*

*The defection of Giant coach Wilbert Robinson, who became Dodger manager in 1914, fanned the flames of the growing rivalry.*

*Boston fans have hated the Yankees since owner Harry Frazee sold Babe Ruth and other top stars to New York about 1920. As in Dodger-Giant competition, several head-to-head pennant fights have intensified the feelings between the two clubs' fans and players.*

## WHY TEAMS FIGHT

*Why do ballplayers engage in fisticuffs on the field? Long-time Pirates' manager Danny Murtaugh had an answer: "During the season, a lot of things happen. The players are bound to get on each other. I've seen guys have it out in our clubhouse—and we were winning. It's just part of our game. It can happen whether you're winning or losing."*

Ebbets Field fans were stunned after a 1940 contest when a fan attacked home plate umpire George Magerkuth.

## TED WILLIAMS BEANED PITCHER

*Ted Williams, known as a dead pull hitter, crossed up the defense one day and slammed a shot off an aluminum plate in the leg of wounded war hero Lou Brissie. The ball resounded with a loud clang, but the pitcher was not injured.*

## MOST RUNS BY A CLUB

*The Boston Red Sox established a scoring record by blasting the St. Louis Browns, 29-4, in the early '50s. The Sox won the previous day, 20-4.*

BASEBALL FIGHTS *continued*

Cardinal catcher Mickey Owen attacked Leo Durocher, player-manager of the Dodgers, after a force-out at second base in an Ebbets Field game in 1940, and bad feeling between the two contenders was smoothed only after Brooklyn general manager Larry MacPhail entered the St. Louis clubhouse to speak to the Cardinal players.

The Red Sox-Yankee feud was too strong for such diplomacy after the Second World War. In 1952, Boston's Jim Piersall scrapped with Yankee infielder Billy Martin, who was manager at New York when Red Sox pitcher Bill Lee was injured in a fight with slugger Graig Nettles in 1976.

Martin was also involved in a giant free-for-all between the Yankees and St. Louis Browns in June 1953. The chief culprit was St. Louis catcher Clint Courtney, called Scrap Iron for his aggressive approach to the game. Courtney and Martin had tangled the previous year, and both were among the fighters after the catcher spiked popular Yankee shortstop Phil Rizzuto in '53.

Courtney paid a $250 fine and Martin $150, as the league assessed $850 in penalties.

Martin was at it again in 1960, when he broke the jaw of Cubs pitcher Jim Brewer during his brief tenure as an infielder for the Reds. Brewer sued for $1,000,000 but eventually settled for $10,000. A beanball had precipitated that fight.

A beanball-in-reverse prompted Giant pitcher Juan Marichal to rap Dodger catcher John Roseboro with his bat in 1965. The pitcher insisted Roseboro's return throw to Sandy Koufax was deliberately close to his head.

Other brawls of note:

* 1902: John McGraw, then player-manager of the Baltimore Orioles (today's Yankees), was spiked at third base by Detroit's Larry Harley. In the ensuing fight, McGraw, 29, suffered a knee injury that ended his playing career.

* 1906: After McGraw's Giants brawled with the Phils on the field, irate Philadelphia fans hurled debris at New York's departing barouches. Roger Bresnahan stood, lost his balance, and fell into the crowd. He ran for his life, barricaded himself in a corner store, and waited to be freed by police. ☞

DO NOT DETACH

THIS CHECK IS IN FULL PAYMENT OF
THE FOLLOWING ACCOUNT, AND THE PAYEE
ACCEPTS IT AS SUCH.

NO OTHER RECEIPT IS REQUIRED

| Date | No. | Amount |
|------|-----|--------|
| | Salary to May 31st | |
| | | 4598.86 |
| | Fine by President | |
| | Johnson XX | 200.00 |
| | | 4398.86 |

| Audited | Approved | Entered |
|---------|----------|---------|

*Old check to Babe Ruth shows withholding of $200 fine imposed by league president Ban Johnson after the slugger entered the stands in pursuit of a heckler.*

* 1909: Ty Cobb spiked Frank (Home Run) Baker of the Philadelphia A's during a hot pennant race between the A's and Tigers. The fans were so angry at the incident that Cobb's life was threatened and he had to be escorted to and from the ballpark.

* 1924: Bert Cole (Tigers) hit Yankee Bob Meusel in the back with a ninth-inning pitch at Detroit, with New York leading, 10-6. In the 30-minute fight that followed, fans ripped out seats and threw them into the fray. Umpire Billy Evans forfeited the game to the Yankees and Meusel and Cole were suspended ten days each. Meusel paid a $100 fine and Cole and Babe Ruth $50 each.

* 1932: When fleet Ben Chapman of the Yankees slid hard into second, Washington second baseman Buddy Myer gave him a friendly kick in the rear as he was leaving. Washington's Earl Whitehill made a sarcastic remark to Chapman, who was on his way to the clubhouse, and a battle began. Fans fought among themselves. Only Babe Ruth and Lou Gehrig remained aloof—not wishing to injure their hands.

* 1937: Cardinal Dizzy Dean collided with base runner Jim Ripple (Giants) at Sportsman's Park, St. Louis. A free-for-all followed.

* 1941: The White Sox and Browns fought after Elden Auker hit the head of Joe Kuhel of Chicago with a pitch.

* 1943: Catchers Mickey Owen of the Dodgers and Walker Cooper of the Cardinals were among combatants in a brawl that erupted when Brooklyn's Les Webber threw some close pitches to Stan Musial.

* 1945: The White Sox and Browns battled again when Chicago's sharp-tongued pitcher Karl Scheel got under the skin of rival George Caster. In retaliation, Caster threw the ball at Scheel in the dugout.

* 1953: Brooklyn's Carl Furillo suffered a broken finger in the fight that followed his confrontation with Giants' manager Leo Durocher. Furillo had been hit by a pitch.

* 1954: Milwaukee slugger Joe Adcock chased diminutive Giants' pitcher Ruben Gomez 500 feet to the clubhouse in dead center field after a beanball. Gomez went inside, grabbed a knife, and warned the lumbering first baseman not to come any closer.

---

# ✳

# FINES

The highest fine in baseball history was leveled against Lenny Randle, infielder of the Texas Rangers, during spring training of 1977. Randle, upset with his failure to win a regular job, punched manager Frank Lucchesi several times in full view of players and fans at the Pompano Beach, Florida ballpark.

Randle was immediately suspended and fined $10,000. He never played for the Rangers again. Dealt to the New York Mets, he enjoyed his finest major league season that year, hitting .304 and stealing 33 bases, a club record.

Babe Ruth and Ted Williams drew $5,000 fines—Ruth for "breaking training rules" and Williams for spitting and making obscene gestures at fans.

Ruth was slapped with the penalty in 1925—the same year he sat out the first month with a giant stomach ache suffered en route home from spring training. Neither he nor the club had been doing well, but Ruth was up to his usual playboy antics during a midwestern swing. Manager Miller Huggins hired a detective to trail him and delivered a complete report to owner Jacob Ruppert, who backed him all the way. The owner sided with the manager when Ruth delivered a him-or-me ultimatum.

Three years earlier, Ruth had lost his appointment as Yankee captain after a heated argument with umpire Tommy Connolly. American League president Ban Johnson slapped a $100 fine on Ruth, suspended him five days, and took away his captain's job.

Among other stiff fines in the game's history was a $1000 assessment against Giant pilot John McGraw early in the century. McGraw also drew a five-day suspension for knocking down umpire Bill Byron during a fight in Cincinnati.

Bill Klem, another umpire of the McGraw period, continued an on-field argument with Tiger outfielder Goose Goslin in a Detroit elevator and was fined $50 for foul language by Commissioner Kenesaw M. Landis.

Arguing with umpire Tom Dunn cost Leo Durocher $25 during his term with the Dodgers, and fans considered it such an injustice that they collected 2500 pennies to pay it.

A fight between umpire George Magerkurth and the Giants' Billy Jurges cost each man $150 in 1939. They contested the call of a home run by Cincinnati's Harry Craft.

In the '30s, Cleveland pitcher Johnny Allen persisted in wearing a tattered sweatshirt which made it difficult for batters to see the ball. The league issued a cease-and-desist order. Lack of action led to a $200 fine.

When the Cardinals' Dean brothers missed an exhibition game in Detroit in 1934, manager Frankie Frisch charged the elder Dizzy $100 and Paul $50. The players contested the fines and took the case to the Commissioner, where they lost easily. The Boston Braves once slapped $300 fines on Al Javery and Tom Nelson for missing a train and the New York Yankees slapped minor levies on stars who skipped a "Welcome Home, Yankees" luncheon before the 1978 season's opener.

Managers of all clubs are frequent targets for fines because it is their responsibility to argue loudest and longest. Even pilots with gentle temperaments run into trouble on occasion.

While Leo Durocher, Eddie Stanky, and Gene Mauch were noted for their "politics of confrontation," one of the champion umpire-baiters in baseball history has to be Earl Weaver. He was ejected 61 times in his first nine-and-a-half years as a big-time pilot. Many times, those ejections were accompanied by fines.

**Commissioner Kenesaw Mountain Landis fined top-rated umpire Bill Klem for using foul language.**

*110*

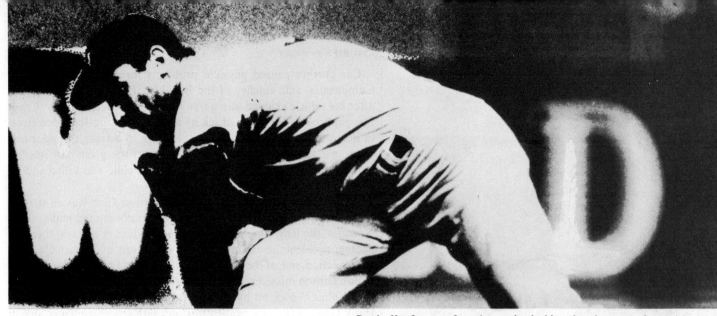
Sandy Koufax was forced to retire in his prime because of arthritis.

# INJURIES

Injuries shape baseball's pennant races and change the course of history. Hank Aaron, free of major injuries after a leg fracture at the end of his rookie year, managed to break Babe Ruth's lifetime home run record by playing often, as well as consistently. Sandy Koufax failed to achieve many pitching milestones because his career was halted by arthritis at age 30. Lou Gehrig, once known as "The Iron Horse" for his durability, was forced to retire at age 36 by amyotrophic lateral sclerosis, the neuromuscular disease that took his life in 1941.

Ray Chapman, Cleveland shortstop, was the only man killed on the field when a Carl Mays pitch struck him in 1920, but dozens of players have been severely injured. Mickey Cochrane's triple skull fracture, also caused by a pitched ball, ended his playing career in 1937, the same season a line drive from Earl Averill's bat fractured Dizzy Dean's toe in the All-Star Game and forced the pitcher into an unorthodox style that ended his career prematurely.

Dodger outfielder Pete Reiser, unmindful of outfield walls even after padding and warning tracks were added, suffered two broken ankles, torn cartilage in his left knee, a broken bone in his right elbow, ripped muscles in his left leg, and countless concussions, contusions, and abrasions. As a rookie, he won the National League batting crown with a .343 mark in 1941 and was running away with another in 1942, with a .381 mark in July. Then he hit the outfield wall in St. Louis. His final mark was .310.

Like Reiser, Ted Williams was hurt when he crashed into a wall. The Red Sox slugger broke his elbow trying to catch a drive by Ralph Kiner in the 1950 All-Star Game.

Off the field, outfielder Lyman Bostock of the California Angels was shot to death shortly before completing his first year with the team in 1978. Visiting relatives in Gary, Indiana during a road trip to Chicago, Bostock was struck by bullets intended for another person in the car he occupied.

Roberto Clemente, a sensational rightfielder for the Pittsburgh Pirates, made his 3000th hit on the last day of the 1972 season, then died in a December plane crash while trying to ferry supplies to victims of an earthquake in Nicaragua.

In 1979, Yankee captain Thurman Munson also lost his life in an airplane crash. His death was even more of a shock than Clemente's because it occurred in mid-season.

## BIG-LEAGUERS CONQUERED HANDICAPS

*Several handicapped players played in the majors. In addition to one-armed Pete Gray, who played with the wartime Browns of 1945, Hugh Daily of the last century had one arm, Tom Sunkel was blind in one eye, Dummy Taylor and Dummy Hoy were deaf mutes, Urban Shocker had heart disease, Sandy Koufax had a circulatory ailment and arthritis, and Catfish Hunter diabetes.*

## STAR SHORTSTOP RECUPERATED

*Marty Marion, shortstop and manager for St. Louis teams, did not walk for a year when he fell off a cliff as a youngster.*

## McDOUGALD LINER STRUCK SCORE

*On May 7, 1957, Gil McDougald of the Yankees—the second batter in the first inning—hit Cleveland pitcher Herb Score in the eye with a line drive. Score, a 20-game winner the previous year, suffered a broken bone and eye damage and was never again the same pitcher. McDougald, hounded by fans after the accident, retired in 1960 at age 32. Score was 29 when he finally gave it up in 1962.*

Car crashes caused physical problems for several players. Roy Campanella, star catcher of the Brooklyn Dodgers, was paralyzed after his vehicle skidded into a tree on an ice-slicked highway. Casey Stengel broke a leg when struck by a driver on a fog-shrouded street in Boston. Art Houtteman's car was struck by a truck during spring training in Lakeland, Florida, and the pitcher was given last rites. He recuperated and resumed his career, but his child was killed and his wife injured in a second crash.

Dizzy Dean once fell out of a car when driver Glen Russell stopped short, but Dean—who fell on his head—was not injured badly. Bobo Newsom, the long-time pitcher, broke both legs in a crash, then had another accident the day his casts were removed; at a South Carolina mule auction, one of the animals kicked him and broke his leg again.

Bob Gibson missed several months of pitching with a fractured leg and Wilbur Wood, hit by a line drive, suffered a shattered kneecap. Hank Greenberg twice beaned pitchers with scorching liners; one of them fractured Jim Wilson's skull and threatened his career. After another line drive broke his leg, Wilson rebounded to throw a no-hitter for the Braves against the Phillies in 1954.

Pitcher Jim Lonborg, whose surprise 22-9 season helped the miracle Red Sox win the wild American League race of 1967, was injured off the field. A ski accident that winter broke his leg, limiting his activities as a pitcher the following season. He was never again the same pitcher that he was in 1967.

Another pitcher, Lou Brissie, narrowly escaped amputation of his left leg when a Nazi shell exploded at his feet during World War II. After 23 operations, he returned to the big leagues—wearing a catcher's shin guard under his uniform.

Gene Bearden, Cleveland's top starter in the pennant year of 1948, also survived war injuries. He was on the deck of the light cruiser *Helena* when Japanese torpedoes struck in 1943. Bearden, with a crushed knee and damaged skull, spent the rest of the war as a patient in naval hospitals.

Bruce Campbell was even more fortunate; he survived spinal meningitis to return to the Cleveland Indians after a year's absence in the '30s. So did Max Alvis, another Indian, in 1964.

Two Braves, Red Schoendienst and Rico Carty, missed seasons nine years apart with tuberculosis. Schoendienst's absence in 1959 cost the team its third consecutive National League pennant, as Felix Mantilla (.215), Casey Wise (.171), and Mel Roach (.097) could not replace the .310 mark Red had compiled before the illness struck late in 1958.

The Braves were victims of a no-hitter by Brooklyn's Ed Head in 1946. What made the feat unusual was the arm Head used—his right. A natural lefthander, he was severely injured in a school bus crash as a youngster. He was determined to play ball anyway and learned how to throw righthanded.

Mordecai Brown's farming machine mishap cost him two fingers but enabled his ball to take a strange hop when thrown. "Three-Finger" Brown won 239 games and a place in the Hall of Fame.

Red Ruffing pitched with only the big toe on one foot; Monte Stratton was successful in the minors on one leg; and Elden Auker's 18-7 record led the American League in 1935 because batters were baffled by his underhand delivery. Auker had thrown normally before an old football injury forced him to make adjustments.

The list of pitchers with serious injuries is almost endless. Every season, tendinitis, sore arms, and elbow bone chips take their toll of

St. Louis Cardinals

Bob Gibson, star righthander, was idled several months with a broken leg.

Wilbur Wood, hit by a line drive, suffered a shattered kneecap.

talented players. One of the most impressive comeback stories was fashioned by Tommy John of the Los Angeles Dodgers in 1976, two years after he had ruptured a ligament in his left elbow. John's injury required complete reconstruction of the arm—a first in medical science.

On July 17, 1974, with a club-leading 13-3 record, John suffered the injury at home against Montreal. A tendon from his right forearm was placed in his left elbow by Dr. Frank Jobe. Recovery was probable, pitching again was doubtful. The southpaw threw out the first ball at the All-Star Game—righthanded.

John missed all of 1975. In 1976, he split 20 decisions. In 1977, he won 20 and lost seven. "It was a miracle," said teammate Bill Russell.

Maybe it was a lucky break—like the one Hank Aaron received as an anonymous rookie in 1954. Bobby Thomson, veteran slugger just acquired by the Braves, broke his leg sliding during spring training. Manager Charlie Grimm named Aaron to replace him. The kid didn't leave the Braves' lineup for twenty-one years.

Tuberculosis put Red Schoendienst out of action in 1959 and cost the Milwaukee Braves a chance to win their third straight pennant.

Tiny Miller Huggins, who managed such musclemen as Babe Ruth, stood just five feet, four inches tall and weighed under 150 pounds. But he lasted 13 seasons as a player and was a well-respected manager.

# PLAYER SIZE AND SEX

Fred Patek , 5-foot, 4-inch shortstop of the Kansas City Royals, started the 1978 All-Star Game for the American League. Patek and one-time American League MVP Phil Rizzuto, a shortstop who stood 5-6, proved size is no obstacle to success in baseball.

If it were possible, an all-star team of short players could be placed on the field. Here's how it might look:

| Pos. | Player | Yrs | Hgt | Wgt | Avg |
|------|--------|-----|-----|-----|-----|
| C | Ray Schalk (1912-29) | 18 | 5:07 | 155 | .253 |
| 1B | Joe Judge (1915-33) | 19 | 5:09 | 155 | .297 |
| 2B* | Miller Huggins (1904-16) | 13 | 5:04 | 148 | .265 |
| SS | Rabbit Maranville (1912-35) | 23 | 5:05 | 155 | .259 |
| 3B | Sparky Adams (1922-34) | 13 | 5:04½ | 151 | .286 |
| OF | Wee Willie Keeler (1892-1910) | 19 | 5:04½ | 140 | .345 |
| OF | Harry Leibold (1913-25) | 13 | 5:06½ | 157 | .267 |
| OF | Hack Wilson (1923-34) | 12 | 5:06 | 190 | .307 |
| P | Bobby Shantz (1949-64) | 16 | 5:06 | 139 | W119 L99 |

(*) also manager

There have not been any women on a team—yet. It's still possible a woman will make the major leagues, and several females have come close to winning professional contracts in Organized Ball.

In July 1952, the Harrisburg Senators of the Class B Interstate League signed a 24-year-old female shortstop named Eleanor Engle. She worked out, wearing uniform No. 11, but her contract was voided by the league office. Earlier, softball star Dorothy Kamenshek, who played first base, was offered a pact by Fort Lauderdale, another Class B club, but the All-America Girls Softball League refused to let her leave.

One woman who did play was Jackie Mitchell, a pitcher used strictly in exhibition games by the Chattanooga Lookouts of the Southern Association in 1932. In one game, she struck out Babe Ruth, Lou Gehrig, and Tony Lazzeri. Lizzie Murphy played an inning at first base for a group of American League All-Stars against the Red Sox in a charity game for the family of Red Sox outfielder Tommy McCarthy on August 14, 1922. She handled one putout cleanly.

# PROLONGED CAREERS

Baseball has always been known as a game for young or old, tall or short, lean or brawny. Many of the game's best players maintained excellent year-round physical condition and managed to play past the age of 35. Some even made it to 40.

In 1897, Cap Anson hit .302 in 114 games for Chicago of the National League. At age 46½, he ended his career on October 3 of that year with two home runs against St. Louis. No other non-pitcher played regularly at such an advanced athletic age.

Sam Thompson, 46, played eight games for the 1906 Tigers and collected several hits—including a triple—when Ty Cobb and others were idled by injuries. Thompson had played in the majors 20 years earlier.

In 1912, when the Tiger players struck in protest of Ty Cobb's suspension (he had hit an abusive fan), manager Hugh Jennings, 43, quickly gathered a team of collegians, semi-pros, and former players, including himself, 41-year-old Joe Sugden, and 48-year-old Jim McGuire. Sugden and McGuire both singled and scored the only two Tiger runs in a 24-2 defeat by the Philadelphia Athletics. By playing in that game, McGuire officially established the record for most years played at 26. Jennings pinch-hit and did so again six years later at age 49.

Spitballer Jack Quinn, 48, won a game for the Dodgers in August 1932 and pitched for the Reds just before his 49th birthday on July 5, 1933. In 1972, knuckleballer Hoyt Wilhelm also just missed spending his 49th birthday in the big leagues; the Dodgers cut him with less than a week to go. For five consecutive seasons after his 40th birthday, Wilhelm managed to keep his ERA below the 2.00 mark.

Satchel Paige was certainly past 50 when he pitched three scoreless innings for the Kansas City A's against Boston as a publicity stunt on September 25, 1965, but he might have been that old—records are uncertain—when he outdueled Detroit's Virgil Trucks, 1-0 in 12 innings, on August 6, 1952.

Paige, then with the Browns, led the American League in relief victories and innings pitched that same season. He was 42 (?) when he broke into the majors with the Cleveland Indians in 1948.

Reliever Don McMahon, winding up with the San Francisco Giants in 1974, was still firing his fastball at age 44, but Warren Spahn prolonged his career by switching from power to finesse.

With pinpoint control and a sharp-breaking screwball, Spahn won 20 or more games in a season 13 different times, pitched his only two no-hitters at ages 39 and 40, and posted a remarkable 23-7 record—with seven shutouts and a 2.60 ERA—as a 42-year-old mound marvel in 1963.

Spahn said he conceded the middle 13 inches of home plate to the batter, but claimed the two inches on either side for himself. He aimed his pitches for those spots.

Another ancient pitcher, 41-year-old Ted Lyons, recorded a fine season at an advanced age in 1942. Working only on Sundays, the White Sox star posted a 14-6 record and 2.10 ERA for a poor ballclub, and completed all 20 of his starts.

Sentiment doesn't last forever and some of the athletes who prospered in their 40s took hard falls. A notable example was Spahn, who suddenly lost his magic overnight and never again had a winning season after his 23-7 record of 1963.

## PLAYER LONGEVITY

*Pitcher Nick Altrock (1898-1933) and outfielder Minnie Minoso (1949-80) played baseball in five different decades.*

*Fifteen others played in four different decades. They are pitchers Kid Gleason, Jack Quinn, Bobo Newsom, Early Wynn, and Jim Kaat; catchers Deacon McGuire, Jack O'Connor, John Ryan, and Tim McCarver; first basemen Dan Brouthers, Mickey Vernon, and Willie McCovey; second baseman Eddie Collins; and outfielders Jim O'Rourke and Ted Williams.*

Early Wynn was one of several players to play in four decades (1939-63). He won a total of 300 games.

# Long Wearing Vets ∴ They're First When It Comes to Lasting

# STUNTS

In addition to strange goings-on before, after, or even during a ballgame, fun-loving players have never been adverse to attempting herculean feats off the field.

Hall of Fame pitcher Walter Johnson, whose 414 victories rank second only to Cy Young's 511, owned a powerful right arm. It was so strong, in fact, that Johnson duplicated George Washington's feat of throwing a silver dollar across the Rappahannock River.

Johnson's catcher, Gabby Street, became one of few men brave enough to catch a ball dropped from the top of the Washington Monument in August of 1908. Drama critic Pres Gibson, a close friend of Street's and a loyal supporter of his outstanding defensive ability, arranged the stunt to prove a bet. Street did not wish to embarrass Gibson, but also wanted to impress Washington fans and writers.

Gibson took 13 balls to the top of the monument, 500 feet in the air, while a crowd gathered to watch Street at the base. Gibson began to throw, but the wind played tricks with the ball. Several hit the side of the structure and bounced away, others were out of reach. Only after Gibson moved to the other side of the monument, away from the wind, did Street have a real chance. He missed several close balls, then grabbed one—the last ball Gibson had.

Eight years later, Brooklyn Dodgers' manager Wilbert Robinson, an old catcher himself, decided to top Street's feat. He arranged to have aviatrix Ruth Law and Dodger trainer Frank Kelly drop a ball from an airplane. The plane was up about 400 feet when Kelly made his drop—but he didn't throw a baseball. Instead, he dropped a red grapefruit.

Unable to distinguish the falling object, Robinson assumed it was a baseball and waited patiently for it to fall into his glove. When the grapefruit hit, it splattered red juice in all directions. "Oh my God!" screamed Robinson. "It broke me open! I'm covered with blood!"

# BENEFITS

Baseball players are as quick to help others as they are to provide laughs. On July 24, 1911, a group of American League stars played the Cleveland Indians in a special game for the benefit of the Addie Joss family. Joss, Cleveland's star pitcher, died suddenly in April from an attack of spinal meningitis. He had been scheduled to pitch the opening game. Had he pitched even part of that game, he would have entered his tenth big-league season and won Hall of Fame eligibility. Despite his spectacular record, Joss was barred from consideration for many years until the ten-year rule was lifted only because of his exceptional case. He was admitted to the Hall in 1978.

The exhibition game in his honor was won by the All-Stars, 5-3. Players included such greats as Ty Cobb, Eddie Collins, Tris Speaker, and Walter Johnson. Among the Indians in action were Cy Young, Joe Jackson, and Napoleon Lajoie.

On June 14, 1937, four major league teams played an exhibition doubleheader at Charleston, West Virginia to raise funds for the Kanawha Valley Children's Tuberculosis Hospital. The Reds played the Athletics and the Senators played the Phillies, raising $17,000 for the hospital fund. On August 16, the St. Louis Cardinals battled Columbus (American Association) in an exhibition before a Charleston-Zanesville (Middle Atlantic) game, adding $10,000 to the hospital fund. ☞

## A DIFFICULT PUTOUT

*Al Schacht, the noted baseball clown, was pitching in a 1928 benefit game for Eddie Plank when he got the first two men out in an inning. He then called in all the fielders but the catcher as batting practice pitcher Ike Powers came to the plate. Powers connected with the ball and unleashed a drive deep to right field. As he circled the bases, Schacht retrieved the ball, fired it home, and nipped Powers by an eyelash.*

## WHY McGRAW FINED INJURED PITCHER

*Giants' manager John McGraw fined pitcher Zeke Barnes $100 after the pitcher reported with a bad ankle and injured wrist —suffered in a bathtub fall. The pitcher profited from the incident when a concern that manufactured bathtub mats gave him $200 to endorse its product.*

Baseball Hall of Fame

Babe Ruth not only loved children but had tremendous influence on them. He was a frequent visitor to children's hospitals.

Throughout the history of the game, clubs and individuals have done considerable charity work. In 1977, for example, several clubs made large contributions to the Jackie Robinson Foundation and National League All-Stars Greg Luzinski and Dave Winfield spent thousands of dollars from their own pockets to purchase game tickets for disadvantaged children.

Such actions usually receive no public exposure.

# OFF THE FIELD

Most baseball people have special hobbies or occupations in the off-season. Many who come from rural backgrounds are wintertime farmers. College-educated players often go into teaching, especially when their classroom assignment coincides with coaching a schoolboy team.

Members of the New York Hilltoppers (later Yankees) in 1905 didn't have to worry about injury on August 4, when the club's winning battery consisted of two doctors—pitcher Jim Newton and catcher Mike Powers.

The Yankees produced two other doctors in infielder Bobby Brown (a lifetime .439 batter in the World Series) and pitcher George (Doc) Medich, who performed in the '70s.

"Baseball gave me the financial opportunity to put myself through medical school," said Brown, a Fort Worth cardiologist who also served the Texas Rangers as an executive. "The experience of playing with those truly great Yankee teams (early '50s) was a tremen-

## THE GAME'S REMARKABLE INFLUENCE

*Eleven-year-old John D. Sylvester of Essex Fells, New Jersey, was given 30 minutes to live by doctors after a severe attack of blood poisoning in October 1926. Young John spent his remaining time listening to the World Series. That was the day Babe Ruth hit three home runs in one game. Amazingly, John began to recover. The New York Times reported that Horace Sylvester, Jr., the boy's father, and the physicians attributed the recovery to messages of encouragement received from Ruth and other stars. When Ruth hit his three home runs, the boy's fever began to break and his recovery began.*

dous influence, enabling me to adapt to all types of crises. The atmosphere of total dedication on those teams will last with me forever."

Record-breaking reliever Mike Marshall, who won the National League's Cy Young Award after working 106 times in 1974, spent his off-season teaching kinesiology—the science of muscle movement in relation to body tissue—to students at Michigan State University.

Juan Marichal, a spectacular Giants' starter of a decade before, became an accomplished skin-diver and once was hired to photograph sharks off the coast of his native Dominican Republic.

In the '40s, Washington's fleet George Case ran a Trenton, New Jersey, sporting goods store and coached the Rutgers University team. Rip Sewell worked for a California motor oil concern. And veteran managers Billy Southworth and Joe McCarthy retired to quiet farm living.

Before Curt Flood challenged baseball's reserve clause in 1969, he had become such an accomplished painter that St. Louis owner Gussie Busch commissioned the outfielder to do a family portrait. Rawly Eastwick, who gained his freedom in the second wave of big-name free agents, also showed talent with a paintbrush.

A Flood contemporary, Jim Bouton, confined his talents to the typewriter and stirred waves of resentment when he penned the inside-baseball book, *Ball Four,* in 1970. He used the book as a springboard to mushroom his career as writer, sportscaster, and television personality.

Yogi Berra and Phil Rizzuto opened a successful bowling alley in Clifton, New Jersey; Red Schoendienst cultivated his interest in a retirement home; and Warren Spahn pitched hay instead of baseballs to the cattle on his ranch near Hartshorne, Oklahoma.

Many Latin players switch uniforms to perform in winter leagues in their native countries. Darrell Evans devotes more time to his relaxing hobby: collecting postage stamps of animals. Garrulous Joe Garagiola escapes the sportscaster stereotype and tackles other broadcast assignments. Mike Marshall plays chess. Maury Wills plays his banjo in nightclubs. Denny McLain appears at the organ.

Big-leaguers plan investments—and watch their weight. Golf, tennis, racquetball, and swimming are popular ways to maintain condition for the coming season.

Some baseball insiders simply relax. They are able to live off their baseball salary, plus money from endorsements and investments.

"I never made a dollar outside of baseball," said long-time coach and manager Charley Dressen. Many others could say the same.

## YOUGEST PLAYER

*Lefthanded pitcher Joe Nuxhall of the Cincinnati Reds was the youngest player to appear in the majors. He made his debut on June 10, 1944, at the age of 15 years and 10 months. He pitched two-thirds of an inning in an 18-0 loss to the Cardinals.*

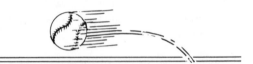

## LONE SENATOR HOMER

*Power production was off sharply in the war-stripped majors of 1945. The Washington Senators hit only 27 home runs as a team—only one in their home park, Griffith Stadium. It was an inside-the-park job by Joe Kuhel.*

# CHAPTER EIGHT

# Famous Faces

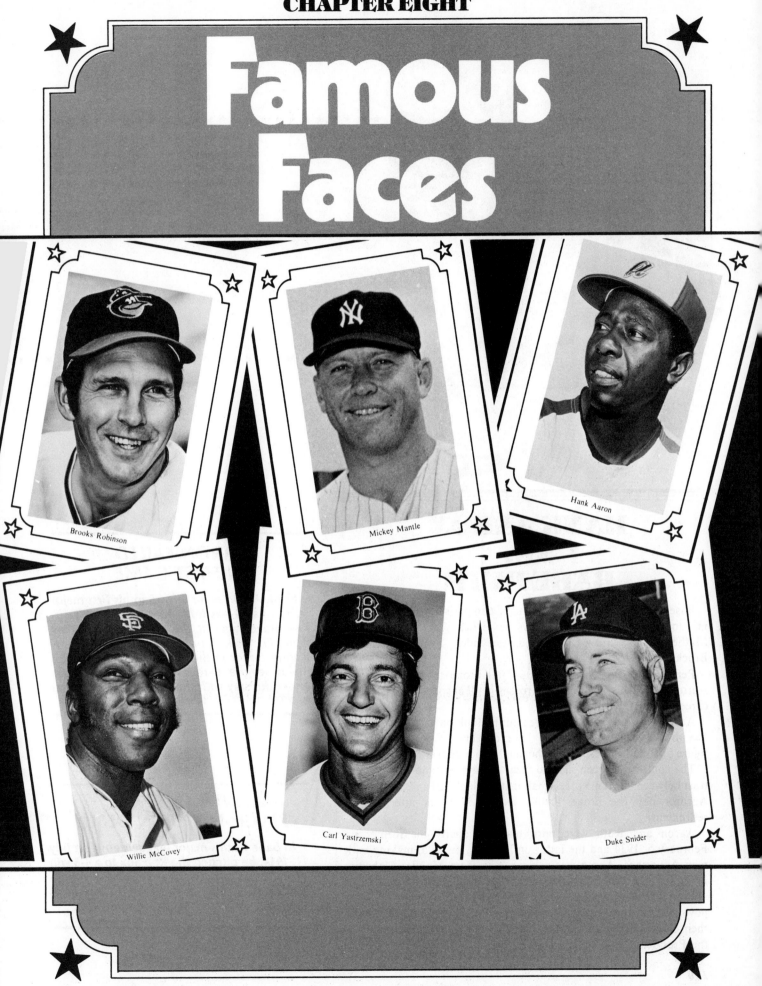

Brooks Robinson

Mickey Mantle

Hank Aaron

Willie McCovey

Carl Yastrzemski

Duke Snider

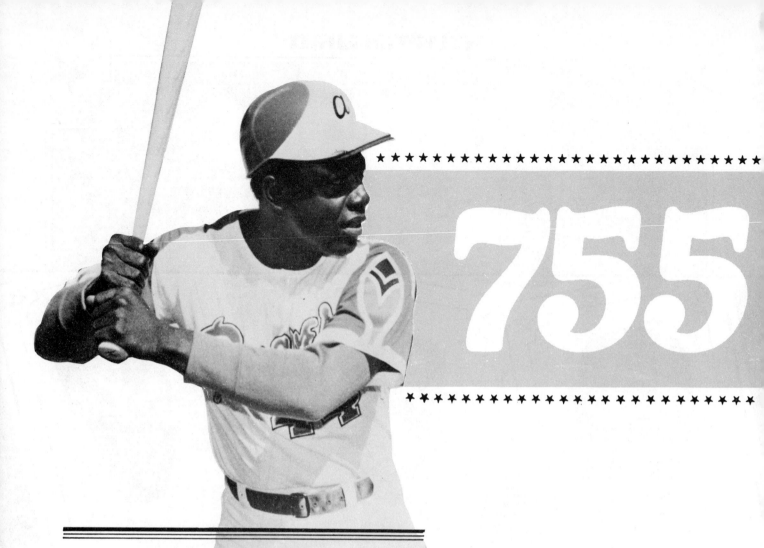

755

# HANK AARON VS. BABE RUTH

Baseball has always been a game of comparisons. Ted Williams *vs.* Joe DiMaggio. Willie Mays *vs.* Mickey Mantle. Christy Mathewson *vs.* Grover Cleveland Alexander. Ty Cobb *vs.* Lou Brock.

Perhaps the biggest argument of all broke loose when Hank Aaron approached the mightiest record in all of sport—Babe Ruth's career total of 714 home runs.

Aaron took on more than a record; he took on a legend. "There has always been a magic about that gross, ugly, coarse, gargantuan figure of a man and everything he did," wrote Paul Gallico of Ruth.

The contrast between the two men was as remarkable as the contrast between the game of baseball that Ruth played and the game of Aaron's day (he broke Ruth's record 39 years after Ruth's retirement).

Aaron and Ruth were born one day apart—the former on February 5, 1934 and the latter on February 6, 1895, making both men Aquarians. Aaron was a black man from Mobile, Alabama; Ruth a white man from Baltimore, Maryland.

Both came into great wealth in baseball after emerging from poverty, both spent little time in the minors, and both spent most of their careers as rightfielders. In addition, both were paid as well as the Presidents who saw them play. ☞

## AARON FAILED IN FIRST GAME

*Hank Aaron went 0-for-5 in his first major league game—as leftfielder for the Milwaukee Braves against the Cincinnati Reds on April 13, 1954. Though he spent his minor-league career in the infield, and most of his major league career in right field, Aaron ended his stay with the Braves as a leftfielder in 1974.*

## RUTH LEFT FOR PINCH-HITTER IN DEBUT

*In Babe Ruth's major league debut on July 11, 1914, he pitched the Red Sox to a 4-3 win over Cleveland, but was lifted for pinch-hitter Duffy Lewis in the seventh inning. A single by Lewis led to the winning run.*

120

# 714

## RUTH BROKE INTO NL WITH BANG

*Babe Ruth had two hits—including a home run—in four at-bats against Carl Hubbell in his National League debut in 1935.*

## RUTH WON $10 FOR NO. 60

*Babe Ruth won a $10 bet from teammate Tony Lazzeri when he hit his 60th home run in 1927.*

## EARLY HOME RUN KINGS

*When Babe Ruth hit 29 home runs in 1919, he broke Gavvy Cravath's record of 24, set in 1915. Ruth replaced Roger Connor as the all-time home run king when he socked No. 138 in 1921.*

Ruth missed the tiring cross-country plane trips required of modern players; St. Louis was the western outpost of the American League when he played.

Because modern managers parade an endless stream of relievers with unorthodox deliveries and unusual pitches, Aaron faced an additional obstacle. Not only did Ruth avoid the phenomenon of relief pitching, but he also played all his games in daylight; the first night game was played in 1935, the same year Ruth retired.

Overall pitching improvement, the advent of night ball, and widespread use of relievers caused the overall major league batting average to fall from .282 in Ruth's heyday to .252 in Aaron's. For that reason, Aaron's National League average of .310 can be favorably compared with Ruth's .342 when the 30-point differential is considered. (In two years as an American League designated hitter, Aaron lost five points off his lifetime average.)

Though Ruth twice stole 17 bases, he never topped the 20 mark, which Aaron did six times. Both men played on teams laden with power. Lou Gehrig batted behind Ruth, forcing pitchers to give Ruth pitches around the plate. A walk might mean a two-run homer by Gehrig.

Aaron also was followed by power hitters—Eddie Mathews, Joe Adcock, Rico Carty, Orlando Cepeda, and others. ☞

The two men became the home run kings of the game with vastly different batting stances. Aaron generated his power with quick, powerful wrists, while Ruth relied on massive shoulders and forearms for strength which moved from arms to bat.

Hall of Famer Eddie Mathews, who formed a devastating 1-2 power punch with Aaron, remembered his style at the plate. "He wasn't a classic hitter and young players shouldn't copy him," said Mathews of Aaron, who batted righthanded—the opposite of Ruth. "He hits off the front foot—a flat-footed stance in any batting textbook. It sounds wrong to say the man who broke Babe Ruth's home run record had a fundamental batting flaw. Let's just say that Hank Aaron hit differently than anybody else."

Both Aaron and Ruth were students of hitting. Ruth had an extra insight because he broke into the majors as a pitcher with the 1914 Boston Red Sox. He won 94, lost 46, and compiled a fine 2.28 lifetime earned run average in six seasons as a pitcher, and for 43 years held the record for most consecutive scoreless innings pitched in the World Series.

Aaron never pitched but, like Ruth, broke into the lineup after conversion from his original post as an infielder. He filled in at second base numerous times in his career.

The greatest Aaron-Ruth controversy stems from the fact that Ruth collected his 714 home runs in 8,399 times at bat, nearly 3,000 fewer than Aaron. Ruth ranks first in the number of home runs per 100 times at bat with 8.5.

A pro-Ruth fan calculated that the Yankee star would have hit an additional 231 home runs with 2,800 more times at bat—for a career total of 945! But the same fan suggested that record-keepers deduct five per cent of that toal because of the home run advantage accorded lefthanded hitters. He came out with a revised total of 898 home runs.

The advantage for a lefty is that there are far more righthanded than lefthanded pitchers in the game, and a lefty has a statistical batting edge against a righthander. ☞

Hank Aaron, then an infielder, always maintained that Jacksonville manager Ben Geraghty was his best boss in baseball.

## WAITE HOYT ON BABE RUTH

*Hall of Famer Waite Hoyt, a Babe Ruth teammate and long-time broadcaster, on Ruth: "I knew and watched most of the baseball greats of the twentieth century, and the Babe was always the one towering above the crowd. We (the Yankees) never ceased being fascinated by the man. He was simple, straightforward, yet so complex and unfathomable. We simply could not characterize him.*

*"He pursued ordinary pleasures hard. His lack of parental guidance was all too evident. He established his own values and they varied greatly. His popularity was a phenomenon of the American scene. He was caught up in an avalanche of hero worship."*

Babe Ruth hit his final home run as a member of the Boston Braves in 1935.

## RUTH'S BATBOY PLAYED RUTH IN MOVIE

*William Bendix, who played the title role in* The Babe Ruth Story, *actually served as Ruth's batboy during the early '20s at the Polo Grounds.*

Ruth definitely benefited by batting lefthanded. After joining the Yankees in 1920, he had the good fortune to play in the old Polo Grounds because Yankee Stadium had not yet been built. The right field fence—just 254 feet away—was an easy mark for the Babe, who smashed 54 home runs that season, 25 more than he had hit in 1919.

He hit 59 the next year but slipped to 35 in 1922 when he spent a third of the season under suspension. In 1923, Yankee Stadium opened and instantly won the nickname, "The House That Ruth Built." Its right field fence was 296 feet away—still one of the easiest targets in the game. From 1926-32, Ruth never hit less than .323 or had fewer than 41 homers in a season.

While Aaron played in Milwaukee and Atlanta ballparks that were also conducive to the long ball, he aimed at fences 330 feet from home.

Aaron faced other problems not encountered by Ruth—the pressure of breaking another man's record, constant media exposure, and the need to maintain prime condition and consistency (Aaron's one-season high was 47 homers, but Ruth topped 54 four times).

"In my mind," said Aaron, "a hitter is always able to hit, but first he must be fit and able to get on the field to play."

The 6-foot, 180-pound Aaron was always in shape, but Ruth wasn't. His record reflected the fact that he was out of shape. After hitting 41 homers at age 37 in 1932, he slipped to 34, then 22, and finally just six in 1935 at age 40. The rotund Yankee slugger was felled by his own insatiable appetite for life's pleasures.

In 1925, when he was just 30, Ruth guzzled countless hot dogs, sodas, and beers during spring training and triggered a gastric revolt in his overworked digestive tract. Teammate Waite Hoyt once joked that if someone sawed Ruth in two, half the concessions of Yankee Stadium would fall out.

Ruth partied late into the night—and sometimes all night. Once, before a big game, Washington's Goose Goslin tried to tire Ruth out by keeping him up 'til sunrise. Goslin limped back to his hotel room to recuperate, but Ruth went to Walter Reed Army Hospital to autograph balls. Later that day, Ruth socked two homers while Goslin went 0-for-5.

"He had to be the greatest power-hitter, the greatest player," said Stan Musial of Ruth. "He was good enough to pitch and bat fourth, like the star of a high school team."

When a young fan asked Ruth if he could hit .400 by concentrating on hits instead of homers, he answered, "Four hundred? Hell, I could hit *five* hundred!"

The young Hank Aaron didn't pay much attention to the Babe Ruth legend. "Why should I have read about a man playing a game I couldn't get into at the time?" Aaron explained.

Aaron certainly did not copy Ruth's home run swing. Ruth's blasts followed great, sweeping curves en route to the outfield seats, while Aaron specialized in line-drive shots. "The Sultan of Swat," for Ruth, and "The Hammer," for Aaron, were fitting nicknames.

Ruth wore a camel-hair coat, dangled a cigar, smiled broadly and easily, and tooled around in a snappy roadster. Aaron, almost an introvert by contrast, drove a Chevrolet Caprice and never drew the attention of the media until he approached Ruth's record. Ruth had charisma; Aaron didn't. But the fans—except for a tiny minority

Henry Aaron didn't read about Babe Ruth because baseball's doors were closed to him as a youngster. "Why should I read about someone playing a game I couldn't get into?" he said.

that scribbled racial hate letters—backed the challenger when he neared the mark.

"I didn't always think 'home run' when I came to the plate," Aaron conceded after the record had fallen. "I was concentrating on getting a hit, trying to win the game. If a home run was needed, then I thought it was my duty to try and get it. First you play baseball, then you play to win, and then you go for home runs. The understanding of the fans is important."

A contemporary of Aaron's, switch-hitting infielder Pete Rose, set many batting records of his own. But he looked at Aaron with admiration.

"I felt like I knew Babe Ruth," he said. "And he was great. But so was Henry Aaron."

# AWARDS

Baseball honors its best players with a series of awards at the end of each season. Members of the media vote for the Most Valuable Player in each league, as well as the Rookie of the Year, Cy Young Award winner, Manager of the Year, and Comeback Player of the Year.

Several publications make their own awards. *The Sporting News* polls the players to pick All-Star lineups based on the entire season, a better perspective than the actual starting teams that clash in the annual mid-summer classic. *The Baseball Bulletin*'s All-Stars and awards are based on the consensus of its staff.

Award-winners invariably come from contending clubs, but there are exceptions. Ernie Banks, who swung a potent bat for the last-place Chicago Cubs in 1958-59, was named the National League's MVP both years.

League leaders in batting and pitching frequently win the writers' attention when ballots are taken. But there are exceptions there too.

Maury Wills was Most Valuable Player of the National League when he broke Ty Cobb's single-season record with 104 stolen bases in 1962, but Lou Brock failed to win the award when he stole 118 times in 1974. Both Wills and Brock played for clubs that narrowly missed the pennant during their big years, but the voters of 1974 handed the award to the leader of the championship club, Steve Garvey.

Willie Stargell, whose Pirates finished 2½ games behind in 1973, was equally deprived when writers named batting champion Pete Rose as the league's MVP. Stargell had hit 44 homers, driven home 119 runs, and recorded a .646 slugging average, while Rose had only five homers and 64 RBI to go with his .338 average. But Cincinnati was a winner.

No one had a more justified complaint than Ted Williams, however. The Boston Red Sox slugger twice won the rare Triple Crown of batting—league leadership in batting average, home runs, and RBI—but failed to win the American League's MVP trophy.

Williams did win the MVP in 1946, when the Red Sox finished first, and in 1949, when they missed by a game, but his 1942 and 1947 Triple Crowns were bypassed by writers who selected Yankees Joe Gordon and Joe DiMaggio, respectively.

Oddly, Lou Gehrig also missed the award in a Triple Crown season. Detroit's catcher-manager Mickey Cochrane hit .320 with

Babe Ruth leaves for spring training in 1930.

## Triple Crown Winners

| Player | Year | HR | RBI | Pct. |
|---|---|---|---|---|
| Carl Yastrzemski | 1967 | 44 | 121 | .326 |
| Frank Robinson | 1966 | 49 | 122 | .316 |
| Mickey Mantle | 1956 | 52 | 130 | .353 |
| Ted Williams | 1947 | 32 | 114 | .343 |
| Ted Williams | 1942 | 36 | 137 | .356 |
| Joe Medwick | 1937 | 31 | 154 | .374 |
| Lou Gehrig | 1934 | 49 | 165 | .363 |
| Jimmie Foxx | 1933 | 48 | 163 | .356 |
| Chuck Klein | 1933 | 28 | 120 | .368 |
| Rogers Hornsby | 1925 | 39 | 143 | .403 |
| Rogers Hornsby | 1922 | 42 | 152 | .401 |
| Henry Zimmerman | 1912 | 14 | 98 | .372 |
| Ty Cobb | 1909 | 9 | 115 | .377 |
| Napoleon Lajoie | 1901 | 14 | 125 | .422 |
| Hugh Duffy | 1894 | 18 | 145 | .438 |
| Tip O'Neill | 1887 | 14 | 123 | .442 |

## HEARTBREAK STATISTICS

*In 1931, Chick Hafey won the NL batting title with a .3489 mark. Bill Terry was second at .3486 and Jim Bottomley third at .3482. The American League's tightest race occurred in '49, when George Kell hit .34291, a narrow edge over Ted Williams' .34276. Had Williams won the batting title, he would have become the only man to win three Triple Crowns.*

## GOLD GLOVES

*With pitchers and hitters recognized through various awards, sure-handed fielders—who contributed handsomely but anonymously to many championships—were given an award of their own. In 1957, the Rawlings Sporting Goods Company, in conjunction with The Sporting News, created the annual Gold Glove Awards. Voting procedure changed several times to include the media, the players, and the managers. One team was selected in '57, but separate teams for each league thereafter. Winners receive a Gold Glove trophy, presented before a game at their home stadium the following year; repeat winners have an additional gold crest attached.*

Rawlings Sporting Goods

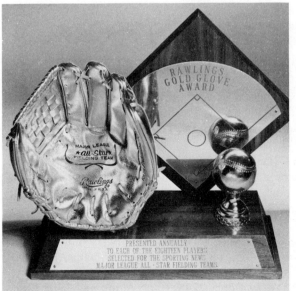

Gold Glove awards for fielding excellence are presented annually.

but two homers and 76 runs batted in for the 1934 season, but brought his club home first. In New York, Gehrig led the league with a .363 average, 49 homers, and 165 runs batted in. His slugging percentage was a resounding .796. But the Yankees finished second, seven games behind.

The first MVPs were World Series opponents Lefty Grove, pitcher of the Philadelphia Athletics, and Frankie Frisch, second baseman of the St. Louis Cardinals. Their selection set a precedent of picking players from champion clubs.

Prior to 1931, when the Baseball Writers Association of America created the Most Valuable Player Award, each league occasionally rewarded its outstanding player on an annual basis. League awards were given from 1922-29 and, prior to that, Chalmers Awards (automobiles) from 1911-14. Neither had the prestige that the baseball writers gave to the MVP.

Since no rookie was considered a bona fide candidate for MVP honors (Fred Lynn of the '75 Red Sox was the only exception), the writers launched a separate award for freshmen in 1947. The first Rookie of the Year was Jackie Robinson, who not only broke the color line, but made a successful conversion from second to first, led the league with 29 steals, and hit .297 to help the Dodgers win the pennant.

Like the rookie award, which was given to one player in each league beginning in 1949, the Cy Young Memorial Award for pitching excellence began as a single citation. Don Newcombe, who had been Rookie of the Year in '49, was the initial winner in 1956, while another Dodger—southpaw Sandy Koufax—was the first unanimous choice seven years later.

Koufax was also a unanimous choice in 1965 and 1966, the last year of his career and also the last year of the single Cy Young Award. In the second year of separate honors, Denny McLain of the Detroit Tigers and Bob Gibson of the St. Louis Cardinals staged the only sweep of Cy Young and MVP honors. McLain, with a 31-6 record for the champion Tigers, was a unanimous choice for both.

The McLain-Gibson victory represented the only example of two pitchers winning MVP awards in the same season.

Only three relief men—Jim Konstanty of the 1950 Phillies, Rollie Fingers of the 1981 Brewers, and Willie Hernandez of the 1984 Tigers—have won the MVP, and only six— Sparky Lyle, Mike Marshall, Bruce Sutter, Steve Bedrosian, Fingers, and Hernandez—have won the Cy Young Award.

Yogi Berra and Jimmie Foxx in the American League and Roy Campanella, Stan Musial, and Mike Schmidt in the National each won three MVP awards. Koufax, Tom Seaver, and Jim Palmer won Young citations as often, while Steve Carlton became the first four-time winner in 1982.

Frank Robinson was the only man to be Most Valuable Player in both leagues, and Gaylord Perry was the only pitcher so honored, with opposite Cy Young trophies. ☆ ☆ ☆ ☆ ☆

# SINGLE-SEASON STARS

**BATTING**—Rogers Hornsby, St. L. NL (1924), .424; Napoleon Lajoie, Phila. AL (1901), .422; George Sisler, St. L. AL (1922) and Ty Cobb, Detr. AL (1911), .420.

**HOME RUNS**—Roger Maris, N.Y. AL (1961), 61; Babe Ruth, N.Y. AL (1927), 60; Ruth (1921), 59; Jimmie Foxx, Phila. AL (1932) and Hank Greenberg, Detr. AL (1938), 58; Hack Wilson, Chic. NL (1930), 56. ☞

Among participants in "The Game of the Century," the first All-Star Game, were National Leaguer Bill Terry (left) and American League stars Joe Cronin and Jimmie Foxx. The game was played in Chicago in 1933.

## 400 TOTAL BASES, SEASON

*Ruth, Babe, Yanks, 1921* .......................... 457
*Hornsby, Rogers, Cards, 1922* ................ 450
*Gehrig, Lou, Yanks, 1927* ...................... 447
*Klein, Chuck, Phils, 1930* ...................... 445
*Foxx, Jimmy, Phila A's, 1932* ................ 438
*Musial, Stan, Cards, 1948* ...................... 429
*Wilson, Hack, Cubs, 1930* ...................... 423
*Klein, Chuck, Phils, 1932* ...................... 420
*Gehrig, Lou, Yanks, 1930* ...................... 419
*DiMaggio, Joe, Yanks, 1937* .................. 418
*Herman, Babe, Dodgers, 1930* .............. 416
*Hornsby, Rogers, Cubs, 1929* ................ 410
*Gehrig, Lou, Yanks, 1931* ...................... 410
*Gehrig, Lou, Yanks, 1934* ...................... 409
*Medwick, Joe, Cards, 1937* .................. 406
*Rice, Jim, Red Sox, 1978* ...................... 406
*Klein, Chuck, Phils, 1929* ...................... 405
*Trosky, Hal, Indians, 1936* .................. 405
*Gehrig, Lou, Yanks, 1936* ...................... 403
*Foxx, Jimmy, Phila A's, 1933* ................ 403
*Aaron, Hank, Braves, 1959* .................. 400

## ALEXANDER'S DEBUT

*Grover Cleveland Alexander won 28 games for the Phillies as a rookie in 1911, thirty-seven years before the creation of the Rookie of the Year Award.*

126

**RUNS BATTED IN**—Hack Wilson, Chic. NL (1930), 190; Lou Gehrig, N.Y. AL (1931), 184; Hank Greenberg, Detr. AL (1937), 183; Gehrig (1927) and Jimmie Foxx, Boston AL (1938), 175; Gehrig (1930), 174.

**RUNS SCORED**—Ruth (1921), 177; Gehrig (1936), 167; Ruth (1928) and Gehrig (1931), 163; Ruth (1920 and 1927) and Chuck Klein, Phila. NL (1930), 158; Rogers Hornsby, Chic. NL (1929), 156.

**STOLEN BASES**—Rickey Henderson, Oak. AL (1982), 130; Lou Brock, St. L. NL (1974), 118; Vince Coleman, St. L. NL (1985), 110; Coleman (1987), 109; Henderson (1983), 108; Coleman (1986), 107; Maury Wills, L.A. NL (1962), 104; Henderson (1980), 100.

**PITCHING VICTORIES**—Jack Chesbro, N.Y. AL (1904), 41; Ed Walsh, Chic. AL (1908), 40; Christy Mathewson, N.Y. NL (1908), 37; Walter Johnson, Wash. AL (1913), 36; Joe McGinnity, N.Y. NL (1904), 35.

**EARNED RUN AVERAGE**—Dutch Leonard, Boston AL (1914), 1.01; Mordecai Brown, Chic. NL (1906), 1.04; Bob Gibson, St. L. NL (1968), 1.12; Mathewson (1909) and Johnson (1913), 1.14.

**GAMES PITCHED**—Mike Marshall, L.A. NL (1974), 106; Kent Tekulve, Pitt. NL (1979), 94; Marshall, Montreal NL (1973), 92; Tekulve (1978), 91; Marshall, Minnesota AL (1979) and Wayne Granger, Cinn. NL (1969), 90; Wilbur Wood, Chic. AL (1968), 88.

**GAMES SAVED IN RELIEF**—Dave Righetti, N.Y. AL (1986), 46; Dennis Eckersley, Oak. AL (1988), Bruce Sutter, St. L. NL (1984), and Dan Quisenberry, K.C. AL (1983), 45; Quisenberry (1984), 44; Jeff Reardon, Minn. AL (1988), 42; Reardon, Mont. NL (1985), 41; Steve Bedrosian, Phila. NL (1987), 40; John Franco, Cinn. NL (1988), 39.

**STRIKEOUTS**—Nolan Ryan, Calif. AL (1973), 383; Sandy Koufax, L.A. NL (1965), 382; Ryan (1974), 367; Rube Waddell, Phila. AL (1904), 349; Bob Feller, Cleve. AL (1946), 348; Ryan (1972), 329.

**WINNING PERCENTAGE** (15 wins minimum)—ElRoy Face, Pitt. NL (1959), .947; Johnny Allen, Cleve. AL (1937), .938; Ron Guidry, N.Y. AL (1978), .893; Fred Fitzsimmons, Brooklyn NL (1940), .889; Lefty Grove, Phila. AL (1931), .886; Preacher Roe, Brooklyn NL (1951), .880.

# LIFETIME LEADERS

**BATTING**—Ty Cobb, .367; Rogers Hornsby, .358; Shoeless Joe Jackson, .356; Ted Williams and Tris Speaker, .344 each; Babe Ruth and Harry Heilmann, .342 each; Bill Terry, .341; George Sisler and Lou Gehrig, .340 each.

**HOME RUNS**—Hank Aaron, 755; Babe Ruth, 714; Willie Mays, 660; Frank Robinson, 586; Harmon Killebrew, 573; Reggie Jackson, 563; Mike Schmidt*, 542; Mickey Mantle, 536; Jimmie Foxx, 534; Ted Williams and Willie McCovey, 521.

**RUNS BATTED IN**—Hank Aaron, 2297; Babe Ruth, 2212; Lou Gehrig, 1991; Stan Musial, 1951; Ty Cobb, 1933; Jimmie Foxx, 1921; Willie Mays, 1903; Mel Ott, 1860; Ted Williams, 1839; Al Simmons, 1827.

**RUNS SCORED**—Ty Cobb, 2245; Hank Aaron and Babe Ruth, 2174 each; Pete Rose, 2165; Willie Mays, 2062; Stan Musial, 1949; Lou Gehrig, 1888; Tris Speaker, 1881; Mel Ott, 1859.

**STOLEN BASES**—Lou Brock, 938; Ty Cobb, 892; Rickey Henderson*, 794; Eddie Collins, 743; Max Carey, 738; Honus Wagner, 703; Joe Morgan, 689; Bert Campaneris, 631; Maury Wills, 586; Davey Lopes, 557. ☞

**PITCHING VICTORIES**—Cy Young, 511; Walter Johnson, 404; Grover Cleveland Alexander and Christy Mathewson, 373 each; Warren Spahn, 363; Steve Carlton*, 329; Eddie Plank, 325; Don Sutton, 324; Phil Niekro, 318; Gaylord Perry, 314; Tom Seaver, 311.

**EARNED RUN AVERAGE** (minimum 1500 innings)—Ed Walsh, 1.82; Addie Joss, 1.88; Smokey Joe Wood, 2.03; Three Finger Brown, 2.06; Christy Mathewson, 2.13; Rube Waddell, 2.16; Walter Johnson, 2.17.

**GAMES PITCHED**—Hoyt Wilhelm, 1070; Kent Tekulve*, 1013; Lindy McDaniel, 987; Rollie Fingers, 944; Gene Garber, 931; Cy Young, 906; Sparky Lyle, 899; Jim Kaat, 896; Don McMahon, 874.

**GAMES SAVED IN RELIEF**—Rollie Fingers, 341; Goose Gossage*, 302; Bruce Sutter*, 300; Dan Quisenberry*, 238; Hoyt Wilhelm, 237; Sparky Lyle, 236; Jeff Reardon*, 235; Gene Garber, 218; Lee Smith*, 209; ElRoy Face, 197.

**STRIKEOUTS**—Nolan Ryan*, 4775; Steve Carlton*, 4136; Tom Seaver, 3640; Don Sutton, 3574; Gaylord Perry, 3534; Walter Johnson, 3509; Bert Blyleven*, 3431; Phil Niekro, 3342; Ferguson Jenkins, 3192; Bob Gibson, 3117.

**WINNING PERCENTAGE** (100 wins minimum)—Spud Chandler, .717; Whitey Ford, .690; Don Gullett, .686; Lefty Grove, .680; Smokey Joe Wood, .669; Christy Mathewson and Vic Raschi, .667; Sal Maglie, .657; Sandy Koufax and Johnny Allen, .655; Three Finger Brown, .653.

*Records through 1988 season (records for modern era only, 1900-present)

## BAT MASTER

*Three-time .400 hitter Rogers Hornsby, whose .424 in 1924 remains the top mark of the modern era, let nothing irk him at bat. Boston Braves' catcher Al Spohrer—a former Hornsby teammate—knew he liked a good steak almost as much as he liked a base-hit.*

*Spohrer started talking food as soon as Hornsby came to the plate. As the Chicago pitcher whizzed across two strikes, the catcher told Hornsby that, his wife had discovered a Boston butcher who provided excellent cuts. He also said his wife had become an excellent cook. He closed with a suggestion that Hornsby stop in for dinner the next time his Cubs came to Boston.*

*Just as Spohrer made his last remark, Hornsby, who took a big stride from a closed stance, stepped into a pitch and hit it far over the left field wall at Wrigley Field. As he reached home, he spotted the frustrated catcher and said, "What night shall we make it, Al?"*

Rogers Hornsby compiled the best lifetime batting average of any National League player. His .358 mark ranked second to Ty Cobb of the American (.367).

National League

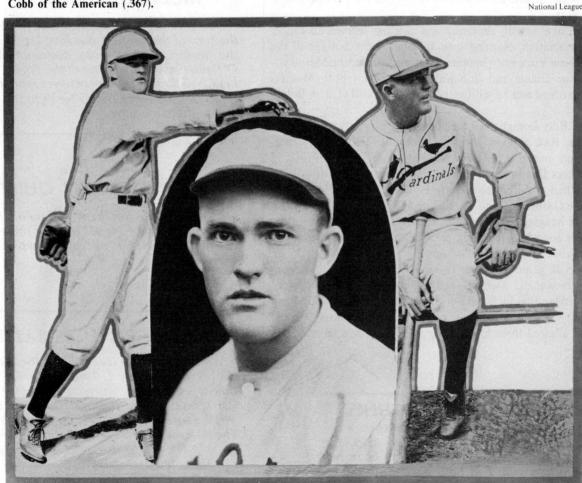

# FAMOUS FAMILIES

Baseball has always been a family game—for players as well as spectators.

For more than a dozen seasons, the Pittsburgh Pirates pounded rivals with two lefthanded hitting outfielders—brothers named Paul and Lloyd Waner. The Waners were in the majors from 1927-45—long enough to hit well over .300 and earn separate plaques in the Hall of Fame. When they hit consecutive homers in 1938, they became the only brothers to do it.

The three DiMaggios never played together; the three Alous and the three Cruz brothers also spent most of their careers with opposing clubs. Paul Reuschel did spend some time with brother Rick of the Cubs, and the two produced the only combined shutout ever thrown by brothers.

Joe Niekro was also teamed with Phil for a spell in Atlanta, but wilted in the bullpen and found himself only after returning to a starter's role elsewhere. Pitcher Ken Brett, who once homered in four consecutive starts, gave younger brother George, a third baseman, various hitting tips, and George won a batting title with the 1976 Kansas City Royals. Lee May and Carlos May were also strong-hitting brothers in the '70s.

Fraternal third basemen were Ken Boyer of the Cardinals and Clete Boyer, who played for the Yankees and Braves. A third brother, Cloyd, pitched for the Cards before Ken came up in 1955. St. Louis also signed a pair of hot pitching prospects in the McDaniels—Lindy and Von—but the latter was curtailed by a sore arm early in his career. Lindy became one of the top bullpen aces in baseball history.

Joe and Luke Sewell, shortstop and catcher, formed an earlier brother combination, teaming their talents for the Indians of the '20s, while New York clubs in opposite leagues owned the Meusels—Irish with the Giants and Bob with the Yankees. Both Meusels played the outfield and hit with authority; Irish ended at .310, Bob at .309.

Tony and Billy Conigliaro, outfielders both, played together briefly with the Red Sox in the '60s, but Joe Torre, a catcher-first baseman, joined the Braves just as brother Frank left.

The brothers Dean proved to be dynamite as pitchers or talkers. Jay Hanna had acquired the nickname "Dizzy" before Paul joined him with the Gashouse Gang Cardinals of 1934. Dizzy was less than successful in hanging the nickname "Daffy" on his younger brother, but he made good his pre-season promise that they would combine for 45 victories.

Dizzy won 30 games and Paul 19—plus two apiece in the winning World Series against Detroit—and engineered a double-shutout against Brooklyn that included a nightcap no-hitter by rookie Paul. "Why didn't you tell me you wuz gonna throw a no-hitter?" asked Dizzy, who allowed three hits in his game. "I woulda throwed one too."

Joe and Dom DiMaggio were part of a three-brother tandem which played in the majors at the same time. Joe was with the Yankees, Dom with the Red Sox, and Vince with the Pirates.

## MULTIPLE BROTHERS

Hall of Famer Ed Delahanty, who played at the turn of the century, had four brothers in the majors, and veteran manager Steve O'Neill, Cleveland catcher of the World War I era, had three. There were never more than three Delahantys or two O'Neills in the majors at the same time.

## WHY TIGERS KEPT QUIET

The Detroit Tigers kept arguments to a minimum on July 14, 1972. The brother of catcher Tom Haller was plate umpire Bill Haller.

## NIEKRO BROTHERS BATTLE

When Phil Niekro (Braves) beat Joe Niekro (Cubs), 8-3, on July 5, 1967, it was the first time brothers had opposed each other as starters since Jesse Barnes (Dodgers) beat Virgil Barnes (Giants), 7-6, on May 3, 1927. The Niekros met several other times—one of them a 1-0 win for Joe with the expansion San Diego Padres of 1969.

## THE FORSCH BROTHERS

When Ken Forsch (Astros) pitched a no-hitter against Atlanta in April 1979, the Forsch family became the first to boast two brothers who had both pitched no-hitters. Brother Bob (Cardinals) had pitched a no-hit game in 1978.

# "LITTLE SHOTS"

Baseball's Hall of Fame is filled with stars—the "big shots" of diamond history. Many "little shots" who won't come close to the Hall without buying a ticket have also made an indelible mark in the game.

Jim Thorpe, track star of the 1912 Olympics at Stockholm, entered pro ball the following year when John McGraw of the Giants offered a $7500 contract—the best of five bids by the majors. Thorpe, an outfielder with no professional experience, had trouble getting along with the fiery McGraw and was sent to the minors in 1916. He promptly led the American Association with 48 stolen bases.

In 1917, Thorpe was sent to the Reds on loan because one-time McGraw ace Christy Mathewson was running that club. Thorpe's timely hit scored the only run in the famous double no-hitter between Fred Toney and Hippo Vaughn.

Two years later, with the Braves, Thorpe hit .327, his career high, in 60 games. His seven-year percentage was .252—not bad for a man who was reputed to have difficulty with the curveball.

Billy Sullivan had trouble with all kinds of pitches; he hit just .212 in his fourteen-year career. But he was such a capable catcher—handling Big Ed Walsh of the White Sox, among others—that he managed to last a long time.

Bob Hazle of the Milwaukee Braves had Sullivan's problem in reverse. Called to replace injured Billy Bruton in July, Hazle's hot bat sparked the team's pennant drive. By August 25, he was hitting .526. Players began to call him "Hurricane" Hazle after the devastating storm of 1954. "Right now the kid is Stan Musial, Mickey Mantle, and Ted Williams all wrapped up in one," said Red Schoendienst, the club's second baseman. Hazle cooled after that but still finished the season with a .403 mark. He went 2-for-13 in the World Series, however, and was even less successful after twice being hit by a pitch the following spring. On May 24, 1958, the Braves shipped Hazle and his .179 batting average to the Detroit Tigers for $30,000. He hit .241 in Detroit, then drifted out of the majors, never to return.

Unlike Hazle, Jack Reed's ticket to the majors was attached to his glove. But the third-string Yankee outfielder picked a perfect time for his only career home run. He hit it in the twenty-second inning to give the team a 9-7 win over Detroit's Phil Regan. Reed's three-year average was .233.

Jimmy Qualls established his niche in history on July 8, 1969. With his Cubs fighting the Mets for the lead in the National League East, Qualls delivered a one-out single in the ninth to deprive Tom Seaver of a perfect game. Seaver settled for a one-hit, 4-0 victory because Qualls, a .223 hitter in a career than spanned just 63 games, had delivered one of his rare hits at an inopportune time.

Seaver could have done worse; he never yielded a hit to Bill Bergen, a catcher with the Reds and Dodgers from 1901-11. He hit over .200 only once (.227 in 1903) and had a lifetime mark of .170! Imagine the reaction of pitchers who allowed him to hit safely.

## SUNDAY WAS A SWIFTEE

*Billy Sunday, later a famous evangelist, stole four bases for the Pirates against the Giants in 1890, the last of his eight seasons. He had a .258 lifetime average.*

## HOW GRIMM HANDLED GRIM GAME

*With his Chicago Cubs down by nine runs, manager Charlie Grimm, coaching at third base, dug a hole and buried his lineup card.*

## THE SPOILERS

*With Billy Pierce one out away from a perfect game in 1958, Ed Fitzgerald doubled. Ted Lyons, also with the White Sox, lost a no-hit bid when Bobby Veach singled with two gone in the ninth in 1925. Pinch-hitter Dave Harris popped a bloop single after Tommy Bridges of Detroit retired the first 26 batters in a row in 1931. Ninth-inning hits by Elston Howard off Bill Rohr (Red Sox) and by Cesar Geronimo off Phil Niekro (Braves) also deprived those pitchers of no-hitters.*

National League

**Olympic star Jim Thorpe (right), who teamed briefly with Chief Meyer as a New York Giant, hit .252 in seven seasons. His biggest hit scored the run which ended the 1917 double no-hitter between Fred Toney and Hippo Vaughn.**

# TWO-SPORT STARS

Overlapping seasons make it difficult for baseball players to tackle another professional sport, but quite a few have tried and succeeded.

Long before Bo Jackson balanced baseball and football careers, baseball players Christy Mathewson, Charlie Dressen, Rube Waddell, and Jim Thorpe also played pro football. George (Pop) Halas, who gained fame as coach of the Chicago Bears of the National Football League, hit .091 in his sole season in the majors—as the last Yankee rightfielder before Babe Ruth. Greasy Neale, who led the Philadelphia Eagles to the NFL title in 1949, hit .259 in seven full seasons as an outfielder, 1916-22.

Baseball-basketball switchers included Ron Reed, Steve Hamilton, Dick Groat, Chuck Connors, Dave DeBusschere, and Gene Conley.

DeBusschere had a 3-4 career record with the White Sox in the '60s, but the 6-6, 220-pound athlete thrived in basketball and eventually became Commissioner of the American Basketball Association. In his first year as a pro, he tried to balance a two-year, $25,000 contract from the Detroit Pistons with a $70,000 signing bonus from the White Sox. Gene Conley, center for several NBA clubs, was also a successful pitcher—and an example for DeBusschere.

"I like all sports," he said. "When it's basketball season, I like basketball, and when it's baseball season, I like baseball."

Had pro football, basketball, or hockey offered the financial promise of baseball before World War II, several key baseball figures might have opted for other sports.

Boston Red Sox slugger Jackie Jensen, American League Most Valuable Player in 1958, was an All-American football player who managed to play in both the Rose Bowl and the World Series. Chuck Essegian, who hit two pinch-homers in the Series for the 1959 Dodgers, was the only man to play in the Rose Bowl *and hit a home run* in the World Series.

In addition to Jensen and Essegian, college football stars who chose baseball as a career included Frankie Frisch, Mickey Cochrane, Jackie Robinson, and Dave Winfield. Frisch was captain of Fordham's baseball, basketball, and football teams, and Winfield starred in the same three sports at Minnesota. Cochrane topped them all; he was a five-way star at Boston University—baseball, football, basketball, track, and boxing.

John Anderson

**Versatile Mickey Cochrane was five-way star in college before becoming a star catcher in the major leagues.**

## RUTH'S ROOMIE

*Ping Bodie, in his first year with the Yankees, drew Babe Ruth as his road roommate. Ruth was seldom in the room, however. When a young writer asked Bodie who his roomie was, he replied, "Babe Ruth's suitcases."*

# BASEBALL'S FUNNY MEN

Joe Garagiola was right when he said baseball is a funny game. Baseball history is filled with practical jokes, hard-to-believe anecdotes, and one-liners that could keep a comic in business for months.

It's possible to pick an All-Star team of funny men: C-Yogi Berra; 1B-Catfish Metkovich; 2B-Germany Schaefer; SS-Rabbit Maranville; 3B-Doug Rader; OF-Babe Herman, Jim Piersall, and Ping Bodie; P-Rube Waddell, Dizzy Dean and Lefty Gomez, starters, and Sparky Lyle, Moe Drabowsky, and Billy Loes, relievers; MGR-Casey Stengel (American) and Charlie Grimm (National).

Berra, a Hall of Fame catcher who was one of three men to manage championship teams in both leagues, has always been the

## CASH WAS CUTE AGAINST ANGEL ACE

*Detroit first baseman Norm Cash, already a strikeout victim twice, tried to break up a no-hitter with a table leg in 1973. Facing the Angels' Nolan Ryan, Cash had come to the plate with the sawed-off leg of an old table in the clubhouse.*

Max Patkin (right), clowning here with lookalike Rusty Riley of the West Palm Beach Braves, never missed a show in a 30-year career that brought him into 4,000 ballparks. Once a Class A pitcher, Patkin began his series of one-night stands in 1951, and traveled more than three million miles since. He gained fame for an uncanny ability to twist his body into many odd positions.

Ray Boetel

subject of kidding because of his short, squat appearance and long nose. When the New York Mets persuaded him to come out of retirement and serve as Warren Spahn's catcher in 1965 (when Berra was 40 and Spahn 44), he was asked if he could remember any older battery. "I don't know if we'll be the oldest, but we'll certainly be the ugliest," Yogi replied.

He always came up with the right comment at the right time. As a youth, someone asked how he liked school. "Closed," Berra responded. When hometown fans honored him during his rookie year of 1947 at St. Louis' Sportsman's Park, he blurted into the mike, "I want to thank everyone for making this night necessary." Twenty-five years later, when presented with a $25 check for a radio interview with long-time announcer Jack Buck, he said, "You've known me all these years and you can't spell my name?" The check was made out to "the Bearer."

In the days of train travel, the Yankees often played "Twenty Questions." On his 19th question, Berra asked, "Is the subject living?" Told that he was, Berra then asked, "Is the subject living *now*?"

In the clubhouse, Yogi once received a message from his wife that she wouldn't be home after the game because she was going to see *Dr. Zhivago*. The catcher wondered aloud, "What's wrong now?"

Relaxing before a game, Yogi wandered up to long-time coach Frank Crosetti. "Remember the first time you saw me?" he asked.

Crosetti responded, "Sure, you were just coming out of the Navy and were wearing a sailor suit."

"I bet you didn't think I looked like a ballplayer," said Berra.

"You didn't even look like a sailor," the coach answered.

In the game, Berra often applied his wit, but he was an alert, aggressive player. One day, he questioned an umpire's call. "Turn around or I'll bite your head off," the ump stormed. "In that case," said Berra, "you'll have more brains in your stomach than you have in your head!"

When he was beaned and X-Rayed in Detroit, a writer seized the opportunity to write, "X-Rays of Berra's head showed nothing."

## RUNNING THE BASES FOR LAUGHS

*Germany Schaefer, a star early in the century, thrilled fans and intimidated rival pitchers by stealing bases in reverse. He'd single, steal second, then steal first again. He did it so often that baseball executives passed a rule requiring that the bases be run only in one direction. With that restriction, Jim Piersall ran them in the right sequence— but faced backwards—to mark his 100th home run in 1963. It was his only homer as a New York Met.*

## RADER WAS RIDICULOUS

*Third baseman Doug Rader of the Astros, interviewed on TV by former teammate Jim Bouton in the early '70s, suggested that kids eat baseball cards. "They should eat the bubblegum, the cards, first base, the mound— things of that nature," he said. "But bad statistics can't be properly digested. So they should only eat the cards of the good players."*

But Berra's proclivity to use the wrong word or say the wrong thing at times did not diminish his stature among opponents or teammates. Stengel once said of him, "Yogi is the smartest baseball man on my club. He can bat against a pitcher once and know more about him than the pitcher's mother."

Babe Herman, who compiled a .323 lifetime average in 13 seasons, had some Yogi Berra in him—plus a lot more. "I'm a serious fellow," he told Brooklyn writers. "I even read books." A reporter was ready. "What did you think of the Napoleonic Era?" he asked. "I think it should have been scored a hit," Herman replied.

The Dodger outfielder, who had a tendency to cause foul-ups on the basepaths, disdained the clown image and told the writers to get off his case. Satisfied, Herman whipped a cigar from his pocket and a writer offered to light it. "Never mind, it's already lit," said Herman, who took a puff to prove the point.

On a steamy summer day in St. Louis, he arrived at the ballpark in a pure white suit. "My, how cool you look!" said a well-dressed, well-built young woman. Herman surveyed her carefully. "You don't look too hot yourself," he replied.

Lefty Gomez, a contemporary of Herman's in the '30s, was not only a great pitcher but also a great talker. One night, he argued with Jimmie Dykes about how to pitch to a hitter with two men on base. They decided to have Mike Kelly settle the argument, but Kelly—asleep in his room—told them, "Go away. Wait until tomorrow." At that point, Gomez said, "What? And leave two men on base??"

Pitching to slugger Jimmie Foxx was easy, according to the Yankee star. "I give him my best pitch and then run to back up third."

In 1934, Gomez dominated American League pitchers, but maintained a weight of only 165 pounds. A club executive told him, "Put on ten pounds and you'll make them forget Jack Chesbro (an earlier Yankee who won 41 games in 1904)." After Gomez listened, but sank to an 11-15 record, he told the official, "Forget Chesbro? Hell, I almost made them forget Gomez."

El Goofy—a nickname he acquired for obvious reasons—went out with a bang. Traded to the lowly Boston Braves, he said, "I'm throwing twice as hard but the ball is only going half as fast."

Pitchers, as a group, seem to have a zany streak. En route to a 25-win season in 1904, Rube Waddell of the Athletics took a 1-0 lead into the ninth against Cleveland. Before anyone was out, the bases were loaded. Waddell waved in his outfielders, instructing them to sit on the fringes of the infield, while he proceeded to strike out the side.

Once, Waddell ran out the side exit of the ballpark in pursuit of a fire engine. The incident occurred between innings of a game he was pitching. When the sides changed, the A's had no pitcher. ☞

## STENGEL GAVE BROOKLYN THE BIRD

*Traded to Pittsburgh in 1918 after six years in Brooklyn, Casey Stengel was booed his first time up. In the outfield, he noticed a sparrow had caught itself on the fence. Seizing the opportunity, he tucked the bird under his cap. When he came up again, the crowd again booed—as expected. Stengel called time, stepped back, and gave a sweeping bow, allowing the bird to escape.*

## HOW MARANVILLE TRIED TO SNAP SLUMP

*Rabbit Maranville, buried in a hitting slump, came to bat against Dazzy Vance with a tennis raquet.*

## ALTROCK'S MIMIC ACT WAS TOPS

*Former pitcher Nick Altrock developed quite a reputation as a baseball clown. A marvelous mimic, he imitated the opposing third baseman from the third base coaching box in Washington.*

132

Another time, Rube woke up in a hospital bed with a monstrous hangover and numerous bandages. Asked how he got there, playful catcher Ossie Schreckengost reconstructed the situation. "You said you could fly so you opened the window and jumped," he said. He would have stopped him, said the catcher, if not for the $100 he bet he could do it.

Dizzy Dean once told his catcher to drop a foul pop. He had bet a friend that he would strike out Vince DiMaggio (Joe's brother) four consecutive times. He was working on No. 4 when DiMaggio popped up. The catcher obliged—while manager Frankie Frisch grew frantic in the dugout—and Dean completed the strikeout, winning a grand total of $80.

Manager Charley Dressen of the Dodgers wondered about one of his pitchers—Billy Loes—before the 1952 World Series against the Yankees. "The paper says you picked the Yankees to beat us in seven games," shouted the irate manager. "I was misquoted," Loes stammered. "I picked them in six games!"

Bill Lee, Red Sox southpaw of the '70s, wore No. 37 but admitted he would have preferred No. 337. "If you turn that upside down, it spells LEE," he said. "Then I could stand upside down and people would know me right away."

Yankee reliever Sparky Lyle sat on birthday cakes, sawed up chairs, and pulled a myriad of other practical jokes, but his best involved rookie pitcher Rick Sawyer. For a week, Lyle watched Sawyer's shower routine. Then, he "borrowed" his towel and

## HOW KLEIN TOPPED OTT

*Chuck Klein of the Phillies edged the Giants' Mel Ott for the home run crown in 1929 because Philadelphia pitchers issued five walks to Ott—one with the bases loaded—in the last game of the season. Klein finished with 43 homers, Ott with 42.*

## BROADCAST AWARD

*The first Ford C. Frick Award for broadcasting excellence was shared by former New York announcers Mel Allen and Red Barber. Their names were inscribed on a plaque which went on permanent display in the Baseball Hall of Fame in 1978.*

Bullpen prankster Sparky Lyle specialized in sawing off chairs.

smeared the underside with black shoe polish. He returned it to the rack exactly the way Sawyer had left it. Finished with his shower, Sawyer first dried his hands, then his face. It took him awhile to figure out why he was suddenly turning black.

Moe Drabowsky, an even more active prankster than Lyle, said he had a definite need for enjoying the lighter side. "If you think about how you're going to pitch to Roberto Clemente with the bases loaded," he said, "you'll go crazy. You have to find humor in the game."

A great imitator, Drabowsky learned the phone numbers of all the bullpens in the league and ordered opposing relievers to warm up at unusual times. He also became a specialist at giving hot-foots.

"We'd put a book of matches down by a guy's shoes, take a can of lighter fluid, and run a trail 35 feet long, around corners," he said. "All of a sudden, you'd see this flame, like a snake, approaching the guy's shoes and then a big puff of smoke. We burned the cuffs on a few pairs of pants that way."

Drabowsky—who once called Hong Kong from the bullpen and ordered takeout food for 40—has many favorite stories. The best involved star shortstop Luis Aparicio, who had a fear of crawling things.

"One day, I put a couple of small snakes into Aparicio's uniform pants pocket before he got to the clubhouse," said Drabowsky. "He put his uniform on and, as he buckled his pants, he felt something squirm in his hip pocket. I think he set an all-time record for getting undressed."

Years earlier, Leo Durocher was a victim twice—the first time as a Cardinal base-runner put out by the hidden ball trick. That night, he dined with the manager of the St. Louis hotel where he was living. Knowing Leo liked chocolate ice cream, his host had two huge portions brought to the table. The delighted Durocher dug in with enthusiasm—until his spoon struck a solid object: a hidden baseball.

Another Cardinal, Joe Medwick, once toured Europe with a group of entertainers. Granted an audience with the Pope, each visitor revealed his occupation: "I'm a singer," "I'm a dancer," and so forth. When Medwick's turn came, he said, "I'm a Cardinal."

Catfish Metkovich, who came up to the majors when Medwick was near the end of his career, also produced a one-liner of note. Returning to the Pirate bench after a strikeout at the hands of Boston's Max Surkont, Catfish complained of the "radio ball." His teammates were incredulous. "Radio ball?" they asked. "Yeah," said Metkovich. "You could hear it but you couldn't see it."

A later Pirate, good-hitting but weak-fielding Dick Stuart, was in the lineup at first base when the stadium announcer blared, "Anyone who interferes with the ball in play will be ejected from the ballpark." Pittsburgh manager Danny Murtaugh said, "I hope Stuart doesn't think that means him."

Fans have a sense of humor too. The Pirates once got a note that read: "I'm enclosing a check for two tickets for myself and my wife. The little woman has been working hard and deserves a rest. However, I'd like one ticket behind first base and one ticket behind third base. After all, I need a rest too."

## TOWEL TRICKS HELP RUNNERS

*In many old parks, bullpen occupants had better perspectives than outfielders on certain plays. The Brooklyn Dodgers assigned the man sitting closest to home on the bullpen bench to signal runners with a white towel when it was safe to advance. The team picked up many extra bases as a result.*

## PERFECT RECORD FOR DROPOUT

*John Paciorek of the 1963 Houston Colts played only one game in the major leagues. He went 3-for-3 with two walks and scored four runs as Houston beat the Mets, 13-4. His brother, Tom, later played for several clubs.*

## HITLESS WONDERS

*Who are the most frustrated batters of all time?*

*Willie Stargell is a candidate. In 1978, he broke Mickey Mantle's record of 1710 lifetime strikeouts. Bobby Bonds, who fanned 189 times for the Giants in 1970, and Dave Nicholson, with 175 for the 1963 White Sox, hold single-season "honors" in the National and American Leagues, respectively.*

*A strikeout represents only a single out—a double-play means two. In 1954, slow-footed Red Sox slugger Jackie Jensen set a one-year standard by grounding into 32 twin-killings. Ernie Lombardi of the 1938 Reds did it 30 times for the NL record.*

*The worst performance on a single day is no contest: Charles T. Pick of the Boston Braves, 0-for-11, on May 1, 1920.*

# CHAPTER NINE
# Managers

Danny Murtaugh

Connie Mack

Joe McCarthy

Walter Alston

Leo Durocher

# THE HAZARDS OF MANAGING

A major league manager is not known for his longevity. When his team fails to win the pennant—or fails to win the World Series—the disappointment of the owner and the fans is invariably vented on the manager. The only other alternative of a vengeful ownership is the outright release of the 25 players.

Managers are hired to be fired. It is the foremost baseball cliche, but also the most accurate one. The most noteworthy exception, Connie Mack, spent fifty-three seasons at the helm of the Philadelphia Athletics, but he also owned the team and certainly would not fire himself.

Not counting Mack, ten men managed in the majors for at least twenty years: John McGraw (33), Bucky Harris (29), Gene Mauch (26), Casey Stengel and Bill McKechnie (25), Joe McCarthy and Leo Durocher (24), Walter Alston (23), Jimmie Dykes (21), and Clark Griffith (20).

Since teams look for experience in selecting a manager, many men have run more than one club. Dykes ran six different teams—a record shared with Dick Williams—and was even traded for another manager when Detroit sent him to Cleveland for Joe Gordon in 1960. He failed to win a single pennant and his managerial career ended when he was axed from the Cleveland job in 1961; the trade of managers had hurt both sides.

More than 40 managers have run three teams each since the turn of the century, and Bucky Harris actually had eight terms as a pilot, including three with Washington and two with Detroit.

In six separate seasons of baseball's century, clubs operated with more than one manager. Early in 1943, Casey Stengel was struck by a car on a rainy night in Boston's Kenmore Square. Idled by a broken leg, Stengel yielded the reins temporarily to co-managers George Kelly and Robert Coleman.

The Chicago Cubs tried a rotating College of Coaches for five seasons, starting in 1961, but junked the idea when players complained they were getting conflicting advice from the rotating head

## Manager's Nightmare
### MOST CONSECUTIVE LOSSES SINCE 1900

#### AMERICAN LEAGUE

| Year | Club | Lost | Home | Rd. |
|------|------|------|------|-----|
| 1988 | Baltimore | 21 | 8 | 13 |
| 1906 | Boston | 20 | 19 | 1 |
| 1916 | Philadelphia | 20 | 1 | 19 |
| 1943 | Philadelphia | 20 | 3 | 17 |
| 1975 | Detroit | 19 | 9 | 10 |
| 1920 | Philadelphia | 18 | 0 | 18 |
| 1948 | Washington | 18 | 8 | 10 |
| 1959 | Washington | 18 | 3 | 15 |
| 1926 | Boston | 17 | 14 | 3 |
| 1907 | Boston (2 ties) | 16 | 9 | 7 |
| 1927 | Boston | 15 | 10 | 5 |
| 1937 | Philadelphia | 15 | 10 | 5 |
| 1972 | Texas | 15 | 5 | 10 |

#### NATIONAL LEAGUE

| Year | Club | Lost | Home | Rd. |
|------|------|------|------|-----|
| 1961 | Philadelphia | 23 | 6 | 17 |
| 1969 | Montreal | 20 | 12 | 8 |
| 1906 | Boston | 19 | 3 | 16 |
| 1914 | Cincinnati | 19 | 6 | 13 |
| 1962 | New York | 17 | 7 | 10 |
| 1977 | Atlanta | 17 | 3 | 14 |
| 1911 | Boston | 16 | 8 | 8 |
| 1944 | Brooklyn | 16 | 0 | 16 |
| 1909 | Boston | 15 | 0 | 15 |
| 1909 | St. Louis | 15 | 11 | 4 |
| 1927 | Boston | 15 | 0 | 15 |
| 1935 | Boston | 15 | 0 | 15 |
| 1963 | New York | 15 | 8 | 7 |

## McGRAW FINED HOMER HITTER

John McGraw of the Giants once fined Sammy Strang $25 for hitting a home run with two men on base. Strang had been ordered to bunt.

## McKECHNIE SERVED BOUDREAU WELL

When Cleveland's young player-manager, Lou Boudreau, signed veteran pilot Bill McKechnie as pitching coach, he made a master stroke. McKechnie joined the Indians in 1946 for the record coaching salary of $20,000 and all but a written affidavit that he would concentrate on pitching and refuse any future managerial offers.

Part of the reason Bill McKechnie lasted 25 years as a major league manager was the good players who surrounded him. At Cincinnati, he had the star battery of Johnny Vander Meer (center) and Ernie Lombardi (right).

coaches. In the last season before owner Phil Wrigley installed the no-manager system, Charlie Grimm began his third term at the helm but switched places with broadcaster Lou Boudreau in mid-season.

When Wrigley unveiled the coaching plan, he explained that the Cubs had tried every type of manager imaginable, from inspirational leader to slave-driver. Since 1945, when the easygoing Grimm won a pennant in his second tour of duty in Chicago, none had succeeded.

The incredible lack of job security facing the big-league manager is underlined by the fact that three pennant-winning pilots were fired after their teams lost the World Series. Bill McKechnie, an outstanding handler of pitchers, was dropped by the Cardinals in 1928, Casey Stengel by the Yankees in 1960, and Yogi Berra by the Yankees in 1964.

Stengel had won ten pennants in twelve years as manager of the Yankees, but was ostensibly dismissed because of old age (70). Never mind that Connie Mack was 88 when he resigned as the active manager of the A's in 1950. Stengel sat out a year, then took over the expansion New York Mets of the National League for their first four seasons. Eight years after Stengel retired, Yogi Berra—who followed him from the Bronx to Queens—became one of three managers to win pennants in both leagues (Joe McCarthy and Alvin Dark were the others).

Common reasons for a manager's dismissal include inability to win, failure to communicate with or control the players, availability of a better man, or less than cordial relations with ownership.

Failure to perform a manager's duties can also quicken the end. A successful pilot must establish cordial relations with the local press, keep 25 players happy even though only nine of them play at the same time, and argue with such haste and diplomacy that neither manager nor players are ejected from the game.

Frankie Frisch seemed to take unusual risks in arguing when his teams played in New York or Brooklyn, and umpires always thought the antics were deliberate so that, following ejection, he could visit his New Rochelle home, 30 minutes away.

Champion umpire baiter Leo Durocher argued loud and long, but was prepared in advance for an early exit. He had pre-arranged signs with sportswriter Barney Kremenko, who always sat in the same seat in the press box. Once thrown out of a game, Durocher would arrive in the press box and take a seat behind Kremenko. Durocher whispered, Kremenko touched his ear, and Bobby Thomson stole second. One day, with Durocher seated behind him, Kremenko innocently adjusted his glasses. The manager blew up. "You've just given the steal sign!"

Durocher lasted twenty-four seasons because he was a fiery, resourceful manager who always managed to out-think his opponent. One of his toughest rivals was Charley Dressen, manager of the Dodgers in the early '50s. Dressen was successful with the veteran Dodgers but—like many before him—struggled when he ran the Washington Senators.

One day, the Senators trailed, 22-1, with two out and nobody on base in the ninth. Pitcher Mickey McDermott suddenly announced, "Don't worry, gang. Charley will think of something!"

It was once said of Dressen, not unkindly, that he talked so much he would finish two games ahead of his club by the time the season ended. But, despite his propensity to jabber endlessly, Dressen joined Billy Martin, Rogers Hornsby, and Bucky Harris as managers of five different teams. Talent is appreciated.

## HOW MACK QUIETED ANGRY GROVE

*Long-time Philadelphia Athletics' manager Connie Mack did not swear—one reason he was not ejected from a game in a career that spanned more than fifty years. In 1929, when star pitcher Lefty Grove got ruffled after consecutive errors by Max Bishop and Jimmie Dykes, Mack decided to remove him from the game. "That will be all for you today, Robert," he said while the A's were batting. Grove, halfway down the bench, replied, "To hell with you, Mr. Mack." With that, the soft-spoken pilot stood up, walked over to Grove, and pointed. "And the hell with you too, Robert," he said. The whole bench— even Grove—laughed. The pitcher departed peacefully, laughing all the way to the clubhouse.*

## UNCLE ROBBIE HAD A FLAIR

*Hall of Famer Dazzy Vance recalled the era of Wilbert Robinson—Uncle Robbie to his players—in Brooklyn: "Robbie was not the smartest baseball man, but he was the best psychologist. His aim was to get his players in the right frame of mind and keep them that way. Before games, he held a relaxation period. He chatted and told stories and poked fun at himself and others until everyone felt at ease."*

## STENGEL GUESSED WRONG

*"You can't say I don't miss 'em when I miss 'em." That's how Casey Stengel recalled his early appraisal of lefthanded pitcher Warren Spahn when both were Boston Braves in the '40s. When Spahn refused to brush back a hitter, Stengel admonished him. "Young man," he said. "You have no guts."*

## CENTURY MARK

*Sparky Anderson and Whitey Herzog are the only managers to guide teams to 100-win seasons in both leagues.*

One of the best player-managers, Lou Boudreau of the Cleveland Indians, led his club's 1948 pennant drive. Here, he's out at the plate as Philadelphia A's catcher Mike Guerra applies the tag. Umpire is Red Jones.

# PLAYER/MANAGERS

In the early years of baseball, most managers were also active players. Some were also full or part owners of their teams, and many handled such general manager functions as trade-making and contract negotiations.

Adrian (Cap) Anson, player-manager of the Chicago National League club from 1879-97, was the game's first great showman. In an effort to attract an audience, he devised unusual uniforms, including colorful Navajo bathrobes, dark blue bloomers, form-fitting pants, and even dress suits for one game. Anson also started the practice of having players parade to the park in open barouches. An early advocate of spring training, he took his charges south in 1886. He also had more than 3,000 hits in his career.

In 1898, Brooklyn owner Charles Ebbets said he did not believe in a bench manager. He preferred a man who could lead by example—and many pilots did just that until the practice faded after the Second World War.

Connie Mack, John McGraw, Miller Huggins, and Bucky Harris were among the great all-time managers who took command while still on the active list. Managers Frank Chance of the first-place Cubs and Fred Clarke of the third-place Giants hit .319 and .309, respectively, as regular players for their teams in 1906.

Cleveland's Tris Speaker hit .388 and won the World Series in 1920.

Rogers Hornsby hit .317 as second baseman and manager of the World Champion Cardinals of 1926 and, one year earlier, hit .403 with 39 homers and 143 runs batted in after replacing Branch Rickey as manager early in the campaign.

Ty Cobb managed the Tigers six seasons without much success, but continued to hit the ball hard. In one of those years, 1922, he hit .401—high mark for a player-manager in the American League.

Other player-managers whose active careers did not diminish immediately after they assumed their double roles included Bill Terry, Gabby Hartnett, and Frankie Frisch in the National League, and Joe Cronin and Mickey Cochrane in the American League. ☞

## SEVEN ROOKIE MANAGERS WERE WORLD CHAMPS

Seven first-year managers won the World Series: Tris Speaker, 1920, Cleveland Indians; Bucky Harris, 1924, Washington Senators; Rogers Hornsby, 1926, St. Louis Cardinals; Bill Terry, 1933, New York Giants; Frankie Frisch, 1934, St. Louis Cardinals; Eddie Dyer, 1946, St. Louis Cardinals; and Ralph Houk, 1961, New York Yankees.

## FROM COLLEGE TO THE MAJORS

Though the minors is the traditional training ground of major league managers, several big-time pilots were recruited from the college ranks. Branch Rickey, coach at the University of Michigan, was named to manage the St. Louis Browns in 1913. Jack Slattery, fresh off the campus, began the '28 campaign as Boston Braves manager. Bobby Winkles left Arizona State for the California Angels in 1973. And Eddie Stanky, a former major league manager, left the University of South Alabama to take the Texas Rangers' managing job in 1977. He got homesick, however, and resigned after one day on the job.

Terry, John McGraw's successor with the New York Giants, zoomed from seventh to first in 1933, his first season as pilot, and kept the team in contention with his strategy as well as batting heroics for two more seasons.

He retired as a player in '36, however, because of bad knees. When the team sank in the standings, 10½ games from the top, in mid-July, Terry disobeyed a doctor's order and went back on the active list. He tripled home the winning run that day—launching a 15-game winning streak—as the Giants went on to win the pennant.

Probably the best example of a player-manager was Lou Boudreau, who took on the Cleveland job at the tender age of 24 in 1942. He'd only been in the majors three seasons, but thought he could translate his enthusiasm and instincts on the field into leadership his teammates would respect. In 1948, his club won the World Championship after copping the American League pennant in a one-game playoff with the Red Sox. In that game, Boudreau slammed two home runs and two singles to spark the 8-3 victory.

Boudreau was the last great player-manager. By the time Cleveland hired Frank Robinson in 1975, he was 39 years old and far off his Triple Crown form of 1966. Phil Cavaretta, with the Cubs of the early '50s; Solly Hemus, who played less than 20 games for the Cardinals in 1959; Joe Torre, who played even less for the Mets after replacing Joe Frazier in 1977; Don Kessinger, manager of the White Sox in 1979; and Pete Rose, who took over the Reds in 1984, were the only player-managers since Boudreau.

Modern baseball has become so specialized and so complex that owners expect managers to devote full attention to the game without having to worry about their own batting averages.

## FRANK ROBINSON'S DEBUT

*Player-manager Frank Robinson—the first black manager hired and later the first fired—slammed a home run in his first at-bat in the double role. The home run, on April 7, 1975, helped the Cleveland Indians defeat the New York Yankees, 5-3.*

John McGraw was called "Little Napoleon" by contemporaries who respected and feared him.

# GREAT MANAGERS

When the Brooklyn Dodgers elevated Walter Alston, the manager of their Triple-A farm at Montreal, to the major league job in November 1953, he explained his philosophy of managing to the press.

An off-season biology and industrial arts teacher in his native Ohio, Alston said: "Teaching students is very much like managing baseball players. You've got to encourage some, you've got to drive others, if you are going to get the best out of every individual."

Alston's technique worked with a variety of Dodger teams. In twenty-three seasons, he won seven pennants and four World Championships—some with good-hitting clubs, others with teams molded around speed, pitching, and defense. His ability to change as the team changed made him a great manager.

The same can be said for John McGraw, Casey Stengel, Connie Mack, and Joe McCarthy—the only managers to win more often than Alston. McGraw and Stengel won ten pennants each, Mack and McCarthy nine. McCarthy and Stengel were World Champions seven times each and Mack five times.

"McGraw, Mack, and McCarthy were the best managers I ever saw," said sportswriter Grantland Rice, a journalistic star of the Babe Ruth era. "Miller Huggins is up there too. You must also include Billy Southworth, Bucky Harris, and Casey Stengel. McGraw was as colorful as any manager in baseball. There were few dull moments at the Polo Grounds when he was leading the Giants. 'Little Napoleon' was a fitting nickname." ☞

Huggins ran the Yankees from 1918 until his death in 1929, and was more referee than manager. The ballclub was populated by talented but independent ballplayers who often disobeyed training rules and directives from management. Babe Ruth was a prime offender.

The 5-6, 140-pound Huggins was no physical match for any of his players—especially the 6-2, 215-pound Ruth. But the manager slapped his star with an indefinite suspension and a $5,000 fine for a series of infractions in 1925.

Ruth rebelled. "People have been asking me what the trouble is with this team," he said. "I haven't wanted to say it before, but I will now. The trouble with the team is Huggins. I think we have the best team in the league this year and look where we are."

Yankee management backed the field pilot—even after Ruth unleashed a him-or-me ultimatum. "Huggins will be the manager as long as he wants to be," said Col. Jacob Ruppert, the team's owner. "You can see where we stand and where Ruth stands."

The team finished seventh that season, but Huggins rallied the troops to win three consecutive pennants. Swirling controversy took its toll on the fragile pilot, however, and he died at age 50 shortly before the end of the 1929 campaign.

Huggins and other successful managers incorporated ideas first advanced by John McGraw with the Giants. The fiery third baseman, with a .334 lifetime average, ran the team thirty years— 1902-32—and preached an aggressive approach, in attitude as well as technique.

His teams used the bunt and hit-and-run, developed defenses on rival hitters, and employed the first pinch-hitters and relief pitchers. A fighter who stuck up for his players but exercised absolute authority over them, McGraw actually developed a hatred of his opponents on the field—though he was friendly with many of them away from the ballpark.

McGraw's driving spirit produced 10 pennants and 10 second-place finishes. He won 2,840 games, more than any National League manager. Connie Mack, eschewing McGraw's stormy technique, led the majors with 3,776 victories in his fifty-three seasons. That may be the safest record in sports.

"Talent comprises 75 per cent of managing," said Mack. "Strategy is 12½ per cent and the other 12½ per cent is comprised of what a manager can get out of his team."

Mack, one of few managers who wore street clothes in the dugout (he preferred high starch collars), thought the gentlemanly approach would produce the best results. Many of his players regarded him as a father figure—especially during the eighteen seasons he managed after the age of 70.

Though he was occasionally sarcastic, he rarely uttered a foul word or even a negative comment about anyone else. The soft-spoken manager called on a computerlike memory and sixth sense of baseball wisdom to win games.

Joe McCarthy won one pennant with the Cubs and eight with the Yankees. He had two near-misses with the Boston Red Sox in 1948-49, ending his career just as Casey Stengel was winning his first of a record five consecutive World Series with the Yankees.

Overloaded with talent on the Yankees, Jimmie Dykes called McCarthy a "push-button manager," implying that anyone could do the job and suggesting that the team probably could win without a manager. ☞

## DYKES SHOVED MACK

*Jimmy Dykes, who became manager of the Philadelphia Athletics in 1951 after Connie Mack ended a tenure that began in 1903, once pushed his predecessor into a pile of bats.*

*It happened during the 10-run explosion of the A's in the seventh inning of the fourth game in the 1929 World Series against the Cubs. Chicago led, 8-0, before the outburst.*

*As the eighth run crossed for Philadelphia, the excited Dykes screamed, "We're tied; we're tied!" He pounded the man next to him so hard that he fell off the bench and into a pile of bats. Only his legs were visible.*

*Dykes, then a 32-year-old utility infielder, suddenly realized who he had pushed. "I pulled him out and said—very apologetically —'Gosh, Mr. Mack, I'm awfully sorry,' " Dykes recalled. "He said, 'Don't worry, Jimmy. Right now anything goes.' "*

## THE VITT REBELLION

*Dissension causes problems for any ballclub, and many teams have lost pennants because players and manager could not get along. "Failure to communicate" is often the rationale for dismissing a manager.*

*In 1940, Cleveland Indians manager Oscar Vitt was so disliked that a band of players asked club owner Alva Bradley to release him. He refused and the team lost the pennant on the last weekend of the season. The following year, with Vitt replaced by Roger Peckinpaugh, the club dropped from a strong second to a weak fourth.*

## FRISCH GOT PAY CUT FOR TWO JOBS

*Frankie Frisch made $18,500 as player-manager of the 1934 St. Louis Cardinals— double the salary of any other player—but considerably below his peak pay of $28,000, which he earned strictly as a player.*

Bucky Harris, who once worked in a coal mine, managed 29 years but lost more often than he won.

But McCarthy, who never played in the majors, preferred a low-key image and developed it to perfection. Controversy was at a minimum under his administration, but winning was at a maximum. Clubhouse disputes were settled quietly, but players who didn't show enough interest in the game were moved quickly.

"Guys who rush in and out of the clubhouse rush in and out of the big leagues," he said.

McCarthy couldn't afford to move Babe Ruth's big bat, but he was often tempted. Ruth resented McCarthy because the slugger coveted the Yankee managing job for himself.

Ted Williams, the great Red Sox star, played three seasons for McCarthy and liked the businesslike pilot. "He was the best manager I ever saw," said Williams, later a manager himself (and winner of the Manager of the Year Award at Washington in 1969). "McCarthy was always on top of the game and knew the limits and abilities of all his players."

McCarthy's .614 winning percentage underscores that point. No manager has ever done better.

# BUCKY HARRIS

Bucky Harris was a 27-year-old second baseman in his fourth major league season when he was appointed manager of the Washington Senators in 1924. When he proceeded to win the pennant and the World Series, the press referred to him as "the boy wonder" and the name remained with him through twenty-nine seasons as a big-league manager.

The 5-9, 155-pound Harris was credited with keeping the Griffith family in baseball because of his heroics as a rookie pilot. Washington attendance jumped from 357,046 in 1923 to 584,310 in 1924 and enabled Clark Griffith, the owner (and manager through 1920), to purchase a $125,000 home—an enormous price in any era. Harris got a $30,000 contract—a vast improvement over the 16 cents per hour he once earned as car-coupler in a coal mine.

He won a second consecutive flag in 1925, but lost a seven-game World Series when he allowed star pitcher Walter Johnson to absorb a 15-hit beating in the finale. Johnson, then 37, was pitching against Pittsburgh on a dark, rainy day but had a 6-4 lead going into the last of the seventh. The Pirates scored twice to tie, but Washington forged ahead, 7-6, in the eighth. In the home half, with the tired Johnson remaining on the mound, Pittsburgh scored three more to win, 9-7.

American League president Ban Johnson wired Harris that he should have replaced the veteran pitcher. The manager responded, "I went down with my best." The line has become a baseball classic.

Harris won another World Championship with the 1947 Yankees, and finished third, 2½ games behind, with the same club the following year, but new ownership replaced him with Casey Stengel, a two-time National League failure. Almost immediately, Harris returned to Washington for his third stint with that club. He had five other terms elsewhere, including two with Detroit.

"I was no genius," he always said. "If you don't have the players, you can't win." Harris' career winning percentage was .493.

# CASEY STENGEL

Stengel sacrificed a potential career as a lefthanded dentist from Kansas City (the "KC" initials inspired his nickname) to become one of the best managers in baseball history.

A disciple of the Giants' John McGraw, his manager in the '20s, Stengel earned a well-deserved reputation as a strategist as well as a showman. He employed McGraw's win-at-all-costs tactics and proved the platoon system practical as manager of the talent-rich Yankees from 1949-60, but relied on his clowning instincts to keep fans happy when he ran bad ballclubs with the Brooklyn Dodgers, Boston Braves, and New York Mets.

Stengel played for five National League clubs, starting with the 1912 Dodgers and ending with the 1925 Braves, and launched his major league managerial career with Brooklyn in 1934. He managed for seven minor league seasons before reaching the majors and returned to the minors for five more years in the '40s before landing the Yankee job in 1949.

Just as Stengel was influenced by McGraw, several modern managers—notably Billy Martin, Ralph Houk, and Whitey Herzog—were influenced by Stengel. That influence stems from Stengel's Yankee years, when he won ten pennants and finished second once and third once.

Under his platoon system, Stengel's daily lineup was unpredictable. A few players—like Joe DiMaggio and later Mickey Mantle—played every day, but most of the others moved up and down the lineup and played a variety of positions. When he had the league's best catchers, Yogi Berra and Elston Howard, Stengel kept both bats in the lineup by using one of them at first base or in the outfield. Hank Bauer batted anywhere from first to eighth but swung a big bat, and Gil McDougald was an infield regular who starred at three different positions.

Though platooned players disliked the concept, many admitted years later that Stengel's maneuvering was wise. The veteran manager had an excellent memory, a mental book on all rival players, and exceptional baseball instincts. He knew when to play percentage baseball—inserting a lefthanded pinch-hitter against a righthanded reliever, for example—and also when to go against "the book." In 1958, Stengel's Yankees became one of the few teams in baseball history to overcome a 3-1 deficit and win the World Series.

Stengel's fractured English, which he poured out in endless interviews with a delighted press corps, coupled with his genius to earn him the nickname, "The Old Perfessor." But he was adept at making himself perfectly clear in the clubhouse.

Far from the buffoon image he projected, Casey was a fighter—a quality inherited from the McGraw years. As Brooklyn manager in the '30s, he battled Leo Durocher, St. Louis shortstop and later a manager himself, after a fierce argument on the field. Stengel said he won by using his "famous punch to the kneecap."

Once, riding the trolley home from Ebbets Field, he saw a Dodger player disciplining one of his children on the sidewalk. The child had swiped some fruit from an open stand, but all Stengel knew was that the player had gone hitless that afternoon. Casey leaned out and yelled, "You go 0-for-4 and take it out on the kid, huh?"

Brooklyn was also the place where Stengel doffed his cap to the crowd in a grand, sweeping gesture as a concealed sparrow flew out. When he slid into second with a man already there, he was fined $50 ☞

Mickey Mantle's batting feats had much to do with Casey Stengel's success as manager of the Yankees. He won 10 pennants in twelve years.

## PLAYER-MANAGERS FACED EXTRA PROBLEM

In addition to the usual job risk faced by any major league manager, player-pilots knew they could be traded at any time. Rogers Hornsby was one of several who lost their managing jobs when they were traded. Hornsby led the St. Louis Cardinals to the World Championship in 1926, but was traded to the New York Giants after the season ended.

## HUGH JENNINGS DEFENDED YOUNG COBB

When young, outspoken Ty Cobb had a hard time with veterans on the Tigers, manager Hugh Jennings—a champion in his first three seasons (1907-08-09)—ended the discussion. "Cobb is going to be a great player," he said, "and he is not going to be driven off this club if I have to fire everybody but him and start over!"

and censured by Brooklyn president Charles Ebbets, who said, "Stengel is the world's greatest ballplayer—from the neck down."

As a minor league outfielder, Casey entertained fans by sliding into his defensive position in center field. An insane asylum was located right behind the ballpark and, after one inning, his manager pointed to the building and said, "It's only a matter of time, Stengel."

It was also in the minors that Stengel encountered a manhole in right field. During one boring game, he climbed in. Almost immediately, the batter hit a high fly to right. Stengel lifted the cover with his bare hand and caught the ball in his glove.

Though Stengel and McGraw formed a mutual admiration society, the dictatorial Giants' manager did not share Casey's penchant for clowning. But Stengel, who compiled a .284 batting average in fourteen seasons, was a solid player. After he hit two key home runs in the 1923 World Series, Casey announced, "The Series stands two games for the Yankees and two for Stengel. What happened to the Giants?"

Fun-loving Stengel spent his nights on the town with Irish Meusel, but the pair deliberately went separate ways when they discovered McGraw had put a tail on them. Stengel told the manager he would have to hire separate detectives. "I ain't gonna save this ballclub no more money by doubling up," he said.

In later years, Casey proved an engaging after-dinner speaker, constantly in demand on the winter banquet tour. He recalled thousands of incidents in detail and hardly needed to exaggerate; his run-on sentences and twisted grammar, known as Stengelese, were entertaining in their own right.

When it came to winning, however, Casey Stengel was all business. Upset with an umpire in Boston, he took off his uniform shirt and thrust it forward. "Wear this and play on our team for a while," he told the startled official.

In Boston and Brooklyn, Stengel twice finished fifth in the eight-team league. (Miraculously, he never finished last.) In New York, he was a roaring success—with the Yankees, who had an excellent farm system and veteran nucleus, and with the Mets, who relied on entertainment and nostalgia in their early years.

Stengel had litle to work with as manager of the original New York Mets in 1962 —but he did provide entertainment for the fans and the news media.

## FRACTURED PERFESSER

One must assess and peruse the talent astutely from out fount of experience we should contrive to assemble an aggregate of proven aptitude, and that's no euphemism we'll imbue spirit and insist on utmost effort and I say, unequivocally, we will finish 'ER-R-R, WOULD YOU MIND REPEATING THAT?'

# LEO DUROCHER

Leo Durocher's 24-year managerial career began with the 1939 Brooklyn Dodgers and ended with the 1973 Houston Astros. In between, he managed the New York Giants and Chicago Cubs.

A fiery competitor who compiled a .247 lifetime average, over fifteen full seasons, Durocher established an early reputation as a fighter when he shoved Babe Ruth into a locker before Ruth could make good on a threat to punch him. The incident occurred when both were with Brooklyn—Durocher finishing his playing career and Ruth serving as a symbolic coach who didn't flash signs.

As a manager, Durocher's name was always in headlines. He was the pilot of the "miracle" New York Giants, who made the most dramatic comeback in the game's history to win the 1951 pennant, and was credited with the development of Willie Mays.

A champion umpire baiter and friend of many celebrities, the erudite and controversial pilot was suspended for the entire 1947 season by Commissioner Happy Chandler for reasons that were never specified. He returned to his job as Brooklyn manager in 1948, but shocked the world in mid-July when he suddenly resigned to become manager of his arch rival, the New York Giants.

In New York, he engineered one of the most stunning upsets in World Series history—a four-game sweep of the Cleveland Indians in 1954.

Durocher transformed the Giants from a collection of slow-footed sluggers to a team with championship defense, adequate speed, and strong pitching to accompany the big bats. The Giants hit 179 home runs in 1951—opposed to 221 in 1947—but won 17 more games.

After an eleven-year hiatus from the field, Durocher became the first manager of the Chicago Cubs after a five-year experiment with the coaching college ended after the 1965 season, and jacked the club into contender status after finishing last in '66.

Chicago seemed to have the National League East championship locked up by August 1969, but the team wilted in the summer heat (the Cubs play only day games at home) and finished second, eight lengths behind the miracle Mets. They were closer in 1970—five games behind Pittsburgh. ☞

Leo Durocher rebuilt the Cubs after the team junked its five-year experiment with a board of rotating head coaches.

## DUROCHER'S ATTITUDE

*"I don't give a hoot whether a guy likes me or not. I don't care what he does off the field or what kind of problems he creates for other people. If he comes to play, that's all I ask."*

*—Leo Durocher on managing*

## DUROCHER DEVOURED LITERATURE

*Leo Durocher was an avid reader who relaxed by reading one mystery and a more serious volume each night.*

Durocher, a teammate of Babe Ruth's with the Yankees, pushed the slugger into a locker after both had moved to Brooklyn.

Durocher didn't have the personnel to win at Houston, where he transferred immediately after leaving the Cubs in mid-season of 1972, and retired the following year with a parting shot at the high-priced modern player.

"When I played," he said, "the manager said 'Sit down, shut up and listen.' Today, the players look you right in the eye and say, 'How dare you talk to me that way? I make $100,000.' "

Durocher, hardly one to be intimidated by his employees, did not like the new breed. He played and managed with military precision, battling opponents as if they were using bullets instead of baseballs.

Once, referring to Mel Ott, the man he later succeeded as Giants' manager, Durocher said, "See Ott? He's a nice guy. And nice guys finish last."

The phrase became baseball's most famous quote, as well as the title of Durocher's book. It is now found in the pages of *Bartlett's Familiar Quotations.*

Durocher was intelligent, articulate, even suave, but could never have been accused of being a nice guy on the field. Umpires expected to do battle with him—though occasionally his encounters were designed for showmanship rather than argument.

"A lot of times," remembered former Brooklyn pitcher Clyde King, "he'd run out, make a lot of motion with his hands, kick the ground, and run back. He felt it would help the club. He wanted to make the umpire bear down. Maybe he was arguing for the *next* close play.

"Leo would do anything to win. I admired him as a manager—he was a good manager—and he was great to me as a young player.

"One day when I was pitching, I was sitting near Durocher and his coaches when there was a close play at first base. I said, 'Hey, Skip, I thought he was safe.' Durocher looked at me and said, 'I thought he was out.'

"That indicated to me that Leo did not argue unless he really thought he was right."

# AL LOPEZ

While Casey Stengel was managing the Yankees to ten pennants in twelve seasons, 1949-60, the only manager who beat him was Al Lopez—first with the 1954 Cleveland Indians, later with the 1959 Chicago White Sox.

A former catcher who was a tremendous handler of pitchers, Lopez patterned himself after Bill McKechnie, his manager with the Boston Braves in the '30s.

"Bill taught me the secret of success is earning the respect of your men," said Lopez, who advocated quiet, stable leadership. "Respect and good pitching. Bill never overworked a pitcher. Whenever a pitcher's turn came up to start, he was well-rested and as ready to work as a man could be.

"McKechnie knew the capabilities of his bullpen better than any manager I ever saw. He knew his relievers so well that he always had the right man ready for the right spot. And the man's arm was always fresh and strong. Bill also had amazing patience. 'A hasty decision,' he used to say, 'is usually a mistake.' "

Lopez made a career of finishing second—he did it ten times—because his teams had pitching that was equal to or better than what

☞

## FRANKIE FRISCH ON JOHN McGRAW

Frankie Frisch, captain of the New York Giants and later a three-time manager of other clubs, said John McGraw was a great influence on him. "We swashbuckled, baited umps, roared, roasted, and rattled our own players and almost everyone else," Frisch recalled. "We swore. Everyone in baseball swore then. McGraw himself was the world's greatest user of four-letter words. When he ran out of the shopworn kind, he invented a few of his own."

## A HUG AT THIRD HURT BROOKLYN

Uncle Wilbert Robinson was managing the Brooklyn Dodgers in the early '20s. One day, with the team in a ninth-inning tie, Zack Taylor hit the ball over the centerfielder's head. As he rounded third, Robinson, coaching there, grabbed him in a big congratulatory bear hug. The throw came to the base and Taylor was tagged out.

## McGRAW BEAT GIANTS IN DEBUT AS PILOT

John McGraw, 26, beat the New York Giants, 5-3, on April 18, 1899, in his debut as manager of the National League's Baltimore Orioles.

Mild-mannered Al Lopez (right) finished second 10 times with the help of players like Herb Score (left) and Ralph Kiner. Lopez went all the way with the 1954 Indians and 1959 White Sox.

the Yankees had. But superior hitting and, occasionally, better defense allowed New York to prevail.

Like McKechnie, Lopez was a sharp judge of talent who maintained a rapid shuttle between majors and minors. He got good mileage out of old arms by telling his pitchers to forget earned run averages and pace themselves. The '59 White Sox featured 39-year-old Early Wynn (22-10) as the top starter and NL rejects Gerry Staley, 38, and Turk Lown, 35, as the top relievers. A punch-and-judy attack led by Nellie Fox and Luis Aparicio paced the offense.

Wynn was 34 and Bob Feller 35 when the Indians rolled up an AL record 111 victories in 1954, but Mike Garcia, 30, and Bob Lemon, 33, were at the top of their game. This foursome—together seven years—was probably the best starting quartet in the history of the game.

In their seven seasons together, Lemon won 20 five times, Wynn three times, Garcia twice, and Feller once. Lopez was their manager in five of those seasons, 1951-55.

The son of a Spanish immigrant who made cigars in Tampa, Lopez said he could not compare his pennant-winning clubs—except in spirit. Lopez had both spirit and pride. He actually declined an offer to manage the talent-rich Yankees in 1961 because he would not succeed his friend, Casey Stengel. Beating him was one thing; taking his job was something else.

Paul Richards, who had two terms as manager of the White Sox, was expert at handling pitchers.

## TEN COMMANDMENTS FOR SUCCESS IN THE MAJORS
### By Joe McCarthy

1. *Nobody ever became a ballplayer by walking after a ball.*
2. *You will never become a .300 hitter unless you take the bat off your shoulder.*
3. *An outfielder who throws back of a runner is locking the barn after the horse is stolen.*
4. *Keep your head up and you may not have to keep it down.*
5. *When you start to slide, slide. He who changes his mind may have to change a good leg for a bad one.*
6. *Do not alibi on bad hops. Anybody can field the good ones.*
7. *Always run them out. You never can tell.*
8. *Do not quit.*
9. *Do not fight too much with the umpires. You cannot expect them to be as perfect as you are.*
10. *A pitcher who hasn't control hasn't anything.*

# PAUL RICHARDS

Like Al Lopez, Paul Richards was a catcher with a reputation for getting the most out of his pitchers.

He inherited a sixth-place club in Chicago when he accepted his first job as manager with the 1951 White Sox, and immediately cut the team's "games behind" column from 38 games to 17. Richards moved the Sox up another notch in 1952 for the first of three consecutive third-place finishes.

Richards was so impressive that the Baltimore Orioles, one year removed from St. Louis, gave him the dual job of manager and general manager before the 1955 season opened. He nurtured the team's young, inexperienced players and developed several stars, including Brooks Robinson, an 18-year-old third baseman who broke in with the O's during Richards' first season there.

"If any man knows more about pitching than Paul Richards, he's in hiding," said White Sox general manager Frank Lane, who gave Richards his first managing job.

When the Orioles emerged as full-fledged contenders in 1960, they did it with a starting rotation whose leader, Chuck Estrada, was 22 years old. Other members of the Big Four were Milt Pappas, Jack Fisher, and Steve Barber, all 21.

Richards taught his "Kiddie Korps" how to pace themselves, how to hold runners on base, and how to throw various pitches. His pet project was the slip pitch, though he knew the ins and outs of the knuckleball too. Veteran Hoyt Wilhelm was 36 when the Orioles finished second in 1960, eight games behind the Yankees, and catcher Gus Triandos reduced his league-leading number of passed balls by using an oversized mitt Richards had developed just for the knuckler.  ☞

Several years earlier, when Richards asked Wilhelm to start, the veteran relief pitcher responded with a 1958 no-hitter against the Yankees and a league-leading 2.19 ERA the following summer.

Richards left the Orioles late in the 1961 campaign to try a new challenge with the Houston Astros, a National League expansion club. He later moved from Houston's front office to Atlanta's, but had problems with veteran stars Joe Torre, whom he traded, and Clete Boyer, whom he released.

When Bill Veeck, an old admirer, purchased the White Sox in 1976, Richards joined the syndicate and agreed to serve as field manager that season before returning to the front office.

## JOE McCARTHY ON MANAGING

*Long-time manager Joe McCarthy, who left the game in 1949, usually enjoyed his job. "Sometimes I think I'm in the greatest business in the world," he said. "Then I lose four straight and want to change places with a farmer."*

# WALTER ALSTON

Only Connie Mack (Athletics) and John McGraw (Giants) managed one club longer than Walter Alston, who guided the Dodgers for twenty-three years from 1954-76.

Alston won the Associated Press Manager-of-the-Year award six times, was the winning manager in a record seven All-Star Games, and finished first or second in fifteen seasons.

Known as "The Quiet Man," Alston was a former schoolteacher who believed in treating his players like men. He scolded when he had to—never publicly—and kept aloof from his athletes.

Alston batted only once in the majors—he struck out with the St. Louis Cardinals in 1936—but was adept at handling other major-leaguers, including "The Boys of Summer" who played for the Brooklyn teams of the '50s. When he became Dodger manager, the New York press asked—in print—"WALTER WHO?"

Charley Dressen preceded Alston as Brooklyn pilot—and won consecutive pennants after the agonizing last-ditch defeat of the 1951 playoffs—but lost his job by insisting on a multi-year contract. Alston held onto his by signing 23 consecutive one-year contracts and surviving even when his coaching staff included former Dodger pilot Leo Durocher.

When the Dodgers finished seventh in 1958, their first Los Angeles season, and eighth in 1967, after the retirement of Sandy Koufax and the trades of Maury Wills and Tommy Davis, the media screamed for Alston's scalp. Calmer—and apparently wiser—heads prevailed.

Alston made the most of his talent, which varied greatly from year to year. He paraded nearly 50 third basemen before discovering Ron Cey and frequently resorted to left-right platoons. "When I had Gil Hodges, Jackie Robinson, and Duke Snider in Brooklyn," he said, "I didn't have to platoon. Give me a lineup like that and I won't."

Alston's outer calm didn't fool his players. The veteran manager commanded respect and performance. Those who didn't do the job were traded, sent to the minors, or even challenged to fist-fights under the stands.

Walter Alston provided such stability that the Dodger organization won a reputation as being the best in baseball. Rivals longed to play in Los Angeles and coaches used their Dodger credentials to jump to vacant managing slots elsewhere.

Among Alston coaches who became major league managers were Preston Gomez, Danny Ozark, and Tom Lasorda.

Walter Alston was almost unknown when he became Dodger manager in 1954, but he lasted 23 seasons in the job.

## TRADE MANDATES SIGNAL CHANGE

*Teams must change their signals—or risk having them stolen—after every trade they make. Many clubs have individual signals for each player. Some use a count sign; the players may receive his signal on the third movement. Others use an indicator signal that something big is coming, while others simply use a key signal followed by the actual signal.*

# MODERN MANAGERS

"Today's manager must be a psychiatrist as well as a baseball strategist. Many games have been won by figuring out what a player is thinking and how a pat on the back is much better than a kick in the rear. Maybe the old-time managers could give an inflexible order, but today's players don't roll over that easily. A manager must think of his player as an individual with completely different problems from any other player."

The words were spoken by Dick Williams, manager of the Montreal Expos and former boss of the Boston Red Sox, Oakland A's, and California Angels. Once a strict disciplinarian, Williams has mellowed in his approach to his players, but not in his approach to winning ball games.

"I was a no-good horse's tail at Boston," he conceded. "I had to be. Hell, I'd been one of them as a player there in '63 and '64. I'd been caught for curfew myself. I didn't win any friends, but nobody turned down the World Series checks."

Williams won again with the Oakland A's of 1972 and 1973—and took those clubs to the World Championship. On national television, 1973 MVP Reggie Jackson indicated Williams and said, "The man on my left taught me to win. He didn't give me pep talks but he taught me to win in the last two years and last two days."

The talented manager has always been sarcastic and outspoken, as well as fiercely independent. He resigned the Oakland job because of constant interference from owner Charles O. Finley, who doubled as general manager.

Another veteran pilot, Gene Mauch, began his managing career at Philadelphia in 1960.

Mauch and Williams are similar types. Both have been accused of "overmanaging," but both dispute the suggestion. Their moves are unpredictable and they want to keep that reputation, since it puts the opposition on the defensive. Williams said a bad manager can cost a team up to two-dozen ball games.

While Williams has used a four-man platoon at second base, a stream of pinch-hitters, pinch-runners, and relief pitchers, and assorted trick plays, Mauch calls on a vast storebank of baseball knowledge. Called "the Little General" when he preceded Williams in Montreal, Mauch is reputed to know the rule book better than most umpires.

"When the game starts, you throw away the book and make your decisions according to the situation," he said in 1973. "There's no cut-and-dried strategy. It varies from game to game and situation to situation."

Mauch keeps constant tabs on rivals by reviewing box scores and digesting past histories, including such statistics as weather information, trends, and other data. He is literally a walking computer, in addition to being a keen student of the game.

"Ask him to recall any situation in a game years ago and he'll tell you the count, where the pitch was, what it was, and who hit it," said Montreal executive Jim Fanning after Mauch left for Minnesota. "He'll not only do it, but he'll use all of that to beat you."

An admiring rival, three-time manager Dave Bristol, once coached for Mauch. "You have to start managing against him when your plane lands in town," Bristol said.

Mauch, like Williams, was a utility infielder for several clubs. Both sat and observed the men calling the shots. ☞

Dick Williams directed "The Impossible Dream" pennant of the 1967 Boston Red Sox and later enjoyed success at Oakland, Montreal, and San Diego.

After a highly successful career as manager of the Cincinnati Reds, one-time infielder Sparky Anderson signed a five-year contract to pilot the Detroit Tigers in June 1979.

Though his record for futility was unmatched among managers (no pennants in 26 years), Gene Mauch was considered a walking computer by dugout rivals.

Earl Weaver, who retired as Baltimore Orioles manager after the 1986 season, recorded a .583 winning percentage during 17 seasons on the job.

Billy Martin is another infielder-turned-manager. A volatile disposition and tendency to cross the front office cost Martin jobs in Detroit, Minnesota, and Texas before he won two consecutive pennants with his old team, the New York Yankees, in 1976-77.

Martin has won divisional championships with the Twins, Tigers, and Athletics, and brought the Rangers home as surprise runners-up, thereby establishing an unchallenged reputation as a winning manager. Martin, like Tom Lasorda of the Los Angeles Dodgers, gets closer to his players than many of his contemporaries.

"Billy Martin is a man's manager," said Jeff Burroughs, who won the Most Valuable Player Award when Martin managed him at Texas in 1974. "He treats you like a man, sticks up for you on and off the field, and teaches you how to win. He was a little peppery second baseman who didn't have all the natural athletic tools to become a superstar, but he worked hard and learned all the little things about the game to help the team win.

"After he became a manager, he just applied his concept of a ballplayer and things worked out real well for him. He's won everywhere he's gone because he makes his team play as a unit. He doesn't really care how the individuals do. The main thing is the team. He loves his ballplayers, but he knows the No. 1 thing is to win."

Frank Quilici, who managed the Twins briefly, also admires Martin. "Billy's the type of guy who just gets enraptured with the ball game," said Quilici, who played for Martin when the Twins won the AL Western flag in 1969. "He's a very smart baseball man, he's very intense, and he's a perfectionist. That's what he tries to get out of his players."

Earl Weaver, who became manager of the Baltimore Orioles in July 1968, is another manager who accomplishes major miracles—sometimes with minor talent. When the Orioles lost regulars Bobby Grich and Reggie Jackson plus 20-game winner Wayne Garland after the 1976 season, the media predicted Weaver's wonders would cease. But the Birds finished second, tied with Boston at 2½ games out of first.

Weaver finished third once—in 1972—in his first ten seasons. In five of those ten, he won a divisional title. Three times, 1969-70-71, Baltimore advanced to the World Series. Weaver won the World Championship in 1970.

"People often talk about how many games a manager can win, but what wins games is how the players perform," Weaver insisted. "When the manager makes out a lineup card, chooses a pinch-hitter or makes a pitching change, he's playing a part in the game.

"Knowing when to get a guy out of the lineup is probably one of the most important, and toughest, parts of managing. If a guy goes hitless in four or five games and you take him out, did you make a mistake only the last time you played him, or every time? Did you make a mistake because he might be ready to break loose? Getting a guy out of the lineup at the right time is important, but it's just as important to have him in at the right time."

Weaver realized the Orioles were changing, and he changed to meet the revised roster of players. He developed exceptional patience with young players, almost reliving his days as a successful minor league pilot in a productive farm system. A major success, in 1977, was pitcher Mike Flanagan, who lost eight of his first ten decisions. Weaver kept him in rotation and watched him win 12 of his next 14, and become an All-Star pitcher in 1978. ☞

*149*

"I just had to have faith," he said. When the Orioles' holdover veterans and half-dozen rookies meshed in 1977, the team surprised all observers and generated two pleasant surprises for Weaver: a three-year contract and the Manager of the Year Award.

Sparky Anderson, like Weaver, became an instant success after taking command of the Cincinnati Reds in 1970. Anderson was one of 19 managers to win a pennant in his first season. He won five divisional titles (four pennants and two World Series) in his first eight years and twice finished second. His Reds averaged 96 wins per year in that span.

## MANAGER TED WILLIAMS

*Former Red Sox slugger Ted Williams was named Manager of the Year in the American League in 1969, his first year as a pilot, when he improved the Washington Senators' winning percentage from .404 to .531. It was the best of his four seasons with the team, including one in Dallas-Fort Worth after the Senators became the Texas Rangers.*

New York Giants manager John McGraw (left) greets counterpart Hal Chase of the Yankees before a game in 1912.

National League

# MANAGERIAL STRATEGY

There are various aspects to managerial strategy. First, the manager must field a team of alert, aggressive players. To keep his athletes that way, curfew rules have become universal in baseball.

John McGraw's early Giants adhered to an 11:30 p.m. curfew on the road and a midnight curfew at home—in season, of course.

Rogers Hornsby devised an ingenious way to catch violators. One night, he handed the only elevator operator a brand-new ball at the stroke of midnight. He bribed the man to get the signature of every player he saw that night—and then hand in the ball the next morning.

Gil Hodges told his players on the Washington Senators that anyone out after curfew the previous evening was to put $100 in the empty cigar box in his office. He said he could name four offenders. When he looked in his box later, he counted $700.

In addition to keeping his team in prime physical condition, a good manager must (1) know the capabilities—as well as the potential—of each man; (2) provide strong, but not overbearing, leadership; (3) have thorough understanding of the rules and how they can be used to best advantage; (4) communicate well with his players—particularly the pitchers; (5) know the weaknesses of rivals; (6) be able to deal with his own front office; and (7) maintain smooth relations with the media.

It is difficult to keep bench-warmers happy, because every player thinks he should play every day. But the manager who can convince an athlete he's more valuable in a reserve role will be better off.

Art Shamsky of the Cincinnati Reds was a prime example of a productive reserve. A lefthanded-hitting outfielder, Shamsky came off the bench on August 12, 1966 to pinch-hit a home run in the eighth. He stayed in the game, and homered again in the tenth and eleventh.

Shamsky didn't play the following day because the opposition started a lefthanded pitcher, but he was back in action a day later, with a righthander working. The slugging substitute connected in his first time up for his fourth consecutive home run, tying a major league record.

Platooning has been part of baseball since George Stallings worked the left-right percentage to his advantage with the World Champion Boston Braves of 1914. Tris Speaker won a world title for Cleveland by platooning at first base and in two outfield spots. And Casey Stengel perfected the art with the Yankees. ☞

Basically, percentages favor a lefthanded batter against a righthanded pitcher, and vice versa. Should the opposition send up a righthanded pinch-hitter for a lefthanded batter, the wise manager would employ a righthanded pitcher to stop him.

On May 15, 1951, rookie White Sox manager Paul Richards used a loophole in the rules to play percentages in the eighth inning of a game against the Red Sox. He moved righthanded pitcher Harry Dorish to third base and brought in star lefthander Billy Pierce to pitch to lefthanded batter Ted Williams. After Williams popped up, Richards brought Dorish back, and he went on to win the game.

Billy Meyer, managing Pittsburgh at the same time, had his own favorite play. With the bases loaded and a 3-1 or 3-2 count on the batter, the runner on third broke for home. He deliberately started slowly so that the pitcher would forget the count and think he had an easy out at the plate. Meyer's idea was to induce the pitcher to lob an outside toss to the catcher for the tag—but the throw would actually be ball four and force a run home.

In the 1972 World Series, Dick Williams used a trick play to strike out Cincinnati slugger Johnny Bench. With the count 3-2, he told catcher Gene Tenace to hold out his hand, the traditional sign for the intentional walk. Tenace would then return to normal position just as reliever Rollie Fingers was set to deliver. Williams conducted his conference on the mound and gestured toward first base, as Fingers nodded in agreement. The pitcher would throw a breaking ball rather than a fastball to camouflage the ruse further.

Bench assumed his stance and the Oakland players did their part in the field. The surprised catcher was called out on strikes.

"Bench was completely fooled," Williams recalled. "The pitch was an excellent one. It caught, maybe, the outside corner of the plate. We got the next man too and saved a run because there was one out with a man on third before Bench came up."

As a rule, managers play to win on the road and to tie at home. Since baseball has a built-in advantage for the home club, the theory is based around the fact that familiar surroundings, partisan fans, and the sudden-death advantage of the home ninth—or subsequent innings—will enable the home team to break the tie and go on to victory.

Another adage for contending clubs is: play .500 against the top teams and murder the tail-enders. A championship cannot be forged without a high winning percentage, and few clubs can maintain a high ratio of wins to losses against top-flight opposition.

Skilled managers gamble by sending runners for extra bases, utilizing the stolen base (and the double-steal), employing the suicide squeeze play and the hit-and-run. In any of these situations, the manager will look bad if the players fail to execute. If anything, the owner or general manager will execute the manager whose strategy doesn't translate into victories.

## CHARLEY DRESSEN USED HIS HEAD

*Charley Dressen, long-time major league manager, was a bundle of excitement during a game. Once, when Gil Hodges was at bat for his Dodgers, Dressen watched the count run to 1-2. The next pitch was high and outside—so far out that the catcher missed it—but the umpire called strike three. When Hodges, assuming the pitch to be ball three, failed to run toward first, Dressen yelled, "Run! Run!" but the first baseman failed to hear him. The screaming manager, jumping up and down in the dugout, banged his head on the ceiling and collapsed. Hodges finally got the idea and made it to first—but for days afterward he avoided Dressen whenever he saw the manager rubbing the sore spot on his head.*

## STENGEL'S QUICK QUIP

*When Tug McGraw was hit hard by the opposition while working for the Mets, manager Casey Stengel came out to the mound. Pointing to the hitter, McGraw said, "I struck out this guy the last time I faced him. Let me stay in." Stengel responded, "I know you struck him out. But it was in this same inning!"*

## CARDINALS' SERIES STRATEGY PAID OFF

*The St. Louis Cardinals walked Babe Ruth 12 times in the 1926 World Series (he still hit four home runs). Ruth, frustrated when Grover Cleveland Alexander walked him with two outs in the ninth inning of Game 7, and the Yankees behind, 3-2, tried to surprise St. Louis by stealing second. He was thrown out easily—ending the World Series—in what baseball experts say was the only stupid play of his career.*

Babe Ruth's biggest blunder was this unexpected attempt to steal a base in Game 7 of the 1926 World Series between the Yankees and Cardinals. Ruth was the last out.

# MANAGERS AND PITCHERS

Handling the pitching staff is generally considered to be the most difficult aspect of managing. A rotation must be established, relief corps assembled, and a special coach chosen to monitor all pitchers.

A little-known aspect of the game is the conference on the mound. What does the manager really say?

When Paul Richards was running the Orioles, he approached Connie Johnson after three hits had loaded the bases. "Connie, it's about time you were getting someone out," Richards offered. "You know," Johnson replied, "I was just thinking about that myself."

Moe Drabowsky remembers an encounter with Fred Hutchinson, the Reds' pilot who once pitched himself. "The bases were loaded—I had just walked a couple of guys—and the score was tied," he related. "All of a sudden I went to 2-0 and with every pitch, I heard a strange noise from the dugout: 'Hmphfff!'

"Throw another pitch and 'Hmphfff!' It was Hutch. When it was a ball, it would upset him so much. Finally, I looked out of the corner of my eye and saw him charging out of the dugout. When he arrived, he said, 'Look around you, what do you see?' I didn't know what he was referring to. He said, 'The bases are loaded now. You better get this next guy.' Then he turned around and went back to the dugout. Fortunately, I got the next guy."

A manager may tell a joke or argue with an umpire to relax a pitcher in a pressure situation, but Clyde King said no one ever asked him where he was going to dinner or what movie he was going to see that night. "I played for Charley Dressen, Leo Durocher, Walter Alston, and Burt Shotton, and those guys were all business," he said.

When King became a manager, he had a club rule that no pitcher could argue about leaving the game.

"I learned you can't depend on the catcher to tell you whether the pitcher is losing his stuff," King reported, "because he might be the roommate or a close friend of the pitcher and it would put him on the spot. As a big-league manager, I believed that if I had to rely on someone else to tell me when a pitcher was losing it, I might not be qualified to be a manager."

## SAIN SAYS MOUND CONFERENCE WASTED

*Veteran pitching coach Johnny Sain says the only purpose of a meeting on the mound with catcher, pitcher, and manager is to stall while a reliever warms up in the bullpen. "If a microphone were placed out there, all you'd hear would be a lot of grunts," he noted.*

## SLEEPLESS NIGHTS

*Bad ballclubs turn managers prematurely gray, raise ulcers, and cause many sleepless nights for field bosses.*

*Burt Shotton, who later found success with the Brooklyn Dodgers, suffered through the nightmare of the 1930 Phillies, a team with eight .300 hitters and a .315 team batting average but a leaky defense and inept pitching staff. The club made 239 errors in 154 games (the '62 Mets made 210 in 162) and posted a 6.71 team-earned run average. Opponents scored 19 runs in a game against the Phils four times!*

## BASEBALL-FOOTBALL TIE

*Hugo Bezdek, who managed the Pirates before 1920, is the only man who managed in the majors and coached in the National Football League—but never played in either.*

Forlorn Babe Ruth, rebuffed in his bid to become a major league manager, spent some time as first base coach for the Brooklyn Dodgers in the late '30s.

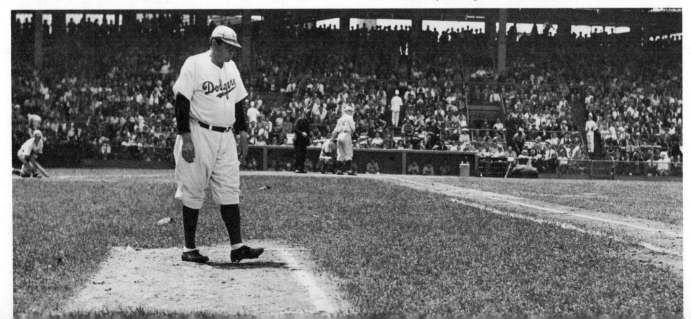

# COACHES

Each major league club carries three or four coaches during the season. Two flash signs to hitters and direct base-runners from coaching boxes behind first and third base when their team bats; another supervises the bullpen; any others share the dugout bench with the manager.

Early baseball managers, including John McGraw, preferred to handle all aspects of running their teams. Substitute players manned the coaching boxes, and non-playing managers frequently filled one of the boxes themselves.

There's always a hitting coach and a pitching coach, though the latter sometimes is a former catcher rather than a former pitcher.

Many of the coaches are former managers seeking to find new jobs as pilots or just-retired players hoping to move into managerial slots without following the traditional route up from the minors.

Coaches use six basic signs: bunt, take, hit-and-run, squeeze, steal, and forget-previous-sign. The third base coach is particularly important because his decisions help—or hurt—the team in scoring runs. Often, he must gamble, and always, decisions must be instantaneous.

In the '20s, KiKi Cuyler of the Cubs threw out Travis Jackson of the Giants at home plate. Jackson had been trying to score from sec-

## WASHINGTON USED FOUR COACHES AT FIRST

*The Washington Senators used four coaches at first base in one game in 1968. Nellie Fox, the normal first base coach, was ejected in the ninth and replaced by utility infielder Bernie Allen. Allen, needed as a pinch-hitter later, was replaced by Cap Peterson, but Peterson had been previously announced as a pinch-hitter and was technically out of the game. The Senators replaced him with pitcher Camilo Pascual. P.S. Washington won in twelve innings.*

Doubling as third base coach, frenetic Leo Durocher, managing the New York Giants, whoops up a storm as Willie Mays heads for home.

ond on a single and had received a green light from third base coach Pancho Snyder. Chicago's bench-jockeys taunted Snyder for letting Jackson go through against Cuyler's powerful arm.

"Never again in a million years," the coach replied.

Later in the game, Cuyler threw out another Giant at home. "Hey, Pancho," the Chicago bench screamed, "time sure flies!"

The good third base coach is automatically the heir apparent to the incumbent manager. When an incumbent goes, and ownership decides not to look outside the organization, the third base coach rates the slight edge over the team's Triple-A manager for the big-league job.

Pitching coach Johnny Sain, unlike many other coaches, was never a drinking buddy of the manager's. Nor was he a candidate to become a manager and hire an unemployed former boss to coach for him.

Sain concerned himself only with pitching, and developed more than a dozen 20-game winners in the '60s and '70s. In both Minnesota and Chicago, he helped Jim Kaat blossom into a top winner.

Like Sain, Art Fletcher, Frankie Crosetti, and Eddie Yost gained reputations as competent, satisfied coaches who did not desire the manager's chair.

The irony of coaching history is that men fired as managers by a certain club frequently return as coaches—and indirect threats to their successors. Charley Dressen and Leo Durocher both returned to the Dodgers, Johnny Pesky to the Red Sox, and Yogi Berra to the Yankees, among others. All were considered excellent aides.

Billy Hunter spent fourteen years as third base coach on the Baltimore Orioles and entertained several managerial offers before joining the Texas Rangers in 1977.

"The third base coach probably can control the game on offense more than the manager can," he said. "He has everything right in his hands. He can hold the runner up or send him in, and it's his judgment that will determine whether a runner is out or safe.

"If you can't be a player, be a third base coach: he's in the game as much as anyone. He has to know not only every outfielder's arm, but every infielder's arm too. When there's a cutoff play, that comes into account. Many times the shortstop is a very good relay man but the second baseman is not. If the first baseman has the ball, he may not throw too well. The leftfielder is usually the worst arm in the outfield.

"A good third base coach will watch infield practice, will watch the outfielders throw, and if somebody's not throwing too well, he might give him a little test during the ballgame."

Hunter coached during the heyday of Frank and Brooks Robinson and Boog Powell—heavy hitters who helped the Orioles become the most successful team of their time. Many Baltimore runners were thrown out because Hunter gambled on their chances of scoring.

"My theory at third," he explained, "was that if you had a 50-50 chance of making it, I sent the runner. You can only do that with a contending club because of the risk involved. I felt that if we made the other team throw, they made more mistakes. When you're cautious, a lot of times you might not score any runs, but when you gamble, you might get two or three."

Charley Dressen, veteran coach and manager, found time for a spring training stroll with young Yogi Berra on February 29, 1948 in St. Petersburg, Fla. Dressen was then a Yankee coach under Bucky Harris.

## DRESSEN A TOP COACH

*Charley Dressen coached for several clubs, including the Yankees and Dodgers, and was highly regarded for his vast storehouse of baseball knowledge. He was an excellent judge of his own pitchers and the enemy's and was particularly adept at stealing signs from other clubs.*

## GRAMMAS EXPLAINS SIGNALS

*Third base coach Alex Grammas, one of the best at his trade, explained how signals are flashed: "A coach usually goes through eight or ten motions, but only one or two mean anything. Each guy has his own individual style. When I was coaching at Cincinnati, I'd go to my cap, my arm, my leg, and back to my arm. I used to use my nose and ears a lot."*

# CHAPTER TEN

# THE GOVERNMENT OF BASEBALL

Since January 12, 1921, organized baseball has been headed by a Commissioner hired by the major league club owners.

He is in the unusual position of wielding power over his employers because he has total authority to protect "the best interests of baseball" by (1) investigating and punishing acts detrimental to the game, (2) resolving interleague disputes, (3) handling serious labor-management problems, and (4) enforcing the five documents governing the game: the Major League Agreement, the Major League Rules, the Major-Minor League Agreement, the Major-Minor League Rules, and the National Association Rules.

Judge Kenesaw Mountain Landis, earning $7500 on the Federal bench in Illinois, agreed to become the first Commissioner only after he was granted the autocratic powers needed to restore the integrity of the game after the Black Sox scandal of 1919.

Landis, who served until his death in 1944, wasted no time in using his powers. Within months, he handed permanent suspensions to the eight White Sox players accused but acquitted of throwing the 1919 World Series to the Reds, and impounded Babe Ruth's World Series share—and suspended him forty days—for illegal post-season barnstorming.

A. B. (Happy) Chandler, Ford Frick, General William D. Eckert, and Bowie K. Kuhn followed Landis as Commissioner, but none ruled with the iron hand of the game's first czar.

The Commissioner's job, now as then, includes presiding over the Executive Council, an advisory group made up of the two league presidents and one additional representative—normally a club owner—from each league. League player representatives are added to the Council when player-related matters are discussed. Majority rules on all votes.

The Commissioner is paid more than $200,000, with salary and office operating expenses drawn from All-Star and World Series receipts. Additional money can be secured by special request from the clubs.

League presidents, like the Commissioner, rely on special executive committees and have powers granted by club owners. They approve player contracts, arbitrate intra-league disputes, and review protested games, in addition to other functions. They also hire, fire, assign, and monitor the umpires.

Before the advent of the Commissioner, league presidents acted arbitrarily in their own selfish interests—as opposed to the best interests of the game. Each was the highest executive in baseball and answered only to the club owners of his own league. As a result, battles between leagues were frequent. In the nineteenth century, battles raged with more intensity off the field than on.

Colonel A. G. Mills, an early National League president, managed to create a calm in the storm when he hammered out a mutually satisfactory arrangement between the National and the new American Association in 1882. This first National Agreement gave the AA official status as a major circuit and protected players and owners in both leagues. For his diplomatic success, Mills won the nickname "the Bismarck of baseball."

A later National League leader, Nick Young, was unsuccessful when he took a kindly, rather than aggressive, stance toward the owners. His umpires were scorned and roughhousing teams dominated timid opponents—often without regard to rules and invariably beyond the bounds of good sportsmanship. ☞

156

## LANDIS HUGGED '31 SERIES STAR

Commissioner Landis embraced 1931 World Series star Pepper Martin and told him he'd like to trade places with him. Martin, earning $4500, replied, "Well, that'll be fine, Judge, if we can swap salaries too!" The baseball czar was then earning $65,000.

## SHOELESS JOE: BLACK SOX SUPERSTAR

Shoeless Joe Jackson was the biggest star banned from baseball in the Black Sox scandal. "He was the finest natural hitter in the history of the game," said Ty Cobb. "He never figured anything out or studied anything with the scientific approach I used —he just swung." Babe Ruth admitted he copied Jackson's batting style. Tris Speaker said Jackson never slumped. Shoeless Joe couldn't read or write, but he could hit. His lifetime average was .356.

The new American League had a tight rein on its umpires and club owners when it launched life as a major league in 1901. President Ban Johnson sought peace and recognition from the National but, when he didn't get it, a two-year war broke out between leagues.

The war, accented by frequent player raids across league lines, ended early in 1903 when Cincinnati Reds president Garry Herrmann helped establish a three-man National Commission to rule the game.

Johnson and NL president Harry Pulliam—both former baseball writers—took two seats, while Herrmann was awarded the third for laying the groundwork.

In effect, Herrmann took the role of an early "Commissioner" because the two leagues often took opposite sides in disputes.

Ironically, one of those disputes later involved Herrmann's position on the Commission. John Heydler, a former umpire who had succeeded Pulliam as NL chief, succumbed to internal pressure and voted against Herrmann's retention on the Commission. But he and Johnson deadlocked on the choice of a successor and the swing seat remained empty in 1920—the same season news of the Black Sox scandal broke.

Staggered by the exposure of the scandal in September, club owners of both leagues realized the importance of hiring a powerful Commissioner to protect the game.

Chicago advertising executive Albert Lasker, who held stock in the Cubs, conceived "the Lasker Plan," which was translated into legal language by White Sox attorney Alfred Austrian and introduced by Sox owner Charles Comiskey. Lasker, Austrian, and NL owners Barney Dreyfuss and William Baker discussed the job with Landis after other candidates—including former President William Howard Taft and Generals John Pershing and Leonard Wood—were rejected.

Though offered $50,000—a huge increase over his jurist's salary—Landis agreed only to consider the job. With teams anxious to prevent further scandals in the game, 11 club owners visited the Landis courtroom en masse while the Judge was trying a bootlegging case. He recognized them when they entered but refused to be interrupted. "There will be less noise in the courtroom or it will be cleared," he announced.

The stunned owners liked the outspoken approach and agreed to grant Landis a contract with the precise wording he specified. The pact granted him absolute power to act "in the best interests of baseball" and has been applied to every Commissioner.

## THE BLACK SOX

*Chick Gandil, one of eight Chicago players banned for life by Judge Landis in the Black Sox scandal of 1919, apparently instigated the plot by contacting gamblers in Boston three weeks before the World Series. Buck Weaver, also in the group, backed out of the plot and played to win but was thrown out of the game because he didn't reveal the conspiracy.*

*Meanwhile, Cincinnati's Edd Roush said gamblers who knew the Sox were going to lose deliberately tried to bribe a Reds' player $5000 to dump a game in favor of Chicago and twist the plot. He informed manager Pat Moran, who verified the attempted bribery.*

*A ninth major-leaguer was banned in the Black Sox scandal: second baseman Joe Gedeon of the St. Louis Browns was handed a lifetime suspension by American League president Ban Johnson for betting on the Reds after learning that the World Series was fixed.*

## RUPPERT PLAYED SANDLOT BALL

*Colonel Jacob Ruppert, beer baron owner of the Yankees during Babe Ruth's heyday, was a sandlot pitcher from New York's East Side who liked to work out with his Yankees in spring training.*

# THE COMMISSIONERS
## JUDGE KENESAW MOUNTAIN LANDIS

Kenesaw Mountain Landis was an ideal choice as the first Commissioner of Baseball. The game needed a strong man and his court record proved him to be just that. In baseball, he was even more authoritarian—actually a benevolent dictator.

Twice the intended victim of bombers in Chicago, Landis won national headlines in 1907 when he fined the Standard Oil Company $29 million in a freight rebate case. He came to the attention of baseball by withholding opinion on an antitrust suit resulting from the collapse of the Federal League in 1915. Seven years later, the case reached the United States Supreme Court, which granted an antitrust exemption to the game.

Landis was remembered by owners for his summary statement: "Both sides may understand that any blows at this thing called baseball would be regarded by this court as a blow at a national institution." ☞

## LANDIS HELD AL TOGETHER

The American League was faced with the threat of secession when Judge Landis was merely a candidate for Commissioner. Boston's Carl Mays, a pitcher under suspension for insubordination, was sold to the Yankees for $50,000 in July 1919, but AL president Ban Johnson canceled the deal and increased the suspension from 10 days to indefinitely. The Yankees won a court injunction against Johnson, and the Red Sox, Yankees, and sympathetic White Sox actually threatened to quit the league with a fourth club and increase the National to a 12-team circuit. Using the threat as a wedge, the rebel clubs forced the other AL owners to subscribe to the Lasker plan, which made Landis Commissioner. He quieted the various factions as soon as he assumed office early in 1921.

## RESPECT FOR LANDIS BLOCKED CUB FARMS

Out of respect for Commissioner Landis, who equated the farm system with slavery, the Chicago Cubs did not develop a minor league chain during his tenure. Instead, the Cubs concentrated on buying players from independent minor league operators.

## HOW LANDIS GOT HIS NAME

Judge Kenesaw Mountain Landis was born in Millville, Ohio, on November 20, 1866, little more than a year after the end of the Civil War. His father, Dr. Abraham Landis, was a Union Army surgeon who suffered a leg wound at the Battle of Kennesaw Mountain, Georgia, on June 27, 1864. The doctor prayed that if his leg could be spared, he would name his son for that beautiful spot. The leg healed and the doctor kept his word—though he dropped an n in the boy's first name.

Judge Kenesaw Mountain Landis had a tough job as baseball's first Commissioner: erasing the memory of the 1919 Black Sox scandal.

The Judge guarded the game zealously after taking the Commissioner's chair. When he was appointed at age 54, Landis was handed a seven-year contract for $50,000, but he accepted only $42,500 because he retained his judgeship for more than a year. The salary was lifted to $65,000 later, but Landis voluntarily sliced his pay to $40,000 during the Depression.

Landis conceded he knew little about baseball when he took the job, but he was well aware of the Black Sox scandal. Throughout his administration, he issued stiff suspensions or lifetime bans to anyone having even the slightest connection with disreputable characters. Among those he banned was Phillies' owner Bill Cox, who bet on his own club.

"Baseball will continue on trial in America as long as baseball is played," Landis announced in his first public appearance as Commissioner. "It is not enough to say that baseball must be as good as any other business. Baseball has got to be better in its morality than any other business."

Landis' first, and most difficult, task was to erase the memory of the Black Sox. He did this with lifetime bans that precluded eight players—five of them regulars—from even buying a ticket at any park of the majors or minors. In addition, their records—including the .356 lifetime batting average of outfielder Shoeless Joe Jackson —were expunged from the official record books.

The Commissioner acted after initial indictments were dropped and the athletes were acquitted of conspiracy charges in a second trial. The Grand Jury records which led to the original indictments were stolen during a change in the state attorney's office in Cooks County.

"Regardless of the verdict of juries," Landis said, "no player who throws a ball game, no player that undertakes or promises to throw a ball game, no player that sits in a conference with a bunch of crooked players and gamblers where the ways and means of throwing games are planned and discussed and does not promptly tell his club about it will ever play professional baseball."

The suspension of the Black Sox was clear evidence that Landis would be a strict and activist Commissioner. He seldom had the patience to rely on his Executive Committee and was criticized for making decisions without them, but scuttled opposition by walking into major league meetings, contract in hand, and threatening to tear it up. The vast majority of owners so respected him—and feared the public reaction if he resigned—that they insisted he stay in office.

Even Babe Ruth, who had no patience for rules or those who tried to enforce them, remained on the good side of the Commissioner when he was suspended for the first forty days of the 1922 season after joining Bob Meusel and another Yankee teammate on an illegal barnstorming tour after the previous fall's World Series. The players' $3000 Series shares were impounded until the suspensions ran out.

Landis had his hand in every aspect of the game. In 1922, he disagreed when umpire George Hildebrand called a World Series game for darkness with the sun still shining and issued an edict that future postponements would have to be cleared with the Commissioner. Twelve years later, he removed Joe Medwick from the Cardinal lineup in the finale of the 1934 World Series at Detroit when Tiger fans showered the outfielder with debris after a controversy on the basepaths. St. Louis led, 11-0, and Landis removed Medwick to keep the peace; a forfeit to the Cardinals could have started a full-fledged riot. 🖝

## SOX "LOSERS" OF 1919 GOT WINNING SHARES

*When the Black Sox scandal of 1919 became public knowledge, Chicago White Sox owner Charles Comiskey fired the seven players accused and gave the remaining athletes on his team bonus checks that represented the difference between winners' and losers' shares in the World Series.*

## FINLEY FIRED PLAYER DURING SERIES

*Charlie Finley attempted to disqualify second baseman Mike Andrews when he made two damaging errors in the twelfth inning of Game 2 in the 1973 World Series. The Oakland owner charged Andrews was injured and sought to replace him with young Manny Trillo. Commissioner Bowie Kuhn objected and Andrews was reinstated. The Andrews case angered the Oakland players.*

## THE COMMISSIONER'S POWERS

*Baseball law gives the Commissioner absolute power to regulate disputes "in the best interests of the game."*

*Dodger owner Walter O'Malley gave this capsule summary: "All the owners are voluntary parties to an agreement stating that the Commissioner has very broad powers and that if he takes jurisdiction in a matter that he deems not to be in the best interests of baseball, holds a hearing for all involved, including lawyers, then his decision is final and binding. We owners have a contract with each other that whatever his decision is, we will not have recourse in the courts."*

The white-maned executive handed year-long suspensions to five players who jumped their contracts to play with independent clubs, banned for life four players in addition to the Black Sox eight, cleared Ty Cobb and Tris Speaker of "fix" charges filed by Dutch Leonard. He ordered clubs to train close to home during World War II to cooperate with wartime travel restrictions, and even had Dizzy Dean removed as broadcaster for the all-St. Louis World Series of 1944 because he feared Dean's clowning and syntax were too undignified for a national audience.

But Landis was regarded as the players' friend. When he took charge of the game, a new form of player's contract was adopted. It gave the athletes the right—for the first time—to appeal any grievances against their club owner. Landis sat in on many cases and handed out rulings as if he were still wearing the black robes of the Federal bench.

Two Cincinnati players, accused of collusion with gamblers by a Chicago racing publication, were cleared, and a number of veterans —along with dozens of minor-leaguers—became free agents under the Landis reign.

Though he maintained a stern exterior that literally made men quake in their boots when he confronted them, Judge Landis also had a lighter side. He entertained friends by impersonating the baseball people at his hearings. His vivid memory for dialogue and dialect made his character acting that much more memorable.

# HAPPY CHANDLER

After Judge Landis died in office on November 25, 1944, the job of Commissioner was inherited by his long-time assistant, Leslie O'Connor, while baseball brass searched for a suitable successor.

Landis had been such an unusual man that no one could fill his shoes. A man was needed who would grow into the job. U. S. Senator A. B. (Happy) Chandler of Kentucky tried, but was voted out of office before his seven-year pact expired in 1952.

Chandler did make history, however, and some baseball insiders suggest he should be enshrined in the Hall of Fame, as were his predecessor, Judge Landis, and his successor, Ford Frick.

Chandler's most noteworthy contribution was throwing the weight of the Commissioner's office behind Branch Rickey's efforts to integrate baseball. All 15 of Rickey's contemporaries in the majors voted against allowing Jackie Robinson—or any other black—to play, but Chandler helped make it possible.

"Rickey came to me and said he couldn't bring in Robinson without my support," Chandler said, "and I told him he had all of my backing and all the backing of my office. The Jackie Robinson decision changed everything about sports. Baseball was first, and the others followed."

Robinson played under Burt Shotton in 1947 because Dodger manager Leo Durocher was under one-year suspension from Chandler for unspecified conduct considered detrimental to the game. The issue came to a boil when he and Rickey advised the Commissioner that Yankee executive Larry MacPhail had gamblers in his box at an exhibition game. MacPhail filed countercharges. After investigating, Chandler fined each club $2000, suspended Yankee coach Charley Dressen thirty days, banned Durocher for a year, and even slapped a $500 fine on Brooklyn road secretary Harold Parrott, who had ghost-written an "objectionable" Durocher column in the *Brooklyn Eagle*. ☞

## SCHEDULE-MAKERS

*Baseball schedules are drawn up by league executives. They plan all day games, then send copies to team traveling secretaries for individual adjustments. These officials, who know plane schedules by heart, plan night games, doubleheaders, and games starting at unusual times. The process takes 90 days.*

*Spring training schedules are drawn up at a meeting of traveling secretaries. The job is done in a day.*

## BREADON HELPED HORNSBY

*Sentimental St. Louis owner Sam Breadon, who sold controversial player-manager Rogers Hornsby from the Cardinals to the Giants after the World Championship season of 1926, rescued Hornsby when the slugger seemed headed out of the majors. Breadon signed Hornsby as a player for the Cards, arranged for him to take the managing job with the St. Louis Browns, and expedited his unconditional release so arrangements could be completed.*

## FAMILIES KEPT CONTROL OF CLUBS

*Many teams have been owned by families who passed the chief executive's job from generation to generation. Clark Griffith passed the role to his adopted nephew, Calvin, with the Washington Senators (later Minnesota Twins). Father-son chains have included William, Philip, and William Wrigley (Cubs); Charles, Lou, and Charles Comiskey (White Sox); Charles and Horace Stoneham (Giants); Walter and Peter O'Malley (Dodgers); and Bob and Ruly Carpenter (Phillies).*

## PRESIDENT'S HALF-BROTHER OWNED PHILS

*Charles P. Taft, half-brother of President William Howard Taft, owned the Phillies for a brief period early in this century.*

Since Chandler ordered all parties involved silenced on the case, the true cause for Durocher's suspension has never been specified.

The Kentucky Commissioner was lenient with Durocher in comparison to the way he treated players who jumped to the outlaw Mexican League a year earlier. Sal Maglie, Mickey Owen, and others faced five-year bans, but Chandler pardoned the players involved after three.

He also was responsible for launching the players' excellent pension plan and signing baseball's first network television contract.

# FORD FRICK

Ford Frick became Commissioner of Baseball in September 1951 —just before Bobby Thomson hit the most dramatic home run in history—but became known as "the asterisk Commissioner" because of another slugger's performance.

In his tenth anniversary in the job, Frick decided to put an asterisk after all baseball records achieved under the new 162-game schedule. Since Babe Ruth had hit his 60 home runs in 154 games, Frick reasoned, Roger Maris did not really surpass him by hitting 61 in 162.

The decision set off a storm of controversy which grew the following fall after Maury Wills stole 104 bases in 162 games, surpassing Ty Cobb's one-season figure of 96. Cobb had stolen 94 bases after 154 games in 1915, but his Tigers had to replay two ties, giving him two extra chances to add to his total. Since Wills swiped 95 in his first 154 games, he actually created a new mark, using Frick's rationale in reverse. After 156 games, Wills had 97—still one more than Cobb over the same period.

Critics contended Frick's asterisk theory stemmed from his one-time friendship with Babe Ruth. Frick, a New York sportswriter and broadcaster, played golf and bridge with Ruth and ghosted several magazine articles under the slugger's byline.

Frick had moved into the busy world of the New York media from Colorado, where he taught journalism and wrote sports in Colorado Springs. Visiting Hearst editor Arthur Brisbane saw his work and brought him east.

Frick became NL public relations director in 1934 and league president a year later. His first notable achievement as an executive was finding funds to bail several clubs out of near-bankruptcy during those Depression days.

A contender for the vacant Commissioner's job after the death of Judge Landis in 1944, Frick had considerable support, but not enough to overcome a late move by Happy Chandler. He remained NL president and took the strongest stance of his career when he blasted clubs, owners, and players who threatened to boycott games which included black players. He sent an especially sharp message to St. Louis Cardinals' owner Sam Breadon, warning that prejudice would be met with lifetime suspensions—even if it hurt the league for five or ten seasons.

With Frick and Commissioner Chandler behind him, Branch Rickey was able to overcome almost unanimous opposition and bring Jackie Robinson into the game in 1947. Robinson won the Rookie-of-the-Year Award that fall.

When he moved into the job of Commissioner, Frick presided over an era of franchise shifts, expansion, and general growth of the game. Though he preferred to be a passive chieftain, Frick did take a major role in seeing that baseball secured good contracts in the young field of television.

Because he had failed to antagonize the club owners in his first seven-year term, Frick won reelection easily. He retired in 1965.

## CARDINAL BOSS SUITED UP

St. Louis Cardinals' owner Sam Breadon worked out in uniform with his team during spring training.

Ford Frick was a key man in ending baseball's color line.

## "STEAMSHOVELS" BOUGHT BRAVES

In the early '40s, a syndicate of Boston businessmen bought the Braves from Charles Adams.

Construction magnates Lou Perini, Guide Rugo, and Joseph Maney, who headed the syndicate, were better known as "The Three Little Steamshovels."

## CUBS' OWNER GOT THE BOOT

Former sportswriter Charles Murphy won four flags in five years as owner of the Chicago Cubs, 1906-10, but tore apart his team in anger when it failed to keep up the pace. He fired and traded stars and managers, berated the uniformed personnel, and angered Chicago fans so much that the National League booted him out after the 1913 season.

# WILLIAM D. ECKERT

Baseball ownership considered 156 candidates to succeed Ford Frick as Commissioner. The list was cut to 15 four months before the choice was announced to the public.

The man who was finally picked was not only anonymous to the baseball fans of America, but he remained so throughout his three-year term in office.

Air Force General William D. Eckert, 56, admitted he knew little about baseball when he was named to preside over the game. His only contribution, aside from an austere image, was his nickname: Spike. But he got it playing basketball.

Eckert's name never appeared on the list of candidates for the job and his selection was a complete surprise. His forced resignation three years later wasn't.

**William D. Eckert**

**Bowie Kuhn tried to keep peace during the free agent revolution, but often found himself the center of controversy.**

## A MAN OF LETTERS

*A. Bartlett Giamatti, 51, took office as the seventh Commissioner of Baseball on April 1, 1989. An Italian Renaissance scholar who was a professor of English and comparative literature before becoming president of Yale University, Giamatti was known to walk around campus with a Red Sox cap and transistor radio. "Men of letters have always gravitated toward sport," he explained. "I've always loved baseball. I wanted to be Bobby Doerr more than anything."*

# BOWIE K. KUHN

Wall Street lawyer Bowie Kuhn had been associated with baseball's legal problems for nineteen years when he was named Commissioner in 1969. Tall, articulate, and soft-spoken, Kuhn projected an image of authority. His dress was all-business and his attitude matched.

Kuhn's decisions were as controversial as any executive rulings in baseball history, but his keen interest in keeping peace in turbulent times proved ideal for management, labor and fans.

Labor-owner disputes by owners marred Kuhn's administration, but the Commissioner succeeded in bringing major league baseball's three prime offices into the same city for the first time. The National and American Leagues, as well as the Commissioner's office, now operate in the same building in midtown New York.

Kuhn was liberal in handing out suspensions—two years to Yankee owner George Steinbrenner for illegal political contributions, a year to Atlanta Braves' owner Ted Turner for tampering with another team's player, and separate three-month and three-week bans to Tiger pitcher Denny McLain in 1969 for association with gamblers and carrying a pistol.

One-time star outfielder Curt Flood, upset by his trade from the Cardinals to the Phillies in 1969, sued the Commissioner in a test of the reserve clause, but his appeal was denied by the U. S. Supreme Court in 1972.

Three years later, however, pitchers Andy Messersmith and Dave McNally became the first players to test the option clause in their contracts. Contending that the clause only bound them to their teams for one year after the expiration of their contracts, the pair deliberately did not sign for 1975 and were ruled free agents by arbitrator Peter Seitz that winter.

The Messersmith decision, twice appealed unsuccessfully by the owners, toppled the traditional reserve system and forced labor and management to reach new understandings regarding player rights and contractual law.

The Kuhn administration created the Major League Baseball Promotion Corporation, engineered the creation of computerized All-Star ballots to return voting to fans in 1970, and produced a flood of news releases and publications designed to give the game greater exposure.

A very positive step in this direction was the syndication of a weekly highlights show for television, *This Week in Baseball*.

Aside from the labor-management situation, the biggest controversy Kuhn faced was his continuing war with the enigmatic owner of the Oakland A's, Charlie Finley. Twice, Kuhn vetoed sales of Oakland pitcher Vida Blue, stating that such million-dollar deals contradicted "the best interests of baseball." Kuhn also canceled sales of star A's Rollie Fingers and Joe Rudi in 1976, then watched the players exercise their newly-won rights as free agents and sell themselves for more money than Finley could have received for them.

# PETER V. UEBERROTH

Peter V. Ueberroth, organizer of the 1984 Los Angeles Olympics, followed that success with a five-year term as Commissioner of Baseball.

When Peter Ueberroth became Commissioner of Baseball in 1984, 21 of the 26 teams were losing money. Ueberroth reversed that trend by preaching "fiscal responsibility" among club owners, adding corporate sponsors, expanding licensing operations, and negotiating lucrative television contracts. Thanks to the increased promotion, total attendance zoomed to a record 56,331,213 in 1988.

"I'm pleased that the game has gone from a financial disaster to something that is financially viable," he said near the end of his term. "And I'm pleased that it went from an immoral, drug-ridden disaster to one of the best slices of society."

During the Ueberroth years, suspensions were issued to more than a dozen star players implicated in drug abuse; efforts were made to visibly increase minority hiring; night baseball became universal in the majors; and cable-TV became an official partner of the game for the first time.

Ueberroth's crowning achievements were negotiation of a four-year, $1 billion network television contract with CBS, effective in 1990, and quick settlement of a potentially devastating 1985 player strike. The two days of games cancelled by that August dispute were later made up. As Ueberroth prepared to leave office, however, labor and management were facing a potential 1990 work stoppage following the expiration of the Basic Agreement the outgoing Commissioner helped negotiate.

Ueberroth's April 1, 1989 departure was timed to coincide with his 10th anniversary as a sports executive. The man he had recommended as his successor, A. Bartlett Giamatti, had been groomed for the post while serving as president of the National League.

## WRIGLEY HIRED FLEXIBILITY EXPERT

*Far-sighted Chicago Cubs' owner Phil Wrigley hired University of Illinois professor Coleman Roberts Griffith to test his team's physical characteristics, including flexibility and reflexes, in 1938. Griffith headed the Bureau of Institutional Research—and the psychology department—at the school.*

## HOW DeWITT STARTED

*Bill DeWitt, who won notoriety for trading managers with Frank Lane in 1960, was involved with the ownership of several clubs, including the Reds, Tigers, Browns, and White Sox. A classic case of a man who worked his way up, DeWitt launched his baseball career by selling soda at Sportsman's Park, St. Louis.*

# TEAM EXECUTIVES

Major league teams are owned by groups or individuals who, as a rule, have made money in other businesses.

Many owners are activists who insist on negotiating their own trades, dealing with players directly, and hiring and firing managers. Others employ general managers to oversee their baseball operations. A business manager may run club finances, while the GM spends his time solely on improving the team and working with big-league players. A farm director runs the minor league network for each big-time club.

Owners have been their own general managers and, at times, even field managers. Chris Von Der Ahe managed the St. Louis Browns (later Cardinals) in 1892 and parts of other years, and Charles Ebbets was in the dugout for the Brooklyn Dodgers when the '98 season ended.

Horace Fogel ran the New York Giants for 42 games when he was part-owner of that club in 1902, and ten years later—as full owner of the Phillies—became the first owner thrown out of the game (he had made wild charges that the 1912 NL race was rigged in favor of the Giants).

Judge Emil Fuchs, New York City magistrate and avid fan who liked to work out in uniform with his Boston Braves, placed himself in the dugout for the 1929 season, relieving Rogers Hornsby, but took a temporary leave in May to try a case in court. Fuchs returned and finished last. Bill McKechnie took over as manager in 1930.

In 1977, Ted Turner of the Atlanta Braves made himself manager after the team had lost 16 games in a row. He lost, 2-1, and had to give up his dual role as owner-manager one day later when National League president Chub Feeney invoked Rule 20 (e): a manager may not have a financial interest in his team without special permission from the Commissioner.

Connie Mack, John McGraw, and Clark Griffith, among others, had been full-time owner-managers for years before baseball brass found any reason to question the idea of one man doing both jobs. But, in 1926, Rogers Hornsby, player, manager, and part-owner of the World Champion St. Louis Cardinals, was traded to the New York Giants.

Since Hornsby owned more than $60,000 worth of Cardinal stock, how could he play for the Giants? The National League ruled that he had to sell it before he could don his new uniform. A dispute arose as to the value of the stock, and a settlement was reached only after other teams pitched in to help the Cards pay Hornsby his asking price for divestiture.

Mack continued as owner-manager of the Athletics until 1950, but he, like Griffith and McGraw, was a player and manager who gained interest in ownership later. A non-playing owner who goes the other way—like Fuchs in 1929 or Turner in 1977—deals with umpires, who are actually his employees as an owner, and can be accused of harming the game, the league, and the club because of his inexperience at the job.

# EARLY OWNERS

Early baseball brass consisted of men like Henry Lucas, who owned the St. Louis Maroons (early Cardinals) in 1885. He had three blacklisted players and decided to raise money for them. Field events, a ballgame, and even a fox chase netted enough revenue to garner $400 a man.

Lucas looked for his players on Saturday nights and handed them impromptu bonuses when they needed spending money. In return, he asked them to come to the park sober and ready to play.

After the Players League rebellion of 1890, ownership could not afford generosity. Nor were owners in the mood to be kind to players who threatened the very existence of the National League.

Rosters were reduced from 15 to 13 men in 1892 and salaries cut 30 to 40 per cent. Cincinnati pitcher Tony Mullane, a 21-game winner, was asked to sign for $3500 after earning $4200 the year before. He refused and joined Butte of the Montana State League. The next spring, he signed with Cincy for $2100.

In 1898, the Robison family owned both the Cleveland and St. Louis clubs of the National League. The following year, the family shifted many of Cleveland's top stars to St. Louis, strengthening the Cardinals but so weakening the Spiders that they finished with a record of 20 wins and 134 losses for a sickly .129 percentage. They had to play most of their games out of Cleveland because they were afraid of their own fans.

Shortly after the turn of the century, 32-year-old Helene Britton became club president through inheritance. An early women's rights advocate, she attended all National League meetings and sought to increase female attendance at games. She succeeded by hiring an attractive male singer to perform between innings. 👉

Phil Wrigley became president of the Cubs in 1934.

## GABE PAUL ON PHIL WRIGLEY

Veteran executive Gabe Paul on the late Cubs' owner Phil Wrigley: "He's the only owner I ever knew who would vote against his own best interests if he thought it was good for baseball."

## THE WRIGLEYS OF CHICAGO

The Wrigley family's association with the Cubs began in 1916, when William Wrigley, Jr., bought stock in the club. His son, Phil, bought a large chunk of club stock in 1926, joined the board of directors three years later, inherited his father's shares in 1932, and became team president in 1934. "I became president because I got all the blame anyway," he said.

## LOYAL OWNER ANSWERS LETTERS

Phil Wrigley, owner of the Chicago Cubs, missed the first three games of the 1945 World Series against Detroit because he was answering letters from fans who couldn't get tickets.

Many of the early owners relied on top executives to make trades, sign players, and run their clubs. Colonel Jacob Ruppert, the beer baron who ran the Yankees in the Babe Ruth era, worked well with long-time baseball man Ed Barrow, while St. Louis Cardinals' owner Sam Breadon depended on the studious Branch Rickey. Tom Yawkey did well with Eddie Collins after the Boston sportsman became Red Sox owner at age 30 in 1933.

Perhaps the most respected old-time owner was Detroit's Frank Navin. When he died at age 64 in 1935, H. G. Salsinger of the *Detroit News* delivered this eulogy:

"More problems were settled in the back room of the Detroit club's headquarters, above the entrance of Navin Field, at Michigan and Trumbull Avenues, than at any other spot in the country. Mr. Navin generally sat there from late morning until late afternoon, and not a day passed but came long-distance calls from base ball men. Kenesaw Mountain Landis leaned heavily on Mr. Navin for advice and guidance.

"He was one of the few owners of major league clubs who knew the playing end of the game as well as the business end. Few of his players ever matched him in technical knowledge.

"He knew more about pitching than most of his pitchers will ever know, and more about batting. No man has ever made as thorough a study of a game as Mr. Navin did of base ball.

"Ballplayers liked to play for him. With all his technical knowledge, he was the most lenient of employers. Because he knew base ball, he understood how breaks figured in decisions; understood how certain happenings over which the player has no control can bring defeat.

"Like the late John Joseph McGraw, he criticized only laziness and stupidity in a player; he never held one responsible for an error."

Connie Mack was owner and manager of the Philadelphia Athletics. He gave up the latter role in 1950.

Giants' owner Horace Stoneham confers with manager Mel Ott in 1946.

## HANEY'S HINTS HELPED HALOS FINISH THIRD

*Former major league manager Fred Haney was voted American League Executive of the Year by* The Sporting News *in 1962 after his second-year expansion club, the Los Angeles Angels, finished third in a 10-team circuit. Haney became general manager of the club soon after cowboy-actor Gene Autry's purchase of the franchise in 1960. Asked for advice, Haney told Autry he should hire a good treasurer, experienced manager who could handle young players, solid farm system director, and top-notch general manager. Autry offered him the supervisory position.*

## HORACE PLAYED HOCKEY

*Long-time Giants' owner Horace Stoneham was a star schoolboy hockey player in New York.*

Tom Yawkey's generosity made him popular with players of the Boston Red Sox.

# FAMOUS TEAM EXECUTIVES

## ★ ★ ★ ★ ★ ★ ★
## BRANCH RICKEY

He that will not reason is a bigot
He that cannot reason is a fool
And he that dares not reason is a slave.

The words appeared on a sign that hung over Branch Rickey's desk in four different team offices: the St. Louis Browns, St. Louis Cardinals, Brooklyn Dodgers, and Pittsburgh Pirates.

Rickey was regarded by many baseball men as the greatest executive in the game's history. He created the concept of the farm system, broke the baseball color line against tremendous odds, developed sliding pits and complex pick-off plays.

Stories about Rickey's dealings at the contract table are almost legendary. "Negotiating with Rickey is like being in on the signing of the Declaration of Independence while taking a course in human relations," said former catcher Joe Garagiola.

Chuck Connors remembered, "It was easy to figure out Rickey's thinking on contracts. He had both players and money and didn't like to see the two of them mix."

Rickey's miserly reputation stemmed from his early days with the Cardinals, when the team was so strapped for finances that it held spring training in St. Louis one year. Rickey once distributed his own salary to help meet the payroll and the team was forced to wear its home uniforms on the road; it couldn't afford to buy a separate set.

Because the Cards couldn't afford to compete with other major league teams for the purchase of top players from the minors, Rickey suggested St. Louis develop its own talent. By 1940, his chain-gang farm system consisted of 32 minor league teams and 8 working agreements with clubs not owned outright. At one point, he controlled the entire player supply of the Nebraska State and

## RICKEY RESTED ON SUNDAY

Branch Rickey, Christy Mathewson, and several other players and managers early in the century did not play ball on Sunday.

## THE GENIUS OF RICKEY

"Rickey's genius was organizational—training, scouting, finding, teaching, developing, always with excellent on-field judgement."
—Leonard Koppett in The Sporting News

## BUSCH LIKED HORSES, BASEBALL

Young Gussie Busch, later owner of the Cardinals, rode horses with humorist Will Rogers in Wyoming and watched the St. Louis Browns play baseball. George Sisler was a favorite.

Arkansas-Missouri Leagues. (Commissioner Landis later limited working agreements to one per league.)

Rickey, who served the Cardinals twenty-five years as president, general manager, and even manager on occasion, moved to the Brooklyn Dodgers' GM post in 1942 and, five years later, brought Jackie Robinson into the majors as the first black player of the modern era.

He earned a reputation for being an astute judge of raw talent, as well as a shrewd trader who peddled veteran players just before their value declined. "It's better to trade one year too early than one year too late," he insisted.

Once, a University of California professor wrote Rickey about a pitcher on his squad. The rookie was invited to camp and promptly hit three 450-foot drives into the center field palm trees. Over the objections of the Cardinal manager, Rickey moved the boy to the outfield. The player—Chick Hafey—turned out to be the National League's batting champion with a .349 average in 1931.

Several years after Hafey's title, Rickey insisted the team keep 18-year-old outfielder Enos Slaughter. Several coaches and scouts objected, saying he couldn't hit. Slaughter went on to compile a lifetime .300 average over 22 seasons. He was the World Series hero of 1946 for the Cards.

Rickey had a bad ballclub with the Pirates of the early '50s, but he laid the groundwork for great Pirate teams to come.

Stubborn, outspoken, shrewd, and exceptionally intelligent, Rickey's last hurrah in baseball was restoring National League baseball in New York.

When he became president of the Continental League—a proposed new major—he so frightened executives of the existing majors that they absorbed several of his cities through expansion. Rickey agreed to abandon plans for the new circuit only after the National League agreed to return to New York, which had been without an NL club since the Dodgers and Giants fled to the West Coast after the 1957 season. In 1962, the New York Mets were born.

★ ★ ★ ★ ★ ★ ★
# LARRY MAC PHAIL

Larry MacPhail's impact on baseball was so strong that his candidacy for the Hall of Fame was fought thirty years after he left the game.

MacPhail finally won election in 1978—forty years after he kept Babe Ruth in baseball by making him a coach with the Brooklyn Dodgers.

A dynamic but often abrasive executive, MacPhail broke into baseball when he purchased Columbus of the American Association in 1931. Three years later, he seized the reins at Cincinnati, one of several National League cities hard-hit by the Depression. He took over Brooklyn in '37 and the New York Yankees in '45.

At all three stops, MacPhail built a reputation as a financial wizard, ingenious promoter, and superb talent scout, but he was accused by critics of enjoying a martini as much as a home run. He battled with commissioners, owners, managers, and players—sometimes firing anyone in sight and rehiring them after he cooled off.

MacPhail is best remembered for bringing night baseball to the major leagues in 1935. When he announced that the Reds would play the first night game, opposition was almost universal, but fan reac-

## FRANTIC FRANK LANE

White Sox general manager Frank Lane—often called Frantic Frank because of his tendency for nonstop talk and rapid-fire trades—was seated in the upper right field stands one day in full view of fans and players. Red Sox rightfielder Jimmy Piersall heard Lane scream at his own second baseman, Nellie Fox, for some minor infraction. Piersall waited for quiet, then yelled to Lane, "Why don't you jump and get it over with?"

## BEER BARON BUSCH STRUCK OUT ON DARK

Beer baron August (Gussie) Busch, owner of the St. Louis Cardinals since 1953, once tried to hire Alvin Dark as manager. Dark, a prohibitionist, said he could not work for the team, which was affiliated with Anheuser-Busch breweries.

## HOW CLUBS MAKE MONEY

Major league teams make money from ticket sales, broadcasting contracts, and advertisements purchased by yearbook and scoreboard sponsors. Many also get income from parking and concessions receipts. World Series money is divided among the clubs, leagues, and Commissioner's office only when the Series lasts more than four games. Proceeds from the first four contests go to the players.

tion was so good that MacPhail also installed lights in Ebbets Field and Yankee Stadium when he arrived there. All other clubs, with the lone exception of the Chicago Cubs, eventually followed suit.

Night ball was intended strictly as a novelty—one of many MacPhail promotions—and the outspoken executive wanted baseball under lights limited to seven games per season. He lived to see clubs adopt schedules calling for more than 60 per cent of their games after dark.

MacPhail was not only adept at promoting but also at building winning teams. These twin talents rescued the Reds and Dodgers from the brink of bankruptcy and restored the Yankee dynasty.

He acquired the players who jelled into the Cincinnati champions of 1939-40, then guided the Dodgers to the '41 flag—their first in more than twenty years. The MacPhail Yankees won the World Championship in 1947, but he left the game on doctor's advice after the season.

MacPhail promoted fashion shows, Old Timers' games, and televised baseball. When he came to Brooklyn from Cincinnati, he brought broadcaster Red Barber with him. He spent $200,000 to refurbish Ebbets Field when the Dodgers were in debt for more than twice that amount; he hired usherettes to attract male fans; and he was the first magnate to have his team travel by air (the Yankees in 1946).

The Stadium Club—another MacPhail innovation—and an announced desire to "make every day Sunday" at the ballpark helped bring crowds to watch MacPhail's clubs. He pioneered the pension plan for executives and helped carve the initial pension plan for players. He also gave long-time executive E. J. (Buzzie) Bavasi his first job in baseball—as an assistant in the office of the Brooklyn Dodgers in 1939.

MacPhail's temper exploded in 1941 when the Dodgers' special train from Boston failed to pick him up at the 125th Street station en route to a team victory party. He blamed manager Leo Durocher—whose career as pilot was launched by MacPhail—and fired him that night. As usual, Durocher was rehired the next morning.

"He and Leo were so much alike there was always fireworks," recalled MacPhail's son, Lee, former general manager for the Orioles and Yankees who became American League president.

MacPhail did fine Joe DiMaggio for missing a Yankee promotion and even accused Commissioner Happy Chandler of slander. His temperament was best reflected in a series of phone calls with his son, then running the Yankee farm at Columbus. When Lee hesitated in following Larry's order to hire Burleigh Grimes as manager, the elder MacPhail threatened him. "If Grimes isn't there by noon tomorrow, clean out your desk," he warned.

MacPhail's arrival in New York was the result of a three-way purchase that also involved Dan Topping and Del Webb. The trio bought the club, the stadium, and the farm system for the ridiculously low price of $2.8 million, $100,000 less than the Yankees gave Reggie Jackson in a multiyear contract that began in 1977.

Topping and Webb purchased MacPhail's holdings for $1.75 million following a tumultuous World Series victory party. He'd been ordered by doctors to leave the game, but MacPhail was also uppity because arch-rival Branch Rickey, chief executive of the Dodgers, had turned his back when MacPhail offered his hand in peace. That confrontation, which occurred just prior to Game 7, soured the taste of victory for MacPhail. ☞

## RUPPERT LOST HIS SHIRT

*Yankee owner Jacob Ruppert literally lost his shirt during his club's World Series victory party on a train headed home from St. Louis in 1928. The players had begun to tear off each other's shirts, and team leaders Babe Ruth and Lou Gehrig—batting stars of the Series—broke into Ruppert's drawing room and ripped off his. Between them, Gehrig and Ruth got 16 hits, 7 home runs, and 13 runs batted in during the four-game sweep of the Cardinals.*

"I'm through!" he screamed at the party. He fired everyone—including himself—but his was the only exit that was for real. No one knew what the doctors had told him. They found out later that a great showman was staging his last act.

★ ★ ★ ★ ★ ★ ★
# BILL VEECK

The most unorthodox and creative owner in the game after World War II was Bill Veeck, son of a baseball writer who became president of the Chicago Cubs in 1919.

Sometimes called "Sportshirt Bill" because of an aversion to ties, Veeck reads four books a week, peg-legs his way around the grandstand to talk to fans, and jots down hundreds of ideas in a bulging card file that his wife says has a value of more than $3 million.

Veeck integrated the American League by bringing Larry Doby and Satchel Paige to Cleveland and introduced the first "home run spectacular"—a scoreboard that shoots flares, Roman candles, and other crowd-pleasing fireworks.

Long known as "the P. T. Barnum of Baseball," Veeck was only 30 when he bought the Cleveland Indians in 1946 and has bought three other clubs since—including the Chicago White Sox twice.

Veeck's antics—which began during his four-year term as president of the Milwaukee Brewers in the American Association—have generated such fan response that he was credited with saving the sagging White Sox franchise for Chicago in 1976. The team had been on the verge of moving to Seattle—filling an American League obligation there—and being replaced by the Oakland A's of Charlie Finley, a Chicago insurance man.

In 1953, two years after he allowed a midget to bat in a regulation game, Veeck's conservative contemporaries translated their dislike of him into a no-vote on his request to move the floundering St. Louis Browns. Faced with losing more money in St. Louis or selling the team, Veeck sold.

He scouted for Cleveland—the team he once owned—in 1955 and, two years later, headed a Cleveland publicity agency and did promotions for the Indians. Attempts to buy the Senators, Tigers, and Pirates failed before Veeck and Hank Greenberg, his close friend, landed the White Sox from the Comiskey family in 1959. The team immediately won its first pennant in forty years.

Ill health knocked Veeck out of the game in '61, but he returned as White Sox owner in 1976, bringing along veteran baseball man Paul Richards as manager and putting Rudie Schaffer back into his job as business manager. Shrewd trades and endless promotion enabled the team to finish a surprising third in 1977 and draw a record Sox attendance of 1,657,135.

Though he lost a leg to a World War II injury suffered at Bouganville, Veeck draws on endless energy to achieve success. His natural sense of humor, expressed so well in his book *Veeck as in Wreck*, makes him a sought-after banquet speaker.

Once, when he accepted back-to-back engagements for a Springfield, Illinois dinner and St. Louis luncheon, he drove all night in a blizzard to keep the lunch date. An hour-and-a-half from the Chase Hotel, he could go no further by car and took to his feet. He was minus coat or hat and restricted to crutches because of recurring leg problems, but he hobbled through the raging storm to reach the hotel exactly at noon. No one was there. ☞

Bill Veeck was only 30 when he became president of the Cleveland Indians in 1946. Within two years, he had integrated the American League.

## VEECK'S TRADING TECHNIQUE

*Bill Veeck's trading technique is simple. "You just don't walk up to another ballclub and tell them you want their shortstop," he said. "If you did that, the price automatically would go up another $50,000. So you begin by talking about their second-string catcher."*

"I had been so intent on making my appointment that it never occurred to me in all that time that nobody else was going to be crazy enough to come out in a blizzard to listen to me talk," he said.

Bill Veeck started in the game as a Wrigley Field vendor, selling peanuts, scorecards, and soft drinks. He became a Cubs' office boy and worked his way up in the organization, becoming treasurer in 1940. A year later, at age 26, Veeck and veteran manager Charlie Grimm bought the Milwaukee Brewers (then a Triple-A club).

"Promotion plus a winning team breaks attendance records " said Veeck. He proved the idea at Cleveland, which drew an American League record 2,620,627 fans during the World Championship season of 1948.

"I can't afford to lose a single fan," Veeck said on several occasions. Often, his ballpark gimmicks are unannounced. Sometimes, the secret is essential—the league might stop some stunts before they start.

## ★ ★ ★ ★ ★ ★ ★
# WALTER O'MALLEY

Had Walter O'Malley convinced New York City politicians to build a domed stadium near Brooklyn's Long Island Railroad depot, both the Brooklyn Dodgers and New York Giants would have stayed in the east.

When city fathers rejected the ideas of O'Malley in 1956, the engineer-attorney-owner sold Ebbets Field and kept the Dodgers there as renters. He even played eight games at Jersey City's Roosevelt Stadium that year—and seven more in 1957—as a "warning" that he was serious about securing better facilities for the Dodgers and their fans.

"I got worried about the location, the vandalism to automobiles, and the molesting of women," he said. A Queens site—now the location of the Mets' Shea Stadium—was suggested but rejected. "If I move from Brooklyn to Queens, I might as well move to the West Coast because we won't be the Brooklyn Dodgers in Queens."

O'Malley convinced Giant owner Horace Stoneham to pull up stakes and go west with him. He said such a move would keep the fabled rivalry alive and help both teams financially.

Los Angeles produced a huge baseball market, and the Dodgers set several attendance records.

O'Malley joined the Dodgers when Wendell Willkie, the 1940 Republican candidate for President, resigned as Dodger attorney. John F. Kennedy might have replaced O'Malley, but Ambassador Joseph P. Kennedy was rebuffed in efforts to buy into the club.

Club president by 1950, O'Malley owned 75 per cent of the team when he went west after the 1957 campaign. He designed Dodger Stadium after finding flaws in other recent parks. O'Malley even scouted the Chavez Ravine site, originally a garbage dump. He used his engineering skills to estimate—accurately—that 8 million tons of earth would have to be moved during construction.

Because of his numerous professional skills, demonstrated baseball expertise, and businesslike approach to the game, O'Malley was frequently called on as advisor during the game's biggest controversies. Several jealous contemporaries had the audacity to charge that O'Malley was the real Commissioner of Baseball.

Under O'Malley and such veteran executives as Buzzie Bavasi, the Dodgers maintained a strong major league club and productive farm system.

## LANE CHALLENGED FAN TO FIGHT

Veteran executive Frank Lane once challenged a fan to a fight. The spectator was attacking Lane for a strategy decision of the manager which Lane also disliked. "I was yelling louder than he was," said the executive. "I didn't mind his yelling at me, but then he called me a stupid so-and-so for having it done. I didn't mind being called a so-and-so, but when he called me stupid, that was going too far!"

## WRIGLEY WAS RILED BY WRITER

Chicago Cubs' owner Phil Wrigley exploded with anger when CHICAGO DAILY NEWS sports editor Lloyd Lewis ran a mid-season box asking Cub fans to vote for a new manager. He had to be restrained from running a Cub-sponsored ad asking for readers to choose a new sports editor.

## ★★★★★★★
# CHARLIE FINLEY

The most controversial executive of the post-war era—and perhaps in the game's history—was Charlie Finley. In the tradition of Larry MacPhail, Finley was a showman, a first-rate talent scout, and a thorn in the side of many others—mostly his own employees.

After several unsuccessful efforts to buy a franchise, Finley purchased the Kansas City Athletics in 1961. Ten years later, as the Oakland A's, the club won the first of five consecutive divisional championships in the American League West. Sandwiched in the middle of that streak were three straight World Series victories.

Finley was an enigma from the start. An absentee owner who ran a Chicago insurance business, he spent hours on the telephone in daily conferences with his manager and was the busiest trader in the game—even when his club was the best in baseball.

He was scorned by contemporaries for many innovations which became standard: colorful uniforms, white shoes, scheduling the World Series on weekend days and weekday nights.

Though he tried working with a general manager in his early days as owner, Finley found—through bitter experience with Frank Lane—that he worked better alone. He also saved money by handling the job, and ran his front office with only a skeleton crew that included several relatives.

Attempts to move the Kansas City franchise to Louisville and the Oakland franchise to Denver did not endear him to the fans of either city, and Finley had to rely on his players to bring spectators to his park. Constant managerial changes and trades kept newspapers and magazines filled with stories about the A's—and such promotions as "Mustache Day" helped. Finley renewed the fashion of mustaches for ballplayers—and even manager Dick Williams went along when Finley offered his uniformed employees a bonus for growing them.

During the lean years in Kansas City, he put bulls in the bullpen, rode mascot mule Charlie O around the diamond, and built a "pennant porch" to imitate the short right field fence of Yankee Stadium. The Kaycee fence violated a rule about minimum distance to the plate and had to be modified.

The major gripe against Finley came from his managers. They said he interfered with their running of the ballclub. Dick Williams, who lasted longer and was more successful than any other manager under Finley, resigned in 1973 after winning three straight divisional flags—two of them resulting in World Championships.

## ★★★★★★★
# TED TURNER

Youthful television magnate Ted Turner, also one of the world's top yachtsmen, bought the Atlanta Braves in 1976 and spent most of the following season under suspension for allegedly tampering with outfielder Gary Matthews, who then belonged to the Giants. ☞

Charlie Finley introduced many new ideas and proved himself an excellent general manager with the Oakland A's—but often ran afoul of the establishment.

## TWO YAWKEYS OWNED TEAMS

Long-time Red Sox owner Tom Yawkey, who purchased the club at age 30 in 1933, was the son of former Tiger owner William Yawkey.

## $400,000 LIMIT SET ON DEALS

Concerned that million-dollar deals contradicted the "best interests of baseball," Commissioner Bowie Kuhn set a $400,000 ceiling on cash involved in any one transaction.

## BING CROSBY HAD A STAKE IN THE PIRATES

*The late Bing Crosby, singer and movie star, spent $250,000 to buy a sizable piece of the Pittsburgh Pirates in 1946. An avid fan who knew both averages and history, Crosby frequently suited up and worked out with the team during spring training in San Bernardino, California. He also visited the Idaho home of young Vern Law in an effort to get his signature on a Pirate contract. Law signed and went on to win 162 games for the team from 1950 through 1967. He was the ace of the staff for the World Championship team of 1960.*

pin-striped collector

GEORGE STEINBRENNER III

Newspaper Enterprise Association

Matthews and pioneer free agent Andy Messersmith, once a top pitcher, were among the big names Turner brought to the Braves in an effort to thrust the team into contention, but the effort failed and Turner tried to unload his high-salaried players almost as quickly as he had signed them.

Turner knew little about baseball until his TV station began carrying the Braves' games in 1975. After his purchase, he became such a prominent fan that President-elect Jimmy Carter, former governor of Georgia, approached him at a Braves' press party in Plains, Georgia and said, "I need to talk to you, Ted, and learn how to become well-known."

The trim, energetic Turner not only attended Atlanta games but stamped himself as the most uninhibited owner in baseball. He jumped fences to greet home run hitters, collapsed on the dugout in a deathlike pose after defeats, threw himself into a collegiate mattress-stuffing contest, finished second in a race of motorized bathtubs, joined a pre-game ostrich race, helped ballgirls sweep the bases between innings, played poker with players, hosted an end-of-season champagne party for fans, and painted THE ENEMY on the roof of the visitors' dugout.

★ ★ ★ ★ ★ ★ ★

# GEORGE STEINBRENNER

The minute he purchased the New York Yankees for $10 million in 1973, Cleveland ship-builder George M. Steinbrenner III replaced Charlie Finley as the game's most controversial and outspoken owner. Through the beginning of the 1989 season, Steinbrenner had changed managers 16 times and pitching coaches two-dozen times—often rehiring men he had fired before (including Billy Martin a record five times).

Steinbrenner showed similar impulsiveness in collecting players, especially high-priced veteran free agents. He signed, among others, Catfish Hunter, Goose Gossage, Tommy John, Reggie Jackson, Don Baylor, Ken Griffey, Dave Winfield, Jack Clark, and Steve Sax.

The team won five divisional crowns, four pennants, and two World Championships from 1976-81 but was never free of controversy. Steinbrenner criticized managers and players so relentlessly that he antagonized many of his own employees and a vast majority of his team's fans. Many found themselves rooting for the Yankees but against Steinbrenner.

The stormiest season to date occurred in 1978, when the beleaguered Martin, caught in a crossfire between Jackson and Steinbrenner, said, "The two of them deserve each other—one's a born liar, the other's convicted." The reference to Steinbrenner's conviction for making illegal campaign contributions to Richard Nixon cost Martin his job.

# CHAPTER ELEVEN

# Trades

# THE ART OF TRADING

Teams trade players—and even managers—more often than kids trade baseball cards.

Revised reserve rules sometimes force executives to secure permission from players before completing deals, but the ritual of constant dealing continues as an integral part of the game.

During baseball's winter meetings, an annual week-long convention, trades happen so frequently that fans have trouble keeping track. The news from those conventions, reflecting the game's continuing position as America's national pastime, invariably dominates other sports news of the week.

"Trading is hoping," according to broadcaster Maury Wills, who was sold or traded three times in his career. "General managers trade for what they hope will happen. There's never been a general manager who's so brilliant he can guarantee a sure-shot trade. Show me a general manager with a reputation as a shrewd trader and I'll show you a man who's been lucky."

Dealing for pitchers is especially risky, Wills said, because an arm can go bad overnight.

No player is immune from trades. Brooks Robinson spent his entire career with the Baltimore Orioles, 1955-77, but he was a rarity. Such superstars as Babe Ruth, Rogers Hornsby, Jimmie Foxx, Hank Greenberg, Warren Spahn, and Hank Aaron experienced at least one trade.

"Being traded is like celebrating your 100th birthday," said NBC commentator Joe Garagiola, a former player. "It might not be the happiest occasion in the world, but consider the alternatives."

## MEDWICK'S RETURN TO THE CARDS

*Slugger Joe Medwick, who first joined the Cardinals in 1932, was treated as an "enemy" after his trade to the Dodgers in 1940, but received a hero's welcome when he rejoined St. Louis seven years later. He received his unconditional release from the Yankees in 1947, but the Cards wanted a righthanded pinch-hitter and signed him. He wasn't recognized in pre-game practice because he wore No. 21 instead of his familiar No. 7, but his name brought wild cheers when it was announced in the late innings with the team behind, 3-1. He smashed a long double in a pinch-hitting role—retiring for a pinch-runner—and, at 35, enjoyed two productive seasons before ending his career.*

## TRADER'S TEMPERAMENT

*Paul Richards on trading: "Gabe Paul, Bill Veeck, and Frank Lane will make a deal and not regret the after-effects in the least. If it turns out bad, they'll go ahead and make another one. That is the attitude you must take if you're going to trade. You've got to wipe it off and keep going. You gamble every time you make a deal. You always know what you've got, but you don't always know what you're getting. The best traders are the ones with the most patience and perseverance."*

## BIG DEALS

There have been two four-club deals in baseball history (in 1953 and 1977), one two-club swap that involved 17 players, and countless big-money transactions. There might have been a complete roster swap between Kansas City and Baltimore in 1958 if Paul Richards hadn't decided to retain Brooks Robinson.

Some of the game's most stunning trades occurred after the advent of the free agent era in the '70s, when executives were forced to rebuild clubs whose stars left voluntarily or to deal players involved in salary haggles. The former case was best illustrated early in 1978, when the Oakland A's sent star southpaw Vida Blue to the San Francisco Giants for seven players and cash. The latter example was shown on the trade deadline of June 15, 1977, when the New York Mets dumped disgruntled pitcher Tom Seaver on the Cincinnati Reds for four players—three of whom became immediate regulars.

Perhaps the most significant "forced trade" occurred on February 9, 1979, when the Minnesota Twins sent seven-time American League batting champion Rod Carew to the California Angels for four young players. The 33-year-old first baseman who had threatened to become a free agent—leaving the Twins with no compensation—quickly parlayed his .334 lifetime batting average into a five-year, $4 million contract.

Minnesota had received better offers for Carew, but the player exercised veto power provided by the five-and-ten rule—giving 10-year major-leaguers who have been with one club for the past five years the right to say no. ☞

Ron Santo of the Chicago was the first to use that right, on December 4, 1973, but later accepted a deal that sent him to the crosstown White Sox.

A no-trade clause, inserted into many players' contracts, has had nebulous significance, just as the five-and-ten rule has done little to discourage trading activity. Generally, when a player finds out his club wants to trade him, he goes. Slugger Jeff Burroughs, dealt from the Rangers to the Braves for five players and $250,000 before the 1977 season, said he had a no-trade clause but did not wish to stay where he wasn't wanted.

Increased player freedom complicates the lives of executives who previously needed to reach agreement only with their contemporaries—without talking to players, agents, and lawyers. But new rules did not prevent the Braves, Pirates, Mets, and Rangers from engineering an 11-man swap on December 8, 1977.

"It was a trade that didn't happen in minutes or hours," said Pittsburgh manager Chuck Tanner. "It took a lot of days and a lot of conferences to get it done."

The swap sent first baseman Willie Montanez from Atlanta to Texas for pitchers Adrian Devine and Tommy Boggs, plus outfielder Eddie Miller. The Rangers, in turn, shipped Montanez and outfielders Tom Grieve and Ken Henderson to the New York Mets for pitcher Jon Matlack, and pitcher Bert Blyleven to the Pirates for outfielder Al Oliver and shortstop Nelson Norman. As part of the deal, the Mets also sent first baseman-outfielder John Milner to Pittsburgh.

In a previous four-team deal, on February 17, 1953, the Philadelphia Phillies sent pitcher Russ Meyer and cash to the Boston Braves for first baseman Earl Torgeson. The Braves sent Meyer to the Brooklyn Dodgers for infielder Rocky Bridges and outfielder Jim Pendleton. Then the Braves sent Bridges and a player to be named later to the Reds for first baseman Joe Adcock.

Trades are made for all kinds of reasons. Sometimes, a bad team will deal in the hope new faces will bring new customers. Salary disagreements and personality clashes force many trades. A player's wish to be closer to home, or a team's desire to hire a new manager are other factors.

Dodger general manager Al Campanis (then farm director) sent his son, Jimmy, to the Kansas City Royals in 1968 because he thought that expansion team would let him catch regularly.

Washington owner Clark Griffith, another man with a baseball family, once acquired his son-in-law from the Cleveland Indians, but made a more successful trade when he sold another son-in-law, shortstop-manager Joe Cronin, to the Boston Red Sox in 1934. He'd been overwhelmed by Tom Yawkey's offer of $250,000—a staggering sum in Depression days—plus Lyn Lary, who would replace Cronin at short. ☞

Oakland owner Charlie Finley sold players for cash when rising salaries and falling attendance curtailed his cash flow.

## BOBO NEWSOM'S TRAVELOG

To say Bobo Newsom was a well-traveled pitcher is an understatement. From 1935 to 1952, he played for, in order, the Browns, Senators, Red Sox, Browns, Tigers, Senators, Dodgers, Browns, Senators, A's, Senators, Yankees, Giants, Senators, and A's. He won 211 games and lost 222.

## JOE TORRE, RAY SADECKI AND ORLANDO CEPEDA

In 1966, the San Francisco Giants traded first baseman Orlando Cepeda to the St. Louis Cardinals for pitcher Ray Sadecki. Three years later, the Cardinals traded Cepeda to the Atlanta Braves for catcher-first baseman Joe Torre. In 1974, they sent Torre to the New York Mets for Ray Sadecki. Cepeda and Torre won MVP awards for St. Louis in 1967 and 1971.

High-salaried stars involved in major trades of the '70s included (left to right) Rod Carew, Willie Montanez, and Tom Seaver.

Player sales were more common in the early part of the century. Trading players for other players became such common practice that huge sales were frowned on by the Commissioner of Baseball.

When Bowie Kuhn canceled the sale of Oakland pitcher Vida Blue to the Reds for $1.75 million and a minor league slugger, he announced, "Public confidence and the integrity of the game could be questioned if a team as strong as the Cincinnati Reds were allowed to buy a pitcher the quality of Blue, with the Oakland club being further weakened. I am sympathetic to the operating problems of Charlie Finley, but there are other ways for him to improve his situation rather than the selling of talent. Player-for-player deals can strengthen a club and help it rapidly to rebuild."

Though Kuhn set an arbitrary ceiling of $400,000 as the maximum amount of cash that may be included in a single transaction, the old practice of selling stars brought financially-strapped Connie Mack some $900,000 in the early '30s. Figuring in the inflationary spiral over forty-plus years, that money would have amounted to $4.5 million by modern standards.

# THE SALE OF BABE RUTH

The first five-figure sale in baseball history occurred before the turn of the century. Mike (King) Kelly, skilled but zany performer who had helped Chicago win five National League pennants in seven seasons, was sold to Boston for $10,000. That started a trend.

After losing the 1914 World Series to the "miracle" Braves, Athletics owner-manager Connie Mack began to break up his team in an effort to keep his stars in the American League rather than the rival Federal League.

Second baseman Eddie Collins, one of those who departed, brought $50,000 into Mack's treasury. Jack Barry and Frank (Home Run) Baker—two other members of the famed $100,000 infield—also went in the supermarket sweep.

The World Champion Boston Red Sox of 1918 followed Mack's lead the following year and began peeling off stars for bank notes. It seems owner Harry Frazee needed funds to underwrite his theater productions, and was willing to sacrifice athletics for dramatics. With the Yankee office two doors from Frazee's New York headquarters, he had a short walk and an eager customer. By 1923, 11 of his stars were Yankees. The biggest was Babe Ruth.

At age 24 in 1919, Ruth hit .322 with 29 home runs and 114 runs batted in, and compiled an 8-5 pitching record for the Red Sox, with two saves and a 2.98 ERA. The power production staggered the baseball world as much as the purchase price—$125,000. The deal was announced on January 3, 1920. Nine months later, Ruth had compiled 54 home runs and the following year enjoyed perhaps the most remarkable season by any player: 59 homers, 171 runs batted in, a .378 batting average, and a 2-0 pitching record.

Harry Frazee lived to see Ruth hit 60 home runs in 1927. The man who got more money but less value in a trade than any of his contemporaries died in 1929.

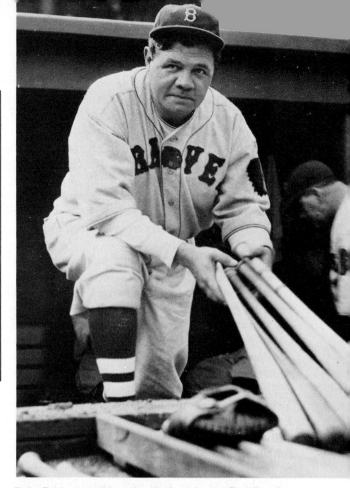

Babe Ruth was sold to the Yankees by the Red Sox for $125,000 on January 3, 1920, then returned to Boston with the National League Braves at the end of his career.

## RUTH'S FIRST SALE WAS A BARGAIN

Babe Ruth reached the majors in 1914 when Jack Dunn, owner of Baltimore (International), sold him to the Boston Red Sox with Ernie Shore and Ben Egan. The price for the trio was $25,000. The Philadelphia A's had earlier declined to purchase Ruth.

## McGRAW SENT MARQUARD TO BROOKLYN

Pressed for cash, John McGraw's last-place New York Giants of 1915 sold pitcher Rube Marquard to the arch-rival Brooklyn Dodgers for $7500.

# ROGERS HORNSBY FOR FRANKIE FRISCH

Rogers Hornsby, who had won six batting crowns by age 30, was player-manager of the World Champion St. Louis Cardinals in 1926. It was his first season as manager and he felt he should be rewarded, but his demands for a three-year, $150,000 contract angered owner Sam Breadon so much that he was dealt from the Cards.

The New York Giants had a well-entrenched incumbent manager in John McGraw, but welcomed the chance to get a hitter of Hornsby's caliber. He was only two seasons removed from his record .424 campaign.

McGraw had to give up local hero Frankie Frisch, who earned the nickname of "Fordham Flash" as a college star, but eagerly made the sacrifice. He also threw in pitcher Jim Ring, who had won 11 games.

Frisch began his long managing career with the Cardinals in 1933 and, while Hornsby never managed the Giants, he did resume directing clubs from the field later. He had two terms with the Browns and one with the Reds.

When the Hornsby-for-Frisch trade was announced, fans were literally stunned. The player-manager of the World Champions was coming to New York, but a hometown favorite had to be sacrificed to get him. The deal made even more headlines than the Yankees' purchase of Babe Ruth six years earlier.

# THE SECOND SELLING OF THE A's

Connie Mack's Philadelphia A's gradually recovered from the economic troubles of the World War I era and slowly returned to contender status. Mack finally found money to make some significant purchases—notably lefthander Bob (Lefty) Grove of the Baltimore Orioles in the International League.

Grove's purchase price was $100,600. He was worth it, as he helped the Athletics jell into one of the most powerful teams in baseball history in 1929, when they won the first of two World Championships and three pennants.

But hard times set in again and Mack was forced to run another fire sale. On December 12, 1933, Grove, Max Bishop, and Rube Walberg were traded to the Boston Red Sox for Harold Warstler, Bob Kline, and $125,000.

Al Simmons, Jimmy Dykes, and Mule Haas had already been sent to the White Sox for $150,000, and Jimmie Foxx arrived in Boston two years later in a $150,000 swap disguised as a four-player trade. Detroit got Mickey Cochrane for $100,000. Pitcher George Earnshaw also wound up with the White Sox.

There were other sales too, bringing Mack a grand total of $900,000. But the deals knocked the A's out of contention and into a long period of snoozing in the basement of the American League. Only after they moved to Oakland (from Kansas City) in 1968 did the A's revive.

## COLLINS OKAYED SALE BY A'S

Secondbaseman Eddie Collins, one of several star players sold by the Philadelphia Athletics during the Federal League raids of 1914-15, accepted his assignment to the Chicago White Sox only after owner Charles Comiskey offered him a five-year contract for $15,000 per season—big money at that time.

## SOX BOUGHT DOERR, DiMAG FROM MINORS

In addition to Ted Williams, the Boston Red Sox also acquired Bobby Doerr and Dom DiMaggio by direct purchase from minor league teams.

One of the best investments in baseball history was made by the Boston Red Sox in December 1937. General manager Eddie Collins sent five players and $25,000 to the San Diego Padres of the Pacific Coast League for Ted Williams.

# THE PURCHASE OF TED WILLIAMS

During the heyday of the independent minor league operator, the majors and minors dealt freely on an open market. Clubs were just learning the nuances of the farm system in the late '30s. Since Commissioner Kenesaw Mountain Landis disliked the concept, several clubs were slow in developing players on their own farms. They relied on dealing—whether for players or cash.

In December 1937, Eddie Collins was considering a deal with the San Diego Padres of the Pacific Coast League. They owned a strong, lefthanded-batting outfielder named Ted Williams. Williams, then 19, had hit .291 that year.

San Diego saw vast potential in Williams and made heavy demands on the Red Sox general manager, asking for five players and $25,000. Collins got over his initial hesitation and agreed to the purchase.

In a career starting in 1939 and ending in 1960, Ted Williams compiled a lifetime average of .345 and slammed 521 home runs. His .406 mark of 1941 has not been surpassed since.

# CUBS PAID HUGE PRICE FOR DIZZY DEAN

Though he was only a shadow of his old self, Dizzy Dean commanded a huge sum when the St. Louis Cardinals put him on the market after the 1937 season.

The Chicago Cubs, seeking to make up the three-game deficit between first and second place that fall, put together an overwhelming package to land Dean the following April.

On April 16, Chicago sent pitchers Curt Davis and Clyde Shoun and outfielder Tuck Stainback, plus $185,000, to the Cardinals for the 27-year-old Dean.

"We knew his arm was questionable," Cub owner Phil Wrigley said years later, "but I thought it was a pretty good deal. We won the pennant and set an attendance record. Dean has a psychological effect on the team, and that's what we wanted him for.

"We'd announce Dizzy Dean was going to pitch and we'd put on extra ticket sellers. People wanted to see whether his arm was good or bad. Baseball is a very controversial game. Take the controversy out and you'd kill it."

Dean posted a 7-1 record and 1.80 ERA for the Cubs—the difference between first and fourth place, as Chicago led the Pirates by two games, the Giants by three, and the Reds by six at season's end.

A 30-game winner for the Gashouse Gang Cardinals of 1934, Dean was never the same after Earl Averill broke his toe with a line drive during the 1937 All-Star Game. But, for that one season, he helped pitch the Cubs to a pennant.

# BASEBALL'S CRAZIEST SWAPS

*By ERNIE HARWELL in Parade Magazine*
*February 26, 1956*

*Under the sun's hot glare down South this week, major-league ball players begin the painful routine of shedding winter fat and limbering up stiffened muscles. Throughout the spring-training grind they'll be lashed on by baseball's ever-present threat: look sharp or be traded. For most of them, the buyer would have to shell out thousands of dollars or other ball players. In baseball's poorer days, however, players were traded for whatever a hard-pressed club owner might need—and he could need almost anything.*

*Take Joe Engel, the president of the Chattanooga Lookouts. During the 1931 season he decided to stage a turkey dinner, but lacked the turkey. He quickly got together with Felix Hayman, who owned the Charlotte, N.C., team and—more important—a butcher shop. The result was a deal which sent Chattanooga shortstop Johnny Jones to Charlotte in return for one of Hayman's chunkier turkeys.*

*Some famous names were pawns in those weird trades. Denton T. (Cy) Young, for instance, won more games (511) than any pitcher in baseball history, but was so lightly regarded as a rookie that the Canton, Ohio, team peddled him to Cleveland for a suit of clothes.*

*Baseball's greatest star, Babe Ruth, came to the New York Yankees in a deal almost as odd. A top pitcher and outfielder with the Boston Red Sox, Ruth was traded in 1919 by the impoverished Sox for $100,000 and a personal loan of $350,000 to the Sox' owner, Harry Frazee (security for the loan: Boston's Fenway Park).*

*Players and plots of land often were tied in during baseball's early days. In the spring of 1913 the St. Louis Browns (now the Baltimore Orioles) trained on the field of the local team in Montgomery, Ala. When time came to break camp, the Browns found they didn't have enough money to pay the rent for the field. After some dickering, they handed over rookie Clyde (Buzzy) Wares to the Montgomery team. (Wares spent a year in Montgomery, but later came up to the big leagues for keeps.)*

*The Browns may have picked up that method of paying rent from the Detroit Tigers. In 1905 they trained in Augusta, Ga., paid on rent day with pitcher Eddie Cicotte (later a star with the Chicago Black Sox).*

*Another great hurler, Robert Moses (Lefty) Grove, got started toward the majors by being exchanged for a center-field fence. Grove was toiling for the Martinsburg, W. Va., club when Jack Dunn, owner of the Baltimore Orioles (then in the International*

League), spotted him. Dunn learned that Martinsburg owed money for the erection of an outfield fence, offered to pay the bill in exchange for Grove. Martinsburg agreed and Grove went off to star at Baltimore, then moved up to the American League and eventually the Hall of Fame.

The strangest trades, though, have stemmed from somebody's being hungry. The Wichita Falls, Tex., team once traded Euel Moore for a plate of beans. Dallas sent Joe Martina to New Orleans for two barrels of oysters, thereby pinning the lifetime nickname of Oyster Joe on the pitcher. San Francisco shipped first baseman Jack Fenton to Memphis for a box of prunes. But when president Homer Hammond of San Antonio agreed to trade infielder Mike Dondero to Dallas for a dozen doughnuts, he managed to keep Dondero and have his doughnuts too; before signing the agreement, he ate them all up.

The hobbies of club owners also have figured in outlandish trades. Barney Burch of Omaha once gave up two players for an air-plane and Nashville's Larry Gilbert traded a set of golf clubs to land Charlie (Greek) George.

At least one owner had to trade a player to get out of a personal jam. After a convention of baseball men, a club president found himself stone broke, unable to pay even his hotel bill. He promptly went down to the lobby, which was full of club owners, and sold one of his pitchers for cash, pocketing enough to pay his bill and train fare home.

But no baseball executive ever traded more cleverly than part-player, part-owner Willis Hudlin. After pitching with Cleveland for 14 years, Hudlin became part owner and pitcher for the Little Rock Travelers. Midway through 1944, owner Hudlin traded pitcher Hudlin to the St. Louis Browns. He pitched only two innings all season long and lost the game, but the Browns won the pennant and Hudlin got a slice of the World Series money. That winter, owner Hudlin bought back pitcher Hudlin from the Browns—and kept the change.

ED. NOTE: Author Harwell left out of this article a trade that he himself was a part of— a trade almost as odd as any that he mentions. In 1948 Harwell was broadcasting the Atlanta Crackers' games. Branch Rickey, then with Brooklyn, heard Harwell and asked Earl Mann, owner of the Crackers, if he would release Harwell from his contract.

"I'll give him to you," replied Mann, "if you give me catcher Cliff Dapper on your Montreal farm. I want him for manager next year."

Rickey agreed, swapping a catcher for a broadcaster, and Harwell went to Brooklyn.

# GREENBERG GOES TO PITTSBURGH

In 1946, Hank Greenberg led the American League with 44 home runs and 127 runs batted in. After the season, he was sold to the Pittsburgh Pirates on waivers.

Waivers are necessary to overcome normal restrictions on trading. Inter-league trading did not exist until the first Inter-League Trading Period opened for three weeks, starting November 21, 1959, and moving of players across league lines had to be accomplished by "waiving a player out of the league."

When all clubs express disinterest in a player who is about to be traded within one league, he can be sold or traded outside the league. Waiver deals have always been easily arranged because owners know who the two dealing parties are, and often look the other way when a talented player finds his way onto the waiver list.

The theory is that if one owner helps another make his trade, the favor will be repaid when the second owner wants to trade.

Ralph Kiner, who played with Greenberg in Pittsburgh, recalled the deal well. "I guess he was making too much money in Detroit and they decided to go for a youth movement," he said.

Greenberg, 35 when the deal was made, teamed with Kiner to give the Pirates a solid one-two power punch, but the club finished last anyway. Kiner led the league with 51 home runs and Greenberg hit 25 in 1947, their first year together.

# HOW VEECK LANDED VERNON AND WYNN

Bill Veeck knew Early Wynn and Mickey Vernon could help his Cleveland Indians win the 1948 American League pennant. But Wynn and Vernon played for Washington under Clark Griffith, who disapproved of Veeck's endless stream of gimmicks and outspoken comments about the game.

Griffith's son-in-law, Joe Haynes, was a sore-armed White Sox pitcher and definitely available. Veeck knew Griffith wouldn't relish the idea of his son-in-law playing in Cleveland, so he sent catcher Joe Tipton to Chicago for Haynes. Griffith sent his adopted nephew, Calvin, to negotiate.

The deal sent Haynes, Eddie Robinson, and reliever Ed Kleimanto to the Senators for Vernon and Wynn. Veeck also agreed to pay for Haynes' surgery. Veeck announced the trade at 4:45 a.m. because, he said, he didn't want to give Griffith time to change his mind.

While Haynes won ten games in four years for Washington, Wynn won 163 for Cleveland and 59 more for Chicago, including 22 in 1959, when newly-named owner Bill Veeck helped the Sox win their first flag in forty years.

The man Veeck yielded for Joe Haynes never amounted to much in the majors. But enterprising White Sox general manager Frank Lane pulled a major coup by sending him to the Philadelphia Athletics for secondbaseman Nellie Fox. Fox, in turn, became the sparkplug of the '59 White Sox and was voted the American League's Most Valuable Player. Wynn won the Cy Young Award for pitching excellence.

It all started because of Joe Tipton.

Roger Maris, acquired from the Kansas City A's, first donned Yankee pinstripes in 1960, then hit 61 homers a year later.

# BRAVES' DEALS WON TWO FLAGS FOR GIANTS

The Braves helped the Giants win their only pennants of the '50s by sending them three stars in two separate transactions. On December 14, 1949, they sent their talented double-play combination —shortstop Alvin Dark and second baseman Eddie Stanky—to New York for third baseman Sid Gordon, outfielder Willard Marshall, infielder Buddy Kerr, and pitcher Sam Webb.

Because the Giants had added speed and defense, and unloaded several slow-footed sluggers, they staged the most dramatic stretch drive in history to win the 1951 National League pennant.

The hero of that season was Bobby Thomson, whose last-of-the-ninth homer erased a Dodger lead and gave victory to the Giants. The Braves, seeking power, made several bids for him and finally succeeded on the eve of the 1954 season.

They sent lefthanded pitchers Johnny Antonelli and Don Liddle, catcher Ebba St. Claire, infielder Billy Klaus and $50,000 to New York for Thomson and catcher Sam Calderone.

Antonelli, 24, immediately blossomed into the ace of the Giants' staff, posting a 21-7 record and league-leading 2.29 ERA. He went all the way in Game 2 of New York's four-game World Series sweep over the favored Cleveland Indians.

Thomson never even made it past spring training. He suffered a broken leg while sliding into a base and was replaced by an unknown 20-year-old rookie named Hank Aaron.

# ROGER MARIS: FROM KAYCEE TO NY

The man who broke Babe Ruth's single-season home run record was, like Ruth, acquired in trade.

Roger Maris, also like Ruth, was a strong lefthanded hitter who had the advantage of Yankee Stadium's short right field porch, only 296 feet from the plate.

He began to notice the fence almost immediately after joining the club, producing 39 home runs and 112 runs batted in to win the American League's Most Valuable Player Award for 1960.

Maris became a Yankee on December 11, 1959, when the club sent outfielders Hank Bauer and Norm Siebern, first baseman Marv Throneberry, and pitcher Don Larsen to the Kansas City Athletics for Maris and two infield substitutes: shortstop Joe DeMaestri and first baseman Kent Hadley.

In 1961, with American League pitching universally weakened by expansion (and Maris having the luxury of not facing the strongest staff in the league), the Yankee rightfielder connected 61 times. It was the only time in his major league career that Roger Maris reached the 40 mark in home runs.

Five years later, at age 31, he hit .233 with 13 home runs as the Yankees dropped to last place in the ten-team American League. After the season, he was traded to the St. Louis Cardinals for little-known third baseman Charley Smith. The one-time superstar of the World Champions enjoyed his last hurrah in the big leagues when he paced the Cardinals to the 1967 World Championship with a club-leading seven runs batted in. In two years with St. Louis, Roger Maris hit a grand total of 14 home runs.

# 17-PLAYER TRADE

General managers Paul Richards of the Orioles and George Weiss of the Yankees engineered the largest two-club deal in the game's history late in the 1954 season.

The Yankees received pitchers Don Larsen, Bob Turley, and Mike Blyzka; catcher Darrell Johnson; first baseman Dick Kryhoski; shortstop Billy Hunter; and outfielders Ted del Guercio and Tim Fridley.

Baltimore acquired nine—pitchers Harry Byrd, Jim McDonald, and Bill Miller; catchers Gus Triandos and Hal Smith; second baseman Don Leppert; third baseman Kal Segrist; shortstop Willy Miranda; and outfielder Gene Woodling.

Larsen, 26, and Turley, 25, proved of immense value to the Yankees. Two years after the trade, Larsen pitched the only perfect game in World Series history and Turley won 21 regular-season games.

Triandos, Woodling, and Miranda became Oriole regulars, making solid contributions as Richards gradually built a strong young club around them.

# INTER-LEAGUE TRADING

Waiver-free inter-league trading was permitted for the first time after the 1959 season. An Inter-League Trading Period was established from November 21 to December 15. Later, these dates were modified to extend the period from five days after the end of the World Series to midnight on the final day of the winter baseball meetings. A spring trading period was added in 1977.

Since the regular trade deadline has remained June 15 for years, several observers suggested the spring period should be fixed for May 15-June 15, thereby allowing teams to turn their talent searches to the other league before all trading ends.

Establishment of the spring period from February 15-March 15 was ineffective for several reasons—primarily because managers have not had ample time to evaluate their squads in spring camp that soon, but also because any deal that could be made then could have also been made the previous fall.

An early spring trading period discouraged trading in the winter and reduced the flow of baseball news when it is needed most—in the off-season, when teams are selling season tickets.

The first trades completed under the new Inter-League Trading Period in 1959 were far from earth-shaking. The Cubs sent first baseman-outfielder Jim Marshall and pitcher Dave Hillman to the Red Sox for first baseman Dick Gernert, and the Reds dealt pitcher Tom Acker to the A's for catcher Frank House.

Dozens of major deals have been made. Jim Bunning went from the Tigers to the Phillies and became the only man to pitch no-hitters in both leagues. Dave Johnson went from the Orioles to the Braves and, in his first season, slammed 43 home runs, a record for a second baseman. Felix Mantilla left the Mets to hit 30 home runs for the Red Sox. Dick Stuart, going to Boston from Pittsburgh, hit 42.

Juan Pizarro, 24-year-old lefthander, became ace of the White Sox staff in 1961 after a three-way deal involving the Reds and Braves gave him his first opportunity to pitch regularly. The same deal sent another little-used Brave, Joey Jay, to the Reds, where he blossomed into a 21-game winner on a pennant-winning staff. ☞

## BRAVES GOT BURDETTE FOR SAIN

*The Braves made a successful waiver deal with the pennant-hungry Yankees in 1951 when they sent Johnny Sain, 33, to New York for Lew Burdette, 24. Burdette went on to win 179 games for the Braves and teamed with southpaw Warren Spahn to give the team an even more formidable left-right punch than the old Spahn-Sain tandem.*

## "PLAYER TO BE NAMED LATER"

*Some baseball deals involve a "player to be named later." In 1964 and again in 1970, players were traded for themselves. Vic Power was dealt to the contending Phillies by the Angels during the stretch drive in 1964, but was given back after the season. Hoyt Wilhelm went from the Braves to the contending Cubs late in 1970 and also was returned.*

## TWO TEAMS, ONE DAY

*In 1922, Max Flack of the Cubs was traded for Cliff Heathcote of the Cardinals between games of a morning-afternoon doubleheader on Memorial Day. They were the only two major-leaguers to play for two different teams on the same day.*

## TIMELY TRADE

*Rick Sutcliffe, who went 16-1 for the 1984 Cubs after arriving from Cleveland, is the only pitcher to be traded in the middle of a season in which he won the Cy Young Award.*

Slugger Frank Howard thrived with Washington after arriving from Los Angeles in a swap for pitcher Claude Osteen. That was clearly a deal that helped both clubs. A one-sided swap across league lines gave the Orioles outfielder Ken Singleton and pitcher Mike Torrez of the Expos in return for pitcher Dave McNally, outfielder Rich Coggins, and a minor-leaguer. All three Montreal additions were washouts.

Tommy John, a quality lefthanded starter, prospered after joining the Dodgers from the White Sox—even though he missed a year-and-a-half with an arm injury. Ken Holtzman, also a southpaw, did well for the Oakland A's after Charlie Finley sent centerfielder Rick Monday to the Cubs to get him. Chicago also was happy with its end of the swap.

After the 1974 season, the Milwaukee Brewers acquired Hank Aaron for a two-year swing around the American League as designated hitter. Aaron was 41 before the '75 campaign opened, but he welcomed the opportunity to close his career in the city where it began. Milwaukee was the home of the National League Braves during Aaron's rookie year in 1954. The Braves got journeyman outfielder Dave May and young pitcher Roger Alexander in the ho-hum deal for their long-time superstar.

Aaron retired in the fall of 1976 and rejoined the Braves as an executive just as the team was landing its first bona fide slugger since his heyday: Jeff Burroughs. The price—five major league players and $250,000—paid off immediately as Burroughs slammed 41 home runs and knocked in 114 runs in his first Atlanta season.

Other sluggers also moved during the Inter-League Trading Period—notably Bobby Murcer and Bobby Bonds, who switched uniforms in a blockbuster trade between the Yankees and Giants after the 1974 season. The Baltimore Orioles, who landed consistent Lee May from Houston for light-hitting rookie infielder Rob Andrews, scored several times in the inter-league market, landing lefthanded pitchers Ross Grimsley from the Reds and Mike Cuellar from the Astros, plus righthander Pat Dobson from the San Diego Padres.

The three worst inter-league trades were engineered by the Mets, Giants, and Reds—the first two within a two-week span. Seeking a thirdbaseman, the Mets opted for long-time California Angels shortstop Jim Fregosi, a 29-year-old power-hitter who had been held to a .233 average in 1971.

To get him, New York sent four players to the Angels, including outfielder Lee Stanton, who became a home run hitter as a regular, and hard-throwing but erratic pitcher Nolan Ryan. Fregosi was a failure and was gone within two seasons, but Ryan became the Angels' ace in his first season, with 19 wins, 329 strikeouts, and a 2.29 ERA.

On November 29, 1971, the San Francisco Giants shipped Gaylord Perry to the Cleveland Indians for Sam McDowell in a trade of pitchers. Perry, 32, was four years older than Sudden Sam when the deal was made, but had much more life left in his arm. McDowell never did a thing for the Giants.

Tom Yawkey... Brought Cronin to Boston

## CRONIN SALE FORCED MANAGER SWAP

*When player-manager Joe Cronin was sold from the Washington Senators to the Boston Red Sox after the 1934 season, the transaction not only included a $250,000 payoff from Tom Yawkey to Clark Griffith, but also a five-year, $30,000 pact for Cronin as Boston's player-manager. Incumbent Red Sox pilot Bucky Harris took the vacant manager's job in Washington.*

Mike Cuellar became a star pitcher after he was acquired by Baltimore from Houston.

## CASEY STENGEL TRADED HIMSELF

*When Casey Stengel was president and player-manager of the Boston Braves farm team at Worcester, Massachusetts, he sold himself to the New York Giants farm club at Toledo, Ohio.*

## FANS REACTED TO KINER TRADE

*New York Mets' broadcaster Ralph Kiner, who witnessed the angry backlash of fans upset with the Mets for dealing Tom Seaver in 1977, recalled a similar reaction by Pirate fans when Branch Rickey traded him to the Cubs in 1953. Kiner, Joe Garagiola, and two others became Cubs in exchange for six players and $100,000.*

## GREENBERG LAUGHED AT VEECK'S PITCH

*During his tenure as boss of the Browns, Bill Veeck always needed money for basic expenses. He tried to convince Cleveland's Hank Greenberg, a close friend, to buy first baseman Hank Arft, but the Indians already had Luke Easter at the position. In his final plea, Veeck's teletype jammed and printed ARFARFARFARFARF. Greenberg wired back, I CAN'T STOP LAUGHING. KEEP THAT DOG IN ST. LOUIS.*

# HOW THE ORIOLES GOT FRANK ROBINSON

In 1965, the Cincinnati Reds finished fourth in the National League, 8 games behind the Los Angeles Dodgers. Their big star was 30-year-old outfielder Frank Robinson, who that year hit .296 with 33 home runs and 113 runs batted in.

During the winter meetings, several Cincinnati executives approached Baltimore's major league scout, Jim Russo, and handed him a slip of paper with Robinson's name on one side and the names of three Orioles on the other side. Those names were Milt Pappas, Jack Baldschun, and Rookie-of-the-Year Curt Blefary.

"I told our people, 'We've got to acquire Frank Robinson in a way that won't cost us Blefary,' " Russo recalled. "I felt we could replace the thirteen games Pappas had won with Jim Palmer, who was 19 years old then. Our manager, Hank Bauer, was a little reluctant to give him up.

"We went back to the Cincinnati people and said we can't make the deal if Blefary is involved, but the day before that we had made a deal for Dick Simpson, and the Reds liked him. They said they had good reports on him from their Triple-A manager in San Diego, Dave Bristol."

That clinched the deal. Bill DeWitt, then the Reds' general manager, sent Robinson away with bitter feelings when he called him "an old 30," and the slugger made up his mind to respond with his most spectacular season. He did just that, winning the Triple Crown of batting with a .316 average, 49 homers, and 122 runs batted in. He homered twice during the four-game World Series sweep over the Los Angeles Dodgers.

Robinson played six seasons in Baltimore and was so brilliant that the team retired his No. 20 after he was traded to the Dodgers for four prospects in the winter of 1971. The Orioles won four pennants in the six Frank Robinson years.

# DEALS OF RECENT VINTAGE

Growing demands by players precipitated an era of "spite trades" in the late '60s and early '70s.

Ken Harrelson was hitting .305, and averaging one RBI every two games, when he got into a haggle with Kansas City Athletics owner Charlie Finley. When manager Alvin Dark was fired in the turmoil, Harrelson called Finley "a menace to baseball" and was summarily fired.

The Boston Red Sox, suddenly in pennant contention after years of lurking near the league basement, jumped at the chance to sign the 25-year-old Harrelson, whose righthanded power was ideally suited to Fenway Park. His signing bonus and salary more than covered his contribution: 3 home runs and 14 runs batted in during the final weeks of a race the Sox won by one game.

That same season, Maury Wills was playing third base for Pittsburgh instead of shortstop for Los Angeles because of a falling out with management the previous fall. After the Dodgers won their second straight pennant, Wills declined to complete a post-season trip to Japan; he left the team in Tokyo, causing owner Walter O'Malley to apologize to the Japanese premier. "A higher degree of devotion was expected," he said of Wills, who called in sick with a knee injury. ☞

## OLD MAN HELPED BRAVES WIN WEST

*With five of the six NL West teams in contention on Labor Day 1969, the Atlanta Braves pulled a coup by acquiring 45-year-old knuckleball reliever Hoyt Wilhelm from the California Angels. In eight appearances, he had a 2-0 record, 4 saves, and 0.75 earned run mark as the Braves won the division by 3 games. As payment for Wilhelm, Atlanta sent minor league outfielder Mickey Rivers to the Angels after the season.*

## HOW MATHEWS HEARD OF DEAL

*Third baseman Eddie Mathews, only man to play for the Braves in Boston, Milwaukee, and Atlanta, was told of his 1966 trade to Houston by a sportswriter. A subsequent letter of apology from the team was addressed to Edward—rather than Edwin—Mathews.*

## PAFKO WAS DISAPPOINTED DODGER

*Cubs outfielder Andy Pafko was disappointed when dealt to the Dodgers in mid-season of 1951. "Nobody bothered me with the Cubs," he said, "but Brooklyn has a Murderers Row with Hodges, Campanella, Snider, and Furillo. When someone ahead of me hits a home run, the next pitch comes at my head. That isn't fun. Dodger-Giant games aren't baseball—they're civil wars."*

## MAAS WAS AMAZED

*Pitcher Duke Maas of the A's didn't know he had been traded to the Yankees that morning when he won a game at Boston's Fenway Park in 1958.*

The St. Louis Cardinals lost two quality lefthanders when salary talks came to an impasse. Steve Carlton, 26, won 20 games in 1971, and Jerry Reuss, 22, won 14 the same season, but both were gone in 1972. Carlton, dealt to Philadelphia for Rick Wise, immediately led the league with 27 victories and a 1.98 ERA. The team won only 59 games.

Gabe Paul, long-time executive with the Reds, Astros, and Indians (twice), deserves much of the credit for restoring the Yankee dynasty through shrewd trades that brought first baseman Chris Chambliss from Cleveland, second baseman Willie Randolph from Pittsburgh, centerfielder Mickey Rivers and pitcher Ed' Figueroa from California, and shortstop Bucky Dent from Chicago.

The Randolph deal was particularly impressive because he was the unknown factor in a deal that brought veteran pitchers Dock Ellis and Ken Brett to New York in exchange for veteran Yankee starter George (Doc) Medich, who went to Pittsburgh. Randolph had excellent minor league credentials but could not budge incumbent second baseman Rennie Stennett.

Charlie Finley, another shrewd dealer, took advantage of entrenched Pirate veterans when he obtained outfielder Mitchell Page, second baseman Mike Edwards, and pitcher Doug Bair (later dealt for first baseman Dave Revering). Seven former Giants arrived in 1978 for veteran Vida Blue; shortstop Mario Guerrero and pitchers John Henry Johnson and Dave Heaverlo were immediately impressive.

Finley even managed to land a quality player for a non-playing manager in 1976, when he sent Chuck Tanner to the Pirates for veteran receiver Manny Sanguillen plus cash. Little more than a year later, he returned Sanguillen to Pittsburgh for several prospects.

Finley wasn't the first to trade active players for bench managers. After the 1967 season, the New York Mets sent pitcher Bill Denehy to the Washington Senators for manager Gil Hodges, a former New York player, and more than fifty years before that, the old New York Giants sent superstar pitcher Christy Mathewson to the Cincinnati Reds as their new manager. The date of that five-player trade —which also made Reds of Edd Roush and Bill McKechnie—was July 21, 1916.

Probably the most lopsided trade of the post-World War II period was made on June 15, 1964, on the eve of the trading deadline.

The St. Louis Cardinals sent 28-year-old righthander Ernie Broglio, an 18-game winner the year before, plus veteran reliever Bobby Shantz and reserve outfielder Doug Clemens to the Chicago Cubs for an erratic but speedy outfielder with a tendency to strike out too often.

Lou Brock went on to become the greatest base-stealer in the long history of the game. He established both single-season and lifetime records.

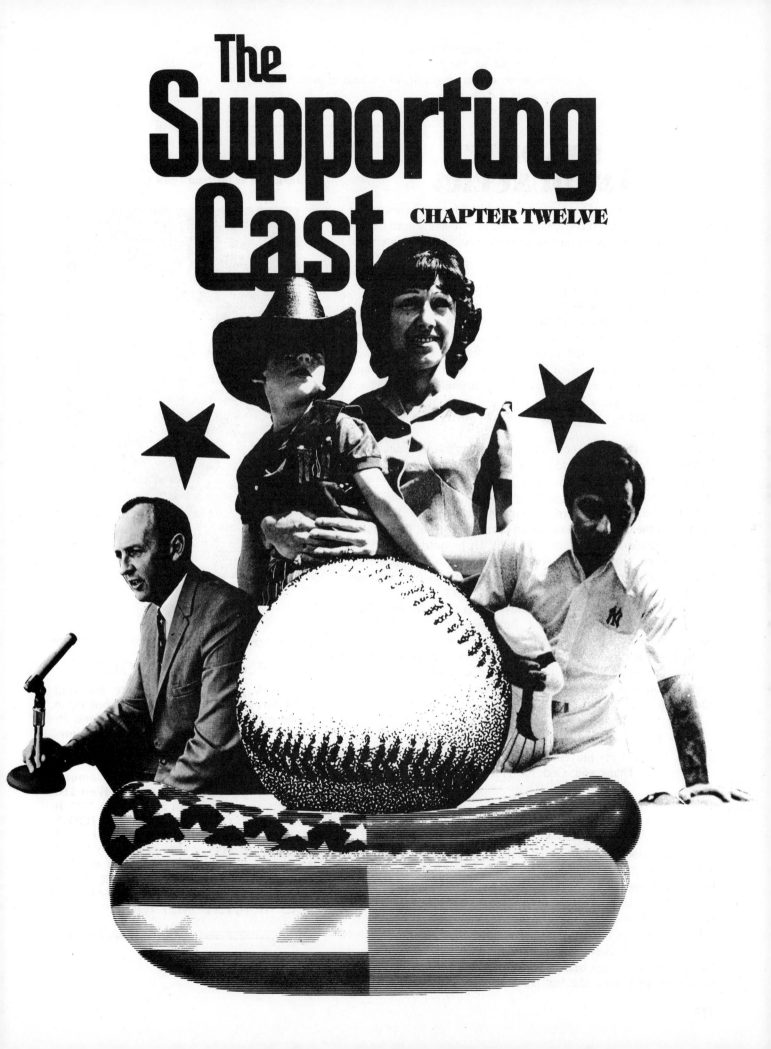

# The Supporting Cast

**CHAPTER TWELVE**

Baseball's supporting cast operates primarily behind the scenes. Few people see the equipment manager, scoreboard operator, team trainer or doctor, organist, or clubhouse man, but they play vital roles on a daily basis.

# STADIUM ANNOUNCERS

Before the advent of sophisticated public address systems, teams employed field announcers, megaphone men who announced lineups to the fans and served as liaison for both press box and scoreboard personnel.

The most famous field announcer was Chicago's Pat Pieper, an announcer at lightless Wrigley Field by day and a waiter at night. Long after electronic systems sent megaphones the route of the buffalo nickel, and stadium announcers to press box locations, Pieper remained on the field. He was known for his drawn-out cry of "Play ball!" which he delivered immediately after giving the lineups. Pieper was to Cub fans what Ed McMahon is to Johnny Carson.

Field announcers weren't paid much, and Brooklyn's Ted Rickard earned just $5 a game for many years. He made up in popularity what he missed in cash. Dodger fans even gave him a "night" at Ebbets Field.

Rickard was one of the best, but he wasn't flawless. One day, coats were hung along the left field railing and the umpire suggested they might interfere with play. Rickard boomed, "Attention please! Will the fans along the left field railing please remove their clothing?"

A close relative of the early megaphone man was the downtown hawker. In the '20s, a San Franciscan proved so good at this job that he won the nickname "Foghorn" Murphy. He paraded up and down Market Street, urging fans to see the San Francisco Seals in action. When the team moved into Recreation Park, with its field level bar in full operation, he didn't have to work as hard.

The coming of the PA system allowed fans in all corners of the park to hear each announcement. Bob Sheppard, the subtle and classical voice of Yankee Stadium, announced many of the game's greatest names through continuous World Series action. But Sheppard's contribution was more than oral; he developed into the team's poet laureate and, in 1961, penned this poem for Roger Maris just after his 61st home run:

> They've been pitching me low and wide and tight
> I've been tense and nervous, drawn and pallid
> But my prayers are full of joy tonight
> Thank you, God, for Tracy Stallard.

# ORGANISTS

Gladys Goodding, the organist at Ebbets Field, Brooklyn, probably was the best-known musician in baseball history. She won her spurs the second day on the job—May 9, 1942—when she played "Three Blind Mice" as umpires Bill Stewart, Ziggy Sears, and Tom Dunn walked onto the field. The fans roared.

Goodding, who also played for boxing matches at St. Nicholas Arena and for hockey, basketball, and fights at Madison Square Garden, knew Stewart because the umpire was a hockey referee in winter. Stewart knew she had taken the organist's job at Ebbets

Bob Sheppard joined the Yankees as public address announcer in 1949 and quickly won a reputation as the team's poet laureate.

Field and had just finished telling his umpiring partners that she was his friend. At that instant, she broke into "Three Blind Mice."

Sears and Dunn looked at Stewart. "I thought you said she was a friend of yours!" they declared.

The talented organist, who began her professional career by playing background music for silent movies, first attracted the attention of sports fans in the winter of 1936-37, when she worked Sunday afternoon hockey at the Garden. A fan suggested she should be working at Ebbets Field and, some time later, Gladys contacted Larry MacPhail. She finally made her debut in 1942, after MacPhail overcame fears that acoustics in the park were not conducive to the organ. Thus, Goodding became the only person to play for the Knicks, Rangers, and Dodgers.

# RUNNING THE SCOREBOARD

Field announcers and organists worked in concert with scoreboard operators. Scoreboards originally were painted wooden billboards with slots where numerals would be placed by hand to indicate runs per inning. The age of electronics, coupled with animation, converted them into complex matrix operations, run by skilled technicians.

The $1.5 million board unveiled at Atlanta-Fulton County Stadium in 1977 is operated by three people.

Animation involves some 900 separate computer steps, and the job involves much more than pushing buttons. Up-to-date statistics are programmed into the computer, lengthy start-up and shut-down procedures are followed, and the chief operator has to know how to handle the system's quirks.

## MANAGER'S WIFE CUT PLAYERS' TIES

*After the Chicago Cubs won 21 consecutive games to clinch the National League pennant in 1935, Lillian Grimm—wife of club manager Charlie Grimm—snipped the players' ties during the victory party. She then wove a rug from the collected material.*

## FAN FAVORITE

*Wendy Stoeker, born without arms, became a fan favorite as an usherette for the Cedar Rapids Giants of the Class A Midwest League in 1976. She also proved valuable to the front office, typing letters and contracts with her toes and answering the telephone.*

Electric scoreboard at Dodger Stadium, Los Angeles.

## THE FIRST CONCESSIONAIRE

*Though Harry M. Stevens was the first large-scale ballpark vendor, he was not the first. Joe Gerhardt, second baseman of Louisville's major league American Association club in 1883, had part of the bar concession, and five years later, third baseman Harry Raymond of the same team had a special arrangement to get extra money tacked onto his salary from scorecard sales.*

## WHEN AND WHY FANS EAT

*Joe McKeller, who runs food operations for ARA at Atlanta Stadium, says, "If the team is winning, they're in a good mood, and more apt to spend money. But if it's losing badly early in the game, people leave. I've never sold a hot dog to an empty seat.*

*"A game that goes into extra innings or a doubleheader is worth 40-60 per cent more than a single game. A loose game compared to a tight game is better for me. A loose score is 10-9 instead of 1-0. In a tight game, people are so interested in the game, they won't leave their seats."*

# THE EQUIPMENT MANAGER

While the scoreboard is the largest piece of equipment owned by a team (excepting those who own their ballparks), smaller items—like bats and uniforms—are carted around by the equipment manager. Minnesota Twins equipment man Ray Crump first joined the team as batboy in 1949, when the Twins were still the Washington Senators.

Because Crump was charged with ordering form-fitting uniforms, complete with players' surnames sewn on the back, anxious athletes flocked to him every spring to learn whether they had made the team. As a result, he and his wife never stayed at the same apartment complex as the ballplayers. Since she did the sewing, she also knew of pending trades or roster cuts before they were officially announced.

Once, the veteran equipment manager disobeyed a request from management not to order a uniform for a player at the end of spring training. Crump's judgment proved correct. "After you've been around, you get to know these things," he said. "You can come close to picking the team."

Pete Sheehy spent so many seasons handling the equipment and running the clubhouse for the New York Yankees that the team named the clubhouse of the new Yankee Stadium in his honor after the refurbished ballpark opened in 1976. That was also Sheehy's 50th year with the club.

Many "characters" ran big-league clubhouses, including one personally scouted by Casey Stengel when his Boston Braves trained in Wallingford, Connecticut during World War II. The rotund but capable Shorty Davis became part of the Boston scene in deed and phrase. He spouted even more fractured English than Stengel.

Watching threatening clouds gather above Bradenton, Florida one spring, he blurted, "Looks like a toronto's coming up." He referred to the fishing paradise of South Florida as "the Evergladiators."

# THE BATBOYS

Baseball batboys hope their proximity to the stars will bloom into full-time jobs too. Sometimes they do, but more often they don't—leaving the batboy with memories he can cherish for life.

Generally, the batboy is little more than a uniformed mascot who depends on tips and possible World Series shares to make up for the paltry pay he receives from his team. In 1955, for example, the New York Giants gave Bobby Weinstein $3.75 for a day game, $4.50 for a night game, and $6 for a doubleheader. Fordham University sophomore Joe Carrieri made only $2.50 per game from the Yankees that season, but had collected more than $1200 in World Series shares, plus royalties from his book *Yankee Batboy* to help pay his tuition.

Carrieri, later a successful lawyer, said at the time he would favor a batboys' union. Like others in his position, he not only handled bats for players, but also shined shoes, answered mail, ran errands, and fetched coffee, Cokes, or hot dogs for hungry athletes.

Batboys specialize in working with bats—smoothing out rough edges, sorting bats by batting order or uniform number in special

## THE HAMBURGER

*Like its close relative, the frankfurter, the hamburger is a meat product developed in Germany and named for its city of origin, Hamburg. The Germans actually imported the idea from the Baltic countries, but refined it, cooking and serving it as a "chopped steak."*

*Dr. J. H. Salisbury popularized the food after its introduction to the U. S. in 1884 and a variation developed with the name of "salisbury steak." By 1912, hamburgers, like hot dogs, were used as fast-food treats in buns and were introduced to ballparks.*

dugout bat racks, and picking up bats dropped by players after they hit the ball.

In addition to bats, they supply sticky substances like pine-tar which enable players to grip bats firmly while swinging.

A number of major league executives began in baseball as bat-boys. Gabe Paul, president of the Cleveland Indians, was once a bat-boy in Rochester. Joe McDonald, general manager of the New York Mets, was once a substitute batboy in Brooklyn. And Donald Davidson, long-time front office man for the Braves and Astros, began as batboy for both Boston clubs at age 14 in 1939.

# BATTING PRACTICE PITCHERS

Many teams employ batting practice pitchers whose sole function is to warm up hitters before the game. They do not count on the roster and never appear in an actual game.

It's one thing to sharpen the eye and the swing against a friendly pitcher who throws what a hitter requests, and quite another to face an enemy pitcher whose mission is the opposite.

The Yankees, first team to carry a batting practice pitcher, hired Paul Schreiber for that job in 1937, but the one-time Brooklyn Dodger hardly anticipated his activation at age 42 in the war year of 1945.

In the first of two appearances, he came on with two outs in the sixth and slammed the door on the Detroit Tigers—allowing just two walks in three-and-one-third innings. He had last pitched in the majors twenty-two years earlier!

# WIVES

Baseball wives must be patient, understanding, and self-sufficient. At home games, they sit together in the stands, rooting for their team and their husbands to do well. When the team is away, most wives stay home, tending to family chores.

Wives know their husbands will be on the road for half the regular season—a total of nearly three months per year. In spring training, families usually accompany their husbands, but not always.

The family of Fred Stanley, a reserve shortstop for the Yankee World Championship team of 1977, moved 43 times in their first nine years of marriage. Others moved even more often.

After a tough defeat and/or a bad game for a player, his wife must avoid criticizing him or the team. Bad press also hurts. In season, wives share in the joy and the despair that naturally accompanies the game.

Veteran New York writer Dan Daniel, writing in *Baseball Magazine* of January 1937, pointed out other facts of life for the baseball wife:

"Managers fear wives of players. They fear grandstand gossip, they are afraid of cabals.

"During the game in the home city, many wives gather in a certain spot in the grandstand. They are sweet, all smiles, when they meet. But once the game gets under way, it is every wife for herself.

"If the pitcher goes along hurling a three-hitter, and the shortstop boots one to lose the game, Mrs. Pitcher may say things unsweet.

# MOST VALUABLE MASCOT
*By Ernie Harwell in The Baseball Bulletin*

*Here's a story about a strange character who had a short career in baseball, but stuck around several seasons with the old New York Giants simply because he was a good-luck charm.*

*The man's name was Faust—Vic Faust. One of the books says he was tall and lanky. Another says he was a midget. Maybe he was somewhere in-between. Anyway, he came along to the manager of the Giants, John McGraw, during the 1911 season. While the team was taking batting practice, Faust told McGraw that a fortune teller had told him that if he pitched for the Giants, they would win the pennant.*

*McGraw had heard some ridiculous stories in his hard-bitten lifetime, but this one was the topper. It sounded even crazier after McGraw watched the would-be pitcher work out. Mr. Faust was no good. In fact, he was awful. But for some strange reason, McGraw took him in as mascot. The only possible explanation could be that, like many old-time baseball men, McGraw was superstitious. Or as the man once said, "I'm not superstitious, I just don't want anything unlucky to happen to me."*

*Anyway, for the rest of the season—home or away—Faust would warm up in his Giant uniform before each game and then take a seat in the dugout. His teammates took a liking to him and began to make him the butt of their many pranks. They would load Faust's suitcase with bricks. They sent him out for a can of striped paint or for the key to the pitcher's box. But he stuck around and he was a good-luck charm. That first season of Charles Victor Faust, the Giants won the pennant. And toward the end of the year, when the pennant was clinched, McGraw put him into two games. He's in the record book . . . two appearances, no wins and no losses.*

*The next season—1912—Faust was back again, warming up every day on the sidelines. And again the Giants won the pennant. In 1913, he was with the team again. By now, he was famous in his own off-beat way, and he signed for a vaudeville tour. He left the team for four games and the Giants lost all four. So, Faust came back and the Giants again went on to win the title.*

*But Faust didn't last much longer. He never returned for the season of 1914. Instead, he spent the season in a mental institution, and in 1914 the Giants did not win the pennant.*

*That was Charles Victor Faust, who appeared officially in only two games, but hung around for three full seasons, because he was lucky. Well, he was lucky for the Giants, but not really lucky for Charles Victor Faust.*

Mrs. Shortstop may retort about the games in which Mr. Shortstop helped Mr. Pitcher with hits and plays—games in which Mr. Pitcher wasn't so hot. These little exchanges sometimes grow into conflagrations, and these little debates sometimes kill pennant chances.

"Mrs. Pitcher goes home and inflames Mr. Pitcher against Mr. Shortstop, and vice versa, and when you get two or three of these things going at the same time, along about September 1, Mr. Manager is tearing his hair and hollering for a rule against marriage in baseball.

"In some cases, managers try to urge and foster marriages. But in most cases, the pilots discourage marriage and try to fight it off as long as they can, on one pretext or another."

Things are different when team officials are involved. Kay O'Malley, whose husband Walter owned the Dodgers, read all 14 New York newspapers (before 11 of them failed) and red-lined anything about the team. She placed them on Walter's desk.

Mrs. O'Malley scored every game for many years, and maintained friendships with the wives of such celebrities as General Douglas MacArthur. She developed a reputation as a very gracious woman.

Mary Frances Veeck always worked closely with husband Bill in his baseball affairs. The Veecks have operated as a partnership since their 1950 marriage and each refers to that arrangement by saying "we" own the White Sox. Mary Frances conceived the idea of building an apartment in the ballpark when they ran the St. Louis Browns and visualized the day nursery in the ballpark and the "Brownie baby" promotion. The latter involved mailing of specially drawn contracts to parents of newborn sons, inviting them for a Browns tryout at age 18.

The Durochers and their two children en-route to their California home after the 1951 world series.

# THE CONCESSIONAIRES

Fans and food have mixed at baseball games since the early days of the game in the late nineteenth century. But the staple of concessions operators—the hot dog—came along two years before ballplayers turned professional for the first time in 1869.

Coney Island pie vendor Charles Feltman, staggering from the competition of boardwalk restaurants that offered both pies and hot sandwiches, devised a charcoal stove and conceived the idea of putting hot sausages in fresh rolls.

The frankfurter, at that point, was just 12 years old; German butchers in Frankfurt first produced it in 1852. Feltman put franks in rolls and Harry M. Stevens, veteran ballpark vendor, sent employees with frank-loaded hot water tanks trudging around stadiums hawking their wares. Cartoonist Tad Dorgan supplied the name "hot dog" to Stevens' 1901 experiment.

Stevens was an active baseball vendor for years before he started the tradition of serving hot dogs to customers. In Columbus, Ohio, he developed an improved scorecard and hired hawkers to yell: "You can't tell the players without a scorecard!" The quote has become as much a baseball classic as the hot dog.

In 1894, Stevens was handling concessions for the Giants at the Polo Grounds, but it took seven years for the "tube steak" to make its mark. The brochure of the modern Harry M. Stevens Company explains what happened:

"One cold spring day at the old Polo Grounds, around 1901, ice cream wasn't selling. Harry M. Stevens went out for sausages, boiled

## UNUSUAL VARIETY OF FOOD

*The most unusual variety of baseball food is served to fans of the Triple-A Hawaii Islanders, who play in Honolulu's Aloha Stadium. They may purchase saimin, manapua, and crack seed in addition to the traditional hot dog or hamburger.*

*Saimin is a Japanese noodle cooked in shrimp broth and topped with slices of Chinese barbecued pork and green onions. It is served in a cardboard bowl and eaten with chopsticks. Manapua is steamed yeast dough stuffed with sweet pork and onions and eaten hamburger-style. Crack seed ranged from Li Hing Mui (salted plum seeds) to sweet-sour cherry seeds or spiced lemon peels.*

them, slipped them lengthwise into rolls, and sent his hawkers through the stands shouting, 'Get 'em while they're hot!' "

Though the term hot dog caught on, some sections of the country called them wieners or red hots. Detroit's Tiger Stadium—built in 1912—has RED HOTS signs above concessions stands.

On May 29, 1930, *The St. Louis Star* described Sportsman's Park hot dogs as "tender as a mother's kiss." The price was still 10 cents six years later, when average concessions prices listed scorecards at a nickel; ice cream soda, or draught beer at a dime; and bottled beer at 20 cents.

Nearly a half-century has elapsed since *The Star* saluted the hot dog in Sportsman's Park; neither newspaper nor ballpark exist, but the hot dog remains vitally important to the success of pro sports franchises. Fans of all sports consume more than $300 million worth of finger food and drinks per year, and the average fan spends more than $1.50 per game at concessions stands.

## HUGE SALES VOLUME

*Running ballpark concessions is a huge job. During the 1971 World Series, concessions stands at Pittsburgh's Three Rivers Stadium, manned by 700 employees, dispensed 70,000 soft drinks, 60,000 hot dogs, 130 kegs and 2,000 cases of beer, 20,000 boxes of popcorn and bags of peanuts, and 5,000 ham and roast beef sandwiches.*

# ALL-STAR VENDORS

Myron O'Brisky earned a spot in the imaginary Hawkers' Hall of Fame in a half-century on the job in Pittsburgh. He estimated that he sold 15 million hot dogs, 20 million soft drinks, and 10 million bags of peanuts to 30 million Pirate fans and another 17 million Pitt and Steeler football fans.

Dodger Stadium peanut vendor Roger Owens became a celebrity because of his ability to make long, accurate throws to patrons. Owens began as a soda vendor when the team moved from Brooklyn to Los Angeles in 1958, then moved up to ice cream and finally peanuts. He met his wife over a bag of peanuts.

Owens claimed an accuracy range of 65 rows with a bag of peanuts weighing one-and-a-half ounces, but he was "benched" for more than a month in 1976 after an ice cream vendor—hoping to emulate his style—hit a woman in the forehead with an ice cream sandwich. All vendors were barred from throwing items after the incident, but a "peanut boycott" ensued as fans refused to buy peanuts without the additional treat of watching Owens uncork his usual variety of trick throws.

After fans flooded the Dodger office with petitions and letters, Owens was reactivated. The Dodgers officially recognized his appeal by letting him throw out the first ball of the 1977 season—from the second-level (loge) section where he works. It was not only the first time a peanut vendor was so honored, but also the longest opening pitch in baseball history.

Owens' one-game peak in sales—1500 bags—helped financially, as he worked strictly on commission.

During an appearance on *The Tonight Show,* Owens invited Johnny Carson to test his throwing skill.

"I can't," said Carson, "I haven't had the training. I'd have to go to Florida for a couple of months for spring peanut training."

**Vendors concentrate on selling instead of watching at the ballpark.**

# THE MEDICAL MEN

Baseball medicine is a highly complex, intricate business with countless unknown factors. Each athlete must be considered as an individual patient, with individual rehabilitation programs to be planned in the event of injury.

When star lefthander Tommy John of the Los Angeles Dodgers tore the inner ligament which supports the elbow (the ligament stressed most by a pitcher), he missed half the 1974 season and all of 1975 before returning in 1976 at less than his usual form.

Thanks to the efforts of Los Angeles surgeon Dr. Frank Jobe, who has treated many ballplayers, John was able to regain his former abilities in 1977. His 20-victory season enabled the Dodgers to win the National League pennant.

Pitcher is the most chronically taxing position because of constant throwing involved, insists Dr. Jim Parkes, team physician of the New York Mets, while catcher is most dangerous because of constant collisions with base runners. First base, where many aging hitters end their careers, is easiest because of minimal movement and throwing. Emotions must also be considered in sports medicine.

"In sports," said Dr. Parkes, "one day you're a hero and the next day you're a bum, and that's hard to take. If somebody had thrown me into an amphitheater with the President of the United States to operate on when I was an intern, I think I might have been a little uptight."

One way to cut the injury toll, the doctor said, is to maintain condition and teach players proper flexibility of the key joints.

Team doctors work closely with trainers—especially when the team is on the road. If an injury occurs, the trainer describes it to the team physician by phone and the doctor gives his recommendations. If the mishap is serious, the home club's doctor provides necessary treatment; he calls the team doctor for further consultation if surgery is needed. Often, a player will return home for an operation.

During trade talks, the physical condition of players involved is of prime importance. "If a team that is going to make a trade for a player requests medical information on him, it is entitled to know," said Dr. Parkes.

## MOVING UP THE LADDER

*Earl Mann, who owned the minor league Atlanta Crackers for more than twenty-five years, began in baseball as a peanut vendor.*

*Many years later, also in Atlanta, usher Bob Hope became vice-president and director of public relations for the major league Atlanta Braves.*

## TED WILLIAMS GAVE AWAY SERIES CHECK

*Generous superstar Ted Williams of the Red Sox gave his entire 1946 World Series check to the clubhouse boy as a tip.*

New York Mets' team physician Dr. Jim Parkes (right) confers with trainer Tom McKenna.

"Our club has the policy that if a trading club requests information, I have the green light to be absolutely objective. My own feeling is that if I were the club requesting information and it was refused, I wouldn't make the trade."

The Major League Physicians Association holds several meetings each year and broaches such subjects as acupuncture, acupressure, and kinesiology—advocated by relief pitcher Mike Marshall—in relation to baseball medicine. Artificial turf is also a subject of controversy.

"When athletes come off AstroTurf, they're like arthritics," said Dr. Parkes. "Their ankles hurt, their shins hurt, their backs hurt. AstroTurf is like concrete; there's no give.

"I am absolutely sure AstroTurf shortens players' careers. I see very good players coming off artificial surfaces in their home parks and I know their backs, knees, and feet suffer."

Vision, essential to success in the game, can be corrected by glasses. Hitters with two-tenths of a second to react to a 90-mile-an-hour fastball can find lenses to help them keep a sharp eye on the ball.

In 1979, bespectacled players in baseball included home run sluggers Reggie Jackson and Jeff Burroughs. The Chicago Cubs' chief power man, Dave Kingman, was one of 50 major-leaguers who wore soft contact lenses, according to The Council on Sports Vision, based in Rochester, New York. The Council reported that 20 per cent of all athletes wore some form of vision correction—more than half of those soft contact lenses.

The role of the baseball doctor, said Dr. Jim Parkes, is to give correct advice to a willing patient. "If you have a player or patient who gets good results, 90 per cent of the credit goes to him," he said. "You must have a dedicated, responsible individual carry through in the treatment you give him."

The Sporting News

## SENATOR SCOUTED SENATOR

*A United States Senator scouted the top slugger in the history of the Washington Senators. The legislator, Herman Welker of Idaho, watched young Harmon Killebrew hit in his hometown of Payette, then notified Washington club owner Calvin Griffith about the prospect. Killebrew collected more than 500 home runs.*

## TRAINER WAS EJECTED

*Milwaukee Braves trainer Joe Taylor recorded a "first" in 1957 when he was ejected from a game after joining a free-for-all on the field.*

Baltimore Orioles superscout Jim Russo recommended trades for Frank Robinson, Mike Cuellar, Pat Dobson, Ken Singleton, Lee May, and others. Robinson won the Triple Crown in 1966, his first year with the club, and the Orioles won the World Series in four straight games from the Los Angeles Dodgers.

# SUPER SCOUTS

It's common knowledge that scouts sign players for teams, but not many fans realize that special assignment scouts prepare advance reports and compile information for future trades on the major league level.

Connie Mack, owner-manager of the Philadelphia Athletics, actually pioneered the idea of the superscout (the widely-used term for major league scout) in 1929, when he sent sore-armed pitcher Howard Ehmke on a scouting mission to follow the Cubs. When the World Series opened between the clubs, Ehmke—not Lefty Grove—opened for the A's and won handily.

The Dodgers were one of precious few clubs that embellished Mack's idea. Clubs went into the World Series cold, hoping for the best, and gambled with every trade they made. Suddenly, baseball became a big business and owners wanted to protect their investments more carefully. The age of the superscout had dawned.

Jim Russo of the Orioles, Frank Malzone of the Red Sox, Howie Haak of the Pirates, Clyde King of the Yankees, and Ray Shore of the Reds were among those who established excellent reputations in the field.

Shore travels one city ahead of the Reds, watching their next opponents and reporting his findings to the team's manager. He files a report on each player's throwing ability, running speed, and hitting, and includes suggestions on how to pitch to each hitter. He also monitors enemy pitchers. ☞

"In advance scouting, the best information is current information," he said. "You might catch a hitter in a slump and pitch him differently or you might run into a strong-throwing outfielder with a sore arm and be able to take an extra base on him.

"When I was watching Atlanta in Houston, Hank Aaron had a collision with the catcher and hurt his arm, but still continued to play. Aaron didn't have an outstanding arm, but it was accurate and he made the throw when necessary. I noticed in the next couple of games they were running on him—and scoring when they wouldn't ordinarily. We capitalized on it in running the bases against the Braves."

Reports are kept simple deliberately; Shore says he believes in being precise and to the point. He follows the same approach in scouting the American League for possible trade material.

"It helps when the manager and superscout have a close relationship and the manager will use the reports," Yankee scout Clyde King reported. "Most managers know the league, but they definitely need help in the opposite league. If there's some particular hitter who's giving the Yankees trouble, our manager will ask me to pay special attention to him and see if there's anything I can detect which will help us get him out."

Russo joined the Oriole organization when it was still operating out of St. Louis as the Browns. Russo recommended a pitcher and catcher from the semipro team he managed and the pair signed with the Browns.

One of his amateur discoveries was Johnny Bench. "We were exchanging information with Cincinnati that year, and I told them about Bench. They had not known about him," Russo revealed.

The Orioles bypassed Russo's recommendation and drafted another player, but the Reds—who by then had seen Bench—waited until the second round of the draft to name him. They gambled on the fact that Bench had played only eight high school games and might sneak by other scouts too. They were right.

Advancing to superscout from his regional assignment in the southwest, Russo prepared the reports which enabled the Orioles to sweep the 1966 World Series over the Dodgers. His analyses of rival clubs helped the Birds to three more pennants (and one world title) in 1969-71.

The '66 sweep was based, in part, on Russo's discovery that Sandy Koufax tended to throw rising fastballs that sailed out of the strike zone—but fooled hitters into swinging. Baltimore batters were told to wait on Koufax and the advice worked; he fanned only two men in six innings of Game 2 and was the losing pitcher.

Russo, who signed Oriole ace Jim Palmer and many other regulars, recommended trades which brought National Leaguers Mike Cuellar, Pat Dobson, Mike Torrez, Ken Singleton, and Lee May.

"My first recommendation in covering the major leagues was that we acquire Frank Robinson," Russo said, beaming with pride. "He was one of the greatest players I've ever seen."

Robinson won the Triple Crown in his first season in Baltimore.

On the amateur level, scouting is no longer a cutthroat proposition. The amateur free agent draft binds each selection to one club. If he chooses not to sign, he goes through the draft six months later.

Scouting, too, has changed. A Central Scouting Bureau serves most teams, though several have refused to join. Scouts of member teams turn their reports in to the bureau rather than to their own club. All members share such information.

Team ticket managers play a key role behind the scenes. Among their chores is distribution of postseason ducats that may never be used. When pennant races are close, several clubs print playoff and World Series tickets. These, issued by the 1977 Chicago White Sox, are now souvenirs of a good team that didn't win.

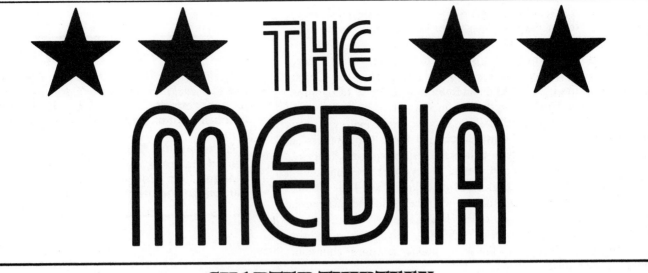

# THE MEDIA

## CHAPTER THIRTEEN

writers---took two seats, while to
laying the groundwork.

In effect, Herrmann took the
because the two leagues often to

Ironically, one of those dispute
the Commission. John Heydler, s
Pulliam as NL chief, succumbe
against Herrmann's retention on
son i͏ the choice o
re͏ ͏ 20---the sa
se͏

͏ posure of
ow͏ realized t
Co͏ the gar
G͏ ecutive
the͏ Lasker
te͏ Sox a
t͏ rles
NL͏ ss and
wit͏ ndid
Wi͏ Gen
W͏

T͏ hug
La͏ t͏
ven͏ an
Can͏ le
case͏
rem͏
clea͏

T͏ ut
gran͏ land͏ e
pac͏ ated͏ owe
baseb͏ nd i͏ applied t

The Com͏
Judge Ke͏ y Mountain Landi͏
Kenesa͏ ountain Landis wa͏
missione͏ seball. The game͏

le͏ mmissioner"
t͏ es.
͏ ion on
͏ eeded
͏ yed
ohn-
seat
Sox
ub
ul

zen
e w
er l
y C
ners

a͏ l choice as the͏ Com-
sec͏ rong man a͏ his court
In base͏ even more
͏ at dictate͏

record proved him to be just that
authoritarian---actually a benevo

Twice the intended victim of
national headlines in 1907 when h
$29 million in a freight rebate c
baseball by withholding opinion c
the collapse of the Federal Leag
case reached the United States Su
titrust a͏ game.

La͏ d by ov
"Bo͏ d tha
base͏ by th
stitut͏

The͏ ame
mission͏ was
handed͏ t fo
$42,9͏ j͏
salary͏ r
pay t͏ re

"I͏ t
remun͏
import͏
life as͏
What͏
directio͏
will be͏ e

Land͏ ec
b, bu͏ e w
dministratio͏
ving͏ en t
mong͏ ose h
own ch͏
ombers t͏ wo
fined the Sta͏ d Oil Company
se. He came͏ he attention of
͏ an antitrus͏ resulting from
͏ e in 1915. Se͏ years later, the
reme Court, ͏ s granted an an-

# THE WRITERS

Baseball writers, unlike broadcasters, are usually distant from the public eye. Newspapers and magazines devote ample space to the game, but readers often fail to remember bylines.

Most writers are known only by their contemporaries and the people they cover, though players who pick up a pen—like Christy Mathewson, Jim Brosnan, and Jim Bouton—do receive recognition.

Because New York is the nation's media center, top members of the city's press corps occasionally do become public figures. At least their names are known: Jimmy Breslin and James (Scotty) Reston, who advanced from sports to politics, and such baseball "lifers" as Maury Allen, Jimmy Cannon, Arthur Daley, John Drebinger, John Kieran, Tom Meany, Sid Mercer, Milt Richman, and Dick Young.

Many writers remained connected with the game after leaving the daily beat. Ken Smith moved to the Hall of Fame, Arthur Richman (Milton's brother) to the New York Mets, Clyde Hirt to editing magazines, and Carl Lundquist to public relations counselor, promoting products through baseball.

The best-known baseball correspondent in the city never got to a game. He existed only on television, as Oscar Madison, sports editor of *The New York Herald* and co-star of Neil Simon's long-running play and television series, "The Odd Couple." Jack Klugman played the TV role with an omnipresent New York Mets' hat, worn backwards.

## "FATHER" HENRY CHADWICK

English-born Henry Chadwick, who took on the nickname "Father" for his many pioneer efforts in the game, is the only baseball writer enshrined in the Hall of Fame.

He wrote the first rule book in 1858, invented the box score, introduced many rules changes, and wrote baseball for fifty years, starting just before the Civil War.

## EXECUTIVES WERE WRITERS

Hall of Fame baseball executives Ford Frick and Ban Johnson began as baseball writers.

# EARLY BASEBALL WRITING

Early baseball writing reflected the journalism of the times. The following flowery account of a National League game appeared in the *Indianapolis Daily Sentinel* on Thursday, May 2, 1878:

The opening game of the season between the Chicagos and Blues was witnessed by about 2,500 people, and resulted in a disastrous defeat to the Blues by a score of 5 to 4. This defeat may be attributed to the poor playing of Williamson on third, in consequence of which the Chicago boys scored three runs in the ninth inning. The managers of the home club would have made the nine much stronger by leaving Warner on third, who played so excellently in that position last season.

The runs were made in the first, fifth, and ninth innings. Each side made their runs in the first inning on errors. In the fifth, the Chicagos scored a run on base hits of Ferguson and Harbridge and slow fielding. In the sixth the Blues made two runs on hits by Flint and Croft and a two baser by Shaffer. In the ninth the Blues made another run, Shaffer taking first on balls, stole second and came home on Nolan's two base hit. The Chicagos got in their work in this inning also. Start made a base hit, taking second on Anson's hit. Each then advanced a base on a muffed ball by Williamson. Start then came home on another fumbler by Williamson and Anson and Ferguson came home on a hit by a Harbridge.

With the exception of Williamson the home club's fielding was all that could be desired. The Chicagos did not do near as well in the field and Harbridge, especially, showing his weakness in throwing to

## CASEY'S CANINE

Writers often develop strong friendships with men in the game. One example was Ed Rumill, who recounted this tale in the May 1977 issue of The Baseball Bulletin:

"My wife and I were invited to spend a day with Casey and Edna Stengel at their home in Glendale, California. Edna had suggested we come for lunch. All through a delicious shrimp salad, Edna's cute little cocker spaniel puppy sat beside my chair, looking up at me with brown loving eyes, its tail wagging constantly.

"When the dessert course came, I said to our hosts, 'I'm not sure, but I think we may have a problem. Your little dog seems to have fallen in love with me. When we leave, we may have to take her with us.'

" 'It's not that,' Casey replied. 'It's just that you're eating out of her dish.' "

second. The batting was good on both sides, but the Blues carried off the honors, the Chicagos only hitting Nolan in the ninth inning after he had weakened on account of the turn of affairs.

With the exceptions mentioned the game was well played and intensely interesting, each individual player trying his best to win for his club.

Shaffer and Nolan deserve special mention for their batting, and before the season is over they will cause all the league pitchers to tremble when they step up to face them.

| INDIANAPOLIS. | Times at bat. | Runs. | First base hits. | Times reach'd first base. | Put out. | Assistances. | Errors. |
|---|---|---|---|---|---|---|---|
| Quest, 2 b............... | 4 | 0 | 1 | 2 | 2 | 1 | 1 |
| Nelson, s.s............... | 4 | 0 | 0 | 0 | 0 | 5 | 0 |
| Clapp, l.f................ | 3 | 1 | 1 | 2 | 1 | 0 | 0 |
| Shaffer, r.f.............. | 3 | 1 | 2 | 3 | 0 | 0 | 0 |
| McKelvey, c.f............ | 5 | 0 | 0 | 0 | 3 | 1 | 0 |
| Nolan, p................. | 5 | 0 | 2 | 2 | 2 | 7 | 2 |
| Williamson, 3 b......... | 4 | 0 | 0 | 0 | 1 | 0 | 3 |
| Flint, c................. | 3 | 1 | 1 | 1 | 9 | 1 | 0 |
| Croft, 1st b............. | 3 | 1 | 1 | 1 | 9 | 0 | 0 |
| Totals ............... | 34 | 4 | 8 | 11 | 27 | 15 | 6 |

| CHICAGO. | | | | | | | |
|---|---|---|---|---|---|---|---|
| Remsen, c.f.............. | 5 | 0 | 1 | 1 | 0 | 0 | 1 |
| Hallinan, l.f............ | 3 | 1 | 0 | 1 | 1 | 0 | 0 |
| Start, 1 b............... | 4 | 1 | 0 | 1 | 13 | 0 | 0 |
| Anson, 2 b............... | 4 | 1 | 1 | 1 | 1 | 2 | 0 |
| Ferguson, s.s............ | 4 | 2 | 1 | 2 | 0 | 3 | 0 |
| Cassidy, r.f............. | 4 | 0 | 0 | 1 | 2 | 0 | 0 |
| Harbridge, c............ | 4 | 0 | 2 | 2 | 9 | 2 | 2 |
| Hankinson, 3 b.......... | 4 | 0 | 1 | 1 | 1 | 3 | 1 |
| Larkin, p............... | 4 | 0 | 1 | 1 | 0 | 7 | 2 |
| Totals ............... | 36 | 5 | 7 | 11 | 27 | 17 | 6 |

| | 1. | 2. | 3. | 4. | 5. | 6. | 7. | 8. | 9. | |
|---|---|---|---|---|---|---|---|---|---|---|
| Indianapolis............. | 1 | 0 | 0 | 0 | 0 | 2 | 0 | 0 | 1—4 | |
| Chicago ................ | 1 | 0 | 0 | 0 | 1 | 0 | 0 | 0 | 3—5 | |

Umpire—Wm. McLain. First Base on Errors—None. Left on Bases—Blues 4, Chicagos 4. Passed Balls—None. Time of Game—2 hours and 20 minutes. Two Base Hits—Shaffer 2, Nolan 1. Bases on Called Balls—Blues 2, Chicagos 1.

# RING LARDNER

Damon Runyon and Grantland Rice became the nation's top chroniclers of baseball in the Babe Ruth era, but it was Ring Lardner who set the stage for writers seeking to employ realism instead of romanticism.

Lardner, out of Chicago, spent a half-dozen years traveling with the Cubs and White Sox of the pre-Ruth, dead-ball period, then began writing short stories for the old *Saturday Evening Post* in 1914.

His "Alibi Ike" concerns a player who could hit, but couldn't field, follow instructions, or get along with other people.

# GRANTLAND RICE MEETS TY COBB

Grantland Rice had many diamond adventures, but listed as his favorite his first encounter with Ty Cobb in 1903. Rice was working for the *Atlanta Journal* when he began to get unsigned letters urging him to watch a young ballplayer named Ty Cobb, then with the Anniston, Alabama team. ☞

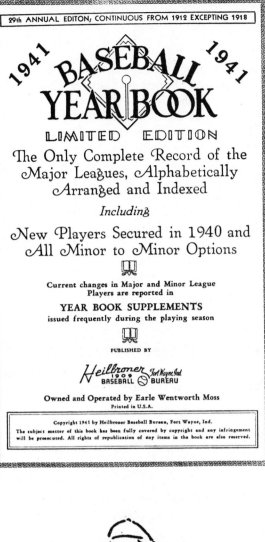

**Noted baseball writer Ring Lardner's chief character, "Alibi Ike."**

197

Rice saw Cobb in Augusta, Georgia, Tris Speaker in Little Rock, Arkansas, and Shoeless Joe Jackson in New Orleans—when all were in their teens shortly after the turn of the century. Years later, Rice said they were the three greatest players he had seen.

The writer also revealed that he had discovered the source of those unsigned letters in Atlanta—Ty Cobb himself.

As a player himself, Rice faced Rube Waddell, the zany pitcher who later made the Hall of Fame. "I first saw Waddell in 1898 when he pitched against me at Vanderbilt University," Rice recalled. "I believe the Rube had a greater combination of speed and curves than any pitcher who ever lived. He was almost as fast as Walter Johnson and had a back-breaking curve. Connie Mack agreed with this estimate."

## ED SULLIVAN WROTE SPORTS

*Famous television host Ed Sullivan was sports editor of* The New York Graphic *in the '20s.*

## FROM BALLBOY TO TYPEWRITER

*New York Mirror sportswriter Ken Smith, later an executive at the Baseball Hall of Fame, once served as ballboy for the minor league club in his hometown of Danbury, Connecticut.*

## FRED LIEB'S LONG TENURE

*Fred Lieb covered baseball for more than sixty-five years, beginning at age 21 with the 1911 New York Press. Lieb, who saw his first major league games in 1904, worked for several newspapers, including* The Sporting News, *before "retiring" to St. Petersburg, Florida, in 1948. Lieb wrote more than a dozen baseball books, including* Baseball as I Have Known It, *a review of his long sportswriting career.*

# HUGH FULLERTON HALTS WORLD SERIES

One of the best early writers, Hugh Fullerton, actually stopped a World Series game in 1911. The Giants-Athletics classic had been delayed five days by rain, but the rains stopped in New York on the night that Game 4 was scheduled in Philadelphia.

Hoping the rain was still falling in Philly so he could keep a dinner date in New York, Fullerton headed for the New York hotel where American League president Ban Johnson was staying. If Johnson was gone, the game was on, Fullerton decided.

When the writer arrived at the president's door, it was open but the room was empty. Discouraged, Fullerton began to leave when the phone rang. "Hello?" said Fullerton. Robby McCoy, Johnson's personal secretary, mistook Fullerton for Johnson but Fullerton recognized McCoy's voice at once.

The secretary reported no rain in Philadelphia but suggested the grounds might be too wet to play. He asked "Johnson" if he should call the game. Seizing the opportunity, Fullerton did his best Ban Johnson imitation: "Call it off, Robby, call it off!"

Leaving the room, Fullerton met the real Johnson. The writer cooly informed him that he had canceled the game—but he didn't reveal his personal interest. Johnson agreed, saying *he* wanted to keep a dinner date that night in New York anyhow!

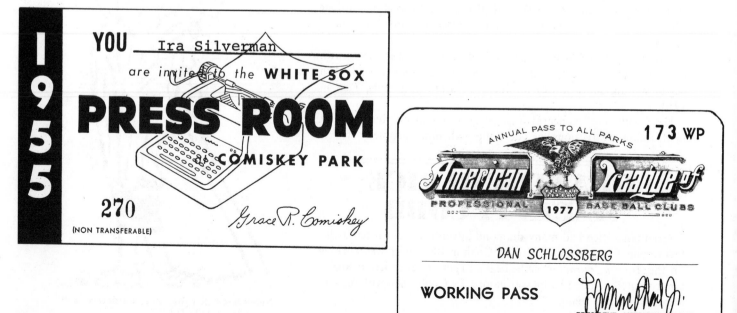

# PRESS REACTION TO RECORD-BREAKERS

In 1927, Ty Cobb achieved a level of excellence that may never be exceeded when he smashed his 4,000th hit. But the press hardly noticed.

Neither the *Detroit Free Press* nor the *Detroit News* paid any attention to the hit—other than a passing reference in the "game notes" column of the former and a small headline in the latter.

H. G. Salinger of the *News* devoted his regular column to boxing and only mentioned Cobb's hit in passing, failing to point out its significance.

Babe Ruth's 714th home run, his last, received little attention in the media, but the number 700 seemed so insurmountable at the time that *The New York Times* of July 14, 1934 printed this headline: "Ruth's Record of 700 Home Runs Likely to Stand for All Time in Major Leagues."

When Hank Aaron approached and finally broke the record forty years later, hundreds of media representatives were on hand. The Braves' clubhouse was sealed off and a special interview room set up to accommodate both Aaron and the press corps he attracted. Aaron's followers included foreign as well as American reporters, males as well as females.

## WOMEN WRITERS

Jeane Hofmann, sportswriter for the *New York Journal-American* in the '40s, was a pioneer who found the press box as closed to her as the players' dressing rooms.

Signs read NO DOGS OR WOMEN in many places and male colleagues plagued Hofmann with endless pranks. A male writer told her Cincinnati outfielders warmed up by carrying sacks of cement on their shoulders so their bats wouldn't feel heavy by contrast.

As a general rule, Hofmann and females who followed her pioneer footsteps got along well with male contemporaries, but requests by "liberated" women to gain admittance to clubhouses ran into numerous roadblocks in the '70s.

Women of the typewriter charged they missed many big stories by not being in locker rooms, while males who were allowed inside received an unfair advantage. A stalemate developed between players seeking privacy and female writers seeking access, but disintegrated in 1979 when Commissioner Bowie Kuhn issued a directive that clubhouses be open to legitimate media representatives—regardless of gender.

Ty Cobb's 4000th hit was almost ignored in the media.

## THE SECRET SCORER

*In 1911, AL president Ban Johnson suggested the identity of scorers be kept secret so they could not be influenced by players to change their decisions.*

*Chicago of the National League employed a mysterious "E. G. Green" as scorer from 1882-91. Only team president A. G. Spalding knew that Mrs. Elisa Green Williams, mother of team treasurer C. G. Williams, was scoring the games.*

## CHANGING STYLES IN COVERING THE GAME

Writers have made various changes in the baseball box score through the years. At one time, box scores revealed when each pinch hitter or pinch runner was used, how he did, who played more than one position, who participated in double-plays, who the umpires were, and how long pitchers lasted when they pitched an inning in which they failed to retire a batter.

By 1979, the traditional box score had deteriorated substantially, so that fans or writers had to be mind-readers to decipher managerial strategy. Position changes were eliminated, so the last position an athlete played was the one that showed in the box score.

Pinch-hitters were listed only if they did not enter the game defensively; if they did, they were listed by the last position played. Nowhere was an indication of how substitutes did. Umpires and names of participants in double-plays were eliminated.

Only *The Sporting News* continued to print more detailed boxes (showing position changes), but that weekly discontinued publication of minor league box scores when it transferred a huge chunk of its baseball space to other sports. Thousands of readers, who had referred to the tabloid as "the Bible of Baseball," objected.

To fill the void created by the vastly reduced coverage of the game by *The Sporting News,* a monthly all-baseball tabloid, *The Baseball Bulletin,* began printing with the January 1975 issue.

*The Sporting News,* operated by the Spink family of St. Louis since 1886, had been known for carrying as much gossip and hearsay information about baseball as actual news. When coverage of other sports began in the '60s, space limitations forced an end to that tradition.

## OFFICIAL SCORERS

*Writers usually serve as official scorers. The job is not easy. On August 29, 1973, a scorer's decision deprived Nolan Ryan of the California Angels of a no-hitter. The New York Yankees made just one hit that day—a pop fly that dropped between two infielders. Both called for it, then both backed away, fearing collision.*

## 1977 WORLD SERIES

### Game 6 at New York

| Los Angeles | AB. | R. | H. | PO. | A. | E. |
|---|---|---|---|---|---|---|
| Lopes, 2b | 4 | 0 | 1 | 0 | 4 | 0 |
| Russell, ss | 3 | 0 | 0 | 1 | 4 | 0 |
| Smith, rf | 4 | 2 | 1 | 1 | 0 | 0 |
| Cey, 3b | 3 | 1 | 1 | 0 | 1 | 0 |
| Garvey, 1b | 4 | 1 | 2 | 13 | 0 | 0 |
| Baker, lf | 4 | 0 | 1 | 2 | 0 | 0 |
| Monday, cf | 4 | 0 | 1 | 3 | 0 | 0 |
| Yeager, c | 3 | 0 | 1 | 4 | 2 | 0 |
| bDavalillo | 1 | 0 | 1 | 0 | 0 | 0 |
| Hooton, p | 2 | 0 | 0 | 0 | 0 | 0 |
| Sosa, p | 0 | 0 | 0 | 0 | 0 | 0 |
| Rau, p | 0 | 0 | 0 | 0 | 0 | 0 |
| aGoodson | 1 | 0 | 0 | 0 | 0 | 0 |
| Hough, p | 0 | 0 | 0 | 0 | 0 | 0 |
| cLacy | 1 | 0 | 0 | 0 | 0 | 0 |
| Totals | 34 | 4 | 9 | 24 | 11 | 0 |
| **New York** | **AB.** | **R.** | **H.** | **PO.** | **A.** | **E.** |
| Rivers, cf | 4 | 0 | 2 | 1 | 0 | 0 |
| Randolph, 2b | 4 | 1 | 0 | 2 | 3 | 0 |
| Munson, c | 4 | 1 | 1 | 6 | 0 | 0 |
| Jackson, rf | 3 | 4 | 3 | 5 | 0 | 0 |
| Chambliss, 1b | 4 | 2 | 2 | 9 | 1 | 0 |
| Nettles, 3b | 4 | 0 | 0 | 0 | 0 | 0 |
| Piniella, lf | 3 | 0 | 0 | 2 | 1 | 0 |
| Dent, ss | 2 | 0 | 0 | 1 | 4 | 1 |
| Torrez, p | 3 | 0 | 0 | 1 | 2 | 0 |
| Totals | 31 | 8 | 8 | 27 | 11 | 1 |

```
Los Angeles ....2 0 1 0 0 0 0 0 1—4
New York .......0 2 0 3 2 0 0 1 x—8
```

| Los Ang. | IP. | H. | R. | ER. | BB. | SO. |
|---|---|---|---|---|---|---|
| Hooton (L) | 3* | 3 | 4 | 4 | 1 | 1 |
| Sosa | 1⅔ | 3 | 3 | 3 | 1 | 0 |
| Rau | 1⅓ | 0 | 0 | 0 | 0 | 1 |
| Hough | 2 | 2 | 1 | 1 | 0 | 3 |
| **New York** | **IP.** | **H.** | **R.** | **ER.** | **BB.** | **SO.** |
| Torrez (W) | 9 | 9 | 4 | 2 | 2 | 6 |

*Pitched to three batters in fourth. aStruck out for Rau in seventh. bBunted safely for Yeager in ninth. cPopped out for Hough in ninth. Runs batted in—Garvey 2, Smith, Davalillo, Chambliss 2, Jackson 5, Piniella. Two-base hit—Chambliss. Three-base hit—Garvey. Home runs—Chambliss, Smith, Jackson 3. Sacrifice fly—Piniella. Double plays—Dent, Randolph and Chambliss; Chambliss, Dent and Chambliss. Passed ball—Munson. Left on bases—Los Angeles 5, New York 2. Umpires—McSherry (N.L.) plate, Chylak (A.L.) first base, Sudol (N.L.) second base, McCoy (A.L.) third base, Dale (N.L.) left field, Evans (A.L.) right field. Time—2:18. Attendance—56,407.

# MR. BASEBALL: J.G. TAYLOR SPINK

Without question, the single most influential journalist in baseball history was J. G. Taylor Spink, who ran *The Sporting News* for more than forty-five years.

"No man has ever done so much in so many ways for the sport than has Mr. Spink," wrote Hugh Bradley of the *New York Journal-American* in 1961. "If he had not existed, Organized Baseball would have been forced to invent him."

Spink, who was called the game's best salesman, its best ambassador, and even "Mr. Baseball," was a dynamo of publishing prowess and baseball ideas who editorialized weekly on the strong and weak points of the game.

He drove his staff hard, and often called contributors with new ideas in the dead of night, but solidified his paper's reputation as "the Bible of Baseball." Only after his death were other sports given any space in *The Sporting News.* Under the J. G. Taylor Spink regime, minor league baseball was much more important than major league football, basketball, or hockey.

Spink ran up $30,000 annual phone bills and spent unlimited sums to improve the paper, which evolved into a tabloid during the '40s.

J. G. Taylor Spink was not often wrong, nor quick to admit his mistakes. One of his biggest occurred in 1948, when Cleveland Indians owner Bill Veeck purchased Satchel Paige, age 42 (at least), from the Negro Leagues. Spink charged repeatedly that Veeck had made a travesty of the game. Veeck answered with wires after each Paige performance.

Veeck's typical telegram read: NINE INNINGS. FOUR HITS. FIVE STRIKEOUTS. WINNING PITCHER PAIGE. DEFINITELY IN LINE FOR THE SPORTING NEWS AWARD AS ROOKIE OF THE YEAR.

Finally, Spink replied: "*The Sporting News* will make no change in its original editorial, except to express its admiration for any pitcher—white or colored—who at Paige's age can gain credit for five victories over a period of six weeks in any league, major or minor. But it cannot express any admiration for the present-day standard of major league ball that makes such a showing possible."

## RADIO IN TWO-TEAM CITIES

*Baseball's two-team cities had unwritten agreements about radio broadcasting, and most of them lasted until shortly after World War II.*

*A key rule stated that the team on the road would broadcast only when the home team wasn't playing. The idea was to convince residents to visit the ballpark of the team in town rather than sit home with an ear tuned to the radio.*

*Most clubs broadcast all or most home games in a promotional venture. When Sam Breadon, Cardinal owner, banned home radio during the Gas House Gang's top year of 1934, attendance dipped alarmingly. With radio back in 1935, with the Depression still a factor, the count went to 517,805 from 334,863. France Laux was the key radio voice in town that year.*

## MIKEMAN MUST SCORE

*Keeping score is part of the broadcaster's job. Since there are many different scoring systems, not all members of broadcast teams can read their partners' scorecards.*

*Ex-player Ralph Kiner did not know how to score when he began in the booth. Fellow announcer Bob Prince taught him.*

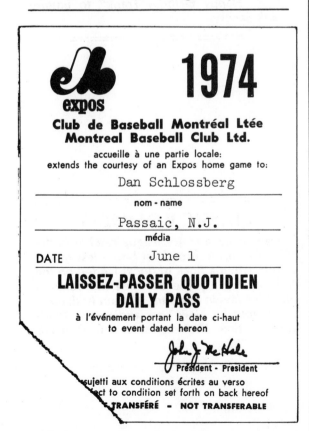

**1974**

**expos**

**Club de Baseball Montréal Ltée**
**Montreal Baseball Club Ltd.**

accueille à une partie locale:
extends the courtesy of an Expos home game to:

Dan Schlossberg

nom - name

Passaic, N.J.

média

DATE      June 1

## LAISSEZ-PASSER QUOTIDIEN
## DAILY PASS

à l'événement portant la date ci-haut
to event dated hereon

*John J. McHale*

Président - President

sujetti aux conditions écrites au verso
act to condition set forth on back hereof

TRANSFÉRÉ — NOT TRANSFERABLE

# THE PUBLICISTS

Increased competition for the entertainment dollar after World War II placed increased emphasis on the role of the baseball public relations man. Because publicity sells tickets, teams consider a good PR staff as vital as a solid infield defense.

Many of the best publicists in baseball culled their files for photos and background information used in preparing this book; they are listed on the acknowledgments page.

Donald Davidson, who became a full-time Braves' employee during the pennant year of 1948, served as clubhouse boy, publicity director, traveling secretary, and special assistant to the president—sticking with the Braves through transfers to Milwaukee and Atlanta before running afoul of turbulent Ted Turner in 1976. He quickly hooked on with the Astros.

Though he never grew more than 4 feet tall, the result of a childhood disease, Davidson has always been as demanding and decisive as he was efficient. Such traits, combined with his size, made him the target of thousands of pranks. He wrote about some of them in his hilarious book *Caught Short*.

One of the best involved his chief tormentors, star pitchers Warren Spahn and Lew Burdette. They arrived early at training camp one spring and warned the new gate attendant to watch out for a midget claiming to be a Braves' executive. When Davidson arrived, the guard refused to admit him.

His patience exhausted, Davidson kicked the guard in the shins. He was about to retaliate when the pranksters, watching from concealed locations, arrived in time to save the executive's life.

On another occasion, with the team staying in a new hotel in Philadelphia, everyone was booked on the 5th floor. Someone came up with the bright idea to change Davidson's room to the 28th floor and bribed the unknowing hotel clerk to do it. Davidson got into the elevator, surrounded by several six-foot Braves who left at the 5th floor without a word. Unable to reach the button for the 28th, Davidson rode up and down several times before someone came to his rescue.

The best-known and best-liked public relations executive, Bob Fishel, spent many years with the Yankees before joining the American League's New York office.

In his assorted assignments in the game, he has handled such PR duties as writing news releases, compiling statistics, running promotions, editing yearbooks, keeping photo files updated, answering media requests for photos, information, or credentials, and—perhaps most important—keeping mum about breaking news stories until they were announced by team officials at news conferences he arranged.

Fishel's connection with baseball began in 1946, after Bill Veeck had purchased the Cleveland Indians. Veeck had heard of Fishel's advertising and promotion prowess and wanted him to handle a huge campaign called, "We're Giving the Indians Back to the Fans."

Broadcasting was a key ingredient of the program and, in 1947-48, Fishel put together a strong Cleveland radio-TV network. He later worked for Veeck with the St. Louis Browns before moving to the Yankees.

# BROADCASTING

Baseball broadcasting did not begin until 1921 on radio and 1939 on television. Electronic communications was so well received by fans that the men behind the mike, like the players they described, soon became celebrities.

Mel Allen, Red Barber, Harry Caray, Bob Prince, and Vin Scully did not play big-league baseball, but became as well-known as fiery manager Leo Durocher or home run king Hank Aaron. The vast audience provided by television allowed many announcers to achieve higher recognition factors than stars who wound up in the Hall of Fame.

Before radio, fans followed the game through newspaper reports. Inning-by-inning scores were posted in the windows of promotion-minded papers and telegraph offices. With competition high, labor costs low, and newsprint plentiful, papers printed multiple editions, including "baseball editions" with partial line scores appearing on the back (or even the front) page.

Radio, and later television, gave fans another outlet—and more immediate results of both the local game and other contests.

Young Mel Allen was at the mike for the Yankees in 1950.

## FIRSTS

Harold Arlin announced the first broadcast baseball game, a Phillies-Pirates contest, on Pittsburgh radio station KDKA, August 5, 1921.

Arlin, a Westinghouse foreman by day and announcer at night, was in the right place at the right time. After KDKA became the first operating radio station in 1920, he delivered broadcast "firsts" in football and tennis, and introduced by radio the voices of Will Rogers, Herbert Hoover, William Jennings Bryan, and Babe Ruth.

Ruth struck out on radio, however. In town for a Yankee-Pirate exhibition game, Ruth was supposed to read a speech prepared by Arlin, but he developed mike fright and couldn't speak. Arlin took his place and the station later got letters praising the quality of "Ruth's" voice.

The novelty of broadcast baseball spread when KDKA linked with two other Westinghouse affiliates, WJZ in New Jersey and WBZ (then in Springfield, Massachusetts), now in Boston, to carry the 1921 World Series between the New York Giants and Yankees. Sportswriter Grantland Rice handled the mike and returned the following fall with another writer, Bill McGheehan, when the same clubs met.

In 1923, New York's WEAF, forerunner of WNBC, introduced a voice that would later make many broadcasting milestones—Graham McNamee. The following year, WMAQ of Chicago became the first station to undertake regular local broadcasts when it aired all home games of the White Sox and Cubs.

## RADIOS AT THE STADIUM

Dodger fans brought radios to the cavernous Los Angeles Coliseum because they were seated far from the field and had trouble seeing the action. They continued the tradition after the team moved to Dodger Stadium in 1962. Announcer Vin Scully tested the number of radios by asking fans to shout "Happy Birthday Frank" to umpire Frank Secory.

## CLASSIC COMMENT

Fran Healy, a major league catcher in the '70s, was in the broadcast booth less than a month when a flock of ducks landed on the field during a game between the Yankees and Blue Jays in Toronto. Without hesitating, Healy told his New York audience: "That's the first time I've ever seen a fowl in fair territory."

Harry Caray captivated fans with his broadcast work in both St. Louis and Chicago.

## THE CARAY WAY

*Harry Caray became an announcer for the St. Louis Cardinals by writing the radio station manager that he could do a better job than the incumbent. Caray and partner Gabby Street won exclusive air rights over several rivals in 1947 and, after the team was purchased by Anheuser-Busch, went to Bavaria to research beer commercials.*

*Always anxious to find a new perspective on the game, he was broadcasting from the bleachers (and sitting with the fans) when he provided a graphic description of Curt Flood's "spectacular catch" at the base of the center field wall. Caray could not actually see the play because it was out of his line of vision.*

## GARAGIOLA'S QUICK WIT

*When the Mets owned the pitching trio of Tom Seaver, Jon Matlack, and Jerry Koosman, they were noted for good pitching but weak hitting. At a banquet, NBC's Joe Garagiola watched a waiter place breadsticks on the table, then announced, "I see the Mets' bats have arrived!"*

# THE EARLY YEARS OF BROADCAST BASEBALL

When radio first became available to ballclubs, some owners argued that broadcast games would reduce home attendance. If fans could hear a play-by-play report, they reasoned, why should they come to the ballpark? The same argument surfaced again years later, when television gave fans the opportunity to hear *and see.*

By 1936, radio broadcasting was universal everywhere in baseball but New York, where the Giants, Dodgers, and Yankees refused to accept it as a valuable promotional tool. The clubs maintained a united boycott until the close of the 1938 season, when the Giants sold exclusive air rights for $150,000 and the Dodgers got a contract for $77,000.

The idea of selling exclusive rights did not take hold until the '30s, more than ten years after the advent of baseball broadcasting. Detroit's WWJ actually refused to sell advertising time for seven years after Ty Tyson began announcing Tiger games in 1927. Even the World Series had no sponsor until Henry Ford signed a four-year, $400,000 pact in 1934.

At first, stations competed with each other not for exclusive rights, but for listeners. Several stations in each city broadcast the games of the home club.

After WMAQ's initial entry in Chicago in 1924, other stations noticed the enthusiastic reaction of the fans and launched rival broadcasts. Among the many voices to announce Chicago games were Joe E. Brown, the film comedian whose son spent many years as general manager of the Pirates, and Ronald (Dutch) Reagan, future actor and politician who "recreated" telegraphed game reports with special sound effects.

Others who earned their broadcast spurs as Chicago pioneers were Bob Elson, who launched a thirty-year run as a baseball voice in 1931; Jimmy Dudley, a WIND employee whose work earned him a long stay as the main mikeman in Cleveland; and Russ Hodges, a one-time Dudley partner whose 1951 shouts of "The Giants win the pennant! The Giants win the pennant!" rank as the most memorable words ever spoken behind a baseball microphone.

# THE RECREATED PLAY-BY-PLAY

Jack Graney, who became the first ex-player to broadcast when he jumped from left field to the Cleveland microphone in 1932, was especially adept at recreating away games. The practice was common in the majors until teams started bringing their announcers on road trips after World War II.

Another former player, Waite Hoyt, and garrulous Les Kieter continued to handle recreations into the late '50s, when the practice ended on the major league level.

Recreating a game was difficult, at best. The announcer worked with a "canned" sound track of cheering fans, which he would raise or lower in volume to indicate their level of excitement. He also had a hollow block of wood, which he would hit with a pencil or stick to represent the sound of bat hitting ball. ☞

The play-by-play came in by teletype: MAYS. B1. S1. B2. ALOU STEALS SECOND. S2. FOUL POP. ERROR CATCHER. TRIPLE. RUN SCORES.

In Cincinnati, Waite Hoyt entertained listeners with a low-key style, frequent use of understatement, and the unusual habit of watching the action and *then* telling his audience what happened in the *past* tense!

Hoyt, a fabled storyteller who played with Babe Ruth on the Yankees, was such a master at filling time during games held up by rain that a record was cut with the title *Best of Waite Hoyt in the Rain*. The album contained stories Hoyt told during a twenty-five-year career as announcer for the Cincinnati Reds.

## A FATHER AND SON BROADCAST TEAM

*Announcers Harry Caray of the White Sox and Skip Caray of the Braves are father and son.*

Star pitcher Sandy Koufax tried his hand at broadcasting, but resigned before completing his contract. By contrast, former pitching sidekick Don Drysdale became adept at describing the action.

## DRYSDALE'S DRILLS PAID OFF

*Pitcher Don Drysdale became an excellent broadcaster after preparing for the transition by "announcing games" while sitting in the bullpen between starting assignments.*

# BALLPLAYERS IN THE BOOTH

Like Waite Hoyt, former players who became broadcasters relied on their baseball experiences to provide insights, and to provide balance when working with professional announcers who were primarily reporters or narrators. Ralph Kiner, a charter member of the New York Mets' air team, had excellent training.

"I heard a lot of Vin Scully when I was in Southern California and liked his style," Kiner recalled. "He's a narrator and storyteller and that's very good. The first year I was broadcasting, my partner was Bob Elson with the Chicago White Sox. He was excellent and probably the best interviewer I ever heard.

"In my early days, I listened to my own and other broadcasters' tapes, trying to figure out what direction to go in. I feel being natural is the answer. I don't listen to my old tapes now because I've developed my own style and don't want to change it.

"One of the secrets of broadcasting is not saying too much. My first broadcast, I said everything I knew in the first two innings and had nothing left."

Pre-game preparation is part of Kiner's daily routine. He talks to home and visiting players and writers, and reads a variety of publications, especially *The Sporting News* and *The Baseball Bulletin*.

"It's easy to find out about Hank Aaron or any other star," he said, "but it's difficult to find out anything interesting about any newcomer—other than where he's played before. Spring training is the place you can pick up a lot of background information."

When the visiting San Francisco Giants were without an announcer one late-summer day in 1977, Kiner took over the chores for KSFO radio. "I had to put the game in perspective for Giants' fans," he said. "It was like being tossed into the water to learn how to swim. I had to make my own way, but I had done my homework ahead of time and it was interesting."

# BLOOPERS ON THE AIR

Even with preparation, no announcer is immune to bloopers. Sooner or later, they strike every broadcast booth. Earl Gillespie of the Milwaukee Braves once said, "Al Deck is in the on-dark circle." And Herb Carneal, with the Springfield Cubs of the International League, contributed this gem: "Syracuse is threatening and, for the Cubs, Tony Jacobs is throwing up in the bullpen."

Early in his career behind the mike, former Yankee shortstop Phil Rizzuto announced, "There's the pitch. Yogi Berra swings and hits a high foul behind the plate. It's coming down . . . and Yogi Berra makes the catch!"

Even Mel Allen, the polished performer who began in 1938 and later won world acclaim as No. 1 announcer for the Yankees, made broadcast boo-boos. In one game, Allen assumed Les Moss was catching for the St. Louis Browns—until Moss appeared as a pinch-hitter in the ninth inning!

## BEFORE SOUNDPROOF BOOTHS

*Early radio men broadcast right from the press box, without the soundproofing provided by booths. During the 10-run uprising by the Philadelphia Athletics in Game 4 of the 1929 World Series against the Cubs, Graham McNamee was at the mike when a writer accidentally played his foil: "McNamee, will you please pipe down?"*

# FAMOUS HOME RUN CALLS

Though Mel Allen's southern drawl, coupled with the Yankees' home run power, popularized the call, "Going, going, gone," the phrase was first used by Cincinnati's Harry Hartman in 1929.

Vin Scully's usual call is a simple, "Forget it," while Ralph Kiner says, "Kiss it goodbye," as the ball disappears over the fence. Russ Hodges said, "Bye, bye, baby," and many broadcasters refer to the home run as a ball that was "hit downtown."

By far the most original call was created by Rosey Rowswell in Pittsburgh, before the advent of television. When Kiner was cracking home runs for the Pirates, Rowswell imagined a little old lady with an apartment window facing Forbes Field. He yelled, "Open the window, Aunt Minnie, here it comes!" and then smashed a light bulb near the microphone when the ball left the park.

Descriptions of home runs which shattered Babe Ruth's one-season and lifetime records were broadcast by Phil Rizzuto of the Yankees on October 1, 1961, and Milo Hamilton, then with the Braves, on April 8, 1974. Both events occurred in the players' home parks.

Rizzuto's reaction:

"Here comes Roger Maris. They're standing up, waiting to see if Roger is going to hit No. 61! Here's the windup . . . the pitch to Roger . . . WAY OUTSIDE, ball one. (Boos) The fans are starting to boo . . . Low, ball two. That one was in the dirt. And the boos get louder. Two balls, no strikes, on Roger Maris. Here's the windup . . . fastball HIT DEEP TO RIGHT, THIS COULD BE IT! WAY BACK THERE! *HOLY COW, HE DID IT!!* 61 HOME RUNS!! They're fighting for that ball out there. Holy cow . . . another standing ovation for Roger Maris!"

Here's how Hamilton handled it:

"Now here is Henry Aaron. This crowd is up all around. The pitch to him . . . bounced it up there, ball one. (Loud round of boos) Henry Aaron in the second inning walked and scored. He's sitting on 714. Here's the pitch by Downing . . . Swinging . . . There's a drive into left-centerfield. That ball is gonna beee . . . OUTA HERE! IT'S GONE! IT'S 715! There's a new home run champion of all time! And it's Henry Aaron! The fireworks are going! Henry Aaron is coming around third! His teammates are at home plate. Listen to this crowd. . . . (thunderous sustained applause and cheers)."

**Phil Rizzuto was at the radio mike for Roger Maris' 61st homer.**

# THE AGE OF TELEVISION

When Larry MacPhail transferred his talents from the Reds to the Dodgers in 1939, he brought broadcaster Red Barber with him. Later that year, on August 26, Barber was the announcer when newborn television station W2XBS aired a doubleheader between the Reds and Dodgers from Ebbets Field. This pioneer baseball telecast reached only a handful of sets in existence then, but paved the way for a new trend in communications. In 1961, the technique became even more sophisticated when two minutes of a Cubs-Phillies game were beamed to Europe via the new Tel-Star satellite.

Early television was often trying. When WGN-TV of Chicago put baseball onto the silver screen in 1948, announcer Jack Brickhouse kept one eye on the field and the other on the monitor. "Viewers don't like you describing things unless they can see what you're describing," he recalled. "At one point, the batter hit a tremendous fly. I described the flight of the ball and the fielder chasing it and was sure I saw him catch the ball as it came down inside the park. On my monitor, the ball was still in flight. The camera followed it over the wall, over housetops, and on until the cameraman realized he was not following the baseball but had picked up a bird in flight."

Announcers making the transition from radio to television had as much trouble as actors switching from silents to talkies. They didn't know whether to talk more or less, and realized their mistakes would become painfully obvious to fans who could see as well as·hear.

They couldn't describe infield pops as long outfield drives. Television personalized the game not only because vision was provided but also because announcers, with less to say about action on the field, began to reveal personal insights about the players.

## PRINCE OF THE PIRATES

*Bob Prince joined the Pirates as a $50-a-week assistant to Rosey Rowswell in 1948 and soon won widespread recognition for his slow, nasal twang, coupled with his knowledge and passion for the game.*

*Prince, equally colorful off-mike, won bets by (1) diving from his third-floor window into the pool of the Hotel Chase in St. Louis, (2) keeping quiet for a solid hour on an airplane trip, and (3) parading in bermuda shorts from the center field clubhouse of the Polo Grounds to home plate, where Giant manager Leo Durocher kissed him on both cheeks.*

## THE GROWTH OF BASEBALL BROADCASTING

*Broadcasting supplied seven per cent of baseball's revenue in 1939, but 10.5 per cent in 1950 and more than 30 per cent by the mid-'70s. Each team will realize nearly $10 million per season under a four-year, $1 billion agreement effective in 1990 between baseball and the CBS-TV network. That agreement dwarfs a previous network package that had increased annual team television revenue from $2 million in 1983 to $7 million for each of six succeeding seasons. An additional cable-TV package, also effective in 1990, will produce an additional $2 million per year for each ballclub. The new network deal allows CBS to telecast 12 weekend games during the regular season, plus the All-Star Game, League Championship Series, and World Series. The largest local cable-TV deal was arranged by Yankee owner George Steinbrenner prior to the 1989 season: a 12-year, $500 million pact with the Madison Square Garden network.*

# NETWORK COVERAGE OF BASEBALL

The National Broadcasting Company pioneered network television coverage of the World Series in 1947 and of the All-Star Game in 1950. The network's New York affiliate handled the first big-league broadcast, in 1939, as well as the first sporting event ever televised—a Princeton-Columbia baseball game announced by Bill Stern that same year. The college game drew an estimated audience of 5,000, while the 1975 World Series colorcast between the Cincinnati Reds and Boston Red Sox had more than 75 million viewers for the decisive seventh game.

The Columbia Broadcasting System won radio rights to the All-Star Game, Championship Series of the two leagues, and World Series in 1976. Those rights extended to 267 affiliates, plus stations in Canada, Puerto Rico, the Dominican Republic, Venezuela, Panama, and other Latin American countries.

Actually, CBS, NBC, and Mutual had all worked All-Star and World Series games on radio as far back as the 1930s, but the rapid growth of the industry in the television era, plus expansion and restructuring of major league baseball, created the modern format which allowed the three major networks to share coverage and provide massive doses of publicity for the game.

Baseball on the air has advanced a long way from Harold Arlin's lonely experimental mike at KDKA.

# CHAPTER FOURTEEN

# Big Moments

**Jubilant Giants greet Bobby Thomson at the
plate after pennant-winning home run of 1951.**

# THE GAME'S MOST MEMORABLE MOMENTS

During the 1975 All-Star Game in Milwaukee, major league baseball began a nationwide campaign to choose its most memorable moments and personalities.

The search ended when Hank Aaron's 715th home run, on April 8, 1974, was voted Most Memorable Moment and Babe Ruth, whose record Aaron broke, was named Most Memorable Personality.

The winners, selected by the media and key baseball officials, were honored at the 1976 All-Star luncheon in Philadelphia. Ms. Julia Ruth Stevens of Conway, New Hampshire, accepted the personality award in memory of her father, who died in 1948.

Winners of the three other Most Memorable Moment categories, revealed at a New York news conference, were: Don Larsen's perfect game in the 1956 World Series; Joe DiMaggio's 56-game hitting streak; and, as the National League's top moment, Aaron's 715th.

The Aaron home run was selected from a list of 72 nominees. As in other categories, the choice could come from a single play, game, series of events, or entire career.

Aaron's historic homer, produced in his home park at Atlanta Stadium, narrowly defeated Bobby Thomson's "shot heard 'round the world" in the competition. The Aaron blow received 485 votes among 2391 cast in the overall category, while Thomson's pennant-winning home run of 1951 received 419.

Larsen's perfect game ranked third with 313, followed by Ruth's "called shot" World Series homer of 1932 and DiMaggio's hitting streak.

Ruth was a runaway winner as Most Memorable Personality with 1176 votes, against 370 for runner-up Casey Stengel. Dizzy Dean had 65. Aaron and Mickey Mantle tied for sixth with 61 each. Forty personalities were nominated. ☞

Chevrolet

## AN UNASSISTED TRIPLE-PLAY

*Cleveland Indians second baseman Bill Wambsganss made an unassisted triple-play to help his team defeat the Brooklyn Robins in the 1920 World Series.*

## WHY GIANTS WON

*The 1951 New York Giants engineered the greatest comeback in a single season because of key player moves by manager Leo Durocher. On May 21, Whitey Lockman took over first base. On May 25, Willie Mays came up from Minneapolis to play center field. On July 20, Bobby Thomson went to third base and Don Mueller began playing right field every day.*

Hank Aaron's 715th home run was voted Most Memorable Moment of baseball history in poll completed in 1976, the year of the U.S. Bicentennial celebration.

Here are the top five finishers (and vote totals) in the World Series/All-Star, American League and National League MMM categories:

| World Series/All-Star | Votes |
|---|---|
| 1. Don Larsen's perfect game in 1956 World Series | 1,037 |
| 2. Bill Mazeroski's series-winning homer in 1960 | 332 |
| 3. Babe Ruth's "called shot" home run in 1932 | 214 |
| 4. Carlton Fisk's game-winning homer in Game 6 of 1975 Series | 127 |
| 5. Mets' miracle W.S. championship in 1969 | 114 |
| **(Leading finishes by All-Star Moments)** | |
| 7. Carl Hubbell's 5 consecutive strikeouts in 1934 | 72 |
| 13. Pete Rose's race home with winning run in 1970 | 23 |

### American League

| | |
|---|---|
| 1. Joe DiMaggio's 56-game hitting streak in 1941 | 1,021 |
| 2. Roger Maris' 61st home run in 1961 | 394 |
| 3. Lou Gehrig's 2130 consecutive game playing streak | 320 |
| 4. Ted Williams' six hits on final day of 1941 season to hit .400 | 126 |
| 5. Ted Williams' homer in final career at-bat in 1960 | 112 |

### National League

| | |
|---|---|
| 1. Hank Aaron's 715th home run in 1974 | 785 |
| 2. Bobby Thomson's playoff-winning home run in 1951 | 781 |
| 3. Johnny Vander Meer's back-to-back no-hitters in 1938 | 271 |
| 4. Jackie Robinson's major league debut in 1947 | 130 |
| 5. Harvey Haddix' 12-inning perfect game in 1959 | 69 |

The club winners were revealed in December 1976. A special panel representing the media and baseball rounded out the final list of nominees in the national competition to make sure events and personalities on clubs no longer in operation were fairly represented.

### MOST MEMORABLE MOMENT NOMINEES
### Regular Season
(In Chronological Order)

#### AMERICAN LEAGUE
1. Ty Cobb's 6-for-6 including 3 home runs—May 5, 1925
2. Lefty Grove's 1-0 loss after 16 straight wins—1931
3. Lou Gehrig's 2130 consecutive game playing streak—June 1, 1925 to April 30, 1939
4. Bob Feller no-hits White Sox on opening day—April 16, 1940
5. Joe DiMaggio's 56-game hitting streak—May 15-July 16, 1941
6. Ted Williams' 6 hits on final day of 1941 season (Sept. 28) puts him over .400
7. Joe Cronin becomes first player to clout a pinch-hit homer in each game of a doubleheader—June 17, 1943
8. St. Louis Browns clinch only pennant—Oct. 1, 1944
9. Lou Boudreau ties major league record and sets AL standard for most long hits in a game (5) with 4 doubles and home run—July 14, 1946
10. Satchel Paige's shutout against Chicago in his first complete major league game—Aug. 10, 1948 ☞

Joe DiMaggio's 56-game hitting streak was Most Memorable Moment in American League voting.

## THE AMAZIN' METS
*Though the Chicago Cubs held first place for 155 straight days in 1969, leading the third-place New York Mets by 9½ games on August 14, the Mets won the NL East title by eight games.*

## '20 INDIANS WON DESPITE TRAGEDY
*The Cleveland Indians won the World Championship in 1920 after overcoming the game's worst tragedy. Shortstop Ray Chapman, batting against submarine righthander Carl Mays of the Yankees on August 16, was struck in the head by a pitch. He died the next day—the only fatality that occurred during play in the major leagues.*

11. Cleveland beats Boston to win only AL playoff—Oct. 4, 1948
12. Allie Reynolds' second no-hitter of 1951—Sept. 28
13. *White Sox win first pennant in 40 years—1959
14. Ted Williams homers in final career at-bat—Sept. 26, 1960
15. Roger Maris' 61st home run—Oct. 1, 1961
16. *Harmon Killebrew's ninth-inning homer beats Yankees and keeps Minnesota in first place—July 11, 1965
17. *Red Sox win 1967 pennant in final game
18. *Jim Hunter hurls perfect game *vs.* Twins—May 8, 1968
19. Denny McLain becomes baseball's first 30-game winner since 1934—Sept. 14, 1968
20. *Baseball returns to Milwaukee—1970
21. *Steve Busby hurls his first no-hitter—April 27, 1973
22. *David Clyde, 18, wins major league debut—June 27, 1973
23. *Frank Robinson's managerial debut, highlighted by his own home run—April 8, 1975
24. *Nolan Ryan ties major league record with fourth no-hitter—June 1, 1975

---

## NATIONAL LEAGUE

25. Boston Braves' miracle finish in 1914
26. Baseball's longest game, the Brooklyn-Boston 26-inning, 1-1 tie—May 1, 1920
27. First major league night game played in Cincinnati—May 24, 1935
28. Babe Ruth's final three homers, hit for the Boston Braves—May 25, 1935
29. *Johnny Vander Meer's consecutive no-hitters—June 11 and 15, 1938
30. Gabby Hartnett's "homer in the dark" gives Cubs NL lead—Sept. 28, 1938
31. Jackie Robinson's major league debut—April 15, 1947
32. Dick Sisler's 10th-inning homer wins pennant for Phils—Oct. 1, 1950
33. Bobby Thomson's ninth-inning playoff homer wins NL championship for Giants—Oct. 3, 1951
34. Stan Musial slugs 5 home runs in doubleheader—May 2, 1954
35. Henry Aaron's home run gives Milwaukee first pennant—Sept. 23, 1957
36. Roy Campanella's testimonial game lures 93,103 in Los Angeles—May 7, 1959
37. Harvey Haddix hurls 12 perfect innings for Pirates, loses in 13th—May 26, 1959
38. *Giants' 1962 playoff victory
39. *Jim Bunning's perfect game—June 21, 1964
40. *Astrodome inaugural—April 9, 1965
41. *Sandy Koufax throws perfect game—Sept. 9, 1965
42. Don Drysdale pitches record 58 2/3 consecutive scoreless innings—May 14-June 8, 1968
43. *Expos' debut in Montreal, first major league game outside of United States—April 14, 1969
44. Tom Seaver's record 10 consecutive strikeouts *vs.* San Diego—April 22, 1970
45. *Ernie Banks' 500th home run—May 12, 1970
46. *Nate Colbert's 5-homer, 13-RBI doubleheader—Aug. 1, 1972
47. *Henry Aaron's record 715th homer—April 8, 1974
48. *Lou Brock's 105th stolen base—Sept. 10, 1974

Star slugger Harmon Killebrew delivered the Most Memorable Moment of the Minnesota Twins with a game-winning, ninth-inning home run, keeping the team in first place in July 1965.

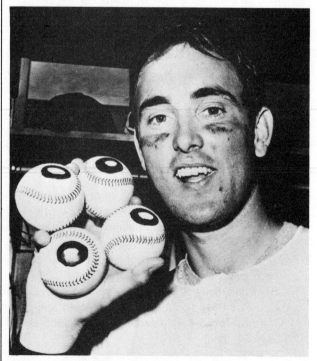

Nolan Ryan carved his niche in baseball history after throwing his fourth no hitter for the California Angels.

## BRAVES BLEW
## '59 PLAYOFF GAME

*In 1959, the Milwaukee Braves took a 5-2 lead into the ninth inning of Playoff Game 2 but could not hold on. The Los Angeles Dodgers tied in the ninth and won, 6-5, when Felix Mantilla made a throwing error in the twelfth.*

## ROOKIE COST BROWNS
## 1922 FLAG

*Connie Mack, manager of the Philadelphia Athletics, was so impressed by semi-pro pitcher Otto Rettig that he signed him to a major league contract. Rettig beat the St. Louis Browns the day he reported for his only major league victory. It was the margin of failure for the Browns, who finished one game behind the Yankees that season.*

Chevrolet

## WORLD SERIES/ALL-STAR GAME

49. Christy Mathewson's three shutouts *vs.* Athletics in 1905 W.S. —Oct. 9, 12, 14
50. Bill Wambsganss makes only unassisted triple play in W.S.— Oct. 10, 1920
51. Walter Johnson's first W.S. victory at age of 36—Oct. 10, 1924
52. Grover Alexander saves 1926 W.S. with bases loaded strikeout of Tony Lazzeri—Oct. 10
53. Athletics overcome 8-0 deficit with 10-run seventh to beat Cubs —Oct. 12, 1929
54. Babe Ruth's "called shot" homer in 1932 W.S.—Oct. 1
55. Carl Hubbell's 5 consecutive strikeouts in 1934 A.S. game— July 10
56. Ted Williams' three-run game-winning A.S. home run in 1941 —July 8
57. Mickey Owen's muff of third strike which opened door to winning Yankee rally in 1941 W.S.—Oct. 5
58. Cookie Lavagetto's double ruins Bill Bevens' no-hit bid in 1947 W.S.—Oct. 3
59. Al Gionfriddo's catch robs Joe DiMaggio in 1947 W.S.—Oct. 5
60. Willie Mays' back-to-the-plate catch off Vic Wertz in 1954 W.S.—Sept. 29
61. Sandy Amoros' catch off Yogi Berra saves Dodgers in 1955 W.S.—Oct. 4
62. *Don Larsen's perfect game in 1956 W.S.—Oct. 8
63. Lew Burdette beats Yankees three times in 1957 W.S.—Oct. 3, 7, 10
64. *Bill Mazeroski's climactic Game 7 homer in 1960 W.S.—Oct. 13
65. Tony Perez wins longest A.S. game for NL with fifteenth-inning home run—July 11, 1967
66. Bob Gibson sets W.S. record with 17-strikeout game—Oct. 2, 1968
67. *Mickey Lolich's three W.S. victories in 1968—Oct. 3, 7, 10
68. *New York Mets' W.S. triumph in 1969
69. Pete Rose's dash to the plate in 12th wins 1970 A.S. game for NL—July 14
70. *Brooks Robinson leads Orioles to 1970 W.S. triumph
71. Roberto Clemente's all-around brilliance in 1971 W.S.
72. Carlton Fisk's twelfth-inning game-winning home run in Game 6 of 1975 W.S.—Oct. 21

*Designates most memorable moment for each club.

## RUTH, GEHRIG
## STAGED POWER SHOW

*Babe Ruth and Lou Gehrig of the Yankees hit two homers each to lead the Yankees to a 7-5 victory in Game 3 of the 1932 World Series against the Chicago Cubs. One of Ruth's home runs was his controversial "pointed shot" against Charlie Root.*

# MOST MEMORABLE PERSONALITIES
### (In Alphabetical Order)

| | | | |
|---|---|---|---|
| Hank Aaron | Frankie Frisch | Connie Mack | Branch Rickey |
| Yogi Berra | Lou Gehrig | Larry MacPhail | Frank Robinson |
| Roy Campanella | Lefty Gomez | Mickey Mantle | Jackie Robinson |
| Roberto Clemente | Lefty Grove | Pepper Martin | Babe Ruth |
| Ty Cobb | Babe Herman | Christy Mathewson | Tris Speaker |
| Dizzy Dean | Rogers Hornsby | Willie Mays | Casey Stengel |
| Joe DiMaggio | Walter Johnson | John McGraw | Rube Waddell |
| Leo Durocher | Al Kaline | Stan Musial | Honus Wagner |
| Bob Feller | Sandy Koufax | Mel Ott | Ted Williams |
| Jimmie Foxx | Judge K. M. Landis | Satchel Paige | Cy Young |

Lou Gehrig

Yogi Berra

Satchel Paige

Mel Ott

# PENNANT RACES

The most exciting aspect of major league baseball is the pennant race. Until 1969, when the American and National Leagues adopted divisional play, there were two races—one in each league—and a World Series between the winners. With split leagues, the number of races doubled, though actual league pennants are awarded only to the winner of the intra-league Championship Series.

Pennant races are often hotly contested, and occasionally end in a tie. Before the creation of East and West divisions in the majors, National League races ended in a dead heat four times—in 1946, 1951, 1959, and 1962—and the AL season ended unresolved once—in 1948. An unusual makeup game decided the National's pennant chase in 1908, but it did not fall into the playoff category.

To advance to the World Series, a best-of-seven affair, today's teams must survive a best-of-five Championship Series. Before 1969, National League ties were settled in a best-of-three playoff, while AL deadlocks were resolved in a single, sudden-death contest. The sudden-death format was used for the first time in divisional play when the Yankees and Red Sox tied for first place in the AL East race of 1978. New York won the Playoff, the Championship Series, and the World Series.

Predicting the pennant winners is a herculean task—even for writers who have been following the game for years. Too many un-

## PLAYOFF RECORDS COUNTED

Under the old playoff rules, individual statistics compiled in league playoffs were considered part of the regular season's averages. The rule allowed Milwaukee Braves third baseman Eddie Mathews to win the NL home run crown when he hit No. 46 against the Dodgers in '59 and broke a tie with Ernie Banks.

## GIANTS REPEATED MIRACLE OF 1951

With star southpaw Sandy Koufax idled by a circulatory ailment in his fingers, the Los Angeles Dodgers were unable to hold the lead in the 1962 National League race. The San Francisco Giants, repeating their miracle finish of 1951, cut the lead to three games with eight to play and finally caught the Dodgers to force a playoff. In the last 13 games, the Giants were 7-6 but the Dodgers 3-10. San Francisco won the best-of-three playoff to win the right to face the Yankees in the World Series.

known factors are involved to make pre-season prognostications reliable. Trades, injuries, unknown rookies, faded veterans, unpoular owners or managers, and countless other possibilities influence each team's chances.

Both the 1967 Boston Red Sox and 1969 New York Mets won the pennant after finishing ninth in a 10-team league the year before. The 1945 Chicago Cubs won, but the same team was 30 games behind in '44. The New York Giants were 35 games behind in 1953, but won the National League pennant of 1954—and swept the favored Cleveland Indians in a four-game World Series.

Should a tie occur under the present divisional format, two playoffs would be necessary—one to dissolve the divisional deadlock, the other to select a league champion.

In 1973, five of the six teams in the National League East were in contention with four days to go in the regular season. There was even a remote chance that all five could wind up tied with identical records of 80-82. The standings at that point:

|            | W. | L. | Pct. | G.B. | Left |
|------------|----|----|------|------|------|
| New York   | 80 | 78 | .506 | —    | 4    |
| Pittsburgh | 79 | 79 | .500 | 1    | 4    |
| St. Louis  | 78 | 81 | .491 | 2½   | 3    |
| Montreal   | 77 | 82 | .484 | 3½   | 3    |
| Chicago    | 76 | 82 | .481 | 4    | 4    |

### Remaining Games
**NEW YORK** (4)—Away Chicago, Sept. 28, 29 (2), 30.
**PITTSBURGH** (4)—Home Montreal, Sept. 28, 29, 30. Oct. 1 make-up game against San Diego if necessary.
**ST. LOUIS** (3)—Home Philadelphia, Sept. 28, 29, 30.
**CHICAGO** (4)—Home New York, Sept. 28, 29 (2), 30.
**MONTREAL** (3)—Away Pittsburgh, Sept. 28, 29, 30.

The need for an intra-divisional playoff never developed; the New York Mets, rebounding from 12-game deficit and last-place standing on July 8, finished on top with an 82-79 record and .509 percentage—lowest ever recorded by a championship team. Moreover, the Mets beat the powerful Cincinnati Reds in the Championship Series and carried the Oakland A's a full seven games before losing the World Series.

## MUSIAL SWITCH WON FLAG FOR CARDS
*Stan Musial's switch from the outfield to first base in June 1946 plugged the only void in the lineup of the St. Louis Cardinals and enabled the team to win the National League pennant.*

## FIRST DIVISIONAL CHAMPS
*In 1969, the New York Mets and Baltimore Orioles became the first pennant-winners to be chosen through the Championship Series format. The Mets, champions of the NL East, swept the Atlanta Braves, champions of the West, despite three home runs from Atlanta slugger Hank Aaron. Baltimore swept three straight from Minnesota in the American League.*

## WINNING LOSERS
*The only players from losing teams to win MVP honors in the Championship Series were Fred Lynn (Angels) in 1982 and Jeffrey Leonard (Giants) in 1987.*

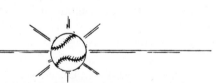

# THE SHOT HEARD ROUND THE WORLD

The drama of the 1951 National League playoff between the Brooklyn Dodgers and New York Giants outmatched all similar battles, including Dodger defeats by the Cardinals in 1946 and Giants in 1962, and a Dodger victory over the Braves in 1959.

Cleveland's 8-3 playoff victory over the Red Sox in 1948—which snuffed out hopes of an all-Boston World Series—also could not compare with the 1951 match between New York's arch-rivals.

The Giants had finished third, five games behind Philadelphia, in '50, but couldn't get untracked in '51. They lost their first 11 games, prompting long time fan Tallulah Bankhead to tell Groucho Marx, "Don't worry about the Giants. Don't forget: Leo Durocher is leading them." Marx twisted his cigar, thought a moment, and snapped, "Yes—but so is everybody else in the National League."

Owner Horace Stoneham and manager Leo Durocher embrace hero Bobby Thomson in victorious Giants' clubhouse after come-from-behind pennant triumph.

**THE SHOT** *continued*

By August 11, the Giants were 13½ games behind the Dodgers. Brooklyn manager Charley Dressen had already pronounced them dead. After the Dodgers swept three straight from New York in early July, he said, "We knocked them out. They'll never bother us again."

While Dressen knew the Giants had a better club than their record showed, he let himself and his players be convinced that they could never be caught. The Giants had other ideas. They posted a 39-8 record down the stretch, while the Dodgers plodded along at .500, and Brooklyn actually had to win its final game or lose the pennant outright.

A bases-loaded catch by Jackie Robinson in the twelfth and his home run in the fourteenth gave the Dodgers a 9-8 win over the Phillies and forced a playoff. The Giants won the opener, 3-1, but the Dodgers took the second, 10-0. The winner of the third game would win the pennant.

Brooklyn pitcher Don Newcombe held a commanding 4-1 lead going into the last of the ninth in the deciding game. Alvin Dark led off with an infield hit, and Don Mueller followed with a solid single. When Monte Irvin popped out, Giants' fans in the Polo Grounds let out a collective groan. A double-play ball would end the game—and the season.

Whitey Lockman, the next hitter, kept New York hopes alive with a solid double to left, scoring Dark to make the score 4-2, but Mueller was hurt sliding into third. He left on a stretcher as Dressen took advantage of the delay to rush Ralph Branca in from the bullpen.

Bobby Thomson—who had hit a home run against Branca in the opening game of the playoffs—was the scheduled hitter, with rookie Willie Mays to follow. Thomson had 31 home runs, more than any other Giant, but Branca elected to pitch to him. ☞

## PRESUMING PIRATES LEFT HANGING

*When Pittsburgh built an eight-game lead over the Chicago Cubs by August 20, 1938, the Pirates anticipated participation in the World Series. The team built a new press box in Forbes Field to accommodate the expected hordes of writers. But the Cubs won 30 of their last 42, as Pittsburgh posted a 20-24 mark, and Chicago capped its drive with a September sweep of the Pirates. The highlight of that sweep—the famous "Homer in the Gloamin'" by Cub player-manager Gabby Hartnett—brought victory to Chicago just before darkness would have halted play.*

## CUBS SHOWED WAY TO WIN IN '35

*The pennant-winning Chicago Cubs of 1935 won 21 in a row, and 23 of 26 (an .885 percentage) in the month of September.*

The first pitch was a high, inside fastball, the type of pitch Thomson could hit for a home run. Catcher Rube Walker—filling in for the injured Roy Campanella—and Branca decided that Thomson would be looking for something low and away—or anything other than the same pitch he had just taken. They were mistaken.

Thomson's three-run home run, known as "the Shot Heard 'Round the World," capped the Giants' pennant drive, called "the Little Miracle of Coogan's Bluff."

"No one ever expected it to happen," recalled Monte Irvin. "When Bobby hit the ball, we were kind of leaning, pulling, trying to *make* the ball go into the left field stands. When it did, we didn't have an instant reaction. We kind of looked at each other and all of a sudden realized we were the champions. Then all bedlam broke loose."

As a footnote to history, Irvin pointed out that Jackie Robinson made sure Thomson touched every base during his trip to home plate. "He was a competitor right to the end," said the Hall of Fame outfielder.

## ROOKIE TOPPED FELLER FOR FLAG

**The Detroit Tigers won the 1940 American League pennant by one game over the Cleveland Indians. Rookie Floyd Giebell pitched the decisive game—a 2-0 victory over Indian superstar Bob Feller at Cleveland. Giebell won only two other games in his major league career.**

**Pitcher Jack Chesbro compiled a record number of victories for a single season.**

# BASEBALL'S GREATEST RACES

Baseball history is filled with exciting pennant races—stories of hope and despair, ecstasy and dejection. The "miracle" Giants of 1951 overcame the greatest deficit in a single season, but the "miracle" tag was first applied to the Boston Braves of 1914, 11½ games behind in July but winners by 10 games at season's end.

Early leads often crumble under the pennant pressure of September. Joe Gordon, star second baseman and manager, described the feeling: "It's impossible to take the last few weeks in stride when you know that one bad bounce or wrong guess can send the entire season down the drain. Contenders crack from mental fatigue, not physical weariness. Experience only makes you more jittery, because you realize how many unexpected things can murder you."

In 1904, the Yankees (then called Highlanders) missed a chance to win their first pennant because pitching ace Jack Chesbro, seeking his record 42nd victory of the season, uncorked a two-out wild pitch in the ninth inning against the first-place Red Sox in an end-of-season doubleheader. A New York sweep would have won the pennant. Instead, Boston won, 3-2, and the second game was unnecessary.

A wild pitch hurt the Chicago White Sox in a heated race four years later. On October 2, 1908, with the Sox fighting Cleveland and Detroit for the pennant, 40-game winner Ed Walsh pitched a four-hitter and struck out 15, but his two-strike, two-out spitball in the third broke off the glove of catcher Ossie Schreckengost and allowed a runner to score. Cleveland's Addie Joss pitched a perfect game to win, 1-0, in a contest experts consider the best-pitched pressure game in history. Detroit eventually won the pennant.

Like the American, the National League featured a three-team chase, involving the Cubs, Pirates, and Giants.

Fred Merkle's base-running boner (described in Chapter 2) had deprived the Giants of an apparent 3-2 victory over Chicago, and the league decided the game would be replayed if necessary when the season ended. Had the Pirates defeated the Cubs on the last day of scheduled play, Pittsburgh would have won the flag. But the Cubs won, forcing a tie with New York, and beat the Giants in the makeup game, 4-2. Mordecai (Three-Finger) Brown was the winning pitcher for Chicago in both victories—the first as a starter and the second as an early reliever.

In 1911, the American League's defending champions, the Philadelphia A's, were mired in the cellar in May, looking up at the Detroit Tigers, who had won 21 of their first 23. A's owner Connie Mack (also the club's manager) entertained his Detroit counterpart, Frank Navin, at dinner and said, "It's too bad you're so far out in front, Frank, you're ruining the race." Navin felt the sting of Mack's gentle needle July 4, when the A's tied for the top, and again in early August, when Philadelphia zoomed past Detroit en route to a pennant margin of 13½ games.

Three years later, the "miracle" Braves, a fifth-place entry that finished 31½ games off the pace the year before, began a pennant march from the National League basement July 18 and knocked off the Athletics in four straight World Series games.

The Yankees started their domination of the American League in the '20s, winning 27 pennants in 42 years from 1923-64, not only because they had great individual stars but also because the collection of talent helped each individual. "When you have great ballplayers playing alongside you, it makes you play so much harder," explained Phil Rizzuto, AL Most Valuable Player in 1950.

Like the Yankees, the Giants had a dynasty of sorts in the National League. Fiery John McGraw had won 10 pennants during his long tenure, and Bill Terry was smug from victory in 1933 when he let his pennant chances stall on a roll of the tongue.

Asked what he thought of the Dodgers, then an also-ran entry, Terry replied, "Oh, is Brooklyn still in the National League?" A group of gathered writers laughed, but the Dodgers laughed last. Brooklyn played the role of spoiler, ruining New York's chance to catch the Cardinals, who finished in front by two games. The Dodgers beat the Giants in the season's finale, 8-5 in ten innings.

By 1942, the Dodgers were strong. Defending the 1941 crown, Brooklyn led St. Louis by 9½ games on August 15, and won 25 of its remaining 42 games, including the final eight. But the Cardinals closed with a 43-9 mark to finish first by two games—just as they had in 1934.

There was an all-St. Louis series in 1944, when the Browns won their only American League pennant by one game over Detroit and six over New York. The Browns finished strong, winning four straight from the Yankees, but went into the final day tied with Detroit. Last-place Washington defeated Dizzy Trout (27-14) as the Browns wrapped up the Yankee series and the pennant.

Detroit got its revenge the following year when Hank Greenberg, just back from a four-year military tour, cracked a ninth-inning grand slam in the opener of a doubleheader against the Browns to clinch the pennant. Had the Tigers dropped both games, they would have had a one-game playoff against Washington.

"My attitude was different from the other players," said Greenberg. "They had lost the pennant on the last day the previous year and were worried they would kick it away again. I was so glad to be back that baseball was just a picnic to me." ☞

## KOUFAX HURLED "MUST-WIN" MATCH

*The Los Angeles Dodgers were forced to use ace Sandy Koufax on the last day of the 1966 season. The Dodgers had a "magic number" of 1 on the final day. Any combination of Dodger wins and Giant losses adding up to one would give them the National League pennant.*

*A Giant win over the Pirates, coupled with a Dodger defeat in a doubleheader with the Phillies, would force a playoff.*

*Manager Walter Alston had hoped to use Koufax in the opening game of the World Series, but pressed him into service in the second game of the doubleheader after San Francisco topped Pittsburgh and Philadelphia beat Los Angeles.*

*Koufax won the game, but was held out of the World Series against Baltimore until Game 2. Don Drysdale pitched and lost the opener as the Orioles won four straight.*

Hank Greenberg's ninth-inning grand slam on the final day of the 1945 campaign enabled Tigers to avert a possible playoff with Washington and enter the World Series against the Chicago Cubs.

The Yankees won their first World Championship in 1923, the same year they moved into Yankee Stadium.

In 1948, the Red Sox eliminated the Yankees on the next-to-last day of the season and earned a playoff berth when Cleveland lost its final game to Detroit while Boston beat New York again. The pitching of rookie Gene Bearden and two home runs by player-manager Lou Boudreau quashed Boston's hopes.

Red Sox fans were also disappointed in 1949, when the Yankees avenged their setback of the previous fall. Boston led by one with two to play against New York, but the Yankees won both games and the championship. Part of the blame was pinned on Red Sox catcher Birdie Tebbetts, who needled Yankee players about the pending pennant party in the Boston clubhouse. Stirred by his remarks, the New Yorkers overcame a 4-0 lead to win, 5-4. New York won, 5-3, the following afternoon.

In the National League, the Brooklyn Dodgers and Philadelphia Phillies hooked up for pennant-deciding battles three years running, 1949-51. In '49, St. Louis beat the Cubs and would have tied for the pennant if Philadelphia had beaten Brooklyn. The next season, the Philadelphia Whiz Kids frittered away a big lead. In the decisive final game, Richie Ashburn's ninth-inning throw nipped Cal Abrams at the plate, sending the game into the tenth inning and setting the stage for Dick Sisler's pennant-winning home run. Had the Dodgers won the season-ending game, the Phils and Dodgers would have gone into a playoff series.

Dodger manager Burt Shotton was criticized for not replacing Abrams, a poor base runner, with fleet Eddie Miksis. Both Shotton and third base coach Milt Stock, who waved Abrams home, were dropped that winter.

In '51, the scenario was reversed. Jackie Robinson's extra-inning homer for Brooklyn beat the Phils and sent the Dodgers into the playoffs with the Giants.

Five years later, the Dodgers opened the campaign defending their first World Championship crown. But Milwaukee and Cincinnati challenged to the end, leaving only two games between first and third place. ☞

## SOUTHPAW SLUGGER

*Switch-hitting shortstop Ozzie Smith had played in the majors for eight seasons before hitting a home run lefthanded. The solo shot in the ninth inning gave the St. Louis Cardinals a 3-2 win over the Los Angeles Dodgers in Game 5 of the 1985 NL Championship Series. A three-run, ninth-inning homer by Jack Clark in Game 6 gave the Cardinals the pennant.*

## RUTH COULD STEAL TOO

*Babe Ruth stole second and third base in the same inning of a 1921 World Series game for the Yankees against the Giants.*

## OLDEST SERIES PLAYER

*Jack Quinn was more than 46 years old when he pitched in the 1930 World Series for the Philadelphia Athletics. He had no record in two innings of work.*

## WILLIE MAYS' LAST HIT

*The final hit of Willie Mays' career drove in one of four runs in the twelfth inning of Game 2 as the New York Mets defeated the Oakland A's, 10-7, in the 1973 World Series.*

On the final weekend, the Braves were up by one with three to play, but lost two of three to the Cardinals while the Dodgers swept the Pirates to win the pennant. After winning the National League title in both '57 and '58, the Braves sought to avenge their one-game deficit of 1956 by beating the Dodgers in a best-of-three playoff. After a three-cornered race, also involving the Giants, the Dodgers won the playoff and, in six games, the World Series over the White Sox.

The 1962 playoff finale bore many similarities to the 1951 classic, won by the Giants with a four-run burst in the last of the ninth. After a devastating late-season slide, the Dodgers lost to NL newcomer Billy Pierce, 8-0, in the opener. They came from behind to win the second, 8-7, and took a 4-2 lead into the ninth inning of the deciding game. The Giants' winning run crossed on a bases-loaded walk.

In 1964, the Philadelphia Phillies suffered the worst collapse of any pennant-bound club. That team has since become synonymous with the word "choke." Leading by 6½ games with 12 to play, the Phils dropped 10 straight, including crucial three-game series to the suddenly-awake Cardinals and Reds.

On October 1, the Cards—with an eight-game winning streak—led the Reds by ½ and the Phillies by 2½. But the hapless Mets knocked off the Cardinals, 1-0 and 15-5, on successive days, while the Phils won one game from the Reds, 4-3. The Cards were now tied with the Reds and one game ahead of the Phils.

Philadelphia beat the Reds again, 10-0, on the final day, but the Cards won. Had they lost, all three teams would have wound up with identical 92-70 marks, forcing the game's first three-way playoff.

Three years after the collapse of the Phillies, the Boston Red Sox pulled off their "Impossible Dream" in the tightest pennant race in American League history.

Named for the lead song in the popular musical, *Man of La Mancha,* the Red Sox championship was forged against 100-to-1 odds with the leadership of rookie manager Dick Williams and Triple Crown winner Carl Yastrzemski.

Boston, Chicago, Detroit, and Minnesota were still serious contenders as the last week opened. The pitching-rich White Sox, with a team batting average of .225, dropped out of the race, but the Twins held a one-game lead as they came to Boston's Fenway Park for their final two games. The Tigers, tied with the Red Sox for second place, were home for back-to-back doubleheaders against the Angels.

The Red Sox won the series opener, reaching a first-place tie, while the Tigers split their doubleheader to pull within a half-game of the lead. On Sunday, Jim Lonborg of Boston won his 22nd game, beating 20-game winner Dean Chance of the Twins, as the Tigers won the first of their doubleheader from the Angels. A Detroit sweep would force a playoff, but the Angels pulled out a come-from-behind 8-5 win in the nightcap, giving Boston the pennant.

In 1974, the Red Sox seemed certain to sew up another flag when they took an eight-game lead into September. Suddenly, the Baltimore Orioles caught fire, posting a 27-6 mark after August 29, while the Sox were 12-21 over the same period. The Yankees wound up second, two games behind, and the Red Sox third, seven games back.

Boston blew yet another pennant in 1978. On July 17, the Red Sox owned a 14-game lead over the New York Yankees, but fortunes quickly changed. A series of injuries slowed the Hub's pennant express to a crawl, while the Yankees regrouped under low-key manager Bob Lemon, who replaced Billy Martin July 25.

Fred Kaplan

**Jim Lonborg won 22 games to spearhead the "Impossible Dream" pennant drive of the 1967 Boston Red Sox.**

## TED WILLIAMS FOILS THE SHIFT

*Red Sox slugger Ted Williams, a notorious lefthanded pull hitter, foiled the "Williams shift" by the St. Louis Cardinals when he bunted safely for one of his five hits in the 1946 World Series.*

## ROBINSONS LAUNCHED '66 SWEEP

*Frank and Brooks Robinson hit consecutive home runs against Don Drysdale in the first inning of the 1966 World Series to start the Orioles toward a four-game sweep.*

## SERIES SWINGER

*Infielder Paul Molitor of the Milwaukee Brewers is the only player to produce five hits in a single World Series game. He did it against the St. Louis Cardinals in the 1982 Series opener.*

# THE WORLD SERIES

Though some players insist the League Championship Series, a product of divisional play, has superseded the World Series in importance, most baseball insiders contend that the best-of-seven classic between league champions retains its traditional role as the highlight of the baseball year.

Stadiums of participating teams are always full—the Dodgers filled more than 92,000 seats at the Los Angeles Coliseum for three games in 1959—and broadcast ratings are high. NBC-TV estimated that 135 million Americans watched at least part of the 1978 World Series.

Interest should be high, because the Series stands as a test of skills between baseball's best teams. Games are played under the glare of the public spotlight, but teams emerging from tight pennant races sometimes tend to let down in the fall classic.

Series history is filled with high drama and bitter disappointment. Don Larsen's perfect game in 1956 was the only no-hitter in the World Series, but Floyd Bevens—another Yankee facing the Brooklyn Dodgers—came within one out of a no-hit game seven years earlier.

Pitcher Ralph Terry of the Yankees pitched a brilliant, 1-0 victory in the seventh game to defeat the Giants in 1962, but two years earlier served a bottom-of-the-ninth home run ball that gave the world championship to Bill Mazeroski and the Pittsburgh Pirates.

Babe Ruth starred as a pitcher and a hitter, twice hitting three home runs in one World Series game (Reggie Jackson did it once) and pitching 29 2/3 consecutive scoreless innings—a record later shattered by Whitey Ford—for the Boston Red Sox. But even Ruth had his Series disappointment; as a rookie in 1915, after winning 18 of 24 decisions for Boston, he was bypassed in post-season play, appearing only in a single pinch-hitting role.

Errors, strikeouts, shutouts, miracle catches, long hits, and stolen bases are taken for granted during the season, but are so important during a short series that few can be forgotten.

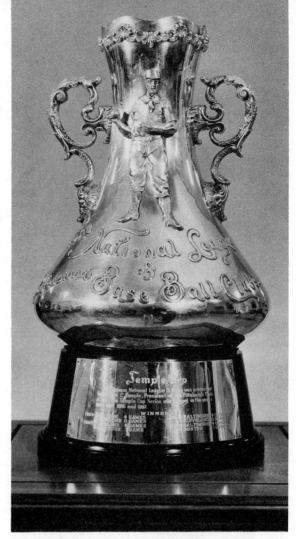

The Temple Cup was given to championship teams before the century changed—and before the World Series began.

## McNALLY'S SURPRISE SLAM

*Baltimore pitcher Dave McNally electrified the baseball world when he hit a grand-slam home run against Cincinnati's Wayne Granger in the sixth inning of Game 3 of the 1970 Series. He won, 9-3.*

# HOW THE SERIES BEGAN

Post-season competition between champions of the major leagues began in 1882, when the American Association joined the 6-year-old National League as a bona fide big-league circuit. Chicago (NL) and Cincinnati (AA) split two games before a series of disputes canceled the rest of the match.

The leagues tried again in 1884, with a best-of-five format, and Providence (NL) beat the old New York Mets (AA) three straight. Nothing formal was arranged between leagues, however, and the 1887 "world series" was exactly that. Detroit (NL) challenged St. Louis (AA) to a 15-game tour that started in St. Louis, shifted to Detroit, then went to Pittsburgh, Brooklyn, New York, Philadelphia, Boston, back to Philadelphia, Washington, Baltimore, Brooklyn again, Detroit again, Chicago, and St. Louis for two final games.

The marathon attracted 51,455 fans who paid $42,000 for the privilege of watching two travel-weary teams playing less-than-championship baseball. Since expenses for the series amounted to $18,000, the clubs divided a pot of $24,000—just $3,000 more than the minimum major league salary in 1978! ☞

## MANTLE'S HOME RUN MARK

*Mickey Mantle, the great switch-hitting centerfielder of the Yankees, hit a record 18 home runs in the World Series.*

Mickey Mantle

HOW THE SERIES BEGAN *continued*

When the Giants and Browns tried a 10-game series after the 1888 season, receipts for the final two games at St. Louis were so discouraging ($411 and $212) that the marathon concept was scrapped.

The American Association, crippled by the Players League revolt of 1890, dissolved after 1891 and the National League took on four of its teams the following year. In 1894, former Pittsburgh Pirates president William Chase Temple created the Temple Cup series between the National League's two top teams.

Without a divisional format, the first- and second-place clubs had already met as often as any other two teams and the significance of the cup was never established.

The first Temple Cup series carried the best-of-seven format that later would be used in the World Series, but the champion Baltimore Orioles dropped four straight to the second-place New York Giants.

Temple was so unhappy with the result that he sold all his remaining stock in the Pirates. His unhappiness turned to distress when word leaked out that five Orioles had agreed in advance to split their shares with the Giants. The greedy Giant players refused to live up their agreement, however, and kept their winner's shares of $564 (losers got 30 per cent less).

Somehow, the Temple Cup survived three more seasons, but it failed to generate enthusiasm among players, fans, or officials.

The first legitimate World Series was played in 1903, two years after the birth of the American League. The Boston Red Sox won a best-of-nine series from the Pittsburgh Pirates, five to three, and 100,000 fans paid double the going rate (50 cents for general admission and $1 for reserved seats) to watch.

There was no World Series in 1904 because John McGraw, manager of the National League champion Giants, refused to acknowledge the major status of the American and shunned its champion. But the Series was renewed to stay in 1905, under the supervision of a three-man National Commission which then governed the game. Revenue would be divided among players, owners, and the commission.

Except for 1903 and 1919-20-21, when a best-of-nine format was used, the World Championship has always been awarded to the first team to win four games.

# THE WILD WINDUP OF 1960

Though Don Larsen's perfect game for the Yankees against the Dodgers in 1956 stands as the finest—and most unexpected—performance by a pitcher in World Series history, the seven-game classic of 1960 had a twist ending that makes it even more memorable.

The Yankees won by scores of 16-3, 10-0, and 12-0, and outscored the Pirates, 55-27, but Pittsburgh won the world championship.

On October 13, the teams were deadlocked at three games each as play unfolded in Game 7. Vernon Law, winner of two games for the Pirates, opposed Bob Turley, who had won once for the Yankees, but neither lasted six innings. Turley, in fact, left in the second.

The Pirates jumped to a quick 4-0 lead, but the Yankees scored one in the fifth and four in the sixth to forge ahead. When New York scored two more in the top of the eighth, Yankee prospects looked good—especially since Bobby Shantz had pitched scoreless ball since entering the game in the third inning. ☞

## TOP SERIES MANAGERS

*Joe McCarthy and Casey Stengel each won seven world championships—a mark unmatched by any other manager.*

## RELIEVERS START SERIES IN '50s

*Relief pitchers Jim Konstanty of the Phillies (1950) and Joe Black of the Dodgers (1952) were surprise starters for their teams in World Series openers. Konstanty lost, 1-0, while Black won, 4-2.*

Bill Mazeroski's dramatic last-of-the-ninth homer gave Pirates a 10-9 victory in Game 7 and made them 1960 World Champions after hard-fought series against the New York Yankees.

But Pittsburgh struck in the last of the eighth. Gino Cimoli, Bill Virdon, and Dick Groat rapped consecutive singles, knocking out Shantz and cutting the Yankee lead to 7-5. Bob Skinner sacrificed, moving the runners to second and third, but Rocky Nelson flied to right without further damage. Roberto Clemente kept the rally going with an infield single to first, scoring Virdon, and second-string catcher Hal Smith—who had replaced Smoky Burgess earlier—strode to the plate.

Jim Coates, who had replaced Shantz, served a fat pitch and Smith socked it over the left-field wall for a three-run homer. Pittsburgh led, 9-7. Ralph Terry came on to retire Don Hoak for the third out.

With all Pittsburgh rabid for revenge against the Yankees—who had beaten the 1927 Pirates four straight in the last Series match between the clubs—Bob Friend took the mound in the top of the ninth. An 18-game winner during the National League season, he had lost twice as a starter earlier in the World Series.

Quick singles by Bobby Richardson (who knocked in 26 runs all season but 12 in the Series) and Dale Long chased Friend, and Harvey Haddix—winner of Game 5—came in. Roger Maris fouled to Hal Smith, but Mickey Mantle singled to score Richardson and send Long to third. Gil McDougald, running for Long, scored on an infield out by Yogi Berra and Bill Skowron hit into a force to retire the side.

Bill Mazeroski led off the last of the ninth. He had hit 11 home runs during the regular season (four of his teammates did better and a fifth did as well) and one in the first game of the World Series. It was a two-run blast that helped the Pirates win, 6-4.

The score was 9-9. A Pittsburgh score would mean the World Championship. Mazeroski studied Terry. On the second pitch from the New York righthander, he swung and sent the ball over the left-field wall to win the game and the Series.

## HOW PLAYERS SHARE PROFITS

*Winners get 60 per cent of the funds set aside for players when World Series proceeds are divided. Losers get 40 per cent. First-division teams and players also receive part of the Series money pie, with the size of the chunk depending on place in the standings.*

## GASHOUSE GANG PLAYED MUSIC TOO

*The World Champion Cardinals of 1934— better known as the Gashouse Gang— formed an excellent hillbilly band called the Mississippi Mudcats.*

## PHILLY FANS BOOED PROHIBITION PRESIDENT

*During the 1931 World Series between the Cardinals and A's, Philadelphia fans booed President Herbert Hoover and chanted repeatedly, "We want beer! We want beer!"*

# SERIES PREDICTIONS IMPOSSIBLE

Matchups between baseball's best teams foil the art of forecasting. Though Las Vegas oddsmakers issue "official lines" on game and Series results, wise baseball observers shy away from bettors.

Who would have bet that none of the three 20-game winners of the 1905 Philadelphia Athletics—Eddie Plank, Rube Waddell, or Andy Coakley—would beat the New York Giants, and that Christy Mathewson and Joe (Iron Man) McGinnity would pitch shutouts for all four victories? Mathewson, with three, was chiefly responsible for New York's record 0.00 team ERA in that classic. The A's plated three unearned runs in Game 2 to win, 3-0, behind Chief Bender.

Mathewson again defied the odds in 1911, when he lost two of three to the Athletics, then powered by the $100,000 infield of Frank (Home Run) Baker, Jack Barry, Eddie Collins, and Stuffy McInnis from third to first. Philadelphia won in six games—its second straight world title—but finished only third the following year.

The new American League champions, the Boston Red Sox, retained the World Championship when the Giants blew a 2-1 lead in the tenth inning by making misplays in the field. With Mathewson on the mound again, Clyde Engle led off with an easy fly to centerfielder Fred Snodgrass. He dropped it, allowing Engle to reach second. Harry Hooper lined to Snodgrass—who caught it this time—but Steve Yerkes walked. Tris Speaker popped up, wide of first, but Fred Merkle failed to move from his position and catcher Chief Meyers could not reach the foul fly. Given another chance, Speaker singled to score Engle. Yerkes went to third and scored when Larry Gardner hit a sacrifice fly to left. Snodgrass' error was labeled "the $30,000 muff" because he denied his 16 teammates (only 17 players were then eligible for the Series) the difference between the winner's share of $4025 and the loser's share of $2566.

Another memorable muff occurred five years later and also involved the Giants, but this time was an error of omission rather than commission. Trailing the White Sox, three games to two, New York literally gave away the decisive Game 6.

In the fourth inning, at the Polo Grounds, third baseman Heinie Zimmerman and outfielder Dave Robertson made consecutive errors, putting runners on first and third with nobody out. Happy Felsch grounded to pitcher Rube Benton, who threw to Zimmerman when base runner Eddie Collins broke for home. Zimmerman fired to catcher Bill Rariden, pushing Collins back toward third, and the catcher threw to Zimmerman, moving Collins closer to home. Ball in hand, Zimmerman chased Collins past Rariden and across the unprotected plate for the first run of the game. Chick Gandil singled for two more runs—all the Sox needed in 4-2 victory.

The following year, an early-September series was scheduled when the regular season was shortened by the war. Babe Ruth and Carl Mays won two games each to help the Red Sox beat the Cubs, but Ruth's record streak of 29 2/3 scoreless innings in the World Series was snapped one day after he hurt the middle finger of his pitching hand fighting with a teammate on the team train.

Events of the 1919 World Series were dictated, in large part, by seven White Sox players who sold out to gamblers in the game's worst scandal. Cincinnati won, five games to three, in an expanded format, and the "Black Sox" conspirators were banned from the game when word leaked out in 1920. ☞

222

Christy Mathewson, as he looked in an ad for Hassan tobacco, shortly before World War I.

## WAGNER ON MATHEWSON

*Honus Wagner, who hit .329 and stole 720 bases in a twenty-year career that ended in 1917, handled even the best pitchers with facility. He hit .324 against Christy Mathewson, whose 373 victories made him the biggest winner (tied with Grover Cleveland Alexander) in National League history.*

*"Mathewson knew more in five minutes about batters than the modern pitcher does in a whole season," said Wagner in 1929. "He had a fastball, slowball, a great curve, a drop, the fadeaway, and the best control I ever saw.*

*"The only pitcher I ever faced who had the control Mathewson had was Grover Cleveland Alexander when he was with the Phillies. Neither Mathewson nor Alex ever let you have a ball in the spot where they knew you could hit."*

*Wagner noted that Mathewson had a faulty delivery which allowed him to steal bases against him with regularity. "When he was throwing his fadeaway, fastball, curve, or floater, he used an easy overarm motion, swinging his arm a little at the top of his pitch.*

*"But with his drop ball, he used a full overarm motion, bringing his arm close to his body, and twisted on his right foot a little to get the necessary twist. This loss of a tenth of a second in the midst of his delivery was all the start I needed."*

In 1923, with the Black Sox scar merely an unpleasant memory to a game revitalized by Babe Ruth and the lively ball, "The House that Ruth Built" opened and the Yankees did so well there that they captured their third consecutive pennant. Many World Series games would be played in Yankee Stadium, but the first was noteworthy not because the Yankees beat the Giants, 4-2, but because the Giants' Casey Stengel—later manager of ten Yankee flag-winners—hit the first two World Series homers in the park.

Ruth hit three homers in that Series—all in the Polo Grounds—and did not hit a World Series homer in Yankee Stadium until 1926.

Two sensational pitchers who won fame as starters became World Series heroes in the '20s. In 1924, Washington won its only World Championship when 37-year-old Walter Johnson—twice beaten by the Giants earlier in the Series—came on in the ninth to hurl four scoreless innings.

In the last of the twelfth, with the score 3-3, Washington's Muddy Ruel hit a foul pop but Giant catcher Hank Gowdy tripped over his mask and dropped the ball. Able to bat again, Ruel doubled. Johnson followed with a grounder to short, bobbled by Travis Jackson, and rookie Earl McNeely grounded to third baseman Fred Lindstrom.

As Lindstrom reached for the routine grounder, the ball struck a pebble and bounded high over his head into left field. Ruel scored the run that won the World Series.

Two years later, Grover Cleveland Alexander pitched the St. Louis Cardinals to a world championship in their first pennant-winning year. Alexander, 39, came to the Cards from the Cubs in mid-season, and proved a valuable addition. In the World Series, he pitched complete-game victories in the second and sixth games, winning 6-2 and 10-2, before he was called on again as a reliever in Game 7.

With the Cardinals leading, 3-2 in the seventh, the Yankees loaded the bases with two outs. St. Louis starter Jesse Haines had developed a blister and player-manager Rogers Hornsby decided it was time to put experience on the line. He called for Alexander, who reputedly had been out into the wee hours celebrating his victory of the day before.

Tony Lazzeri—second to Babe Ruth in home runs and runs batted in during the regular season—was the hitter. Alexander went to a 1-1 count, then threw a pitch which Lazzeri laced hard down the left field line—just foul. After taking a deep sigh of relief, the grizzled veteran fired a third strike to end the rally.

Alexander retired the next five batters, then walked Babe Ruth with two outs in the ninth and the score still 3-2, St. Louis. Bob Meusel, another slugger, came to bat when Ruth suddenly broke for second, trying to steal. Catcher Bob O'Farrell fired a bullet to Hornsby to retire Ruth and bring the World Championship to St. Louis. In two-and-a-third innings, Alexander had yielded no hits, no runs, and one walk.

The 1927 Yankees, perhaps the greatest team of all time, had an easy time with their competition that fall, the Pittsburgh Pirates. New York won four straight, but even before the Series began, in spacious Forbes Field, Yankee sluggers had terrorized the Pirates with a long-ball display in batting practice. The all-righthanded Pittsburgh pitching staff had to deal with an array of lefthanded hitters, including Babe Ruth (.356, 60 HR, 164 RBI that season) and Lou Gehrig (.373, 47, 175). Even the statistics were scary. ☞

**Long-time Phillies' star Grover Cleveland Alexander was the key man in the first World Championship of the St. Louis Cardinals, in 1926.**

## SANDY AMOROS
## SAVED WORLD TITLE

*A spectacular catch by little-known outfielder Sandy Amoros in the sixth inning of Game 7 enabled the Brooklyn Dodgers to beat the New York Yankees, 2-0, and win their first World Championship. Amoros, who had replaced Junior Gilliam in left at the start of the inning, easily doubled baserunner Gil McDougald after the catch. Lefthanded pull hitter Yogi Berra almost foiled the Dodger defense by slicing the ball down the left field line.*

Many experts insist the Philadelphia Athletics of 1929 were even stronger than the '27 Yankees. Surely the Chicago Cubs would agree; they won the National League pennant by 10½ games but lost the World Series, four games to one.

Enterprising A's manager Connie Mack sent sore-armed pitcher Howard Ehmke to scout the Cubs during the season, then pulled a surprise by naming him the opening-game pitcher. He won, 3-1, fanning 13 in the process.

Game 4 destroyed Chicago's hopes for good. Leading 8-0, going into the home seventh, the Cubs used four pitchers as the A's erupted for ten runs—the biggest inning of World Series history—and copped the game, 10-8. Part of the scoring resulted from a fly ball lost in the sun by Chicago centerfielder Hack Wilson. The misplayed fly became a three-run, inside-the-park homer for Mule Haas.

In 1930, the A's tripped the Cards with two wins each from Lefty Grove and George Earnshaw, but rookie Pepper Martin reversed the results when the same clubs met again the following fall.

In the greatest World Series performance by a freshman, Martin collected 12 hits (including a homer and four doubles) in 24 at-bats, scored five runs, knocked in five, and stole five bases with the leaping, head-first slide that won him the nickname "Wild Horse of the Osage." In Game 4, his single and double were the only hits off A's ace George Earnshaw. Martin also shone afield, gloving a low liner by Max Bishop to save the decisive seventh game for veteran spitballer Burleigh Grimes.

Martin had been moved from center field to third base when the "Gashouse Gang" Cardinals won their only pennant, in 1934, and he pounded 11 hits to share the team lead with Rip Collins and Joe Medwick as the Cards beat the Tigers, 4-3. But the real stars of that Series were the Dean brothers; Dizzy and Paul won two each to account for all the Cardinal victories. Old Diz won Game 7, 11-0, after boasting to the Tiger hitters that he would use only fastballs against them.

Dean wasn't so lucky in 1938, when he lost Game 2 during a four-game sweep of the Cubs by the Yankees. In the second inning, Dean retired two straight after a single by Joe DiMaggio and walk to Lou Gehrig. Joe Gordon's easy roller rolled into left field, for two bases, after Cub infielders Billy Herman and Stan Hack collided, and Dean had to run out to left field to retrieve it. Two runs scored and things never got better for Dean or the Cubs.

In '39, the Yanks engineered another sweep—this time against the Reds—and the end of the Series was marked by an unusual play. After a walk, a bunt, and an error, Joe DiMaggio singled to right for a run, but Ival Goodman kicked the ball around and Charley (King Kong) Keller tried to score too. He arrived just as burly catcher Ernie Lombardi was taking Goodman's belated throw. Accidentally kicked in the groin, Lombardi lay stunned—the ball beside him—as Keller and DiMaggio plated two insurance runs in the tenth inning of the fourth game.

Another catcher—Mickey Owen—made the most famous error in World Series history in 1941 when he failed to hold the game-ending third strike for the Dodgers against the Yankees in Game 4 at Brooklyn. Instead of a 3-2 Dodger win, knotting the Series at two games each, the Yankees scored four runs and took a 3-1 lead. They wrapped up the World Championship the next day.

In 1946, Enos Slaughter led the National League with 130 runs batted in, but his legs won the World Series for the Cardinals. In the seventh game against the Red Sox, he led off the eighth with a single.

Cardinal stars Pepper Martin (left) and Chick Hafey helped St. Louis beat the favored Philadelphia A's in the 1931 World Series. Martin, a rookie that year, managed 12 hits in 24 at-bats.

## COMPARISON COSTS

*Winner's shares in the 1973 World Series between the Oakland A's and New York Mets were $24,617.57. Losing shares were $14,950.18. In 1903, winning shares for the Boston Pilgrims were $1,182. Losers received $1,316.25 because Pittsburgh owner Barney Dreyfuss, loyal to his troops, donated his share of the receipts to the players.*

## BROCK'S FEET FLEW

*Lou Brock of the Cardinals twice stole three bases in a single World Series game and seven in an entire Series. The years: 1967-68.*

One out later, with St. Louis needing a run to break a 3-3 deadlock, Slaughter and Harry Walker worked a perfect hit-and-run play.

Slaughter—told to take any risk in an effort to score—broke for second with the pitch and Walker dropped a Texas Leaguer between shortstop Johnny Pesky and substitute centerfielder Leon Culberson. Slaughter had reached second while the ball was still in the air and took third easily. Then, remembering Culberson did not have the throwing arm of injured regular Dom DiMaggio, he streaked for home.

Shortstop Pesky, receiving the relay throw, had his back to the infield during Slaughter's dash and was stupefied when he wheeled and saw him approaching the plate.

Pesky hesitated just slightly—giving Slaughter the split-second he needed—before throwing home. Slaughter's run gave the Cardinals a 4-3 victory and the Series crown.

The '47 World Series had a little of everything. Brooklyn's Al Gionfriddo made a sensational catch to rob Joe DiMaggio of a home run. New York's Yogi Berra hit the first pinch-homer in a World Series. And Cookie Lavagetto ruined Floyd Bevens's no-hitter.

New York led in games, two to one, as Lavagetto came to bat with two men out, two men on base, and the Yankees leading Game 4 by a 2-1 score. Lavagetto, a utility infielder who hit .261 during the regular season, found a pitch he liked and rammed a double off the right field wall. Both runners scored and the Dodgers won, 3-2.

Don Larsen succeeded where Bevens failed. In his 14-year career, Larsen won only 81 games—an average of less than six per season—and posted an embarrassing 3-21 record with the 1954 Baltimore Orioles (nee St. Louis Browns). But he thrived with the Yankees, with 45 wins and 24 losses in five Yankee years.

After Dodger bats knocked him out in the second inning of Game 2, Larsen returned in Game 5, on October 8, 1956. He threw only 97

Don Larsen . . . brilliant against Brooklyn

## NO SCOUTING REPORT FOR CUELLAR

*Baltimore Orioles superscout Jim Russo delivered advance reports on the Reds in 1970, and discussed the National League champions with all pitchers except Mike Cuellar. Asked why, Russo responded, "You don't tell Leonard Bernstein how to conduct the New York Philharmonic and we don't tell Mike Cuellar how to pitch. He's an artist."*

## THE GREATNESS OF GIBSON

*Bob Gibson pitched eight straight complete games, winning the first seven, in World Series play. The star Cardinal right-hander fanned a record 17 in a game and 35 in a seven-game Series against Detroit in 1968. Previously, Dodgers Sandy Koufax (1963) and Carl Erskine (1953) held one-game strikeout records—recorded against the Yankees—with 15 and 14, respectively.*

Bob Gibson . . . Series strikeout king

Casey Stengel shows ball Don Larsen used for final strikeout in 1956 perfect game against Dodgers in World Series. Yankees won, 2-0, and went on to the World Championship.

*( 1949 photo W.S. )*

## SERIES PREDICTIONS IMPOSSIBLE *continued*

pitches in retiring all 27 batters who faced him. Pinch-hitter Dale Mitchell, batting for Dodger starter Sal Maglie, swung and missed twice, hit a foul into the left field stands, then took a called third strike to end the game. The score was 2-0.

Larsen said later he was nervous only in the ninth, when Dodger manager Walter Alston hesitated in selecting his pinch-hitter. None of the Yankees—including manager Casey Stengel—talked to Larsen during the game for fear of upsetting him. Jackie Robinson's liner to third, knocked down by Andy Carey and fielded by Gil McDougald, was the most serious threat to the million-to-one gem. Most experts regard Larsen's achievement as the World Series record least likely to fall.

A rookie reliever, Larry Sherry of the Dodgers, was the hero in 1959 when he won two and saved two other World Series victories over the White Sox. Sherry threw hard and slow sliders—perfected in the Venezuelan Winter League—to complement a fastball, curve, and changeup. His 0.71 ERA in 12 2/3 World Series innings matched his season-long standard. In relief, he was 7-0 with a 0.74 ERA; he lost twice as a starter and had an overall earned run mark of 2.18. Sherry also won one of the Dodgers' two playoff wins against Milwaukee with 7 2/3 shutout innings of relief in Game 1.

Seldom-used outfielder Chuck Essegian helped the Dodgers win in six games by slamming two pinch-hit home runs. His emergency heroics recalled the performance of the Giants' Dusty Rhodes during a 1954 sweep of the Cleveland Indians. In addition to two pinch-singles, Rhodes beat Bob Lemon in the opener with one gone in the last of the tenth, when he hit a 260-foot fly ball over the short right field wall.

The Dodgers could have used Dusty Rhodes in 1966, when they were blanked three times in four straight losses to the Baltimore Orioles. Twenty-year-old Jim Palmer became the youngest man to hurl a Series shutout, but the great surprise of the Series was the yeoman work of veteran Moe Drabowsky, a journeyman who pitched the best game of his career as a Game 1 reliever.

After the Dodgers scored their only two runs of the Series against Dave McNally, Drabowsky came out of the bullpen to strike out 11 men and yield only one hit and two walks in 6 2/3 innings of shutout relief. ☞

## WORLD SERIES WORKHORSE

*Reliever Darold Knowles of the Oakland A's appeared in all seven games of the 1973 classic against the New York Mets.*

## MAYS MADE MIGHTY CATCH IN '54

*His back to the plate, Willie Mays of the Giants hauled down a 460-foot drive by Vic Wertz of the Indians during the 1954 World Series at the Polo Grounds in New York. The play stifled a Cleveland rally in the eighth inning of the opening game.*

## WORLD SERIES SLAUGHTER

*The Yankees beat the Giants, 18-4, in Game 2 of the '36 Series.*

## CATFISH HUNTER'S VIEW OF SERIES

*"The best thing about the World Series," according to Catfish Hunter of the 1978 World Champion Yankees, "is getting that World Series ring. There's no way you can buy one of them. You have to win it. Winning any World Series game has to rank as one of the biggest achievements of my life."*

Los Angeles knew the end was near when star centerfielder Willie Davis made three errors in the fifth inning of Game 2. He dropped two consecutive flies and, seeking to repair the damage, threw the ball over the third baseman's head. The Dodgers also made three other errors that day.

Five years later, the Orioles were at Pittsburgh for the first night game in World Series history, on October 13, 1971. The Pirates won, 4-3, and went on to take a seven-game match behind the spirited play of Roberto Clemente, whose .414 mark included a Game 7 homer that made the difference in a 2-1 score.

The Oakland A's won the first of three straight World Championships in 1972 when Dick Williams—guiding hand of the "Impossible Dream" Red Sox of 1967—deployed his pinch hitters and relief pitchers with uncanny success.

Rollie Fingers won one, saved two, had a 1.74 ERA, and struck out 11 batters in 10 1/3 innings over six games. Second-string catcher Gene Tenace, who hit .225 with five homers for the season, became the first man to homer in his first two World Series at-bats and struck four during the seven-game set against Cincinnati. And pinch-hitters Gonzalo Marquez, Don Mincher, and Angel Mangual all singled to spark a two-run, last-of-the-ninth rally that won Game 4 by a 3-2 score.

One of the most dramatic Fall Classics of baseball history occurred when the Cincinnati Reds met the Boston Red Sox in 1975. After the teams split two games, they cracked six homers in Game 3, but a disputed bunt marred the Reds' 6-5 victory.

In the last of the tenth, Cesar Geronimo led with a single for Cincinnati. Pinch-hitter Ed Armbrister dropped a bunt in front of the plate, but Armbrister blocked catcher Carlton Fisk's path and his throw to second sailed into center field. Umpire Larry Barnett refused to heed Boston's charge of interference.

With Geronimo on third and Armbrister on first, and none out, Pete Rose was intentionally walked to set up a force at home. Merv Rettenmund struck out but Joe Morgan singled over the head of centerfielder Fred Lynn to end the game.

Another last-ditch single by Morgan ended the World Series eight days later. Boston manager Darrell Johnson foolishly inserted inexperienced rookie Jim Burton as a ninth-inning reliever with Game 7 tied at 3-3. He immediately walked leadoff hitter Ken Griffey. A sacrifice, infield grounder, and single by Morgan plated the winning run.

The most exciting game of the '75 classic was the sixth. Boston led, 3-0, through four innings, but the Reds surged ahead, 6-3, in the eighth. Former Red Bernie Carbo then delivered his second pinch-homer of the Series—trying Chuck Essegian's 1959 record—to tie the score. Boston's Dwight Evans leaped to snag a probable home run by Joe Morgan in the eleventh, and Carlton Fisk won the game for the Sox with a leadoff homer in the twelfth.

## FORD'S SCORELESS STRING

**Yankee southpaw Whitey Ford pitched a record 33 2/3 consecutive scoreless innings in the World Series.**

**Roberto Clemente hit .414 for Pirates in 1971 World Series, including a decisive home run in Game 7 against Orioles.**

| 1933 | AL 4 | NL 2 | | 1961 | NL 1 | AL 1 |
|---|---|---|---|---|---|---|
| 1934 | AL 9 | NL 7 | | 1962 | NL 3 | AL 1 |
| 1935 | AL 4 | NL 1 | | 1962 | AL 9 | NL 4 |
| 1936 | NL 4 | AL 3 | | 1963 | NL 5 | AL 3 |
| 1937 | AL 8 | NL 3 | | 1964 | NL 7 | AL 4 |
| 1938 | NL 4 | AL 1 | | 1965 | NL 6 | AL 5 |
| 1939 | AL 3 | NL 1 | | 1966 | NL 2 | AL 1 |
| 1940 | NL 4 | AL 0 | | 1967 | NL 2 | AL 1 |
| 1941 | AL 7 | NL 5 | | 1968 | NL 1 | AL 0 |
| 1942 | AL 3 | NL 1 | | 1969 | NL 9 | AL 3 |
| 1943 | AL 5 | NL 3 | | 1970 | NL 5 | AL 4 |
| 1944 | NL 7 | AL 1 | | 1971 | AL 6 | NL 4 |
| 1946 | AL 12 | NL 0 | | 1972 | NL 4 | AL 3 |
| 1947 | AL 2 | NL 1 | | 1973 | NL 7 | AL 1 |
| 1948 | AL 5 | NL 2 | | 1974 | NL 7 | AL 2 |
| 1949 | AL 11 | NL 7 | | 1975 | NL 6 | AL 3 |
| 1950 | NL 4 | AL 3 | | 1976 | NL 7 | AL 1 |
| 1951 | NL 8 | AL 3 | | 1977 | NL 7 | AL 5 |
| 1952 | NL 3 | AL 2 | | 1978 | NL 7 | AL 3 |
| 1953 | NL 5 | AL 1 | | 1979 | NL 7 | AL 6 |
| 1954 | AL 11 | NL 9 | | 1980 | NL 4 | AL 2 |
| 1955 | NL 6 | AL 5 | | 1981 | NL 5 | AL 4 |
| 1956 | NL 7 | AL 3 | | 1982 | NL 4 | AL 1 |
| 1957 | AL 6 | NL 5 | | 1983 | AL 13 | NL 3 |
| 1958 | AL 4 | NL 3 | | 1984 | NL 3 | AL 1 |
| 1959 | NL 5 | AL 4 | | 1985 | NL 6 | AL 1 |
| 1959 | AL 5 | NL 3 | | 1986 | AL 3 | NL 2 |
| 1960 | NL 5 | AL 3 | | 1987 | NL 2 | AL 0 |
| 1960 | NL 6 | AL 0 | | 1988 | AL 2 | NL 1 |
| 1961 | NL 5 | AL 4 | | | | |

**TOTALS**
**Tie 1 (1961)**     NL—38   AL—21

# THE ALL-STAR GAME

With Chicago hosting the Century of Progress exposition in 1933, *Chicago Tribune* sports editor Arch Ward decided a baseball game between National and American League "all-star" squads would be a worthy added attraction.

Though many club owners opposed a three-day break in mid-season for what they considered to be an exhibition game, Ward refused to abandon the thought. He approached Commissioner Kenesaw Mountain Landis who, in turn, contacted NL president John Heydler and his AL counterpart, Will Harridge.

The executives agreed and the idea was born, though its original purpose was strictly to stage a high caliber contest for the 1933 exposition. There was no thought given to an annual All-Star Game until overwhelming fan reaction mandated continuation of the matchup.

An informal fan poll conducted by the *Tribune* provided "guidelines" for managers Connie Mack of the American League and John McGraw, called out of retirement to manage the National League team. But Mack, the 70-year-old owner-manager of the Philadelphia Athletics, and McGraw, winner of 10 pennants with the Giants, were free to choose their own 18-man squads.

Fourteen of the 36 players named eventually found their way to the Hall of Fame gallery at Cooperstown, and the brightest star of all—Babe Ruth—wasted no time in showing that the players took the contest seriously.

Ruth's two-run home run in the third inning paced the American League to a 4-2 triumph on July 6, 1933 at Comiskey Park. Forty-seven thousand fans—all that fire marshals would allow—generated more than $51,000 for the retired players' fund and spread the exciting news about a possible "inter-league all-star series."

**Dizzy Dean won the first All-Star game for the National League after the AL won three in a row.**

# CHOOSING THE ALL-STARS

In 1934, the second year of the All-Star Game, baseball again used an informal fan poll to "suggest" players to managers who were not bound to take any advice. Since both circuits were guided by player-managers that season, NL manager Bill Terry named himself the starting first baseman and AL pilot Joe Cronin doubled as his league's starting shortstop.

Realizing the fan vote was a farce, it was scrapped, leaving total selection in the hands of the managers. The pilots themselves were the pennant-winners of the previous fall. Blatant favoritism resulted, but AL manager Joe McCarthy countered his critics when he deliberately kept his six Yankee All-Stars on the bench while beating the Nationals without contribution from his powerful club.

From 1947-57, fans were given total control of player selection for the first time. The Associated Press tabulated the results, but AP's crack sportswriters joined the national protest when Cincinnati fans stuffed the ballot box in 1957 and "elected" seven of the eight Red starters.

Commissioner Ford Frick vetoed the choice of Gus Bell and Wally Post, inserting Willie Mays and Hank Aaron into the National League lineup and ending the fan balloting.

In 1958, a more objective system was introduced when players, coaches, and managers voted only for their own league's representatives. They were barred from voting for teammates—a device that worked in sending fairly-chosen squads to the All-Star Game.

Though player voting was successful—and respected by fans—new Commissioner Bowie Kuhn returned the vote to the fans again in 1970. Problems flared immediately.

A computerized ballot was prepared so early that nominees at each position were frequently traded, injured, or converted to other positions by the time the season opened in April.

That very first year, the "experts" who compiled the listing of 24 National League outfielders did not have the intelligence to include Rico Carty, who had hit .342 the previous season and personally guided the Atlanta Braves to the NL West championship with a sensational September streak.

When Carty opened the 1970 campaign with his bat still smoking, baseball's brass was embarrassed, but the fans saved the day by picking the star outfielder through a difficult write-in process. Only one other write-in—first baseman Steve Garvey of the 1974 Dodgers—won election in the ballot's first eight seasons.

Instead of promoting All-Star teams made up of the game's best players, the fan voting has degenerated into a popularity contest. Teams urge their fans to vote for hometown favorites. Too often, sentimental choices or well-known names appear instead of true All-Stars.

If fans were prohibited from voting for local players, the balloting would certainly become more objective. Even so, fans are poor selectors because of limited knowledge of the game. They cannot judge the true value of top players because they don't watch baseball daily.

In 1974, 74.2 per cent of fans responding to a poll in *The Sporting News* agreed with the idea that players—not fans—should choose the All-Stars.

Perhaps the best way to retain fan interest but guarantee fair elections is to establish a One-Third Plan whereby fan votes would count for one-third; the player-coach-manager vote for one-third; and the media vote for a final third. That way, two-thirds of the ballots would be cast by people who watch baseball every day.

Wayland Moore/Atlanta Braves

**Fans have picked baseball's All-Stars at various times, but their selections have often been criticized.**

## BALLOT DRAWS RESPONSE

*In 1976, 8,370,145 All-Star ballots were returned by fans—more than the total number of votes President Abraham Lincoln received in both his victories plus the total population of the United States at the time the Constitution was ratified.*

## ARE FAN PICKS UNWISE?

*Bill Freehan, a catcher playing first base with less than smashing success for the Tigers in 1974, ranked second in the fans' All-Star voting for catchers. "I've got no business being second this year," he said. "It's the fans' game and they ought to be able to pick who they want, but that's no guarantee they're going to pick the most deserving players."*

229

## 15 TOP FEATS IN GAME'S HISTORY

1—Ty Cobb, Tigers, winning 12 American League batting championships in 13 years, nine in succession.
2—Ed Walsh scoring 40 victories for 1908 "Hitless Wonder" White Sox.
3—Joe DiMaggio's 56-game batting streak with 1941 Yankees.
4—Rogers Hornsby's .424 batting average with 1924 Cardinals.
5—Babe Ruth's 60 home runs with 1927 Yankees.
6—Cy Young gaining 511 major league victories.
7—Grover Alexander pitching 16 shutouts for 1916 Phillies.
8—Jack Chesbro's 41 victories with 1904 Yankees.
9—Christy Mathewson's three shutouts in six days in 1905 World Series.
10—Bob Feller's 348 strikeouts with 1946 Indians.
11—Johnny Vander Meer's two successive no-hit games with 1938 Redlegs.
12—Rube Marquard's 19 straight victories with 1912 Giants.
13—Walter Johnson's 56 consecutive scoreless innings with 1913 Senators.
14—Harry Stovey stealing 156 bases with 1888 Philadelphia Athletics.
15—Lou Gehrig's major league consecutive game record of 2,130 games.

—The Sporting News
Dec. 5, 1956

# ALL-STAR HIGHLIGHTS

When the best players of both leagues meet in head-to-head competition, unusual feats occur.

Though a starting pitcher is barred from working more than three innings, Carl Hubbell put on the most dazzling pitching exhibition in All-Star history in less than three on July 10, 1934.

Working before 48,363 fans in the Polo Grounds, his home park, the crafty southpaw used his screwball to perfection in striking out five straight future Hall of Famers—Babe Ruth, Lou Gehrig, Jimmie Foxx, Al Simmons, and Joe Cronin.

Hubbell had given up a single and walk to start the game, but was all business with the American League's big bats. He seemed unruffled even when the two runners pulled a double-steal.

The Giants' star nearly had seven straight strikeouts—he had two strikes on Bill Dickey before the Yankee catcher singled, and he whiffed New York pitcher Lefty Gomez. Hubbell held a 4-0 lead when he left after three frames, but the Americans eventually won, 9-7.

Ted Williams of the Boston Red Sox staged the most dramatics by a hitter in 1941. The NL took a 5-3 lead into the last of the ninth at Detroit, but the Americans scored a run when Billy Herman made a bad throw on a double-play grounder that would have ended the game.

With two outs and two on, Williams worked the count to 2-1 against Claude Passeau. Then he smashed a long, game-winning home run against the facade of the third tier in right field. The Williams blast wrested the hero's laurels from NL shortstop Arky Vaughan, who had hit two homers earlier in the game.

Williams hit a pair in '46—along with two singles—as the Americans coasted to a 12-0 triumph after a one-year hiatus caused by wartime travel restrictions. The Boston leftfielder actually batted five times in that game, but received a walk the first time up—from Claude Passeau, his victim in 1941.

The second Williams homer came on a high, arcing blooper pitch thrown by Rip Sewell. "Before the game," Sewell said later, "I'd been talking to Williams and he asked if I would throw that pitch in the game. I said I would. When he came up, he was shaking his head as if to say, 'Don't do it.' I answered back with a nod that said, 'You're going to get it.'

"The first pitch was a blooper. He fouled it off as the crowd roared. They loved it. So I gave him another one. Too high. Then a fastball down the middle. He was surprised and let it go over for a strike. Our eyes met. He grinned because we both knew another blooper would be coming. It was a perfect strike but he timed it and sent it into the bullpen. The crowd went wild."

National League

Carl Hubbell of the Giants fanned five straight superstars in '34 All-Star Game at the Polo Grounds, his home park.

Infielders Dick Bartell, Frankie Frisch, and Pepper Martin discuss strategy before "Game of the Century" at Chicago in 1933. AL prevailed, 4-2.

Braves' Field, Boston, was the setting for the 1936 All-Star Game, won by the National League. Contributing to the victory were (left to right) pitchers Van Lingle Mungo, Dizzy Dean, Lon Warneke, Carl Hubbell, and Curt Davis. All but Mungo pitched.

The pitch, delivered like a fastball, was so deceptive that Sewell led the National League with 21 victories in 1943. He developed it after a gunshot wound to his toe forced him to take an awkward stance on the mound, with both feet pointed directly toward the batter. He changed his motion from three-quarters to overhand and released the ball earlier than he released a straight fastball. In ten years, Williams was the only hitter to bat the blooper over the fence.

There are many cases of timely home runs in All-Star competition. In 1950, a blast by Ralph Kiner tied the AL in the ninth and set the stage for spray-hitting Red Schoendienst to deliver a totally-unexpected clout in the fourteenth.

Stan Musial's shot in the twelfth inning won the 1955 classic, 6-5, for the Nationals, and Johnny Callison's three-run homer off fire-baller Dick Radatz capped a four-run ninth that brought victory to the NL in 1964. Tony Perez gave the NL a 2-1, fifteen-inning triumph with a 1967 home run. Al Rosen of the AL in 1954 and Willie McCovey (1969) and Gary Carter (1981) of the NL joined Williams and Vaughan as players with two homers in one All-Star Game.

Enos Slaughter, 37, singled twice, walked once, stole a base, and made a spectacular catch in the outfield to bring victory to the Nationals in 1953, and Willie Mays collected three hits in each of two 1960 games (two All-Star Games were played from 1959-62 to speed payment of player's pension fund indebtedness but failing fan interest caused a return to one game in 1963).

Mays, the third-ranked home run hitter in baseball history, ranks as king of the All-Stars. He compiled 23 hits, 20 runs, 40 total bases, and 6 stolen bases in 24 All-Star games. He often batted from the unfamiliar leadoff spot in the mid-summer classic, as National League managers enjoyed the luxury of overabundant power in the lineup.

Hank Aaron, the career home run leader, was a mysterious failure in All-Star play until 1971, when he finally hit a home run for the Nationals, at Detroit. Aaron saved his most dramatic All-Star show for his hometown Atlanta fans the following year when his sixth-inning blast off old nemesis Gaylord Perry gave the NL a 2-1 lead. It eventually prevailed, 4-3.

Unusual events have marked a number of All-Star contests. In 1961, a stiff wind at San Francisco's Candlestick Park played havoc with fielders and pitchers. National League reliever Stu Miller made the first balk of his long career when he was blown off the mound in the middle of his windup. Seven errors marked the fray, won by the Nationals with a two-run burst in the tenth, 5-4. Willie Mays thrilled 44,115 hometown fans when he plated the tying run with a double and scored the winning marker on a single by Roberto Clemente.

In 1942, the only National League run in a 3-1 defeat came on a pinch-hit homer by Mickey Owen, who did not hit another in 133 games that season.

There was one tie—a 1-1 game rained out after nine innings at Boston in 1961—and one game curtailed by rain—a 3-2 win for the Nationals, ended after five innings at Philadelphia in 1952.

**Rival catchers of 1933 All-Stars were Bill Dickey (Yankees) of the American League and Gabby Hartnett (Cubs) of the National League.**

## THE PHANTOM SHORTSTOP

*In 1974, Luis Aparicio was listed on the All-Star ballot even though he had been released by the Red Sox before the season opened.*

## ALL-STAR INJURY IDLED KILLEBREW

*Harmon Killebrew, first baseman of the Minnesota Twins, was out for the year after suffering a severe hamstring pull in the 1968 All-Star Game. He bounced back to enjoy his best season in 1969: 49 home runs and 140 runs batted in.*

## ALL-STAR HAYMAKER

*Fred Lynn's grand slam, the only bases-filled home run in All-Star history, allowed the American League to trounce the National, 13-3, in the 50th anniversary All-Star Game at Chicago's Comiskey Park on July 8, 1983. The AL's run total is an All-Star record.*

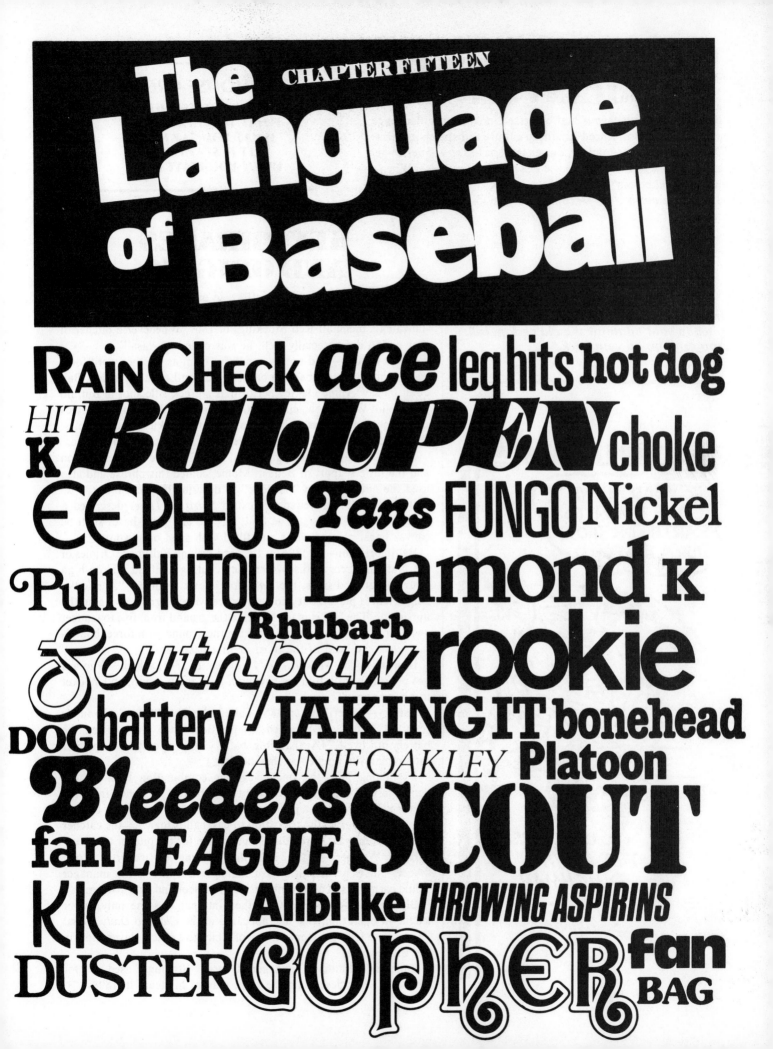

# CHAPTER FIFTEEN
# The Language of Baseball

# BASEBALL WORDS IN AMERICAN CULTURE

Baseball's rich heritage is best expressed in its colorful language, which has greatly influenced American culture and speech patterns.

When a businessman fails at a given task, he has *struck out*. When a girl rejects a boy's advances, he *can't get to first base*. When a luncheon speaker can't keep his date, he asks for a *rain check* and tries to find a *pinch-hitter*. A competitor who loses a bidding is *shut out*.

## THE NECKTIE BALL

*Interviewed with slugger Ernie Banks on the radio, Satchel Paige said, "Know how I'd pitch to you? I'd throw the old necktie ball. You can't hit on your back."*

# NICKNAMES

TOO BAD I HAVE TO COME DOWN TO EARTH FOR THOSE DURN BASES!

...OF COURSE, THE FLYING DUTCHMAN...

Renderings by Jim Berryman, The Sporting News, Nov. 18, 1943.

# KEY PHRASES AND ORIGINS

**Ace**—The star of any team effort, in or out of sports, is the ace, named for the great Asa Brainard, who pitched every game for the unbeaten Cincinnati Red Stockings of 1869. Whenever a pitcher of that period did especially well, he was called an "asa."

**Annie Oakley**—Old-timers recall this term as another word for a walk, which is a free base on balls. American League president Ban Johnson saw Annie Oakley perform as a crack rifle shot in Buffalo Bill's Wild West Show, circa 1900, and compared the punched holes in complimentary baseball tickets to Annie Oakley's bullet holes. Ballplayers eventually extended the name to cover anything free.

**At bat**—A sailor, keeping score at an 1872 game between Boston and the little seaport of Belfast, Maine, coined this phrase and also used the nautical term "on deck" to describe the next hitter.

**Bag**—In 1857, a newspaper called *Spirit of Times* described a baseball rule this way: "The first, second, and third bases shall be canvas bags, painted white and filled with sand or sawdust."

**Baltimore chop**—In 1896, as the hard-driving Baltimore Orioles of the National League discovered they could get infield hits on high bouncing ground balls, the *Baltimore News* reported: "A middle-height ball is picked out and is attacked with a terrific swing on the upper side. The ball is made to strike the ground from five to ten feet away from the batsman and, striking the ground with force, bounds high over the head of the third or first baseman."

**Baseball**—The *New Orleans Picayune,* in 1841, asked, "Who has not played Barn Ball in his boyhood, Base in his youth, and Wicket in his manhood?"

**Battery**—Describing an 1867 batter, the *Ball Players' Chronicle* reported, "He soon resumed his position, once more facing the battery of Lovett." (At that time, battery referred only to the pitcher rather than the pitcher-catcher tandem.)

Explaining how the pitcher-catcher combination took on the name, several experts suggest the term "battery" extends from the military. Since one man provides ammunition for an artillery battery but another fires it, the transition to baseball is logical—the catcher is the "commander" providing ammunition for the pitcher to "fire."

**Bench Warmer**—A 1912 *Saturday Evening Post* reporter wrote: "A certain rich man offered a manager $10,000 if the manager would carry his son as a combination of mascot and bench-warmer."

**Big League**—In 1899, when the National was the only major league in operation, this line appeared in the *Chicago Daily News:* "They were telling a story on one of Chicago's crack players now in the Big League."

**Bonehead**—Phillies' manager George Stallings used it for emphasis when describing the inept play of his team in 1898. ☞

**Bullpen**—The most popular theory, dating back to the turn-of-the-century, indicates that the area where pitchers warm up won its name because almost every ballpark in the country featured a large outfield billboard advertisement for Bull Durham tobacco. Not only did pitchers warm up under the sign—usually in fair territory deep in the outfield—but the company popularized its name by offering $50 to any player who hit the bull when he batted.

The actual word pre-dates baseball. Bullpen was once known as a log enclosure used by pioneers attacked by Indians before they could reach the fort. It was later used to describe any makeshift jail—hence the transition to baseball when Connie Mack began the practice of having his pitchers warm up in a secluded area in 1909.

There are also other interpretations:

In bullfighting, the bulls are kept in separate pens. One is led out, bouts with the matador and eventually dies. The pen opens and another comes out, and so on until the matinee is completed. In baseball, when a pitcher is routed, a gate opens to introduce another.

Some railroad fans insist bullpen was introduced to baseball by Bill Friel, utilityman for the American League's Milwaukee Brewers of 1901 and a former rail employee. There were shanties with benches at intervals along the roadbed and workers would sit and talk there during work-breaks. When Friel played, pitchers who weren't working sat on a similar bench, in right field foul territory. He referred to it as the bullpen because the railroad bench had the same name.

**Bunt**—A derivation of butt, as a goat will do—to push with the head. The 1767 *Boston Gazette:* "The black ram will sometimes . . . give him a paultry bunt at unawares." When Dick Pearce of the Brooklyn Atlantics was unable to connect with his regular swing, he tried the approach for the first time in baseball. His 1866 bunt succeeded.

**Bush league**—First used in 1910 to describe any baseball league outside the majors, as in an *American Magazine* quote: "The scouts returned from the deepest parts of the bushes proclaiming that the crop was poor." The same magazine, two years later, referred to players from such leagues as "bushers."

**Charley Horse**—This reference to leg injury came into regular usage by 1890, but definitely originated with a lame horse named Charley. Which one is not certain.

On a summer day in Chicago in 1886, the National League's White Stockings (who gave their name to the American League's White Sox but remained a National League franchise as the Cubs) were scheduled to play, when heavy morning rains forced a postponement. One of the players reported that the racetrack seven miles south was dry, and the team departed in unison.

Another player reported a "hot tip" on a horse named Charley and his teammates placed their bets on him. The inevitable happened. Charley broke last from the gate, stayed last, and finished far to the rear. After making the appropriate derogatory comments to their bookie-teammate, most of the team left.

The next day, when a Chicago player pulled up lame, one quick-witted companion called him "Charley horse."

Another horse named Charley, overworked from pulling a cab in the days before the automobile, helped drag the infield for the Sioux City club of the Western League in 1889. The aged, tired horse seemed to suffer from arthritis—moving each leg with difficulty. It wasn't long before players started referring to any limp or leg injury as a "charley horse." ☞

## SATCHEL PAIGE'S RULES FOR STAYING YOUNG

Satchel Paige was at least 62 years old when he pitched one inning of an exhibition game in Atlanta Stadium and retired Hank Aaron, Ken Boyer, Junior Gilliam, and three other hitters with 12 pitches—only two of them called balls.

Paige, whose career included 2500 games (153 of them in one season) attributed his longevity to his rules for staying young. "If you're over six years of age, follow these rules closely," he said.

1. Avoid fried meats which anger up the blood.
2. If your stomach disputes you, lie down and pacify it with cool thoughts.
3. Keep the juices flowing by jangling around gently as you move.
4. Go very light on the vices, such as carrying on in society—the social ramble ain't restful.
5. Avoid running at all times.
6. And don't look back. Something might be gaining on you.

## ON RUTH'S 60TH

Looking back on the growing significance of Babe Ruth's 60th home run in 1927, Washington pitcher Tom Zachary, who threw the pitch, admitted, "If I'd a known it was gonna be a famous record, I'd a stuck it in his ear."

**Chinese home run**—Used primarily to describe the short home runs at New York's Polo Grounds, which was just 258 feet down the line in right field and 280 in left, the term, like many others, is of disputed origin.

*New York Tribune* sports editor Bill McGeehan used it in the early '20s after noting that the close right field looked thick, low, and not very formidable—like the Great Wall of China.

T. A. Dorgan of the *Journal,* also in the '20s, meant the phrase to mean a home run that wasn't worthy of being a home run. He disliked the Giants in general, and manager John McGraw in particular, and enjoyed deprecating Giant victories. His point of reference was his hometown of San Francisco, which had the largest Chinese population in the U.S. but did little to make it feel welcome. Chinese immigrants were barred from voting during that period.

Probably the most logical source of the term was the vast Coolie (Chinese) labor force, which would work for small wages. A natural evolvement: Chinese (cheap) labor, Chinese (cheap) home run.

**Diamond**—When Alexander Cartwright sketched his first "regulation" baseball field, with bases 90 feet apart, in 1845, it was immediately called a diamond—even through it was actually a square. A true diamond has two acute and two obtuse angles, but the infield has four 90-degree angles. Since the diamond is best viewed from the catcher's perspective, however, the diamond reference is apparent.

Baseball's use of the term also stems from the urban planning of the nineteenth century. Towns were generally built around a square, featuring public buildings. In the east, that square was called a diamond.

**Doubleheader**—Two engines on the same train or two games on the same day. No dispute here. The first baseball twinbill was played October 9, 1886, Philadelphia at Detroit.

**Eephus**—Later used to describe a pitch which was a high arc that slipped through the strike zone, the term's originator was Lefty Gomez, zany Yankee star who eventually made the Hall of Fame. He described it as that certain something that marked fine pitching from poor. "Eephus is that little extry you have on your good days," he said.

**Fan**—During the late 1880s, German-born Chris Von der Ahe, owner of the St. Louis Browns in the American Association, was discussing a St. Louis spectator who never missed a game. "Dot feller is a regular FAN-a-tic," he said, accenting the first syllable of the last word. Sportswriter Sam Crane picked up on it.

**Foot in the Bucket**—A hitter who fails to pivot properly when swinging because he's afraid the pitch will come too close to his body has "his foot in the bucket."

Shirley Povich of *The Washington Post* first used the tag after hearing a sailor, watching such a batsman at the Norfolk Air Base, say, "There's a great hitter for you. He's got his heart and soul in the game and his rear end in the dugout."

**Fungo**—Pioneer baseball writer Henry Chadwick referred to it in his *Baseball Reference,* published in 1867: "Fungo is a preliminary practice game in which one player takes the bat and tosses the ball up, hits it as it falls, and if the ball is caught on the fly the player catching it takes the bat. It is useless as practice in batting, but good for taking fly balls." ☞

---

## THE TEN COMMANDMENTS OF PITCHING

*By Carl Hubbell*

1. *You must have a limber arm*
2. *You must have a rugged physique*
3. *A good repertoire is a must (fastball, breaking ball, change-of-pace, perhaps one other)*
4. *Control is essential*
5. *You must have competitive courage*
6. *You must have stamina and endurance*
7. *You must be intelligent*
8. *Know how to size up a hitter*
9. *Be confident*
10. *Make sure you can field your position*

---

## THE GASHOUSE GANG

*The wild, fun-loving Cardinals of 1934 won the nickname "the Gashouse Gang" when they wore unwashed uniforms during a game in New York. With no clean suits available, and no time to wash the uniforms they wore in a Boston doubleheader on Saturday, the Cards donned the same outfits for their Sunday game against the Giants. Writer Garry Schumacher, referring to the rundown Gashouse area of New York, said, "They look like a gang from the Gashouse district! A real Gashouse gang!"*

In modern baseball, coaches use special fungo bats to hit practice balls to fielders before the game. The bat is lighter and thinner than a regular bat, and some historians suggest its resiliency contributed to the term—fungus, fungeous, fungo. Others say the game of hitter hitting and fielder chasing formed the phrase through a combination of "run" and "go."

**Hit and Run**—The *Chicago Daily News* of 1899 made reference to this practice of starting the base runner while ordering the batter to swing at the oncoming pitch, regardless of its location in the strike zone. The result may be (1) a stolen base for the runner if the batter misses the ball, (2) advancement from first to third on a single, (3) avoidance of a double-play if the batter hits a grounder.

**Holdout**—First used by the *New York Press* (1888), to describe a player who delayed in accepting salary terms, it caught on when Brooklyn pitcher Tommy Lovett held himself out of the game for the entire 1893 season in a salary dispute.

**Hot corner**—After Reds' third baseman Hick Carpenter caught seven line drives, a Cincinnati writer of 1889 wrote, "The Brooklyns had Old Hick on the hot corner all afternoon and it's a miracle he wasn't murdered."

**K**—Used to designate a strikeout victim, especially in scoring, the single initial was introduced by *New York Herald* baseball writer M. J. Kelly in 1868. Kelly, who used a system of letters to cover most situations in the game, hit upon "K" because it is the last letter of the word "struck." He said "S" could not be used because it might be confused with shortstop.

**Ladies Day**—The tradition of admitting women free when accompanied by male escorts was one of the game's first promotions. It began when executives of the 1889 Cincinnati Reds noticed more females in the stands whenever handsome hurler Tony Mullane worked. The team advertised he would pitch every Monday, which would be Ladies Day. Mullane, who had black, wavy hair and a waved mustache, won 283 games in his career—helped, in part, by his loyal band of female supporters.

**Murderer's Row**—Great slugging teams, like the 1927 Yankees, are said to have a "Murderer's Row" (hitters who kill pitchers), but the phrase dates back to 1858, when an early baseball writer borrowed it from the isolated Death Row at The Tombs prison in New York.

**Night Ball**—First referred to by name in *Morrison's Chicago Weekly*, 1910, it reached the majors at Cincinnati in 1935 after an earlier trial in the minor leagues.

**On Deck**—A nautical term used to refer to the next hitter, its origin recalls the 1872 Belfast, Maine sailor who also coined "at bat."

**Rain check**—Both theories of origination have merit. In pre-1900 baseball, heavy cardboard tickets were sold, but collected during each game and used again. When a game was shortened by rain one day in 1889, New Orleans owner Abner Powell saw numerous fence-jumpers and complimentary guests join the paying customers in line for new tickets. He devised the idea of a perforated rain-check stub, and the innovation was so successful it is still in use.

In the majors, the Detroit Baseball Association came up with the first rain checks, circa 1890. They read: "Rain check. In case rain interrupts game of this date before three innings are played, this check will admit bearer to grounds for next league game only."

**Rhubarb**—Garry Schumacher of *The New York Journal-American* used this word from his boyhood to describe a 1938 Dodger-Giant brawl. He explained that winners of fights in Brooklyn would invariably force the losers to swallow terrible-tasting rhubarb tonic. ☞

## MINOR LEAGUE NICKNAMES

*Minor league clubs and nicknames undergo constant change, but many minor nicknames are worth remembering for their originality.*

*Here's a sampling from May 1936:*

**AMERICAN ASSOCIATION**—*Columbus Red Birds, Indianapolis Indians, Kansas City Blues, Louisville Colonels, Milwaukee Brewers, Minneapolis Millers, St. Paul Saints, Toledo Mud Hens.*

**INTERNATIONAL LEAGUE**—*Albany Senators, Baltimore Orioles, Buffalo Bisons, Montreal Royals, Newark Bears, Rochester Red Wings, Syracuse Chiefs, Toronto Maple Leafs.*

**PACIFIC COAST LEAGUE**—*Los Angeles Angels, San Francisco Missions, San Francisco Seals, Oakland Oaks Portland Beavers, Sacramento Solons, San Diego Padres, Seattle Indians.*

**SOUTHERN ASSOCIATION**—*Atlanta Crackers, Birmingham Barons, Chattanooga Lookouts, Knoxville Smokies, Little Rock Travelers, Memphis Chicks, Nashville Volunteers, New Orleans Pelicans.*

**TEXAS LEAGUE**—*Beaumont Exporters, Dallas Steers, Fort Worth Cats, Galveston Buccaneers, Houston Buffaloes, Oklahoma City Indians, San Antonio Missions, Tulsa Oilers.*

**NEW YORK-PENNSYLVANIA LEAGUE**—*Allentown Brooks, Binghampton Triplets, Elmira Pioneers, Hazleton Mountaineers, Scranton Miners, Wilkes-Barre Barons, Williamsport Grays, York Roses.*

**WESTERN LEAGUE**—*Cedar Rapids Raiders, Davenport Blue Sox, Des Moines Demons, Omaha Robin Hoods, Sioux City Cowboys, Waterloo Hawks.*

**PIEDMONT LEAGUE**—*Asheville Tourists, Durham Bulls, Norfolk Tars, Portsmouth Cubs, Richmond Colts, Rocky Mount Red Sox.*

**SOUTH ATLANTIC LEAGUE**—*Augusta Tigers, Columbia Senators, Columbus Red Birds, Jacksonville Tars, Macon Peaches, Savannah Indians.* ☞

# NICKNAMES

AH, GOOD MORNING, SISTER JONES,... AND WASN'T THE SERMON FINE?

DEACON McKECHNIE REALLY IS ONE——

**COTTON STATES LEAGUE**—*Clarksdale Ginners, Cleveland Athletics, El Dorado Lions, Greenville Bucks, Greenwood Little Giants, Helena Seaporters, Jackson Senators, Pine Bluff Judges.*

**EAST TEXAS LEAGUE**—*Gladewater Bears, Henderson Oilers, Jacksonville Jax, Kilgore Braves, Longview Cannibals, Marshall Orphans, Palestine Pals, Tyler Trojans.*

**MIDDLE ATLANTIC LEAGUE**—*Akron Yankees, Charleston Senators, Dayton Ducks, Huntington Red Birds, Canton Terriers, Portsmouth Pirates, Zanesville Greys, Johnstown Jawns.*

**WESTERN ASSOCIATION**—*Bartlesville Mustangs, Hutchinson Larks, Joplin Miners, Muskogee Seals, Ponca City Angels, Springfield Cardinals.*

**ARKANSAS-MISSOURI LEAGUE**—*Bentonville Mustangs, Cassville Blues, Fayetteville Bears, Monett Red Birds, Rogers Lions, Siloam Springs Travelers.*

**EVANGELINE LEAGUE**—*Abbeville Athletics, Alexandria Aces, Jeanerette Blues, Lafayette White Sox, Lake Charles Skippers, New Iberia Cardinals, Opelousas Indians, Rayne Rice Birds.*

**FLORIDA STATE LEAGUE**—*Daytona Beach Islanders, DeLand Reds, Gainesville G-Men, Palatka Azaleas, Sanford Lookouts, St. Augustine Saints.*

**NORTHERN LEAGUE**—*Crookston Pirates, Duluth Dukes, Eau Claire Bears, Fargo-Moorhead Twins, Jamestown Jimmies, Superior Blues, Wausau Lumberjacks, Winnipeg Maroons.*

**GEORGIA-FLORIDA LEAGUE**—*Albany Travelers, Americus Cardinals, Cordele Reds, Moultrie Packers, Tallahassee Capitals, Thomasville Orioles.*

**PENNSYLVANIA STATE ASSOCIATION**—*Monessen Indians, Charleroi Tigers, Greensburg Red Wings, Jeannette Little Pirates, McKeesport Tubers, Butler Yankees.*

# NICKNAMES

NO SIR, MY NAME AIN'T RUBE... ..IT'S ELMER

A NATURAL HANDLE FOR BOYS FROM THE TALL CORN....

**Rookie**—First mentioned in print by the *Chicago Record-Herald* in 1913, this term for a freshman player may have stemmed from chess, where the rook must wait its turn and is often the last piece to be used as the game opens. In the early days of the game, older players shunned first-year players, who were the last to receive the attention of their teammates.

**Scout**—The modern baseball scout recommends players for his team, but the original scout—before the Cartwright rules of 1845—was something else. He was a second catcher who played far to the rear of the regular catcher. He grabbed passed balls and wild pitches, and fielded "hits" that landed near him. (Fouls were then unknown and batters could run on hits behind the plate as well as in front of it.)

**Seventh-Inning Stretch**—A popular legend says President William Howard Taft accidentally launched the practice in 1910 when he stood to stretch his legs at an opening game in Washington and the crowd, thinking he was departing, stood out of respect for the office. But old-time star Harry Wright wrote a friend in 1869 that fans stood in the seventh to gain momentary relief from the hard wooden benches of nineteenth-century ballparks.

**Shutouts**—Scoreless games had been called "Chicago's" because a White Stockings pitcher hurled the first one, but a Troy, New York writer came up with this more appropriate term—borrowed from the world of horse racing—in 1879.

**Southpaw**—In a world of righthanded people, lefthanders have always stood out—because they are a small minority. Righthanders seeking to coin an appropriate phrase to describe them derived "southpaw" because most ballparks are laid out in such a way that the afternoon sun is behind the batter and usually in the eyes of the rightfielder. Such an alignment makes the home-to-first base line run almost directly east and west. Therefore, a lefthander pitches with an arm that faces south.

**Texas Leaguer**—When Art Sunday, a player with Houston of the Texas League, joined Toledo of the International League in 1889, he immediately proceeded to collect a series of bloop hits that were too far out for the infielders but too far in for the outfielders. Because he had just come from the Texas League, his scratch hits were dubbed "Texas Leaguers."

Former Vice President John Nance Garner presented another theory in 1940; he said he himself created the term during his ballplaying days in Texas. Unable to hit the ball hard, Garner concentrated on popping the ball over the infielders' heads. Others followed suit and the practice became known as "hitting Texas leaguers"—or so Garner said.

**Umpire**—In its original Middle English form, "noumper" means an extra man, called in when two persons disagreed. The third party was considered not to be an equal or peer of the disagreeing persons. The "n" was eventually dropped, and "umpire" became part of baseball's phraseology when the rules were written for the original Knickerbocker club in 1845.

**Whitewash**—Its current double meaning includes the old context of a shutout victory. The old *Ball Players' Chronicle* used the term first in 1867 when it reported, "A blank score in Albany, New York is called a blind; in Connecticut, it is called a whitewash." A white wash, as in laundry, is said to be pure as a pitcher's shutout—because a run-less game leaves the pitcher's record untainted.

# QUOTES

"Nice guys finish last." It came from baseball—from Leo (the Lip) Durocher, long-time player and manager, in 1948. Never at a loss for words, Durocher was talking to a group of Brooklyn writers when he gazed across the field and noticed his contemporary, Giants' manager Mel Ott.

"Look at Ott," he told the reporters. "He's such a nice guy and they'll finish eighth for him." Spying Bobby Thomson, Sid Gordon, and other Giant home run stars, Durocher added, "All nice guys and they'll finish eighth."

The National League had eight teams until 1962, when expansion swelled the circuit to ten, but it wasn't long after he made the statement that writers had delivered the classic quote to the American public. Since its quick adoption into everyday usage, the substitution from "eighth" to "last" was immediate. But the meaning never changed.

Baseball is a gold mine which could start its own version of *Bartlett's Familiar Quotations*.

Take this one, from writer Grantland Rice: "It's not whether you win or lose, it's how you play the game."

Connie Mack, whose worst season in a 50-year managerial career might have been 1916, when his A's lost 117 games, contributed another classic: "Well, you can't win them all." The 1914 A's finished first.

And Babe Ruth, after an embarrassing strikeout, summarized the game succinctly: "You're a hero one day and a bum the next."

Not all baseball quotes have found their way into common use, but most make common sense—and are worth recording as part of the game's legacy.

# FAMOUS LINES BY MANAGERS

Executive Branch Rickey, talking about the controversial Durocher, described the fiery manager in no uncertain terms: "He can take a bad situation and make it immediately worse."

Managers are eventually fired—scapegoats when their teams go bad—but Birdie Tebbetts put the thought into words: "This is pure insanity. We strive desperately to become managers of big-league clubs, and all the time we're fully aware it's a job from which we have to be fired."

Joe Kuhel, one of many men whose managing could not lift the Washington Senators out of the American League cellar, made a profound pronouncement the day he was axed: "You can't make chicken salad out of chicken feathers."

Solly Hemus, who managed the Cardinals years later, agreed. "I'd say managing makes the difference in about 10 games," he said.

When he ran the Yankees, Joe McCarthy didn't have to do anything, according to rival pilot Jimmie Dykes. "He's just a push-button manager," Dykes declared.

Casey Stengel, who absorbed similar charges years later, said, "I couldn't have done it without my players."

On his deathbed, George Stallings imagined himself still in the dugout, watching his pitcher struggle to throw the ball over the plate. "Oh, those bases on balls," he moaned. Frankie Frisch picked up the cry when he left the Cardinals and went to the Pirates.

Sometimes it's best not to say anything. New York Giants' field boss Bill Terry learned that lesson in 1934, when writers asked what

## CHUG HANDLE

The 1944 Southern Association featured one entry with a historic name: the Chattanooga Choo-Choos. The team wore an artist's rendition of the famous Civil War engine, "The General," on its uniforms that season.

## "THE BIG TRAIN"

Walter (the Big Train) Johnson threw such a lively fastball that its speed was compared to steam locomotives—the fastest form of transportation in the '20s.

## THE FRENCH CONNECTION

Players with red hair invariably acquire the nickname "Red," as in Red Schoendienst, Red Ruffing, or Red Lucas. Daniel J. (Rusty) Staub, whose hair could stop traffic, was such an immediate hit when traded from Houston to Montreal in 1969 that French-speaking Expos' fans came up with the endearing term, "Le Grand Orange."

he thought of the cross-borough Dodgers. "Oh, is Brooklyn still in the league?" he asked. The Dodgers were nothing more than spoilers that year and the next—but they used the statement as a war cry and helped knock the Giants out of at least one sure pennant.

In the '50s, the Dodgers used double-talk to knock out their own credibility in town—but they didn't need any with a move to Los Angeles in the offing. Owner Walter O'Malley told the press shortly before the shift, "My roots are in Brooklyn, so why should I move?"

Branch Rickey, Dodger executive, inspired a player, Chuck Connors (who traded baseball for television stardom), to talk about his reputation for tight economics: "It was easy to figure out Mr. Rickey's thinking about contracts. He had both players and money and didn't like to see the two of them mix."

Stingy with the dollar, Rickey was quick with the compliment—particularly for one of his own men. Of Eddie Stanky, the scrappy Dodger infielder who later managed several clubs, Rickey said, "He can't hit, he can't run, and he can't throw—all he can do is beat you."

A shrewd trader, Rickey is sometimes credited with saying, "The trades you don't make are your best ones."

Umpire Bill Klem might have been thinking of Rickey when he said, "There are 154 games in a season and you can find 154 reasons why your club should have won every one of them."

Of umpires, American League president Ban Johnson noted, "A good umpire is the umpire you don't even notice. He'll be there all afternoon, but when the game is over, you won't recall his name."

One-time National League president Harry Pulliam had one of sports' classic quotes printed on a placard he kept on his desk. It read, "Take nothing for granted in baseball." That meant ninth-inning uprises, surprising pennant races, unusual trades, and classic quotes from colorful characters.

## O'ROURKE WHO?

*Of the two O'Rourkes who starred in the pre-1900 National League, James Henry won the nickname "Orator" while Timothy Patrick was called "Voiceless."*

## THE MAHATMA

*Branch Rickey's nickname, "The Mahatma," was a creation of well-known writer Tom Meany. The journalist had been reading Inside Asia, wherein John Gunther described Mohandas (Mahatma) Ghandi as "an incredible combination of Jesus Christ, Tammany Hall, and your father."*

*Meany noted that Rickey was part paternal, part political, and part pontifical. He applied the Ghandi monicker, and it stuck.*

## NEW NICKNAMES OF NOTE

*Nicknames of recent vintage worth remembering: Orlando Cepeda (the Baby Bull), Jim Wynn (the Toy Cannon), Zoilo (Zorro) Versalles, George (the Stork) Theodore, Willie Mays (the Say Hey Kid), Doug Rader (the Red Rooster), Larvell (Sugar Bear) Blanks, Greg Luzinski (the Bull), Roderick Edwin (Hot Rod) Kanehl, Frank (Hondo) Howard, George Scott (the Boomer), Ralph Garr (the Roadrunner), Fred (Chicken) Stanley, Tim (Crazy Horse) Foli, Ed Charles (the Glider), Bob Coluccio (the Macaroni Pony), Marshall Bridges (Sheriff), Tom Hall (the Blade), Al Hrabosky (the Mad Hungarian), Bob (Hoot) Gibson, Sherman (Roadblock) Jones, Bill Lee (the Spaceman), Bill Singer (the Singer Throwing Machine), J.R. Richard (High Rise), Phil Regan (the Vulture), and Rick (Buzz) Sawyer.*

# THE THINGS PLAYERS SAY

Joe Garagiola, player and broadcaster, knew the truth of Pulliam's placard. Here's how he describes the sport: "Baseball is just a boy's game that men play to make a living."

Other players have also contributed to the quotebook.

Wee Willie Keller, whose flood of hits between 1890 and 1910 seemed to have eyes, was ready with a quip when questioned about his proficiency at the plate. "I hit 'em where they ain't," he said.

Ty Cobb, who also began before the century changed, once fought with a roommate over first rights to the hotel bathtub. "I got to be first—all of the time," said Cobb, whose .367 lifetime batting average ranks at the head of the list.

Shoeless Joe Jackson, White Sox star, was first in the hearts of Chicago youngsters who approached him as he emerged from the room where game-fixing charges were being heard in 1920. One of them blurted, "Say it ain't so, Joe."

Yankee pitcher Lefty Gomez was more fortunate. Finding success and a receptive press in the '30s, he announced, "I'd rather be lucky than good."

Not long afterward, a young catching prospect joined the club and received valuable tips from the star who preceded him. Yogi Berra admitted, "Bill Dickey is learning me all his experiences."

Ralph Kiner, who made the Hall of Fame on the strength of his home run heroics, always maintained, "Home run hitters drive Cadillacs, singles hitters drive Fords."

Strikeout victims don't last long, umpire Bill Byron told a rookie one day: "You'll have to learn before you're older, you can't hit the ball with the bat on your shoulder." ☞

Roger Maris and Mickey Mantle kept swinging in 1961, and closed with home run totals of 61 and 54, respectively, the best teammates have done in one season. Talking about his senior partner, Maris said, "It's smarter to give the big man four balls for one base than one ball for four bases."

Maris and Mantle were fine on defense as well as offense, but many major-leaguers aren't. Some are good-field, no-hit, others are good-hit, no-field. Mike Gonzalez coined this phrase when he looked at a new prospect: "This player—she's good field, no hit."

Feminine references are common in baseball. Durocher, when a player, once said, "If I were playing third base and my mother were rounding third with the run that was going to beat us, I'd trip her. Oh, I'd pick her up and brush her off and say, 'Sorry, Mom.' But nobody beats me."

During a 1934 radio interview, Detroit pitcher Schoolboy Rowe suddenly thought of his fiancee and casually remarked into the mike, "How'm I doin', Edna?" The media and rival dugouts never let him forget it, and the words live today.

So does Babe Herman's statement about his young son's upcoming birthday. "Buy an encyclopedia for my kid?" he said. "He'll learn to ride a two-wheeler or walk!"

As a broadcaster in wartime, Dizzy Dean was not allowed to give weather conditions. So he said, "I can't tell you why this game is stopped, but if you'll stick your head out the window you'll know what it's all about."

The loquacious Dean closed with this rejoinder: "Don't fail to miss tomorrow's game!"

After Dean won 30 games in 1934, the next pitcher to reach that almost-insurmountable plateau was Denny McLain, who was 31-6 for the pennant-winning Detroit Tigers of 1968. That spring, the 24-year-old righthander wondered aloud how many games an above-average pitcher could win in a year. Pitching coach Johnny Sain quoted author Norman Hill: "Anything you can conceive or believe, you can achieve."

Pitcher Mudcat Grant, who won 20 games for the 1965 Twins after some tips from Sain, praised the coach: "That man Sain sure puts biscuits in your pan."

Lefty Gomez also did well financially, but recognized the signs of age late in his career. "I'm throwing twice as hard," he said, "but the ball is getting there half as fast."

Ping Bodie wasn't fast enough either; he was thrown out trying to steal second, prompting a remark from witness Bugs Baer: "His head was full of larceny, but his feet were honest."

Mike (King) Kelly of the Chicago White Stockings, who popularized the hit-and-run play, was successful 53 times in 1886 and hit .388 as Chicago beat Detroit in the race for the National League flag. Enchanted by his flamboyance, fans couldn't wait for him to run so they could scream, "Slide, Kelly, slide!"

Kelly never played for Brooklyn, which would have loved to add the slide slogan to its all-star collection of one-liners. About the loud-mouthed but losing Dodgers of the '30s, Eddie Murphy cracked, "If the Dodgers aren't careful, overconfidence might cost them seventh place."

The bumbling Bums of that period developed the famous line —"Wait 'til next year!"—which has been plagiarized hundreds of times.

## TOBACCO ROAD GOES TO SPRING TRAINING

Baseball fan Erskine Caldwell, author of Tobacco Road and other classics, often traveled around Florida spring training camps with his broadcasting friend, Ernie Harwell.

**NICKNAMES**

IT'S BAD 'NUFF T'BE BLIND...BUT Y'URE ALSO DUMB!

LIPPY DUROCHER IS EASY ENOUGH TO FIGURE...

# BASEBALL TALK

While terms and quotes from the game are widely known, the language of the players themselves is not. Communication on the field is an art as much as discussions among doctors behind closed hospital doors. Moreover, it is constantly changing.

For years, a player who was hit on the hands "pulled a Brenegan," after an obscure third-string catcher who played for the Pirates in 1914. The receiver in question, Sam Brenegan, spent almost all his time in the bullpen, but broke into occasional regular games. Once, when inserted in a close contest, he was hit on the thumb with a pitched ball. Instead of chasing the ball, which rolled back to the screen, he shook his thumb at the plate while a run scored. He was returned to the minors soon afterward.

Likewise, an "Arlie Latham" was a too-hot-to-handle infield smash, named after a pre-1900 infielder who would practice safety first rather than risk injury on hard shots.

A "Big Bill," named for Bill Bradley of the Indians, was a high infield bounder, later called a Baltimore chop. Bradley specialized in hitting such balls when called upon as a pinch-hitter.

Many phrases have survived the test of time. Walter Johnson's fastball was called "the pneumonia ball" because hitters were said to feel a rush of cold air after the pitch passed them. The modern equivalent would be "Johnson is *bringing it*" or *"throwing aspirins."*

When a hitter or fielder is *handcuffed,* he is unable to get around on an inside fastball. A *gopher* is a long hit (especially a home run) because the batters "go for" four bases.

Good fielders *can pick it* but bad fielders often *kick it.* Fast batters who bunt *lay one down* and weak hitters, unable to hit anything hard, can't even manage a *loud foul.*

*In the doghouse* means in trouble—in or out of baseball—and one way pitchers can get there in the eyes of rival hitters is to *stick it in their ears,* or throw close to their heads. Such a pitch is commonly called a *beanball* or *duster.* Pitchers who disagree with their catcher's calls *shake them off* in an effort to try to hang *Size 4 collars* on enemy hitters (no hits in four at-bats).

*Pull* hitters will come around on the ball and hit it to their natural side of the diamond with consistency—righthanded batters to left and lefthanded batters to right. But *spray* hitters cannot be classified. Batters who hit for high average generally *go with the pitch* even if it means *hitting to the opposite field* (hitting the ball where it's pitched even though a righthanded hitter may sacrifice power to hit the ball to right field instead of left).

*Taking a cut* means two things: swinging the bat or finishing on the wrong end of a contract discussion. A *hot dog* or *showboat* is a player with ability who likes to show off, usually a fielder. If he's not talented, he'll probably get little more than a *cup of coffee* (brief trial) in the majors. That's especially true of players who *choke in the clutch* (fold under pressure).

A *bad-ball hitter* reaches for pitches outside the strike zone but may very well be successful (Yogi Berra is a noted example). Curveballs come in good and bad variety—*jughandle* and *nickel,* respectively. Managers play *percentage baseball,* or *go by the book,* if they *platoon* extensively, using only righthanded batters against lefthanded pitchers and vice versa. A hitter who refers to a pitcher as his *cousin* means he hits the hurler well; most modern hitters prefer to keep their boasting to a minimum for fear of riling their favorite pitcher. ☞

# NICKNAMES

PIE TRAYNOR WAS ACTUALLY NUTS ABOUT ... PIE....

SLUP SLUP

242

Base-runners don't take liberties with an outfielder who has a *gun* for an arm, but fast men often outrun infield grounders to make *leg hits.* Players who prefer privacy are *loners,* while colorful characters are often branded as *flaky.* A *scatter-arm* infielder frequently makes wild throws on balls he reaches but is often victimized by *seeing-eye balls,* or *bleeders,* which find their way through the infield, converting certain outs into hits.

Before air travel became commonplace, leagues which did most of their travel by bus were known as *horse leagues* and a player who complained about conditions—or anything else—was known as *Alibi Ike,* as in the Ring Lardner story of that name.

Then, as now, athletes were required to *bear down* and play *heads-up baseball* or be accused of *jaking it* (loafing)—the most serious accusation that can be hurled at a player.

# TEAM NICKNAMES

Nicknames have always been an integral part of baseball—both for teams and persons connected with the game.

Alexander Cartwright's Knickerbocker Baseball Club of New York in 1845 supplied the nickname of New York's National Basketball Association team a century later and paved the way for other early clubs to adopt an appropriate monicker.

Even before the Civil War, newspapers were reporting baseball, with writers referring to teams like the New Yorks, the Brooklyns, or the Bostons. Nicknames were badly needed—especially after professional baseball introduced the concept of placing more than one team in a given city.

In 1864, the Athletic club of Philadelphia was formed—and the name Athletics remained with the team after it joined the American League in 1901 and through franchise shifts to Kansas City and Oakland. Because the club wore a script "A" on its uniform hat and shirt writers eventually adopted the abbreviated "A's."

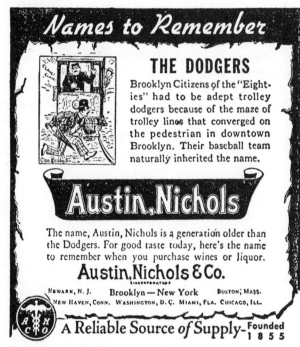

The name Cincinnati Reds also pre-dates the start of organized ball in 1876. The club was known as the Red Stockings two years before it began paying players in 1869, and press box occupants, seeking to save time and space, shortened that to Reds, though Redlegs was used during periods when it was politically dangerous to be identified as "Reds."

Another historic name—and a logical one—is Baltimore Orioles, from the bird. It was applied whenever that city had a big-league club—even though it erased the nickname Browns when St. Louis moved to Baltimore in 1954. Nor could "Orioles" be retained when the original O's shifted to New York after the 1902 campaign.

Team nicknames have long, colorful histories. Of the original 16 clubs that existed before expansion in 1961, only the Pittsburgh Pirates retained its original monicker, though writers sometimes refer to them as Bucs, a shortened version of Buccaneers.

Here's a closer look at club nicknames: ☞

# NATIONAL LEAGUE

**Atlanta Braves**—Braves, also used in Boston and Milwaukee, began in 1912 when owner Jim Gaffney was a Tammany Hall chieftain. Previously, the team was called Doves (after president George B. Dovey) and Beaneaters. After a disastrous 1935 season, management changed the name of Braves to Bees, hoping for a fresh start, but it never caught on.

**Chicago Cubs**—Originally called White Stockings (assumed and shortened by the AL team of 1901), the nickname became Colts after manager Cap Anson appeared on stage in Syracuse, New York, in a play specially written for him in 1896, *A Runaway Colt.* Cowboys and Broncos, natural derivatives, followed, and Rainmakers was used briefly. Sportswriters Fred Hayner and George Rice coined Cubs (and the Little Bears image) when the team had many young players in 1901.

**Cincinnati Reds**— Red Stockings, Redlegs, Reds.

**Houston Astros**— This '62 expansion team was first Colts and Colt .45s before moving into the Astrodome three years later. The transition to Astros was a natural, since Houston is the home of the Manned Space Flight Center.

**Los Angeles Dodgers**— Called Bridgegrooms because three 1888 players got married, the team won the 1889 American Association flag and took the title Superbas after a vaudeville troupe: "Hanlon's Superbas." Also called Atlantics, Kings, and Robins—after colorful manager Wilbert Robinson—the name Dodgers is an abbreviated version of Trolley Dodgers, an unkind nickname given turn-of-the-century Brooklynites by New Yorkers.

**Montreal Expos**—This '69 expansion club was named after Expo '67, World's Fair exposition retained and renamed "Man and His World."

**New York Mets**—This 1962 addition to the NL, officially called Metropolitan Baseball Club of New York, actually borrowed its abbreviated nickname from the American Association team of the 1880s.

**Philadelphia Phillies**—Once spelled Fillies, as in horses, the club was called Quakers briefly and is often referred to as Red Quakers—a nickname for a nickname—because of their uniforms. In 1944, exasperated team officials who had heard their club called the "Futile Phillies" for too many years, conducted a name-change contest and renamed the team Blue Jays. The winning entry in a contest that produced 5,064 letters and 635 different suggestions, was submitted by a Philadelphia woman who received a $100 war bond as a prize. Mrs. John L. Crooks picked the name, she said, "because it reflects a new team spirit. The blue jay is colorful in personality and

PIRATES

plumage. His plumage is a brilliant blue, a color the Phillies could use decoratively and psychologically." One of the more appropriate losing names was "Stinkers." Anyhow, the name Blue Jays failed to stick.

**Pittsburgh Pirates**—Because their players had a fearsome look, and because management successfully signed a deserting Players League star who rightfully belonged to another club, the monicker took in 1891. Writers also called the team Bucs, derived from Buccaneers. When the team made a surprise pennant march in 1960, broadcaster Bob Prince keyed the fans' war cry of "Beat 'em, Bucs!"

**St. Louis Cardinals**—Often called Cards or Redbirds, the nickname changed from the original Maroons when the team uniforms changed just before the turn-of-the-century. A female fan, near the press box, noticed the new suits and declared, "What a lovely shade of cardinal!" Writers heard her and the name stuck.

**San Diego Padres**—This 1969 expansion franchise assumed the name of the old Pacific Coast League team it replaced. The name reflects the region's Spanish heritage.

**San Francisco Giants**—The nickname traveled west from New York, where its 17 pennants established a tradition that could not be broken by a franchise shift. Manager Jim Mutrie, in 1885, was thrilled with a particular play and jumped to his feet shouting, "My Giants!" The club had previously been called Green Stockings and, after making its NL debut in red-tinged uniforms in 1876, the Mutuals.

# AMERICAN LEAGUE

**Baltimore Orioles**—As St. Louis Browns before 1954, the club was named for the brown trimmings on its outfits, but often dubbed "Brownies" because of its inept play.

**Boston Red Sox**—Once called Pilgrims, then Puritans, then Somersets (after owner Charles Somers), the Red Sox nickname is still one of the oldest in baseball. Bosox is a common abbreviation.

**California Angels**—The 1961 expansion club took the name of the Los Angeles Angels, the Pacific Coast League team it replaced in the "City of Angels." When it moved down the freeway to Anaheim, it retained the nickname but took a state ID. The team is sometimes referred to as "Halos" because of a halo decoration on its uniforms.

**Chicago White Sox**—Once the Invaders, the club assumed the discarded nickname of its NL counterpart early in the century, but reverted to a shortened form created by sportswriters Carl Green and I. E. Sanborn. They knew headline-writers would have a tough time; even now, many newsmen call the club Chisox.

**Cleveland Indians**—First called Forest City, later Molly McGuires (for many Irish players), Blues (for uniforms), Spiders (for players' dexterity), and Naps (for player-manager Napoleon Lajoie) before writers labeled the club Indians in an informal poll. Indians once lived on the shores of Lake Erie.

**Detroit Tigers**—Because Michigan is the Wolverine State, the Tigers had that nickname before *Detroit Free Press* newsman Phil J.

Reid noticed the blue-and-orange striped stockings on the 1901 club. Reminded of the Princeton colors, he gave the team the monicker of the Ivy League college's clubs.

**Kansas City Royals**—Fans nicknamed the '69 expansion club.

**Milwaukee Brewers**—A time-honored name for minor league clubs in Milwaukee, the capital of the brewing industry, the Seattle Pilots assumed it when they transferred to Wisconsin from Washington State in 1970, just one year after their creation. The Pilots had been named for the area's giant aircraft manufacturing industry.

**Minnesota Twins**—When the original Washington Senators moved to the twin cities of Minneapolis-St. Paul in 1961, they didn't wish to offend either, nor did they play in either—since their stadium is located in Bloomington. So they incorporated both into their name. In Washington, they had been known variously as the Senators and the Nationals—for obvious reasons. Writers called them "Nats" for short. Some called them "Griffs" after owner Clark Griffith.

**New York Yankees**—For 11 years after their transfer from Baltimore after the 1902 season, this club was called Highlanders because of the elevation of their park at the entrance to Manhattan Island. They were also called Hilltoppers for a spell before moving from that park into the Polo Grounds, which they shared with the Giants before Yankee Stadium opened in 1923. *New York Press* sports editor Jim Price and *New York Globe* newsman Mark Roth, later a Yankee official, decided either name was too long to fit into a headline and created the name Yankees.

**Oakland A's**—Merely an abbreviation of the ancient Athletics, the ancestral name from Philadelphia. The A's were called White Elephants for a spell because an elephant balancing a ball was the club's symbol for many years.

**Seattle Mariners**—The 1977 expansion team honors the nautical tradition of the Pacific Northwest.

**Texas Rangers**—The modern baseball team, inhabiting the Dallas-Fort Worth area after vacating Washington following the '71 season, had a similar problem as that faced by the Minnesota Twins, who left Washington 11 years earlier: it did not wish to offend either "host" city but actually played elsewhere (in Arlington). So it took the traditional name of the state's famous lawmen.

**Toronto Blue Jays**—A fan contest provided the handle for this new '77 entry, but the name was not new, as the Phils of the mid-'40s used it without much fan enthusiasm before reverting to tradition.

## MICHENER PUSHED ROBERTS FOR HALL

*Philadelphia-based author James Michener, an unabashed fan, campaigned in print for the election of Phillies pitcher Robin Roberts to the Hall of Fame. Roberts eventually won entry.*

# PLAYER NICKNAMES

Player nicknames come mostly from the animal kingdom. They are too numerous to list in a single chapter, as they merit an entire book of their own, but a sampling of the best should illustrate the point.

Strong players were named after strong animals. Broad-shouldered slugger Jimmie Foxx was not only known as "Double-X" because of his name but also "The Beast" because of his brawn. Charlie (King Kong) Keller and Dave (Kong) Kingman also were strongmen of the batting box.

Jim (Hippo) Vaughn, who weighed 230 and pitched half of the famed double no-hit game of May 2, 1917, was opposed in the classic by 260-pound Fred Toney, the Man Mountain from Tennessee.

Mike (Bear) Garcia and Fred (Big Bear) Hutchinson were two burly pitchers of note, while Dick (the Monster) Radatz dazzled rivals with a sizzling fastball as a Red Sox reliever of the '60s.

Lou Gehrig, the Yankees' durable slugger of the '30s, was "The Iron Horse," while New York Giants catcher Harry (the Horse) Danning took his name from a Damon Runyon character. Early in the century, Boston Braves pitcher Charley Pittinger was called "Horse Face" and the name became widely known because of its extensive use by Philadelphia writer Horace Fogel, later Phillies' president. A female fan objected, writing that she found Pittinger one of the more handsome athletes, but Fogel answered in print, "Lady, can I help it if he looks like a horse?"

Charles (Old Hoss) Radbourn, who won 60 games in 1884, won his name because of his willingness to work, and perform well, whenever asked.

Iron Man McGinnity, who pitched for the Orioles and Giants a decade later, also did yeoman service, pitching three doubleheaders —and winning them all—in August 1903. Few fans knew his name was Joe.

The most famous baseball mule, a close relative of the horse, was George (Mule) Haas, fleet centerfielder for the Philadelphia A's and Chicago White Sox. Jimmie Dykes, veteran manager who pinned the name on him, usually referred to him as "Donkey" or "The Donk." The Mule name fit so well that even Haas' wife used it. An ironic footnote: the name Haas, translated from German, means rabbit.

Frank Thomas, with the Pirates and Cubs in the '50s, was known as "Donkey" because of his big ears, Ken (Hawk) Harrelson because of his nose, and Turkey Mike Donlin was nicknamed after his walk —or waddle—as was Ron Cey, "the Penguin," more than 50 years later.

Donlin, a star outfielder, missed two seasons when he joined his wife in a vaudeville act in 1909-10, but returned to the New York Giants in 1911, delighting *New York Times* sportswriter Harry Cross. He wrote, "Turkey Mike has been dancing the boards with his wife for two seasons but he still does the turkey trot when he walks on the diamond." Donlin, who hated the monicker, warned Cross not to use it again.

Joe (Ducky) Medwick, a Hall of Fame outfielder who starred with the Gashouse Gang Cardinals, acquired his nickname in the St. Louis farm system when the press overheard an excited Medwick fan scream, "Isn't he a ducky wucky of a ballplayer!"

Goose Goslin's nickname seemed to fit his last name better than his given name of Leon Allen; while Choo-Choo Coleman, lifetime .197 hitter who chugged after pop fouls as an early-'60s catcher, had a much better calling card than Clarence. Coleman would be entirely forgotten if not for that alliterative nickname.

So would catcher Frank House, if not for his monicker, "The Pig." As a little boy, Frank had a natural lisp but considerable size. When someone would say, "You're big as a house," he would repeat "Pig House."

Tris Speaker, prematurely gray, was "The Gray Eagle" in the press but "Spoke" to teammates. The media referred to Ted Williams as "The Splendid Splinter," to Joe DiMaggio as "The Yankee Clipper," and to Tom Seaver as "The Franchise," but the names did not catch on among ballplayers.

The athletes preferred one or two words: George (Highpockets) Kelly, John (Tight Pants) Titus, Harry (Stinky) Davis, "Get-

# NICKNAMES

HAROLD REISER WAS A FAN OF MOVIE-SERIAL DAREDEVIL, *TWO-GUN PETE...*

247

tysburg" Eddie Plank, Fred (Cy) Williams, Hazen (KiKi) Cuyler, Edwin (Duke) Snider, Mike (Pinky) Higgins, Derrel (Bud) Harrelson, Edward (Whitey) Ford, Willie (Stretch) McCovey, Everett Lamar (Rocky) Bridges, Lawrence Peter (Yogi) Berra, and so many more.

© 1974 R. D. PARKER

"2nd BEST"
by BOB PARKER

GAVVY Cravath
· PHILLIES ·

...AVERAGED .341 FOR THE 1913 SEASON AND STILL FINISHED SECOND IN THE NATIONAL LEAGUE RACE !!

A SLUGGER, GAVVY SOCKED 34 DOUBLES, 14 TRIPLES AND LED BOTH LEAGUES WITH 19 HOME RUNS

JAKE Daubert
· BROOKLYN ·

...BATTED .350 FOR 139 GAMES AND CAPTURED THE BATTING CROWN !

JOY TO DODGER TOWN

*Nicknames have always been a baseball tradition. "Jake" Daubert was simply a shortened version of Jacob, but "Gavvy" Cravath was born Clifford Carlton Cravath and sometimes called "Cactus."*

248

# STORIES BEHIND THE NICKNAMES

There's always a story behind the name. Charles Arthur (Dazzy) Vance dazzled the opposition with a great curve to go with a great fastball. Norman Lewis Newsom was known as "Bobo" because he called anyone he met by that Spanish term for fool. Sal Maglie was "The Barber" because he would "shave" hitters with inside pitches. Walter (Boom-Boom) Beck was a pitcher so battered by enemy batters that he won an appropriate nickname. Hollis John (Sloppy) Thurston was an immaculate dresser. William Ellsworth (Dummy) Hoy was a deaf-mute who lasted fourteen years.

John Henry Wagner, considered the greatest shortstop of all, was best known as "Honus," the German word for John, but also called "The Flying Dutchman." Harold (Pee Wee) Reese was a whiz with marbles. Charles Leo (Gabby) Hartnett talked a lot; Emil (Dutch) Leonard was one of four Washington knuckleballers on the same staff in the '40s; and Harold Joseph (Pie) Traynor used to run grocery errands for his mother and read a list that invariably ended in "pie."

Perry Werden was called "Peach Pie Perry" because of an amusing incident from the 1880s.

Making his rounds of St. Louis on a pie wagon, Werden spotted a game in progress, stopped, and tied up his horse. When a player was injured, Werden got into the game and hit two home runs to help his team win. But a wild throw, just before game's end, struck the horse and the frightened animal bolted, spilling the pies. His bakery job obviously gone, Werden's good performance in the game began his baseball career. He played for the St. Louis club of the Union Association, which folded after the single season of 1884, and then played some in the minors before becoming an umpire.

An umpire of the same era won himself a nickname by arranging a phony presentation in his honor from "appreciative" Cleveland fans. The ump, rookie George Burnham, had taken a beating from abusive Chicagoans and wanted to counteract the bad publicity. He bought a watch, had it inscribed with a "message of appreciation," and arranged for it to be presented to him before a game on July 25, 1883. Word later leaked out and the ump became known as "Watch" Burnham.

Perhaps the best-known nickname, next to Babe Ruth's, was Rabbit Maranville's. His size dictated the name—and the size of his ears didn't hurt. Even his wife used it. Few fans knew his true name was Walter. On a 1931 post-season tour of Japan, Rabbit was the most popular player; Japanese fans wiggled their hands like a rabbit's ears and the impish Rabbit responded to their delight.

Baseball had such felines as Harry (the Cat) Brecheen and Harvey Haddix and Felix Millan, both known as "The Kitten." Millan was named after Felix the Cat, a cartoon character, but was thought too small to be called a cat. "Catfish" Hunter, created by A's owner Charley Finley, added color to an excellent pitcher with the rather ordinary first name of Jim.

Mark (the Bird) Fidrych, who didn't have to worry about cats, was nicknamed both for his abundance of curly hair, which resembled a nest, and for his pecking motions around the pitching mound. ☞

# NICKNAMES

AN OOM-PAH SERENADE TO THE TIGERS BEFORE HE PITCHED TO THEM IN A WORLD SERIES IS TYPICAL OF WHY *DEAN* WAS TAGGED *DIZZY....*

Jim Berryman

**George Robert (Birdie) Tebbetts:** The Reds' new manager was the victim of a backfiring nickname. He used to call his older brother Birdie.

**Willie (Puddin' Head) Jones:** He was nicknamed for a song popular when he was a boy, "Wooden Head, Puddin' Head Jones."

**Wilmer (Vinegar Bend) Mizell:** That's the name of his home town—Vinegar Bend, Ala.

**Harry (Peanuts) Lowrey:** When he was three months old, an uncle looked at him and commented, "No bigger than a peanut."

**Denton T. (Cy) Young:** When Young, an Ohio farm boy, tried out for the Canton, O., team, he repeatedly fired his fast ball past a Canton batter. Each time it smashed into the wooden grandstand behind home plate and splintered it.

The batter told his manager later, "Boss, you'd better sign that kid. He did more damage to your grandstand than a cyclone."

He was "Cyclone" Young for a while. Then the name was shortened to "Cy."

**Omar (Turk) Lown:** Nicknamed not for his nationality, but because he loves that Thanksgiving bird.

249

Johnny Murphy, Yankee reliever of the '30s, also had pecularities as a pitcher; his wind-up reminded observers of a rocking chair and he took on the nickname "Grandma." Needless to say, he didn't like it.

A later New York relief man, Albert Walter (Sparky) Lyle, was nicknamed because a series of bullpen and clubhouse pranks created the need for a more appropriate first name. The game has seen other Sparkys too—notably Detroit Tigers manager George (Sparky) Anderson.

Sandy Koufax hung the nickname "Bad Henry" on Hank Aaron because he was bad for pitchers. Aaron was one of many players also called strictly by their uniform numbers; in his case "No. 44."

There have been many Mickeys (George Stanley Cochrane and Arnold Malcolm Owen are two notable examples), Rubes (George Edward Waddell and Richard Marquard are best-known), and dozens of Docs—medical doctors like Bobby Brown and George Medich, dentists like old White Sox star G. Harry White and Phillies' manager James Prothro, and even a relief pitcher—Otis Crandall—who bore the monicker because he took care of sick ballgames.

Elwin Charles (Preacher) Roe was also a pitcher—primarily for the Brooklyn Dodgers of the early '50s—while Lynwood Thomas (Schoolboy) Rowe toiled for the Tigers of the '30s. The former was quiet and serious, the latter a cutup who never seemed to grow up.

Jim (Bad News) Galloway entered baseball from telegraphy, where he acquired the nickname by arranging with a friend in another office a trick to free him for ballgames. The friend would wire Galloway that a relative was sick and, armed with the perfect excuse, he would leave work.

Emil Frederick (Irish) Meusel, who played for Irishman John McGraw with the New York Giants of the early '20s, was Irish only in appearance; in reality, he was of German extraction. McGraw, equipped with an Irish temper to match his savvy as a manager, didn't mind Meusel's nickname, but hated the one stuck to him: Muggsy.

The monicker was taken from a Baltimore politician of questionable morals.

The best ever in the nickname department? The vote goes to Bob (Death to Flying Things) Ferguson, who led the National League with 24 walks in 1880. That year, a walk was changed from nine to eight called balls.

# CHAPTER SIXTEEN
# SUPERSTITIONS
## AND OTHER TRADITIONS

# SUPERSTITIONS IN BASEBALL

Though eighteenth-century writer Edmund Burke called superstition "the religion of feeble minds," ballplayers have practiced strange rituals—designed to bring them good luck and ward off evil spirits—since the game began.

The most prominent superstition requires players doing well to wear the same clothes while their hot streaks continue. Some maintain the same daily routine—eating, driving, and even sleeping the same way during hot streaks. Many follow widely accepted routines of not stepping on the foul lines, but deliberately touching a base while running out to a defensive position.

Almost all players—and many broadcasters and fans—feel they will "hex" a spectacular achievement by discussing a no-hitter in progress, and "the sophomore jinx" is an imaginary curse stalking second-year players—particularly those who enjoyed fine rookie years.

Baseball is rich in superstition of varied origins and nationalities. Concern over unseen hexes and jinxes blankets the game, extending into every major and minor league ballpark.

Traditionally, it is good luck in baseball to (1) knock on wood, (2) carry a charm like a rabbit's foot or four-leaf clover, (3) swing two bats with the regular bat while warming up, (4) see empty barrels, (5) put on the left shoe first, (6) have the pitcher receive the ball from the same man each inning, (7) find a lucky hairpin that is supposed to bring hits, (8) step on third base—or another base—before taking a fielding position, and (9) wear the same clothes, eat the same food, and do the same things while in a hot streak.

Players say it is bad luck to (1) chew gum instead of tobacco, (2) walk between catcher and umpire when coming to bat, (3) step on the foul lines, (4) put a hat on a hotel bed, (5) open an umbrella in a room, (6) see a black cat, or (7) have anything to do with the No. 13.

Pitchers are superstitious sorts. As a group, they don't like to be bothered before a start. They think it is "bad luck" to do anything that will disturb their concentration.

Satchel Paige was one of many players who brought superstition with him to the majors from the Negro Leagues. On July 30, 1949, umpire Bill Summers made Paige remove a lucky string bracelet from his right wrist. But the pitcher wore another under his stocking and beat the Boston Red Sox, 10-6 in 10 innings.

Well-traveled Bobo Newsom, who pitched in the majors for more than twenty years starting in 1929, had a fear of paper on the pitching mound. He always made a show of picking up every scrap he could find, and opposing players took advantage by scattering reams of turn-up sheets as they left the field after each inning.

Newsom began his day at the ballpark by touching both fair and foul territory, avoiding the dividing foul line, and during the game kept his glove on the ground, face up, with the thumb pointing exactly the same way each time. He also had a water cooler ritual: he took a sip before he went to the mound each inning—well aware of how he was holding his hands, feet, and head—and returned to drink exactly the same way whenever he retired the side in order. ☞

St. Louis Browns manager Luke Sewell believed that his luck improved when he kept infielders' gloves in the third base coaching box while the team hit. Current rules prohibit batting team from leaving equipment on the field.

## ONE FOR THE BOOKS

*The Montreal Expos should have stayed home on Friday the 13th of May 1977. They lost, 5-3, at Olympic Stadium to the Chicago Cubs, evening their record at 13-13. The Cubs had 13 hits, and left 13 runners on base. The game's winning run was driven in by the Cubs' Larry Biittner, whose number 26 is 2 x 13. The losing pitcher, Dan Warthen, wore 39, or 3 x 13.*

## PITCHERS USED VOODOO

*Philadelphia Athletics' pitcher Russ Christopher tried to break a slump by appearing in a straw hat and carrying a big key and other charms on his person. Urban Shocker, ace of the Browns, and Bobo Newsom, who pitched for several clubs, practiced voodoo rites before a game.*

The Sporting News

LUKE SEWELL LAYS IT DOWN

SAL MAGLIE WOULDN'T SHAVE THE DAY HE PITCHED

MOOSE MORYN TIES A RABBIT-FOOT TO HIS SPIKES.

ERNIE BANKS TWIDDLES HIS RIGHT THUMB.

Another pitcher, Ewell Blackwell of the Reds, alternated red and white sweatshirts. If he won while wearing a certain color, he stuck with it until he lost. Hugh Casey, Vic Raschi, and Chief Bender were among the more adamant of the hurlers who refused to be photographed before a game—and Bender grew so indignant when the ban was broken that he smashed the offender's camera.

Ace Yankee reliever Johnny Murphy always sat in the same spot on the dugout bench while working in a game, and Bob Shawkey wore his "lucky" red sweatshirt no matter what the weather.

A handful of athletes risked wearing No. 13, but one who did—Ralph Branca—threw the most infamous pitch in the history of the game. His last-of-the-ninth pitch to Bobby Thomson with one out and two men on became a three-run homer that erased a 4-2 Dodger lead and gave the New York Giants their miracle pennant of 1951.

Branca, then just 25, was crushed. Slowed by a sore arm the next season, he was never again the pitcher he had been before the Thomson home run. He was through before he turned 30.

Sal Maglie, ace of the '51 Giants, had a superstition that was shared by numerous contemporaries: he didn't shave before he pitched. Maglie was called "The Barber" not only because his pitches passed ominously close to rival hitters' heads but also because he needed one.

Hitters also have their idiosyncracies. Five of the game's stars—Hal Chase, Eddie Collins, Baby Doll Jacobson, Frank Crosetti, and Phil Rizzuto—regularly removed the gum from their mouths and perched it on their cap buttons for safe-keeping. Collins kept it there until the pitcher had two strikes on him, then replaced the wad in his mouth. With the White Sox, Collins went through this ritual one day when he suddenly discovered—to his chagrin—that playful teammates had placed pepper on the top of his cap. The gum absorbed the pepper in the few seconds it was placed on the button.

Many players had similar "good luck" mannerisms which they did almost without thinking. Frankie Frisch—even as a manager—rubbed his right shoe up and down his left stocking. Babe Ruth knocked the dirt out of his spikes after every strike. Robin Roberts fiddled with the ends of his uniform pants after each pitch. Gil Hodges blew a kiss to his wife whenever he hit a home run in Brooklyn. Tony Taylor crossed himself vigorously each time he stepped into the batter's box. Willie Mays never went to center field without touching second base. Sherm Lollar stuffed his locker with four-leaf clovers. Marty Marion picked up imaginary pebbles. ☞

Ralph Branca, who flaunted superstition by wearing No. 13, kids nemesis Bobby Thomson (in uniform) at the 1951 World Series. New York's slugger delivered a pennant-winning homer against Brooklyn's Branca in the last inning of the NL playoff.

Two players—Bill Nicholson and Harry Walker—earned nicknames for their well-known routines at the plate. Nicholson swished his bat several times while waiting for the pitch, and Walker frequently stepped out, putting his hat off and on numerous times. Harry (the Hat) Walker went through three or four caps a year, while Swish Nicholson enjoyed some big seasons with the Phillies.

Even Ted Williams had a regular ritual. He tucked his bat under his arm and pulled down hard on his cap whenever he had two strikes against him. Jackie Robinson, a fellow Hall of Famer, walked to the plate by passing in front of the catcher; if the catcher was in conference when Robinson's turn came up, Jackie waited until the meeting was over to take his customary stroll.

Minnie Minoso conceived what he thought was the sure cure for anemic achievement: he showered in full uniform—spikes included—during his days as player for the Chicago White Sox.

Old-time players believed that empty beer barrels were a portent of good-hitting days to come—and John McGraw subscribed to the theory while running the Giants. Just before the 1905 World Series, he hired a mule team to drag a wagon of barrels past the Polo Grounds, where the Giants were playing the Philadelphia Athletics. New York won the World Series, four games to one.

Stan Hack, former Cubs' third baseman, tried to cull good fortune by spending the first inning on the coaching lines at third before managing the rest of the game from the dugout.

George Stallings, like Bobo Newsom, was a paper fanatic who used to frighten Rochester batboy Gabe Paul (later general manager of several major-league clubs) with shouts to clear paper scraps from the dugout area. "If one little scrap escaped me," Paul said years later, "Mr. Stallings' roar scared the life out of me."

When managing the Browns, Luke Sewell coached at third base full-time and kept the gloves of his shortstop and third baseman in the coaching box with him. He then handed each to the rightful owner when the sides changed.

An early Cubs' manager, Fred Mitchell (1917-20), enjoyed a long winning streak after finding a hairpin on a sidewalk near Wrigley Field the day the streak started. Mitchell, honoring the long tradition that a hairpin will bring hits, searched for hairpins every day and found them for 17 more days. On the 19th day, he was unable to locate a hairpin and the Cubs lost.

During the 1924 season, Washington Senators' manager Bucky Harris learned that his team won every time an 11-year-old schoolboy named Bradley Willson was in the ballpark. During the World Series that fall, Harris arranged for the youngster to attend every game by sending a chauffered limousine to bring him to the stadium.

St. Christopher's medals, crosses, six-pointed Stars of David, and other religious items were worn by old-time and modern players hoping for good fortune.

General Manager Al Campanis of the Los Angeles Dodgers collected pins in anticipation of hits when he played for Brooklyn and maintained his hobby of collecting Greek charms after his active career ended. Campanis hid the charms in peta (pies) to bring good luck to guests who found them in their portions. When Campanis found them himself, in 1965 and 1966, the Dodgers won pennants.

The Sporting News

## ROBIN ROBERTS PULLS HIS PANTS DOWN BEFORE EACH PITCH.

**Hall of Famer Robin Roberts had a regular routine on the mound.**

## 44 FOR "4"

*Hank Aaron wore No. 5 during his first year, 1954, with the old Milwaukee Braves, but switched to No. 44 the next season. The hard-hitting outfielder, who became the all-time home run king by avoiding injury and producing with consistency, hit a one-season high of 47 homers, and hit 45 once, but hit the total represented by his numerals four times en route to a career mark of 755 round-trippers.*

## THE WHITE LINES

*Ralph Kiner never stepped on a white line. "It didn't help or hurt me," he said. "I just didn't want to take any chances."*

President William Howard Taft, attending the Washington opener in 1910, may have inadvertently started the tradition of the seventh-inning stretch.

# TRADITIONS

Every aspect of baseball—professional and amateur—has a long tradition. A radical rules change, such as the introduction of the designated hitter by the American League in 1973, may seem the exception, but even that idea was brewing for forty-five years (since its conception by NL president John Heydler in 1928).

Intercollegiate baseball pre-dates the turn of the century. As long ago as 1882, the Manhattan College team played under the watchful eye of a coach named Brother Jasper. Before each game, he told the student-spectators not to move or leave their seats with the game in progress. One hot afternoon, however, the fans got restless and, as the team came to bat in the seventh inning, Brother Jasper told them to stand and stretch their legs.

Manhattan College often played in the park of the New York NL club and Giant fans picked up on the "seventh inning stretch," according to a news release from the school's office in 1958.

Other sources say the seventh-inning stretch began when fans of the Cincinnati Red Stockings, the first professional team in 1869,ˑ stood to gain temporary relief from the hard wooden benches of the day.

Some historians insist President William Howard Taft, attending the 1910 opener in Washington, inadvertently started the tradition when he rose to stretch in the seventh inning. Thinking he was leaving, fans stood out of respect for the office. When they saw Taft stretch they stretched—and continued to do so from that game forward.

There are other traditions associated with fans. Until the home run era triggered by Babe Ruth in the '20s, they returned balls hit into the stands. The practice of returning balls was reinstated during the Second World War to benefit the Army relief fund. ☞

## TAFT PLEASED BOTH SIDES

President William Howard Taft, passing through St. Louis on May 4, 1910—a rare day when both the Cardinals and Browns were at home—did not wish to offend either team. He managed to see parts of each game.

## HOW TO CHANGE LUCK

Some players tried to change bad luck by changing numbers; Roger Craig switched to No. 13 in his second year as a New York Met and lost 22 of 27 decisions after a 10-24 mark the year before. Jake Powell believed hairpins represented hits, collected 241 of them one season, and produced exactly that many hits for his team in the minors. Ron Northey, Pete Reiser, and Al Rosen were among several who made "X" marks at home plate before they batted.

The "traditional" Sunday doubleheader is a relatively new development. When the American League was founded in 1901, only Chicago played games on Sunday. St. Louis allowed Sunday ball the next year, but Boston didn't approve until 1929 and Philadelphia until 1934.

Like Sunday ball, the tradition of retiring uniform numbers is relatively young in comparison to the long history of the game. Babe Ruth's No. 3 was not retired at the end of his Yankee career in 1934; in the thirteen years it remained active, it was worn by George Selkirk, Allie Clark, Bud Metheny, Cliff Mapes, and (in spring training) Joe Medwick.

Before regular games begin, players sometimes play "pepper," a practice of one man bunting to a row of fielders whose return tosses serve as "pitches." Pepper games were played for Cokes; anyone who made an error was charged a Coke. When Cardinal owner Gussie Busch (of Anheuser-Busch) was playing pepper with his employees during the early '50s, slugger Stan Musial quipped, "What do you play for, breweries?"

SHERM LOLLAR STUFFS FOUR-LEAF CLOVERS INTO HIS LOCKER.

The Sporting News

## PENNY PINCHER

**Washington Senators first baseman Mickey Vernon picked up pennies he found on the field; he regarded them as omens of base hits to come.**

**"I can't recall a time that I found a penny and did not get a hit," he said. "Why doesn't the manager throw pennies onto the field near first base? That's the catch. The penny had to be found by accident. You can't fool around with this superstition stuff and get away with it."**

WHAT'S THAT—YOUR MARK?

The Sporting News

# THE ART OF CHEWING

Chewing is a well-established baseball tradition. Players chew gum, licorice, tobacco, and a variety of other items because they need constant moisture (especially in the field, where there is no access to a drinking fountain), because constant exercise of the jaw muscle helps athletes concentrate on the game, and because chewing relaxes the nerves.

By far the most widespread "chew" is bubble gum—usually unadulterated but sometimes intertwined with a wad of chewing tobacco. The Brooklyn-based Topps Chewing Gum Company even held a national bubble-blowing tournament in 1975, with the finals shown on television. Managers frown on players blowing bubbles during the national anthem, however, and at least one big-league club has imposed a rule against it.

The pitcher is the most obvious gum-chewer, as he frequently makes exaggerated chewing gestures while studying the catcher's signal for the next pitch.

Babe Ruth, Roy Campanella, and Johnny Mize were three of the more prominent former sluggers who enjoyed tobacco almost as much as a home run, but the tradition did not retire with them.

Perennial All-Stars Johnny Bench and Rod Carew chew today, along with pitchers Tug McGraw, Luis Tiant, and Sparky Lyle. Countless other major-leaguers also pursue the habit, but few dare to swallow even a drop of the foul-tasting juice.

Some players say they prefer chewing tobacco to smoking because chewing is far less harmful to their health and does not jeopardize the welfare of non-users in the vicinity. But finding spittoons is difficult—society frowns on constant spitting—and as a result many tobacco-chewers confine their activities to ballparks, where grass, dirt, dugout steps, and the white shoes of unsuspecting reporters serve as ample targets.

# OPENING DAY

Though each major league team plays 162 games during the regular season, plus two dozen spring exhibitions, and up to 12 more for pennant-winners, the highlight of the year for many is Opening Day.

On that festive day in early April, all teams are equal. The worst team and the best team have the same 0-0 records, and the feeling of hope that prevailed through the six-week spring training period still exists.

For many Americans, Opening Day is the official start of spring, a signal that the miseries of winter are over. Temperatures are still low in many major league cities (and snow is still falling in Canada), but fans, players, and team executives have a special warmth inside on the eve of the season.

Bands play, flags wave, teams are introduced one-player-at-a-time, and a celebrity—maybe even a President—throws out the first pitch.

When Washington had a team, it would always open at home, one day ahead of the other American League teams. Cincinnati enjoys annual advance-opener honors in the National League—a tradition that began in 1876, the league's first season.

The Reds (then Red Stockings) missed opening at home only once in their long NL tenure (the team was out of the league 1881-89). The exception occurred in 1877, when rain forced cancellation of the opener for three days and the team boarded a boat for Louisville to open the season there.

Opening Day games have been marked by unusual events on the field. In 1900, the Phillies beat the Braves, 19-17, the highest score ever recorded in an NL opener. A year later, in the first American League game for both clubs, Detroit scored 10 runs in the ninth inning to beat Milwaukee, 14-13.

Leon (Red) Ames of the New York Giants no-hit the Brooklyn Dodgers for the first nine innings in a 1909 opener, but lost in the thirteenth, 3-0. The next season, Walter Johnson won the

## PITCHER BATTED SEVENTH

*In the 1952 opener of the Boston Red Sox, manager Lou Boudreau placed pitcher Mel Parnell seventh in the batting order.*

## NEAR-MISS FOR LEMON

*Cleveland pitcher Bob Lemon allowed only a single in a 6-0 opening victory over the White Sox in Municipal Stadium on April 14, 1953.*

## GEHRIG'S LAST OPENER

*Lou Gehrig played his last opening game at Yankee Stadium on April 20, 1939. He had no hits and was charged with an error.*

Opening Day is usually a festive occasion, but the serious faces of Dodger players indicate some knew that the 1957 Ebbets Field lidlifter would be Brooklyn's last.

Los Angeles Dodgers

Washington lid-lifter, but lost a no-hitter because rightfielder Doc Gessler tripped over a child who was sitting in front of an overflow crowd behind outfield ropes. The ball, which would have been a routine out, dropped for a double.

When Yankee Stadium opened in 1923, a throng of 74,000 swamped the ballpark and more than 25,000 more fans were turned away at the gates. Bob Shawkey beat Boston, thanks to a three-run home run by Babe Ruth, who wasted no time in showing why the park was called "the House that Ruth Built."

In '25, the Cleveland Indians scored the biggest Opening Day rout, a 21-14 victory over the St. Louis Browns. Cleveland also registered the only no-hitter on Opening Day, a 1-0 triumph pitched by Bob Feller over the Chicago White Sox in 1940. Lefty Grove of the Boston Red Sox nearly upstaged Feller by pitching seven perfect innings at Washington before giving up a one-out single to Cecil Travis in the eighth.

The 1946 openers were marked by the return of the stars from World War II and 1947 was important because Jackie Robinson's debut in Brooklyn ended the game's color line.

**Huge throngs swamped Yankee Stadium for the 1923 opener. More than 25,000 fans were turned away.**

Baseball Hall of Fame

**President Herbert Hoover risked the wrath of Depression-bound fans to throw out the first ball of the 1930 season.**

# PRESIDENTS AT THE BALLPARK

The President of the United States has always had a close association with "America's national pastime," particularly when a club was located in the nation's capital at Washington, D.C.

More than 40 openers were preceded by Presidents throwing out the first ball from a box adjacent to the field, and an even dozen Presidents took part in the ceremonies.

Former President U. S. Grant smoked cigars while watching New York beat Boston, 7-5, at the Polo Grounds on May 1, 1883, but the first incumbent President to watch a game was Benjamin Harrison, who watched Cincinnati edge Washington, 7-4 in eleven innings, on June 6, 1892 (Washington was then in the National League).

William Howard Taft, once a standout pitcher at Yale University, was a fan of Walter Johnson in particular and the Washington Senators in general when he threw out the first Presidential pitch—on April 14, 1910.

His successor, Woodrow Wilson, not only threw out the first ball three times but also attended games regularly, even after leaving office. Warren Harding, an Ohio sportswriter turned senator, succeeded Wilson in office and maintained an avid interest in the game, but Calvin Coolidge considered the first-ball assignment a task rather than a privilege and once left a game in the second inning.

Herbert Hoover, a Yankee fan, had managed his college baseball team at Stanford. Harry Truman rooted for the St. Louis Browns and—like a good Missouri senator—wished well for the Cardinals too, though Bess Truman developed a definite interest in the Kansas City A's and later the Kansas City Royals, who played near her home in Independence. ☞

Truman probably was the most unorthodox of Opening Day pitchers, as he threw two balls—one with each arm. The Kennedy-Johnson ticket, elected in 1960, knew baseball thoroughly. Kennedy discussed detailed aspects of the game with George Selkirk, general manager of the "new" Senators, when the baseball executive presented the President with the traditional gold season's pass in 1963. Kennedy attended all three Opening Day games during his short-lived administration.

Jimmy Carter, an excellent softball pitcher, twice threw out the first ball for the Atlanta Braves when he was Governor of Georgia, and Senator Henry Jackson—an unsuccessful candidate for the Presidential nomination—had the unusual distinction of making the first pitch for the 1969 Seattle Pilots, who lasted only that one season, and the new Seattle Mariners, in 1977.

## LEFTY GROVES

*Hall of Fame pitcher Lefty Grove spelled his last name "Groves" when he made his major league debut for the Philadelphia A's in the 1925 opener.*

# FAREWELLS

While season openers—especially Presidential openers—are festive, happy occasions, farewells are invariably sad, whether the retiring star enjoys a good final season or a bad one.

There was a touch of irony in the final game of Cy Young, whose 511 pitching victories may never be duplicated. Young, at age 45, pitched a masterful game in his last appearance with the Boston Braves on September 7, 1911, but wound up on the short end of a 1-0 score. The winning pitcher, Philadelphia rookie Grover Cleveland Alexander, not only won 28 games that year but went on to win 373 lifetime, tied with Christy Mathewson for tops in the National League.

Two other all-time pitching stars, Mordecai (Three-Finger) Brown and Mathewson, ended their careers in a specially-arranged final duel on September 4, 1916. Brown, 37, was working for the Cubs, while Mathewson, 39, was manager of the Reds, a club he took over after leaving the New York Giants in mid-season. ☞

## PRESIDENTS USED REAL "BODY" GUARD

*Presidents attending baseball games are assigned a "body" guard to protect them from foul balls or bad throws. The guard was usually a utility player from the home team.*

Lou Gehrig, wearing his Yankee uniform, prepares to make a sad farewell speech during "Lou Gehrig Day" ceremonies in 1939.

Mathewson beat Brown, 10-8, to register his only decision in a Cincinnati uniform.

Walter Johnson, second to Young with 414 lifetime wins, was 39 when he made his final appearance, but his farewell was unusual for two reasons. First, the great righthander came up as a pinch-hitter for pitcher Tom Zachary in the ninth inning, and flied out to right-fielder Babe Ruth. Second, that was the same game in which Babe Ruth hit his record-smashing 60th home run! The date was September 30, 1927.

Two Hall of Fame hitters, Ted Williams and George Sisler, hit .300 while playing at least 100 games in their final seasons. Williams and Hank Greenberg also hit more than 20 home runs in their last campaigns as active players.

The widely-accepted baseball adage, "He knew when to quit," applies most appropriately to Ted Williams. In 1960, he hit .316 with 29 homers in just 310 at-bats—including a home run in his last trip to the plate.

## THE FIRST HALL OF FAME VOTE

*In the first vote for the Hall of Fame, on February 3, 1936, Ty Cobb drew 222 of 226 votes, Babe Ruth and Honus Wagner finished second with 215 each, followed by Christy Mathewson with 205. Walter Johnson, with 189, was the only other man to have the required three-quarters majority for election in the voting, then conducted by players and writers.*

## INJURY FORCED KOUFAX TO QUIT

*Star pitcher Sandy Koufax of the Los Angeles Dodgers took the advice of doctors and retired at age 30 in November 1966. Though he had just won 27, lost 9, and posted a 1.73 earned run average, Koufax revealed that continued pitching could result in permanent disability because of an arthritic left elbow.*

A Personal Reaction to

# BASEBALL'S HALL OF FAME

### By Mike Schuman
### The Baseball Bulletin

As a kid, after I continually pestered my parents to take me to Cooperstown, they finally relented. My mother was bored, my father was interested but preoccupied, and I was fascinated. Ten years later, I went back to the Baseball Hall of Fame, and was still fascinated.

Sure, kids love the place. But only a true baseball fan realizes that the museum is far more than a place to take the Little Leaguer for the summer. In fact, it's possible that the youngsters may not fully appreciate the history and the tradition of the sport that is preserved in the Hall.

"The first scheme for playing baseball, according to the best evidence obtainable to date, was devised by Abner Doubleday at Cooperstown, New York, in 1839." So said the final report of the Commission to determine the origin of baseball, which was organized around the turn of the century. This is now generally accepted as fiction rather than fact, but like all such legends, it has

Baseball Hall of Fame

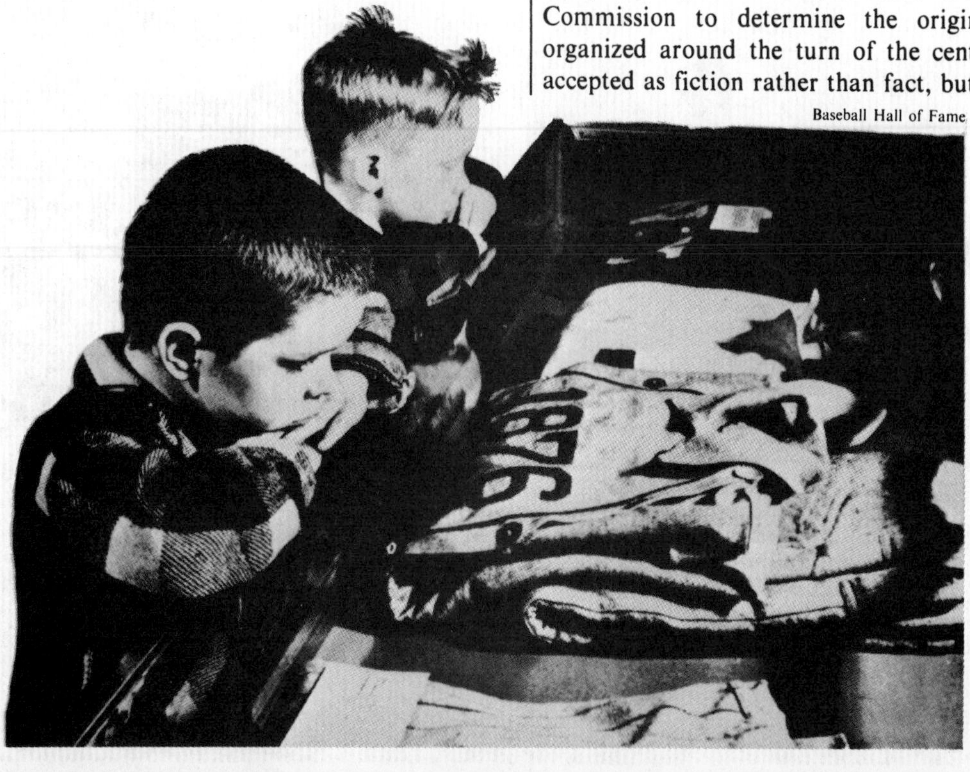

**Old-time exhibits intrigue young visitors at Cooperstown.**

How the National Baseball Hall of Fame and Museum looked when it was opened in 1939.

stuck. It was the adherence to this finding which placed America's first museum entirely devoted to a sport in Cooperstown, New York.

Scenic, sleepy, charming, sedate—they're all various epithets used and overused to describe baseball's home. The village was named for the father of James Fenimore Cooper, who lived in that region most of his life and felt justified in naming at least one town after himself. Cooperstown is located halfway between Schenectady and Utica, accessible only through a maze of back roads. To put it bluntly, it's in the middle of nowhere. So when baseball fans drive through the wilds of upstate New York simply to see the Baseball Hall of Fame, there must be something there worth seeing.

The Hall of Fame itself, that is the special wing which so grandly displays the plaques of the members, takes up only a small portion of the building. The museum occupies the rest—all four floors worth. The displays are such that one can see and enjoy everything in one afternoon, but could discover something new and different every day for a year.

First of all, some displays consist of statistics, which not only take time to sink in, but are constantly changing. The all-time top ten leaders in major categories are listed smartly on wall displays. The leaders in home runs, RBI's, and runs scored change quite often. Some categories, like top ten at bats, which include Henry Aaron along with other active players, change from day to day.

Certain exhibits could take a year alone to see wholly. Current and old baseball cards are shown under glass cases, and if I were to examine every card to study its style or to see whose picture is on it, I'd still be there now. For a fanatic card collector, this single display is worth the trip in itself.

Nostalgia freaks—they'd be right at home, too. In fact, one wouldn't even have to be an avid fan to appreciate the collection of memory bogglers. Even my mother got a kick out of seeing Joe DiMaggio's old uniform. And my father relived the day, many moons ago, when he saw Mickey Owen drop the infamous "third strike." "I was there," he boasted, as he had boasted about it many times before. "I remember that like I remember Pearl Harbor," he recollected, gazing at a last remnant of the Ebbets Field wall.

Younger nostalgia freaks would not be left out. Reading through a list of every no-hitter pitched since 1940, I remembered exactly where I was and what I was doing when Dave Morehead pitched his

## THE HALL OF FAME GAME

Each summer, two major league teams hook up in an exhibition contest at Cooperstown's Doubleday Field on the day of the Hall of Fame inductions. In the first such contest, on June 12, 1939, two players from each of the 16 clubs journeyed to Cooperstown. Honus Wagner and Eddie Collins chose up sides, with leagues mixing, and Babe Ruth—long retired as a player—fouled out in his only at-bat.

## 10-YEAR RULE WAIVED FOR JOSS

To be eligible for the Hall of Fame, a player must have performed in 10 major league seasons. The requirement was waived for Addie Joss, who was one game short when stricken by tubercular meningitis just as he was to pitch the first game of the 1911 season for Cleveland. Joss, who died a week later at age 31, had 160 victories and a 1.88 lifetime ERA, second only to Ed Walsh's 1.82. The wily righthander had an uncanny ability to predict the score ahead of time. Before his perfect game against Walsh and the White Sox on October 2, 1908, he announced, "They ain't gonna score." They didn't.

hitless game for the Red Sox ten years back. And I remembered watching on television as Tom Phoebus threw his gem against the Bosox.

Ah, Morehead and Phoebus. Where are they now? Which leads me to another point. Hall of Famers aren't the only ballplayers represented in the museum. A lot of everyday guys are there, too. Of course, there is an entire wing devoted to Babe Ruth, and there is Stan the Man's uniform, along with Ty Cobb's first contract. But there's also a tribute to Harvey Haddix for pitching the most famous of all heartbreakers; and each of the players who endured baseball's longest game are part of the National Baseball Museum, if only in a blown-up box score.

A pocketless baseball glove? Maybe. But a fingerless baseball glove? No way. That's what I would have imagined if I had not seen the thing before my eyes. But there it was—a glove with no fingers, in its little glass-enclosed home, staring me in the face. A most primitive piece of baseball equipment, it was used in the late 1870s. Gloves with no pockets, such as those used by John McGraw and Cy Young, were right there too, keeping its primitive ancestor company.

I also came across a 17-foot bat. But, rest easy. I'm not going to tell you it was used by an original New York Giant. It was a present for Ted Williams made by some admirers. What a potent weapon though, if it ever were to be used. All we'd need is a batter twice the size of Frank Howard.

Mementoes of baseball past do not control the building. A room, which did not exist during my first visit, has been set aside to show the goings-on in "Baseball Today." Carpeted in Astroturf, a highlight of this room are 26 displays, one devoted to each team in the majors. Featured here are press guides, uniforms, pictures and pennants. Also included in this colorful room are special exhibits about current players and recent events.

Walking into the actual Hall of Fame is not unlike entering the Rotunda of the Capitol or Independence Hall. The designers of the Hall didn't monkey around when building this shrine to the immortals. Solemnity overtakes the atmosphere as one enters the wing, with its 25-foot high ceiling and its marble columns. The plaques belonging to each of baseball's greats line the walls to the right and left. On each plaque are the player's greatest accomplishments in nutshell form. Whether it's the facts and figures on the walls, or seeing the names and faces of the best of the best, or simply the monumental architecture of the place, one can't leave the Hall without being just somewhat inspired.

I'm looking forward to visiting the epitome of quaintness again and again and again. If for nothing else, simply to see my favorite exhibit in the place: the front page of *The Boston Record* dated October 2, 1967—no headline, no article, just a picture of two big red socks.

## Hall of Famers Receiving Highest Percentage of Votes

| Rank | Year | Player | Ballots Cast | Votes Received | Omitted | % Received |
|------|------|--------|--------------|----------------|---------|------------|
| 1. | 1936 | Ty Cobb | 226 | 222 | 4 | 98.2 |
| 2. | 1982 | Henry Aaron | 415 | 406 | 9 | 97.8 |
| 3. | 1989 | Johnny Bench | 447 | 431 | 16 | 96.4 |
| 4. | 1936 | Honus Wagner | 226 | 215 | 11 | 95.1 |
| 5. | 1936 | Babe Ruth | 226 | 215 | 11 | 95.1 |
| 6. | 1979 | Willie Mays | 432 | 409 | 23 | 94.7 |
| 7. | 1989 | Carl Yastrzemski | 447 | 423 | 24 | 94.6 |
| 8. | 1962 | Bob Feller | 160 | 150 | 10 | 93.8 |
| 9. | 1966 | Ted Williams | 302 | 282 | 20 | 93.4 |
| 10. | 1969 | Stan Musial | 340 | 317 | 23 | 93.2 |

## NATIONAL LEAGUE

| Number | Player | Club |
|--------|--------|------|
| — | Christy Mathewson | New York Giants |
| — | John McGraw | New York Giants |
| 1 | Pee Wee Reese | Brooklyn |
| 1 | Rich Ashburn | Philadelphia |
| 1 | Billy Meyer | Pittsburgh |
| 3 | Bill Terry | New York Giants |
| 4 | Ralph Kiner | Pittsburgh |
| 4 | Mel Ott | New York Giants |
| 4 | Duke Snider | Los Angeles |
| 5 | Johnny Bench | Cincinnati |
| 6 | Stan Musial | St. Louis |
| 8 | Willie Stargell | Pittsburgh |
| 9 | Bill Mazeroski | Pittsburgh |
| 11 | Carl Hubbell | New York Giants |
| 14 | Ernie Banks | Chicago |
| 14 | Ken Boyer | St. Louis |
| 14 | Gil Hodges | New York Mets |
| 17 | Dizzy Dean | St. Louis |
| 19 | Junior Gilliam | Los Angeles |
| 20 | Lou Brock | St. Louis |
| 20 | Pie Traynor | Pittsburgh |
| 21 | Roberto Clemente | Pittsburgh |
| 21 | Warren Spahn | Milwaukee |
| 24 | Willie Mays | San Francisco |
| 24 | Walter Alston | Los Angeles |
| 26 | Billy Williams | Chicago |
| 27 | Juan Marichal | San Francisco |
| 32 | Sandy Koufax | Los Angeles |
| 32 | Jim Umbricht | Houston |
| 33 | Honus Wagner | Pittsburgh |
| 35 | Phil Niekro | Atlanta |
| 36 | Robin Roberts | Philadelphia |
| 37 | Casey Stengel | New York Mets |
| 39 | Roy Campanella | Los Angeles |
| 40 | Danny Murtaugh | Pittsburgh |
| 40 | Don Wilson | Houston |
| 41 | Eddie Mathews | Milwaukee |
| 41 | Tom Seaver | New York Mets |
| 42 | Jackie Robinson | Los Angeles |
| 44 | Henry Aaron | Atlanta |
| 44 | Willie McCovey | San Francisco |
| 45 | Bob Gibson | St. Louis |
| 53 | Don Drysdale | Los Angeles |

## AMERICAN LEAGUE

| Number | Player | Club |
|--------|--------|------|
| 1 | Bobby Doerr | Boston |
| 1 | Billy Martin | New York |
| 2 | Nellie Fox | Chicago |
| 2 | Charlie Gehringer | Detroit |
| 3 | Earl Averill | Cleveland |
| 3 | Harmon Killebrew | Minnesota |
| 3 | Babe Ruth | New York |
| 4 | Luke Appling | Chicago |
| 4 | Joe Cronin | Boston |
| 4 | Lou Gehrig | New York |
| 4 | Earl Weaver | Baltimore |
| 5 | Lou Boudreau | Cleveland |
| 5 | Hank Greenberg | Detroit |
| 5 | Brooks Robinson | Baltimore |
| 5 | Joe DiMaggio | New York |
| 6 | Al Kaline | Detroit |
| 7 | Mickey Mantle | New York |
| 8 | Yogi Berra | New York |
| 8 | Bill Dickey | New York |
| 9 | Roger Maris | New York |
| 9 | Minnie Minoso | Chicago |
| 9 | Ted Williams | Boston |
| 10 | Phil Rizzuto | New York |
| 10 | Dick Howser | Kansas City Royals |
| 11 | Luis Aparicio | Chicago |
| 15 | Thurman Munson | New York |
| 16 | Whitey Ford | New York |
| 16 | Ted Lyons | Chicago |
| 19 | Bob Feller | Cleveland |
| 19 | Billy Pierce | Chicago |
| 20 | Frank Robinson | Baltimore |
| 22 | Jim Palmer | Baltimore |
| 26 | Gene Autry | California |
| 29 | Rod Carew | Minnesota |
| 29 | Rod Carew | California |
| 32 | Elston Howard | New York |
| 37 | Casey Stengel | New York |
| 44 | Hank Aaron | Milwaukee |

# CHAPTER SEVENTEEN

# Spring Training

# SPRING TRAINING

Spring training has always been an integral part of baseball. Clubs routinely worked out under the stands of their home parks, even before A. H. Roden took his Boston Nationals to New Orleans, the first stop of an 1884 pre-season swing.

New Orleans was actually a pre-season training site twice; the first for a newly-organized touring club from Chicago in February 1870.

In an effort to beat the Cincinnati Red Stockings, who had gone undefeated in 1869, Tom Foley found considerable semi-pro talent and put it together under the name Chicago White Stockings (a name later applied to the Chicago club which was a charter member of the National League in 1876). Foley and star second baseman Jimmy Wood, imported from Brooklyn, took their squad to Louisiana for training. Other teams of the National Association (the loosely-organized circuit which began a five-year existence the next season) also practiced in New Orleans.

Following the 1884 appearance of the Boston NL club, Pittsburgh and Louisville of the American Association, then a major league, staged several practices in the warmer climes of the southeast.

The first journey southward for the specific purpose of entering a period of pre-season training didn't occur until 1886, when White Stockings manager Cap Anson, concerned about his team's portly condition, decided to force off the suet with sweat under the broiling sun—and in the therapeutic baths—of Hot Springs, Arkansas.

CAP ANSON STARTED IT ALL IN 1886 WHEN HE BOILED THE BEER OUT OF HIS CHICAGO WHITE STOCKINGS AT HOT SPRINGS, ARK.

OOH—ALL THAT LOVELY BREW (CHOKE) J-JUST EVAPORATIN'!

## THE "GOOD" OLD DAYS?

*Long-time manager and executive Branch Rickey attended his first training camp in Dallas as a rookie with the 1906 St. Louis Browns. There was no permanent camp— just a traveling road show to Fort Worth and Houston. Three of the 20 players had to be cut by opening day; when they were, the team had seven pitchers, three catchers, three outfielders, and four infielders. In camp, everyone played except manager Jimmy McAleer, road secretary Lloyd Rickert and trainer Kirby Samuels. There were no coaches, team doctors, scouts, or newsmen with the ballclub.*

# EARLY ACCOMMODATIONS

In 1888, the Washington Senators, with Connie Mack as a catcher, went south for the spring with a 15-man contingent. Overnight accommodations were in third-class hotels because the better inns refused ballplayers, in those days regarded as a rowdy bunch. Two men were assigned to a lower berth when the team traveled during its two weeks of training.

When the Washingtons found a lone top hotel that would take them in, they booked their players on the American plan, with rooms and meals included. That meant second-class meals and scant attention from waiters—but Ted Sullivan overcame that by slipping out a shiny silver dollar and placing it alongside his plate at the start of each meal. The waiters, thinking it was a tip, provided excellent service, but Sullivan never left it; he pocketed it at meal's end and pulled the same trick in other restaurants.

In 1890, Brooklyn's prelude to its first National League season featured a swank boat ride to St. Augustine, Florida, where a game was played against Anson's Chicago club March 11. Brooklyn lost that contest and eight of ten overall but capped the tour with a 28-1 win over a choose-up local nine.

The 1903 Philadelphia A's, with Connie Mack as manager, slept on cots in a Jacksonville barracks during the training period, and ate at a second-rate establishment named Wolfe's.

Three years later, John McGraw's New York Giants became the first team to train in California, but the experiment was short-lived. Heavy rains had made fields in the Los Angeles area unplayable, and McGraw reluctantly headed east in search of suitable surroundings. He finally set up headquarters in San Antonio. ☞

Finding Texas to their liking, the Giants established the first permanent training base in Marlin Springs in 1908. The team received not only an annual subsidy from the town but also the deed to the ballpark. Not long after, the Chicago Cubs pitched camp on Catalina Island, off Los Angeles. Theirs was the second regular spring training site.

Florida was far from becoming the spring hub of activity which hosted 18 clubs in 1978. In fact, there were only 16 teams in existence when Branch Rickey brought the St. Louis Browns to St. Petersburg for a one-year stand in 1914, succeeded by the Phillies the following spring.

Rickey's Florida initiative was the result of a series of letters from former Pittsburgh resident Al Lang, a baseball insider who had gone south for his health in 1911 at age 41. Lang had been batboy, clubhouse boy, and errand boy for ballplayers in his youth and, as owner of a successful laundry business, retained his ties with people from the game.

His closest friend was Pirate owner Barney Dreyfuss, whose club trained in Hot Springs, Arkansas. When Lang read that snow kept the team out of action for three straight days, he wrote Dreyfuss that he should join him at St. Pete, which was then a sleepy fishing village of 3,000 residents. Dreyfuss didn't bite.

At first, few fans turned out for St. Petersburg games. But Al Lang—and the growing town—struck gold in 1922, when the Boston Braves moved there from Galveston, Texas. Freezing New Englanders, seeking to cut their winter short, came to see them work out and the city prospered.

In 1927, the Braves were joined by the powerful New York Yankees, shifting sites from New Orleans to Florida.

The Cubs, Pirates, White Sox, and St. Louis Browns spent long stretches of spring training seasons in California, while most other clubs concentrated on Florida and other southeastern states.

Some sites were chosen for rather frivolous reasons—Augusta, for example, was a Detroit spring base because it was the hometown of manager Ty Cobb. When Cobb left Detroit, Detroit left Augusta.

Foreign capitals—Mexico City, Havana, Ciudad Trujillo, and Panama City—also had at least one season in the baseball sun.

Hall of Fame exhibit shows 1907 Red Sox en route by trolley to spring camp at Hot Springs, Arkansas.

## FISHING FOR TIPS

When Bucky Harris was running the Washington Senators one spring, he drew special attention from owner Clark Griffith. Standing in the outfield with a young player, Harris appeared to be teaching the art of proper throwing.

"Look at Harris," said Griffith. "He's never too busy to teach a young fellow the right way."

In truth, Harris was getting tips from the rookie, who had been champion flycaster in his home state of Mississippi.

Red Sox training exercises at Hot Springs involved strenuous leg work.

# SPRING TRAINING TODAY

By 1980, there were 18 clubs training in Florida, seven in Arizona, and one in California. Growth of the Cactus League, as the western half of spring training is called, began some 30 years earlier, when the New York Giants joined the Cleveland Indians, who came to Tucson in 1947. Games played by Florida clubs are listed in standings as the Grapefruit League, but none of the games has a bearing on the championship races.

Spring is a time when all managers predict pennants, optimism reigns supreme, and autographs are as plentiful as hot dogs. The atmosphere is so relaxed that established players often get time off and frequently are excused from long bus trips during the exhibition schedule of roughly 25 games.

All fields have natural grass and most games are played in daylight—factors which change when play begins for real in April—and experimentation is plentiful. Players work at new positions, freshmen get a chance to impress the manager, pitchers loosen their arms by working three innings in their first outings, and veterans seek to hang on for one more season.

Teams could not always afford spring training. In 1919, for example, the St. Louis Cardinals could not pay for the trip south, so Branch Rickey moved them indoors—to the Washington University gymnasium in St. Louis. Out-of-town players tripled up at a nearby hotel, while residents commuted by trolley.

When weather permitted, the Cards practiced on the college's outdoor diamond, which did not have an outfield fence.

Eight years before the Cards trained at home, the Phillies returned from the south with an internal squabble over a rookie pitcher who had been purchased from Syracuse for $500.

Manager Charlie Dooin wanted to return the young player and get his money back, but Pat Moran, whose "B" squad included the man in question, insisted he be kept. The rest is history: Grover Cleveland Alexander went on to win 373 games, as many as Christy Mathewson and more than any other National League pitcher.

## THE MEANING OF SPRING TRAINING

*Hall of Famer Ralph Kiner, home run king of the Pirates and New York broadcaster, on spring training:*

*"Spring training is made for the owners, managers, and general managers. It's the only time they can really go down and relax, enjoy what's going on, and not worry about whether their team won or lost.*

*"As a player, I looked on spring training as an experiment—a chance to try, for maybe 20 or 30 days, to come up with some new theory that I might work on and see if it held up. Sometimes it would be completely different from what I had been doing.*

*"Probably the biggest thing I ever did in spring training was to go to a much heavier bat. It worked well; I stayed with it and used it the rest of my career. I used a 42-ounce bat and then dropped down to 37, which is extremely heavy compared to what the average player uses (anywhere from 30 to 32 ounces).*

*"I couldn't have cared less about what I hit during the spring, but I did have to play all the ballgames because I was the so-called 'attraction' of the Pittsburgh Pirates."*

Manager Connie Mack, who preferred a business suit to baseball flannels, instructs prospects at 1949 Philadelphia A's spring camp. From left are pitcher Bobby Shantz (soon to be the club's top star), infielder Todd Davis, catcher Joe Astroth, and pitchers Jim Wilson and Clem Hausman.

# AT THE CAMPS

Though many madcap adventures have transpired during spring training, the pre-season period was—and is—a serious time for players and clubs.

"I looked forward to spring training," said Clyde King, a Brooklyn Dodgers' pitcher of the '40s and '50s who later managed the San Francisco Giants and Atlanta Braves.

"I actually couldn't wait to get there. I was not a great player, so I had to work hard and utilize everything I had to make the ballclub. Some players didn't like training and would make excuses to get there late. On the Brooklyn club, there weren't that many jobs open. We had Gil Hodges, Roy Campanella, Pee Wee Reese, and others.

"We went down to Vero Beach and lived together in the barracks. The guys played pool at night, and they had movies sometimes. We ate together in the cafeteria—another one of those togetherness things. If you had your family, you could live out.

"One year, we trained in the Dominican Republic. Leo Durocher was our manager and his wife, Laraine Day, was an actress who would bring current movies to our hotel one night a week. There were so many things they did for us that we appreciated—even though we didn't say so."

The tradition of off-the-field entertainment during the spring is almost as old as the game itself. One spring, John McGraw offered Ted Sullivan $50 to bring the movies of the 1913-14 round-the-world baseball tour from Dallas to Marlin, Texas where the Giants were training.

Sullivan came and, with McGraw's approval, hired a piano player to provide background music. The musician was instructed to play "The Marseillaise" when the film showed the group arriving in France and "God Save the King" when it got to England. Rehearsals went perfectly, with Sullivan reading his text to the musical background. But McGraw managed to bribe the pianist to switch national anthems—playing the German anthem for the arrival in Paris and "The Marseillaise" for England. Sullivan tried to outshout the music as McGraw & Co. howled.

**Roy Campanella puts on catching gear at Vero Beach, Fla.**

**Graceful fielders at Philadelphia A's spring camp included (from left) Eddie Collins Jr., Bob Johnson, Dee Miles, and Sam Chapman.**

The concept of spring exercises hasn't changed much since the Philadelphia Athletics worked out in West Palm Beach in 1946.

# THE IMPORTANCE OF CONDITIONING

There were smiles among the Yankees of the Babe Ruth era—until the slugger nearly ate himself out of the league at the end of spring training in 1925. Fined $5000 by manager Miller Huggins for breaking training rules, Ruth endured a miserable season. Absent for long spells, he lost 88 points from his 1924 batting average, hit 21 fewer home runs, and knocked in 55 fewer runs than the year before.

Ruth paid careful attention to his physical condition that winter and he engineered a mighty comeback in 1926, returning the Yankees—who had fallen to seventh in '25—to the top of the league.

Ten years later, Lefty Gomez told writers covering the Yankee spring camp, "I'm going to stay at 160 pounds. A couple of years ago, Joe McCarthy told me if I could take on 15 pounds, I'd make people forget Lefty Grove. I took 'em on and people almost forgot Lefty Gomez."

Weight is the first thing managers discuss in the spring. When players report, they march to the scales almost before they do anything else. Often, they are asked to report at a specific weight and may be fined $100 a pound for every pound exceeding the limit.

Ty Cobb lasted twenty-four years mainly because he maintained a constant vigil on his physical condition, running 10 miles per day in the winter and wearing weighted shoes during spring training. At Detroit's training camp, he habitually installed steel plates into his shoes when he reported—an effort to strengthen his leg muscles. On opening day, the plates were removed.

Cobb, Tris Speaker, Honus Wagner, and other Hall of Famers enjoyed long careers because they safeguarded their legs. (Often, when a pitcher retires, he is forced to quit because his legs can no longer take the strain; the arm may still be sound.)

Managers have always emphasized running and nutrition as keys to conditioning, and flexibility has won such recognition from clubs that several have hired special flexibility coaches for spring training. The theory is that flexible athletes—who know how to reach, twist, and even fall—are less likely to suffer injuries.

Since throwing is an unnatural act, pitchers must prepare themselves slowly, building up strength and endurance not only in their arms but also in their legs. When durable Ed Walsh, a 40-game winner for the 1908 White Sox, failed to do this one spring, he began a premature backslide from the pitching heights. ☞

## CURRENT TRAINING SITES
*Where the big-league clubs hold spring training today:*

### NATIONAL LEAGUE

**Atlanta—West Palm Beach, Florida**
**Chicago—Mesa, Arizona**
**Cincinnati—Plant City, Florida**
**Houston—Kissimmee, Florida**
**Los Angeles—Vero Beach, Florida**
**Montreal—West Palm Beach, Florida**
**New York—Port St. Lucie, Florida**
**Philadelphia—Clearwater, Florida**
**Pittsburgh—Bradenton, Florida**
**St. Louis—St. Petersburg, Florida**
**San Diego—Yuma, Arizona**
**San Francisco—Scottsdale, Arizona**

### AMERICAN LEAGUE

**Baltimore—Miami, Florida**
**Boston—Winter Haven, Florida**
**California—Palm Springs, California**
**Chicago—Sarasota, Florida**
**Cleveland—Tucson, Arizona**
**Detroit—Lakeland, Florida**
**Kansas City—Baseball City, Florida**
**Milwaukee—Chandler, Arizona**
**Minnesota—Orlando, Florida**
**New York—Fort Lauderdale, Florida**
**Oakland—Phoenix, Arizona**
**Seattle—Tempe, Arizona**
**Texas—Port Charlotte, Florida**
**Toronto—Dunedin, Florida**

Sliding practice is an important element of spring training. Keeping legs in shape has always been the secret of baseball longevity.

Philadelphia Phillies

On the first day of training at Paso Robles, California, in 1913, Walsh was on the diamond behind the hotel when he spied fellow pitcher Jim Scott throwing hard to catcher Ray Schalk. Scott had played ball during the winter and was already in prime condition, so he was able to throw at top velocity without any trouble.

Walsh hadn't thrown since the final game of the Chicago City Series the previous fall, but a tang of jealousy gave him an urgent desire to throw as hard—or harder—than Scott.

Since manager Jim Callahan and coach Kid Gleason weren't around to stop him, Walsh began to throw as hard as he could. The sore arm which followed ruined his career.

## TRAINING CAMP TRADE

*One of the most unusual trades in baseball history occurred in 1951, when the New York Yankees and New York Giants swapped training camps for one year only. The Giants trained in St. Petersburg, Florida, and the Yankees in Phoenix, Arizona, in '51, met in the World Series that fall, then reverted to their original sites in 1952.*

## AL LANG'S LEGACY

*The dream of the late Al Lang, who put Florida on the baseball map, lives on in the form of $3.2 million Al Lang Field in St. Petersburg, spring home of the New York Mets and St. Louis Cardinals.*

*The field, several blocks east of the National Association of Professional Baseball Leagues (minor league headquarters), also hosts the St. Pete Cardinals of the Florida State League (Class A) in the summer and Florida Instructional League teams in the fall.*

## MUSIAL'S VIEWS

*Hall of Famer Stan Musial, a dud in spring training as a rookie with the 1942 Cardinals, suggests pre-season workouts are not accurate indicators of player potential.*

*"I think there is a tendency to overrate pitchers and underrate hitters down there," he said. "In most of the parks, the background for a hitter is terrible and you really notice the difference when you get home and see those double-decked stands."*

# IN THE NORTH

In 1897, the New York Giants abandoned their spring training headquarters in Jacksonville in favor of Lakewood, New Jersey. In 1943, bowing to wartime travel restrictions, they again gave up Florida (Miami this time) for Lakewood.

The 1897 move was engineered by team owner Andrew Freedman, a Tammany Hall bigwig who wanted to see his club in action without missing council meetings in New York.

The mid-'40s transfer was dictated by the Landis Line, wartime spring training directive issued by Baseball Commissioner Kenesaw Mountain Landis. Landis ruled that no club could train south of the Ohio or Potomac Rivers nor west of the Mississippi (with the exception of the St. Louis Browns and Cardinals.).

Long training trips by the 16 big-league teams had tied up transportation vital to the nation's war effort, making the Landis Line mandatory for the springs of 1943, 1944, and 1945.

All but six of the 16 teams chose close-to-home sites and trained there all three seasons. The others shifted around—the Braves jumping to Washington, D.C., in 1945 after two springs in Wallingford, Connecticut, and the Phils switching to Hershey, Pennsylvania the same year from Wilmington, Delaware.

The Philadelphia Athletics, who shared Wilmington in '43, transferred to Frederick, Maryland, and the Yankees moved from Asbury Park to Atlantic City, New Jersey, at the same time. The Red Sox and White Sox relocated for the final year of training in the north—Boston moving from Medford, Massashusetts, to Atlantic City and Chicago switching from French Lick to Terre Haute, Indiana.

At Lakewood, the Giants were the sole occupants of a 45-room hotel. Incredible as it may seem in retrospect, the players traveled to their practices by horse-and-buggy because it was the most practical means in view of wartime gas rationing and rubber shortages.

That first day of training in 1943, the club began its journey to the South Jersey pinelands by assembling in the team's New York office on West 42nd Street. They crossed the Hudson River by ferry, rode the rails to the Lakewood depot, and then boarded the horse-drawn tally-ho to reach the Hotel de Brannick. The hotel had been shut all winter, but was made ready for the invading ballplayers.

New York's other National League entry, the Brooklyn Dodgers, made Bear Mountain, New York their spring port o' call. The club also had an option to use the West Point fieldhouse for a minimum of three hours per day—and did just that when bad weather prevailed. Even when the weather was fair, it was a far cry from the warmth of the south.

Asked what the players wore, former pitcher Clyde King answered, "Everything we had! We wore turtlenecks and more than one sweatshirt—sometimes heavy long sweatshirts. I don't remember long-johns. I do know there wasn't a whole lot of complaining even though it was cold. They had great food there.

"On the real bad days, we'd go to West Point, but there weren't too many of those," King continued. "The cold really doesn't stand out in my mind as a discomfort; maybe my enthusiasm for the game made me overlook that. I do remember working out on the field at Bear Mountain and seeing Hessian Lake—behind the lodge—frozen over.

"We played some exhibitions at Bear Mountain and some on the Army field at West Point. We were ready by the time the season opened—as ready as anyone else because everyone trained in the north. Our site was a perfect one; it was close to New York and we enjoyed it. Mrs. McKeever, whose husband was a former owner of the Dodgers, used to play the piano in the inn at night. We'd all gather around and sing songs."

King recalled a classic moment involving team president Branch Rickey. "Mr. Rickey believed in running speed and pacing," he said. "We had a pitcher named Claude Crocker who was a roomate of mine at the University of North Carolina. We signed at the same time, but he threw a lot harder than I did. Mr. Rickey worked very hard on trying to teach him to control the ball.

"One day, he was coaching him while the whole team was around him. Mr. Rickey took off that hat he used to wear, laid it down on home plate, and said to Crocker, 'You haven't thrown a strike in your last 15 pitches. If you hit that hat one time out of three pitches, I'll give you $25.' ☞

## HOPE SPRINGS ETERNAL

*Spring is a time of hope—especially among young players seeking permanent jobs in the big leagues. Sometimes, deserving players don't make it because veteran incumbents block the way.*

*Former Cleveland slugger Al Rosen remembers, "I was sent out three years in a row. I was really down. I had been Most Valuable Player in every league I played in. There wasn't much more that I could prove."*

*In 1950, things changed. Ken Keltner, starting to deteriorate in the field, couldn't play regularly anymore. "Lou Boudreau, the manager, didn't want to let him go," Rosen said. "He had strong feelings of loyalty to his old players. But Hank Greenberg, the general manager, wanted me."*

The Sporting News

"So Crocker wound up and hit that hat on the first pitch. That's one of the few times I've ever seen Mr. Rickey speechless. He didn't know *what* to do. After he recovered, he said, 'You see what concentration will do for you?' I'll never forget that, after being stunned and speechless, he came back with the perfect answer."

Like the Dodgers, the Pittsburgh Pirates learned to cope with unpredictable conditions. Manager Frankie Frisch told his crew the first day at Muncie, Indiana: "If you can see your breath when you walk out of the hotel in the morning, don't go to the field. Go to the high school gymnasium. We'll play basketball instead of baseball."

On tolerable days, the Pirates worked out at the city park, which had an acceptable diamond, complete with grandstand and bleachers, and a stone house that served as team clubhouse. Fortunately, the stone building had an ample fireplace and team trainer Doc Jorgensen kept it burning. Fresh wood became an important part of the trainer's equipment.

It was at Muncie that each rostered player was asked how much of his salary he wanted withheld for purchase of war bonds. It was also at Muncie that pitcher Rip Sewell found a potted palm in the window of a local barber shop and transported it to the team's hotel—an effort to remind the athletes of brighter days to come.

En route to one exhibition game, the team rode 100 miles in an unheated baggage car because the coaches were packed with soldiers. Diners were often too full to accommodate them—if there were any on the trains at all. But no one complained. The war had a searing impact on individuals as well as ballclubs.

When wounded soldiers took over the Yankees' indoor headquarters at the 112th Field Artillery Armory in Atlantic City, the club moved without a whimper. The Boston Red Sox, who trained outdoors in Pleasantville, six miles away, also sought new quarters for bad-weather days because they had agreed to use the armory on a rotating basis with the Yankees.

Some clubs had more serious problems. In Cairo, Illinois, which did not have the variety of facilities offered by Atlantic City, the St. Louis Cardinals suddenly found their field under four feet of water—levee seepage from the swollen Ohio and Mississippi Rivers.

On March 26, 1945, the Cardinals packed their gear for St. Louis and completed training in Sportsman's Park.

In 1946, with the war over, every club in the majors returned to the typical tropical climes of spring training—the adventures in the north reduced to an unusual footnote in the long history of the game.

## MILWAUKEE BLOOMS IN SPRING

*The City of Milwaukee has twice won teams during spring training. On March 18, 1953, the Boston Braves announced their franchise would become the Milwaukee Braves that season—the first change in the baseball map since 1903. The Braves moved again, to Atlanta, after the 1965 season but in March 1970, with little more than a week before opening day, the Seattle Pilots, a 1969 expansion team with financial woes, became the Milwaukee Brewers.*

## SPRING GAMES DRAW WELL

*Major league teams drew 1,146,579 fans during their spring training exhibition season of 1978, an 8 per cent increase over the record attendance achieved in 1977.*

*A total of 955,608 fans attended games at regular training sites, while 190,989 more passed through the gates when games were played in Puerto Rico, the Dominican Republic, Mexico, and major league parks in Atlanta, Houston, Los Angeles, San Diego, and Anaheim, California.*

*Eleven teams reported new spring attendance peaks.*

*The New York Yankees, 1977 World Champions, with 75,395 fans in 12 dates at Fort Lauderdale, Florida, had an average of 6282 per game. Nine of the Yankees' 11 road games drew standing-room-only crowds, while the Cincinnati Reds had SRO audiences at 12 of 13 contests.*

The Sporting News

*Where Clubs Will Kindle Camp-Fires*

**NATIONAL LEAGUE**
(Figures in black circles)
1—Cardinals, Cairo, Ill.
2—Reds, Bloomington, Ind.
3—Dodgers, Bear M'tain, N. Y.
4—Pirates, Muncie, Ind.
5—Cubs, French Lick, Ind.
6—Braves, Washington, D. C.
7—Phils, Wilmington, Del.
8—Giants, Lakewood, N. J.

**AMERICAN LEAGUE**
(Figures in outlined circles)
1—Yankees, Atlantic City, N. J.
2—Senators, College Park, Md.
3—Indians, Lafayette, Ind.
4—White Sox, Terre Haute, Ind.
5—Tigers, Evansville, Ind.
6—Red Sox, Pleasantville, N. J.
7—Browns, Cape Girardeau, Mo.
8—Athletics, Frederick, Md.

# HEADING HOME

Rising hotel and transportation costs killed the concept of spring barnstorming by teams headed home to open the season. Current clubs keep their home bases in operation almost to the eve of their openers, playing exhibition game schedules that extend into April.

By 1951, the barnstorming routine was already on the decline. The Yankees, training in Phoenix that spring, played dates in Los Angeles and San Francisco—minor league cities then—on an 11-game jaunt to the west, but made only a $4000 profit after packing parks at every stop. Smaller crowds produced larger profits—encouraging annual baseball tours—during the Babe Ruth era.

Small towns had small diamonds—with stands often seating 3000 or less—and an appearance by Ruth (whose fame spread through the print media) guaranteed an overflow. Fans stood behind roped-off sections of the outfield and daredevil youngsters clung to trees beyond the outfield fence—if indeed there was a fence.

In one southern park, Ruth homered into an imposing oak tree just beyond the right field barrier. The tree was crammed with young fans yearning for a look at the living legend of the Yankees, but Ruth's blast—hit like a shot—cleared the branches in record time.

Ruth was a tremendous drawing card. The touring Yankees of 1928, sweeping through Texas and Oklahoma after leaving St. Petersburg, compiled a total spring attendance of 128,000 and made a handsome haul of $60,000—a lot of money in those days. Ruth received 10 per cent of the gate receipts—an arrangement unique in baseball history.

The first whistle-stop spring trip undertaken by special agreement between two major league clubs occurred in 1918, when the Giants and Tigers trained in Texas.

John McGraw's Giants had agreed to barnstorm with Ty Cobb's Tigers, but Detroit's temperamental star scrapped with his rivals, left the tour, and completed his training with the Cincinnati Reds. Cobb's departure, coupled with attendance already hindered by World War I, posed financial problems for McGraw.

The two-team tour of the longest duration involved the New York Giants and Cleveland Indians, who first locked horns in 1934, when the Giants trained in Miami and Cleveland in New Orleans. When the clubs became the first teams to invade Arizona in the late '40s, their barnstorming became even more practical, and continued for more than twenty-five years—even after the Giants' shift to San Francisco made scheduling more difficult.

Barnstorming did have advantages: welcoming crowds at every depot, hero-worshipping fans packed into every park, and enough attention and affection in town to cover not only the players but the entire traveling party—even the writers.

Spring training is still fun, but it has changed.

Barnstormers Babe Ruth and Lou Gehrig (left), here advancing the cause of a world's championship rodeo in 1928, enabled the Yankees to rake in huge crowds en route home from spring camp.

## PITCHERS AHEAD OF HITTERS

*Early in the baseball season, pitchers have the edge on hitters. Some hurlers have rounded into mid-season form long before the hitters have sharpened their batting eyes.*

*In 1944, Chicago Cubs' manager Jimmie Wilson explained why:*

*"Any manager can get his pitchers into condition to start off the season at an effective clip, regardless of whether his club trains in the south or in the north. The manager can make the pitchers do the right amount of running and throwing to be ready to hurl at top speed when the bell rings.*

*"But the manager cannot train his hitters. They must train themselves. He can see to it that they get lots of running and also lots of hitting practice, but he cannot do a single thing about perfecting their timing. That must come from actual competition and even in a long southern training season many hitters do not get enough of this sort of preparation to match the pitchers in being ready to play for keeps. So the pitchers annually start with an edge."*

# CHAPTER EIGHTEEN

# Other Leagues Other Lands

# THE NATIONAL ASSOCIATION

The minor leagues, widely known as the training ground for the majors, provide a place for talented players to polish their skills and garner valuable experience that will eventually enable them to compete against the best ballplayers in the world.

The National Association of Professional Baseball Leagues has been representing minor league baseball since September 1901, when it was created to protect minor league operators against wanton raids of their players by major league teams.

With rare exceptions (Sandy Koufax is one) every big league player reaches the majors only after spending time in the minors. Ty Cobb, Rogers Hornsby, and Babe Ruth were among the superstars who began their professional careers in the minor leagues.

The first minor league, the International Association, was organized in Pittsburgh on February 20, 1877.

Other leagues sprang up quickly. In 1887, three of them merged to form the International League, but an unwieldy ten-club structure was plagued by numerous franchise shifts and all but extinguished during the Players League revolt of the majors in 1890 (the only year since its founding that the International failed to finish a season).

In 1902, the league launched an eleven-year period of stability thanks in part to construction of new ballparks by prosperous streetcar companies. The lines hoped to make money from fans riding trolleys to the parks.

NATIONAL ASSOCIATION · PROFESSIONAL BASEBALL LEAGUES

1901
The American way
BASEBALL TODAY
1951

## CHALLENGES TO THE MINORS

The Federal League, an attempted third major league in 1914-15, weakened the International League by invading many of its cities and World War I so strickened the minors in 1918 that only the IL finished its season.

Since that time, the International has prospered despite much shifting of clubs, usually in proportion to growth or decline of cities along the eastern seaboard.

Along with other minor leagues, the IL survived raids from the majors by enforcing the National Agreement, originally a ten-year pact, that promised to punish players and clubs who violated contracts; established salary limits; fixed a reserve rule which bound each player to his club; and classified leagues according to levels of play.

Top circuits were classified as Double-A, then A, B, C, and D in declining order of ability. Later, the three top categories were changed to AAA, AA, and A. In 1963, all bottom categories were dropped and leagues were changed to AAA, AA, or A with the sole exception of the Rookie Leagues, the modern equivalent of Class D.

Minor leagues are often called "bush leagues," because of the long bus rides, or "hamburger leagues," because players don't receive enough meal money to buy more expensive meat.

With rare exceptions, travel and hotel accommodations are well below major league standards, ballparks have poor lighting systems, and opportunity for recognition is non-existent.

After escaping the minors, some players often laugh at conditions they left behind: shower heads that only came up waist high in Leesburg, a four-headed shower stall that flooded the clubhouse in Statesville, a movie theater with rocking chairs in the same town, a community washroom in the hotel at Dubuque, and steamy, deteriorating hotels that invariably were in worse condition than the ballparks.

## WORKHORSE

*In 1878, Buffalo Bisons pitcher Jim Galvin had a record of 75 wins, 25 defeats, and three ties. He completed 96 of 101 games, threw 17 shutouts, and had a 10-5 mark in exhibition play against the National League. He started and finished his club's first 23 games and relieved in the 24th. Buffalo then belonged to the International Association.*

## HIGH-SCORING SERIES

*From June 9-11, 1978, the Reno Silver Sox and Visalia Oaks of the Class A California League combined for 101 runs. The games, played at Reno, Nevada, set several league records for offensive production. Reno won the opener, 24-12. Then Visalia won by consecutive scores of 27-17 and 14-7.*

**Minor-league life brings fans closer to the players. Tight budgets forced countless promotions, including this Ball Day giveaway by the old Toronto Maple Leafs. Sparky Anderson, soon to be a major-league manager, was the key attraction.**

# THE TIGHT ECONOMY

Money, always hard to come by in minor league baseball, was especially scarce during the Depression years. Members of the Los Angeles Angels were happy to get winners' shares of $210 per man for beating the Pacific Coast League All-Stars after the 1934 season. Losing shares were worth $122.

Things became so tight that the Northern League allowed its clubs the use of only one ball per game. One team conserved so well that it had two-dozen balls left to sell to the local school system when the season ended.

In the heyday of the independent operator, Chattanooga owner Joe Engel was trying to sign a player. The athlete sent him a message: "Double your offer or count me out." Engel wired back, "1, 2, 3, 4, 5, 6, 7, 8, 9, 10."

As late as 1972, minor leaguers in the Class A Midwest League got only $3.50 per day for meal money, as opposed to $18 given major-leaguers. The average minor league salary was little more than $1,000 per month.

In 1926, the St. Louis Cardinals, with Branch Rickey at the controls, sought to purchase a player from the Joplin, Missouri club. Their interest became known and a small bidding war ensued. The Cardinals, already operating on a shoe-string, were knocked out quickly.

"If we can't buy the contracts of players," Rickey told team owner Sam Breadon, "we'll have to raise our own."

When Cardinal scouts started signing large numbers of players, other teams jumped into the act. But Baseball Commissioner Kenesaw Mountain Landis never liked the idea, called it "slavery," and predicted the farm system would ruin the independence of the minors.

Development of the farms did not hurt the minors, since major league organizations poured their own resources into player development, hired the managers, and maintained the ballparks of their minor league teams. Many of the major-minor links were by "working agreement," giving the minor league team the chance to retain local ownership while having a big-league affiliation.

Rickey cultivated his farm system concept so thoroughly that by 1946, when he was running the Brooklyn Dodgers, the club had the amazing total of 20 farm teams, including two each at the Triple-A and Double-A levels.

Three years later, there were 448 teams in 59 minor leagues—the National Association's largest roll call. Independents and farms thrived; minor league attendance was 26 million, while major league attendance was 10 million.

By 1963, the minors were reduced to 130 teams in 18 leagues. The farm system idea had taken over and external factors forced reductions in the minor leagues. An agreement between majors and minors stipulated that every major league club must own or have an affiliation with at least one team at each of the three classifications in the minors, AAA, AA, and A. ☞

"What killed the minors? The answer is simple," said Bobby Bragan, president of the National Association in 1978. "Television and air-conditioning were the big things. A fan can sit home and watch a big-league game in the comfort of his living room on a hot summer night instead of spending $1 or $2 to come out to the ballpark."

Bragan said that minor league teams can counteract such drawbacks by promoting heavily. "Three things are essential for a successful team," he insisted. "Geography, a good operator, and a facility."

The largest crowd ever to attend a minor league game turned out in Denver for Fireworks Night, an Independence Day celebration, in 1982. A total of 65,666 fans passed through the turnstiles of Mile High Stadium. Denver held the previous minor league mark with more than 59,000 for Fireworks Night 1981.

Jersey City sold 65,391 tickets to the 1940 opener at Roosevelt Stadium (capacity 40,000), thanks in large measure to the extensive footwork of men working for Mayor Frank Hague. In 1948 and 1949, opening games in the city reported ticket sales of 52,000.

There were 52,833 fans in Baltimore Memorial Stadium for a Little World Series game against Louisville on October 9, 1944.

Of the many top teams in minor league history, the 1937 Newark Bears, an affiliate of the New York Yankees, were probably the strongest. Sixteen of seventeen Newark players made the majors—nine of them in 1938. The club's record for 1937 was 109 wins and 43 losses.

Jack Dunn's Baltimore Orioles, also an International League team, ranks second to Newark. From 1919-25, they won seven straight pennants. The 1920 race was especially exciting when Baltimore and Toronto went into the final month separated by only one game, the Maple Leafs on top. Toronto won 20 of its last 22 but Baltimore won 25 in a row to win the pennant.

The best of the Pacific Coast League's clubs was the Los Angeles Angels of 1934, which recorded a league record .733 winning percentage with 137 wins and 50 defeats. Among the circuit's top stars was Joe DiMaggio, who put together a 61-game hitting streak for San Francisco in 1933.

The Baseball Hall of Fame is very much aware of the contributions that minor league baseball has made to the game. At the original dedication of the museum on July 9, 1939, each of 41 existing minor leagues sent one star player to participate in a minor league all-star game. The "Doubledays" beat the "Cartwrights," 9-6.

Baseball owes a debt to the Western League for introducing runs batted in (1911) and earned run average (1913) as regular statistics. It also owes a debt to the minors for providing the stage for stars to make their final farewells.

Lefty O'Doul, 1929 National League batting champion, went to bat as a pinch-hitter for Vancouver (Pacific Coast) at age 59 in 1956 and belted a triple! He was followed by 51-year-old coach Eddie Taylor, who singled him home.

Warren Spahn, the most successful southpaw in National League history, made token appearances for Tulsa and Mexico City after leaving the NL at age 44 in 1965. Those games came back to haunt Spahn; they delayed his candidacy for the Hall of Fame. Rules stipulate that eligible players must have been retired five years from professional baseball—minors as well as majors. ☞

## AN UMPIRE GOES TO BAT

*An umpire was used as a pinch-hitter in a Pioneer League game on June 17, 1945, at Great Falls, Montana. When one of the regular umps failed to arrive, one player from each team was assigned to umpire at the infield corners. Jim Keating, "designated umpire" for Great Falls, was used as a pinch-hitter—another man replaced him as umpire—and singled to help his team beat Ogden, 11-10.*

## DISEASE HALTED NEW ORLEANS

*An outbreak of yellow fever in New Orleans in 1905 forced that city's Southern Association club to play all its games on the road.*

## LOW PURCHASE PRICE

*In 1909, Chattanooga bought the franchise and players of Little Rock for $12,000.*

## OUTFIELD OBSTACLE

*Atlanta's Ponce de Leon Park, home of the powerful Crackers, had a magnolia tree in center field. Though the park was last used in 1964, and subsequently replaced by a shopping center, the magnolia tree was left untouched.*

## LONGEST GAME

*Pawtucket (International) beat Rochester, 3-2, in a 1981 AAA contest that consumed 33 innings, the most in professional baseball history. The game, which took 8:25 to play, began April 18, was suspended, then concluded June 23. The longest previous game, a 29-inning affair in 1969, occurred in the Florida State League.*

## AN UNORTHODOX STOLEN BASE

*On June 21, 1917, Ray McKee of San Francisco stole third base with the bases loaded—and was exonerated when the umpire called a balk on the pitcher.*

## HIGH SCORE CAUSES CONFUSION

*When Corsicana swamped Texarkana, 51-3, at Ennis, Texas, on June 15, 1902, disbelieving telegraph operators reported the score as 5-3.*

## EQUAL HONORS

*Each player on the Douglas (Arizona) Copper Kings hit exactly one home run in a game on August 18, 1958.*

Among perennial minor-leaguers of the past were Ox Eckhardt of the San Francisco Seals, Nick Cullop and Tom Winston of Columbus, slugger Joe Bauman, and Smead Jolley, who led six different leagues in hitting.

Steve Bilko, hefty firstbaseman of the Los Angeles Angels in the mid-'50s, twice hit more than 50 home runs in a season at tiny Wrigley Field, the team's home park, and seemed disappointed when the Reds finally called him to the majors.

Bauman, only man to hit more than 70 home runs in a season (he hit 72), never got the call. Gene Rye, who hit three homers in an inning on August 6, 1930, did—and hit .179 with no homers in a quick cup-of-coffee with the 1931 Red Sox.

Babe Ruth hit exactly one home run in the minors—a three-run blast for Providence (International) on September 5, 1914. Ruth, then a pitcher, also hurled a one-hitter against Toronto that day, winning 9-0.

Billy Martin, scrappy Yankee infielder of the '50s, wasn't a feared hitter in the majors, but he was in the minors. At Phoenix of the Texas League in 1947, the 19-year-old Martin hit .392 with 174 runs batted in, with 230 hits in 130 games. He also made 55 errors at third base; he became a quality secondbaseman later.

**Joe DiMaggio (second from left) made San Francisco Seals manager Ike Caveney (right) a happy man with a 61-game hitting streak in the minors. He also brought smiles to team officials Charles (Doc) Strub (left) and Charles Graham.**

# THE MODERN MAJOR-MINOR RELATIONSHIP

The firm establishment of the farm system has led to certain rules regarding treatment of players owned by one organization.

Each major league player is subject to six options. He may be included on the big-league team's forty-man "protected" list during the off-season and be sent back to that team's minor league system six times. Once those options expire, the major league team must keep him or risk losing him to another organization through the annual winter draft of minor-leaguers (1) who were not included on their parent team's 40-man "protected list" or (2) whose options have expired, leaving them "frozen" in the minors and ineligible for recall by the parent club.

Should a "frozen" player pass through the draft untouched, he may rejoin the parent team only through purchase—and only after all other clubs have waived their right to claim him.

Draft sessions are conducted in reverse order of the standings, so that the weakest teams will have the chance to obtain the best players in the minor leagues. By the '70s, however, the best minor league talent was invariably included on the 40-man lists, which become effective September 1, leaving slim pickings from the rest of the minors.

# THE FEDERAL LEAGUE

Though player records from the two-year Federal League are included in major league lifetime statistics, many historians insist the Federal was not a major at all, but a glorified minor circuit which dreamed it had made the big time.

The league began as the financially unstable United States League in 1912, with clubs in such unlikely places as Richmond and Lynchburg, Virginia and Reading, Pennsylvania. By June, the league had folded, but its remains spawned the first Federal League the following year. Superstar pitcher Cy Young managed Pittsburgh, but the 1913 FL was strictly a minor league which received little attention.

Late that year, however, Chicago coal magnate James Gilmore reorganized the League and began to pursue top caliber players. He and other industrialists built new ballparks in each of the eight FL cities and used the facilities as bait to attract major-leaguers. One of the parks, Wrigley Field, remains in use today as home of the Chicago Cubs.

A Cub star of 1912, shortstop Joe Tinker, was the first "name" player to jump from the majors. After he signed as manager of the Chicago Whales, others followed suit: Hal Chase, Danny Murphy, Jack Quinn, and later Chief Bender and Eddie Plank.

But the Federal League failed to attract the quantity of talent it sought and was forced to rely primarily on top minor-leaguers and second-liners from the majors.

Though Ty Cobb was offered a five-year, $75,000 contract in the Federal League, he didn't want to risk his career on an uncertain venture, and chose to retain his $12,000 deal with Detroit. But Chief Bender and Eddie Plank, ace pitchers of the Philadelphia Athletics, jumped after winning 33 games for the champion A's of 1914. ☞

## NO-HITTER PRODUCES BIG TAB

*In January 1971, lefthander Ken Frailing pitched a no-hitter for Mazatlan in the Mexican Winter League. More than 50 fans—of whom he knew only a handful—took him out to celebrate the city's first no-hitter. They went to six bars and partied into the wee hours. The next morning, Frailing found the bill for the entire group in his mailbox. Each person in the party had signed his name at the bars, running up a total tab of more than $500.*

## RETREAT

*When a number of International League clubs moved out of cities invaded by the new Federal League in 1914-15, the league won the uncomplimentary nickname "the Belgium of Baseball."*

## EARLY EXCITEMENT

*When Baltimore made its Federal League debut in April 1914, a crowd of 27,000 stood 15 rows deep in the outfield to watch the Terrapins whip Buffalo, 3-2.*

## DOUBLE-TEAMING

*Indianapolis, home of the first Federal League pennant, had two teams in 1914, as the Indianapolis Indians of the American Association also played there. The Feds had no nickname until the results of a fan poll were made known a week after the season opened. Though the fans picked "Hoosier Federals," the media invariably referred to the team as "Hoosiers" or "HooFeds."*

"We lost the World Series because our team was divided into factions," insisted owner-manager Connie Mack. "Half wanted to jump to the Federal League and the other half wanted to stay."

Mack decided to sell his stars before they left him without compensation (the same argument advanced by Oakland A's owner Charley Finley after the advent of free agency in 1976).

Indianapolis won the first FL flag in 1914, but the franchise moved to Newark, New Jersey the following year. Other Federal teams were located in Chicago, Baltimore, Brooklyn, Buffalo, Kansas City, Pittsburgh, and St. Louis. The owner of Ward Baking owned the Brooklyn club and hinted he would name it the Tip-Tops after his well-known bread, but New York writers quickly quashed the idea. The team became the Brookfeds.

Robert Ward's untimely death, coupled with several court actions and failing finances, forced the Federals to fold after the 1915 season. The National League struck a secret deal to buy out the circuit, but the refusal of American League president Ban Johnson to give a dime to the upstart owners delayed a negotiated peace until December 22.

As part of the deal, Chicago Whales' owner Charles Weeghman took over the Chicago Cubs and Phil Ball of the St. Louis Feds acquired ownership of the St. Louis Browns. Federal contracts were assumed by the league for sale to other teams, with the exception of the Chicago and St. Louis players, who remained with their owners. Players who jumped Organized Ball were allowed to return immediately.

Unhappy with the sudden sellout, Baltimore of the Federal League filed a million-dollar suit against baseball. It won in the lower courts but lost when the United States Supreme Court handed down its 1922 decision exempting the game from antitrust laws.

## CONDITIONS IN MEXICO

*Vic Davalillo was earning $3000 a month for the five-month Mexican League season in 1977 when the Los Angeles Dodgers bought his contract for $2500. "It was a good league with good parks and good fans," he said. "The pitchers threw junk balls—sinkers and sliders. The only bad thing was travel. It wasn't always easy to find a restaurant. Sometimes, we'd finish a game and ride ten hours in the bus on an empty stomach."*

## MINNIE MINOSO'S LAST HURRAH

*Minnie Minoso, long-time American League outfielder, celebrated his 50th birthday as a Mexican League player. Still a solid performer, Minoso was 53 years old in 1976 when he became a player-coach for the White Sox late in the year. He delivered a solid single in six at-bats.*

Renata Galasso, Inc.

**Sal Maglie, back from outlaw Mexican League, helped pitch New York Giants to 1951 pennant.**

# THE MEXICAN LEAGUE

Because the little man can succeed in baseball, Mexicans took an instant liking to the game after it was introduced with a visit by the Chicago White Sox in 1906. In a country where bullfighting is king, and customers eat tacos instead of hot dogs, fans love their "beisbol" as much as their American counterparts.

Professional baseball began in Mexico in 1925, but the country did not enter the structure of Organized Ball until thirty years later, when the Mexican League officially became a Double-A circuit.

Mexican interest in the game became most apparent to American fans in 1946, when Jorge Pasquel and four brothers induced several major league stars to play south of the border.

Mickey Owen, Sal Maglie, Max Lanier, and Vern Stephens were among those Giants' manager Mel Ott called "jumping beans," but Stephens changed his mind when Commissioner Happy Chandler warned that he would impose a five-year ban from Organized Ball on anyone who did not return at once.

The Pasquels promised better salaries, newer ballparks, and pennant races guaranteed to be competitive by rules which barred trades but permitted talent to be distributed equally among teams (with the worst served first.)

Miami Amigos began as lone U.S. entry in Inter-American League, independent AAA circuit, in 1979.

MEXICAN LEAGUE *continued*

Spicy food, stifling heat, foreign customs, and thin mountain air made life difficult for American imports—and "Montezuma's revenge" and other ills also gave jumpers second thoughts. Most returned within two years. Even after joining Organized Ball in 1955, Mexican clubs maintained independence from the major leagues; owners were free to sign or sell players at will. Latin stars Rico Carty and Vic Davalillo, thought to be through in the majors, regained their batting eyes in Mexico and were purchased by big-league teams.

# LATIN WINTER LEAGUES

Mexico is one of many Latin countries which host professional baseball during the off-season of Organized Ball in the United States. Caribbean leagues were operating before World War II, but became more prominent in 1949, when champions from Cuba, Puerto Rico, Panama, and Venezuela competed in the first Caribbean Series.

Fidel Castro's ascension to power eliminated Cuba from such competition, but Nicaragua, the Dominican Republic, and Mexico joined. The series, suspended from 1966-69, resumed in 1970 as a full-fledged championship pageant, *Las Series del Caribe*.

Caribbean winter ball gives Latin stars the chance to play before fans of their native countries, and also gives major- and minor-leaguers an opportunity to improve their game.

Umpires and managers from the United States, like the players, sharpen their skills in the winter leagues. Appearances by major league umpires or managers are rare, but the minors send a steady stream of hopefuls bent on following in the footsteps of Sparky Anderson, Earl Weaver, or Tom Lasorda—who became major league managers after they garnered additional experience in the winter leagues.

The caliber of play in the Caribbean ranks somewhere between Triple-A and the majors, but pitching is erratic and umpiring spotty at best. In Venezuela, for example, all arbiters are natives whose only experience is the winter league games. The mismatch of major league players with minor league (and worse) umpires causes constant arguments, many of them justified.

League and team rules, plus regulations of the Commissioner of Baseball, force the winter league manager to be a juggler, mind-reader, and often a magician.

At playoff time, gamblers, ticket-scalpers, overexcitable fans, and peddlers-turned-vendors swamp the stadiums, causing so many problems that police protection frequently must be provided for visiting teams. Betting, prohibited in Organized Ball, runs rampant in the Caribbean leagues.

American players and officials look at the league as a training ground where young athletes learn new positions, injured regulars test their healing power, and all players perform under conditions that approach major league standards. Fans cheer not only the natives of their country but also their favorite foreigners.

Though some baseball executives insist athletes who play in the winter are too tired to perform well the following season in the majors, veteran Caribbean leagues' manager Ozzie Virgil disagrees. "There's no such thing as too much baseball," he said.

## THE FANS OF THE WINTER LEAGUES

Caribbean baseball fans know the game and are as enthusiastic as fans in Philadelphia or New York, according to veteran manager and coach Preston Gomez. "Everybody waits for the winter leagues because winter baseball is the main sport of the countries involved," he said. "The fans demand that the players perform. They have a short schedule, so every game is important."

## ELIAS SOSA ON DOMINICAN BASEBALL

Relief pitcher Elias Sosa, righthander with several teams in the '70s, insists winter baseball in his native Dominican Republic is better than that. played in Puerto Rico, Venezuela, or Mexico. "We have lots of big league and Triple-A players," he said. "We don't play guys who played in Mexico during the summer or who are retired from the major leagues."

## OZZIE VIRGIL ON VENEZUELAN LEAGUE

Ozzie Virgil, major league player and coach, managed in the Venezuelan Winter League. "On our club," he said, "There always had to be at least four natives on the field. This really limits you in late-inning situations; you have to check your lineup card at all times. Also, because of the attitude of some of the Americans, you could wake up any morning and find you're two or three players short. If you're in a playoff fight, that could kill you."

# THE NEGRO LEAGUES

Before Jackie Robinson broke baseball's "color line" in 1947, black players displayed their talents in the Negro National League and Negro American League, six-club circuits with uncertain schedules.

Record-keeping was difficult because games were played not only against league rivals but also against semi-pro clubs or any other opposition which would generate enough revenue to keep a Negro League team solvent.

When Monte Irvin first joined Newark in 1937, he made $150 a month plus one dollar per day meal money. In certain towns, no hotels would accept blacks and the players were housed in private homes. People renting rooms were glad to get some extra money and enjoyed proximity to players whose devotion to the game was not soured by long bus rides, cold meals at odd hours, or lack of recognition.

Many Negro league stars followed Jackie Robinson to the majors: Satchel Paige, Roy Campanella, Willie Mays, Ernie Banks, and Elston Howard among them. Others, like Josh Gibson, were too old when the gates finally opened.

## SATCHEL PAIGE

Satchel Paige, called "the black Matty" after Hall of Famer Christy Mathewson, was probably the most remarkable pitcher in the game's history. The owner of a resilient right arm, which allowed him to work more than 2500 games and throw at least 100 no-hitters, he first appeared in a Negro League contest in 1926. He ended his active career by pitching three innings in a major league game in 1965—thirty-nine years later!

The 6-3, 150-pound pitcher with size 12 shoes pitched 30 straight games, in 30 days, for the 1941 Kansas City Monarchs. Five years later, he threw 64 consecutive scoreless innings (and yielded two runs in 93 frames) to help that club win the pennant.

Paige first played for the Chattanooga Black Lookouts at $50 a month, then went on to countless other cities. Near the end of his career, he pointed to his face and said, "We seen some sights, it and I."

Paige was the king of the barnstormers. He sometimes grossed $35,000 per year—about $1 per mile—on the barnstorming circuit. He was advertised as "Satchel Paige, World's Greatest Pitcher, Guaranteed to Strike Out the First Nine Men."

He demonstrated his pinpoint control by throwing a strike over the top of a Coke bottle.

In 1934, Paige spent the season pitching for a Bismarck, North Dakota team that won 104 of its 105 games. That fall, he was the starting pitcher in a Hollywood, California exhibition game against Dizzy Dean, who had just won 30 games for the St. Louis Cardinals. Dean struck out 15 and yielded one run in thirteen innings. Paige fanned 17 and pitched a shutout.

The following fall, Paige fanned 15 and yielded only three hits to a team of major-minor stars that included Joe DiMaggio. Backed only by a pick-up club, Paige lost, 2-1.

Convinced he had to pitch a shutout to win, the righthander scored a spectacular 8-0 victory over Bob Feller's All-Stars in Los Angeles in the fall of 1947. Paige, who went up to the majors the next season, struck out 16 members of a squad that included Charlie (King Kong) Keller, Phil Rizzuto, Jeff Heath, Ken Keltner, and Bob Lemon.

## THE 1946 NEWARK EAGLES

The 1946 Newark Eagles were one of the best black teams of all time. "We had four really good pitchers," recalled Monte Irvin. "If we could have added another four or five, we could have put our club—intact—right into the major leagues. We were that good."

## SECOND-CLASS CONDITIONS PREVAILED

Life in the Negro leagues was not easy. The average salary was $18-$20 per week and the small, cramped, steamy buses broke down frequently. The Newark Eagles became the first team to buy a large, air-conditioned bus, but did not do so until after World War II.

Satchel Paige . . . barnstorming king

As early as 1930, major-leaguers knew about Paige. That year, Hack Wilson hit an NL record 56 homers and drove home a major league record 190 runs. But he couldn't handle Paige with an all-star team headed by Babe Ruth. "That was some pitching," said Wilson. "It looked like you were winding up with a baseball and throwing a pea."

☆ ☆ ☆

# JOSH GIBSON

Josh Gibson, the Babe Ruth of black baseball, was a catcher who hit more than 70 home runs in a season several times. In his first season, at age 19 in 1930, he hit the only fair ball over the Yankee Stadium roof. His shots were known for distance as well as frequency—and he could hit anyone.

With the Homestead Grays, Gibson faced Kansas City's Satchel Paige in a game at Wrigley Field in Chicago. Gibson hit three home runs and a triple off the top of the fence in right center field.

From 1933-45, Gibson was chosen for the East-West (All-Star) Game every year but 1941, when he played in Mexico. Roy Campanella, the All-Star catcher when Gibson was out of the league, said later, "I couldn't carry Josh's glove. Anything I could do, he could do better."

Gibson hit .457 in 1936 and .440 in 1938, became adept at stealing bases, and worked hard to improve his catching. In the Negro Leagues, freak pitches banned in the majors were legal; many were as hard to catch as they were to hit. Common deliveries included the spitball, emery ball, mud ball, and shine ball—a pitch smeared so thick with Vaseline it caught the glare of the sun on its flight to the plate.

## MANY NEGRO LEAGUE RECORDS LOST

*Records were not kept in all Negro League games because the media paid little attention to them. Several black newspapers did make an attempt, however. The Pittsburgh Courier kept tabs on the Homestead (Pennsylvania) Grays and the Baltimore AfroAmerican and Chicago Defender followed other Negro League teams. When The Courier went out of business, many of the records—haphazard to begin with—were lost.*

## HARD TO BEAT

*John Beckwith, an outstanding hitter who consistently finished second to Oscar Charleston as batting king of the Negro Leagues, finally won the crown himself by hitting .546 in 1930.*

Monte Irvin collection

**Josh Gibson, best hitter in the Negro Leagues, was an exceptional all-around player who constantly won All-Star catching honors over Roy Campanella.**

Backbone of the Pittsburgh Crawfords, greatest Negro League team ever assembled, were (left to right) Oscar Charleston, Josh Gibson, Ted Paige, and Judy Johnson. Photo was taken in 1935.

# OTHER NEGRO LEAGUE STARS

Though Satchel Paige and Josh Gibson were the most famous stars of the Negro leagues, countless others could have been major league standouts had the door been open.

Oscar Charleston, a centerfielder who broke in with the Indianapolis ABC's of 1915, was considered the peer of Willie Mays on defense. As player-manager of the Harrisburg Giants in 1925, he led the Eastern Colored League with a .430 average and 14 home runs.

Cool Papa Bell also played center, though he began as a pitcher for the St. Louis Stars in 1922. Bell, who was active for 29 summers and 21 winters of baseball, was compared to Tris Speaker by observers who saw them both. A switch-hitter with exceptional speed, he stole more than 175 bases with the 1933 Pittsburgh Crawfords.

Pitcher Leon Day was the equal of Bob Gibson and Ray Dandridge the equal of Brooks Robinson, according to Monte Irvin, who spent ten years in the Negro Leagues before signing with the New York Giants.

Bell, Charleston, Gibson, Irvin, and Paige, plus W. Julius (Judy) Johnson, Marty Dihigo, Buck Leonard, and Pop Lloyd won enshrinement in the Hall of Fame for their accomplishments in the Negro Leagues. Of the group, only Paige and Irvin played in the majors.

# BARNSTORMING

Prior to the advent of television, baseball enthusiasts who lived far from major league cities got a chance to see stars in action through the post-season ritual of barnstorming.

Teams of players from various clubs banded together to earn extra money by bringing the game to small towns—usually farming communities—dotted with barns. The invasion of baseball stars became known as "barn storming."

Both major league and Negro League players regarded barnstorming as an economic necessity. For a little extra money, athletes played under tough lights in county fair ballparks and lived out of suitcases on trains.

## STRANGE POTION HELPED SATCHEL PAIGE

Satchel Paige maintained that he was able to avoid injury and maintain top condition through regular application of an ointment called "deer oil," after the daughter of a Sioux chief he met during his North Dakota days. The mixture, the Indian's remedy for snake-bite, did wonders for Paige. "It sends curative sensations vibrating about the muscles," he said.

**Monte Irvin**

Barnstorming can trace its origin to 1888, when the Chicago White Stockings of A.G. Spalding and a team of all-stars headed by John Montgomery Ward of the New York Nationals headed west on a round-the-world tour. They played in such places as Cedar Rapids, Omaha, St. Paul, Colorado Springs, Salt Lake City, Los Angeles, and San Francisco before boarding a boat for the Kingdom of Hawaii.

After games under the palms in the future Fiftieth State, the Spalding-Ward group played in Sydney and Melbourne, Cairo, Naples and Rome, Paris, and London. In Egypt, the baseball contingent paraded through the streets with the White Stockings on donkeys, the all-stars on camels, and their wives in carriages. Games were played with the pyramids as backdrop.

In 1913 and again in 1924, Giants' manager John McGraw participated in similar winter tours. Coupled with Chicago White Sox owner Charles Comiskey on the first trip, McGraw brought the game to Japan and China for the first time. The final game of the 1913 junket was played before 35,000 Britons, including the King of England.

## KINER HAD PREVIEW OF JACKIE ROBINSON

*Slugger Ralph Kiner played barnstorming baseball games against Jackie Robinson before Robinson made the majors in 1947. "Actually, baseball was his worst sport," said Kiner, like Robinson a Californian. "He was a fantastic football player and track star who got into baseball as a third sport. I don't think I've ever seen a better competitor than Jackie Robinson."*

## MANAGER STEALS FIRST BASE

*Frank Peters, manager of Portland (Northwest), was so angry at an umpire's decision one day that he stole first base—literally—and took it to his hotel room. The team forfeited the game.*

## THE FAIRBANKS GOLDPANNERS

*The Fairbanks (Alaska) Goldpanners, a semi-pro club made up of collegians looking for a summer place to play ball, dominated the National Baseball Congress in Wichita, Kansas, through the '60s. Alumni who made the majors included Tom Seaver, Andy Messersmith, Rick Monday, Dave Kingman, and Graig Nettles.*

# THE GAME IN JAPAN

Because there is no football, basketball, or hockey to distract the Japanese sports fan, baseball is well established as the national game.

American missionary Horace Wilson taught it to his pupils in 1869 (the same year the Cincinnati Red Stockings became the first professional team), and Hiroshi Hiraoka brought back a translation of American rules in 1877.

Visits by American all-stars in 1913, 1922, 1931, 1932, and 1934 fanned developing Japanese interest and the island's first professional league was founded in 1936.

The 1934 All-Star team was overwhelmed by admiring fans when it reached Tokyo by train from the port of Yokohama. They shouted "Banzai Babe Ruth!" and "Banzai Lou Gehrig!" (Long Live Ruth, Long Live Gehrig) until they were hoarse. Police estimated swirling masses in the eight-block Ginza district at one million persons.

Ruth, as popular in Japan as he was at home, poked 13 long home runs to help the '34 stars win all 16 games from Japanese college opposition, but fans didn't care as long as they could see him play. They went so far as to knock on his hotel room door for autographs.

A plaque outside Osaka's Koshien Stadium was erected in memory of the visit, which Ruth spiced with such antics as holding a Japanese parasol to fend off the rain while playing first base.

Babe Ruth was the only non-Japanese name on a list of the nation's best-known personalities over a forty-year period. The game was promoted in Japan through an annual Babe Ruth Day, and Japanese soldiers taunted Americans in World War II with the cry, "To hell with Babe Ruth !"

At first glance, Americans might not understand the game in Japan. Spring training is a rigorous two-month training grind that includes eight-hour conditioning sessions of weight-lifting, running, calisthenics, and even wood-chopping.

Pitchers work often (Tadashi Sugiura was 38-4 one season) and don't go to the showers when knocked out; instead, they head for the bullpen and throw until meeting the fans' approval. ☞

During pre-game practice, Japanese coaches determine which regulars look rusty and withhold those men from the game. Fans shy away from foul balls in the stands and ushers return them to the umpire.

Beer, peanuts, an import called the *hotto dogu*—plus noodles and seaweed—keep concessions stands busy, and spectators spend more time booing each other than the men on the field. Fans sit in rooting sections for the team of their choice. Average annual attendance is 12 million, but the Yomiuri Giants get close to 25 per cent of that total.

Fans pick players for three All-Star Games, which provide one million dollars for the player pension fund—60 per cent of the annual input. At age 50, players with ten years' service (major or minor league) receive annual stipends of $1000, about one-eighth of what their American counterparts earn.

An iron-clad reserve clause forbids player shifts at will, but most athletes seem satisfied with an average wage of $20,000, though American imports average twice as much. Only two foreigners are permitted on each team's 60-player "control list," which includes an active roster of 28 names. Contracts, by league rule, are for one year only, but bonus clauses are accepted and widely used.

The very best Japanese players are enshrined in an impressive Hall of Fame, near Tokyo. The gallery includes artifacts tracing the history of the game in Japan, and the prized possessions are photos of the 1934 tour of American stars.

## IS BASEBALL A MARTIAL ART?

*When baseball was first brought to Japan, sportsmen interpreted the game as an American version of a martial sport—much like judo or karate. The game was played under extremely adverse conditions until the Japanese learned that baseball was primarily a test of skill, not endurance.*

## MOE BERG'S SECRET MISSION

*Though Babe Ruth was the biggest draw on the 1934 tour, the key man was actually light-hitting catcher Moe Berg. This Princeton graduate, a master of languages, had done little to distinguish himself with two clubs that season, but was added to the "all-star team" by the United States government.*

*After learning Japanese in a two-month cram course, Berg presented numerous lectures on the game and became a popular figure. But his mission, which he accomplished with relative ease, was to photograph the Japanese capital. Berg's movies were the principal reference for General Jimmie Doolittle's air raids over the city, which began on April 18, 1942.*

# JAPANESE BASEBALL IN WARTIME

The war had a tremendous impact on the game. Early in the conflict, the militarist government ordered that only Japanese terms could be used to describe baseball action. Previously, the terms "safe," "out," and "play ball" had been incorporated into the language. American team names (Senators, Tigers, Giants, etc.) were also banned and ordered replaced with Japanese titles.

Encounters between Americans and Japanese often involved their most common tie: baseball. In December 1941, Dr. Alexander Paul, a missionary in China, was subjected to a search by Japanese soldiers. In his home, they spotted copies of *The Sporting News.* "Baseball!" they shouted, then argued how to divide the captured newspapers.

At Guadalcanal, PFC John Mooney, Jr., of Worcester, Massachusetts recalled taking a Japanese prisoner who asked, in plain English, "Who won the World Series?"

Games in the Central League, then Japan's only major circuit, were suspended from September 1944 to November 1945, as World War II drew to a close.

With the war over, eight teams opened the 1946 Japanese season. Two years later, night ball was introduced at Gehrig Stadium in Yokohama. Warming relations with the Americans allowed a goodwill visit by the San Francisco Seals of the AAA Pacific Coast League in 1949. Japan's second league, the Pacific, began play in 1950.

# SADAHARU OH:
## THE JAPANESE BABE RUTH

In 1959, a lefthanded-hitting firstbaseman named Sadaharu Oh broke into the Japanese leagues with the powerful Yomiuri Giants, one of four clubs in Greater Tokyo. In 1977, Oh became the "world" home run champion when he smashed his 756th ball over the wall.

Oh, whose name means "king" and who wears No. 1, is best known for his Mel Ott batting style; he lifts his front foot high in the air before he swings. A typical year for Oh, whose team plays a 130-game schedule, occurred in 1976: 49 home runs, 123 runs batted in, and a .325 batting average.

The six-foot, 174-pound slugger, unquestionably the national hero of Japan, helped the Giants win nine straight pennants, 1965-73, but he lost a televised home run derby to Hank Aaron, 10-9, late in 1974.

Oh had many advantages over Aaron in his pursuit of the home run record:

* Japanese stadiums are smaller than those in the U.S., with typical dimensions 300 feet to the foul lines and 395 feet to center.

* Pitchers never throw brushback pitches common in the States; when a pitch slips and becomes a duster by accident, they apologize. Thus, Oh can "dig in" and take a comfortable hitting position.

* Because fans support the Giants so heavily, umpires obviously favor that club, giving Yomiuri pitchers a large strike zone but hitters a small strike zone. Oh gets pitches exactly where he wants them or he doesn't swing. He walked 166 times in 1974.

* Smaller Japanese pitchers can't throw as hard as their American counterparts.

* Fans of both teams prefer an Oh home run to victory by their favorite nine.

# AMERICAN PLAYERS
## IN JAPAN

Only one player from the Japanese leagues made the majors; lefthanded pitcher Masanori Murakami of the San Francisco Giants (4-1 with eight saves in 1965).

Numerous Americans went the other way, and one—Davey Johnson—was the only U.S. import to make the Japanese All-Star team, as well as the only major-leaguer to resume his career after playing in Japan (until Willie Davis joined the California Angels).

Johnson established a one-season standard for secondbasemen with 43 home runs as an Atlanta Brave in 1973, became a Japanese All-Star in 1976, then returned as a valuable part-timer for the NL East champion Philadelphia Phillies of 1977.

Other Americans who did well in Japan were Daryl Spencer, Larry Doby, Willie Kirkland, George Altman, Don Blasingame, Roger Repoz, Bob Chance, Jim Lefebvre, Don Buford, Walt (No-Neck) Williams, Adrian Garrett, Leron Lee, and Clyde Wright. Don Newcombe, always a strong hitter as a Brooklyn Dodger pitcher, thrived as a firstbaseman in Japan.

None of these imports came close to surpassing Babe Ruth as a cherished baseball immortal among Japanese fans. But they did enhance the game in a country that has unbounded enthusiasm for an imported pastime.

Sadaharu Oh became a Japanese home run hero by adopting Mel Ott's unorthodox batting style.

CHAPTER NINETEEN

# fans

# THE MASTER PROMOTER: BILL VEECK

Bill Veeck was the best of several promotion-minded owners who advanced the theory which helped bad teams prosper without natural fan-drawing power. The theory was "Give 'em a show if you can't give 'em a ballclub."

Veeck, the P.T. Barnum of baseball, believed in both shows and giveaways. And he used his creative genius at every opportunity.

The most outlandish stunt in baseball history involved Veeck's 3-foot, 7-inch midget, Eddie Gaedel, age 26. On August 19, 1951, at St. Louis, Gaedel emerged from a birthday cake between games of a doubleheader. He wore a Browns' uniform with the numerals 1/8 stitched on the back.

In the last of the first inning in the second game, Gaedel was sent to the plate as a pinch-hitter for leadoff man Frank Saucier. At first, umpires Ed Hurley and Art Passarella balked. But, when manager Zack Taylor produced the official player's contract Gaedel had signed (for $100 per game), they waved him into the batter's box.

The midget went into the crouch Veeck had taught him in secret session and walked on four pitches. He was immediately replaced by a pinch-runner and never appeared in the majors again. American League president Will Harridge ruled him ineligible and also killed a Veeck plan to employ a 9-foot, 3-inch giant from Great Britain.

Five days after the Gaedel caper, more than 1000 "grandstand managers," selected from applicants who wrote local newspapers, voted on strategy while manager Taylor sat in the stands in street clothes. They split 60-40 on all decisions but the majority was right consistently and the Browns beat the Philadelphia Athletics, 5-3.

In the first inning, when St. Louis ace Ned Garver was hit hard, Veeck groaned when the grandstand managers voted against warming up a new pitcher, but Garver pitched out of trouble and won the game. The night ended with a "skywriting" display in fireworks. It read: "Thank you, G.S. Managers, for a swell job. Zack manages tomorrow."

Veeck considered each individual fan to be very important. He even staged a "day" for night watchman Joe Early in Cleveland.

In a letter to the *Cleveland Press*, Early asked why teams were always giving "days" to well-paid stars who really didn't need the money instead of to loyal fans like him, who did. He signed the letter "Good Old Joe Early."

Veeck, then running the Indians, realized Early had logic on his side. He called the paper for Early's address and told him to be at the ballpark.

On the appointed night, gifts were given to fans before Early took center stage. First, he got a series of gag gifts, including an outhouse, a backfiring Model-T, and assorted animals. Then, he received a new Ford convertible, a refrigerator, washing machine, luggage, watch, clothes, stereo system, and more. An instant celebrity, he became quite successful from that day on.

Each Veeck promotion was greeted with charges that he was making a travesty of the game. But who could argue with success? In 1948, the Indians smashed previous attendance records with a season's draw of 2,620,627. Against Chicago on August 20, the club drew 78,382.

Manager Zack Taylor tackles new challenge: tying the shoelaces of 3'7", 50-pound midget Eddie Gaedel. Wearing No. ⅛, Gaedel pinch-hit for Bill Veeck's Browns against Detroit. He walked on four pitches, then left the game.

## A VEECK FIASCO

*Master promoter Bill Veeck was the victim of one of his own gags when fans ran wild during "Anti-Disco Night" festivities at Comiskey Park in 1979. A mass record-burning in the outfield, plus the unruly fans, made the field unplayable for the second half of a scheduled doubleheader. The umpires forfeited the game to the visiting Detroit Tigers.*

# GRANDIOSE PROMOTIONS

Minor league history is filled with unusual promotions staged by enterprising operators. Chattanooga's Joe Engel, tired of giving away automobiles, hit the jackpot when he auctioned off his popular radio announcer before thousands of cheering women. The winner used him to mow the lawn, wash the dishes, and do other household chores.

The Miami Beach nine gave away orchids, animals, and bicycles on a night that also featured the traditional cow-milking contest. For players with non-farming backgrounds, the cow contest often ended in udder confusion.

With the help of sponsors and local businesses, major league teams took a cue from the minors and planned clever promotions in numbers that increased in direct proportion to the rise of player salaries in the '70s.

Many teams hosted Fan Appreciation Days, with multiple giveaways, at season's end, and most promoted heavily throughout the year. In Philadelphia, team sponsor Tastykake printed its slogan, "All the good things wrapped up in one," on halter-tops distributed to female fans by the ballclub.

The 1979 Phillies gave away sweatshirts, batting gloves, gym shorts, pennants, ladies tote bags, wristbands, jackets, tube socks, caps, ponchos, shirts, notebooks, and ski caps—all on different days. Fireworks displays were also part of the promotional calendar.

One Phillies event marked by ingenuity was Music Night. Fans were invited to bring their own instruments (or receive a free kazoo) and play "Take Me Out to the Ball Game" in the seventh-inning stretch. Certificates were awarded to participants stating that they had played with "the world's largest orchestra."

## DALLAS DUMPED USHERETTES

*Attractive red-haired usherettes served patrons of the Dallas ballpark for two years, starting in 1938, but club president George Schepps eventually fired them. "They detracted too much from the game," he said. "The men didn't even know the score."*

## FAN COLLECTS BASEBALL SONGS

*Collecting baseball items is a hobby that takes many shapes and forms. Perhaps the most unusual collection ever assembled was the baseball music library put together by J. Francis Driscoll of Brookline, Massachusetts. He obtained the music to more than 50,000 songs, including "Take Me Out to the Ball Game," in a hobby that spanned forty years.*

*The collection included George M. Cohan's "Take Your Girl to the Ball Game" and John Philip Sousa's "The National Game," dedicated to Commissioner of Baseball Kenesaw Mountain Landis in 1925. Neither caught on.*

Nick Altrock and Al Schacht, long-time baseball clowns, stage pre-game match, entertaining crowd during the '30s.

# LADIES DAY

Promotions to swell attendance have long been part of the game. There is dispute about the exact origin of Ladies Day, but the idea of admitting women free—whether accompanied by a paying male escort or not—definitely rates as the oldest promotion in baseball.

New York of the National League used the idea once in 1883, but it was not adopted on a regular basis in the majors until 1889, in Cincinnati. Women gained free admission only with a paid escort.

Two years earlier, the New Orleans club allowed women to enter free, even if unaccompanied, one day per week. The practice violated prevailing social mores and brought waves of protests.

Major leagues teams eventually discovered the value of admitting females "for a smile." The idea was twofold: to hook women on baseball so that they might become regular paying customers and to lure male fans who would welcome the presence of females who shared their interest in the game.

In 1937, the New York Giants reported the ratio of female guests to paying males was four to ten. The Chicago Cubs did even better business on Ladies Day. After more than 30,000 free females flooded Wrigley Field one day, the team imposed a maximum of 20,000 free tickets for Ladies Day promotions. Those who exceeded the limit were given priority for the following Ladies Day game.

A 1930 New York City subway sign tells the story about Ladies Day.

# "DAYS" FOR PLAYERS

"Days" for players were accepted as a common way to honor stars.

Appreciative Tiger fans saluted Charlie Gehringer with "Charlie Gehringer Day" in Detroit on August 14, 1929, and The Mechanical Man responded with a home run, three singles, and a steal of home.

In 1930, Rabbit Maranville Day was held at Braves' Field, Boston. More than 32,000 fans watched as the city and the ballclub presented the star shortstop with a car, tea set, reading lamp, cigar box, and assorted other gifts—including a gray rabbit that looked very much like the player himself.

While most "days" were happy occasions, the two saddest in the game's history were held at Yankee Stadium. In 1939, Lou Gehrig, wracked by disease which would kill him two years later, addressed the crowd: "Today, I consider myself the luckiest man on the face of the Earth. I might have been given a bad break, but I've got an awful lot to live for. Thank you."

In 1947, it was Babe Ruth Day. He too was dying. "You know how pained my voice sounds," he said. "Well, it feels just as bad. You know this baseball game of ours . . . the only real game, I think, in the world—baseball."

Sad Babe Ruth said goodbye during tearful "Babe Ruth Day" ceremony.

## MANY MOTHERS DISCARDED CARDS

*The common complaint of collectors starts at home. They say their mothers, while cleaning attics and bedrooms of assorted debris, discarded old shoe boxes bulging with baseball cards. Today, many of those old cards have significant value.*

## DIZZY DEAN'S LAST GAME

*Colorful Dizzy Dean, Cardinals' star of the '30s, was retired six seasons when the St. Louis Browns reactivated him for one game as a publicity stunt in 1947.*

*Dean, then a popular St. Louis broadcaster, was not only out of condition but also overweight. But he still had his baseball instincts; he pitched four scoreless innings against the Chicago White Sox, lined a hit to left, and later slid into second while on the basepaths.*

*When the 36-year-old righthander got up limping at second, his wife Pat leaned over the dugout rail and hailed Browns' manager Muddy Ruel. "He's proved his point," she said. "Now get him out of there before he kills himself!"*

*In the four-inning stint that closed his career, Dean yielded three hits and one walk. He thoroughly enjoyed his unexpected last hurrah as an active player.*

# OLD TIMERS' DAY

When Ruth was playing, the Yankees used the slugger in a typical end-of-season promotion: they let him pitch—twice. In 1930 and again in 1933, the ex-pitcher took to the mound with no preparation on the season's last day and stopped his former Red Sox teammates 9-3 and 6-5, respectively.

With fan interest on the wane for clubs not involved in pennant races, activating an old-time hero helps fill the stands. The practice evolved into the regular once-a-year promotion, Old Timers' Day.

Before the Yankees introduced the first "official" Old Timers' Day in 1947, retired players returned to action for fleeting appearances in the final stages of the season.

On September 30, 1934, the St. Louis Browns employed catcher Grover Hartley, 46, and shortstop Charlie O'Leary, 52. Though he had been out of the majors since 1913, O'Leary slammed a pinch-single and scored a run.

St. Louis Cardinals' manager Gabby Street, 49, caught three innings on September 20, 1931, when Sylvester Johnson was on the mound. The Johnson-Street battery was supposed to remind fans of the famous tandem of Walter Johnson and Street, Washington Senators stars more than twenty years before.

The Senators brought back pitcher Nick Altrock, 53, as a right-fielder on October 6, 1929, and he managed to get a hit. Coach Minnie Minoso of the Chicago White Sox was also 53, but several months younger than Altrock, when he singled once in six at-bats late in the 1976 season.

Jimmy Austin doubled and stole home at age 46 in 1926 and played three innings for the Browns three years later. Johnny Evers, 47, played one inning for the Boston Braves in 1929.

Another old man of September was James (Orator) O'Rourke, who caught a full game for Iron Man McGinnity of the New York Giants on September 22, 1904. O'Rourke had been out of the majors eleven years but got a hit and scored a run; he also made an error.

After George Weiss established Old Timers' Day—the Yankees' lone promotion for years—other clubs quickly followed suit.

# THE KNOTHOLE GANG

Though long-time executive Branch Rickey is credited with launching "The Knothole Gang" concept in the majors, the idea was actually the brainchild of minor league player-manager Abner Powell, who also conceived the rain check (1887) and the tarpaulin (1889).

When Powell came to Sportsman's Park, New Orleans, during the 1889 campaign, he often encountered a ragged band of boys who loved baseball in general and Powell in particular. They hung around in front of the park, unable to come up with 10 cents for a bleacher seat, and then migrated to the wooden outfield wall when the game started. They punched out a knothole to get a good view of the action inside.

Powell suggested to team owner Toby Hart that he admit the youths free, seating them in a special section of the ballpark. The reluctant owner agreed only after Powell promised he would be responsible for their behavior and pay for any damage. The thoughtful Powell, the team's player-manager, arranged twice-weekly free admissions for the group, but asked them to be neat in appearance and behavior once inside. Beards and tobacco were prohibited.

## THE PIONEER PROMOTER

*Frank Bancroft, business manager of the Cincinnati Reds from 1892-1921, was the first baseball official to promote the game heavily. He staged the first homeplate wedding, led major league squads to Cuba, and arranged baseball Olympics, featuring long-distance throwing, races, fungo-hitting, and home run derbys. A one-time field manager in the early days of the National League, Bancroft had a background as advance man for the circus and vaudeville tours.*

# SHOW BIZ ON THE DIAMOND

Though giveaway days are guaranteed fan favorites, pre-game or post-game spectacles have definite pulling power. The Atlanta Braves appealed to a male blue-blooded audience with their Wet T-Shirt Night of 1977, but ran into repercussions when the winner's father turned out to be a Methodist minister.

The Braves countered with such innocent entertainment as ostrich races, bathtub races, fireworks and laser shows, and a look-alike contest for blonde actress Farrah Fawcett-Majors. Wedlock and Headlock Night was something special—mass weddings at home plate before the game and professional wrestling matches afterward.

"What we're trying to do," explained Atlanta promotion chief Bob Hope, "is stimulate the feeling that it's fun to come to the ballpark. We want people to say they had a good time even if the home team gets clobbered."

The Browns used a pitcher per inning as a last-game gimmick in 1949; fans entering Brooklyn's Ebbets Field were given candles before the lights were dimmed in birthday tribute to Pee Wee Reese; and John "Hans" Lobert of the Phillies raced a horse around the bases in 1913.

Lobert had been timed at 13 4/5 seconds—exceptionally fast by any standard—in circling the bases, but lost his race when the horse violated an agreement to race on the outside of the basepaths and crowded him at third base. It won by a nose.

# CROWDS

Promotions pull fans into ballparks, but other key factors are good weather, an interesting opponent, a reasonable chance the home team will win, and overall interest in baseball by local residents.

Only 17 fans—6 of them paying customers—watched a Pittsburgh Pirate game in 1890, the year of the Players' League revolt, and just 26 saw Baltimore of the International League play a 1914 game; that city had a Federal League team that year.

But the Los Angeles Dodgers drew more than 90,000 spectators four times—three of them during the 1959 World Series against the Chicago White Sox. The team then was in the second of four seasons at the Los Angeles Coliseum, a football bowl which housed the team before Dodger Stadium could be built. ☞

Atlanta Braves

Female fans—and male admirers—flocked to Farrah Fawcett-Majors lookalike contest in Atlanta Stadium.

## BROOKLYN 1920

The Brooklyn Dodger fan of 1920 could root his team to the National League pennant while eating a nickel hot dog and reading a nickel program. School children got a bleacher seat for a quarter on Friday afternoons.

## OPENING DAY LONGEVITY

George Doerzbach saw 55 consecutive Cleveland openers.

Fans crowd center field section of Philadelphia's Veterans Stadium.

Laura Gaynor

While tenants of the Coliseum, the Dodgers drew the largest crowd ever to watch a game—93,103 for Roy Campanella Night on May 7, 1959. The New York Yankees provided the oppositon for an exhibition game which followed pre-game tributes to the Dodger catcher whose career was shortened by a winter auto mishap in New York.

The Coliseum allowed the Dodgers to establish National League standards for day and night crowds, but it was after the move to Dodger Stadium that the club drew a record 3,000,000 fans in one year. The Dodgers' day record was 78,672 (vs. the Giants on April 18, 1958) and night mark was 72,140 (vs. the Reds in a twilight-night doubleheader on August 16, 1961).

Both the Cleveland Indians and New York Yankees drew more than 80,000 fans on a single day, with doubleheaders (two games for the price of one) as added incentive. Cleveland had 84,587 paid (86,563 in the park) against the second-place Yankees on September 12, 1954, while New York drew 81,841 on Memorial Day 1938 against the arch-rival Boston Red Sox.

The Indians, occupants of a ballpark with a capacity of more than 76,000, also established a major league record when they drew 78,382 fans for a night game (against the White Sox on August 20, 1948) and an American League opening day mark with 74,420 against the Tigers on April 17, 1973. The Dodgers had drawn 4,000 more for their first game in Los Angeles in 1958.

Rather than turn customers away, many early club executives roped off sections of outfield and allowed fans to stand on the field behind the ropes. This practice made it necessary to set up special ground rules for balls hit into the crowd and also created additional problems for groundskeepers who had to cope with cigarette butts and all kinds of other debris. The Washington Senators were roundly criticized for allowing field crowds in 1941 and 1949, after the practice had gone out of general use in the major leagues.

One of the most popular modern promotions is Father-and-Kids Day, featuring a game between baseball dads and their offspring. Slugger Steve Garvey enjoyed this 1977 encounter at Dodger Stadium.

## FAN GOES ON THE ROAD

*Philadelphia Athletics fan Hyman Pearlstone made at least one roadtrip with the club for 44 straight seasons.*

## RED SOX RECORD

*The largest crowd to see the Red Sox play in Boston came not to Fenway Park, but to Braves' Field, borrowed from the National League as site of the 1916 World Series. The Sox drew 42,620 as they won the World Series in five games over the Brooklyn Dodgers. Score of the October 12 clincher was 4-1.*

# THE ADVENT OF USHERS

Feelings invariably ran high in crowds, with the displeasure of the majority vented on the few who dared root against the home team. Intense rivalries between the New York Yankees and Boston Red Sox of the American League, and Brooklyn Dodgers and New York Giants of the National League, frequently flared into confrontations. The practice of using ushers to police the stands began after rowdyism in New York so infuriated Detroit star Ty Cobb in 1912 that he jumped into the stands and attacked Claude Lucker.

A suspension resulted and sympathetic teammates pulled a one-day strike which forced the Tigers to recruit a group of semi-pros as last-minute replacements. The Philadelphia Athletics won, 24-2, and the regular Detroit players, having made their point, then returned.

After Cobb charged the fan, warning posters went up around the majors to remind fans that rowdyism would not be tolerated. Ushers were hired and, where necessary, special police were assigned to stadium duty.

# THE SEASON TICKET

The advent of the season ticket proved a lifesaver to numerous teams. The business community pitched in to purchase blocks of seats. With 81 home dates under the 162-game format launched in 1961, clubs could guarantee an attendance of 405,000 simply by selling 5000 season tickets. Most important of all was the fact that money used to purchase season tickets was immediately available to the team.

Providence, a National League team in 1884, pioneered the season ticket concept. Its prices were $15 if purchased before March 15, $20 before April 15. Boston charged $15 for a season ticket, but cut $5 off that figure if the tickets were purchased by or for a woman.

To illustrate how times changed, in 1978, a fan could have purchased a seat for himself and his wife in the deluxe loge area of Candlestick Park, San Francisco, for $14.20—just 80 cents less than the price of a season's ticket in 1884.

# FAMOUS FANS

Fans watched, and listened, and became infatuated with baseball. Songwriter George M. Cohan wrote "Yankee Doodle Dandy" but was an ardent fan of the New York Giants. So were famous New York restauranteurs Toots Shor and Dinty Moore. Jack White of the 18 Club and actress Tallulah Bankhead were known to be distraught when the Giants lost.

Pearl Yount and Dorothy Wolff formed a team of passionate St. Louis Cardinal rooters, attending all weekend and holiday games at Sportsman's Park in the '30s and heading out of town to follow the Redbirds on roadtrips. The Yount-Wolff tandem became so well known by the Cardinal players and management that an article was written about them in the four-page team house organ.

Another well-known St. Louis fan, Mary Ott, dominated the bleachers of Sportsman's Park during the war years. Her trademark was a piercing laugh which could best be described as a whinny. The rotund Mrs. Ott had a fine arrangement with her second husband; he cooked the meals while she went to the games.

Mrs. Ott looked down upon those who entered free of charge on Ladies Day. "They don't know baseball or how to behave at ballgames," she said.

# "THE BELL OF EBBETS FIELD"

Brooklyn's Hilda Chester, accompanied by her cowbell, was the head cheerleader of the Ebbets Field faithful at the same time that Ott operated in St. Louis. She was called "The Bell of Ebbets Field" with good reason.

The one-time player for the New York Bloomer Girls developed rheumatism in her arm and received a doctor's advice that she should exercise the arm in the sun. What better way than to ring a four-pound cowbell at the ballpark?

Hilda's act began in batting practice and Dodger players responded with waves as soon as they heard it. She sat in the center field bleachers, earning money for tickets by selling songsheets at the corner of DeKalb Avenue and Flatbush Extension.

While Hilda Chester was ringing her cowbell, a five-piece band provided a stream of music—or sounds approaching music—from behind the Dodger bench. Broadcaster Red Barber named the group

# ... AND A WORD ABOUT STICKBALL

There are dozens of different ways to play stickball, best-known as the New York City street sport played with a rubber spaldeen and sawed-off broomstick.

In most games, there are just two players—batter and pitcher. The pitcher throws against a wall which may or may not be decorated with a hand-drawn rectangular "strike zone." He also calls balls and strikes—though arguments are frequent.

The pitcher's distance from the plate and prevailing ground rules depend on the game site, which may be a schoolboy's backyard or driveway, or a handball court in a nearby park. In the street game, it is often necessary to expand the sides to two players each so that a catcher can serve as backstop.

In some versions of stickball, there is no pitcher at all—only a batter and an outfielder. The hitter bounces the ball and swings for the same "automatic" doubles, triples, or home runs that prevail in stickball games that use pitchers.

Either way, youthful players frequently make out lineups of their favorite teams and keep league records. The same youngster who hit home runs as Hank Aaron and Eddie Mathews could also pitch a shutout for Warren Spahn—between 1954 and 1964, when that trio was together.

In the winter, when basketball was king, some hardy baseball loyalists in North Jersey invented "base-basketball," whereby successful shots from designated spots represented hits and misses were outs. This game was also played with lineups and league records—and it was played in icy weather.

"the Dodger Sym-Phony" and it was so well-received that the drummer had the name emblazoned on his instrument.

The Sym-Phony specialized in mocking the actions of rival players with music. When a visiting player approached the water fountain, the band played a chorus of "How Dry I Am." When he returned to his seat on the bench, his act of seating himself was greeted by a clash of the cymbals.

## HOW TEAM FIGURES GREW

| NL team | 1977 | 1957 | 1937 |
|---|---|---|---|
| Atlanta | 872,464 | 2,215,514* | 385,339** |
| Chicago | 1,439,834 | 670,629 | 895,020 |
| Cincinnati | 2,519,670 | 1,070,850 | 411,221 |
| Houston | 1,109,560 | — | — |
| Los Angeles | 2,955,087 | 1,028,258# | 482,481# |
| Montreal | 1,433,757 | — | — |
| New York | 1,066,825 | — | — |
| Philadelphia | 2,700,070 | 1,146,230 | 212,790 |
| Pittsburgh | 1,237,349 | 850,732 | 459,679 |
| St. Louis | 1,659,287 | 1,183,575 | 430,811 |
| San Diego | 1,376,269 | — | — |
| San Francisco | 700,056 | 653,923## | 926,887## |

*Milwaukee  **Boston
#Brooklyn  ##New York

| AL team | 1977 | 1957 | 1937 |
|---|---|---|---|
| Baltimore | 1,195,769 | 1,029,581 | 123,121# |
| Boston | 2,074,549 | 1,181,087 | 559,659 |
| California | 1,432,633 | — | — |
| Chicago | 1,657,135 | 1,135,688 | 589,245 |
| Cleveland | 900,365 | 722,256 | 564,849 |
| Detroit | 1,359,856 | 1,272,346 | 1,072,276 |
| Kansas City | 1,852,603 | — | — |
| Milwaukee | 1,114,938 | — | — |
| Minnesota | 1,162,727 | 457,079* | 397,799* |
| New York | 2,103,092 | 1,497,134 | 998,148 |
| Oakland | 495,599 | 901,067## | 430,738** |
| Seattle | 1,338,511 | — | — |
| Texas | 1,250,722 | — | — |
| Toronto | 1,701,052 | — | — |

*Washington  **Philadelphia
#St. Louis  ##Kansas City

# FANS ON THE FIELD

As Hilda Chester and the Dodger Sym-Phony illustrated, Brooklyn fans made the most noise and did the craziest things. On July 31, 1935, with the Cardinals in town, a woman named Kitty Burke jumped out of the stands, grabbed a bat, ran to home plate, and took a swing at one of Dizzy Dean's warmup pitches. The ball went bounding back to the pitcher, who was speechless for the first time in his career.

Eleven years later, a Boston fan decided to try the defensive end of the game. Before 28,000 Fenway Park patrons on August 26, 1946, a midget hopped over the fence, picked up a glove, and took up position at third base. Ted Williams was the hitter and the entire Cleveland infield, in the Boudreau Shift, had moved to the right side of second base, leaving shortstop and third base wide open. The midget was later identified as vaudevillian Marco Songini.

It wasn't long after Montreal joined the National League in 1969 that Quebec fans found their way into history's footnotes. During an unusual fall fog, a streaker appeared just long enough to be seen before disappearing into the mist. A musically-inclined spectator whipped out a violin, jumped on top of the home dugout, and gave Montreal a living "Fiddler on the Roof." Mrs. Bob Bailey, appearing with other wives in a fashion show, was booed because her husband was in a batting slump. And Expos fans gave umpires crash courses in the off-color words of the French language.

# CHICAGO'S BLEACHER BUMS

The same year the Expos started, the National League's oldest franchise, the Chicago Cubs, appeared headed for the pennant playoffs. Their unexpected achievements of mid-summer so excited their fans that they developed an addiction to the game. Bedecked in bright yellow hard-hats, they vocally destroyed opponents

"I would have hated being an opposing player in Wrigley Field at that time," said Randy Hundley, who played for the Cubs then. "They didn't hold anything back. If they knew something personal about a guy, they'd let it rip. They used to get on Willie Davis about his ex-wife. He was ready to go into the stands to fight them."

The team actually had to erect a chicken-wire fence in front of the bleachers because overenthusiastic fans paraded around on a narrow cement walk on top of the outfield wall. The nickname of Bleacher Bums stuck when Cub fans used it with a certain pride during the abortive pennant chase of 1969.

**Unruly fans stormed onto field in last inning of the final game in Washington in 1971, causing the Senators to forfeit a game they were winning. Team transferred to Texas.**

295

# TRUE BELIEVERS

Many fans are as devoted as the man whose letter helped slugger Chuck Klein escape a batting slump in 1935. Klein smashed 17 hits in 50 trips (.340) immediately after receiving the letter from N.L. Silver. The four-paragraph note, written in very humble style, explained a flaw the fan had detected in the slugger's swing.

Jimmie McCullough of Atlantic City, New Jersey devoted himself not to a player but to an event. In 1926, he began a remarkable streak of watching the World Series in person. He did it for more than fifty years! The streak involved travel of more than 100,000 miles, purchase of $50 tickets from scalpers on occasion, and acquisition of press credentials wherever possible.

Since McCullough had a background as publicist and press agent, he sometimes had little trouble joining the huge series press corps. An AP dispatch dubbed McCullough "the Babe Ruth of baseball fans."

The "sign man" of the New York Mets, advertising executive Carl Ehrhardt, could also contend for the title. His hand-lettered signs, held aloft at dramatic moments in the game, became such a hit at Shea Stadium that he was even interviewed on Ralph Kiner's postgame television show.

Ehrhardt's signs were direct descendants of the ragged but clever banners which decorated both the Polo Grounds, home of the Mets in 1962 and 1963, and the Flushing ballpark. Zealous young fans displayed their enthusiasm over the new, struggling expansion team by painting bedsheets and parading them around the park.

Mets' management realized the promotional potential in the banners, and the resulting Banner Day—with prizes awarded in various categories—proved a smashing success.

Lou Mercurio

**Blind radio reporter Ed Lucas of Jersey City, N.J. has parlayed his love for the game into his profession, impressing such sighted colleagues as former player Ron Swoboda (left). Lucas, subject of many interviews himself, represents several stations—including outlets for the blind—and often asks players to describe parks or plays his audience cannot see.**

Tom Reid, Bloomfield, NJ

# HOW TO CATCH FLIES

TAKE IT BABE ALL YOURS

If another Fielder also yells for the catch, don't fight him. Holler "take it" and give him plenty of room.

If you know you can catch it, yell "mine."

ALL MINE!

HIGH FLY

LOW BALL

Never point fingers at ball. Take a high ball with hands this way. Low ball, this way.

DIAMOND STARS GUM
Mfg'd by The Goudey Gum Co.
Boston; Mass., U.S.A.

# COLLECTORS

Many fans express their love for baseball by collecting memorabilia ranging from cards to yearbooks, magazines, buttons, photos, press pins, press guides, uniforms, and even broken bats used by big-leaguers.

Collecting mushroomed into a major industry with the nostalgia wave of the '70s. Adults became so adept at the child's game of buying, selling, and trading cards that they established full-time businesses. Publications sprang up strictly to serve this new industry.

By far the most popular collectors' items were baseball cards. The Topps Chewing Gum Company of Brooklyn, New York began to issue complete sets of players cards in 1951, changing the basic design each year.

By the '70s, the Topps name had become synonymous with baseball cards. The company sold more than 250 million each year and gave awards to outstanding players.

Though Topps became the leading manufacturer of baseball cards, it actually borrowed the idea from earlier tobacco, bread, publishing and even chewing-gum firms.

Old Judge Cigarettes made the first baseball cards in 1886 by photographing players swinging at a ball on a string inside a studio. Cracker Jack candy issued a handsome series during the dead-ball era before 1920, and Babe Ruth adorned the face of a Big League Chewing Gum card issued after that date. Three other gum companies—Goudey, DeLong, and National Chicle—were active in the '30s, while Bowman and Fleer's were the main competitors when Topps entered the field.

# CHAPTER TWENTY

# Baseball Today

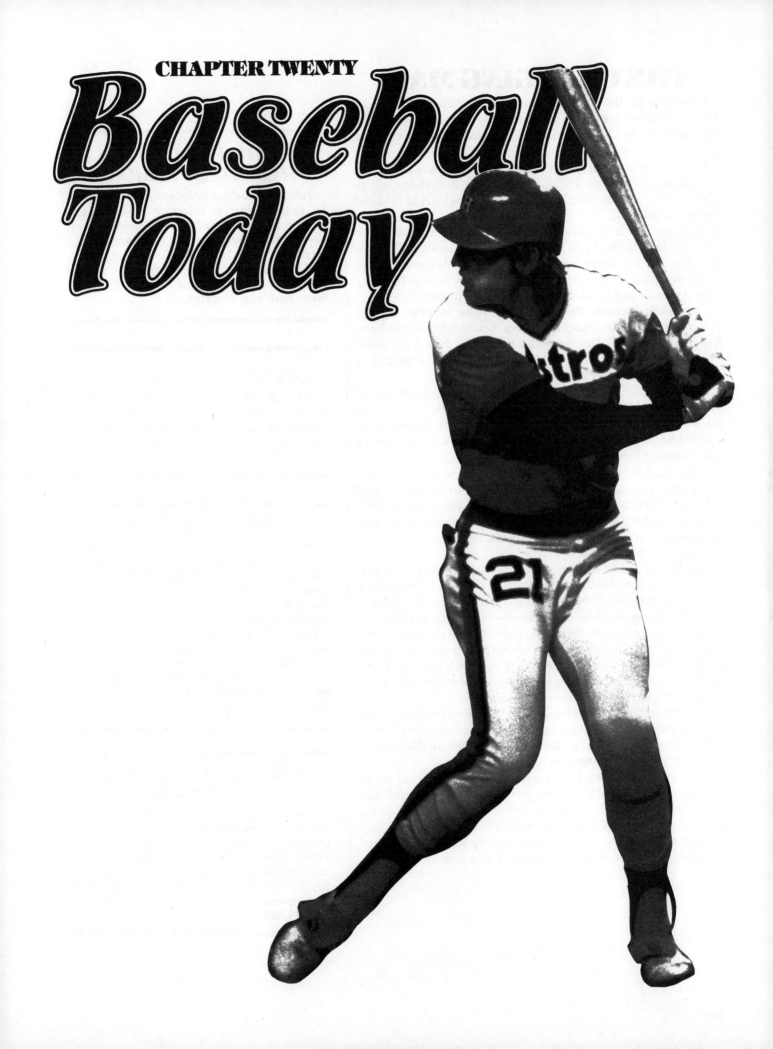

# THE CHANGING MAP

From 1903-53, there were no changes in the baseball map. Both the American and National Leagues contained eight cities each, and five towns (New York, Boston, Philadelphia, St. Louis, and Chicago) had two clubs.

The first move that broke up the fifty-year status quo in baseball was engineered by Lou Perini, owner of the Boston Braves, on March 18, 1953. Only 281,278 fans visited Braves Field in 1952 and Perini lost $600,000.

With the Braves in Milwaukee, where they immediately drew 1,826,397 fans, the St. Louis Browns had to look elsewhere for a new site. The club was operating on a shoe string budget and realized things would get worse after the Cardinals received fresh financing from Anheuser-Busch, which bought the team in 1953.

The Browns became the Baltimore Orioles in 1954 and the Philadelphia Athletics, under new owner Arnold Johnson, moved to Kansas City in 1955. The three-team situation in New York ended after the 1957 season when the Brooklyn Dodgers moved to Los Angeles and the New York Giants to San Francisco.

After the 1960 campaign, the Washington Senators moved to Minneapolis-St. Paul, where they became the Minnesota Twins, and the American League replaced them with an expansion team of the same name. Another new club was established in California as the Los Angeles Angels.

The American League repeated the mistake of placing two teams in one city when its owners okayed the transfer of the Kansas City Athletics to Oakland, across the bay from San Francisco, in 1968. As in the Washington move of 1960, the league replaced the A's with an expansion team, the Kansas City Royals, and added a second new franchise, the Seattle Pilots.

Seattle ran into bad weather and bad financing, and gave up after that single season. During spring training of 1970, it became the Milwaukee Brewers, filling a stadium vacated when the National League Braves made their second move—to Atlanta in 1966.

Milwaukee's return to the majors ended that city's pending lawsuit against baseball, but newly-abandoned Seattle jumped in where the city fathers of Milwaukee left off. The AL silenced the suit by sending Seattle another team in 1977, when the Mariners and Toronto Blue Jays swelled the league to 14 members.

One gap remained: Washington. The capital was without a club after the expansion Senators, plagued by bad concessions and broadcast contracts plus falling attendance, switched to Dallas-Fort Worth as the Texas Rangers in 1972.

The National League's first four expansion entries turned out to be welcome additions: New York and Houston in 1962 and San Diego and Montreal in 1969. For a time, the Padres had severe financial problems which almost ended in a cross-county shift to new ownership in Washington, but hamburger king Ray Kroc delivered the eleventh-hour monetary infusion which kept them in San Diego.

## CONTINENTAL LEAGUE FORCED EXPANSION

Talk of a third major league, the Continental League, forced reluctant major league owners to expand in 1961-62. Branch Rickey, president of the proposed Continental, had targeted New York as his key objective. Rickey's circuit collapsed when the majors agreed to add several of its sites, including New York and Houston.

## INFLATION AND BABE RUTH

Babe Ruth's record $80,000 contract of 1932 was worth $454,000 in 1968, according to economist Lawrence Ritter, author of The Glory of Their Times.

## ARTIFICIAL TURF

Fields with artificial surfaces look prettier, guarantee sure hops for fielders, and reduce rainout prospects because water can be swept off minutes before game time. Ground balls zip through the infield, forcing fielders to play back.

However, artificial turf is a hard surface which causes wear and tear on knees and legs. Over the long term, it may shorten careers. The zippered turf also gets unpleasantly hot in the sun. Athletes must wear special shoes to play on it.

## HOW MEDIA REVENUE CHANGED

Radio supplied seven per cent of baseball's revenue in 1939, while radio-TV provided 10.5 per cent in 1950 and 30 per cent by the mid-'70s. In 1978, the Boston Red Sox led the majors with an annual haul of $2,450,000 for broadcast rights. Total broadcast revenue for the game amounted to $52,510,000.

# EXPANSION

Expansion was a difficult process. When the AL added Washington (replacing Minnesota) and Los Angeles for the 1961 season, the new clubs received players through a special expansion draft from the rosters of established teams.

Each existing team made 15 players available from its 40-man roster and drafting clubs made 28 selections for $75,000 each.

After the 1961 season, National League expansion teams in New York and Houston drafted 20 players each, 16 priced at $75,000 and four at $125,000.

The price of NL draftees was $200,000 in the fall of 1968, as opposed to $175,000 in the American. The AL imposed the same purchase price for the third wave of expansion late in 1976.

After widespread criticism of the "talent" available in the 1961-62 drafts, the selection system was altered so that existing clubs could protect only 15 players when drafting began.

Drafts were conducted in rounds so that established teams would share the burden of stocking new entries.

The history of expansion indicates that it takes seven years for a newborn ballclub to win a championship. That's the time span demonstrated by the 1969 World Champion New York Mets and the 1976 AL West champion Kansas City Royals.

All 10 expansion teams finished at, or near, the bottom in their first year. All lost at least 91 games and five lost 100 or more. The best first-year team was the Los Angeles Angels of 1961, which won an expansion record 70 games and zoomed from eighth to third in 1962. Good fortune didn't last, however, as the Angels duplicated their initial 70-91 record during a ninth-place season in '63.

## EXPANSION RECORDS

| YEAR | TEAM | WON | LOST | PCT. | POS. | ATTENDANCE |
|------|------|-----|------|------|------|-----------|
| 1961 | *Los Angeles Angels | 70 | 91 | .435 | 8 | 603,510 |
| 1961 | #Washington Senators | 61 | 100 | .370 | 9 | 597,287 |
| 1962 | @Houston Colts | 64 | 96 | .400 | 8 | 924,456 |
| 1962 | New York Mets | 40 | 120 | .250 | 10 | 922,530 |
| 1969 | Kansas City Royals | 69 | 93 | .426 | 4W | 902,414 |
| 1969 | xSeattle Pilots | 64 | 98 | .395 | 6W | 677,944 |
| 1969 | Montreal Expos | 52 | 110 | .321 | 6E | 1,212,608 |
| 1969 | San Diego Padres | 52 | 110 | .321 | 6W | 512,970 |
| 1977 | Seattle Mariners | 64 | 98 | .395 | 6W | 1,338,511 |
| 1977 | Toronto Blue Jays | 54 | 107 | .335 | 7E | 1,701,052 |

*became California Angels in 1966
#became Texas Rangers in 1972
@became Houston Astros in 1965
xbecame Milwaukee Brewers in 1970

### 1st Met Box Score
ST. LOUIS, APRIL 11, 1962

| METS | ab | r | h | rbi | CARDS | ab | r | h | rbi |
|------|----|----|----|----|-------|----|----|----|----|
| Ashburn, cf | 5 | 1 | 1 | 0 | Flood, cf | 4 | 3 | 2 | 1 |
| Mantilla, ss | 4 | 1 | 1 | 0 | Javier, 2b | 5 | 3 | 4 | 1 |
| Neal, 2b | 4 | 1 | 3 | 2 | White, 1b | 4 | 1 | 2 | 3 |
| Thomas, lf | 3 | 0 | 0 | 1 | Musial, rf | 3 | 1 | 3 | 2 |
| Bell, rf | 3 | 0 | 1 | 0 | Landrum, rf | 1 | 0 | 0 | 0 |
| Hodges, 1b | 4 | 1 | 1 | 1 | Boyer, 3b | 4 | 0 | 1 | 2 |
| Zimmer, 3b | 4 | 0 | 1 | 0 | Minoso, lf | 4 | 0 | 1 | 1 |
| Landrith, c | 4 | 0 | 0 | 0 | Oliver, c | 4 | 1 | 2 | 0 |
| Craig, p | 1 | 0 | 0 | 0 | Gotay, ss | 4 | 1 | 0 | 0 |
| Bouchee, p | 0 | 0 | 0 | 0 | Jackson, p | 4 | 1 | 1 | 1 |
| Moorhead, p | 1 | 0 | 0 | 0 | | 37 | 11 | 16 | 11 |
| Moford, p | 0 | 0 | 0 | 0 | | | | | |
| Labine, p | 0 | 0 | 0 | 0 | | | | | |
| Marshall, ph | 0 | 0 | 0 | 0 | | | | | |
| | 33 | 4 | 8 | 4 | | | | | |

New York ......... 0 0 2 1 1 0 0 0 0— 4
St. Louis ...... 2 0 3 0 1 4 0 1 X—11

E—Neal, Landrith, Mantilla, Boyer. DP—St. Louis, 2. LOB—New York, 7; St. Louis, 5. 2B—Mantilla, Musial, Boyer, Oliver. HR—Hodges, Neal. SB—Flood, 2, Javier. SF—Thomas, Flood, White.

#### PITCHING SUMMARY

| | IP | H | R | ER | BB | SO |
|---|----|----|----|----|----|----|
| Craig, L, (0-1) | 3 | 8 | 5 | 5 | 0 | 1 |
| Moorhead | 3 | 6 | 5 | 2 | 1 | 1 |
| Moford | 1 | 1 | 0 | 0 | 0 | 0 |
| Labine | 1 | 1 | 1 | 0 | 0 | 0 |
| Jackson, W, (1-0) | 9 | 8 | 4 | 4 | 4 | 2 |

Balk—Craig. Attendance—16,147.

## SIX-YEAR DEAL IS HAUL FOR HISLE

*Are the contracts given free-agent stars astronomical? Larry Hisle signed a six-year Milwaukee Brewers pact for $3.15 million, starting in 1978. Exactly twenty years earlier, the players in the entire eight-club American League earned a collective $3.7 million.*

## THE AMAZING METS

The 1962 Mets, with their 40-120 record, were the most pathetic expansion club, but the return of National League baseball to New York, coupled with the nostalgic appeal of the club's aging stars, generated an amazing emotional response among the fans.

With Casey Stengel as manager, and former Dodgers Gil Hodges and Roger Craig two of the mainstays, the team substituted memories for hitting, pitching and fielding.

Positive contributions by Frank Thomas and Richie Ashburn were overshadowed by Marv Throneberry's attempts at fielding, Craig Anderson's 16-game losing steak, Don Zimmer's 0-for-34 batting slump, and the 44 losses suffered by the two "best" starters, Roger Craig and Alvin Jackson.

During a clubhouse birthday party, a cake was carved and Stengel handed the pieces to everyone but Throneberry. "What about me?" the firstbaseman asked. "We wuz gonna give you a piece," the manager replied, "but we wuz afraid you'd drop it." ☞

The first Mets' winning pitcher was Jay Hook, a mechanical engineer who could explain the dynamics of a curveball but couldn't throw one. With an 8-19 record, he was one of the team's better pitchers.

A disappointment to the Mets—but probably a hero to their fans—was Bob Miller, the team's first choice in the expansion draft. He lost 12 games in succession and seemed headed for a winless season when he won a game just before the season ended.

To add to the confusion on the ballclub, the Mets had another pitcher named Bob Miller! Bob G. Miller was lefthanded and little more than a journeyman ballplayer. Bob L. Miller, the righthander whose losing ways drew the fans' sympathy, went on to a successful career with the Dodgers, Twins, and seven other clubs.

# BEST PICKS
# IN EXPANSION DRAFTS

Not all expansion clubs suffered the setbacks incurred by the Mets' over-the-hill gang. Many new teams went for youth in expansion drafts and recruited fine prospects.

Pitcher Dean Chance and shortstop Jim Fregosi, selected by the Angels, blossomed into American League All-Stars. Fregosi was so highly regarded by the club that he became manager of the team when his playing career ended in 1978.

The Senators scored with versatile Chuck Hinton, twice a .300 hitter, while outfielder Jim Hickman of the Mets and third baseman Bob Aspromonte and pitcher Dave Giusti of the Astros proved to be positive picks in the first National League draft.

The best choices of 1968 were made by the San Diego Padres, who named first baseman Nate Colbert and outfielders Cito Gaston and Downtown Ollie Brown. That same year, Montreal selected pitcher Bill Stoneman and outfielders Mack Jones and Manny Mota (Mota and fellow draftee Maury Wills were traded to the Dodgers for Ron Fairly); Kansas City tabbed pitchers Jim Rooker and Dick Drago; and Seattle drafted outfielders Lou Piniella (immediately traded to Kansas City) and Tommy Harper.

Harper stole 73 bases for the Pilots, then became a sudden power-hitter and joined the select few players who have hit 30 homers and stolen 30 bases in the same season. He turned the trick after the Pilots became the Milwaukee Brewers in 1970.

Colbert of San Diego became a consistent home run hitter and All-Star whose biggest day in the majors occurred in Atlanta on August 1, 1972. He hit five home runs and knocked in 13 in a doubleheader against the Braves.

The biggest mistake made by the 1969 expansion teams was Seattle's unloading of pitcher Mike Marshall, who lost ten games but pitched a shutout for one of his three victories. He stopped in Houston before becoming the game's outstanding relief pitcher with Montreal and later Los Angeles.

The second Seattle franchise was more careful when it made its selection in 1976. Its first pick, also the first pick in the draft, was a budding young star named Ruppert Jones, a speedy outfielder. Selected from Kansas City, Jones slugged 24 homers as a rookie and represented the Mariners in the All-Star Game.

Toronto also chose wisely, naming Baltimore farmhand Bob Bailor, who played both infield and outfield and swung the bat with authority. His .310 rookie average represented the best mark ever recorded by a player on a new expansion club.

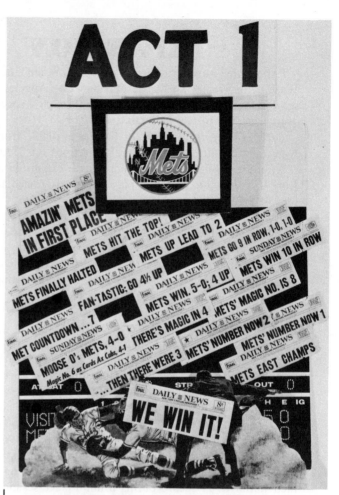

New York Mets, after years of agony, rocketed to the pennant with a late summer drive in 1969.

| YEAR | TEAM | FIRST DRAFT CHOICE |
|------|------|--------------------|
| 1960 | Los Angeles Angels | Fred Newman, pitcher, Boston |
|  | Washington Senators | Dick Donovan, pitcher, Chicago |
| 1961 | Houston Colts | Joey Amalfitano, 2b, San Francisco |
|  | New York Mets | Bob Miller, pitcher, St. Louis |
| 1968 | Kansas City Royals | Roger Nelson, pitcher, Baltimore |
|  | Seattle Pilots | Don Mincher, 1b, California |
|  | Montreal Expos | Manny Mota, of, Pittsburgh |
|  | San Diego Padres | Ollie Brown, of, San Francisco |
| 1976 | Seattle Mariners | Ruppert Jones, of, Kansas City |
|  | Toronto Blue Jays | Bob Bailor, ss-of, Baltimore |

# THE ADVENT OF THE AMATEUR DRAFT

Each January and June, major league clubs draft negotiating rights to high school and college players. The first free-agent draft, on June 9, 1965, was held to stop bidding wars by teams pursuing the same players. These wars caused huge bonuses to be given amateurs before they spent an inning in the major leagues. Many of them never made it that far.

Under rules of the amateur draft, teams picked negotiating rights in reverse order of the previous year's standings.

That first year, Rick Monday, outfielder from Arizona State, was the Number One pick in the nation. Other future major-leaguers selected at the 1965 session were Ray Fosse, Bernie Carbo, and Billy Conigliaro.

The free-agent draft was created to equalize talent among teams and cut off high-priced bidding which threatened to raise ticket prices and anger the fans. The "reentry" draft, created by baseball after the fall of the reserve system in 1976, had just the opposite effect.

## A LEFTHANDED CATCHER

*When Dale Long caught two games for the 1958 Cubs, he became the first lefthanded catcher in the majors since 1902. Southpaws seldom catch because their throws have a natural spin that make them "sail" away from second base—a handicap in catching base-stealers. "We really do live in a righthander's world," said Long, who had to use a first-baseman's mitt in one catching assignment because the team had no lefthanded catcher's mitt.*

Mel Bailey

**Pioneer free agent Andy Messersmith signed with Atlanta after challenging reserve clause in court.**

# CURT FLOOD VS. BASEBALL

The beginning of the end for the reserve system can be traced to Curt Flood's suit against baseball, filed after his trade to the Philadelphia Phillies by the St. Louis Cardinals in 1969.

Flood, who had spent twelve years with the Cardinals, refused to accept the deal and did not report in 1970. Instead, he challenged baseball's antitrust exemption, which had been upheld by the United States Supreme Court in 1922 and not seriously challenged since.

At that time, the court ruled baseball was a sport, not a business, and therefore not subject to laws which governed the business world.

Flood, with his suit to protect, missed the game after his 1970 sit-down strike and signed a traditional contract—with the reserve clause included—with the Washington Senators in 1971. He agreed to play only with the stipulation that such action would not hurt his case. After getting off to a bad start, however, he left the game for good.

The Flood challenge was denied by the Supreme Court in 1972, exactly fifty years after the first baseball decision by the high court, but events were already in motion which would accomplish Flood's objective.

In 1975, pitcher Andy Messersmith "played out his option" by refusing to sign a Dodger contract (the club renewed his 1974 pact under the option clause provided). After the season, he was declared a free agent by Peter M. Seitz, the same man who had granted free agency to Oakland A's pitcher Catfish Hunter on a contract technicality the previous year.

The effort by club owners to overturn the Seitz ruling failed in federal court. The old reserve system was dead.

# LABOR UNREST IN BASEBALL

Before management was forced to hack out the historic 1976 agreement that revamped the reserve system, there were two unpleasant incidents in player-owner relations.

On April 1, 1972, the Major League Baseball Players Association, headed by former steelworkers adviser Marvin Miller, staged a strike over retirement benefits and increased medical premiums. The 12-day strike ended when owners agreed to pay the estimated $1.2 million asked by the players in exchange for cancelation of all games missed to that point. Teams lost up to $200,000 and a player making $75,000 lost more than $1500 in take home pay.

Four years later, with another dispute brewing, owners smarting from the Messersmith decision decided they would not open camps and risk another walkout. The Basic Agreement between players and owners had expired and, without resolution in sight, management feared labor would strike to force an unfair agreement under pressure.

Finally, the players agreed not to strike while negotiations continued. A new three-year agreement was reached in July.

## MEGABUCKS CONTRACTS

*Baseball's average salary, with all post-season bonuses figured in, was $430,688 in 1988. The average salary on the New York Yankees, the best-paying team in baseball, was $708,487. The average salary had been $22,500 in 1966, $32,500 in 1972, and $150,000 in 1980. Baseball minimums have escalated from $7,000 in 1966 to $13,500 in 1972, $32,500 in 1980, and $62,500 in 1988. Top salaries have risen from $200,000 in 1972 to $1.5 million in 1980 and $2.4 million in 1988.*

## THE RE-ENTRY SYSTEM

Terms of the July 1976 agreement replaced the old reserve rule with the reentry system. Experienced stars could exercise their newly-won right to "play out the option year" in their contracts and sell their services to the highest bidder. Such "free agents" hardly deserved that title after 14 of them received $22 million in long-term deals after the 1976 season.

Teams drafted negotiation rights to free agent stars in the reentry draft, held several weeks after the World Series. Since more than a dozen clubs could draft rights to a single star, the bidding wars which followed were predictable well in advance.

Critics charged the reentry system allowed teams in the best cities, as well as those with the most money, to corner the market on top talent and buy a championship.

The New York Yankees did that in 1976, with the help of 17-game winner Catfish Hunter, and in 1977, when Reggie Jackson yielded free agency for Yankee dollars.

Wealthy owner George Steinbrenner added other quality free agents in reliever Rich Gossage, starters Tommy John and Rudy May, and sluggers Bob Watson and Dave Winfield.

## BIGGEST LOSERS OF THE RE-ENTRY SYSTEM

The Wayne Garland case was one of several which underlined the danger of the reentry system, which dictated long-term, big-money contracts—many of them guaranteed agreements with no-cut, no-trade provisions.

Garland won 20 and lost 7 while playing out his option with the Baltimore Orioles in 1976. Though that had been the only winning season in Garland's three-year career, the Cleveland Indians gambled that the 26-year-old pitcher would continue to produce with similar results. They gave him a ten-year contract for $2.15 million —an annual salary of $215,000, or $191,500 more than he received from Baltimore the year before. ☞

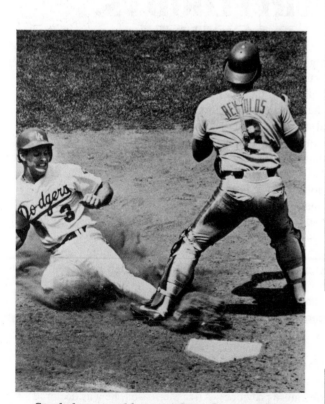

Sparkplug second baseman Steve Sax, one of only two players to hit safely in all five games of the 1988 World Series, used free agency to defect from the World Champion Los Angeles Dodgers. Sax became the latest prize in George Steinbrenner's free-agent stable when he inked a three-year, $4 million deal with the New York Yankees.

Garland lost 19 in his first year at Cleveland and three of five, pitching in pain, in 1978. Doctors diagnosed a torn rotator cuff and had to preform surgery.

The Indians, crippled by Wayne Garland's physical problems, weren't the only losers in the free-agent sweepstakes. The Oakland A's, champions of the American League West five straight seasons from 1971-75 (and World Champions in 1972-73-74), lost the heart of their club because of the new freedom given the players.

Oakland stars who played out their options were Joe Rudi, Rollie Fingers, Gene Tenace, Bert Campaneris, Sal Bando, and Don Baylor. Two long-time A's who threatened to do so were traded— Ken Holtzman and Reggie Jackson went to the Orioles in April. Oakland owner Charles O. Finley, seeking compensation for other stars before they became free agents, sold Rudi and Fingers to the Red Sox and Vida Blue to the Yankees in million-dollar deals on June 15, 1976. But Commissioner of Baseball Bowie Kuhn nullified the sales on the grounds they were against "the best interests of baseball."

After the season, Finley's fears were realized when Rudi and Fingers joined the mass exodus from the A's. Blue was eventually traded twice more by Finley—once in a canceled million-dollar transaction with Cincinnati and finally in a swap that brought seven players and an estimated $400,000 from San Francisco.

One-time Oakland World Series hero Rollie Fingers, a newcomer to the 1981 Milwaukee Brewers, became the first relief pitcher to win the Most Valuable Player and Cy Young awards in the same season. With six wins and 28 saves in the strike-shortened season, Fingers figured in 34 of his team's 62 victories—most in the AL East—and saved both Brewer wins in the divisional series against the Yankees. The career leader in saves posted a microscopic 1.04 earned run average in 47 appearances at age 35.

# RUNAWAY SALARIES

All teams felt the sting of the free-agent revolution. Clubs were forced to jack up the salaries of athletes who stayed put as a preventative measure. Between 1976 and 1977, the average salary rose from $51,501 to $76,066, and the Phillies alone added one million dollars to their payroll.

The team attracted 2.7 million fans but expenditures exceeded income and the team made money only because it participated in the NL Championship Series. *The Los Angeles Times* reported that the Phils paid $3,497,900 in salaries—an average of $139,916—while the Yankees paid an average of $138,973.

Biggest winner among the players at that time was Larry Hisle, 31, the AL's runs batted in champion of 1977. Hisle hit .302 with 28 homers and 119 RBI, and stole 21 bases, for the Minnesota Twins, who paid him $47,200. With the Milwaukee Brewers, who signed him for six years, his average annual salary jumped to $525,000!

Hisle's neighbor in Minnesota's outfield, Lyman Bostock, made $20,000 for hitting .336 (second in the league) with 14 home runs, 90 runs batted in, and 16 stolen bases—easily the best marks of his three-year career. At age 27, the California Angels gave him a package worth $450,000 annually. Bostock never finished the season; he was murdered in Gary, Indiana in September.

Bostock died only months before National League MVP Dave Parker became the game's first $1-million-a-year player. The 28-year-old rightfielder of the Pittsburgh Pirates signed a five-year pact worth an estimated $5 million.

Just previous to his signing, American League MVP Jim Rice, 26, agreed to remain with the Boston Red Sox for a multi-year deal worth $700,000 per season, and former MVPs Rod Carew of the California Angels and Pete Rose of the Philadelphia Phillies won $800,000-a-year contracts from their new clubs.

Barbara Morgen

Pete Rose played 16 years for Cincinnati, then left via reentry to sign an $800,000-per-year contract with Philadelphia. In 1978, his last year with the Reds, Rose tied a National League record with a 44-game hitting streak. A year later, he became the first player to produce ten 200-hit seasons and played his fifth different position in the All-Star Game.

# PLAYER AGENTS

The advent of huge contracts with deferred payments and complex clauses was accompanied by an increase in the number of players using agents to negotiate for them.

Agents became part of baseball in 1970, when owners agreed that players could use a representative in salary negotiations. In 1973, the same year binding arbitration was first used to settle salary and contract disputes, Jerry Kapstein entered the field with one client: Richie Zisk.

In 1976, the Providence, Rhode Island agent handled 10 of the 14 free-agent stars and earned more than $700,000 in fees for arranging spectacular salary packages in their behalf.

Another prominent agent, Ed Keating, placed Gary Matthews with the Braves and earned $200,000 for that transaction alone. Keating was so admired by Atlanta owner Ted Turner that he was retained to represent Turner in various commercial enterprises.

# HOW CONTRACTS HAVE CHANGED

The seller's market of high-priced free agents in the '70s produced countless cases of salary increases or bonuses equal to the $80,000 Babe Ruth made in 1932.

The figure stood as the top salary for years. Dizzy Dean, one of the game's greatest pitchers, earned just $3000 per season in both 1932 and 1933, jumped to $7500 in 1934, and was raised to $18,500 after his 30-win season the year before. Dean was paid $27,500 in both 1936 and 1937.

After one of his greatest seasons, Joe DiMaggio asked the Yankees for a raise from $25,000 to $35,000. When they refused, he said, "I insist upon it." The team responded, "If you insist, go home and we'll see you later."

Even Ty Cobb owner of the highest lifetime batting average, failed to get rich from baseball. He became wealthy after investing in a small soda company in his native Georgia. The name of the firm was Coca-Cola.

A Cobb contemporary, Ed Walsh of the White Sox, won 27 and saved 10 other games in 1911, but took home only $300 per month. Top stars were up to $700 a month by the Depression era.

There were no official minimum salaries until 1947, when the bottom line was established at $5000. Ten years later, it was $7000, and twenty years after that it was $19,000. In 1979, the minimum player's salary was $21,000.

**Dick Allen was the game's highest-paid player with the White Sox in the early '70s, but his $225,000 pact was passed by dozens of players with the advent of reentry.**

## HOW '27 YANKEES WERE PAID

| | |
|---|---:|
| Ed Barrow, general manager | $25,000 |
| Miller Huggins, manager | 37,000 |
| Babe Ruth, outfield | 70,000 |
| Herb Pennock, pitcher | 17,500 |
| Urban Shocker, pitcher | 13,500 |
| Bob Meusel, outfield | 13,000 |
| Joe Dugan, third base | 12,000 |
| Dutch Ruether, pitcher | 11,000 |
| Waite Hoyt, pitcher | 11,000 |
| Bob Shawkey, pitcher | 10,500 |
| Earle Combs, outfield | 10,500 |
| Tony Lazzeri, second base | 8,000 |
| Bennie Bengough, catcher | 8,000 |
| Lou Gehrig, first base | 8,000 |
| Pat Collins, catcher | 7,000 |
| Mark Koenig, shortstop | 7,000 |
| Ben Paschal, outfield | 7,000 |
| Myles Thomas, pitcher | 6,500 |
| John Grabowski, catcher | 5,500 |
| John Gazella, infield | 5,000 |
| Joe Giard, pitcher | 5,000 |
| George Pipgrass, pitcher | 4,500 |
| Credic Durst, outfield | 4,500 |
| Ray Morehart, infield | 4,000 |
| Jules Wera, infield | 2,400 |
| Wilcy Moore, pitcher | 2,500 |

## TOP TEN SALARIES: 1950

| | |
|---|---:|
| Ted Williams, Red Sox | $125,000 |
| Joe DiMaggio, Yankees | 100,000 |
| Ralph Kiner, Pirates | 65,000 |
| Lou Boudreau, Indians | 65,000 |
| Hal Newhouser, Tigers | 50,000 |
| Stan Musial, Cardinals | 50,000 |
| Bob Feller, Indians | 45,000 |
| Tommy Henrich, Yanks | 45,000 |
| George Kell, Tigers | 35,000 |
| Jackie Robinson, Dodgers | 35,000 |
| Pee Wee Reese, Dodgers | 35,000 |

# WHY TRADING IS TOUGHER TODAY

Long-term, complex contracts make trading difficult. Unfortunately for the general managers, who make most of the deals, most players are tied up for more than one year.

"Before," said Harry Dalton, Milwaukee Brewers' general manager, "all you did was trade a service contract, usually an obligation for one year. There were very few, if any, other restrictions.

"Now you have long-term guaranteed financial commitments, in some cases four or five years, and in many cases a million dollars. First, it's tough for teams to take on that obligation and second, within the service contract itself, the player has the right to say no. Paul Owens of the Phillies might come up to me and offer a player. I'll say, 'What's his contract like?' He'll tell me and I'll say, 'I'm not interested.'"

# MAJOR CHANGES IN THE GAME

Expansion, free agents, and runaway salaries were three of the many changes baseball encountered following the Second World War.

The electronic era, marked by television and air-conditioning, hurt the minors and forced the majors into widespread promotional campaigns. Night ball, once considered a novelty, became a necessity—though energy shortages of the '70s threatened to curtail excess use of electricity and, in the cases of domed stadiums, giant air-conditioning systems.

Artificial turf replaced grass in many parks (mostly in the National League), starting in 1965, and upset the same critics who contended that the designated hitter, first used by the AL in 1973, had destroyed the traditional concept of baseball.

Records established by Babe Ruth and Ty Cobb, the game's greatest stars, were wiped out, and teams in California—out of the majors until 1958—produced the only pitchers to throw four no-hitters (Sandy Koufax and Nolan Ryan).

A storm of controversy greeted the entry of the first modern black player in 1947, but Jackie Robinson performed so well for Brooklyn that he won the first Rookie of the Year Award. Pitchers had a hard time winning points in Most Valuable Player voting, but the oversight was corrected when the Cy Young Award was created in 1956—and split into separate awards, one for each league, in 1967; four of its first eight winners won entry to the Hall of Fame.

Divisional play began with the second wave of expansion in 1969, and the majors increased their fan appeal with four pennant races instead of two.

The cultivation of relief pitching into a highly-technical science was definitely a development of the modern age. The Philadelphia "Whiz Kids" of 1950 raised eyebrows all over the majors when they won the pennant primarily because of 33-year-old bullpen ace Jim Konstanty. He worked 74 games—a record that stood more than ten years—and won 16 while saving 22 others. Konstanty was voted the league's Most Valuable Player.

There have been dozens of top relievers since, including Hoyt Wilhelm—one of two to pitch more than 1000 games in his career—and Mike Marshall—the only man to pitch more than 100 in a season.

Relief pitching spread so quickly in the '50s that *The Sporting News* launched an annual "Fireman of the Year" competition in 1960, giving awards to pitchers who compiled points derived from adding relief wins and "games saved."

Saves—given to relievers who face the tying or winning run but preserve the victory—became an official statistic in 1969.

## LONG STRETCHES WITHOUT DEFEAT

*Relievers often work long stretches without losing. Roy Face went 98 games without defeat, recording a 22-0 record, from May 30, 1958 to September 11, 1959. Wes Stock went 100 games without a loss, with a 12-0 mark, from July 12, 1962 to July 19, 1964.*

## HOYT WILHELM ON MIKE MARSHALL

*After Mike Marshall worked 106 games for the Dodgers in 1974, veteran bullpen star Hoyt Wilhelm said, "If somebody had come along fifteen years ago and told me a guy would some day work 100 games while throwing a fair amount of fastballs, I'd have said it was a ridiculous statement. In fact, I'd have said it was about as ridiculous as the breaking of Babe Ruth's lifetime home run record!"*

## WHY KNUCKLER WORKED WONDERS FOR WILHELM

*When Hoyt Wilhelm broke into the majors with the 1952 New York Giants, he challenged his teammates to catch three knuckleballs out of five. None—including Willie Mays—could do it. Wilhelm, who broke in at 29, was just short of his 49th birthday when he retired as a player in 1972.*

Hoyt Wilhelm, whose 21-year career ended with the Dodgers, compiled numerous relief pitching records.

# RECORD-BREAKERS

The game's two most talked-about records—Ruth's one-year and career home run highs—were erased by Roger Maris, with 61 in 1961, and Henry Aaron, who passed Ruth's 714 in 1974 and retired two years later with a final count of 755.

Sixty-one home runs would not have been as surprising if produced by Harmon Killebrew, Rocky Colavito, or Jim Gentile, but Maris never hit more than 39 in any other season. He received a steady diet of good pitches to hit—and was never intentionally walked—because Mickey Mantle, batting directly behind him, was en route to his best home run year; he ended with 54.

In the National League in 1961, the most noteworthy performance was registered by 40-year-old Warren Spahn, pitcher for the Milwaukee Braves. He led the league with 21 victories, 21 complete games, four shutouts, and a 3.01 earned run average.

Spahn, Early Wynn, Whitey Ford, and Sandy Koufax were the Cy Young Award winners, 1956-63, who advanced to the Hall of Fame. Had he not been forced to retire with arthritis at age 31, Koufax could have challenged Spahn's position as the "winningest" lefthander in National League history (363).

In his last five years, Koufax won 111, lost 34, led NL pitchers in earned run average each year, and struck out 1,444 men. In 1966, pitching in pain, he was 27-9 with 317 strikeouts in 323 innings pitched. He completed 27 of 41 games and recorded a 1.73 earned run average.

Koufax's teammate, Maury Wills, proved the value of speed to managers around the league. The art of base-stealing had virtually disappeared in 1950, when Dom DiMaggio led the American League with 15, but Wills revived it and refined it to the point where he could run at will.

In 1962, when the NL pennant was decided in a best-of-three playoff between the Dodgers and Giants, Wills stole 104 bases, a one-season high that eclipsed Ty Cobb's 96 in 1915.

Lou Brock of the St. Louis Cardinals stole 118 bases, shunting Maury Wills to second place and Ty Cobb to third, in 1974. Brock went on to pass Cobb's lifetime standard of 892 stolen bases.

There was a post-season controversy in 1974 when Brock lost the Most Valuable Player designation to Steve Garvey of the champion Dodgers. Wills had won the honor in 1962, and other record-breakers had also been voted the MVP: Roger Maris in 1961, Frank Robinson and Carl Yastrzemski for their Triple Crowns in 1966 and 1967, Denny McLain for his 31-6 record and Bob Gibson for his 1.12 earned run average and 13 shutouts in 1968.

Lou Brock's feat of 118 steals in 1974 was overshadowed by the yeoman relief pitching of Mike Marshall, righthander of the Los Angeles Dodgers. He won 15 games, saved 21 others, finished 83 times in 106 appearances, and posted a 2.42 earned run mark for a record 208 relief innings. From June 18 through July 3, Marshall pitched in 13 consecutive games.

Marshall not only owned a rubber arm but knew its stress limitations. He had become an authority on kinesiology, the study of anatomy in relation to human movement. The 31-year-old reliever abstained from smoking and drinking, ate only nutritious foods, never wore the traditional sweatshirt, and frequently pitched batting practice to keep his arm in tune.

After the 1974 season, Marshall became the first relief man to win the coveted Cy Young Award. Sparky Lyle of the Yankees became the second in 1977.

## THE ROOKIE RACE OF 1975

*Teammates Fred Lynn and Jim Rice of the champion Boston Red Sox staged the closest Rookie of the Year race in 1975. Lynn led the league in runs scored, doubled, and slugging percentage, was second in batting, and third in runs batted in. But Rice, his fellow outfielder, almost matched him. Their statistics:*

|      | G   | AB  | R   | H   | HR | RBI | SB | BA   |
|------|-----|-----|-----|-----|----|-----|----|------|
| Lynn | 145 | 528 | 103 | 175 | 21 | 105 | 10 | .331 |
| Rice | 144 | 564 | 92  | 174 | 22 | 102 | 10 | .309 |

## WEST COAST FIRST

*The Giants blanked the Dodgers, 8-0, in the first game on the West Coast, April 15, 1958, at Seals Stadium, San Francisco. The ballpark, which held 22,900, served the Giants two seasons before the opening of Candlestick Park in 1960.*

## WAY TO WIN

*In 1975, Pirate pitcher Ken Brett shut out San Diego in the first game of a Memorial Day doubleheader, then batted for the shortstop and slugged a two-run triple to tie the nightcap. Pittsburgh won that too.*

Nolan Ryan, the career strikeout leader and the only man to pitch five no-hitters, proved that life begins at 42 when he signed a guaranteed $1.6 million contract to pitch for the Texas Rangers in 1989. Ryan had previously pitched for the New York Mets, California Angels, and Houston Astros.

The Perry brothers, Gaylord (left) and Jim, created an unusual record in 1970, when both enjoyed 20-victory seasons—the first time brothers had won 20 games each in the same year. One year earlier, the Perrys performed another first when they won three games on the same day, July 20, 1969.

## SWEET 'N SOUR DEBUTS

*Superstar righthander Juan Marichal of the Giants broke in with a bang by one-hitting the Phillies, 2-0, on July 19, 1960, but team-mate Willie Mays had opposite luck in his 1951 debut. Mays went 0-for-5, a dubious debut that Hank Aaron would also suffer—three years later.*

## A'S QUARTET HURLED NO-HITTER

*Four Oakland A's pitchers combined for a no-hitter against the California Angels on the last day of the 1975 season. The only no-hitter thrown by more than a pair of pitchers was thrown by Vida Blue, Glen Abbott, Paul Lindblad, and Rollie Fingers.*

## LOSING NO-HITTERS

*Baltimore Pitchers Steve Barber and Stu Miller combined for a no-hitter against Detroit in 1967, but lost, 2-1. Barber walked 10, hit a batter, made a wild pitch, and committed an error in 8 2/3 innings. Houston's Ken Johnson lost a 1-0 no-hitter to the Reds in 1964 when he made an error in the ninth inning.*

# UNUSUAL ACHIEVEMENTS

The twenty-five-year period beginning in 1953, when the Braves fled Boston for Milwaukee, made many contributions to the lore of the game.

## PENNANT RACES

The 1964 Phillies will be remembered forever as the team that blew a pennant by losing ten straight games in September after mounting a six-and-a-half-game lead with two weeks to play.

On the plus side, the 1967 Red Sox and 1969 Mets will be remembered as "miracle teams" who beat long odds by jumping from ninth place to the pennant.

## PERFECT GAMES

Don Larsen's perfect game in the 1956 World Series was followed by regular-season duplicates: Jim Bunning in 1964, Sandy Koufax in 1965, and Catfish Hunter in 1968, Mike Witt in 1984, and Tom Browning in 1988.

## NINE POSITIONS IN ONE GAME

Two players—shortstop Bert Campaneris and third baseman Cesar Tovar—proved their versatility by playing nine positions in one game. Campy did it for the 1965 Kansas City A's and Tovar three years later for the Minnesota Twins. The former dropped a fly ball in right field and, as a pitcher, walked two and yielded a run-scoring single. But Tovar, starting the game on the mound, not only blanked the opposition but struck out slugger Reggie Jackson. He also induced the first man he faced—Bert Campaneris—to hit a soft foul fly for an out.

## SEVEN-FOR-SEVEN

One of the game's all-time oddities occurred June 21, 1970, when weak-hitting Detroit Tigers shortstop Cesar Gutierrez, wearing No. 7, became the first modern player to get seven hits in seven times at-bat (twelve innings). The uniform had been temporarily retired after the death of its former wearer, manager Charlie Dressen, but the club's equipment man accidentally gave it to Gutierrez when he reported to the team. Gutierrez hit just .243 for the season, his only one as a regular in the major leagues.

Five years later, Rennie Stennett of the Pirates went 7-for-7 as Pittsburgh devastated the Chicago Cubs, 22-0, in the regulation nine innings. It was the most lopsided shutout in modern baseball history, erasing 21-0 games of 1901 and 1939.

The record for most hits in a game remained 9—by Cleveland shortstop Johnny Burnett in an eighteen-inning affair in 1932. Burnett's hits were not consecutive. Like Gutierrez, he was a regular only that one season.

## BENTON FACED RUTH AND MANTLE

*Al Benton was the only pitcher to face Babe Ruth and Mickey Mantle in regular-season American League competition.*

# DAVE JOHNSON'S HOME RUN RECORD

The National League's comeback choice in 1973, Dave Johnson, proved that injuries could be overcome. Therapy and isometric exercises cured an ailing left shoulder and Johnson, in his first year with the Atlanta Braves, hit 43 home runs, one more than any second-baseman had hit in a season before (Rogers Hornsby had 42 in 1922). In seven previous seasons with Baltimore, Johnson had never hit more than 18 home runs and his 1972 total was only five.

# FOUR CONSECUTIVE HOME RUNS

Hitters found another unusual niche in baseball history. On June 8, 1961, the Milwaukee Braves hit four consecutive home runs—a big-league first—in the seventh inning of a game against the Cincinnati Reds. The batters were Eddie Mathews, Hank Aaron, Joe Adcock, and Frank Thomas.

Two years later, on July 31, 1963, this extremely difficult achievement was duplicated in a highly unexpected manner. The Cleveland Indians did it against the California Angels with power provided by the 8-9-1-2 hitters in the batting order! Woodie Held, pitcher Pedro Ramos, Tito Francona, and Larry Brown bombed Paul Foytack for all four home runs.

A third team hit four consecutive homers less than a year later when Tony Oliva, Bob Allison, Jimmie Hall, and Harmon Killebrew of the Minnesota Twins unloaded in the eleventh inning of a May 2, 1964 contest against the Kansas City Athletics.

Four home runs in a row, three times in four seasons, but never before or since—further illustration of the oft-proved adage: "Take nothing for granted in baseball."

Hank (44) and Tommie Aaron, teammates with the Braves in the '60s, hold the record for home runs by brothers. Hank hit 755 and Tommie 13.

## FINE FAREWELL

Joe Pignatano hit into a triple-play in his last at-bat in the majors.

## RECORD-SETTING SLUGGERS

The 1977 Los Angeles Dodgers were the only team with four 30-home run men. Four years earlier, the Atlanta Braves became the only team to have three 40-home run men.

## THE YEAR OF YAZ

Red Sox outfielder Carl Yastrzemski had a remarkable year in 1967. Leading his club to a photo-finish pennant against 100-to-1 odds, Yaz won the Triple Crown with a .326 batting average, 44 home runs, and 121 runs batted in. He led in hits, runs, total bases, and slugging average. Down the stretch, he poked 10 hits in his last 13 at-bats, including four in the pennant-clinching finale against Minnesota and three the previous day.

## SEAVER SMOTHERED SAN DIEGO

Tom Seaver fanned the last 10 San Diego Padres, running his game total to 19, as the Mets won, 2-1, on April 22, 1970. He yielded only two hits in tying the single-game strikeout record, shared by contemporaries Nolan Ryan and Steve Carlton.

## AARON'S BALL BROUGHT GOOD LUCK

Obscure lefthanded reliever Tom House of the Braves enjoyed his only superlative season in 1974 after catching Hank Aaron's 715th home run in the Atlanta bullpen on April 8, 1974.

## DOUBLE TROUBLE

*Rivals pitchers have twice hurled back-to-back no-hitters in the same series. It happened first on September 17-18, 1968, when Gaylord Perry of the San Francisco Giants no-hit the St. Louis Cardinals the day before Ray Washburn of the Cards no-hit the Giants. On April 30, 1969, Jim Maloney of the Cincinnati Reds pitched a hitless game against the Houston Astros—one day before Houston's Don Wilson no-hit the Reds.*

## BRETT'S BONANZA

*Since Ted Williams hit .406 in 1941, baseball's best single-season batting average has been a .390 mark by George Brett of the Kansas City Royals in 1980. Brett, a third baseman who later moved to first, also had 118 RBI in 117 games that season.*

## BASEPATH BANDITS

*In 1980, Montreal's Ron LeFlore became the first man to lead both leagues in stolen bases as he combined with Rodney Scott to steal 160 times, a two-man record.*

## MEXICAN MARVEL

*Lefthanded screwball specialist Fernando Valenzuela, discovered by the Dodgers in the Mexican League, won both the Rookie of the Year Award and the Cy Young Award—an unprecedented double citation—in 1981. He pitched eight shutouts while winning 16 games, including three in post-season play, and became the first rookie to start the All-Star Game.*

## STANLEY SWITCH HELPED '68 TIGERS

*Manager Mayo Smith, seeking to insert more punch in his lineup, switched outfielder Mickey Stanley to shortstop for the 1968 World Series against the Cardinals. With southpaw Mickey Lolich victorious three times, and Stanley playing well at short, the Tigers won in a seven-game contest.*

## PITCHERS HOLD SWAP RECORD

*Pitchers Bob Miller and Dick Littlefield both worked for ten different major league clubs.*

Slugging outfielders Kirk Gibson (left) of the Los Angeles Dodgers and Jose Canseco of the Oakland Athletics won Most Valuable Player awards after leading their teams into the 1988 World Series. Gibson, in his first National League season, hit 25 regular-season homers before adding three (including a World Series game-winner) in post-season action. Canseco led the majors with 42 homers and 124 RBI while becoming the game's first 40/40 player.

# A NEW ERA

The period from 1978-87 was marked by great competitive balance in baseball. During that span, baseball produced 10 different World Champions in as many years. Even divisional winners had a tough time stringing together successive titles.

Through the 1988 campaign, only three of the 26 clubs—the Seattle Mariners, Texas Rangers, and Cleveland Indians—had not finished first at least once since the 1969 advent of divisional play.

Both teams and individuals rewrote the record book.

The 1982 Atlanta Braves and 1987 Milwaukee Brewers won their first 13 games of the season, while the 1988 Baltimore Orioles lost their first 21; the Kansas City Royals twice recovered from 3-1 deficits in games to become World Champions of 1985, the first year that the League Championship Series became a best-of-seven event; the Minnesota Twins became 1987 World Champions (defeating the St. Louis Cardinals) when the home team won every World Series game for the first time; and the Chicago Cubs ended their all-daylight menu when they played the New York Mets in the first official Wrigley Field night game on August 9, 1988.

Longevity helped Steve Garvey play in 1,207 games, a National League record; Pete Rose become the career leader in hits (4,192); Kent Tekulve join Hoyt Wilhelm as the only men to pitch in 1,000 games; and Nolan Ryan wrest career strikeout leadership. But the retirements of Carl Yastrzemski, Willie Stargell, Rose, and Phil Niekro indicated that the torch had passed to a new generation in baseball.

Though a seven-week player strike resulted in a controversial "split-season" format in 1981, Rickey Henderson was ready when the game resumed normal operations a year later: Henderson, then with the Oakland Athletics, stole a record 130 bases. ☞

# 4 MAY
## TODAY IN HISTORY

1910 — The Browns and Cardinals each played home games in St. Louis and U.S. President William Howard Taft, not wanting to offend either club, saw parts of both games at Robinson Field and Sportsman's Park.